Datsun Owners Workshop Manual

by J H Haynes
Member of the Guild of Motoring Writers

and Ian Coomber

Models covered:

UK: Datsun 140J Mk III Saloon 1397 cc
      Datsun 160J Mk III Saloon 1595 cc
      Datsun 160J Mk III Coupe/Hatchback 1595 cc

USA: Datsun 510 Sedan 119 cu in (1952 cc)
      Datsun 510 Coupe/Hatchback 119 cu in (1952 cc)
      Datsun 510 Station Wagon 119 cu in (1952 cc)

Covers manual and automatic transmission versions

ISBN 0 85696 430 1

Printed in England   *(430 - 2F1)*

**HAYNES PUBLISHING GROUP
SPARKFORD YEOVIL SOMERSET ENGLAND**
distributed in the USA by
**HAYNES PUBLICATIONS INC
861 LAWRENCE DRIVE
NEWBURY PARK
CALIFORNIA 91320
USA**

Acknowledgements

Thanks are due to the Nissan Motor Company Limited of Japan for the provision of technical information and certain illustrations. The Champion Sparking Plug Company supplied the illustrations showing the various spark plug conditions. The bodywork repair photographs used in this manual were provided by Lloyds Industries Limited who supply 'Turtle Wax', 'Dupli-Color Holts', and other Holts range products.

Lastly thanks are due to all those people at Sparkford who helped in the production of this manual. Particularly Brian Horsfall and Les Brazier, who carried out the mechanical work and took the photographs respectively; Lee Saunders who planned the layout of each page and David Nielson who edited the text.

About this manual

Its aim

The aim of this manual is to help you get the best value from your car. It can do so in several ways. It can help you decide what work must be done (even should you choose to get it done by a garage), provide information on routine maintenance and servicing, and give a logical course of action and diagnosis when random faults occur. However, it is hoped that you will make full use of the manual by tackling the work yourself. On simpler jobs it may even be quicker than booking the car into the garage, and having to go there twice, to leave and collect it. Perhaps most important, a lot of money can be saved by avoiding the costs the garage must charge to cover its labour and overheads.

The manual has drawings and descriptions to show the function of the various components so that their layout can be understood. Then the tasks are described and photographed in a step-by-step sequence so that even a novice can do the work.

Its arrangement

The manual is divided into twelve Chapters, each covering a logical sub-division of the vehicle. The Chapters are each divided into consecutively numbered Sections and the Sections into paragraphs (or sub-sections), with decimal numbers following on from the Section they are in, eg 5.1, 5.2, 5.3 etc.

It is freely illustrated, especially in those parts where there is a detailed sequence of operations to be carried out. There are two forms of illustration: figures and photographs. The figures are numbered in sequence with decimal numbers, according to their position in the Chapter: eg Fig. 6.4 is the 4th drawing/illustration in Chapter 6. Photographs are numbered (either individually or in related groups) the same as the Section or sub-section of the text where the operation they show is described.

There is an alphabetical index at the back of the manual as well as a contents list at the front.

References to the 'left' or 'right' of the vehicle are in the sense of a person facing forwards in the driver's seat.

Whilst every care is taken to ensure that the information in this manual is correct no liability can be accepted by the authors or publishers for loss, damage or injury caused by any errors in, or omissions from, the information given.

Introduction to the Datsun 140J/160J Violet and 510 Series

The Datsun models covered by this manual are the 140J and 160J Violet series for the European markets and the 510 Series for the USA market.

The 140J models use an overhead valve engine of 1397 cc whilst the 160J models are fitted with a single overhead camshaft engine of 1595 cc and the 510 models an engine of 1952 cc (119·1 cu in).

The transmission system varies according to model and requirement, and can be a four-speed manual gearbox (full synchromesh), a three-speed fully automatic transmission with floor control selector or a five-speed manual gearbox with full synchromesh.

All models are fitted with independent front suspension and 4 link coil spring at the rear except the Estate Car which has a semi elliptic rear suspension for greater load carrying.

Drive to the rear axle is via a single or two piece (depending on model) propeller shaft.

The diaphragm spring clutch fitted to all manual transmission models is hydraulically operated except on the 140J models where a cable is used.

The brakes are hydraulically operated and are servo assisted on all models. The front brakes are of the disc type and the rear are of the drum type. The handbrake which is cable operated, operates on the rear wheels only.

Models manufactured for the USA have a wider range of accessories available and in order to comply with the regulations, a sophisticated emission control system is fitted to reduce the poisonous exhaust gases being freely released into the atmosphere. The emission control equipment fitted to California models differs slightly to comply with the additional regulations of that State.

Contents

Datsun 160J Mk III Saloon

Datsun 160J Mk III Hatchback

Datsun 510 5-door Wagon

Datsun 510 2-door Saloon

Buying spare parts
and vehicle identification numbers

Buying spare parts

Spare parts are available from many sources, for example: Datsun garages, other garages and accessory shops, and motor factors. Our advice regarding spare parts is as follows:

Officially appointed Datsun garages – This is the best source of parts which are peculiar to your car and otherwise not generally available (eg complete cylinder heads, internal gearbox components, badges, interior trim etc). It is also the only place at which you should buy parts if your car is still under warranty; non-Datsun components may invalidate the warranty. To be sure of obtaining the correct parts it will always be necessary to give the storeman your car's engine and chassis number, and if possible to take the old part along for positive identification. Remember that many parts are available on a factory exchange scheme – any parts returned should always be clean! It obviously makes good sense to go straight to the specialists on your car for this type of part for they are best equipped to supply you.

Other garages and accessory shops – These are often very good places to buy material and components needed for the maintenance of your car (eg oil filters, spark plugs, bulbs, fan belts, oils and grease, touch-up paint, filler paste etc). They also sell general accessories, usually have convenient opening hours, charge lower prices and can often be found not far from home.

Motor factors – Good factors will stock all of the more important components, (eg. pistons, valves, exhaust systems, brake cylinder/pipes/hoses/seals/shoes and pads etc). Motor factors will often provide new or reconditioned components on a part exchange basis – this can save a considerable amount of money.

Vehicle identification numbers

Modifications are a continuing and unpublished process in vehicle manufacture quite apart from major model changes. Spare parts manuals and lists are compiled upon a numerical basis, the individual vehicle numbers being essential to correct identification of the component required.

The car identification number plate is located in the centre of the bulkhead at the top, being visible on opening the bonnet (photo).

The chassis number is stamped into the top of the cowling in the engine compartment.

The car serial number (510 models) is stamped into the bulkhead directly behind the engine.

The engine serial number is on the right-hand side of the cylinder block (photo).

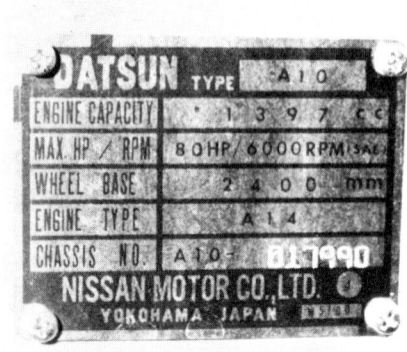

Car identification plate

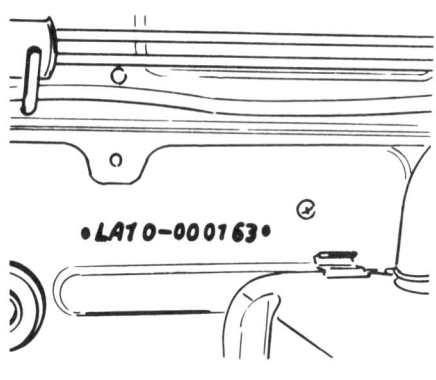

Chassis number

Car serial number (510 models)

Engine number

Use of English

As this book has been written in England, it uses the appropriate English component names, phrases, and spelling. Some of these differ from those used in America. Normally, these cause no difficulty, but to make sure, a glossary is printed below. In ordering spare parts remember the parts list will probably use these words:

English	American	English	American
Aerial	Antenna	Layshaft (of gearbox)	Countershaft
Accelerator	Gas pedal	Leading shoe (of brake)	Primary shoe
Alternator	Generator (AC)	Locks	Latches
Anti-roll bar	Stabiliser or sway bar	Motorway	Freeway, turnpike etc
Battery	Energizer	Number plate	License plate
Bodywork	Sheet metal	Paraffin	Kerosene
Bonnet (engine cover)	Hood	Petrol	Gasoline
Boot lid	Trunk lid	Petrol tank	Gas tank
Boot (luggage compartment)	Trunk	'Pinking'	'Pinging'
Bottom gear	1st gear	Propeller shaft	Driveshaft
Bulkhead	Firewall	Quarter light	Quarter window
Cam follower or tappet	Valve lifter or tappet	Retread	Recap
Carburettor	Carburetor	Reverse	Back-up
Catch	Latch	Rocker cover	Valve cover
Choke/venturi	Barrel	Roof rack	Car-top carrier
Circlip	Snap-ring	Saloon	Sedan
Clearance	Lash	Seized	Frozen
Crownwheel	Ring gear (of differential)	Side indicator lights	Side marker lights
Disc (brake)	Rotor/disk	Side light	Parking light
Drop arm	Pitman arm	Silencer	Muffler
Drop head coupe	Convertible	Spanner	Wrench
Dynamo	Generator (DC)	Sill panel (beneath doors)	Rocker panel
Earth (electrical)	Ground	Split cotter (for valve spring cap)	Lock (for valve spring retainer)
Engineer's blue	Prussian blue	Split pin	Cotter pin
Estate car	Station wagon	Steering arm	Spindle arm
Exhaust manifold	Header	Sump	Oil pan
Fast back (Coupe)	Hard top	Tab washer	Tang; lock
Fault finding/diagnosis	Trouble shooting	Tailgate	Liftgate
Float chamber	Float bowl	Tappet	Valve lifter
Free-play	Lash	Thrust bearing	Throw-out bearing
Freewheel	Coast	Top gear	High
Gudgeon pin	Piston pin or wrist pin	Trackrod (of steering)	Tie-rod (or connecting rod)
Gearchange	Shift	Trailing shoe (of brake)	Secondary shoe
Gearbox	Transmission	Transmission	Whole drive line
Halfshaft	Axleshaft	Tyre	Tire
Handbrake	Parking brake	Van	Panel wagon/van
Hood	Soft top	Vice	Vise
Hot spot	Heat riser	Wheel nut	Lug nut
Indicator	Turn signal	Windscreen	Windshield
Interior light	Dome lamp	Wing/mudguard	Fender

Miscellaneous points

An 'oil seal' is fitted to components lubricated by grease!

A 'damper' is a 'shock absorber', it damps out bouncing, and absorbs shocks of bump impact. Both names are correct, and both are used haphazardly.

Note that British drum brakes are different from the Bendix type that is common in America, so different descriptive names result. The shoe end furthest from the hydraulic wheel cylinder is on a pivot; interconnection between the shoes as on Bendix brakes is most uncommon. Therefore the phrase 'Primary' or 'Secondary' shoe does not apply. A shoe is said to be 'Leading' or 'Trailing'. A 'Leading' shoe is one on which a point on the drum, as it rotates forward, reaches the shoe at the end worked by the hydraulic cylinder before the anchor end. The opposite is a 'Trailing' shoe, and this one has no self servo from the wrapping effect of the rotating drum.

Tools and working facilities

Introduction

A selection of good tools is a fundamental requirement for anyone contemplating the maintenance and repair of a motor vehicle. For the owner who does not possess any, their purchase will prove a considerable expense, offsetting some of the savings made by doing-it-yourself. However, provided that the tools purchased are of good quality, they will last for many years and prove an extremely worthwhile investment.

To help the average owner to decide which tools are needed to carry out the various tasks detailed in this manual, we have compiled three lists of tools under the following headings: *Maintenance and minor repair, Repair and overhaul,* and *Special.* The newcomer to practical mechanics should start off with the *Maintenance and minor repair* tool kit and confine himself to the simpler jobs around the vehicle. Then, as his confidence and experience grows, he can undertake more difficult tasks, buying extra tools as, and when, they are needed. In this way, a *Maintenance and minor repair* tool kit can be built-up into a *Repair and overhaul* tool kit over a considerable period of time without any major cash outlays. The experienced do-it-yourselfer will have a tool kit good enough for most repair and overhaul procedures and will add tools from the *Special* category when he feels the expense is justified by the amount of use to which these tools will be put.

It is obviously not possible to cover the subject of tools fully here. For those who wish to learn more about tools and their use there is a book entitled *How to Choose and Use Car Tools* available from the publishers of this manual.

Maintenance and minor repair tool kit

The tools given in this list should be considered as a minimum requirement if routine maintenance, servicing and minor repair operations are to be undertaken. We recommend the purchase of combination spanners (ring one end, open-ended the other); although more expensive than open-ended ones, they do give the advantages of both types of spanner.

Combination spanners - 6, 7, 8, 9, 10, 11, & 12 mm
Adjustable spanner - 9 inch
Engine sump/gearbox/rear axle drain plug key (where applicable)
Spark plug spanner (with rubber insert)
Spark plug gap adjustment tool
Set of feeler gauges
Brake adjuster spanner (where applicable)
Brake bleed nipple spanner
Screwdriver - 4 in long x $\frac{1}{4}$ in dia (flat blade)
Screwdriver - 4 in. long x $\frac{1}{4}$ in dia (cross blade)
Combination pliers - 6 inch
Hacksaw, junior
Tyre pump
Tyre pressure gauge
Grease gun (where applicable)
Oil can
Fine emery cloth (1 sheet)
Wire brush (small)
Funnel (medium size)

Repair and overhaul tool kit

These tools are virtually essential for anyone undertaking any major repairs to a motor vehicle, and are additional to those given in the *Maintenance and minor repair* list. Included in this list is a comprehensive set of sockets. Although these are expensive they will be found invaluable as they are so versatile - particularly if various drives are included in the set. We recommend the $\frac{1}{2}$ in square-drive type, as this can be used with most proprietary torque wrenches. If you cannot afford a socket set, even bought piecemeal, then inexpensive tubular box spanners are a useful alternative.

The tools in this list will occasionally need to be supplemented by tools from the *Special* list.

Sockets (or box spanners) to cover range in previous list
Reversible ratchet drive (for use with sockets)
Extension piece, 10 inch (for use with sockets)
Universal joint (for use with sockets)
Torque wrench (for use with sockets)
'Mole' wrench - 8 inch
Ball pein hammer
Soft-faced hammer, plastic or rubber
Screwdriver - 6 in long x $\frac{5}{16}$ in dia (flat blade)
Screwdriver - 2 in long x $\frac{5}{16}$ in square (flat blade)
Screwdriver - 1$\frac{1}{2}$ in long x $\frac{1}{4}$ in dia (cross blade)
Screwdriver - 3 in long x $\frac{1}{8}$ in dia (electricians)
Pliers - electricians side cutters
Pliers - needle nosed
Pliers - circlip (internal and external)
Cold chisel - $\frac{1}{2}$ inch
Scriber (this can be made by grinding the end of a broken hacksaw blade)
Scraper (this can be made by flattening and sharpening one end of a piece of copper pipe)
Centre punch
Pin punch
Hacksaw
Valve grinding tool
Steel rule/straight edge
Allen keys
Selection of files
Wire brush (large)
Axle-stands
Jack (strong scissor or hydraulic type)

Special tools

The tools in this list are those which are not used regularly, are expensive to buy, or which need to be used in accordance with their manufacturers' instructions. Unless relatively difficult mechanical jobs are undertaken frequently, it will not be economic to buy many of these tools. Where this is the case, you could consider clubbing together with friends (or a motorists' club) to make a joint purchase, or borrowing the tools against a deposit from a local garage or tool hire specialist.

The following list contains only those tools and instruments freely available to the public, and not those special tools produced by the vehicle manufacturer specifically for its dealer network. You will find occasional references to these manufacturers' special tools in the text of this manual. Generally, an alternative method of doing the job without the vehicle manufacturer's special tool is given. However, sometimes, there is no alternative to using them. Where this is the case and the relevant tool cannot be bought or borrowed you will have to entrust the work to a franchised garage.

Valve spring compressor
Piston ring compressor
Balljoint separator
Universal hub/bearing puller
Impact screwdriver
Micrometer and/or vernier gauge
Carburettor flow balancing device (where applicable)
Dial gauge
Stroboscopic timing light
Dwell angle meter/tachometer
Universal electrical multi-meter
Cylinder compression gauge
Lifting tackle
Trolley jack
Light with extension lead

Buying tools

For practically all tools, a tool factor is the best source since he will have a very comprehensive range compared with the average garage or accessory shop. Having said that, accessory shops often offer excellent quality tools at discount prices, so it pays to shop around.

Remember, you don't have to buy the most expensive items on the shelf, but it is always advisable to steer clear of the very cheap tools. There are plenty of good tools around at reasonable prices, so ask the proprietor or manager of the shop for advice before making a purchase.

Care and maintenance of tools

Having purchased a reasonable tool kit, it is necessary to keep the tools in a clean serviceable condition. After use, always wipe off any dirt, grease and metal particles using a clean, dry cloth, before putting the tools away. Never leave them lying around after they have been used. A simple tool rack on the garage or workshop wall, for items such as screwdrivers and pliers is a good idea. Store all normal spanners and sockets in a metal box. Any measuring instruments, gauges, meters, etc, must be carefully stored where they cannot be damaged or become rusty.

Take a little care when tools are used. Hammer heads inevitably become marked and screwdrivers lose the keen edge on their blades fom time to time. A little timely attention with emery cloth or a file will soon restore items like this to a good serviceable finish.

Working facilities

Not to be forgotten when discussing tools, is the workshop itself. If anything more than routine maintenance is to be carried out, some form of suitable working area becomes essential.

It is appreciated that many an owner mechanic is forced by circumstances to remove an engine or similar item, without the benefit of a garage or workshop. Having done this, any repairs should always be done under the cover of a roof.

Wherever possible, any dismantling should be done on a clean flat workbench or table at a suitable working height.

Any workbench needs a vice: one with a jaw opening of 4 in (100 mm) is suitable for most jobs. As mentioned previously, some clean dry storage space is also required for tools, as well as the lubricants, cleaning fluids, touch-up paints and so on which become necessary.

Another item which may be required, and which has a much more general usage, is an electric drill with a chuck capacity of at least $\frac{5}{16}$ in (8 mm). This, together with a good range of twist drills, is virtually essential for fitting accessories such as wing mirrors and reversing lights.

Last, but not least, always keep a supply of old newspapers and clean, lint-free rags available, and try to keep any working area as clean as possible.

Spanner jaw gap comparison table

Jaw gap (in)	Spanner size
0·250	$\frac{1}{4}$ in AF
0·275	7 mm AF
0·312	$\frac{5}{16}$ in AF
0·315	8 mm AF
0·340	$\frac{11}{32}$ in AF; $\frac{1}{8}$ in Whitworth
0·354	9 mm AF
0·375	$\frac{3}{8}$ in AF
0·393	10 mm AF
0·433	11 mm AF
0·437	$\frac{7}{16}$ in AF
0·445	$\frac{3}{16}$ in Whitworth; $\frac{1}{4}$ in BSF
0·472	12 mm AF
0·500	$\frac{1}{2}$ in AF
0·512	13 mm AF
0·525	$\frac{1}{4}$ in Whitworth; $\frac{5}{16}$ in BSF
0·551	14 mm AF
0·562	$\frac{9}{16}$ in AF
0·590	15 mm AF
0·600	$\frac{5}{16}$ in Whitworth; $\frac{3}{8}$ in BSF
0·625	$\frac{5}{8}$ in AF
0·629	16 mm AF
0·669	17 mm AF
0·687	$\frac{11}{16}$ in AF
0·708	18 mm AF
0·710	$\frac{3}{8}$ in Whitworth; $\frac{7}{16}$ in BSF
0·748	19 mm AF
0·750	$\frac{3}{4}$ in AF
0·812	$\frac{13}{16}$ in AF
0·820	$\frac{7}{16}$ in Whitworth; $\frac{1}{2}$ in BSF
0·866	22 mm AF
0·875	$\frac{7}{8}$ in AF
0·920	$\frac{1}{2}$ in Whitworth; $\frac{9}{16}$ in BSF
0·937	$\frac{15}{16}$ in AF
0·944	24 mm AF
1·000	1 in AF
1·010	$\frac{9}{16}$ in Whitworth; $\frac{5}{8}$ in BSF
1·023	26 mm AF
1·062	$1\frac{1}{16}$ in AF; 27 mm AF
1·100	$\frac{5}{8}$ in Whitworth; $\frac{11}{16}$ in BSF
1·125	$1\frac{1}{8}$ in AF
1·181	30 mm AF
1·200	$\frac{11}{16}$ in Whitworth; $\frac{3}{4}$ in BSF
1·250	$1\frac{1}{4}$ in AF
1·259	32 mm AF
1·300	$\frac{3}{4}$ in Whitworth; $\frac{7}{8}$ in BSF
1·312	$1\frac{5}{16}$ in AF
1·390	$\frac{13}{16}$ in Whitworth; $\frac{15}{16}$ in BSF
1·417	36 mm AF
1·437	$1\frac{7}{16}$ in AF
1·480	$\frac{7}{8}$ in Whitworth; 1 in BSF
1·500	$1\frac{1}{2}$ in AF
1·574	40 mm AF; $\frac{15}{16}$ in Whitworth
1·614	41 mm AF
1·625	$1\frac{5}{8}$ in AF
1·670	1 in Whitworth; $1\frac{1}{8}$ in BSF
1·687	$1\frac{11}{16}$ in AF
1·811	46 mm AF
1·812	$1\frac{13}{16}$ in AF
1·860	$1\frac{1}{8}$ in Whitworth; $1\frac{1}{4}$ in BSF
1·875	$1\frac{7}{8}$ in AF
1·968	50 mm AF
2·000	2 in AF
2·050	$1\frac{1}{4}$ in Whitworth; $1\frac{3}{8}$ in BSF
2·165	55 mm AF
2·362	60 mm AF

Jacking and towing

Jacking points

The pantograph type jack supplied with the car must only be used at the positions below the body sills. Other types of jack should be located below the front crossmember or rear axle differential casing. If axle-stands are to be used, then they must be positioned under the bodyframe sidemembers or rear axle casing. No other positions should be used for jacking or support purposes.

When jacking up the car always chock a wheel on the opposite side, in front and behind.

Towing points

If the vehicle has to be towed, any rope or cable should be connected to the hook attached to the front sidemember. On vehicles equipped with automatic transmission, the towing speed should not exceed 20 mph (30 km/h) nor the towing distance 6 miles (10 km) otherwise the transmission may be damaged due to lack of lubrication. If towing distances are excessive, disconnect the propeller shaft from the rear axle pinion flange and tie the shaft up out of the way.

When towing another car, connect the rope to the rear towing hook on saloon and hardtop models, and to the rear leaf spring shackle on estate cars.

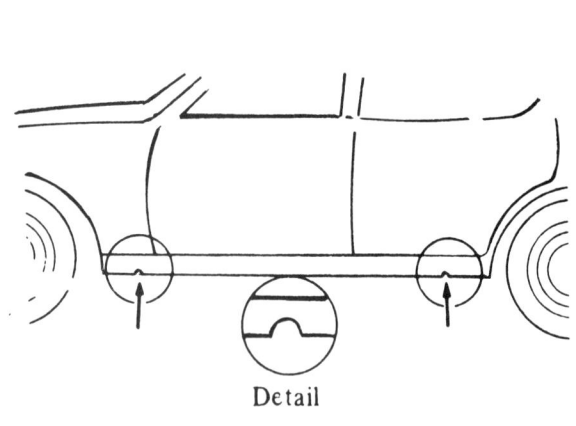

Detail

Jacking points for Saloon and Coupe

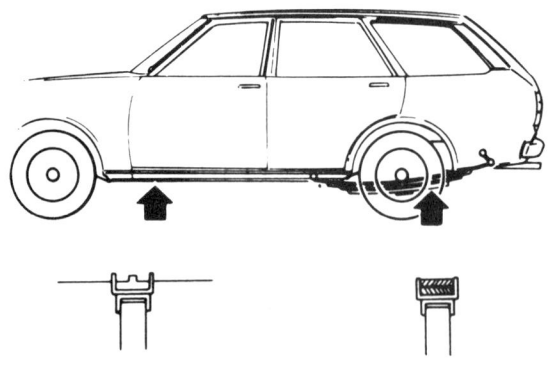

Jacking points for Estate Car

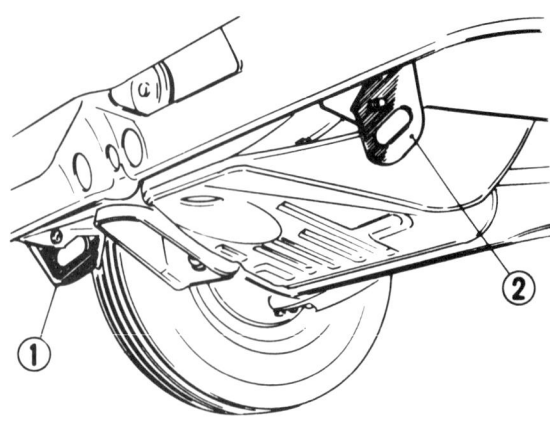

Front towing hook (1) and tie down hook (2)

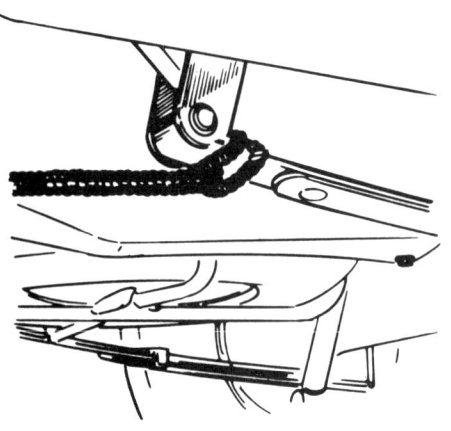

Rear towing point – Estate Car

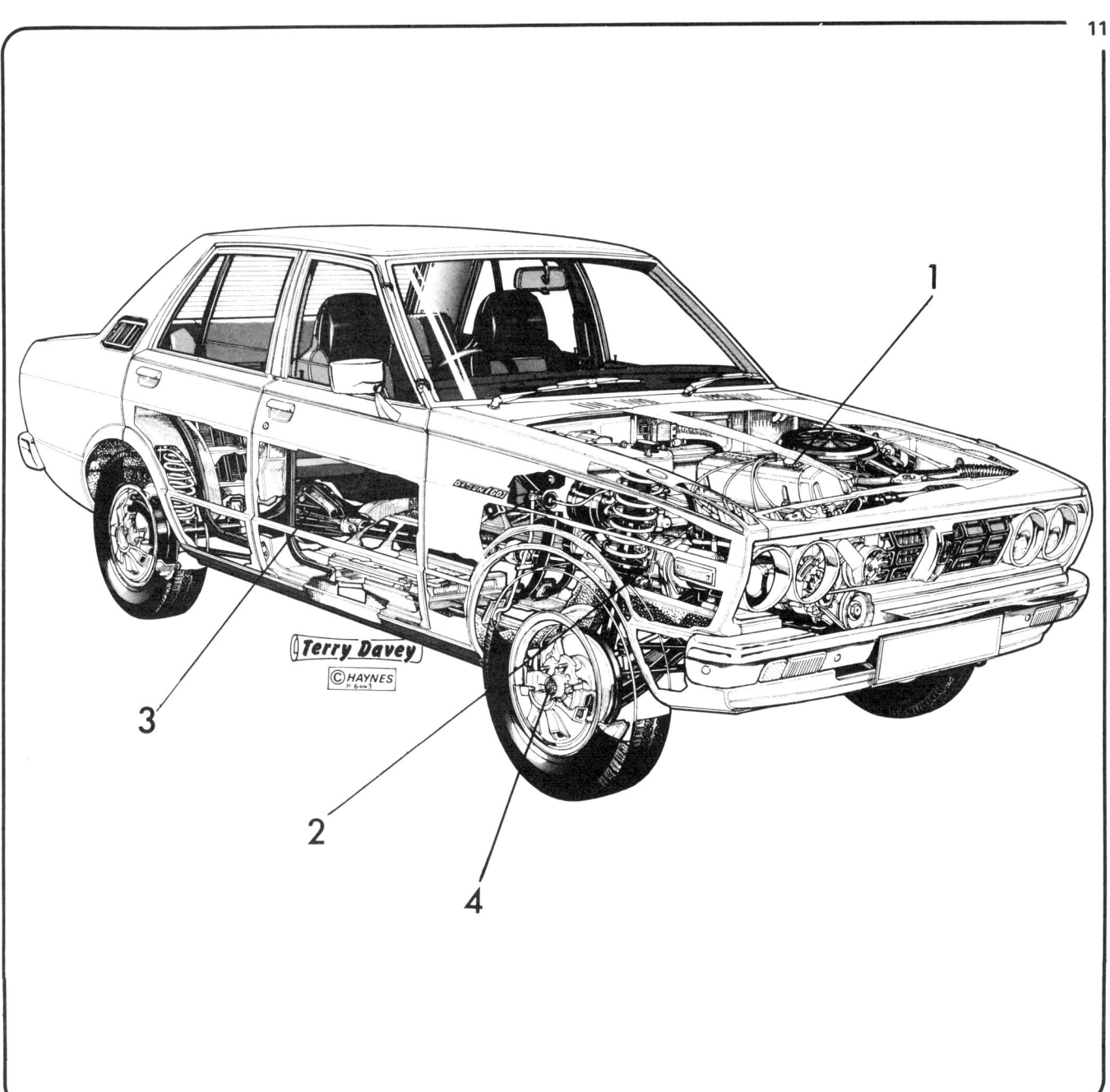

Recommended lubricants

Component	Castrol Product
Engine (1)	Castrol GTX
Gearbox (2)	
Manual	Castrol Hypoy Light (80EP)
Automatic	Castrol TQ Dexron ®
Rear axle (3)	Castrol Hypoy B (90 EP)
Front wheel bearings (4)	Castrol LM Grease
Clutch and brake fluid	DOT 3, DOT 4, or SAE J1703F

Note: *The above are general recommendations only. Lubrication requirements vary from territory to territory and depend on vehicle usage. Consult the operators handbook supplied with the car.*

Routine maintenance

Maintenance is essential for ensuring safety and desirable for the purpose of getting the best in terms of performance and economy from the car. Over the years the need for periodic lubrication – oiling, greasing and so on – has been drastically reduced if not totally eliminated. This has unfortunately tended to lead some owners to think that because no such action is required, the items either no longer exist, or will last for ever. This is certainly not the case and it is essential to carry out regular visual examination as comprehensively as possible in order to spot any possible defects at an early stage before they develop into major and expensive repairs.

The maintenance information given in this Section is not of a detailed nature as the information required to carry out the necessary tasks is to be found in the appropriate Chapters throughout this manual.

140J and 160J models

Every 250 miles (400 km) or weekly – whichever comes first

Engine
Check the sump oil level; top-up if necessary
Check the radiator coolant level, top-up if necessary
Check the level of the electrolyte in the battery, top-up as necessary

Steering
Check the tyre pressures
Examine the tyres for wear or damage

Brakes
Check the reservoir fluid level
Check the efficiency of service brake and handbrake

Lights, wipers and horns
Check that all lights work at the front and rear
Check the windscreen washer reservoir fluid level

Every 3000 miles (5000 km)

Engine
Change the engine oil

Every 6000 miles (10 000 km)

Engine
Check drivebelts for cracks, fraying and wear. Check for correct tension
Renew engine oil filter
Drain and flush cooling system if filled with water
Clean carburettor air cleaner (dry paper type)
Clean spark plugs and check gap
Check distributor cap, rotor, contact points and condenser
Check and adjust dwell angle, ignition timing and idling speed
Clean battery terminals and check specific gravity of electrolyte
Check level of oil in carburettor damper
Check condition of cooling, fuel and vacuum hoses
Check exhaust system for security and leaks
Check the air conditioning system hoses and connections for leaks

Steering
Examine all steering linkage rods, joints and bushes for signs of wear or damage. Check steering wheel play
Check front wheel hub bearing
Check tightness of steering box mounting bolts
Check level of oil in steering box
Check wheel alignment

Brakes
Examine disc pads and drum shoes for wear
Examine all hydraulic pipes, cylinders and unions for signs of chafing, dents or leaks
Check handbrake lever travel
Adjust drum type brakes if necessary

Suspension
Examine all nuts, bolts and balljoints securing the front and rear suspension, and tighten as necessary
Examine rubber bushes for signs of wear or deterioration
Check operation of shock absorbers

Transmission and differential
Check oil level and top-up if necessary
Check for oil leaks
Check security of propeller shaft and driveshaft bolts

Clutch
Check fluid reservoir level and top-up if necessary
Check pedal free movement and adjust if necessary
Check for fluid leakage

Body
Lubricate all locks and hinges
Check that water drain holes at bottom of doors are clear
Check windscreen wiper blades
Check seat belts, buckles, retractors, anchor points and adjuster

Every 12 000 miles (20 000 km)

Engine
Check positive crankcase ventilation system
Check fuel storage evaporation emission control system
Check cylinder head bolts, manifold nuts and carburettor securing nuts for correct torque
Check operation of automatic temperature control air cleaner
Fit new distributor breaker points
Fit new spark plugs
Lubricate distributor shaft and cam
Check exhaust emission control system

Steering
Check wheel balance

Brakes
Change brake fluid

Every 24 000 miles (40 000 km)

Engine
Drain and flush cooling system. Refill with antifreeze mixture
Renew carburettor air cleaner filter (viscous paper type and dry paper type)
Check ignition wiring and coil

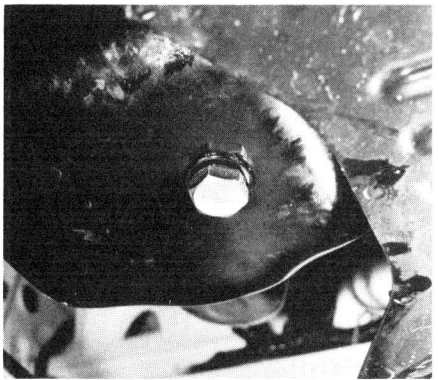
Engine sump drain plug (typical)

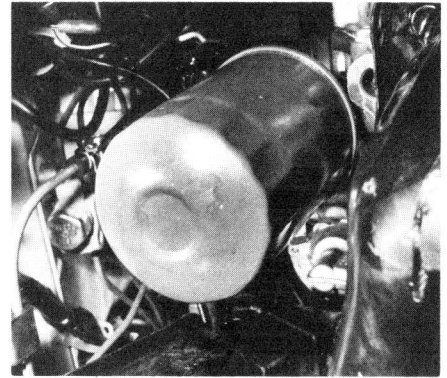
Engine oil filter (typical)

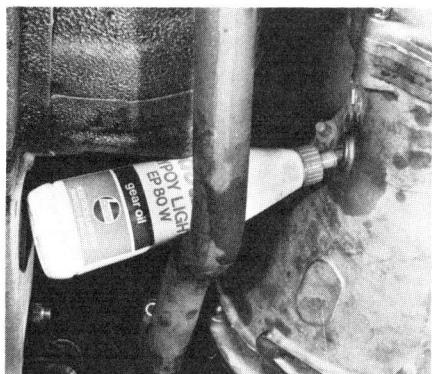
Topping-up the manual transmission

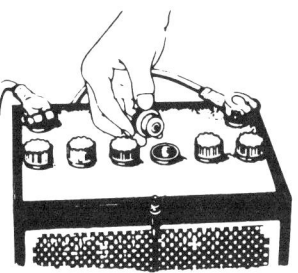
Checking battery electrolyte level

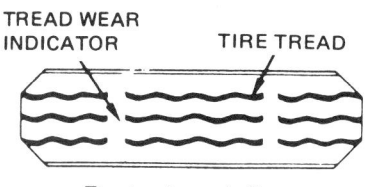
Tyre tread wear indicator

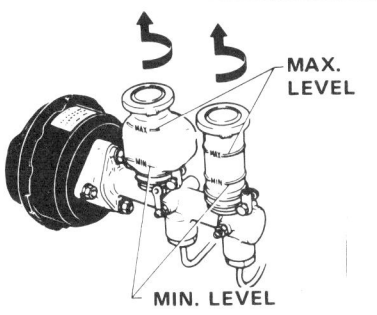
Checking hydraulic fluid level

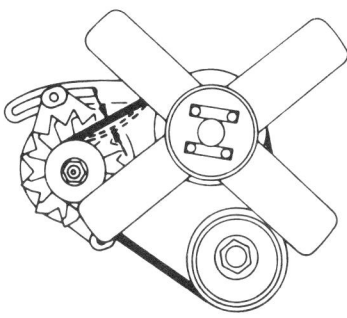
Checking fan belt tension

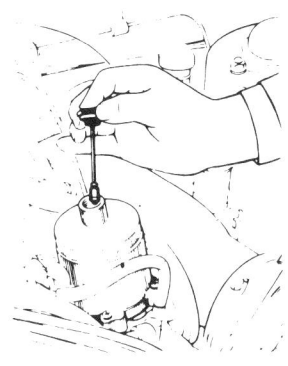
Checking carburettor oil level

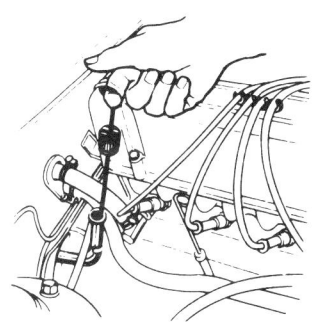
Checking automatic transmission fluid level

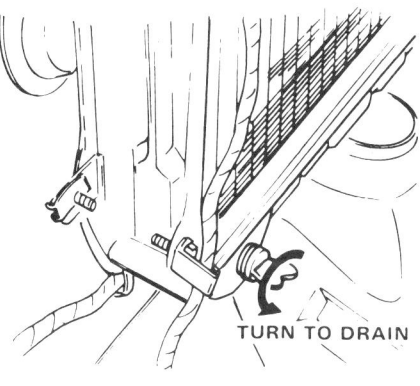
Radiator drain plug

Center lever type

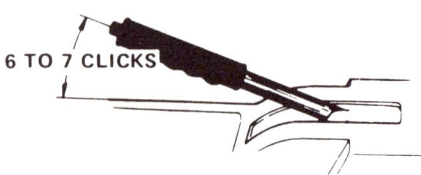

Stick lever type

Checking handbrake adjustment

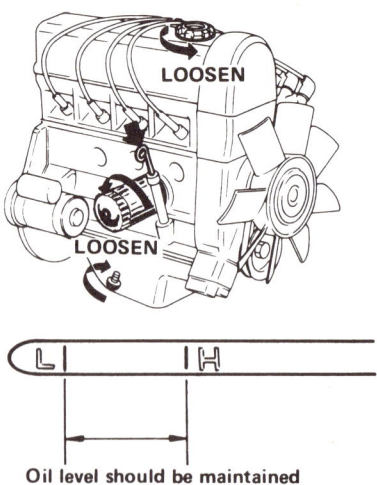

Oil level should be maintained
within this range.

Engine oil dipstick, filler cap, drain plug and filter

Rear axle oil level plug and drain plug

Renew fuel filter
Renew positive crankcase ventilation valve and filter
Renew fuel evaporative system carbon canister filter
Brakes
Change brake fluid (models with only drum brakes)
Suspension
Repack front wheel bearings with grease

Every 30 000 miles (50 000 km)

Transmission
Drain manual gearbox and refill with fresh oil
Drain differential unit and refill with fresh oil
Grease rear axle driveshaft joints
Steering
Grease steering linkage and front suspension balljoints

510 models

Every 250 miles (400 km) or weekly – whichever comes first

Engine
Check the sump oil level; top-up if necessary

Typical underbody fuel line and cable retainers

Check the radiator coolant level, top-up if necessary
Check the level of the electrolyte in the battery, top-up as
necessary
Steering
Check the tyre pressures
Examine the tyres for wear or damage
Brakes
Check the reservoir fluid level
Check the efficiency of service brake and handbrake
Lights, wipers and horns
Check that all lights work at the front and rear
Check the windscreen washer reservoir fluid level

Every 3000 miles (5000 km) or 3 months – whichever comes first
---

In hot dusty operating conditions the specified mileage intervals
between oil changes is reduced to the above mileage. Also in
these conditions, inspect the brakes system, steering and suspension components for wear and lubricate as required

---
Every 7500 miles (12 000) or 6 months – whichever occurs first
---

Engine
Renew the engine oil and filter

Inspect the exhaust system for leaks and security
Inspect the fuel lines for leaks
Steering
Check the steering gear oil level
Brakes and clutch
Inspect the brake and clutch hydraulic fluid levels and top-up if necessary
Check the brake system for leaks, excessive wear and adjust the rear brakes if necessary. Check the disc pads for wear and renew if worn beyond the specified limit
Transmission and differential
Check the automatic and manual transmission fluid level
Check the rear axle oil level

Every 15 000 miles (24 000 km) or 12 months – whichever comes first

---

Engine
Check and adjust the valve clearances
Renew the spark plugs
Check the ingition timing
Check the engine idle speed
Inspect and adjust the drivebelts
Inspect the cooling system and vacuum fitting hoses
Inspect the automatic temperature control air cleaner
Brakes
Renew the brake fluid

Check the brake lining for wear
Steering
Inspect the steering and suspension components for wear

Every 30 000 miles (48 000 km) or every 2 years – whichever comes first

---

Engine
Drain and renew the engine coolant and renew the antifreeze
Renew the fuel line filter
Check the fuel lines for security and any signs of leakage
Renew the carburettor air filter element
Emission control
Renew the air compressor filter (where fitted)
Check the emission control equipment ventilation hoses, vapour lines and the fuel tank vacuum relief valve where applicable
Renew the crankcase ventilation valve and filter
Renew the carbon canister filter
Air conditioning
Inspect the air conditioning system hoses and connections for condition and security. Look for any refrigerant leaks or defective hoses and have any suspect components checked out by your Datsun dealer or refrigeration engineer.
Steering
Check all steering and suspension joints for excess wear and grease the front wheel bearings

Chapter 1 Part A Overhead camshaft engines

Contents

Specifications

Engine (general)

Engine type	Four cylinder, in-line overhead camshaft (ohc)	
	L16	**L20B**
Displacement	1595 cc (97.3 cu in)	1952 cc (119.1 cu in)
Bore	3.27 in (83.0 mm)	3.35 in (85.0 mm)
Stroke	2.90 in (73.7 mm)	3.39 in (86.0 mm)
Compression ratio	8.5 : 1	
Firing order	1 - 3 - 4 - 2 (No 1 cylinder nearest radiator)	
Oil pressure (warm) @ 2000 rpm	50 to 57 lbf/in² (3.5 to 4.0 kgf/cm²)	

Crankshaft

Journal diameter	2.1631 to 2.1636 in (54.942 to 54.955 mm)
Max. taper or out-of-round	0.0004 in (0.01 mm)
Crankshaft endplay	0.0020 to 0.0071 in (0.05 to 0.18 mm)
Max. crankshaft endplay	0.0118 in (0.3 mm)
Crankpin diameter	1.966 to 1.967 in (49.961 to 49.974 mm)
Max. taper or out-of-round	0.0004 in (0.01 mm)
Main bearing thickness (standard)	0.0717 to 0.0722 in (1.822 to 1.835 mm)

Main bearing clearance . . . .   0.0008 to 0.0024 in (0.020 to 0.062 mm)
Max. main bearing clearance . . . .   0.0047 in (0.12 mm)
Max. permissible crankshaft bend . . . .   0.0020 in (0.05 mm)

Camshaft
Journal diameter . . . .   1.8877 to 1.8883 in (47.949 to 47.962 mm)
Bearing inner diameter . . . .   1.8898 to 1.8904 in (48.000 to 48.016 mm)
Journal to bearing clearance . . . .   0.0015 to 0.0026 in (0.038 to 0.067 mm)
Max. permissible camshaft bend . . . .   0.0007 in (0.02 mm)
Camshaft endplay . . . .   0.0032 to 0.0150 in (0.08 to 0.38 mm)
Camshaft lobe lift:
    Inlet . . . .   0.276 in (7.0 mm)
    Exhaust . . . .   0.276 in (7.0 mm)

Pistons

	L16	L20B
Piston dia. (standard)	3.2671 to 3.2691 in (82.985 to 83.035 mm)	3.3459 to 3.3478 in (84.985 to 85.035 mm)
Piston dia. (oversize 0.0197 in/0.50 mm)	3.2860 to 3.2880 in (83.465 to 83.515 mm)	3.3648 to 3.3667 in (85.465 to 85.515 mm)
Piston dia. (oversize 0.0394 in/1.00 mm)	3.3057 to 3.3077 in (83.965 to 84.015 mm)	3.3844 to 3.3864 in (85.965 to 86.015 mm)
Piston to bore clearance	0.0010 to 0.0018 in (0.025 to 0.045 mm)	0.0010 to 0.0018 in (0.025 to 0.045 mm)
Piston ring groove widths:		
Top compression	0.0787 in (2.0 mm)	0.0799 to 0.0807 in (2.030 to 2.050 mm)
Second compression	0.0787 in (2.0 mm)	0.0795 to 0.0803 in (2.020 to 2.040 mm)
Oil control	0.1575 in (4.0 mm)	0.1581 to 0.1591 in (4.015 to 4.040 mm)

Piston rings

	L16	L20B
Thickness:		
Top compression	0.0788 in (1.977 mm)	0.0778 to 0.0783 in (1.977 to 1.990 mm)
Second compression	0.0778 in (1.977 mm)	0.0776 to 0.0783 in (1.970 to 1.990 mm)
Clearance in groove:		
Top compression	0.0016 to 0.0031 in (0.040 to 0.080 mm)	0.0016 to 0.0029 in (0.040 to 0.073 mm)
Second compression	0.0012 to 0.0028 in (0.030 to 0.070 mm)	0.0012 to 0.0028 in (0.030 to 0.070 mm)
Piston ring endgap:		
Top compression	0.0098 to 0.0157 in (0.25 to 0.040 mm)	0.0098 to 0.0157 in (0.25 to 0.040 mm)
Second compression	0.0059 to 0.0118 in (0.15 to 0.30 mm)	0.0118 to 0.0197 in (0.30 to 0.50 mm)
Oil control	0.0118 to 0.0354 in (0.30 to 0.90 mm)	0.0118 to 0.0354 in 0.30 to 0.90 mm)

Gudgeon pins
Diameter . . . .   0.8265 to 0.8268 in (20.993 to 21.000 mm)
Length . . . .   2.8445 to 2.8740 in (72.25 to 73.00 mm)
Pin to piston clearance . . . .   0.0001 to 0.0006 in (0.003 to 0.015 mm)
Pin to connecting rod bushing (interference fit) . . . .   0.0006 to 0.0013 in (0.015 to 0.033 mm)

Connecting rods

	L16	L20B
Distance between centres of small-end connecting rod (big-end) bearings	5.25 in (133.0 mm)	5.748 in (146.0 mm)
Bearing thickness	0.0588 to 0.0593 in (1.493 to 1.506 mm)	0.0588 to 0.0593 in (1.493 to 1.506 mm)
Sideplay	0.0079 to 0.0118 in (0.20 to 0.30 mm)	0.0079 to 0.0118 in (0.20 to 0.30 mm)
Bearing clearance	0.0010 to 0.0022 in (0.025 to 0.055 mm)	0.0010 to 0.0022 in (0.025 to 0.055 mm)

Valves
Clearance

	L16	L20B
Cold:		
Intake	0.008 in (0.20 mm)	0.008 in (0.20 mm)
Exhaust	0.010 in (0.25 mm)	0.010 in (0.25 mm)
Warm:		
Intake	0.010 in (0.25 mm)	0.010 in (0.25 mm)
Exhaust	0.012 in (0.30 mm)	0.012 in (0.30 mm)

	L16	L20B
Valve head diameter:		
Intake	1.6535 in (42.00 mm)	1.654 to 1.661 in (42.0 to 42.2 mm)
Exhaust	1.2992 in (33.00 mm)	1.378 to 1.386 in (35.0 to 35.2 mm)
Valve stem diameter:		
Intake	0.3136 to 0.3142 in (7.965 to 7.980 mm)	0.3136 to 0.3142 in (7.965 to 7.980 mm)
Exhaust	0.3128 to 0.3134 in (7.945 to 7.960 mm)	0.3128 to 0.3134 in (7.945 to 7.960 mm)
Valve length:		
Intake	4.524 to 4.535 in (114.9 to 115.2 mm)	4.524 to 4.535 in (114.9 to 115.2 mm)
Exhaust	4.555 to 4.567 in (115.7 to 116.0 mm)	4.555 to 4.567 in (115.7 to 116.0 mm)
Valve lift:		
Intake	0.413 in (10.5 mm)	0.413 in (10.5 mm)
Exhaust	0.413 in (10.5 mm)	0.413 in (10.5 mm)
Valve spring free-length (intake and exhaust):		
Inner	1.766 in (44.85 mm)	1.766 in (44.85 mm)
Outer	1.968 in (49.98 mm)	1.968 (49.98 mm)
Valve spring coil dia:		
Intake		
Inner	0.862 in (21.9 mm)	0.953 in (24.2 mm)
Outer	1.157 in (29.4 mm)	1.150 in (29.4 mm)
Exhaust:		
Inner	0.862 in (21.9 mm)	0.0953 in (24.2 mm)
Outer	1.157 in (29.4 mm)	1.150 in (29.4 mm)
Valve guide length	2.323 in (59.0 mm)	2.323 in (59.0 mm)
Valve guide height from surface of cylinder head	0.417 in (10.6 mm)	0.417 in (10.6 mm)
Valve guide inner diameter	0.3150 to 0.3154 in (8.000 to 8.018 mm)	0.3150 to 0.3154 in (8.000 to 8.018 mm)
Valve guide outer diameter	0.4733 to 0.4738 in (12.023 to 12.034 mm)	0.4812 to 0.4817 in (12.223 to 12.234 mm)
Valve stem to guide clearance:		
Intake	0.0008 to 0.0021 in (0.020 to 0.53 mm)	0.0008 to 0.0021 in (0.020 to 0.53 mm)
Exhaust	0.0016 to 0.0029 in (0.0040 to 0.0073 mm)	0.0016 to 0.0029 in (0.0040 to 0.0073 mm)
Seat width:		
Intake	0.055 in 1.4 mm	0.0551 to 0.0630 in 1.4 to 1.6 mm
Exhaust	0.0512 in 1.3 mm	0.0709 to 0.0866 in 1.8 to 2.2 mm
Seat angle (inlet and exhaust)	45°	45°
Valve seat interference fit:		
Intake	0.0032 to 0.0044 in (0.081 to 0.113 mm)	0.0032 to 0.0044 in (0.081 to 0.113 mm)
Exhaust	0.0025 to 0.0038 in (0.064 to 0.096 mm)	0.0025 to 0.0038 in (0.064 to 0.096 mm)
Valve guide interference fit	0.0011 to 0.0019 in (0.027 to 0.049mm)	0.0011 to 0.0019 in (0.027 to 0.049 mm)

Engine lubrication (L16, L20B)

	Standard tolerance	Wear limit
Oil pump:		
Rotor side clearance (outer to inner rotor)	0.0016 to 0.0032 in (0.04 to 0.08 mm)	0.0079 in (0.20 mm)
Maximum rotor tip clearance	0.0047 in (0.12 mm)	0.0079 in (0.20 mm)
Outer rotor to body clearance	0.0059 to 0.0083 in (0.15 to 0.21 mm)	0.0197 in (0.5 mm)
Rotor to bottom cover clearance	0.0012 to 0.0051 in (0.03 to 0.13 mm)	0.0079 in (0.20 mm)
Oil pressure regulator valve:		
Oil pressure at idling	11 to 40 lbf/in² (0.8 to 2.8 kgf/cm²)	11 to 40 lbf/in² (0.8 to 2.8 kgf/cm²)
Regulator valve spring:		
Free length	2.067 in (52.5 mm)	2.067 in (52.5 mm)

Regulator valve opening pressure	50 to 71 lbf/in² (3.5 to 5.0 kgf/cm²)	50 to 71 lbf/in² (3.5 to 5.0 kgf/cm²)
Oil pressure warning light illuminates at	5.7 to 8.5 lbf/in² (0.4 to 0.6 kgf/cm²)	5.7 to 8.5 lbf/in² (0.4 to 0.6 kgf/cm²)

Torque wrench settings

	lbf ft	kgf m
Cylinder head bolts	60	8.3
Connecting rod big-end nuts	40	5.5
Flywheel bolts	110	15.2
Main bearing cap bolts	40	5.5
Camshaft sprocket bolt	85	11.8
Sump drain plug	20	2.8
Rocker pivot locknuts	40	5.5
Carburettor mounting nuts	40	5.5
Crankshaft pulley bolt	100	13.8
Clutch housing to engine bolts	35	4.8
Torque connector housing to engine bolts	35	4.8
Driveplate to torque connector	35	4.8
Clutch to flywheel bolts	20	2.8
Cylinder block reinforcement plate	24	3.3
Engine front mounting to bracket	20	2.8
Engine front mounting bracket to crankcase	20	2.8
Rear mounting crossmember to bodyframe	20	2.8
Oil pump bolts	9.4	1.3
Oil pump cover bolt	6.1	0.85
Oil pump regulator valve cap nut	33	4.6

1 General description

Both the L16 and L20 type engines are of the four cylinder in-line type, with valve operation by means of an overhead camshaft.

The cast iron cylinder block contains the four bores and acts as a rigid support for the five bearing crankshaft. The machined cylinder bores are surrounded by water jackets to dissipate heat and control operating temperatures.

A disposable oil filter is located on the right-hand side of the cylinder block and supplies clean oil to the main gallery and various oilways. The main bearings are lubricated from oil holes, which run parallel with the cylinder bores. The forged steel crankshaft is suitably drilled for directing lubricating oil so ensuring full bearing lubrication.

To lubricate the connecting rod small-end, drillings are located in the big-ends of the rods so that the oil is squirted upwards.

Crankshaft endfloat is controlled by thrust washers located at the centre main bearings.

The pistons are of a special aluminium casting with struts to control thermal expansion. There are two compression and one oil control ring. The gudgeon pin is a hollow steel shaft which is fully floating in the piston, and a press fit in the connecting rod small-end. The pistons are attached to the crankshaft via forged steel connecting rods.

The cylinder head is of aluminium and incorporates wedge type combustion chambers. A special aluminium bronze valve seat is used for the inlet valve whilst a steel exhaust valve seat is fitted.

Located on the top of the cylinder head is the cast iron camshaft which is supported in four aluminium alloy brackets. The camshaft bearings are lubricated from drillings which lead from the main oil gallery in the cylinder head.

The supply of oil to each cam lobe is through an oil hole drilled in the base circle of each lobe. The actual oil supply is to the front oil gallery from the 3rd camshaft bearing. These holes on the base circle of the lobe supply oil to the cam pad surface of the rocker arm and to the valve tip end.

Two valves per cylinder are mounted at a slight angle in the cylinder head and are actuated by a pivot type rocker arm in direct contact with the cam mechanism. Double springs are fitted to each valve.

The camshaft is driven by a double row collar chain from the front of the crankshaft. Chain tension is controlled by a tensioner which is operated by oil and spring pressure. The rubber shoe type tensioner controls vibration and tension of the chain.

On L20 engine models fitted with an air conditioning system, special care must be taken before dismantling or removing any part of the system circuit. Contact your Datsun dealer or refrigeration engineer who has the specialised knowledge and equipment required to depressurize the system before any engine overhauls are undertaken that necessitate the removal of part of the air conditioning system. *Never* disconnect any of the air conditioning supply lines until they are depressurized! Do *not* heat or weld in the vicinity of the supply lines. Do *not* bend or distort the supply lines.

2 Major operations possible with the engine fitted

1 Removal and refitting of the cylinder head.
2 Removal and refitting of the oil pump unit.
3 Removal and refitting of timing cover, timing chain and sprockets and tensioner.
4 Removal and refitting of the camshaft (after removing the cylinder head).

3 Major operations only possible on removal of the engine

1 Renewal of the crankshaft main bearings.
2 Removal and refitting of the crankshaft.
3 Removal and refitting the sump, pistons and connecting rods.

4 Engine – method of removal

1 The engine can be removed from the vehicle either on its own or as a combined unit with the gearbox.
2 Although depending on the work to be carried out, it is usually preferable to remove the engine/transmission combined as it is easier to separate them out of the car.
3 Lifting tackle of suitable capacity will be required and if removing both engine and transmission combined, allow for sufficient height when at full lift as they must be tilted to clear the bulkhead tunnel and front radiator attachment panel.

5 Engine and transmission – removal

1 Disconnect the battery cables.
2 Mark the bonnet hinge location on the underside using a soft lead pencil. This will assist in correctly realigning it on assembly.
3 Drain the radiator coolant, referring to Chapter 2 if necessary. If the engine is to be dismantled, the engine oil must be drained at this stage.
4 Disconnect the upper and lower coolant hoses from the engine/radiator connections.
5 On automatic transmission models, detach the lower splash panel

and disconnect the oil cooler hoses from their installation at the lower end of the radiator. Drain the automatic transmission fluid (see Chapter 6).

6   Where applicable remove the radiator shroud.

7   Disconnect and carefully remove the radiator and grille (see Chapter 2).

8   Detach the air cleaner hoses and withdraw the air cleaner.

9   The following wires must be disconnected but make a note of their respective locations so that there is no confusion on reassembly:

    (a)   Starter motor wires and cable from the battery
    (b)   Ignition coil to distributor HT lead
    (c)   Distributor lead at the body terminal, and also the earth wire to the terminal on the vacuum diaphragm retaining screw. The wires are the same colour so label them to differentiate
    (d)   The oil pressure switch wire which is located on the filter unit
    (e)   The alternator wires, and the carburettor choke wire (when fitted)
    (f)   The temperature gauge wire from the front of the cylinder head at the right-hand side
    (g)   The engine earth cable from the front bolt retaining the oil filter unit
    (h)   From underneath the car, disconnect the reverse light switch wire from the transmission terminal, and on automatic transmission models, detach the inhibitor switch and down-shift solenoid wires.

10   On models fitted with Emission Control equipment the following items must also be disconnected:

    (a)   Detach the automatic choke heater wire
    (b)   On air conditioned models disconnect the fast idle control device (FICD) magnet valve hose at the dashpot and the three way connector
    (c)   Detach the combined air control (CAC) valve hose on California models, or the air control valve hose on other models (except Canada)
    (d)   The air pump air cleaner hose
    (e)   The boost controlled deceleration device (BCDD) vacuum control valve hose on California models
    (f)   The carbon cannister hose on the engine connection

11   Disconnect the heater hoses, (inlet and outlet), and the Master-Vac vacuum hose from the inlet manifold (where applicable).

12   Disconnect the fuel hose from the fuel pump and plug or clamp it to prevent spillage or the ingress of dirt. Tie back out of the way to prevent damaging.

13   Detach and withdraw the accelerator linkage from its bracket.

14   On models fitted with a mechanically operated clutch disconnect the cable from the withdrawal lever at the clutch housing. On models fitted with a hydraulically operated clutch, disconnect the slave cylinder (operating cylinder) from the clutch housing. Further information on both systems is given in Chapter 5.

15   On models fitted with air conditioning equipment, slacken the compressor drivebelt idler pulley nut and bolt and with the tension released, remove the drivebelt. Unscrew and remove the compressor securing bolts and relocate the compressor away from the engine so that it will not get in the way during engine withdrawal. Do *not* under any circumstances detach the hoses or allow the gas to discharge from the system.

16   The following operations are carried out underneath the car and therefore it must be over a work pit or raised sufficiently clear of the ground to enable the respective components to be disconnected. Do not rely purely on the jack supplied with the car – supplement with axle-stands and/or suitable blocks to make secure.

17   Unscrew and detach the speedometer cable from its location in the transmission.

18   Detach the manual or automatic transmission control lever or linkage as applicable, refer to Chapter 6 if necessary.

19   Unscrew the exhaust pipe to manifold flange nuts and detach the pipe, secure it safely to one side using a piece of wire.

20   Scribe a matching mark across the flange faces of the propeller shaft and companion flange joints to ensure correct alignment on reassembly. Now detach the propeller shaft from the differential carrier companion flange.

21   On propeller shafts fitted with centre bearings, support the propeller shaft and unscrew the centre bearing bracket retaining bolts.

22   Lower the propeller shaft at the rear and withdraw it rearwards

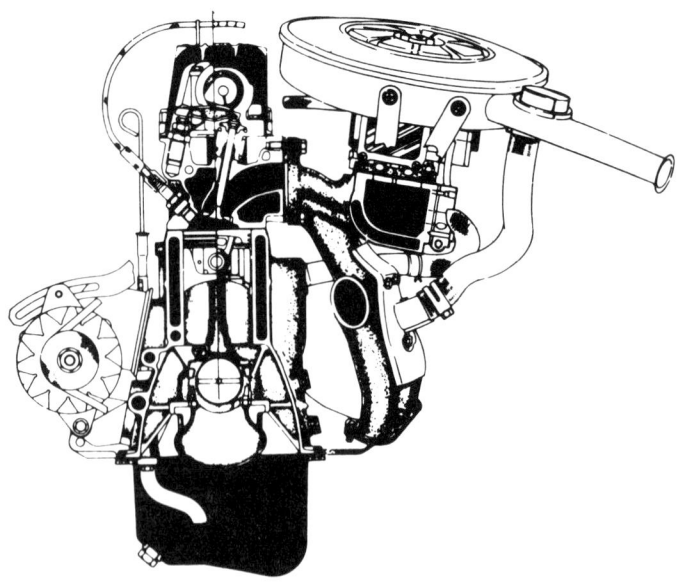

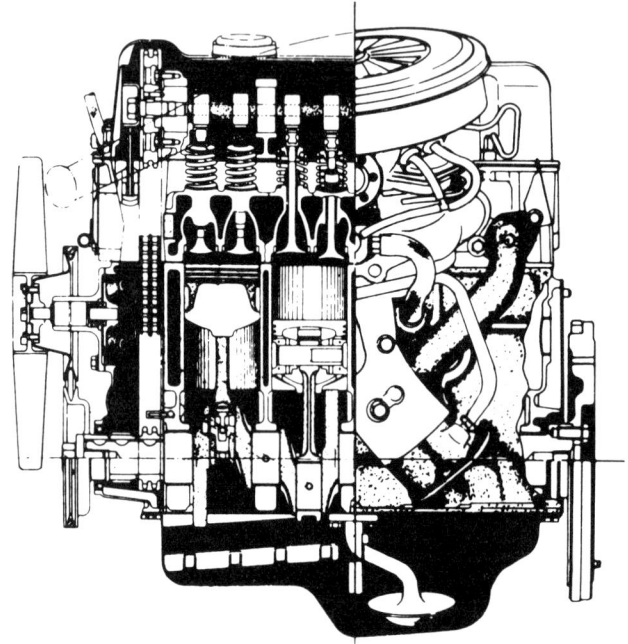

Fig. 1.1 Sectional views of OHC engine

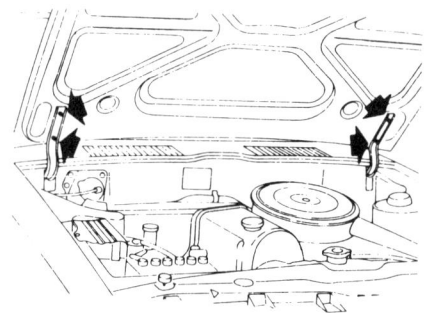

Fig. 1.2 Bonnet attachment bolts (arrowed)

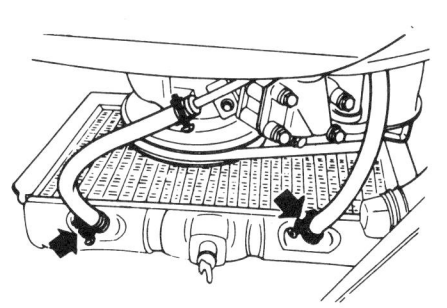

Fig. 1.3 Disconnect the oil cooler hoses

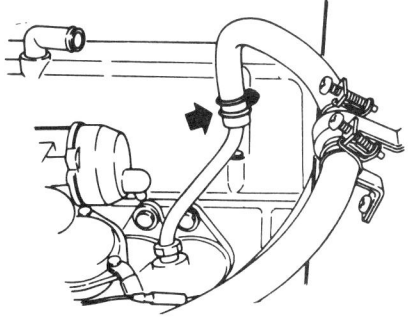

Fig. 1.4 Disconnect the Master-Vac hose

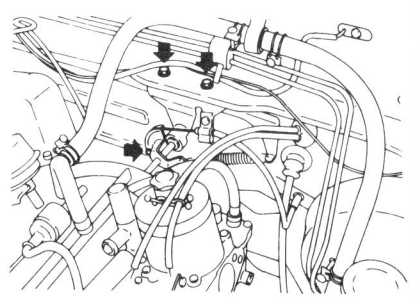

Fig. 1.5 Detach the accelerator linkage

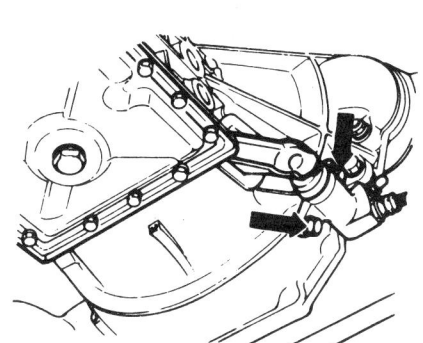

Fig. 1.6 Disconnect the clutch slave cylinder

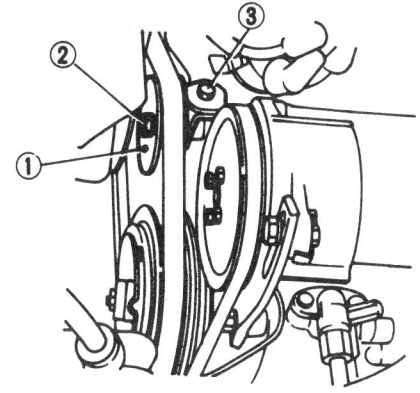

Fig. 1.7 The compressor drivebelt pulley

1 Idler pulley   3 Adjustment
2 Idler pulley   bolt
   locknut

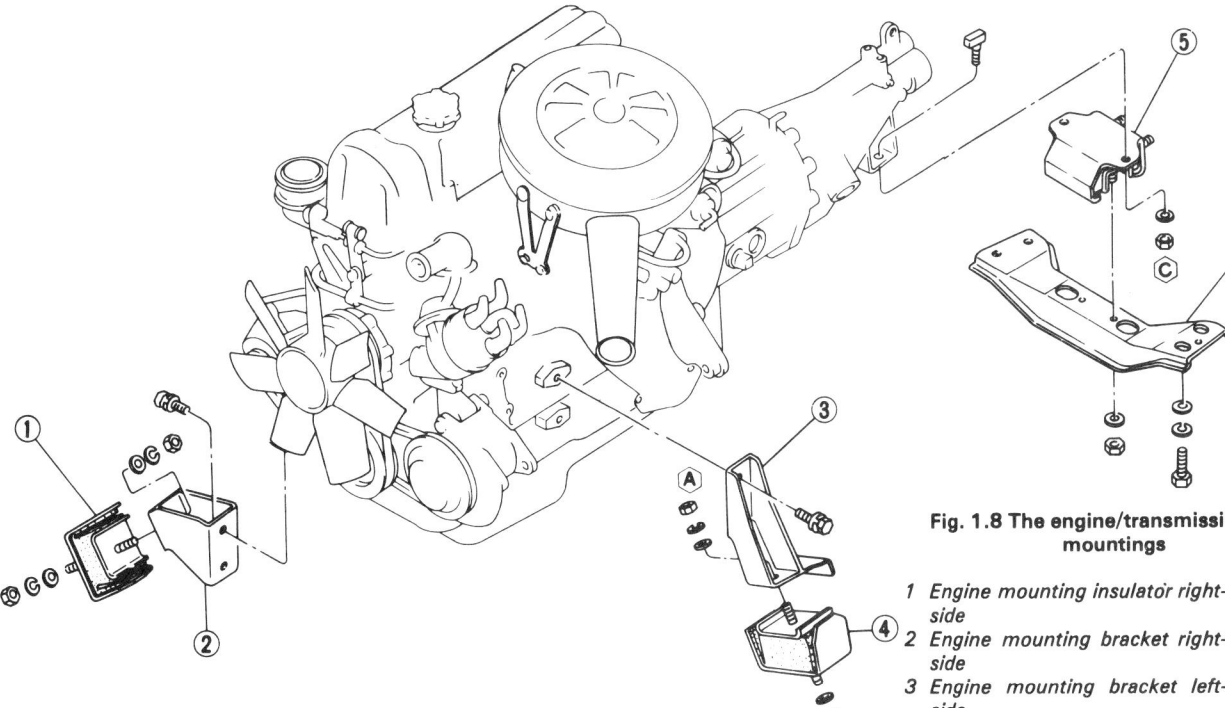

Fig. 1.8 The engine/transmission
mountings

1 Engine mounting insulator right-hand
   side
2 Engine mounting bracket right-hand
   side
3 Engine mounting bracket left-hand
   side
4 Engine mounting insulator left-hand
   side
5 Transmission mounting insulator
6 Transmission mounting bracket

from the gearbox extension housing to remove. Plug the end of the extension housing or locate a plastic bag over the end to prevent oil spillage, especially during removal.

23 Position a jack under the transmission and raise to just support it.

24 Unscrew and remove the bolts/nuts securing the transmission supporting crossmember and remove it. Note the respective bolt positions and lengths.

25 Carefully locate the lifting sling around the engine and arrange it so that the front of the engine can be 'hinged' upwards to provide the necessary angle required for the removal of the engine and transmission unit. Raise the engine just sufficiently to allow the weight to be relieved from the engine mountings and then remove the nuts/bolts from the insulators.

26 Before lifting the engine/transmission units check that all adjacent and interconnecting fittings and attachments are free and clear of the engine.

27 Raise the engine slowly and tilt it to enable the front end and sump to clear the radiator crossmember and the transmission to clear the bulkhead tunnel. When clear of the car, lower the engine/transmission and remove to a workbench or clean floor area so that the respective ancillary components can be removed as necessary.

---

6 Engine – separation from manual transmission

1 With the engine and transmission now removed from the vehicle, unscrew and remove the bolts which connect the clutch bellhousing to the engine block.

2 Unbolt and remove the starter motor.

3 Pull the transmission from the engine in a straight line, at the same time supporting the transmission so that its weight does not hang up on the primary shaft, even momentarily, whilst the shaft is still engaged with the clutch mechanism.

4 It is recommended that the clutch is removed also at this stage if the engine is undergoing repair. This is to prevent contamination by cleaning solvents when cleaning the engine (Section 8). Refer to Chapter 5 for further information on clutch removal.

---

7 Engine – separation from automatic transmission

1 Remove the rubber plug from the lower part of the engine rear plate.

2 Unscrew and remove the bolts which secure the driveplate to the torque converter. The crankshaft will have to be turned by means of

the pulley bolt so that each driveplate comes into view in turn.

3 With all the driveplate bolts removed, mark the relative position of the driveplate to the torque converter. This is best achieved by placing a dab of coloured paint around one bolt hole in the driveplate and also on the torque converter hole top threads.

4 Remove the starter motor and the fluid filler tube support bolt.

5 Unscrew and remove the bolts which secure the torque converter housing to the engine.

6 Withdraw the automatic transmission in a straight line; expect some loss of fluid as the torque converter moves away from the driveplate.

---

8 Engine dismantling – general

1 It is best to mount the engine on a dismantling stand but if one is not available, then stand the engine on a strong bench so as to be at a comfortable working height. Failing this, the engine can be stripped down on the floor.

2 During the dismantling process the greatest care should be taken to keep the exposed parts free from dirt. As an aid to achieving this, it is a sound scheme to thoroughly clean down the outside of the engine removing all traces of oil and congealed dirt.

3 Use paraffin or a good grease solvent. The latter compound will make the job much easier, as, after the solvent has been applied and allowed to stand for a time, a vigorous jet of water will wash off the solvent and all the grease and filth. If the dirt is thick and deeply embedded, work the solvent into it with a wire brush.

4 Finally wipe down the exterior of the engine with a rag and only then, when it is quite clean should the dismantling process begin. As the engine is stripped, clean each part in a bath of paraffin.

5 Never immerse parts with oilways in paraffin (eg the crankshaft) but to clean, wipe down carefully with a paraffin dampened rag. Oilways can be cleaned out with wire. If an air-line is present all parts can be blown dry and the oilways blown through as an added precaution.

6 Re-use of old engine gaskets is false economy and can give rise to oil and water leaks, if nothing worse. To avoid the possibility of trouble after the engine has been reassembled always use new gaskets throughout.

7 Do not throw old gaskets away as it sometimes happens that an immediate replacement cannot be found and the old gasket is then very useful as a template for making up a replacement. Hang up the old gaskets as they are removed on a suitable hook or nail.

8 To strip the engine it is best to work from the top down. The oil sump provides a firm base on which the engine can be supported in an

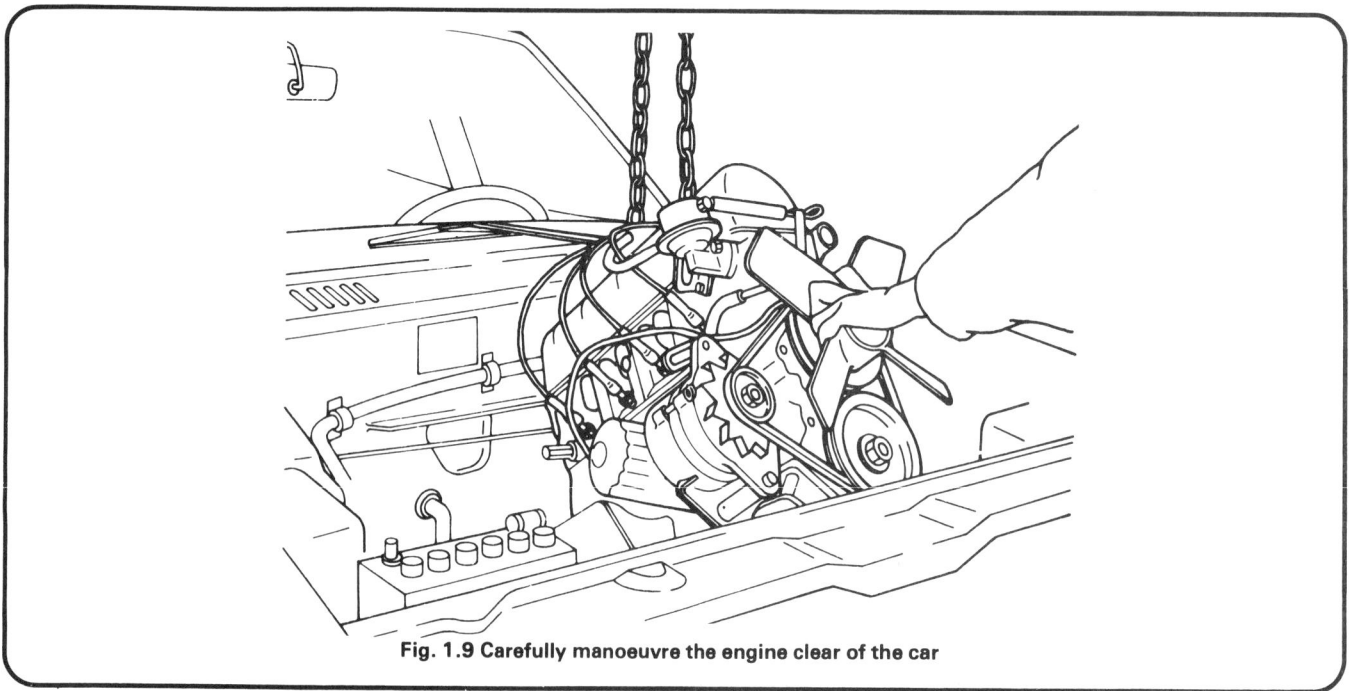

Fig. 1.9 Carefully manoeuvre the engine clear of the car

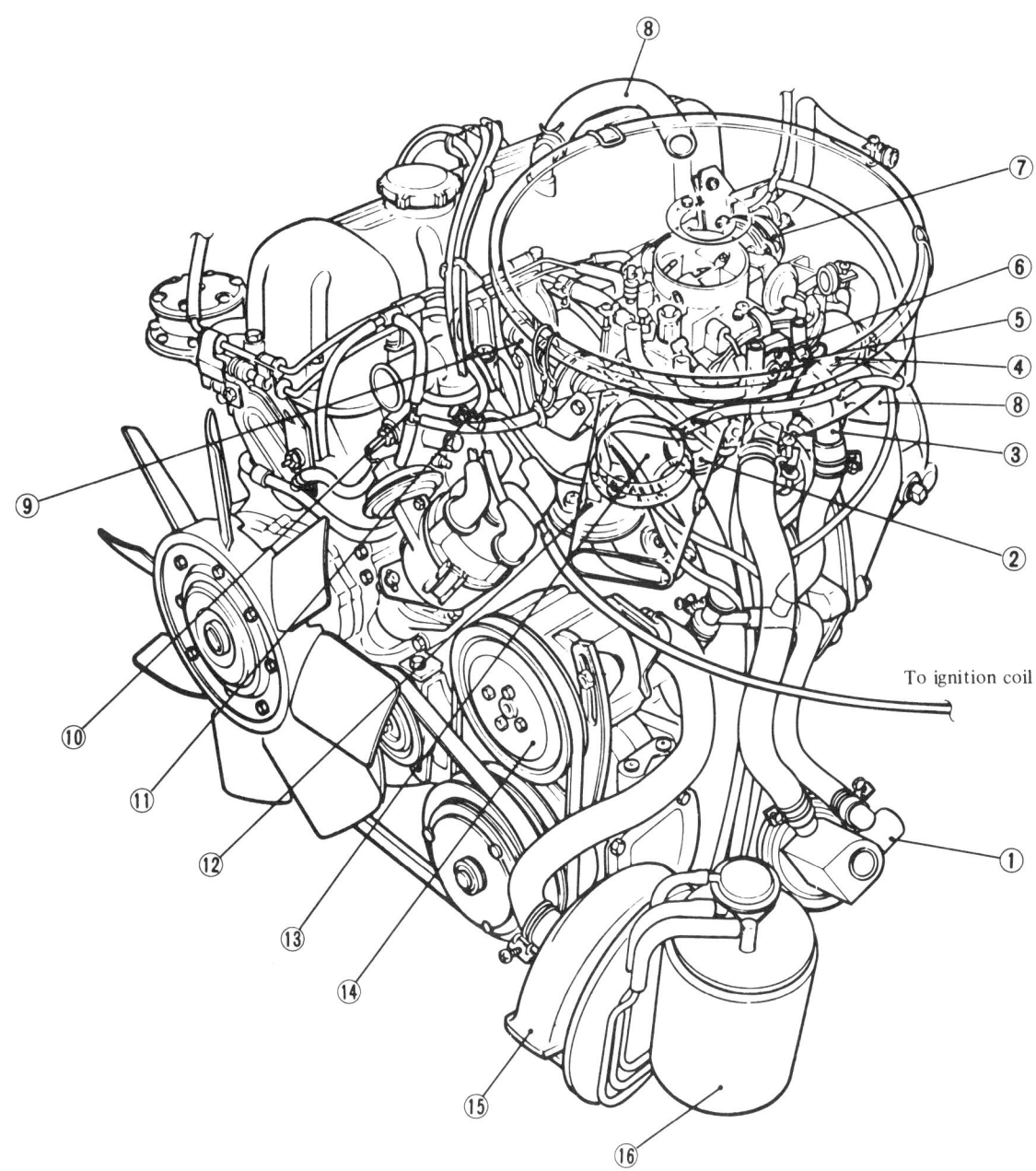

To ignition coil

Fig. 1.10 Emission control system component locations – Non-California models shown

1 Air control valve	7 Auto-choke	12 BPT valve
2 EGR control valve	8 PCV hose	13 ATC air cleaner
3 Air relief valve	9 Check valve (for AIS)	14 Air pump for AIS
4 AB valve	10 3-way connector (Manual	15 Air pump air cleaner
5 BCDD solenoid valve	transmission models)	16 Canister
6 BCDD	11 Thermal vacuum valve	

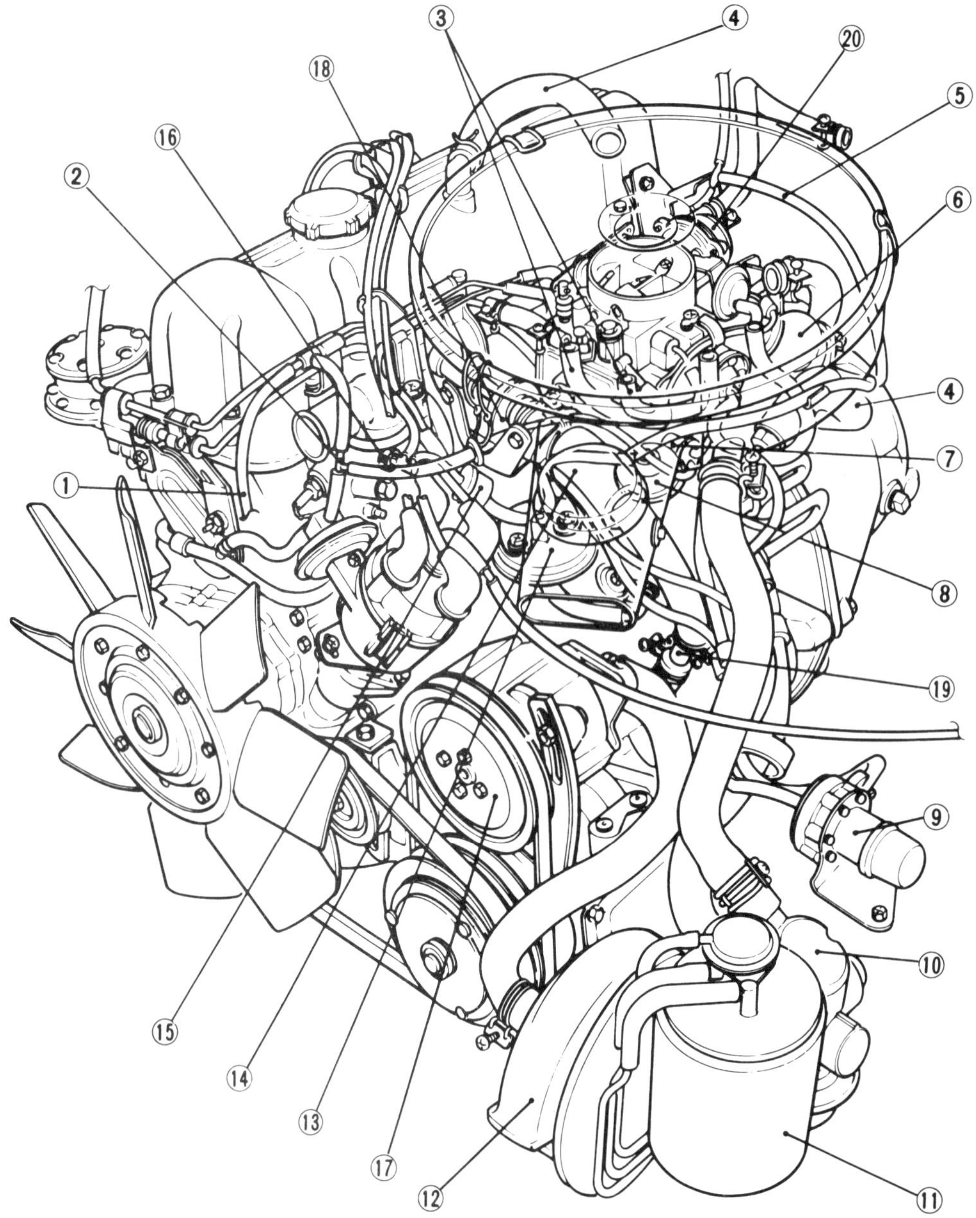

Fig. 1.11 Emission control system component locations – California model

1	Vacuum tube for carbon canister	
2	3-way connector (Manual transmission)	
3	Altitude compensator hose	
4	PCV hose	
5	Vacuum tube for AB valve	
6	AB valve	

7	Vacuum switching valve (Manual transmission)
8	EGR control valve
9	BCDD vacuum control valve
10	CAC valve
11	Carbon canister
12	Air pump air cleaner

13	BPT valve
14	ATC air cleaner
15	Vacuum delay valve
16	Thermal vacuum valve
17	Air pump for AIS
18	Check valve (For AIS)
19	3-way connector for AIS
20	Auto-choke

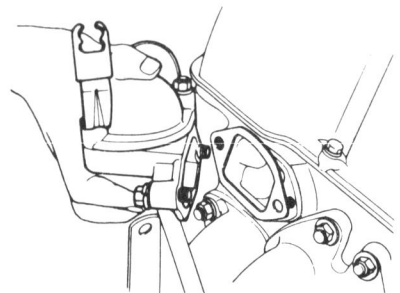

Fig. 1.12 Remove the thermostat

upright position. When the sump stage where the sump must be removed is reached, the engine can be turned on its side and all other work carried out with it in this position.

9 Wherever possible refit nuts, bolts and washers fingertight from wherever they were removed. This helps avoid later loss and muddle. If they cannot be refitted then lay them out in such a fashion that it is clear from where they came.

10 Even though the engine may not have to be completely dismantled, it is a good system to clean it thoroughly whilst removed from the car.

9 Ancillary components – removal

1 If you are stripping the engine completely or preparing to fit a reconditioned unit, all the ancillaries must be removed first. If you are going to obtain a reconditioned 'short' motor (block, crankshaft, pistons and connecting rods) then obviously the cam, cylinder head and associated parts will need retention for fitting to the new engine. It is advisable to check just what you will get with a reconditioned unit as changes are made from time to time.

2 Remove the fan assembly, noting that the shallow recess of the fan boss faces the radiator.

3 Remove the right-hand engine mounting bracket.

4 Unscrew and remove the oil filter and discard it. The use of a chain wrench or similar tool wrench or similar tool will probably be required to remove the filter.

5 Unscrew and remove the oil pressure switch.

6 Withdraw the engine oil dipstick.

7 Unscrew the crankshaft pulley bolt. To prevent the engine turning during this operation, jam the flywheel starter ring gear by passing a sharp cold chisel or large screwdriver through the starter motor aperture in the engine rearplate.

8 Withdraw the crankshaft pulley. The insertion of two tyre levers behind the pulley will usually extract the pulley but if it is exceptionally tight, use an extractor but take care not to distort the rims of the pulley.

9 Disconnect the HT leads from the spark plugs then remove the distributor cap complete with leads.

10 Unscrew and remove the spark plugs.

11 The next step is to detach the fuel, water, air and suction hoses. These vary considerably on the different engines and the only satisfactory way of doing the job is to attach identity labels so that refitting can be readily carried out. The connections will typically be:

(a) *Crankcase PCV hoses*
(b) *Fuel pump-to-carburettor hose*
(c) *Rocker cover-to-air cleaner hose*
(d) *Intake manifold water hoses*
(e) *Vacuum tube to carburettor hoses*
(f) *Air control valve hoses*
(g) *EGR valve vacuum hose*
(h) *EGR tube*
(i) *Anti-backfire valve hose*

12 Having removed the hoses, the associated emission control or engine ancillary items can be removed. Typically these will be:

(a) *EGR valve, tube and passage (Fig. 1.10 and 1.11)*
(b) *Fuel pump*
(c) *Air pump and idler pulley*
(d) *PCV valve*
(e) *Dashpot bracket*
(f) *Check valve*
(g) *Air control valve (Fig. 1.12)*

13 Remove the thermostat housing.

14 Unbolt and remove the manifold assemblies complete with carburettor.

15 Remove the engine left-hand mounting bracket.

16 Remove the water pump.

17 Unscrew and remove the distributor clamp plate bolt from the crankcase and withdraw the distributor from its recess. Refer to Chapter 4 for further information.

18 Remove the rocker cover.

19 The engine should now be stripped of its ancillary components, and dismantling proper may be carried out as described in Section 10 onwards.

10 Cylinder head – removal

1 If the cylinder head is to be removed with the engine in the car, then the following procedures must first be carried out:

(a) *Disconnect the battery*
(b) *Drain the radiator*
(c) *Remove all HT leads from the rocker cover*
(d) *Remove all connections to the carburettor and remove the air cleaner assembly*
(e) *Remove the exhaust downpipe from the exhaust manifold*
(f) *Remove all hoses connected to the cylinder head*
(g) *Remove the crankcase ventilation hose from the inlet manifold*
(h) *Remove the rocker cover*
(i) *Remove the two bolts which secure the cylinder head to the timing chain cover*

2 Position the crankshaft at TDC with no. 1 piston on the compression stroke and the timing chain and camshaft sprocket relative positions marked, to ensure correct reassembly. It is also most important to ensure that when removing the cylinder head that tension is maintained on the timing chain so that it does not become disengaged from the crankshaft sprocket. A long tapering wooden wedge can also be inserted to overcome the pressure of the chain tensioner. Should the timing chain become disengaged from the crankshaft sprocket, then the timing cover will have to be removed to correctly refit the chain.

3 From the front of the camshaft, remove the centre bolt and withdraw the fuel pump eccentric cam.

4 Remove the camshaft sprocket complete with chain from the camshaft. Slip the sprocket out of the loop of the timing chain and then support the timing chain with a piece of wire pending removal of the cylinder head.

5 Unscrew and remove the cylinder head bolts in the sequence shown. **Do not unscrew the camshaft bearing housing bolts by mistake** (Fig. 1.14).

Note: *A special tool may be required (tool no ST10120000) to remove and refit the cylinder head bolts. Alternatively, one can be made up from a 10 mm AF hexagon wrench (Allen key) suitably adapted for use with a standard torque wrench.*

11 Camshaft – removal

1 If the engine is still in the car remove the cylinder head as described in Section 10. If the engine has been removed from the car remove the camshaft sprocket.

2 Extract the valve rocker springs by lifting them from the rocker arm grooves.

3 Release the pivot locknuts and unscrew the pivots.

4 Compress each valve spring in turn using a large screwdriver and withdraw the rocker arms, taking care to retain the rocker guides (photo).

5 Remove the camshaft locating plate and withdraw the camshaft, taking care not to damage the bearings as the camshaft lobes pass through them. **Note:** *On no account screw the camshaft bearing housing bolts. The bearings are line-bored and alignment will be ruined if they are disturbed.*

12 Engine sump, timing gear and oil pump – removal

1 With the engine upside-down standing on the top face of the cylinder block, unbolt and remove the sump.

2 Unbolt and remove the oil pick-up tube and screen.

3 Unbolt the oil pump and withdraw it complete with the drive spindle.

4 Unbolt and remove the timing cover.

5 Unbolt and remove the timing chain tensioner and guide.

6 Remove the timing chain.

7 From the crankshaft front end, remove the oil thrower and the oil pump worm drivegear, then draw off the crankshaft sprocket (photo).

13 Piston/connecting rod assemblies – removal

1 Examine the big-end bearing caps and connecting rods. They

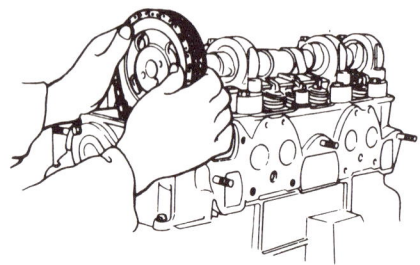

Fig. 1.13 Disengaging the camshaft sprocket

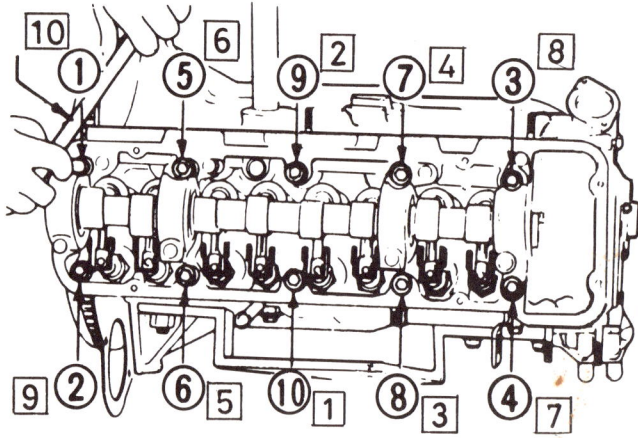

Fig. 1.14 The cylinder head bolt loosening/tightening sequence

Loosening sequence ◯   *Tightening sequence* ▢

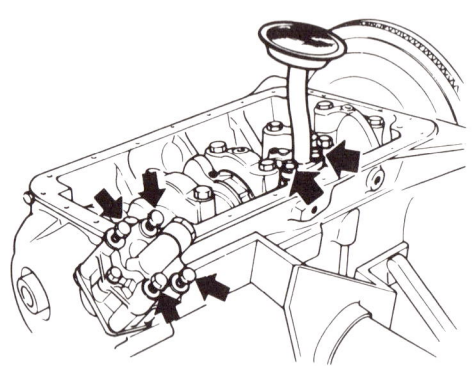

Fig. 1.15 The pick-up tube, strainer and coil pump retaining bolts

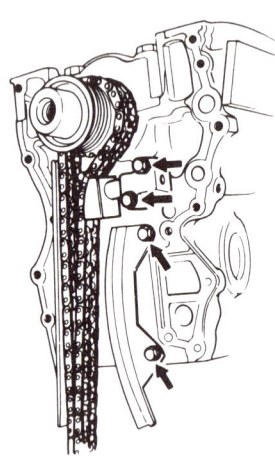

Fig. 1.16 Remove the tensioner and timing chain guide

11.4 Removing rocker arms

12.7 Removing the crankshaft sprocket

should be match-marked from 1 to 4 from the front of the engine. If they are not, dot punch the caps and rods at adjacent points, noting carefully to which side of the engine the numbers or punch marks face so that they can be refitted in their same original relative positions.

2   Unbolt No. 1 big-end (connecting the rod bearings) cap and, using the wooden handle of a hammer, carefully tap the piston/connecting rod assembly from the top of the cylinder bore. It is unlikely that the original shell bearings will be used again but should this be the case, retain them in exact order, identifying them in respect of connecting rod and cap sections.

3   Extract the remaining three piston/connecting rod assemblies.

14 Flywheel (or driveplate – automatic transmission) – removal

1   Mark the position of the flywheel in relation to the crankshaft flange and unbolt the flywheel.

2   In order to prevent the flywheel from turning while the securing bolts are being unscrewed, wedge one of the crankshaft webs with a piece of wood.

15 Crankshaft and main bearings – removal

1   Examine the main bearing caps for numbers and directional fitting arrows. If they are not marked, dot punch them 1 to 5 from the front of the engine and note which way round the caps are fitted. The centre main bearing incorporates thrust washers.

2   Unbolt and remove each of the main bearing caps. The centre and rear caps may be very tight and will require tapping out or the use of an extractor, a threaded hole being provided for the purpose.

3   Extract the side seals from the rear bearing cap also the crankshaft rear oil seal. Note which way round they are fitted.

4   Lift the crankshaft from the crankcase. It is unlikely that the original shell bearings will be used again but should this be the case, retain them in the exact order, identifying them in respect of crankcase and cap sections.

5   Remove the baffle plate and mesh block which is part of the crankcase breather system.

16 Piston rings - removal

1   Each ring should be sprung open only just sufficient to permit it to ride over the lands of the piston body.

2   Once a ring is out of its groove, it is helpful to cut three $\frac{1}{4}$ in (6 mm) wide strips of tin and slip them under the ring at equidistant points.

3   Using a twisting motion this method of removal will prevent the ring dropping into an empty groove as it is being removed from the piston.

17 Gudgeon pin – removal

1   The gudgeon pins are a finger pressure fit (at room temperature) in the pistons but are an interference fit in the connecting rod small-end.

2   It is recommended that the removal of the gudgeon pins is left to a local dealer having a suitable press.

3   Where such facilities are available to the home mechanic, the body of the piston must be supported on a suitably shaped distance piece into which the gudgeon pin may be ejected. Ensure that each gudgeon pin remains with its correct piston.

18 Lubrication system – description

Oil is drawn from the engine sump through an oil strainer by a trochoid-type oil pump. This is driven by a spindle which in turn is driven from the crankshaft. The upper end of the spindle drives the distributor. Oil is passed under pressure through a renewable canister type oil filter and onto the main oil gallery. It is then distributed to all the crankshaft bearings, chain tensioner and timing chain. The oil that is supplied to the crankshaft is fed to the connecting rod big-end bearings via drilled passages in the crankshaft. The connection rod little-

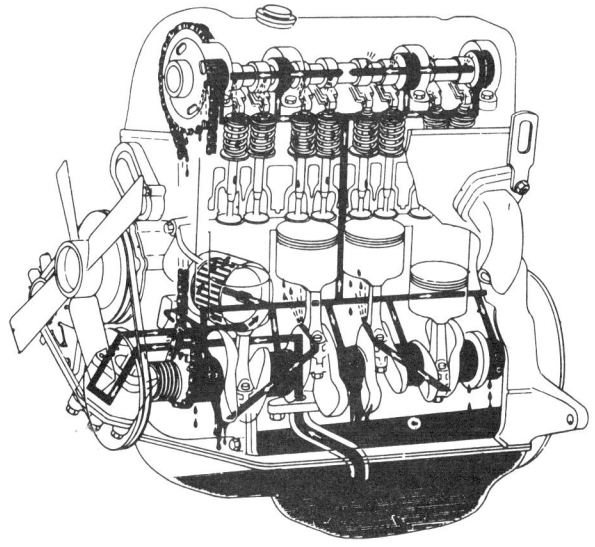

Fig. 1.17 The engine lubrication circuit

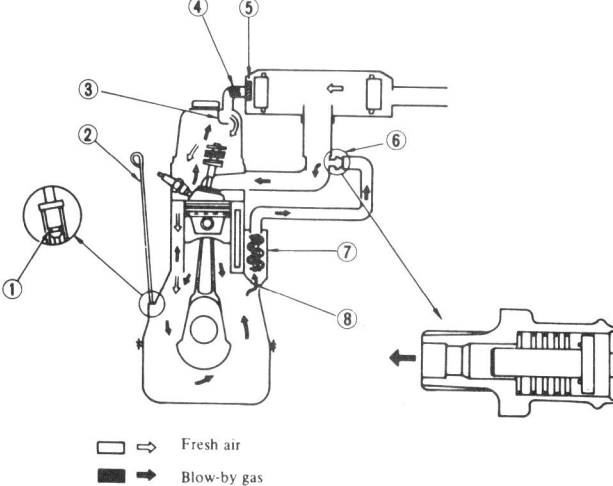

Fig. 1.18 Crankcase emission control system – typical

⬜ ⇨   Fresh air
⬛ ➡   Blow-by gas

1	O-ring	5	Filter
2	Dipstick	6	PCV valve
3	Baffle	7	Steel net
4	Flame trap	8	Baffle

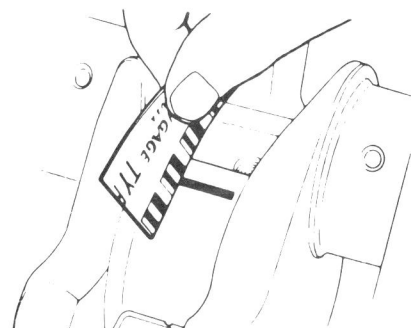

Fig. 1.19 Measuring main bearing clearances using Plastigage strip

ends and underside cylinder walls are lubricated from jets of oil issuing from little holes in the connection rods.

Oil from the centre of the main gallery passes up to a further gallery in the cylinder head. This distributes oil to the valve mechanism, and to the top of the timing chain. Drillings pass oil from the gallery to the camshaft bearings. Oil that is supplied to number 2 and 3 camshaft bearings is passed to the rocker arm, valve and cam lobe by two drillings inside the camshaft and small drillings in the cam circle of each arm.

The oil pressure relief valve is located in the oil pump cover, and is designed to control the pressure in the system to a maximum of 80 lbf/in² (5.6 kgf/cm²).

19 Crankcase emission control system

The closed type of crankcase emission control system fitted to models covered by this manual draws air from the air cleaner and passes it through a mesh type flame trap to a hose connected to the rocker cover.

The air is then passed through the inside of the engine and back to the intake manifold via a hose and regulating valve. This means that fumes in the crankcase are drawn into the combustion chambers, burnt and passed to the exhaust system.

When the vehicle is being driven at full throttle conditions, the inlet manifold depression is not sufficient to draw all fumes through the regulating valve and into the intake manifold. Under these operating conditions the crankcase ventilation flow is reversed with the fumes drawing into the air cleaner instead of the intake manifold.

To prevent the engine oil being drawn into the intake manifold, a baffle plate and filter gauze pack is positioned in the crankcase.

Maintenance of the system simply involves inspection of the system, and renewal of any suspect parts. Check the condition of the rocker cover to air cleaner hose and the crankcase to intake manifold hose. Check for blockage, deterioration or collapse; should either be evident, new hoses must be installed.

Inspect the seals on the engine oil filler cap and dipstick. If their condition has deteriorated renew the seals.

Operation of the ventilation regulation valve may be checked by running the engine at a steady idle speed and disconnecting the hose from the regulation valve. Listen for a hissing noise from the valve once the hose has been detached. Now position a finger over the inlet valve, and a strong depression should be felt immediately as the finger is placed over the valve.

Should the valve prove to be inoperative, it must be renewed as it is not practical to dismantle and clean it.

Other symptoms showing a faulty or inoperative valve are:

(a) *Engine will not run smoothly at idle speed*
(b) *Smoky exhaust*
(c) *Engine idle speed rises and falls, but engine does not stop*
(d) *Power loss at speeds above idle*

20 Examination and renovation – general

With the engine stripped, and all components thoroughly cleaned, it is now time to examine everything for wear and damage.

Parts and assemblies should be checked and, where possible, renovated or otherwise renewed as described in the following Sections.

21 Crankshaft and main bearings – examination and renovation

1   Examine the crankpin and main journal surfaces for signs of scoring or scratches. Check the ovality of the crankpins at different positions with a micrometer. If out-of-round by more than the specified amount, the crankpin will have to be reground. It will also have to be reground if there are any scores or scratches present. Also check the journal in the same fashion.

2   If it is necessary to regrind the crankshaft and fit new bearings your local Datsun garage or engineering works will be able to decide how much metal to grind off and the size of the new bearing shells required.

3   Full details of crankshaft regrinding tolerances and bearing

undersizes are given in the Specifications.

4   The main bearing clearances may be established by using a strip of Plastigage between the crankshaft journals and the main bearing/shell caps. Tighten the bearing cap bolts to a torque of between 33 and 40 lbf ft (4.6 and 5.5 kgf m). Remove the cap and compare the flattened Plastigage strip with the index provided. The clearance should be compared with the tolerances in the Specifications.

5   Temporarily refit the crankshaft to the crankcase having positioned the other halves of the shell main bearings in their locations. Refit the centre main bearing cap only, complete with shell bearing and tighten the securing bolts to between 33 and 40 lbf ft (4.6 and 5.5 kgf m) torque. Using a feeler gauge, check the endplay by pushing and pulling the crankshaft. Where the endplay is outside the specified tolerance, the centre bearing shells will have to be renewed (photo).

6   Finally examine the clutch pilot bearing (bush) which is located in the centre of the flywheel mounting flange at the rear end of the crankshaft. If it is worn, renew it by tapping a thread in it and screwing in a bolt. Carefully press in the new bush so that its endface will lie below the crankshaft flange surface by between 0.18 and 0.20 in (4.5 and 5.0 mm). Lubrication of the bush is not required.

22 Connecting rods and connecting rod (big-end) bearings – examination and renovation

1   Big-end bearing failure is indicated by a knocking from within the crankcase and a slight drop in oil pressure.

2   Examine the bearing surfaces for pitting and scoring. Renew the shells in accordance with the sizes specified in the Specifications. Where the crankshaft has been reground, the correct undersize shell bearings will be supplied by the repairer.

3   Should there be any suspicion that a connecting rod is bent or twisted or the small-end bush no longer provides an interference fit for the gudgeon pin then the complete connecting rod assembly should be exchanged for a reconditioned one but ensure that the comparative weight of the two rods is equal within 0.25 oz (7 gm).

4   Measurement of the big-end bearing clearances may be carried out in a similar manner to that described for the main bearings in the previous Section. The running clearances are given in the Specifications.

5   Finally check the big-end thrust clearance which should be between 0.008 and 0.012 in (0.2 and 0.3 mm) with a maximum wear limit of 0.024 in (0.6 mm).

23 Cylinder bores – examination and renovation

1   The cylinder bores must be examined for taper, ovality, scoring and scratches. Start by carefully examining the top of the cylinder bores. If they are at all worn, a very slight ridge will be found on the thrust side. This marks the top of the piston ring travel. The owner will have a good indication of the bore wear prior to dismantling the engine, or removing the cylinder head. Excessive oil consumption accompanied by blue smoke from the exhaust is a sure sign of worn cylinder bores and piston rings.

2   Measure the bore diameter just under the ridge with a micrometer and compare it with the diameter at the bottom of the bore, which is not subject to wear. If the difference between the two measurements is more than 0.008 in (0.2 mm) then it will be necessary to fit special pistons and rings, or to have the cylinders rebored and fit oversize pistons.

3   The standard clearance between a piston and the cylinder walls is between 0.0010 and 0.0018 in (0.025 and 0.045 mm). The easiest way to check this is to insert the piston into its bore with a feeler blade 0.0016 in (0.04 mm) in thickness inserted between it and the cylinder wall. Attach the feeler blade to a spring balance and note the force required to extract the blade while pulling vertically upwards. This should be between 0.4 and 3.3 lb (0.2 and 1.5 kg). The ambient temperature during this test should be around 68°F (20°C).

4   Where less than specified force is required to withdraw the feeler blade, then remedial action must be taken. Oversize pistons are available as listed in the Specifications.

5   These are accurately machined to just below the indicated measurements so as to provide correct running clearances in bores bored out to the exact oversize dimensions.

6   If the bores are slightly worn but not so badly worn as to justify

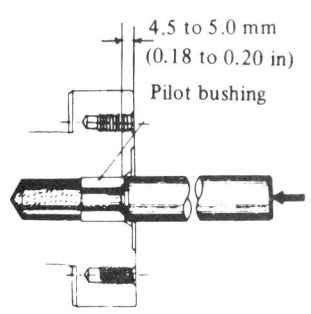

Fig. 1.20 Clutch pilot bearing (bush) installation

4.5 to 5.0 mm
(0.18 to 0.20 in)
Pilot bushing

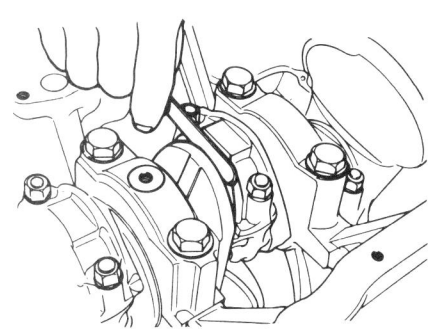

Fig. 1.21 Checking connecting rod (big-end) bearing side thrust clearance

21.5 Checking the crankshaft endfloat

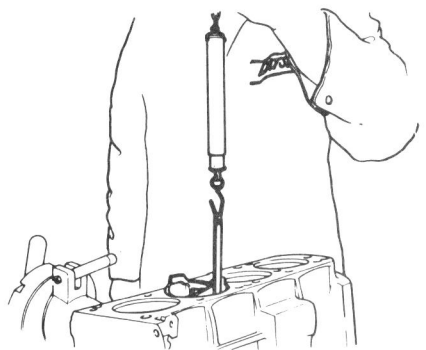

Fig. 1.22 Measuring piston clearance in bore

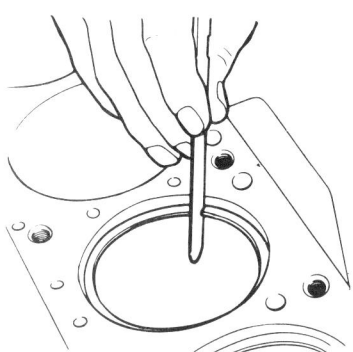

Fig. 1.23 Check piston ring endgap

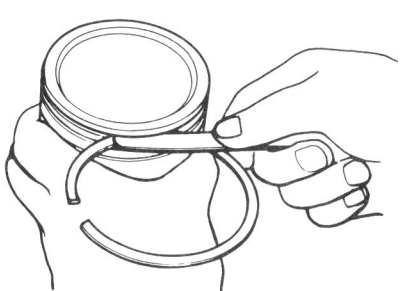

Fig. 1.24 Check piston ring side clearance

reboring them, then special oil control rings and pistons can be fitted which will restore compression and stop the engine burning oil. Several different types are available and the manufacturer's instructions concerning their installation must be followed closely.

7 If new pistons are being fitted and the bores have not been reground, it is essential to slightly roughen the hard glaze on the sides of the bores with fine glass paper so that the new piston rings will have a chance to bed in properly.

24 Crankcase, cylinder block and mountings – examination and renovation

1 Examination of the cylinder block and crankcase should be carried out in conjunction with examination of the cylinder bores. Obviously if any faults or damage are visible, it will be a waste of money having the block rebored.

2 Check for cracks especially between the cylinder bores. Repair of cast iron is a specialized job and it may be more economical to purchase a new assembly or one in good condition from a car breaker.

3 Examine stud and bolt holes for stripped threads. New spiral type thread inserts can often be used to overcome this problem, but the manufacturer's fitting instructions must be strictly observed.

4 Probe all oil and water passages with a piece of wire to ensure freedom from obstruction.

5 Now is the time to examine the engine mountings. Although the mountings can be renewed with the engine still in position in the vehicle by taking its weight on a hoist, now is the best opportunity to check for perished rubber or deformation, and to purchase or order new ones.

25 Pistons and piston rings – examination and renovation

1 Where new pistons have been supplied to match the rebore

diameter, new sets of piston rings will also be provided but it is worthwhile checking the ring clearances, as described in the following paragraphs.

2 Of the original pistons are being used, carefully remove the piston rings as described in Section 16.

3 Clean the grooves and rings free from carbon, taking care not to scratch the aluminium surfaces of the pistons.

4 If new rings are being fitted to old pistons (cylinders not rebored) then order the top compression ring to be stepped to prevent it impinging on the 'wear ring' which will almost certainly have been formed at the top of the cylinder bore.

5 Before refitting the rings to the pistons, push each ring in turn down its cylinder bore (use an inverted piston to do this to keep the ring square) and then measure the ring endgap. The gaps must be given in the Specifications according to engine type and should be measured with a feeler blade.

6 Piston ring endgaps can be increased by rubbing them carefully with carborundum stone.

7 The piston rings should now be tested in their respective grooves for side clearance. The clearances must be as listed in the Specifications.

8 Where necessary, a piston ring which is slightly tight in its groove may be rubbed down holding it perfectly squarely on a carborundum or a sheet of fine emery cloth laid on a piece of plate glass. Excessive tightness can only be rectified by having the grooves machined out.

9 The piston pin should be a push fit into the piston at room temperatire. If it appears slack, then both the piston and piston pin should be renewed.

26 Camshaft and camshaft bearings – examination and renovation

1 Carefully examine the camshaft bearings for wear. If the bearings are obviously worn or pitted then they must be renewed. This is an

operation for your local Datsun dealer or local engineering works as it demands the use of specialized equipment. The bearings are removed with a special drift after which new bearings are pressed in, and line-bored, care being taken to ensure the oil holes in the bearings line-up with those in the pedestal brackets.

2   The camshaft itself should show no signs of wear, but, if very slight scoring on the cams is noticed, the score marks can be removed by very gently rubbing down with very fine emery cloth. The greatest care should be taken to keep the cam profiles smooth.

3   Check the camshaft sprocket for hooked teeth or distortion and renew if evident.

4   When refitting, the camshaft endplay must be between 0.003 and 0.015 in (0.08 and 0.38 mm). If above the maximum, the locating plate must be renewed.

27 Timing chain, gears and tensioner – examination and renovation

1   Wear in the timing chain can be compensated for by adjusting the position of the camshaft sprocket as described in the reassembly operations but if the chain is obviously very badly worn or stretched, and a high mileage has been covered, renew it.

2   Check the condition of the chain tensioner and guide, and renew them if necessary.

3   Examine the crankshaft and camshaft sprocket teeth for wear and damage, renewing as necessary.

28 Cylinder head and valves – servicing and decarbonising

1   With the cylinder head removed, use a blunt scraper to remove all traces of carbon and deposits from the combustion spaces and ports. Remember that the cylinder head is aluminium alloy and can be damaged easily during the decarbonising operations. Scrape the cylinder head free from scale or old pieces of gasket or jointing compound. Clean the cylinder head by washing it in paraffin and take particular care to pull a piece of rag through the ports and cylinder head bolt holes. Any dirt remaining in these recesses may well drop onto the gasket and cylinder block mating surface as the cylinder head is lowered into position and could lead to a gasket leak after reassembly is complete.

2   With the cylinder head clean, test for distortion, especially if a history of coolant leakage has been apparent. Carry out this test using a straight edge and feeler gauges or a piece of plate glass. If the surface shows any warping in excess of 0.0039 in (0.1 mm) then the cylinder head will have to be resurfaced which is a job for a specialist engineering company.

3   Clean the pistons and top of the cylinder bores. If the pistons are still in the block then it is essential that great care is taken to ensure that no carbon gets into the cylinder bores as this could scratch the cylinder walls or cause damage to the piston and rings. To ensure this does not happen, first turn the crankshaft so that two of the pistons are at the top of their bores. Stuff rag into the other two bores and seal them off with paper and masking tape. The waterways should also be covered with small pieces of masking tape to prevent particles of carbon entering the cooling system and damaging the water pump.

4   Before scraping the carbon from the piston crowns, press grease into the gap between the cylinder walls and the two pistons which are to be worked on. With a blunt scraper carefully scrape away the carbon from the piston crown, taking great care not to scratch the aluminium. Also scrape away the carbon from the surrounding lip of the cylinder wall. When all carbon has been removed, scrape away the grease which will be contaminated with carbon particles, taking care not to press any into the bores. To assist prevention of carbon build-up the piston crown can be polished with a metal polish. Remove the rags or masking tape from the other two cylinders and turn the crankshaft so that the two pistons which were at the bottom are now at the top. Place rag or masking tape in the cylinders which have been decarbonised and proceed as just described.

5   The valves can be removed from the cylinder head by the following method. Compress each spring in turn with a valve spring compressor until the two halves of the collets can be removed. Release the compressor and remove the spring and spring retainer.

6   If, when the valve spring compressor is screwed down, the valve spring retaining cap refuses to free to expose the split collet, do not

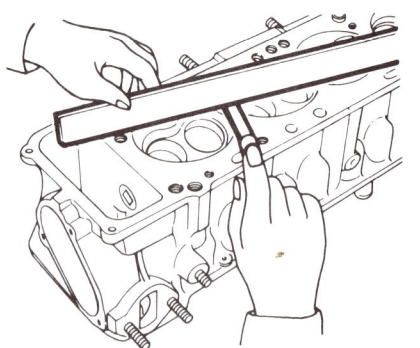

Fig. 1.25 Check the cylinder head for distortion using a straight edge and feeler gauge

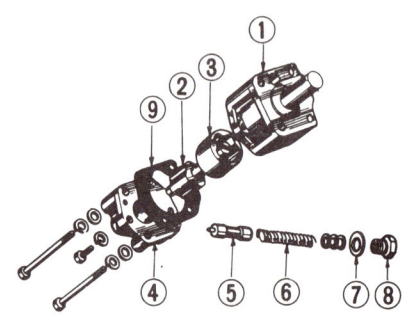

Fig. 1.26 The oil pump components

1	Pump body	6	Spring
2	Inner rotor and shaft	7	Washer
3	Outer rotor	8	Regulator cap
4	Pump cover	9	Cover gasket
5	Regulator valve		

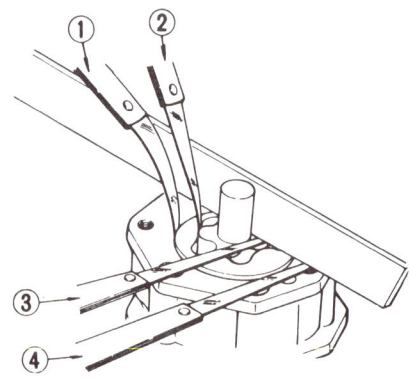

Fig. 1.27 Check the pump rotor clearance

1	Outer rotor to body	3	Side
2	Tip	4	Rotor to body

continue to screw down the compressor as there is a likelihood of damaging it.

7   Gently tap the top of the tool directly over the cap with a light hammer. This will free the cap. To avoid the compressor jumping off the valve spring retaining cap when it is tapped, hold the compressor firmly in position with one hand.

8   Slide the rubber oil control seal off the top of each valve stem (where applicable) and then drop out each valve through the combustion chamber.

9   It is essential that the valves are kept in their correct sequence unless they are so badly worn that they are to be renewed.

10   Examine the heads of the valves for pitting and burning, especially the heads of the exhaust valves. The valve seatings should be examined at the same time. If the pitting on valve and seat is very slight the marks can be removed by grinding the seats and valve together with coarse and then fine, valve grinding paste.

11   Where bad pitting has occurred to the valve seats it will be necessary to recut them and fit new valves. If the valve seats are so worn that they cannot be recut, then it will be necessary to fit new valve seat inserts. These latter two jobs should be entrusted to the local Datsun agent or engineering works. In practice it is very seldom that the seats are so badly worn that they require renewal. Normally, it is the valve that is too badly worn to be refitted, and the owner can easily purchase a new set of valves and match them to the seats by valve grinding.

12   Valve grinding is carried out as follows:

Smear a trace of coarse carborundum paste on the seat face and apply a suction grinder tool to the valve head. With a semi-rotary motion, grind the valve head to its seat, lifting the valve occasionally to redistribute the grinding paste. When a dull matt even surface finish is produced on both the valve seat and the valve, wipe off the paste and repeat the process with fine carborundum paste, lifting and turning the valve to redistribute the paste as before. A light spring placed under the valve head will greatly ease this operation. When a smooth unbroken ring of light grey matt finish is produced, on both valve and valve seat faces, the grinding operation is complete.

13   Scrape away all carbon from the valve head and the valve stem. Carefully clean away every trace of grinding compound, taking great care to leave none in the ports or in the valve guides. Clean the valves and the valve seats with a paraffin soaked rag then with a clean rag, and finally, if an air-line is available, blow the valves, valve guides and valve ports clean.

14   Test each valve in its guides for wear. After a considerable mileage, the valve guide bore may wear oval. This can best be tested by inserting a new valve in the guide and moving it from side to side. If the tip of the valve stem deflects by about 0.0080 in (0.2 mm) then it must be assumed that the tolerance between the stem and guide is greater than the permitted maximum.

15   New valve guides (oversize available) may be pressed or driven into the cylinder head after the worn ones have been removed in a similar manner. The cylinder head must be heated to 392°F (200°C) before carrying out these operations and although this can be done in a domestic oven, it must be remembered that the new guide will have to be reamed after installation and it may therefore be preferable to leave this work to your Datsun dealer.

16   Finally check the free-length of the valve springs and renew them if they are much less than specified or if they have been in operation for 30 000 miles (48 000 km) or more.

29 Oil pump – examination and renovation

1   Unbolt the pump cover, remove the gasket and slide out the internal rotors.

2   Remove the regulator valve threaded plug and extract the valve and spring.

3   Clean all components and carry out the following checks for wear using a feeler gauge:

(a)   *Check the clearance between the outer rotor and the oil pump body. This should be between 0.0059 and 0.0083 in (0.15 and 0.21 mm) with a wear limit of 0.020 in (0.5 mm)*

(b)   *Check the clearance between the high points of the inner and outer rotors. This should be less than 0.005 in (0.12 mm) with a maximum of 0.008 in (0.20 mm)*

(c)   *Using a straight-edge, check outer to inner rotor clearance.*

This should be 0.0016 to 0.0032 in (0.04 to 0.08 mm) with a wear limit of 0.008 in (0.20 mm)

(d)   *Using a straight-edge, check the gap between the rotor and the bottom cover face. This should be 0.002 to 0.005 in (0.05 to 0.12 mm) with a wear limit of 0.008 in (0.20 mm)*

4   Where any of the clearances are outside the specified tolerances, renew the oil pump complete.

30 Flywheel – servicing

1   Examine the clutch driven plate contact area on the flywheel for scoring or cracks. If these are severe or extensive then the flywheel should be renewed. Surface grinding is not recommended as the balance of the crankshaft/flywheel assembly will be upset.

2   If the teeth on the flywheel starter ring are badly worn, or if some are missing then it will be necessary to remove the ring and fit a new one, or preferably exchange the flywheel for a reconditioned unit.

3   Either split the ring with a cold chisel after making a cut with a hacksaw blade between the teeth, or using a soft headed hammer (not steel) to knock the ring off, striking it evenly and alternately at equally spaced points. Take great care not to damage the flywheel during this process.

4   Heat the new ring in either an electric oven to about 392°F (200°C) or immerse in a pan of boiling oil.

5   Hold the ring at this temperature for five minutes and then quickly fit it to the flywheel so the chamfered portion of the teeth faces the transmission side of the flywheel.

6   The ring should be tapped gently down onto its register and left to cool naturally when the contraction of the metal on cooling will ensure that it is a secure and permanent fit. Great care must be taken not to overheat the ring, indicated by it turning light metallic blue, as if this happens the temper of the ring will be lost.

31 Driveplates – servicing

1   This component, fitted instead of the flywheel in conjunction with automatic transmission should be checked for distortion and elongation of the bolt holes which secure it to the torque converter.

2   Examine the starter ring gear teeth for wear or chipping.

3   Where any of these faults are evident, renew the driveplate complete.

32 Oil seals – renewal

1   At the time of major overhaul, renew the timing cover oil seal and the crankshaft rear oil seal as a matter of routine.

2   Make sure that the lips of the seals face the correct way as shown (photo).

3   Removal and installation of the timing cover oil seal should be carried out using a piece of tubing as a drift.

33 Engine reassembly – general

1   Before commencing reassembly, gather together the necessary tools, gaskets and other small items.

2   Observe absolute cleanliness during reassembly and lubricate each component before refitting with clean engine oil. In particular, blow through all oil ways and lubricate them to ensure that they are clear of dirt and metal swarf.

3   Do not use unnecessary force to install a part, but re-check clearances and tolerances where difficulties are encountered.

4   Where applicable always use new lockwashers, gaskets and seals, and tighten all fittings to the specified torques.

34 Crankshaft and main bearings – reassembly

1   Install the upper halves of the main bearing shells into the crankcase and oil them liberally. Note that the centre shell incorporates the thrust washers. Shell bearings (nos. 2 and 4) are similar and interchangeable. The front and rear bearing shells are

32.3 Timing cover oil seal

34.1a Oiling crankcase bearing shells

34.1b Main bearing shell incorporating thrust washer

34.1c Front main bearing with timing chain oil spray hole

34.2 Crankcase breather baffle

34.3 Refitting crankshaft

34.4 Refitting centre main bearing cap and shell

34.6 Rear main bearing cap side seal

34.7 Crankshaft rear oil seal

35.1 Engine rear plate

36.1 Piston directional fitting mark

36.3 Refitting a connecting rod bearing shell

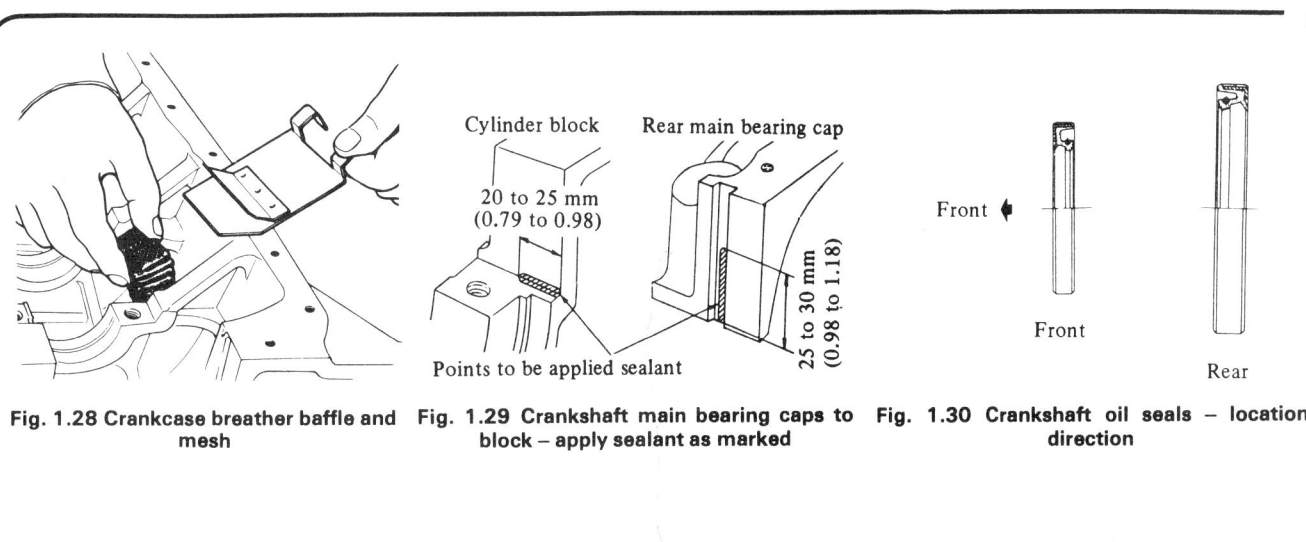

Fig. 1.28 Crankcase breather baffle and mesh

Fig. 1.29 Crankshaft main bearing caps to block – apply sealant as marked

Fig. 1.30 Crankshaft oil seals – location direction

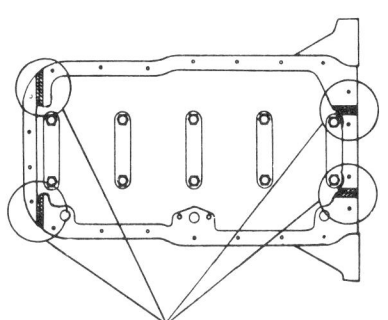

Fig. 1.31 Apply sealant to indicated joint areas

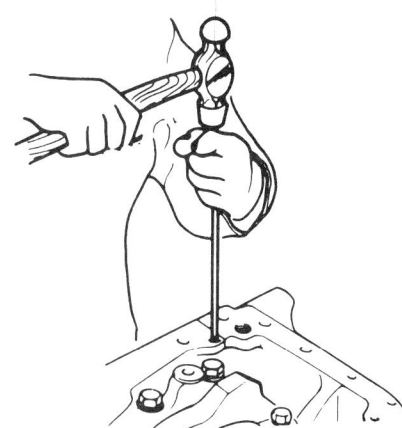

Fig. 1.32 Tap in the new main bearing cap side seal

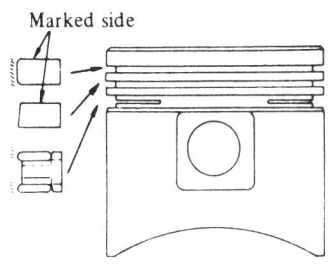

Fig. 1.33 Main bearing cap bolt tightening sequence

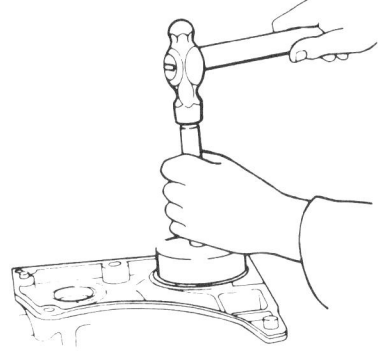

Fig. 1.34 Fitting the crankshaft rear oil seal

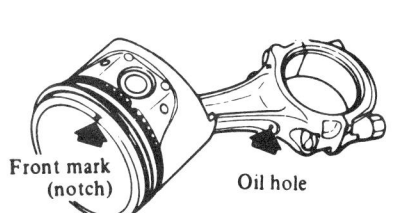

Fig. 1.35 Piston assembly position to connecting rod

Fig. 1.36 Piston rings – fitted positions

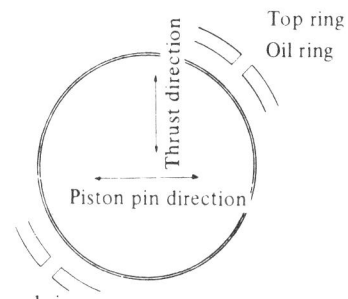

Fig. 1.37 Piston rings – the offset endgap positions

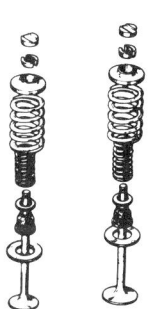

Fig. 1.38 The inlet and exhaust valve components

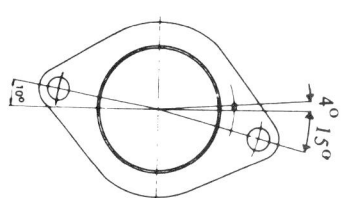

Fig. 1.39 The fitted position for the camshaft locating plate

similar but they are not interchangeable as only the front bearing incorporates an oil hole for the timing chain oil spray. All upper and lower bearing halves of similar type are interchangeable (photos).

2   If the crankcase breather baffle and mesh were removed, refit them now before refitting the crankshaft (photo).

3   Lower the crankshaft carefully into the crankcase (photo).

4   Install the main bearing caps complete with shells making sure they go back in their numbered sequence and also the correct way round (photo). Smear the caps and block with a sealant as shown (Fig. 1.29).

5   Tighten the main bearing cap bolts to the specified torque, progressively and in the sequence shown (Fig. 1.33).

6   Check that the crankshaft rotates freely without binding and also check the crankshaft endfloat using a feeler gauge.

7   Smear jointing compound on the new rear main bearing cap side seals and tap them into their recesses (photo).

8   Install the crankshaft rear oil seal tapping it into position with a piece of tubing (photo).

---

35 Flywheel (or driveplate) – refitting

1   Bolt the engine rear plate to the crankcase (photo).

2   Bolt the flywheel (or driveplate - automatic transmission) to the crankshaft rear mounting flange.

3   Tighten the bolts to the specified torque.

---

36 Pistons, rings and connecting rods – reassembly and refitting

1   As previously recommended, the pistons will probably have been assembled to their connecting rods by the dealer supplying the new components. When correctly assembled, the notch on the piston crown (on some pistons an 'F' mark is used adjacent to the gudgeon pin boss) must face the front of the engine while the oil hole in the connecting rod will be towards the right-hand side of the engine (photo).

2   Install the piston rings by reversing the removal procedure described in Section 16. When correctly installed, the markings on the rings must be facing upwards. The top compression ring is chromium plated while the second compression ring is tapered towards the top. The oil control ring has two rails which can be interchanged and located at the top and bottom of the groove. Stagger the piston ring gaps as shown (Fig. 1.36).

3   Install the bearing shells to the connecting rod and big-end cap (photo).

4   Compress the piston rings with a suitable compressor and, having well lubricated the rings and the cylinder bore with engine oil, tap the piston/connecting rod assembly into the cylinder (photo).

5   Engage the connecting rod with the crankshaft when the crankpin is at its lowest point of rotational travel. Lubricate the exposed part of the crankpin.

6   Install the big-end cap complete with shell bearing making sure that the numbers are adjacent and in their correct sequence (photo).

7   Tighten the big-end nuts to specified torque.

8   Repeat the operations to refit the remaining three piston/connecting rod assemblies, and check the endfloat of each connecting rod big-end using a feeler gauge.

---

37 Cylinder head and timing gear – reassembly and refitting

1   Insert each valve in turn into its respective guide, applying a little engine oil to the stem (photo).

2   Fit a new oil seal to the valve stem if one was originally fitted and with the aid of a spring compressor, assemble the springs (outer spring has close coils nearest cylinder head), retainers and split collets. The latter can be retained in the valve stem cut-out with a dab of thick grease. **Note:** *The narrow spring coil section is also painted red for further clarification.*

3   Oil the camshaft bearings and insert the camshaft carefully into

36.4 Refitting a piston

36.6 Refitting a connecting rod (big-end) cap and shell

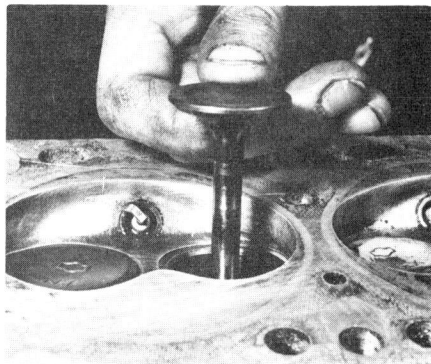
37.1 Refitting a valve

37.2a Refitting a valve spring retainer

37.2b Compressing a valve spring

37.3 Refitting the camshaft

37.6 Engaging the rocker spring with rocker arm

37.7 Refitting the camshaft locating plate

37.9 Refitting a timing chain guide

37.10 Cylinder head gasket located in block

37.11 Lowering cylinder head into position

37.12a Refitting crankshaft sprocket

37.12b Refitting the oil pump/distributor drivegear

37.12c Refitting the crankshaft oil thrower

37.14a Engaging timing chain with camshaft sprocket

37.14b Refitting camshaft sprocket bolt and fuel pump eccentric

37.14c Crankshaft sprocket timing mark aligned with chain 'bright' link

37.14d Camshaft sprocket timing mark aligned with chain 'bright' link

position (photo).

4 Screw the valve rocker pivots complete with locknuts into the pivot bushes.

5 Refit the rocker arms and guides by depressing the valve springs with a screwdriver.

6 Engage the rocker springs.

7 Refit the camshaft locating plate to the camshaft so that the horizontally engraved line is visible from the front and is positioned at the top of the plate (photo).

8 Rotate the camshaft until the valves of no 1 cylinder are fully closed (equivalent to no 1 piston at TDC) and then turn the crankshaft (by means of the flywheel or driveplate) until no 1 piston is at TDC.

9 Bolt the two timing chain guides into position (photo).

10 Clean the mating surfaces of the cylinder block and head, and locate a new gasket on the face of the block; do not use gasket cement (photo).

11 Lower the cylinder head into position and insert the two centre bolts finger-tight only at this stage (photo).

12 To the front of the crankshaft, refit the sprocket, oil pump/distributor drivegear and the oil thrower. Make sure that the timing marker on the sprocket is visible from the front (photos).

13 On no account turn the crankshaft or camshaft until the timing chain is installed, otherwise the valves will impinge upon the piston crowns. Install the chain to the crankshaft sprocket and draw the chain through the opening in the cylinder head.

14 Engage the camshaft sprocket within the upper loop of the timing chain, then engage the chain with the teeth of the crankshaft sprocket and bolt the camshaft sprocket to the camshaft ensuring that the following conditions are met:

> (a) The keyways of both the crankshaft and camshaft sprockets must point vertically
>
> (b) The timing marks ('bright' link plates) on the chain should align with those on the two sprockets, and be positioned on the right-hand side when viewed from the front

On L20B type engines there should be 21 black plates between the two bright plates, while L16 engines have 20 black plates between them. Where a timing chain has stretched, this can upset the valve timing and provision is made for this by alternative dowel holes drilled in the camshaft sprocket. With no 1 piston at TDC (compression stroke) check whether the notch in the camshaft sprocket (with chain correctly engaged) appears to the left of the engraved line on the locating plate. If this is the case, disengage the camshaft sprocket from the chain and move the sprocket round so that when it is re-engaged with the chain it will locate with the camshaft flange dowel in its no 2 hole. Where this adjustment does not correct the chain slack, repeat the operation using no 3 hole of the camshaft sprocket to engage with the flange dowel. Where no 2 or 3 sprocket holes are used, then the no 2 or 3 timing marks must be used to position the chain. Where this adjustment procedure still will not correct or compensate for the slackness in the timing chain, then the chain must be renewed (photos).

15 When the timing is satisfactory, tighten the camshaft sprocket bolt to the specified torque.

16 Install the chain tensioner so that there is the minimum clearance between the spindle/slipper assembly and the tensioner assembly (photo).

17 Thoroughly clean the mating faces of the front cover and cylinder block.

18 Locate a new gasket on the front face of the engine, applying gasket cement to both sides of it.

19 Apply gasket cement to the front cover and cylinder block as indicated.

20 Offer up the front cover to the engine and insert the securing bolts finger tight. Take care not to damage the head gasket which is already in position (photo).

21 The top face of the front cover should be flush with the top surface of the cylinder block or certainly not more than 0.0059 in (1.5 mm) difference in level.

22 Tighten the front cover bolts to the correct torque.

23 Install the water pump (photo).

24 Oil the lips of the front cover oil seal and push the pulley onto the crankshaft. Tighten its securing bolt to the specified torque (photo).

25 Insert the remaining cylinder head bolts noting carefully the position of the longer bolts (A) and the shorter ones (B).

26 Tighten the bolts to the specified torque progressively and in the

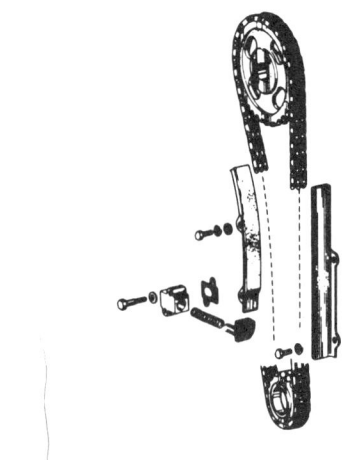

Fig. 1.40 The camshaft drive chain and related parts

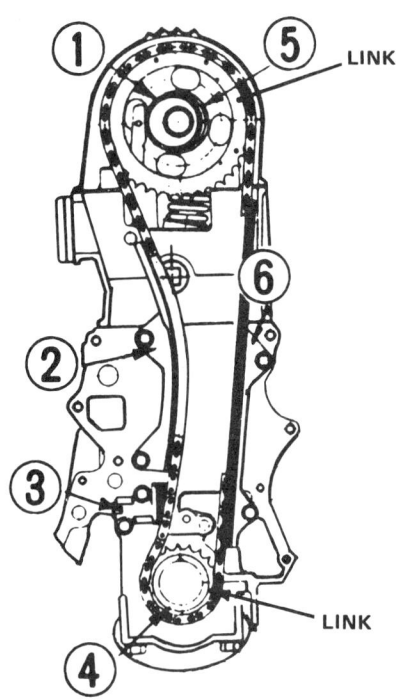

Fig. 1.41 The fitted position of the timing chain. L16 engines 21 links. L20B engines 22 links

1 Fuel pump drive cam	4 Crank sprocket
2 Chain guide	5 Cam sprocket
3 Chain tensioner	6 Chain guide

37

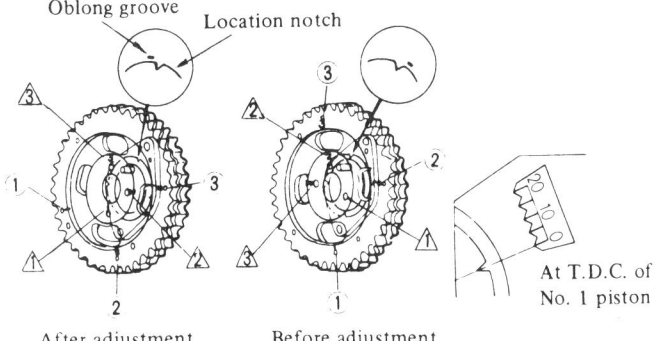

Oblong groove   Location notch

△3   △3   △2

1   3   2

△1   △2   △3

2   1

After adjustment   Before adjustment

At T.D.C. of
No. 1 piston

Fig. 1.42 The camshaft sprocket adjustment positions to compensate for timing chain stretch. The numbers in the circles indicate the timing marks. The numbers in the triangles are the dowel location hole positions

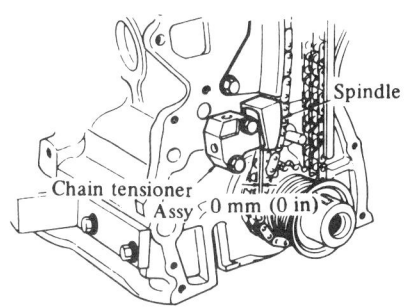

Spindle

Chain tensioner
Assy   0 mm (0 in)

Fig. 1.43 Adjust the chain tensioner spindle protrusion to take up any play

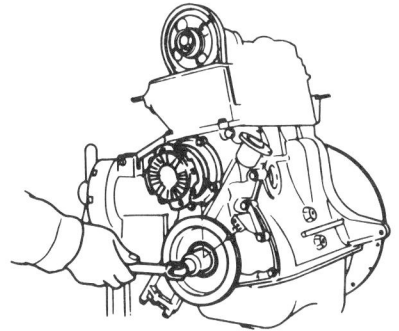

Fig. 1.44 Refit the crankshaft pulley and bolt

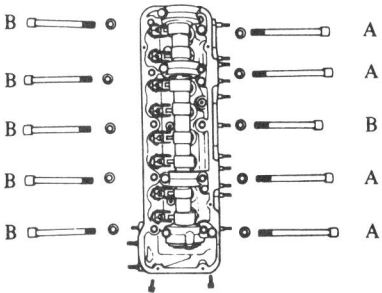

B   A
B   A
B   B
B   A
B   A

Fig. 1.45 The long and short cylinder head bolt locations

A = Long   B = Short

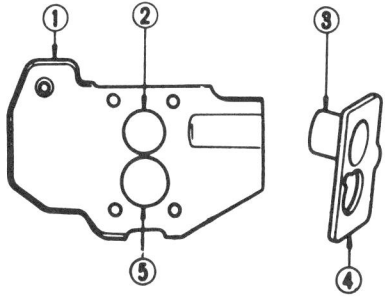

Fig. 1.46 Carburettor joint components
(L20B type engine)

1 Heatshield plate   4 Joint seat
2 Primary hole   5 Secondary hole
3 Duct

37.16 Refitting timing chain tensioner

37.20 Refitting the front cover

37.23 Refitting the water pump

37.24 Refitting the crankshaft pulley

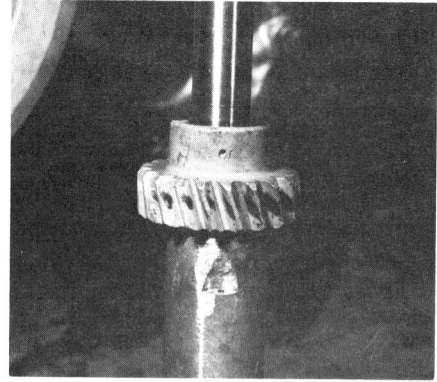

38.3 Oil pump driveshaft alignment marks

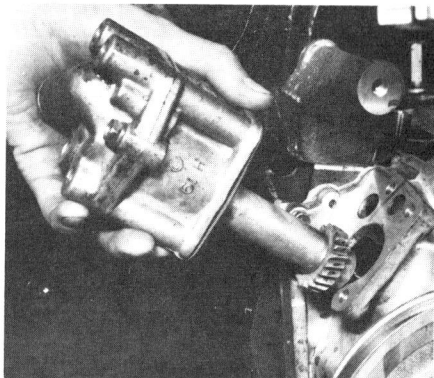

38.4a Refitting the oil pump

38.4b Correct position of distributor drive tongue after refitting the oil pump

38.6 Refitting the distributor

39.1 Oil pick-up tube and strainer fitted

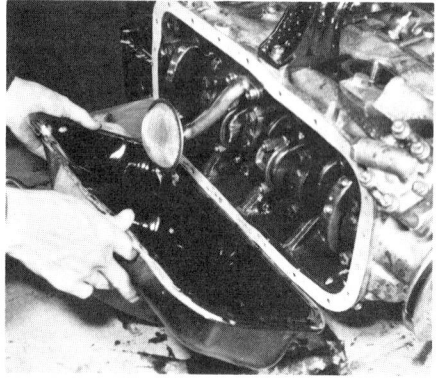

39.3 Refitting the oil pan

40.1a Checking an inlet valve clearance

40.1b Adjusting a valve clearance

sequence shown in Fig. 1.14. **Note:** *Where the cylinder head is being installed with the engine in the vehicle, tension must be applied to the timing chain in an upward direction at all times in order to prevent the chain becoming disengaged from the crankshaft sprocket (See Section 10).*

38 Oil pump and distributor – refitting

1   Set the engine so that No. 1 piston is at TDC on its compression stroke.
2   Lubricate the oil pump assembly with clean engine oil.
3   Align the punch mark on the oil pump driveshaft with the oil hole just below the driven gear (photo).
4   Use a new flange gasket and insert the oil pump into its recess so that as its driveshaft meshes with the drivegear on the crankshaft the distributor drive tongue will take up a position as shown being at 5° to a line drawn through the centres of the bolt holes of the distributor

mounting flange (when viewed from above) and having the smaller segment towards the front of the engine (photo).
5   Tighten the oil pump securing bolts.
6   Without moving the crankshaft, insert the distributor into its recess so that the large and small segments of the driveshaft engage correctly, then tighten the clamp plate bolt at its original position in the elongated hole (photo).
7   The ignition timing should be precisely checked and adjusted, as described in Chapter 4.

39 Oil strainer and oil pan – refitting

1   Bolt the oil strainer and pick-up tube assembly to the flange of the crankcase (photo).
2   Clean the mating surfaces of the crankcase and oil pan. Apply gasket cement at the points indicated, then smearing a film of cement

to the crankcase flange, stick the oil pan gasket to the crankcase.
3   Smear the flange of the oil pan with gasket cement then bolt it to the crankcase. Do not overtighten these bolts (photo).

40 Valve clearances – adjustment

1   To adjust the valve clearance, turn the crankshaft until no 1 piston is at TDC on its compression stroke. In this position the high points of the cam lobes will be furthest from the rocker arms. Check the clearance between the base of the cam profile and the rocker arm by inserting the appropriate feeler blade. The blade should be a stiff sliding fit. To adjust the clearance, release the locknut and turn the pivot screw. The valve clearances are given in the Specifications (photos).
2   As the firing order is 1-3-4-2 it will reduce the amount of the crankshaft rotation required if the valve clearances are adjusted in accordance with the firing order. To obtain a better appreciation of the valve clearance it is recommended that the rocker arm springs are detached. Numbering from the front, the inlet valves are 2-3-6-7 and the exhaust valves 1-4-5-8.
3   When carrying out valve clearance adjustment with the engine in the car, the crankshaft can most easily be turned by engaging top gear, jacking-up and turning a rear roadwheel (manual transmission). On vehicles with automatic transmission a wrench will have to be applied to the crankshaft pulley bolt which makes the adjustment procedure somewhat more protracted. With either method, the work will be facilitated if the spark plugs are first removed.

41 Ancillary components – refitting

1   This is essentially the reverse of the removal procedure described in Section 9. However, for L16 engines, ensure that the carburettor flange insulator is fitted on the manifold so that its marking is visible from above. For L20B engines, remember to fit the heat shield plate to the carburettor; note that the joint seat duct is inserted into the primary hole in the carburettor.
2   Lubricate the oil filter seal with engine oil and fit hand-tight only.
3   Refer to Figs 1.10 and 1.11 and Chapter 3 for information on pipe-runs for the emission control items.

42 Engine/transmission – refitting

1   Install the clutch (where applicable) by following the procedure given in Chapter 5.
2   Reconnect the engine to the manual or automatic transmission by reversing the procedure given in Section 6 or 7.
3   Using the hoist and slings, refit the engine/transmission in the vehicle by reversing the removal procedure given in Section 5.
4   When fitting is complete, check and adjust the fan belt tension as described in Chapter 2.
5   Refill the engine with the correct grade and quantity of oil (where applicable).
6   Refill the cooling system (Chapter 2).
7   Check the level in the manual or automatic transmission, and top-up if necessary.

43 Initial start-up after major repair

1   With the engine refitted in the vehicle, make a final visual check to see that everything has been reconnected and that no loose rags or tools have been left within the engine compartment.
2   Turn the idling speed adjusting screw in about $\frac{1}{2}$ turn to ensure that the engine will have a faster than usual idling speed during initial start-up and operation.
3   Start the engine. This may take a little longer than usual as the fuel pump and carburettor bowls will be empty and will require priming.
4   As soon as the engine starts, allow it to run at a fast-idle. Examine all hose and pipe connections for leaks.
5   After the engine has been run for several minutes check the tightness of the cylinder head bolts.
6   Operate the vehicle on the road until normal engine temperature is reached, then remove the rocker cover and adjust the valve clearances hot, as described in Section 40.
7   Where the majority of engine internal bearings or components (pistons, rings etc) have been renewed then the operating speed should be restricted for the first 500 miles (800 km), and the engine oil changed at the end of this period.
8   Check and adjust if necessary the ignition timing (Chapter 4).
9   Check and adjust the carburettor and all exhaust emission control equipment as far as is practicable (Chapter 3).

44 Fault diagnosis – engine

Refer to Section 84, Part B of this Chapter.

Chapter 1 Part B Overhead valve engines

Contents

Specifications

Engine (general)

Engine type	4 cylinder, in-line (ohv)
Firing order	1 - 3 - 4 - 2
Displacement	1397 cc (85.24 cu in)
Compression ratio	8.5 : 1
Bore	2.992 in (76 mm)
Stroke	3.031 in (77 mm)
Engine idle speed	650 rpm
Oil capacity (with filter)	$2\frac{7}{8}$ Imp qt (3.2 litre, $3\frac{3}{8}$ US qt)

Valves

Valve clearances – inlet and exhaust:	
Cold	0.010 in (0.25 mm)
Hot	0.014 in (0.35 mm)
Valve head diameter	
Inlet	1.46 in (37 mm)
Exhaust	1.18 in (30 mm)
Stem diameter	
Inlet	0.313 to 0.314 in (7.970 to 7.985 mm)
Exhaust	0.312 to 0.313 in (7.945 to 7.960 mm)
Valve length	4.07 to 4.09 in (103.5 to 104.1 mm)
Valve spring free length	1.831 in (46.5 mm)

Valve guides
    Length .... 1.929 in (49.0 mm)
    Height from head surface .... 0.709 in (18.0 mm)
    Inside diameter .... 0.3150 to 0.3156 in (8.000 to 8.015 mm)
Stem clearance
    Inlet .... 0.0006 to 0.0018 in (0.015 to 0.045 mm)
    Exhaust .... 0.0016 to 0.0028 in (0.040 to 0.070 mm)
Valve seat angle .... 45°
Valve seat width
    Inlet .... 0.071 in (1.8 mm)
    Exhaust .... 0.087 in (2.2 mm)

Cylinder block

Top face warp limit .... 0.004 in (0.10 mm)
Bore diameter standard .... 2.9921 to 2.9941 in (76.000 to 76.050 mm)
Bore wear limit .... 0.0079 in (0.20 mm)
Maximum ovality in bores .... 0.0006 in (0.015 mm)
Maximum taper in bores .... 0.0006 in (0.015 mm)

Camshaft

Endfloat .... 0.0004 to 0.0020 in (0.01 to 0.05 mm)
Lobe lift
    Inlet .... 0.2224 in (5.65 mm)
    Exhaust .... 0.2331 in (5.92 mm)
Camshaft journal diameters:
    No 1 .... 1.7237 to 1.7242 in (43.783 to 43.796 mm)
    No 2 .... 1.7041 to 1.7046 in (43.283 to 43.296 mm)
    No 3 .... 1.6844 to 1.6849 in (42.783 to 42.796 mm)
    No 4 .... 1.6647 to 1.6652 in (42.283 to 42.296 mm)
    No 5 .... 1.6224 to 1.6229 in (41.208 to 41.221 mm)
Camshaft distortion (max) .... 0.0006 in (0.015 mm)
Camshaft bearing to journal clearances
    No 1 .... 0.0015 to 0.0024 in (0.037 to 0.060 mm)
    No 2 .... 0.0011 to 0.0020 in (0.027 to 0.050 mm)
    No 3 .... 0.0016 to 0.0025 in (0.040 to 0.063 mm)
    No 4 .... 0.0011 to 0.0020 in (0.027 to 0.050 mm)
    No 5 .... 0.0015 to 0.0024 in (0.037 to 0.060 mm)
Camshaft bearing inside diameter
    No 1 .... 1.7257 to 1.7261 in (43.833 to 43.843 mm)
    No 2 .... 1.7056 to 1.7060 in (43.323 to 43.333 mm)
    No 3 .... 1.6865 to 1.6868 in (42.836 to 42.846 mm)
    No 4 .... 1.6663 to 1.6667 in (42.323 to 42.333 mm)
    No 5 .... 1.6243 to 1.6247 in (41.258 to 41.268 mm)

Connecting rods and bearings

Bearing clearance .... 0.0004 to 0.0024 in (0.010 to 0.060 mm)
Wear allowance (max) .... 0.0039 in (0.10 mm)
Big-end endplay .... 0.004 to 0.008 in (0.1 to 0.2 mm)

Pistons and piston rings

Diameter
    Standard .... 2.9908 to 2.9927 in (75.967 to 76.017 mm)
    0.50 Oversize .... 3.0105 to 3.0125 in (76.467 to 76.517 mm)
    1.00 Oversize .... 3.0302 to 3.0322 in (76.967 to 77.017 mm)
Piston ring side clearances
    Top .... 0.0016 to 0.0028 in (0.04 to 0.07 mm)
    2nd .... 0.0012 to 0.0024 in (0.03 to 0.06 mm)
    Oil ring .... Combined
Ring gap
    Top .... 0.0079 to 0.0138 in (0.20 to 0.35 mm)
    2nd .... 0.0059 to 0.0118 in (0.15 to 0.30 mm)
    Oil .... 0.0118 to 0.0354 in (0.30 to 0.90 mm)

Crankshaft and main bearings

Journal diameter .... 1.9666 to 1.9671 in (49.951 to 49.964 mm)
Taper and ovality limit .... −0.0002 in (−0.005 mm)
Endfloat .... 0.0020 to 0.0059 in (0.05 to 0.15 mm)
Maximum endfloat .... 0.0118 in (0.30 mm)
Crankpin diameter .... 1.7701 to 1.7706 in (44.961 to 44.974 mm)
Crankpin ovality and taper (Max) .... 0.0002 in (0.005 mm)
Crankpin clearance .... 0.0008 to 0.0024 in (0.020 to 0.062 mm)
Crankpin wear limit .... 0.0039 in (0.10 mm)

Torque wrench settings

	lbf ft	kgf m
Main bearing cap bolts	36 to 43	5 to 6
Connecting rod bolts	23 to 27	3.2 to 3.8

Cylinder head bolts	51 to 54	7.0 to 7.5
Flywheel bolts	58 to 65	8.0 to 9.0
Rocker shaft support bolts	14 to 18	2.0 to 2.5
Camshaft sprocket bolt	29 to 35	4.0 to 4.8
Crankshaft pulley bolt	108 to 145	15 to 20
Manifold nuts	11 to 14	1.5 to 2.0
Engine mounting bolts	14 to 18	1.9 to 2.5
Location plate (camshaft)	2.9 to 3.6	0.4 to 0.5
Oil drain plug	14 to 22	2.0 to 3.0
Oil pump bolt	6.5 to 10	0.9 to 1.4
Sump bolts	2.9 to 3.6	0.4 to 0.5
Timing case bolts	2.9 to 4.3	0.4 to 0.6

45 General description

The engine is a four cylinder in-line type with overhead valves operated from the camshaft via pushrods and a rocker arm assembly.

The cast iron cylinder block has integral cylinders and waterways.

The crankshaft is located in five main bearings and has drilled oilways to provide the necessary lubrication to the respective main bearings and connecting rod big-end journals.

The H section connecting rods have oil jets to supply a splash feed lubrication to the respective cylinder walls.

Aluminium alloy cast pistons are used and are located on the connecting rods by a gudgeon pin which is an interference fit in the small-end.

The camshaft is located in five bearings which are lubricated via holes intersecting the main oil gallery in the cylinder block. Each cam lobe is lubricated via a hole in its base from the integral passages.

The cylinder head is manufactured in aluminium alloy and is of conventional layout having the inlet and exhaust valves in line, with the respective inlet and exhaust ports and manifolds on the left-hand side.

The pushrod operated valve system uses single valve springs and the valves to rocker arm clearances are fully adjustable via a ball head stud and locknut. The tappets are located within the cylinder block and can only be withdrawn with the camshaft removed, as they cannot be extracted or inserted from the top of the block.

The camshaft is driven from a double row chain which is automatically adjusted between the crankshaft and camshaft sprockets by a spring loaded chain tensioner.

The engine oil pump unit is externally mounted and the housing incorporates the oil filter location. The pump, which is a trochoid type, is driven by a shaft from the camshaft, and distributes oil to the various engine components via the respective internal oilways.

The inlet manifold is aluminium and the exhaust manifold is cast iron and incorporates a quick warm up valve.

46 Major operations possible with engine fitted

The following operations can be carried out with the engine still in the vehicle.

1 Removal and refitting the cylinder head assembly.
2 Removal and refitting the timing case, timing chain and sprockets.
3 Removal and refitting the oil pump unit.

47 Major operations only possible with engine removed

1 Removal and refitting the crankshaft.
2 Removal and refitting the flywheel.
3 Renewal of the crankshaft rear oil seal.
4 Removal and refitting the camshaft.
5 Removal and refitting the pistons, connecting rods, and big-end bearings.

48 Engine and transmission – removal

1 It is generally recommended that the engine and transmission units are removed together and separated when out of the vehicle. Although it is possible to remove the engine on its own, this can be a more time consuming operation in the long run.

2 The general removal instructions for the ohv engine are basically the same as those given for the ohc versions in the 160J and 510 models in Section 5 of Part A.

3 Certain instructions may not be applicable and in particular those concerning the emission control items and associate parts, and these instructions should therefore simply be ignored if your vehicle is not so equipped.

49 Engine – separation from transmission

1 Refer to Section 6 in Part A.

50 Engine dismantling – general

1 Refer to Section 8 in Part A.

51 Ancillary components – removal

1 Refer to the instructions given in Section 9 of Part A but note that for most applications the reference to emission control items can be ignored.

52 Cylinder head – removal

The operations given in Section 10 paragraph 1 must first be carried out before the cylinder head can be removed with the engine in the car.

1 With the rocker cover removed, progressively loosen the rocker shaft bracket bolts. Lift the rocker shaft assembly clear when free. Note that the end bolts retain the rocker arms and springs on the shaft and therefore unless the shaft assembly is to be dismantled, leave the bolts in their locations in the brackets.

2 Withdraw the pushrods, keeping them in order so that they can be refitted to their respective locations on re-assembly. A piece of wood or thick cardboard with two rows of holes drilled in it and numbered accordingly will provide a suitable rack for the pushrods.

3 Progressively loosen the cylinder head retaining bolts in the order shown in Fig. 1.48.

4 Carefully lift the cylinder head clear. If it appears to be stuck do not attempt to prise it free but tap it lightly all round using a soft head mallet or wooden block. Remove the cylinder head gasket.

53 Valves – removal

1 The valves can be removed from the cylinder head by the following method. Compress each spring in turn with a valve spring compressor until the two halves of the collets can be removed. Release the compressor, and remove the spring and spring retainer.

2 If, when the valve spring compressor is screwed down, the valve spring retaining cap refuses to free to expose the split collet, do not continue to screw down on the compressor as there is a likelihood of damaging it.

3 Gently tap the top of the tool directly over the cap with a light hammer. This will free the cap. To avoid the compressor jumping off

48.2 Lifting the engine and transmission unit clear

55.5 The crankshaft and camshaft pulleys ready for withdrawal together with the chain. Note and check the sprocket timing marks prior to removal

56.2 The oil feed pipe and strainer

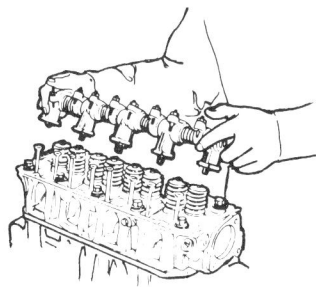

Fig. 1.47 Removing the rocker shaft assembly

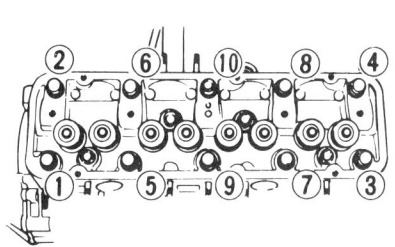

Fig. 1.48 The cylinder head bolt loosening sequence

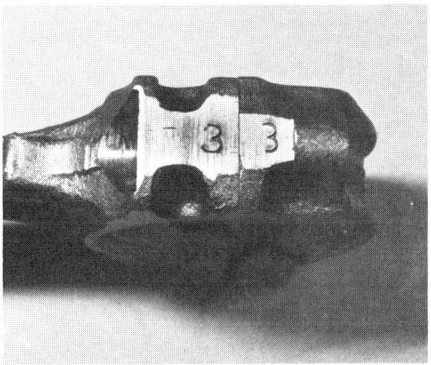

59.3 The connecting rod and cap showing rod number

the valve spring retaining cap when it is tapped, hold the compressor firmly in position with one hand.
4   Slide the rubber oil control seal off the top of each valve stem and then drop out each valve through the combustion chamber.
5   It is essential that the valves are kept in their correct sequence unless they are so badly worn that they are to be renewed.

54 Rocker assembly – dismantling

1   Withdraw the end bolts from the rocker brackets and simply slide the brackets, springs, and rocker arms off the shaft, keeping them in order of sequence.

55 Timing chain cover, timing chain and gears – removal

1   Remove the bolts from the timing chain cover, then take off the cover and gasket.
2   Remove the oil thrower disc from the crankshaft, noting which way round it is fitted.
3   Unbolt and remove the chain tensioner.
4   Unscrew and remove the bolt and washers retaining the camshaft sprocket in position. Jam the flywheel to prevent the engine from turning when applying pressure to loosen the bolt.
5   Remove the camshaft and crankshaft gearwheels simultaneously, complete with double roller chain. Use tyre levers behind each gear, and lever them equally a little at a time. If they are stuck on their shafts, the use of a puller may be required (photo).
6   When the gearwheels and chain are removed, extract the Woodruff keys from the crankshaft and camshaft. Note that there are two keys for the crankshaft sprocket. Take care not to damage any shims fitted between the crankshaft sprocket and flange (if fitted).

56 Sump and oil pipe/strainer – removal

1   Unscrew in a progressive manner the respective sump securing

bolts and remove the oil sump and gasket.
2   Unscrew the two retaining bolts from the oil pipe and remove it (photo).

57 Flywheel – removal

1   If the clutch has not been removed refer to Chapter 5 and detach it from the flywheel.
2   Unscrew the six special bolts retaining the flywheel to the crankshaft. To prevent the crankshaft from turning, block a crankshaft web. Lift the flywheel clear taking care not to drop it (photo).
3   If the engine is being completely stripped, remove the rear plate and gasket at this stage.

58 Camshaft and tappets – removal

1   Unscrew and remove the two camshaft retaining plate bolts and remove with washers. Note which way round the plate faces.
2   Lay the engine on its side and carefully withdraw the camshaft. Special care is needed during removal to avoid damaging the camshaft journals with the corners of the lobes.
3   The respective tappets can now be extracted from inside the block. If stuck poke them down from above using a screwdriver, but on removal keep them in sequence so that they can be refitted into their respective positions.

59 Pistons and connecting rod assemblies – removal

1   With the cylinder head and sump removed, undo the connecting rod (big-end) retaining bolts.
2   The connecting rods and pistons must only be lifted out from the top of the cylinder block.

3   Remove the big-end caps one at a time, taking care to keep them in the right order and the correct way round. Also ensure that the shell bearings are kept with their correct connecting rods and caps unless they are to be renewed. Normally, the numbers 1 to 4 are stamped on adjacent sides of the big-end caps and connecting rods, indicating which cap is fitted on which rod, and which way round the cap is fitted (photo). If no numbers or lines can be found, then, with a sharp screwdriver or file, scratch mating marks across the joint from the rod to the cap. One line for connecting rod No. 1, two for connecting rod No. 2 and so on. This will ensure there is no confusion later, as it is most important that the caps go back in the correct position on the connecting rods from which they were removed.
4   If the big-end caps are difficult to remove they may be gently tapped with a soft hammer.
5   To remove the shell bearings, press the bearings opposite the groove in both the connecting rod, and the connecting rod caps and the bearings will slide out easily.
6   Withdraw the pistons and connecting rods upwards and ensure they are kept in the correct order so that they can be refitted in the same bore. Reassemble the connecting rod, caps and bearings to the rods if the bearings do not require renewal, to minimise the risk of getting the caps and rods mixed up.

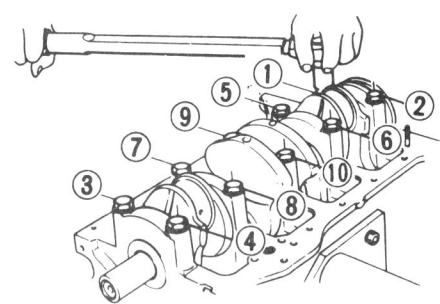

Fig. 1.49 The main bearing cap bolts loosening sequence

60 Main bearings and crankshaft – removal

1   Unscrew and remove the securing bolts from the main bearing caps. The caps are numbered 1 to 5 starting from the timing cover end of the engine and arrows are marked on the caps. These point towards the timing cover to ensure correct orientation of the caps when refitting. If arrows are not visible, dot punch the caps on the side nearer the camshaft. Unscrew the securing bolts in the sequence shown (Fig. 1.49).
2   Withdraw the bearing caps complete with the lower halves of the shell bearings.
3   Remove the rear oil seal.
4   Lift the crankshaft from the crankcase and then remove each of the upper halves of the shell bearings.
5   Unscrew the baffle plate retaining screws and remove the plate. Extract the wire gauze from its recess in the crankcase to complete its dismantling.

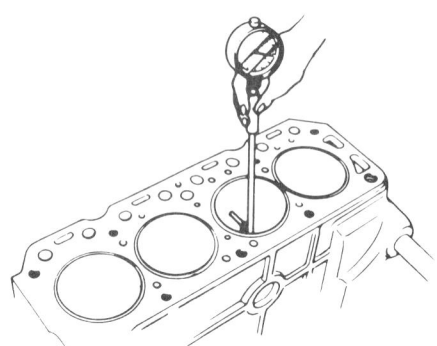

Fig. 1.50 Measuring the cylinder bores for wear

61 Piston rings – removal

1   Refer to the procedure given in Section 16 of this Chapter.

62 Gudgeon pin – removal

1   Refer to the procedure given in Section 17 of this Chapter.

63 Lubrication system – description

1   A force-feed system of lubrication is fitted with oil circulated around the engine from the sump below the cylinder block. The level of engine oil in the sump is indicated by the dipstick which is fitted on the right-hand side of the engine.
2   The oil pump is mounted on the side of the crankcase and is driven by a helical gear and spindle from the camshaft. Oil is drawn from the sump through a gauze screen in the oil strainer, and is sucked up the pick-up pipe and drawn into the trochoid type oil pump. From the pump it is forced under pressure along a gallery on the right-hand side of the engine, and through drillings to the big-end, main and camshaft bearings. A small hole in each connecting rod allows a jet of oil to lubricate the cylinder wall with each revolution.
3   From the camshaft central bearing, oil is fed through drilled passages in the cylinder block and head to the rocker bracket where it enters the hollow rocker shaft. Holes drilled in the hollow rocker shaft allow for lubrication of the rocker arms, the valve stems and pushrod ends. Oil from the front camshaft bearing also lubricates the timing gears and timing chain.
4   Oil returns to the sump by various passages, the tappets being lubricated by oil returning via the pushrod drillings in the block.

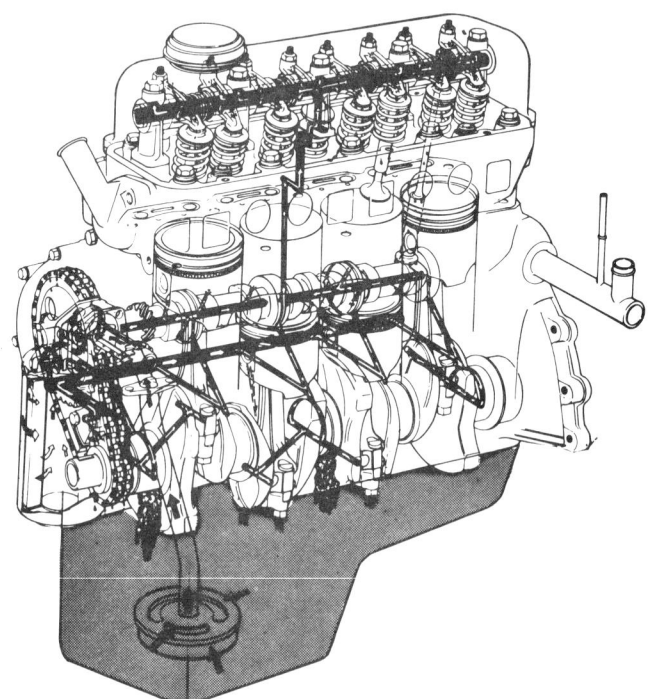

Fig. 1.51 The lubrication circuit

63.6 The oil filter and pump body. Note the oil pressure switch and the engine earth strap retained under the securing bolt head at the front

66.1 The shell bearing identification mark on its rear face

69.1 Check the ring to piston clearance using a feeler gauge

5   A full flow cartridge type filter is fitted and oil passes through this filter before it reaches the main oil gallery. The oil is passed directly from the oil pump to the filter.
6   An oil pressure relief valve and warning switch are located in the pump unit body (photo).

64 Examination and renovation – general

1   With the engine stripped, and all components thoroughly cleaned, it is now time to examine everything for wear and damage.
2   Individual parts and assemblies should be checked and, where possible, renovated or otherwise renewed, as described in the following Sections.

65 Crankshaft and main bearings – examination and renovation

1   Refer to the procedure given in Section 21, but note the following differences:

    (a) *The torque wrench setting for the main bearing cap bolts when using Plastigage is 36 to 43 lbf ft (5 to 6 kgf m)*
    (b) *The fitted depth of the clutch pilot bearing is 0·110 in (2·8 mm)*

66 Connecting rods and connecting rod (big-end) bearings – examination and renovation

1   Refer to the procedure given in Section 22 but note that the comparative weight of new connecting rods must be equal within 0·176 oz (5 gm).
2   The big-end endplay differs and should be 0·004 to 0·008 in (0·1 to 0·2 mm).

67 Cylinder bores – examination and renovation

1   Refer to the procedure given in Section 23, but not the following differences:

    (a) *When measuring the bore diameter, the difference between the two measurements should be a maximum of 0·008 in (0·20 mm)*
    (b) *The standard clearance between a piston and the cylinder walls is between 0·0009 and 0·0017 in (0·023 and 0·0043 mm)*
    (c) *The extracting force for a feeler blade 0·001 in (0·03 mm) should be between 0·020 and 0·059 lb (0·5 and 1·5 kg)*

68 Crankcase, cylinder block and mountings – examination and renovation

1   Refer to the procedure given in Section 24 of this Chapter.

69 Pistons and piston rings – examination and renovation

1   Refer to the procedure given in Section 25 of this Chapter.

70 Camshaft and camshaft bearings – examination and renovation

1   The procedure is generally as described in Section 26, remembering that the camshaft bearings are in the cylinder block rather than the cylinder head.
2   Camshaft endplay should be less than 0·004 in (0·10 mm). If above the maximum, the locating plate must be renewed.
3   Check that the oilways are clear.

71 Timing chain, gears and tensioner – examination and renovation

1   Examine the teeth on both the crankshaft gear wheel and the

70.3 Check that the camshaft oilways are clear

74.1a Using feeler gauges to check the rotor tip clearance

74.1b Using feeler gauges to check the rotor side clearance

74.1c The oil pressure relief valve removed for inspection

78.1 Insert the gauze filter

78.2 Refit baffle plate

78.3 Refit the tappets

78.4 Refit the camshaft (carefully)

78.5 Refit the camshaft retaining plate as shown

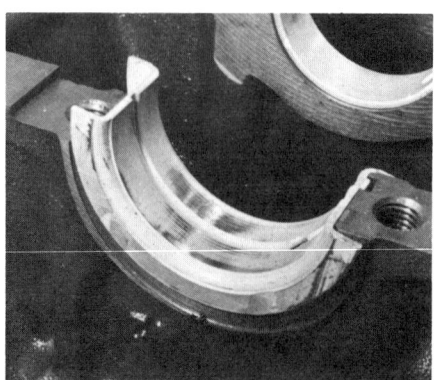

78.6 The central main bearing cap incorporating side thrust washers

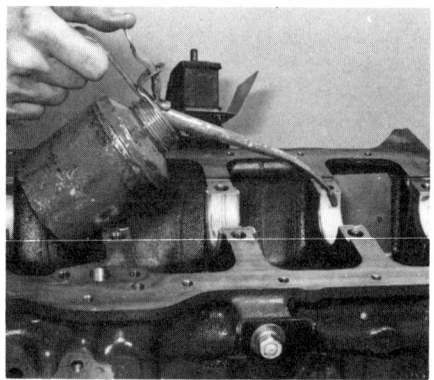

78.7a Lubricate the bearings and ...

78.7b ...refit the crankshaft

camshaft gearwheel for wear. Each tooth forms an inverted 'V' with the gearwheel periphery, and if worn the side of each tooth under tension will be slightly concave in shape when compared with the other side of the tooth (ie; one side of the inverted 'V' will be concave when compared with the other). If any sign of wear is present the gearwheels must be renewed.

2 Examine the links of the chain for side slackness and renew the chain if any is noticeable when compared with a new chain. It is a sensible precaution to renew the chain at about 30 000 miles (48 000 km) and at a lesser mileage if the engine is stripped down for a major overhaul. The actual rollers on a very badly worn chain may be slightly grooved.

3 Examine the chain tensioner for wear, and ensure that the slipper pad and plunger move smoothly under the action of the spring. Renew as necessary.

72 Cylinder head and valves – servicing and decarbonizing

1 Refer to the procedure given in Section 28.

73 Valve operating gear – examination and renovation

1 Thoroughly clean the rocker shaft and then check the shaft for straightness by rolling it on plate glass. It is most unlikely that it will deviate from normal, but if it does, purchase a new shaft. The surface of the shaft should be free from any worn ridges caused by the rocker arms. If any wear is present, renew the shaft.

2 Check the rocker arms for wear of the rocker bushes, for wear at the rocker arm face which bears on the valve stem, and for wear of the adjusting ball ended screws. Wear in the rocker arm bush can be checked by gripping the rocker arm tip and holding the rocker arm in place on the shaft, noting if there is any lateral rocker arm shake. If shake is present, and the arm is very loose on the shaft, a new bush or rocker arm must be fitted.

3 Check the tip of the rocker arm where it bears on the valve head for cracking or serious wear on the case hardening. If none is present re-use the rocker arm. Check the lower half of the ball on the end of the rocker arm adjusting screw.

4 Check the pushrods for straightness by rolling them on the bench. Renew any that are bent.

5 Examine the bearing surface of the tappets which lie on the camshaft. Any indentation in this surface or any cracks indicate serious wear and the tappets should be renewed. Thoroughly clean them out, removing all traces of sludge. It is most unlikely that the sides of the tappets will prove worn, but, if they are a very loose fit in their bores, and can readily be rocked, they should be exchanged for new units. It is very unusual to find any wear, and any wear is likely to occur only at very high mileages.

74 Oil pump – examination and renovation

1 Refer to the procedure given in Section 29 of this Chapter.

75 Flywheel – servicing

1 Refer to the procedure given in Section 30 of this Chapter.

76 Oil seals – renewal

1 Refer to the procedure given in Section 32 of this Chapter.

77 Engine reassembly – general

1 Refer to the procedure given in Section 33 of this Chapter.

78 Engine – reassembly

1 If removed, refit the engine mounting brackets.

2 Reinsert the gauze filter into its recess in the crankcase and refit the baffle plate locating with screws and washers (photos).

3 Lubricate and insert the respective tappets into the crankcase (photo).

4 Lubricate the camshaft bearings and lobes and carefully insert the camshaft into position in the crankcase (photo). Do not force it if it gets stuck during insertion but carefully manoeuvre it through the respective bearings until it is fully home.

5 Locate the camshaft retaining plate with its 'lower' marking facing outwards (photo). Refit and tighten the plate bolts and washers and tighten to the specified torque.

6 Check that the main bearings, caps and shells are perfectly clean, then position the shell halves in the block saddles and bearing caps. Note that the centre bearing shell is the flanged one which takes up the endfloat (photo). Check that the oil holes are in alignment when fitted to those of the cylinder block.

7 Lubricate the bearings and crankshaft journals and oilways using clean engine oil (photo). Carefully lower the crankshaft into position (photo).

8 Before fitting the bearing caps, apply some suitable sealant to the rear main bearing contact corners of the block as indicated in Fig. 1.52.

9 Apply some clean engine oil to the lip of the oilseal and carefully locate it on the rear end of the crankshaft (photo). Use a suitable tube drift to locate it on the shaft.

10 Now locate the respective bearing caps and bolts (photo). Tighten the bolts in the sequence shown in Fig. 1.53 progressively to the specified torque. On completion check the crankshaft endfloat and also that it rotates freely (photo). Note that the arrow marks on the cap faces must point to the front of the engine. Check the crankshaft end-float using a suitable feeler gauge as shown in the photo.

11 The piston and connecting rod assemblies are now to be fitted and it is important that they are clean and well lubricated prior to assembly (photo).

12 Locate the connecting rod bearing shells into the rods and caps and lubricate with clean engine oil.

13 Clean and lubricate with clean engine oil both the piston assemblies and the cylinder bores, then insert each piston and rod assembly into its respective bore. Note that the piston number and small notch on its top outer edge must face to the front (photo). As a further check the oil jet hole in the connecting rod must face to the crankcase right-hand side.

14 Compress the piston rings with a suitable ring compressor and carefully tap the piston crown with the end of a hammer handle to press the piston home into its bore (photo).

15 Engage the connecting rod with the crankshaft when the crankpin is at its lowest point of rotational travel. Lubricate the exposed part of the crankpin.

16 Install the big-end cap complete with shell bearing, making sure that the numbers are adjacent and in their correct sequence (photo).

17 Tighten the nuts to the specified torque then repeat the procedure for the remaining pistons/connecting rods and bearings.

18 The crankshaft and camshaft sprocket must now be checked for alignment. Relocate any shim washers originally fitted over the respective shafts and refit the Woodruff keys and sprockets (photo). Now check using a depth gauge that the sprocket alignment heights are within 0·020 in (0·5 mm). Any further adjustment can be made by the use of the special shim washers which are available and are 0·006 in (0·15 mm) thick.

19 When the sprocket alignments are correct, withdraw the sprockets from their shafts and locate them in the timing chain, so that the timing dot on each sprocket are in direct alignment.

20 Now relocate the sprockets and chain onto the crankshaft and camshaft, keeping the timing dots in alignment (photo). Refit the camshaft sprocket retaining bolt with spring and flat washer (photo). Tighten to the specified torque.

21 Check that the timing chain tensioner oil feed hole is clear (photo) and relocate the chain tensioner, securing with the two bolts and spring washers. Now check that the gap between the tensioner body and guide is within 0·6 in (15 mm). If over this tolerance renew the spindle.

22 Relocate the dished washer over the crankshaft with the concave side facing outwards (photo).

23 Smear a liberal proportion of sealant solution over the faces of the timing case and front mating cylinder block faces. Locate the gaskets over the dowels.

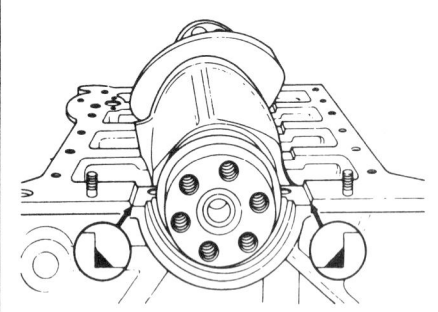

Fig. 1.52 Apply some sealant to the areas shown

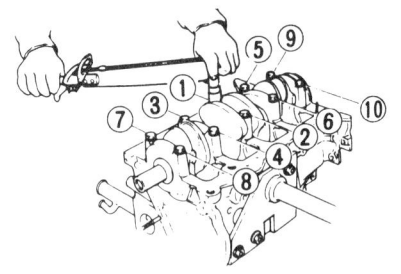

Fig. 1.53 Main bearing cap bolt tightening sequence

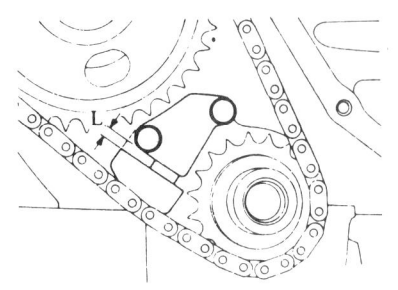

Fig. 1.54 Measure the tensioner spindle projection, 'L'

78.9 Refit the oil seal

78.10a Locate the bearing caps and secure

78.10b Check the crankshaft endfloat using feeler gauges

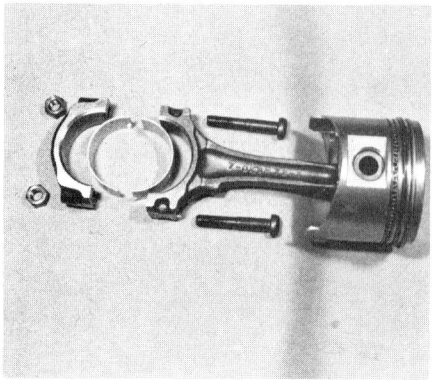

78.11 Piston and connecting rod components laid out ready for reassembly

78.13 The notch on the outer edge of the piston crown indicates the front

78.14 Using a ring compressor to refit the piston

78.16 Refit the big-end caps and bearings

78.17 Tighten to the specified torque

78.18 Crankshaft sprocket shim and Woodruff keys in position

78.20a The sprocket alignments dot clearly marked and in alignment

78.20b Refit the retaining bolt and washers to the camshaft

78.21a Ensure that the timing chain tensioner oil feed hole is clear and ...

78.21b ... refit the tensioner

78.22 Relocate the dished washer onto the crankshaft

78.24 Refit the timing case

78.26 Fit the rubber seals and the sump gaskets

78.27 Refit the sump

78.28 Relocate the backplate and ...

78.29 ... refit the flywheel and securing bolts

78.30 Refit the crankshaft pulley

79.2 The valve lip seals fitted over the guides

24 Check that the oilseal is fully located in the timing case and lubricate its seating lip. Carefully refit the timing case into position (photo) and secure with the retaining bolts tightened to the specified torque.
25 Refit the oil feed suction pipe and gasket, retaining with the two bolts and spring washers.
26 Apply some sealant to the front and rear sump groove seal corners and carefully locate the rubber seals into position with the thick seals at the front and thin to the rear. Fit the sump flange gasket halves into position over the studs and check that the securing bolt holes are in line (photo).
27 Refit the sump and secure with bolts and nuts (photo).
28 Locate the backplate over the two dowels (photo).
29 Refit the flywheel and secure with the six bolts. Note that the bolt holes are not equi-distant and therefore the flywheel will only fit in one position. Tighten the bolts to the specified torque (photo).
30 Refit the crankshaft pulley and secure with bolt and washer (photo).

79 Cylinder head and rocker shaft – reassembly and refitting

1 Fit the valve spring seat over the valve guide.
2 Fit the valve lip seal over the guide using special drift number KV10104800 if available (photo).
3 Lubricate the stem and fit the valve into the guide (photo).
4 Refit the spring with the white painted coil section to the cylinder head and fit the retainer and collets with the aid of a valve spring compressor. The collets can be retained in the valve stem groove with a dab of grease.
5 Reassemble the rocker shaft assembly in the reverse sequence to dismantling. Lubricate the respective components as they are assembled.
6 Position the cylinder head gasket onto the top of the block locating it over the dowels. Use a non-setting sealant on the joint faces of the head and block if desired.
7 Carefully place the cylinder head into position locating onto the dowels (photo).
8 Insert the respective cylinder head bolt (photo). Note that the longer bolt fits in the centre on the opposite side to the valves. Progressively tighten the bolts to the torque specified in the sequence shown (Fig. 1.56).
9 Lubricate and insert the pushrods into their respective locations (photo).
10 The rocker assembly can now be fitted into position and the ball-pins located in the pushrod dwells (photo). Tighten the bolts to the specified torque (Fig. 1.57).
11 Readjust the valve clearances.

80 Valve clearances – adjustment

1 To check the valve clearances, the engine must be turned over and this is best achieved by applying a ring spanner or socket onto the crankshaft pulley bolt and rotating the crankshaft to the positions required. If the engine is in the vehicle it will be easier to turn it over if the spark plugs are removed (to reduce the compression).
2 The valve clearances should normally be checked when the engine is hot, but if it has been standing and cooled off or is being reassembled, they can be adjusted to the cold clearance specifications initially and checked again later when the engine has been run to warm it up. The clearances are as given in the Specifications.
3 The correct valve clearances are essential for the efficient running of the engine. If the clearances are set too open, the efficiency of the engine is reduced as the valves open late and close earlier than was intended. If, on the other hand the clearances are set too close there is a danger that the stems will expand upon heating and not allow the valves to close properly which will cause burning of the valve head and seat and possible warping.
4 If the engine is in the car to get at the rockers it is merely necessary to remove the rocker cover, and then to lift the rocker cover and gasket away.
5 It is important that the clearance is set when the tappet of the valve being adjusted is on the heel of the cam, (ie opposite the peak). This can be done by carrying out the adjustments in the following order, which also avoids turning the crankshaft more than necessary.

Valve fully open	Check & adjust
Valve No. 8	*Valve No. 1*
Valve No. 6	*Valve No. 3*
Valve No. 4	*Valve No. 5*
Valve No. 7	*Valve No. 2*
Valve No. 1	*Valve No. 8*
Valve No. 3	*Valve No. 6*
Valve No. 5	*Valve No. 4*
Valve No. 2	*Valve No. 7*

6 The correct valve clearance is obtained by slackening the hexagon locknut with a spanner while holding the ballpin against rotation with the screwdriver (photo). Then, still pressing down with the screwdriver, insert a feeler gauge in the gap between the valve stem head and the rocker arm and adjust the ballpin until the feeler gauge will just move in and out without nipping, and, still holding the ballpin in the correct position, tighten the locknut.
7 On completion of all the valve clearance adjustments, refit the rocker cover using a new gasket (when necessary).

81 Engine – external component assembly after major repair

1 Refit the fuel pump using new gaskets, and secure with nut, spring and flat washers.
2 Refit the oil pump unit using a new gasket (photo). The two short bolts are fitted at the rear of the pump. The single long bolt is fitted at the front but do not tighten this bolt at this stage if the engine is out of the vehicle. If the engine is fitted then the earth strap can be fitted under the long bolt head and it can be tightened. (Note that the top rear bolt also retains a wire clip.)

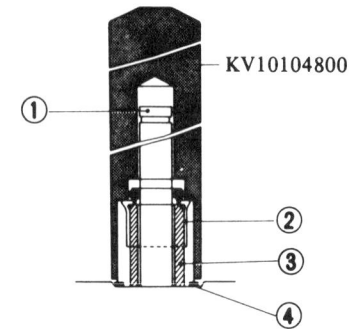

Fig. 1.55 The special drift, tool no KV10104800 used to fit the valve lip seal over the guide

1	Valve	3	Valve guide
2	Lip seal	4	Spring seat

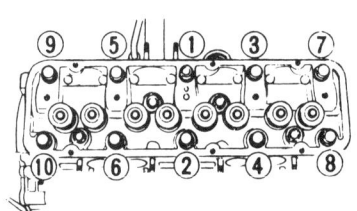

Fig. 1.56 The cylinder head bolt tightening sequence

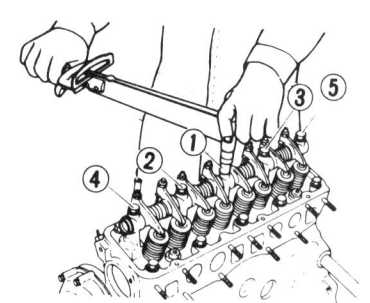

Fig. 1.57 The rocker pedestal bolt tightening sequence

79.3 Refit the valves

79.4a Locate the spring (painted portion downwards) and retainer

79.4b Compress retainer and refit the collets in the valve groove

79.7 Refit the cylinder head — note location dowels in block

79.8 Refit the retaining bolts

79.9 Insert the respective pushrods

79.10 Refit the rocker arm assembly

80.6 Adjusting the valve clearances

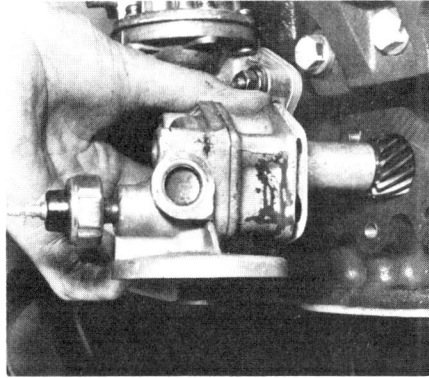

81.2 Install the oil pump

81.5 Refit the inlet and exhaust manifolds using new gasket

81.8 Locate the fuel line with clips at points 1, 2 and 3. Note also the locations of the engine lift bracket (4) and air filter support bracket (5)

3   Refit the water pump unit. Clean off any old gasket from the mating surfaces and fit a new one. Secure the pump with three nuts and two bolts.

4   Refit the thermostat with the 'pip' at the top (see Chapter 2) and secure the housing. Note that the bolt on the top right-hand side retains the fuel line clip.

5   Locate the new inlet/exhaust manifold gasket, making sure that the mating surfaces are clean. Refit the manifolds (photo) and secure with nuts and washers. Remember that the air cleaner support bracket fits over the second stud from the rear, and the engine lifting bracket fits over the front stud of the exhaust manifold. The front stud of the inlet manifold retains the fuel line clip.

6   Refit the alternator, but do not fully tighten the bracket and stay nuts at this stage.

7   Refit the distributor. Refer to Chapter 4 for the correct procedure.

8   Locate the fuel line retaining clip on the alternator side of the cylinder head (photo) using the special bolt. Reconnect the feed tube from the fuel pump.

9   Refit the carburettor using new gaskets and check that the mating surfaces are perfectly clean. Reconnect the fuel line.

10 Refer to Chapter 5 and refit the clutch assembly.

11 Refer to Chapter 6 and refit and secure the gearbox (if removed).

12 Relocate and secure the starter motor unit.

13 The engine is now ready for fitting but first check that all external components are secure and correctly attached.

82 Engine/transmission refitting

1   Refer to the procedure given in Section 42 but ignore those items which do not apply. These are principly the automatic transmission and emission control components.

83 Initial start-up after major repair

1   Refer to the information given in Section 43 but when checking the valve clearances refer to Section 80.

84 Fault diagnosis – engine

Symptom	Reason/s
Engine will not turn over when starter switch is operated	Flat battery Bad battery connections Bad connections at solenoid switch and/or starter motor Starter motor jammed Defective solenoid Starter motor defective
Engine turns over normally but fails to start	No spark at plugs No fuel reaching engine Too much fuel reaching the engine (flooding)
Engine starts but runs unevenly and misfires	Ignition and/or fuel system faults Incorrect valve clearances Burnt out valves Worn piston rings
Lack of power	Ignition and/or fuel system faults Incorrect valve clearances Burnt out valves Worn out piston rings
Excessive oil consumption	Oil leaks from crankshaft rear oil seal, timing cover gasket and oil seal, rocker cover gasket, oil filter gasket, oil pan gasket, oil pan plug washer Worn piston rings or cylinder bores resulting in oil being burnt by engine Worn valve guides and/or defective valve stem seals
Excessive mechanical noise from engine	Wrong valve to rocker clearances Worn crankshaft bearings Worn cylinders/pistons (piston slap) Slack or worn timing chain and sprockets

NOTE: *When investigating starting and uneven running faults do not be tempted into snap diagnosis. Start from the beginning of the check procedure and follow it through. It will take less time in the long run. Poor performance from an engine in terms of power and economy is not normally diagnosed quickly. In any event the ignition and fuel systems must be checked first before assuming any further investigation needs to be made.*
On later model vehicles pay particular attention to the connections of the emission control system, and also refer to the Fault Diagnosis Section in Chapter 3.

Chapter 2 Cooling system

Contents

Specifications

Type	Pressurised system assisted by pump and fan

Coolant capacity
With heater
140J model . . . . $4\frac{1}{2}$ Imp qt (5.1 litre, $5\frac{3}{8}$ US qt)
160J model . . . . $6\frac{1}{8}$ Imp qt (7.0 litre, $7\frac{3}{8}$ US qt)
510 model . . . . $7\frac{7}{8}$ Imp qt (8.9 litre, $9\frac{3}{8}$ US qt)
Without heater
140J model . . . . $3\frac{7}{8}$ Imp qt (4.4 litre, $4\frac{5}{8}$ US qt)
160J model . . . . $5\frac{1}{2}$ Imp qt (6.3 litre, $6\frac{5}{8}$ US qt)
510 model . . . . $7\frac{1}{4}$ Imp qt (8.2 litre, $8\frac{5}{8}$ US qt)

Fan	Belt driven, 4 blades normal or 7 blades on vehicles with air conditioner

Radiator
Type . . . . Corrugated fin and tube
Radiator cap pressure . . . . 13 lbf/in² (0.9 kgf/cm²)

Thermostat opening temperature
Normal use . . . . 80.5 to 83.5° C (177° to 182° F)
Cold use . . . . 86.5 to 89.5° C (188° to 193° F)
Tropical use . . . . 75° to 78° C (167° to 172° F)

1 General description

The principle items of the engine cooling system are the radiator, top and bottom water hoses, water pump, and thermostat. The heater system also operates from the cooling system.

The system operates in the following manner. Cold coolant in the lower part of the radiator is circulated up through the bottom hose to the water pump. The pump impeller then circulates the water through the waterways of the cylinder block and head to cool the cylinder bores and cylinder head components. When the engine has reached its normal operating temperature, the thermostat, which is located in the front face of the cylinder head, opens and the coolant then flows via the top hose into the radiator header tank. The hot coolant then flows down through the radiator core tubes and is cooled by the forward motion of the vehicle. When the engine is running with the car stationary, the cooling fan blades draw air through the radiator to retain the air flow through the core. The flow cycle of the coolant is then repeated through the system.

To assist the engine in reaching its normal operating temperature quickly, the thermostat, which controls the flow rate of coolant dependent on temperature, remains in the closed position and progressively opens as the temperature increases.

If for any reason the coolant temperature rises beyond the normal and boils, the pressure build up in the system will increase and therefore the radiator cap incorporates a pressure valve seal which will open at the specified pressure to relieve the system.

On the 510 models a torque coupling is fitted to the fan and regulates the fan speed to 2500 rpm on standard models or 1800 rpm on models fitted with air conditioner. This unit contains a special silicone oil and it is this which actually controls the operating speed of the fan. There is no facility for topping-up this oil should it ever leak out therefore a new unit must be obtained should this be the case.

Before undertaking *any* operations necessitating the removal of part of the air conditioning equipment, refer to the special notes on this system given in Chapter 1, Part A, Section 1.

2 Cooling system – draining

1   Should the system have to be left empty for any reason both the

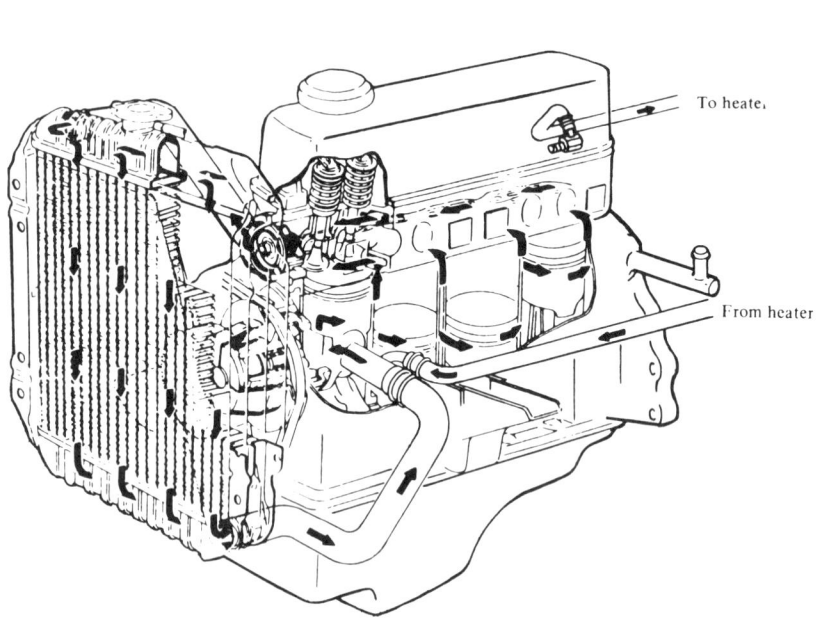

Fig. 2.1 The cooling system circuit – A14 engine

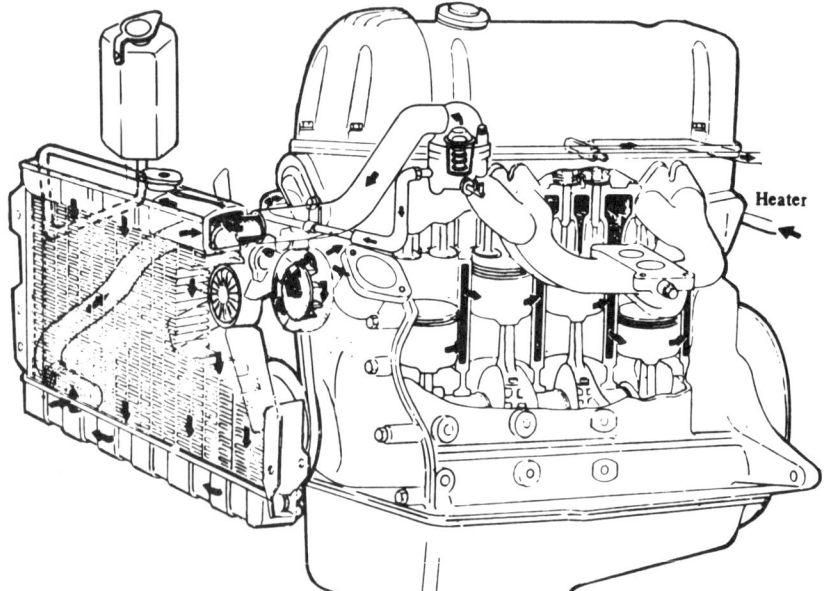

Fig. 2.2 The cooling system circuit – L16 and L20 engines

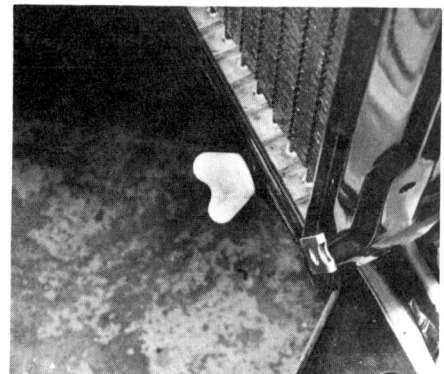

2.4a The radiator drain tap

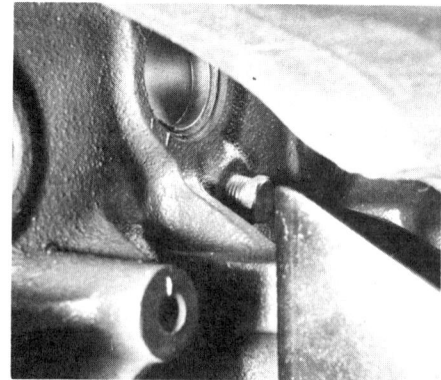

2.4b The cylinder block drain plug (140J)

6.3 Remove the shroud (140J)

6.4 Lift the radiator carefully and remove (140J)

cylinder block and radiator must be completely drained, otherwise with a partly drained system corrosion of the water pump impeller seal face may occur with subsequent early failure of the pump seal and bearing.
2   Place the vehicle on level surface and have ready a container having a capacity of approximately two gallons (9 litres, 2.4 US gals) which will slide beneath the radiator and sump.
3   Move the heater control air lever to 'HOT' and unscrew and remove the radiator cap. If hot, unscrew the cap very slowly, first covering it with a cloth to prevent the danger of scalding when the pressure in the system is released.
4   Unscrew the radiator drain tap (photo) at the base of the radiator then, when coolant ceasesd to flow into the receptacle, repeat the operation by unscrewing the cylinder block plug located on the side of the engine (photo). Retain the coolant for further use. If it contains antifreeze.

3   Cooling system – flushing

1   The radiator and waterways in the engine after some time may become restricted or even blocked with scaler or sediment which reduces the efficiency of the cooling system. When this condition occurs or the coolant appears rusty or dark in colour the system should be flushed. In severe cases reverse flushing may be required as described later.
2   Place the heater control air lever to the 'HOT' position and unscrew fully the radiator and cylinder block drain taps.
3   Remove the radiator filler cap and place a hose in the filler neck. Allow water to run through the system until it emerges quite clean and clear.
4   In severe cases of contamination of the coolant or in the system, reverse flush by first removing the radiator cap and disconnecting the lower radiator hose at the radiator outlet pipe.
5   Remove the top hose at the radiator connection end and remove the radiator as described in Section 6.
6   Invert the radiator and insert the hose in the bottom outlet pipe. Continue flushing until clear water comes from the radiator top tank.
7   To flush the engine water jackets, remove the thermostat as described later in this Chapter and place a hose in the thermostat location until clear water runs from the water pump inlet. Cleaning by the use of chemical compounds is permitted, but the product used must be suitable for use with aluminium-alloy components.

4   Cooling system – filling

1   Place the heater control air lever to the 'HOT' position.
2   Screw in the radiator drain tap and close the cylinder block drain tap.
3   Pour coolant slowly into the radiator so that air can be expelled through the thermostat pin hole without being trapped in a waterway.
4   Fill to the correct level with 1 in (25 mm) below the radiator filler neck and refit the filler cap.
5   Run the engine at about 2000 rpm check for leaks and recheck the coolant level.

5   Antifreeze mixture

1   The cooling system should be filled with antifreeze solution in early autumn. The heater matrix and radiator bottom tank are particularly prone to freeze if antifreeze is not used in air temperature below freezing. Modern antifreeze solutions of good quality will also prevent corrosion and rusting, and they may be left in the system to advantage all year round, draining and refilling with fresh solution every two years.
2   Before adding antifreeze to the system, check all hose connections and check the tightness of the cylinder head bolts as such solutions are searching. The cooling system should be drained and refilled with clean water as previously explained before adding antifreeze.
3   The quantity of antifreeze which should be used for various levels of protection is given in the table below, expressed as a percentage of the system capacity.

Antifreeze volume	Protection to	Safe pump circulation
25°	−26°C (−15°F)	−12°C (10°F)
30%	−33°C (−28°F)	−16°C (3°F)
35%	−39°C (−38°F)	−20°F (−4°F)

4   Where the cooling system contains an anti-freeze solution any topping-up should be done with a solution made up in similar proportions to the original in order to avoid dilution.

6   Radiator – removal, inspection and refitting

1   Drain the cooling system as described in Section 2.
2   Unscrew the respective retaining clips and detach the top and bottom hoses.
3   Unscrew the radiator shroud retaining screws and remove the shroud (photo).
4   On automatic transmission models, detach the inlet and outlet cooler lines from the base of the radiator.
5   Unscrew the two retaining screws on each side of the radiator whilst supporting the radiator. With the screws removed lift the radiator clear (photo) and store in a safe place where the core will not get damaged.
6   Inspect the radiator for leaks or signs of deterioration prior to refitting. The core will probably be partially blocked with road dirt and dead insects in which case hose the core through with water and then blow through using an air line. If the radiator is suspected of leaking, seal off the bottom hose connection temporarily and insert the drain plug/tap, then fill with water. If no leaks are apparent and the radiator appears to be in good order, a further test can be carried out using a pressure tester. This can easily be carried out by your local garage or Datsun dealer but is best done in the car. In this way any other leak points in the system will be detected.
7   Small radiator leaks can be repaired using a solution such as 'Radweld' which is diluted into the coolant, but the manufacturers instructions must be closely followed for maximum results.
8   Badly leaking or damaged radiators can only be properly repaired by a specialist or exchanged for a new/reconditioned unit.
9   Refitting is a reversal of the removal procedure but check that the hoses and connections are good. Renew the hoses if they are at all suspect. When the engine is restarted check the cooling system components for any signs of leakage. If an air conditioner is fitted, check that when refitted there is a minimum clearance of 0.71 in (18 mm) between the compressor and hose.

7   Thermostat – removal, testing and refitting

1   Partially drain the cooling system to allow the top hose to be disconnected without spillage, (about ½ gallon or 2.2 litres should be sufficient).
2   Disconnect the top hose from the thermostat.
3   Unscrew the two retaining bolts and carefully remove the thermostat housing from the front of the cylinder head. Note the position of the thermostat and remove it.
4   To test whether the unit is serviceable, suspend the thermostat on a piece of string in a pan of water being heated. Using a thermometer, with reference to the opening temperature in the Specifications, its operation may be checked. The thermostat should be renewed if it is stuck open or closed or if it fails to operate at the special temperature. The operation of the thermostat is not instantaneous and sufficient time must be allowed for the movement during test. Never refit a faulty unit – leave it out if a new unit is not immediately available.
5   To refit the thermostat and housing, reverse the above procedure but check that the thermostat is correctly positioned as shown in the photograph. Ensure that the mating surfaces of the cylinder head and thermostat housing are clean and in good condition. If the surface is badly corroded, fit a new housing and always use a new gasket.

8   Water pump – removal and refitting

1   Drain the cooling system and retain for further use if an antifreeze

7.5 Install the thermostat with the air release pin positioned at the top as shown. Note also the housing face – cleaned and ready for new gasket

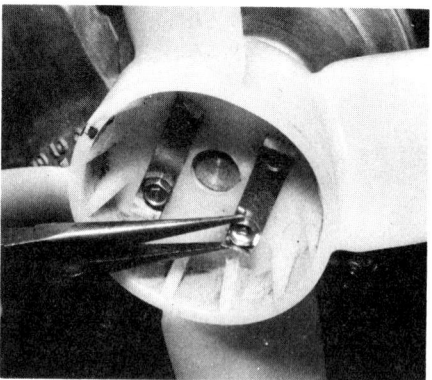

8.4 Fan bolts and lock tabs

8.7 Refit the water pump using a new gasket

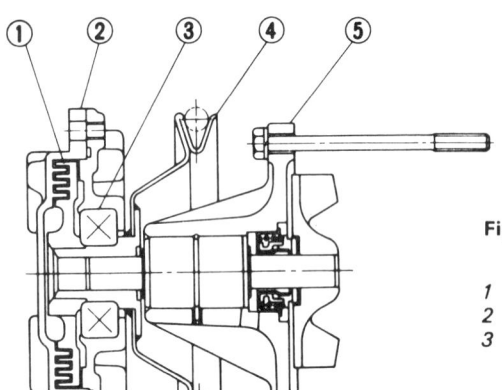

Fig. 2.3 The torque coupling as fitted to 510 models

1 Coupling wheel   4 Pulley
2 Coupling cover   5 Water pump
3 Bearing

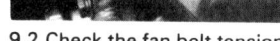

9.2 Check the fan belt tension

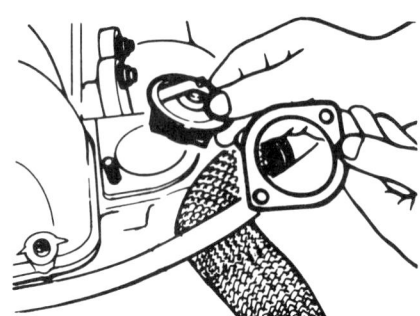

Fig. 2.4 Refitting the thermostat and gasket on the L16 and L20 engines

Fig. 2.5 Removing the water pump (L16 and L20 engines)

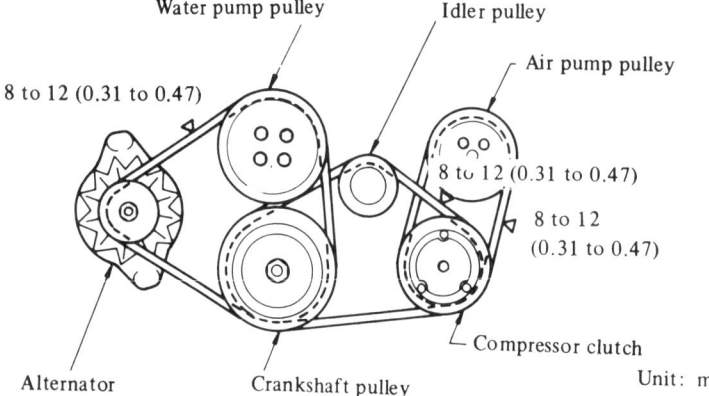

Water pump pulley

Idler pulley

Air pump pulley

8 to 12 (0.31 to 0.47)

8 to 12 (0.31 to 0.47)

8 to 12 (0.31 to 0.47)

Compressor clutch

Alternator

Crankshaft pulley

Unit: mm (in)

Fig. 2.6 Layout of fan, air pump and air conditioning compressor drivebelts showing their respective tension adjustments

solution is used.

2   If necessary, remove the shroud from the radiator.

3   Loosen the alternator mounting bolts and adjustment bolts just sufficiently to allow the alternator to be pivoted towards the engine. Remove the fan belt from the water pump pulley.

4   Bend back the lock tabs retaining the four fan securing bolts and unscrew them. Remove the fan, spacer and pulley from the flange of the water pump (photo).

5   Unscrew the retaining nuts and bolts and withdraw the water pump unit from the cylinder block. Try not to break the gasket in case a new one isn't readily available. If the water pump is stuck tight, tap it gently away using a soft head hammer to break the seal.

6   Where there is evidence of a leaking seal or where severe corrosion of the impeller blades has occurred, do not attempt to repair the water pump but renew it for a reconditioned exchange unit.

7   Refitting is a reversal of the removal procedure, but whenever possible use a new gasket (photo). Readjust the fan belt tension (see Section 9) and refill the cooling system. Check for any signs of leaks

when the engine is running.

9   Fan belt adjustment

1   In order to ensure efficient operation of the alternator and water pump, the fan belt must be correctly tensioned at all times.

2   The fan belt tension is correct when there is a deflection of 0.3 to 0.47 in (8 to 12 mm) midway betweem the alternator and water pump pulleys under an applied force of 22 lb (10 kg). As a rough guide apply finger pressure as shown (photo).

3   If adjustment is required, loosen the alternator pivot and adjusting link bolts, and reposition the alternator as necessary. Tighten the bolts again afterwards.

4   If a new belt is fitted, recheck the tension after about 200 miles (300 km) of driving.

5   Adjustment of the air pump and compressor drivebelts is achieved by repositioning the idler pulleys. The belt layout is shown in Fig. 2.6.

10 Fault diagnosis – cooling system

Symptom	Reason/s
Heat generated in cylinders not being successfully dissipated by radiator	Insufficient wear in cooling system
	Fan belt slipping (accompanied by a shrieking noise on rapid engine acceleration)
	Radiator core blocked or radiator grille restricted
	Bottom water hose collapsed, impeding flow
	Thermostat not opening properly
	Ignition advance and retard incorrectly set (accompanied by loss of power and perhaps misfiring)
	Carburettor incorrectly adjusted (mixture too lean)
	Exhaust system partially blocked
	Oil level in sump too low
	Blow cylinder head gasket (water/steam being forced down the radiator overflow pipe under pressure)
	Engine not yet run-in
	Brakes binding
Too much heat being dissipated by radiator	Thermostat jammed open
	Incorrect grade of thermostat fitted allowing premature opening of valve
	Thermostat missing
Leaks in system	Loose clips on water hoses
	Top or bottom water hoses perished and leaking
	Radiator core leaking
	Thermostat gasket leaking
	Pressure cap spring worn or seal ineffective
	Blown cylinder head gasket (pressure in system forcing water/steam down overflow pipe)
	Cylinder wall or head cracked

Chapter 3 Fuel, exhaust and emission control systems

Contents

Specifications

Air cleaner type . . . .   Viscous or dry paper element. USA models incorporate air temperature control device

Fuel pump
Type . . . .   Diaphragm type mechanically operated from camshaft eccentric
Pump capacity per minute @ 1000 rpm . . . .   1700 cc (103.73 cu in)
Fuel pressure . . . .   3.0 to 3.9 lbf/in^2 (0.21 to 0.27 kgf/cm^2)

Fuel tank capacity . . . .   11 gallons (13$\frac{1}{4}$ US gallons, 50 litres)

Carburettor application
A14 engine models DCG306-80
L16 engine models:
    Manual transmission   213282-331
    Automatic transmission   213282-341
L16 engine models (Twin carburettors) . . . .   HJT38W-7 (Hitachi)

L20 engine models (Non-California)
    Manual transmission DCH340-93A
    Automatic transmission DCH340-94A
L20 engine models (California)
    Manual transmission DCH340-99
    Automatic transmission DCH340-92A

Carburettor data

DCG306-80 carburettors

	Primary	Secondary
Venturi diameter – large	0.87 in (22 mm)	1.06 in (27 mm)
Venturi diameter – small	0.31 to 0.51 in (8 to 13 mm)	0.28 to 0.39 in (7 to 10 mm)
Main jet	104	150
Main air bleed	65	60
Slow air bleed	170	100
Power jet	60	
Engine slow idle speed	650rpm	
Fuel level	0.75 in (19 mm)	

213282-331 and 213282-341 carburettors

	Primary	Secondary
Outlet diameter	1.1024 in (28 mm)	1.2598 in (32 mm)
Venturi diameter	0.8661 x 0.2756 in (22 x 7 mm)	1.1417 x 0.3937 in (29 x 10 mm)
Main jet	102	165
Main air bleed	60	60
1st slow air bleed	0.0394 in (1.0 mm)	—
2nd slow air bleed	180	100
Slow economiser	0.0630 in (1.6 mm)	—
Main nozzle	0.0906 in (2.3 mm)	0.0984 in (2.5 mm)
Power jet	45	
Float level	0.8661 in (22 mm)	
Engine vacuum idle speed	600 rpm	

HJT38W-7 carburettors

Bore . . . . . 1.4961 in (38 mm)
Piston lift . . . . . 1.1417 in (29 mm)
Jet needle M87
Nozzle jet diameter . . . . . 0.0921 in (2.34 mm)
Suction spring 23
Float chamber needle valve inner diameter . . . . . 0.0591 in (1.5 mm)
Float level
    Front . . . . . 0.98 in (25 mm)
    Rear . . . . . 0.79 in (20 mm)
Throttle valve opening . . . . . 0.024 in (0.6 mm)

DCH340-93A carburettors

	Primary	Secondary
Main jet	104	160
Main air bleed	60	60
Slow jet	48	70
Power valve	43	
CO emission at 600 rpm	$1 {+1 \atop -0.7}$ %	
Fuel level	0.91 in (23 mm)	
Bi-metal setting	Centre of index marks	
Fast idle gap – throttle valve to body	0.0524 to 0.0579 in (1.33 to 1.47 mm)	
Fast idle speed at 2nd cam step	1900 to 2800 rpm	
Vacuum break gap	0.0689 in (1.75 mm)	
Choke unloader gap	0.0965 in (2.45 mm)	
Primary/secondary throttle valve interlock opening	0.2906 in (7.38 mm)	
Dashpot adjustment	1900 to 2100 rpm	
BCDD at set pressure (sea level)	-21.65 ± 0.79 in Hg (-550 ± 20 mm Hg)	
BCDD mixture setting (CO% air off)	2 ± 1	

DCH340-94A carburettors
Carburettor details are as listed for the DCH340-93A model, except as given below:
Fast idle gap – throttle valve to body . . . . . 0.0622 to 0.0677 in (1.58 to 1.72 mm)

Fast idle speed at 2nd cam step	2200 to 3200 rpm
	(transmission in N position)
Dashpot adjustment	1650 to 1850

DCH340-99 carburettors
Carburettor details are as listed for the DCH340-93A model except as given below:

	Primary	Secondary
Main jet	103	158
Main air bleed	70	60
Power valve	35	
Vacuum break gap	0.0638 in (1.62 mm)	
BCDD at set pressure (sea level)	−22.44 ± 0.79 in Hg	
	(−570 ± 20 mm Hg)	

DCH340-92A carburettors
Carburettor details are as listed for the DCH340-93A model except as given below:

	Primary	Secondary
Main jet	102	158
Power valve	40	
Fast idle gap – throttle valve to body	0.0622 to 0.0677 in	
	(1.58 to 1.72 mm)	
Fast idle speed at 2nd cam step	2200 to 3200 rpm	
	(transmission in N position)	
Vacuum break gap	0.0591 in (1.50 mm)	
Dashpot adjustment	1650 to 1850 rpm	
BCDD at set pressure (sea level)	−22.44 ± 0.79 in Hg	
	(−570 ± 20 mm Hg)	

Torque wrench settings

	lbf ft	kgf m
Carburettor nuts	3.6 to 7.2	0.5 to 1.0
BCDD	17 to 35	20 to 40
Anti-dieseling solenoid	13	1.8
Accelerator pedal stop bolt	2.7 to 3.2	0.38 to 0.45
Fuel tank drain plug	36 to 43	5.0 to 6.0
Fuel tank securing bolt	5.8 to 8.0	0.8 to 1.1
Reservoir tank securing bolt	2.3 to 3.2	0.32 to 0.44
Exhaust manifold to front tube nut	14 to 18	1.9 to 2.5
U-bolt nut	14 to 15	1.9 to 2.1
Mounting bracket bolt	7 to 9	1.0 to 1.2
Front tube mounting bracket bolt (California)	14 to 15	1.9 to 2.1
Catalytic converter-to-tube bolts (California)	19 to 25	2.6 to 3.4
Top detecting switch	14 to 22	1.9 to 3.0
BPT valve mounting screw	2.7 to 3.7	0.38 to 0.51
Thermal vacuum valve	16	2.2
Air gallery flare nut	36 to 43	5.0 to 5.9

1 General description

All models are equipped with a rear mounted fuel tank, a mechanically operated fuel pump and a carburettor with the necessary pipe lines. The type of carburettor depends upon the engine type and vehicle model (see Specifications).

Emission control systems vary considerably according to the engine type, vehicle model and operating territory. The system components are dealt with in the appropriate Sections towards the end of this Chapter.

Before removing any components necessitating dismantling or disturbing part of the air conditioner system, turn to Chapter 1, Part A, Section 1 and take note of the special precautions necessary regarding the air conditioner system.

2 Automatic temperature control air cleaner

1 This type of air cleaner is fitted on models which have a full emission control system.
2 The air cleaner incorporates a sensor and valve device which 'mixes' the air being drawn into the carburettor to maintain the air temperature at a predetermined level thus preventing icing of the carburettor, reduction of exhaust emission and reduced condensation within the rocker cover.

3 Hot air is drawn from the interior of a deflector plate attached to the exhaust manifold.
4 When the engine is operating under full load, a vacuum diaphragm connected to the intake manifold opens the control valve fully to exclude hot air and override the sensor 'mixing' device.
5 Renewal of the paper type element is carried out by unscrewing the wing nut, springing back the clips (where applicable), and removing the air cleaner lid (still with all connecting hoses attached).
6 If the air cleaner assembly is to be removed complete, then disconnect the following, as applicable:

    (a) Main air inlet hose
    (b) Hot air inlet hose
    (c) Sensor to inlet manifold hose
    (d) The inlet manifold to carbon cannister hose
    (e) CAC valve to air cleaner hose (California models)
    (f) The air control valve hose (Non-California)
    (g) Air pump to air cleaner hose (Non-California)
    (h) AB valve hose
    (i) BCDD hose (Non-California)
    (j) Air cleaner to rocker cover blow-by hose
    (k) Altitude compensator hose (California)

7 Unbolt the air cleaner from its supports and remove.
8 In the event of a fault developing which may be reflected in poor idling, increased fume emission or carburettor icing, or the formation

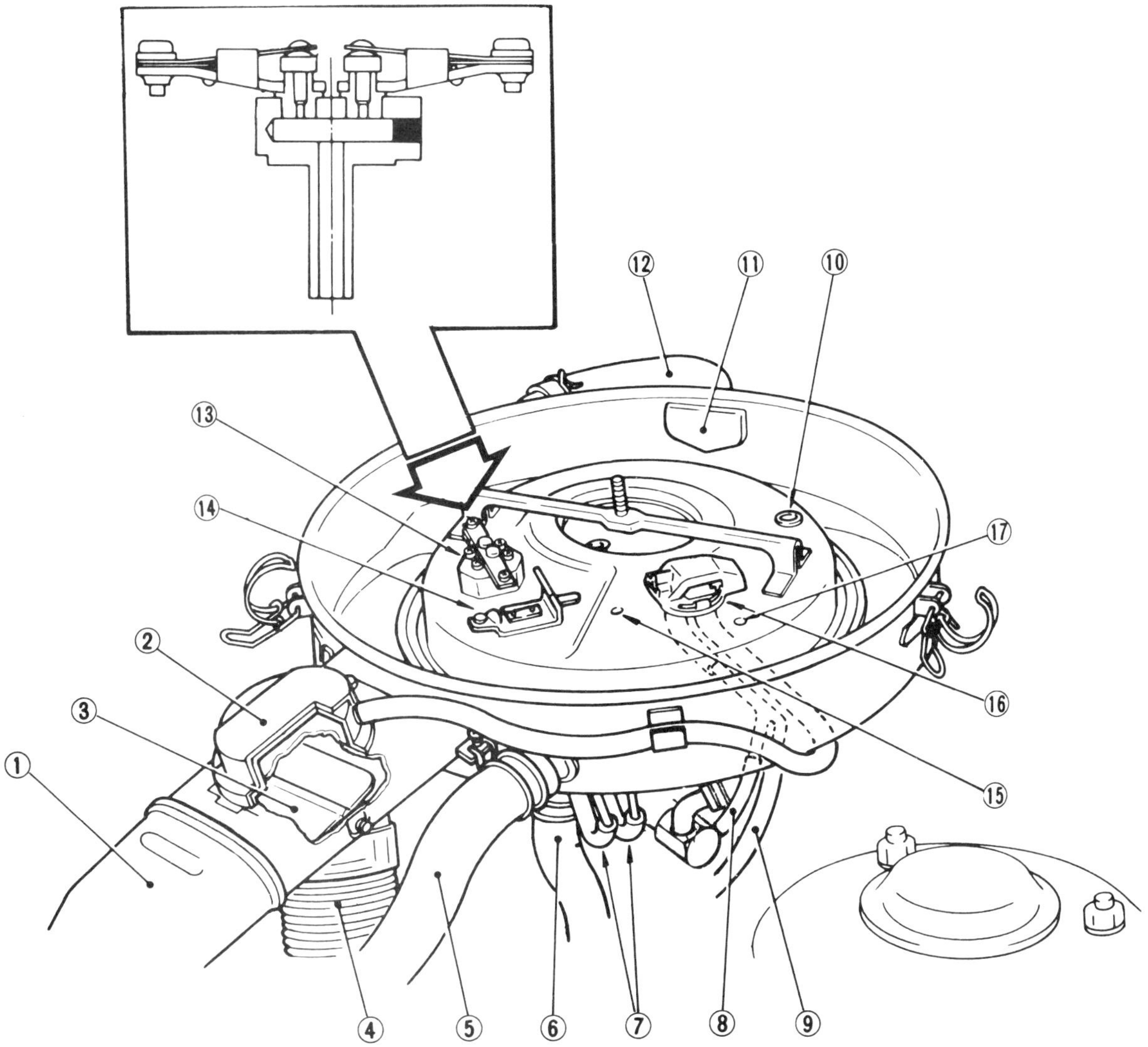

Fig. 3.1 Air cleaner unit as fitted to USA models incorporating an air temperature control

1	Fresh air duct		canister
2	Vacuum motor	6 Air relief valve for air pump (Non-California models)	10 Air inlet for AB valve
3	Air control valve	7 Air tubes for altitude compensator (California models)	11 Blow-by gas filter
4	Hot air duct		12 Blow-by hose
5	Air hose (AIS) From CAC valve (California models) From Air control valve (Non-California)	8 Vacuum tube from intake manifold	13 Idle compensator
		9 Vacuum tube from carbon	14 Altitude compensator (California models)

1 Fresh air duct
2 Vacuum motor
3 Air control valve
4 Hot air duct
5 Air hose (AIS) From CAC valve (California models) From Air control valve (Non-California)

6 Air relief valve for air pump (Non-California models)
7 Air tubes for altitude compensator (California models)
8 Vacuum tube from intake manifold
9 Vacuum tube from carbon

canister
10 Air inlet for AB valve
11 Blow-by gas filter
12 Blow-by hose
13 Idle compensator
14 Altitude compensator (California models)

15 Air hole for TCS system – M/T only (From vacuum switching valve)
16 Temperature sensor assembly
17 Air hole for BCDD (Non-California models)

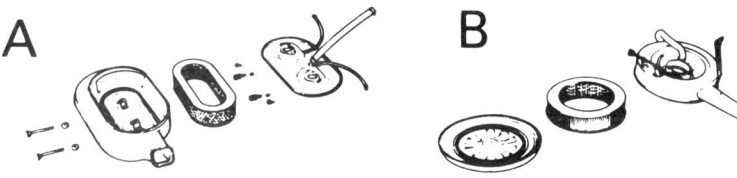

Fig. 3.2 The standard air filters for twin (A) and single (B) carburettor models

of condensation within the rocker cover, carry out the following checks:

9   Inspect all air cleaner hose connections for security and correct location. Check that they are not damaged, distorted or split.

10   Run the engine until normal operating temperature is reached and then allow the engine to idle for a few minutes with the bonnet closed. Switch off the engine and, with the aid of a mirror, inspect the position of the air control valve within the air cleaner intake nozzle. The valve should be closed against exhaust manifold heated air. Conversely, with the engine cold and under bonnet temperature below 100°F (38°C), the valve should be open to exhaust manifold heated air.

11   Where these tests prove the sensor unit to be faulty, flatten the retaining clips and disconnect the hoses by pulling them from their nozzles. Note the relative positions of the two hoses.12   Remove the sensor but leave the gasket which is bonded to the air cleaner body.

13   An idle compensator is fitted in the base of the air cleaner assembly and its purpose is to direct air into the intake manifold to compensate for abnormal enrichment which can occur at high ambient temperature when idling.

14   The compensator has a dual bi-metal valve unit as shown in Fig. 3.1. One valve opens at a temperature of 140 to 158°F (60 to 70°C). The second valve opens at 158 to 194°F (70 to 90°C).

15   This compensator may well be suspect if erratic idling persists.

16   To test the compensator valve, ensure that the ambient temperature is below the opening level and blow and suck through the connecting hose. Any escape of air will mean that the compensator must be renewed.

17   Access to the compensator is obtained after removing the air cleaner cover.

18   If removed, a second test can be undertaken on the compensator by immersing in a bowl of water which is then heated. The respective valves should open at the specified temperature ranges, if not the compensator should be renewed.

19   Refitting of the air cleaner element and component parts is the reverse of the removal procedure.

3   Alternative type air cleaners

1   For some markets, a dry paper element air cleaner is fitted. This requires no maintenance other than periodic cleaning with a compressed air blast and renewal at the specified intervals.

2   A viscous paper element is fitted for some markets, the only maintenance being renewal at the intervals given in the Routine Maintenance Section at the beginning of the manual.

3   For most applications a summer/winter level is incorporated to enable the intake air to be drawn from the engine compartment (summer setting) or from a heat stove around the exhaust manifold (winter setting).

4   To remove an air cleaner element, unscrew the wing nut, spring back the cover clips (where applicable) and lift off the cover.

5   Lift off the air cleaner element, taking care that dirt does not fall into the carburettor.

6   If the air cleaner base is to be removed, undo the clamp screw and remove the screws from the support brackets. Remove the hose to the heat stove. Remove the air cleaner hose.

4   Fuel line filter – renewal

1   The filter is of cartridge, disposable type and should be renewed at intervals not greater than 24 000 miles (40 000 km).

2   The condition of the element can be seen through its transparent bowl (photo).

3   The filter is located on the inner wing panel, and is removed and refitted simply by disconnecting the hoses from it and then pulling it from its retaining clip.

4   It is recommended that the filter fuel lines are not disconnected when there is a high level of fuel in the tank. In any event, the supply hose from the tank should be raised and plugged immediately it is removed from the fuel filter.

5   Fuel pump – description and testing

1   The fuel pump is actuated by the movement of its rocker arm on a

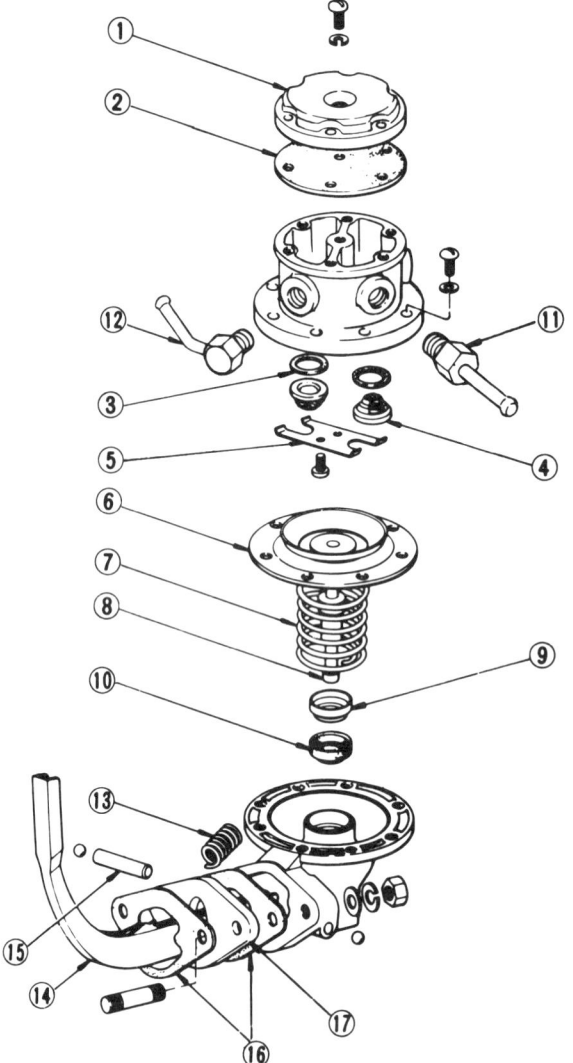

Fig. 3.3 The fuel pump components

1	Pump cap	10	Lower body seal
2	Gasket	11	Inlet connector
3	Valve packing assembly	12	Outlet connector
4	Fuel pump valve assembly	13	Rocker arm spring
5	Valve retainer	14	Rocker arm
6	Diaphragm	15	Rocker arm side pin
7	Diaphragm spring	16	Fuel pump packing
8	Pull rod	17	Spacer-fuel pump to
9	Seal washer		cylinder block

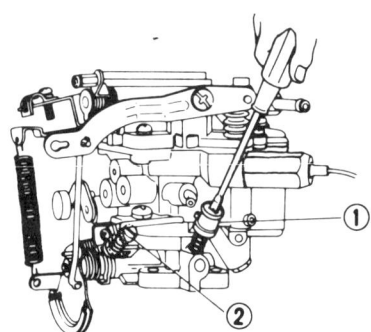

Fig. 3.4 Adjusting the idle screw (1) Also shown is the throttle adjustment screw (2) (DCG306-80 carburettor)

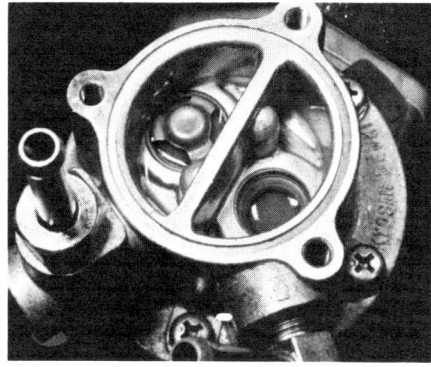

4.2 The fuel line filter

6.2 Removing the fuel pump – note spacer and gaskets

7.5 The fuel pump valves

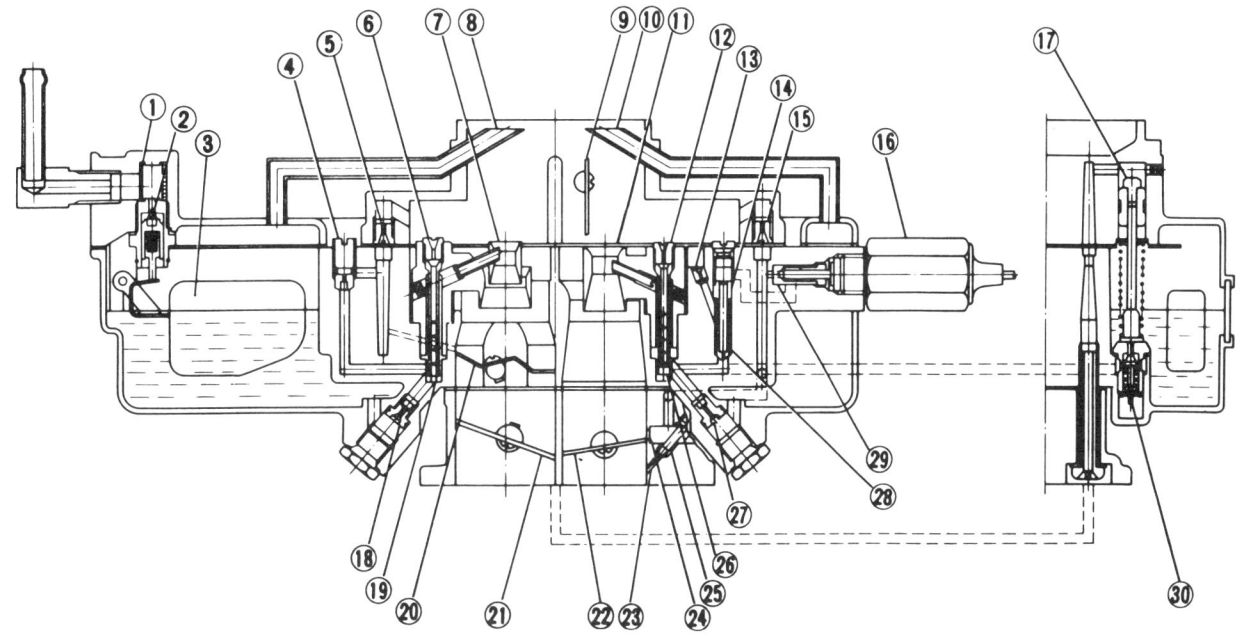

Fig. 3.5 The DCG306-80 carburettor – sectional view

1	Filter	9	Choke valve
2	Needle valve	10	Primary air vent
3	Float	11	Primary small venturi
4	Secondary slow jet	12	Primary main air bleed
5	Secondary slow air bleed	13	Economizer bleed
6	Secondary main air bleed	14	Primary slow jet
7	Secondary small venturi	15	Primary slow air bleed
8	Secondary air vent pipe	16	Solenoid valve

17	Vacuum piston	23	Idle hole
18	Secondary main jet	24	By-pass hole
19	Secondary emulsion tube	25	Idle adjuster screw
20	Auxiliary valve	26	Primary emulsion tube
21	Secondary throttle/ butterfly valve	27	Primary main jet
22	Primary throttle/butterfly valve	28	Economizer hole
		29	Slow economizer
		30	Power valve

camshaft eccentric. This movement is transferred to a flexible diaphragm which draws the fuel from the tank and pumps it under pressure to the carburettor float chamber. Inlet and outlet valves are incorporated to control the flow of fuel irrespective of engine speed. To check the pump proceed as follows.

2   Check that the fuel lines are in good condition, including their unions and also that there is a reasonable quantity of fuel in the tank.

3   Disconnect the fuel pipe at the carburettor inlet union, and the high tension lead to the coil, and with a suitable container or a large rag in position to catch the ejected fuel, turn the engine over on the starter motor solenoid. A good spurt of fuel should emerge from the end of the pipe every second revolution.

6   Fuel pump – removal and refitting

1   Disconnect the hoses from the pump inlet and outlet nozzles. It is recommended that the fuel lines are not disconnected when the fuel

tank is fairly full and in any event the supply pipe from the tank should be raised above the level of fuel in the tank and plugged as soon as it is removed from the pump.

2   Unscrew and remove the securing nuts from the fuel pump flange and remove the pump. Note the sequence of gaskets and spacer. Note that on some models a heat shield is fitted (photo).

3   Refitting is the reverse of the removal procedure.

7   Fuel pump – dismantling, inspection and reassembly

1   Prior to removing the top cover, scribe a mark across the edges of the upper and lower body flanges so that they can be reassembled in the same relative position.

2   Now unscrew the cover retaining screws and carefully remove the cover and gasket. Try to avoid damaging the gasket if possible – a new gasket may not be readily available.

3   Unscrew and remove the screws from the body flange.

4   Unscrew and remove the inlet and outlet elbows.
5   Unscrew and remove the screws from the valve retainer and remove the two valves (photo).
6   Unhook the diaphragm pushrod from the fork at the end of the rocker arm by depressing the diaphragm against the action of its spring and then tilting the diaphragm/rod assembly until the bottom of the rod can be felt to touch the inside of the pump body.
7   Take care not to damage the oil seal as the diaphragm and pushrod are released.
8   If necessary, the rocker arm pivot pin can be driven out with a small drift.
9   Examine all components for wear or cracks and the diaphragm for porosity or deterioration and renew as appropriate.
10   Reassembly is a reversal of dismantling but use new gaskets and other components from the appropriate repair kit.
11   Grease the rocker arm and pivot before assembly.
12   When the reassembly is complete, place a finger over the inlet port and depress the rocker arm fully. A strong suction noise should be heard which indicates that the pump is operating correctly.

8 Carburettor (DCG306–80) – general description

This is a downdraught, twin choke carburettor comprising a primary, secondary and main jet system with a mechanically operated accelerator pump.

The choke is manually operated via a cable. When in operation the choke closes one of the venturi choke tubes and this then opens the throttle valve plate just sufficiently to enrich the fuel mixture entering the inlet system, and increasing the slow running speed when the engine is cold.

For idling and slow running, the fuel passes through the slow running jet, the primary slow air bleed and the secondary slow air bleed. The fuel is finally ejected from the bypass and idle holes (Fig. 3.4).

The accelerator pump is synchronized with the throttle valve. During periods of heavy acceleration, the pump which is of simple piston and valve construction, provides an additional metered quantity of fuel to enrich the normal mixture. The quantity of fuel metered can be varied according to operating climatic conditions by adjusting the stroke of the pump linkage.

The secondary system provides a mixture for normal motoring conditions by means of a main jet and air bleed. The float chamber is fed with fuel pumped by the mechanically operated pump on the crankcase. The level in the chamber is critical and must at all times be maintained as specified. The power valve system utilizes the vacuum in the intake manifold to open or close the valve. During light load running the valve is closed, but is opened during full load running or acceleration, thus furnishing more fuel.

9 Carburettor (DCG306–80) – slow running adjustment

1   Run the engine to normal operating temperature and then set the throttle adjusting screw to provide an engine speed of 600 rpm. If the vehicle is fitted with a tachometer then the setting of engine speed will be no problem. Where an instrument is not available then a useful guide may be obtained from the state of the ignition zarning lamp. This should be just going out at the correct idling speed.
2   Setting of the mixture screw may be carried out using 'Color-tune' or a vacuum gauge attached to the inlet manifold. In either case follow the equipment manufacturer's instructions.
3   In certain territories, the use of a CO meter is essential and if this is used then the throttle adjusting screw and the mixture screw must be turned to provide a reading on the meter as given in the Specifications at the specified engine idling speed.
4   As a temporary measure, the adjustment screws may be rotated progressively, first one and then the other until the engine idles at the correct speed without any 'hunting' or stalling. Turning the mixture screw clockwise weakens the mixture and anti-clockwise enriches it. Never screw the mixture screw in too far so that it forced into its seat or damage to the needle point of the screw will result. On later types carburettors this cannot happen as a travel stop is fitted.
5   If it is found difficult to set the adjustment at the specified idle speed without the engine stalling, hunting or running erratically, then a check should be made on the ignition timing and the other associate

component adjustments, both in the carburettor and engine. Items such as the distributor contact breaker points, spark plugs and valve clearances must all be as specified in good working condition, and the carburettor float level adjustment must be correct.
6   It may be necessary to occasionally 'blip' the throttle to clear the carburettor during adjustment.

10 Carburettor (DCG306–80) float level adjustment

1   Where the appropriate adjustments have been carried out and there is evidence of fuel starvation or conversely, flooding or excessively rich mixture, the float level should be checked.
2   Remove the carburettor, as described in Section 12.
3   Disconnect choke connecting rod, accelerator pump lever and return spring (photo).
4   Unscrew and remove the five securing screws which secure the upper choke chamber to the main body.
5   Turn the float chamber upside down and check the dimension H with the float hanging down under its own weight. This should be 0·59 in (15·0 mm) (Fig. 3.6).
6   Now gently push the float upwards to the full extent of its travel and check the clearance between the endface of the inlet needle valve and the float tongue. This should be 0·051 to 0·067 in (1·3 to 1·7 mm). Adjustment to correct either of these dimensions is carried out by bending the float tongue or the stopper tag.
7   Reassemble in the reverse order but use a new gasket. Do not overtighten the retaining screws and on completion recheck the idle adjustments.
8   If the float level has been correctly adjusted the fuel level should be 0·75 in (19 mm) from the centre body to choke chamber flange as in Fig. 3.7.

11 Carburettor (DCG306–80) primary and secondary throttle butterfly valves – adjustment of interlock opening

1   Remove the air cleaner unit from the carburettor.
2   Check that the choke and throttle controls are fully operational and not sticking.
3   Refering to Fig. 3.8, open the primary throttle butterfly valve so that it is 48° from the closed position. Now measure the gap between the butterfly and the chamber wall as indicated by G1. The correct clearance should read 0·2295 in (5·83 mm).
4   If adjustment is necessary, retain the butterfly in position and carefully bend the connecting rod to suit. On completion check that the link mechanism operates freely.
5   When the primary valve butterfly is opened to 48° from the closed position the secondary throttle butterfly should be just ready to open.
6   When the air cleaner is refitted, run the engine up to its normal operating temperature and recheck the idle adjustments.

12 Carburettor (DCG306–80) – removal and refitting

1   Disconnect the battery earth cable.
2   Remove the carburettor air cleaner.
3   Unscrew the choke cable connection clamp screw, and loosen the outer cable clamp screw.
4   Depress the throttle cable attachment plate and release the cable nipple. Unscrew and release the outer cable clamp (photo).
5   Pull the distributor to carburettor vacuum pipe free from the carburettor.
6   Unscrew and release the petrol feed pipe clip. Pull the pipe free.
7   Detach the cable from the anti-dieseling solenoid valve at the snap connector.
8   Unscrew the four carburettor to manifold retaining nuts, and carefully lift clear taking care not to damage the gasket if possible.
9   Refitting is a reversal of the removal procedure but check that all connections are correctly made, and whenever possible use new flange gaskets. Readjust the carburettor.

13 Carburettors, dismantling and reassembly – general

1   With time the component parts of the carburettor will wear and

"G1": 5.83 mm (0.2295 in)

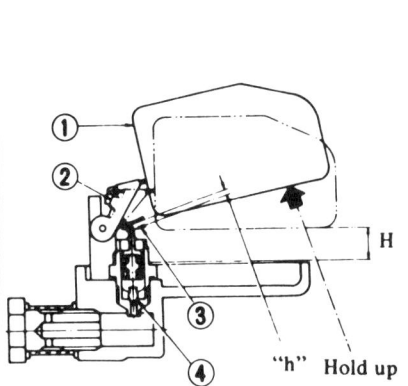

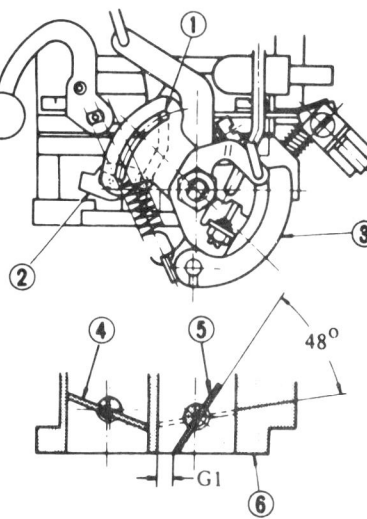

Fig. 3.6 Float adjustment (DCG306-80 carburettor)

1 Float
2 Float stop
3 Float stop
4 Inlet needle valve

Fig. 3.7 Fuel level check via window in float chamber (DCG306-80 carburettor)

Fig. 3.8 Check the primary throttle butterfly valve clearance (DCG306-80 carburettor)

1 Connecting rod
2 Secondary connecting rod
3 Throttle lever
4 Secondary throttle butterfly valve
5 Primary throttle butterfly valve
6 Throttle chamber

Fig. 3.9 The DCG306-80 model carburettor component parts

1 Throttle return spring
2 Starting lever
3 Connecting rod
4 Choke connecting rod
5 Secondary slow jet
6 Primary slow jet
7 Economizer bleed
8 Power jet
9 Main air bleed – secondary
10 Main air bleed – primary
11 Small venturi – primary and secondary
12 Slow air bleed – primary
13 Slow air bleed – secondary
14 Needle valve
15 Float
16 Main jet – primary
17 Main jet – secondary
18 Idle adjusting screw
19 Throttle adjusting screw
20 Throttle valve – primary
21 Throttle valve – secondary
22 Accelerating pump rod
23 Accelerating pump lever
24 Accelerating pump
25 Injector weight
26 Choke valve
27 Auxiliary valve
28 Anti-dieseling solenoid valve

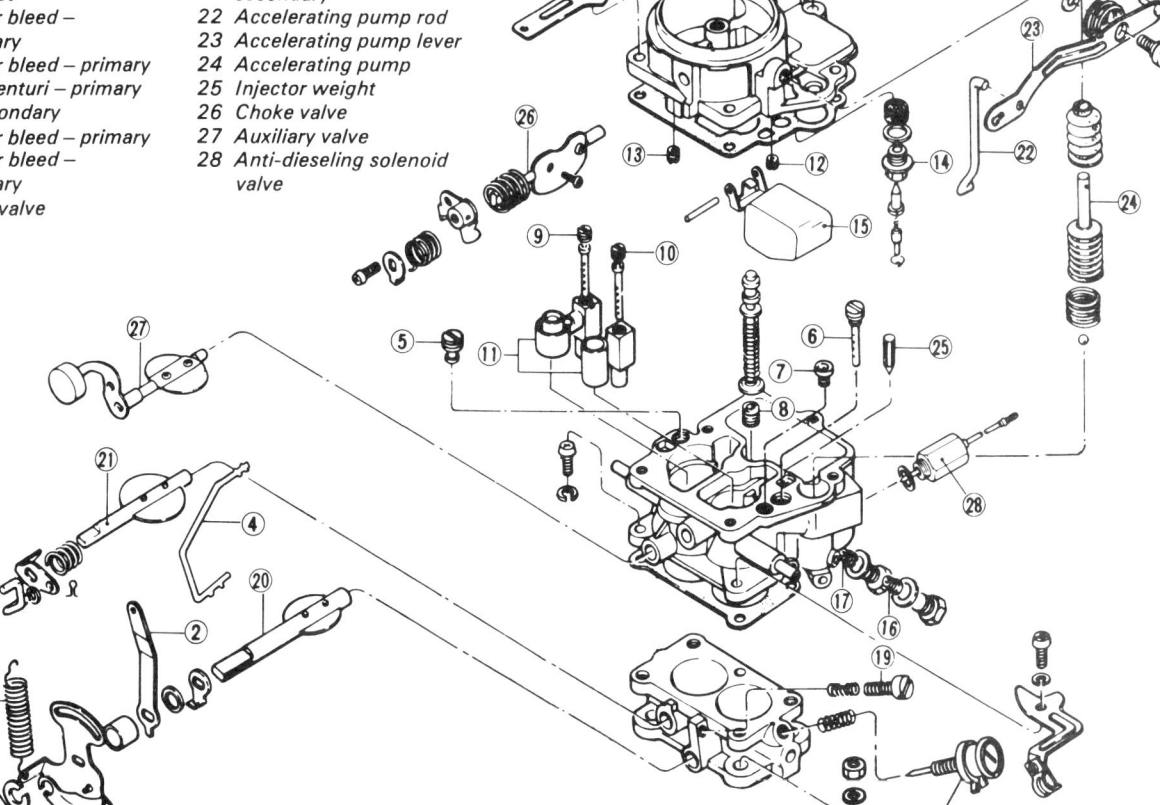

66

10.3 The DCG306–80 carburettor
A Choke connecting rod
B Accelerator pump rod
C Return spring

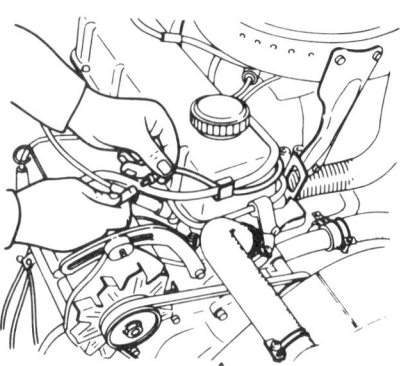

Fig. 3.10 Disconnect the solenoid wire

12.4 The DCG306–80 carburettor throttle cable connection
A Cable clamp
B Nipple

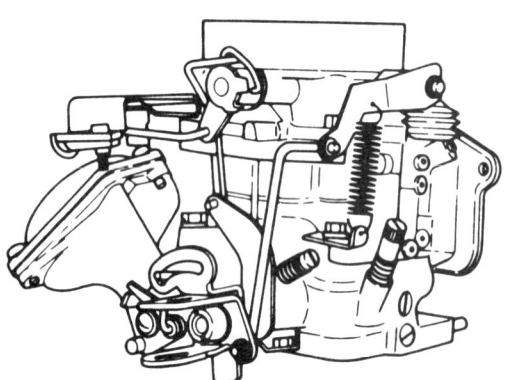

Fig. 3.11 The 213282-331 carburettor fitted to engine with manual transmission

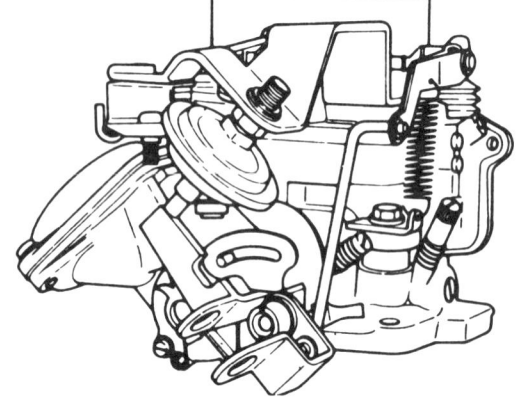

Fig. 3.12 The 213282-341 carburettor fitted to engine with automatic transmission

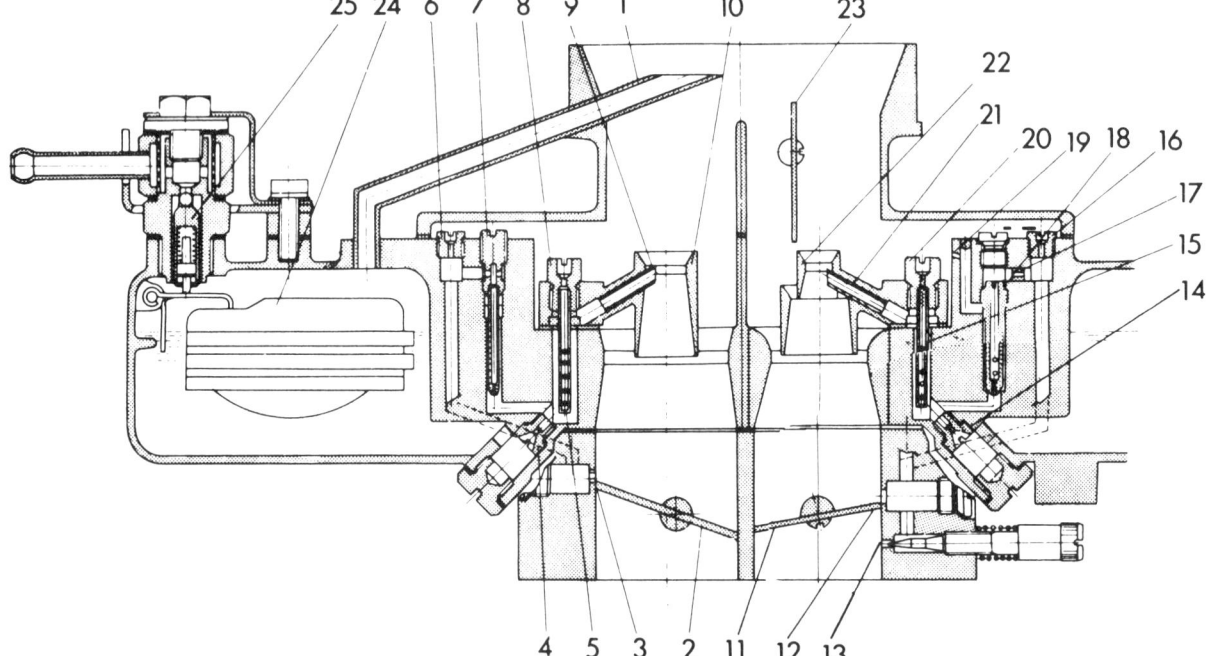

Fig. 3.13 Sectional view of the 213282 type carburettor

1 Air vent pipe	8 Secondary main air bleed	14 Primary main jet	20 Primary main air bleed
2 Secondary throttle valve	9 Secondary main nozzle	15 Primary emulsion tube	21 Primary main nozzle
3 Step hole	10 Secondary small venturi	16 2nd slow air bleed	22 Primary small venturi
4 Secondary main jet	11 Primary throttle valve	17 Slow economizer jet	23 Choke valve
5 Secondary emulsion tube	12 Bypass hole	18 Slow jet	24 Float
6 Step air bleed	13 Idle nozzle	19 1st slow air bleed	25 Float valve
7 Step jet			

petrol consumption will increase. The diameter of drillings and jet may alter, and air and fuel leaks may develop round spindles and other moving parts. Because of the high degree of precision involved it is recommended that an exchange rebuilt carburettor is purchased. This is one of the few instances where it is better to buy a new component rather than to rebuild the old one.

2　The accelerator pump itself may need attention and gaskets may need renewal. Providing care is taken there is no reason why the carburettor may not be completely reconditioned at home, but ensure a full repair kit can be obtained before you strip the carburettor down. *Never* poke out jets with wire or similar to clean them but blow them out with compressed air or air from a car tyre pump. Always use suitable tools and new gaskets.

14 Carburettor (DCG306–80) – dismantling and reassembly

1　The main jets and needle valves are accessible from the exterior of the carburettor.
2　These should be unscrewed, removed and cleaned by blowing them through with air from a tyre pump; *never* probe a jet or needle valve seat with wire.
3　Detach the choke chamber by removing the connecting rod, accelerator pump lever, return spring and the five securing screws.
4　The primary and secondary emulsion tubes are accessible after removing the main air bleeds.
5　Remove the accelerator pump cover, retaining the spring, piston and ball valve carefully.
6　Separate the centre body from the throttle housing by unscrewing and removing securing screws. Slide out the float pivot pin and remove the float.
7　Unless imperative, do not dismantle the throttle butterfly valves from their spindles.
8　Take great care when disconnecting the interlock rods that they are not bent or twisted or the settings and adjustments will be upset.
9　With the carburettor dismantled, clean all components in clean fuel and blow through the internal body passages with air from a tyre pump.
10　Inspect all components for wear and the body and chamber castings for cracks.
11　Clean the small gauze filter and if corroded or clogged, renew it.
12　If wear is evident in the throttle spindle, the carburettor should be renewed on an exchange basis.
13　Check all jet and air bleed sizes with those specified in Specifications in case a previous owner has changed them for ones of incorrect size.
14　Check the ejection of fuel when the accelerator pump is actuated.

15　Reassembly is a reversal of dismantling using all the items supplied in the repair kit.
16　When the carburettor is being reassembled, check the float movement (Section 10) and when it is refitted to the engine, carry out all the checks and adjustments described in this Chapter.

15 Anti-dieseling solenoid valve – testing, removal and refitting

1　To check the operation of the dieseling solenoid run the engine at its normal idle speed and detach the solenoid wire (Fig. 3.10). If the engine fails to stop running the solenoid is suspect and a check should be made on its wiring for continuity.
2　The valve is not repairable and must therefore be renewed if faulty.
　　To remove simply unscrew it from the carburettor. Screw in the new valve and tighten to the setting given in the Specifications.

16 Carburettor (213282–331 and 213282–341) – general description

These carburettors are of a dual barrel downdraught design which incorporate a primary and secondary system.

Each system shares a common top cover but each has a separate main nozzle and throttle valve.

The function of the primary system is to supply a suitable petrol air mixture for low speeds, cruising speeds and acceleration. It will also provide the correct mixture for engine starting when the choke disc is in the closed position. There is a special power mechanism which will discharge fuel into the primary system under full load or acceleration.

Carburettors fitted to automatic transmission models differ in that they are fitted with a dashpot device which is designed to prevent the engine stalling. The dashpot works in conjunction with the primary throttle butterfly valve via a linkage. When the butterfly is to within 11° of being closed, the throttle lever contacts the dashpot stem and the primary butterfly valve is then progressively closed.

A step port regulates the change of fuel supply from primary to secondary system which comes into operation when the primary valve butterfly is opened to about 50°.

The change over between primary and secondary systems is controlled by a special diaphragm, one side of which is open to the atmosphere and the other side connected through a small drilling to air jets in both the primary and secondary systems.

When induction depression is increased at the venturis the diaphragm is pulled against its spring and to the secondary throttle valve via a linkage from the diaphragm. The secondary throttle valve now comes into operation.

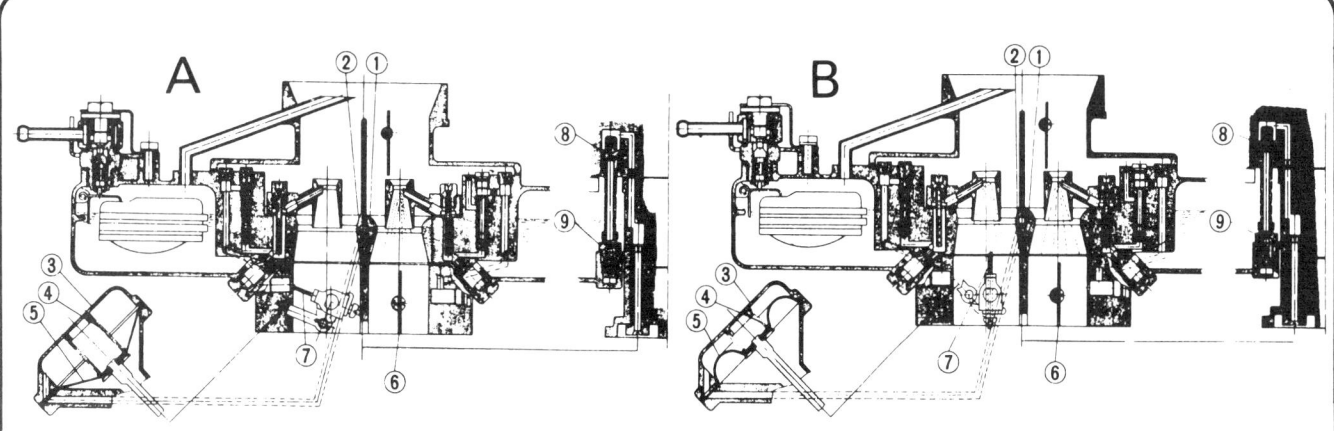

Fig. 3.14 Views showing the fuel flow at full throttle – low speed (A), and (B) shows the flow at full throttle – at high speed (213282 type carburettor)

1 *Primary vacuum port*	4 *Diaphragm spring*	6 *Secondary throttle valve*	8 *Vacuum piston*
2 *Secondary vacuum port*	5 *Diaphragm*	7 *Primary throttle valve*	9 *Power jet*
3 *Diaphragm chamber cover*			

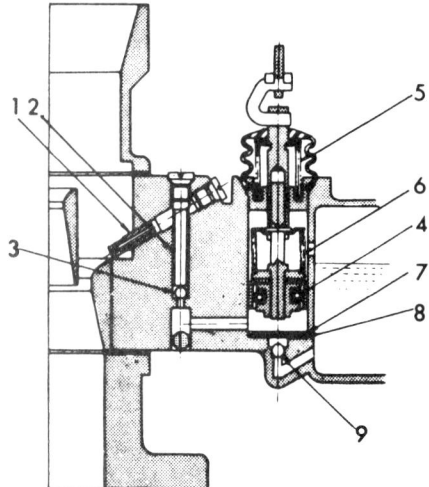

Fig. 3.15 The accelerator pump components (213282 type carburettor)

1 Pump injector	6 Piston return spring
2 Weight	7 Clip
3 Outlet valve	8 Strainer
4 Piston	9 Inlet valve
5 Damper spring	

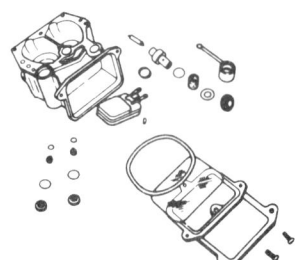

Fig. 3.16 Float chamber components
(213282 type carburettor)

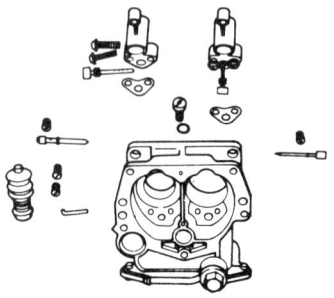

Fig. 3.17 Removal of emulsion tubes
(213282 type carburettor)

Fig. 3.18 Removal of choke
(213282 type carburettor)

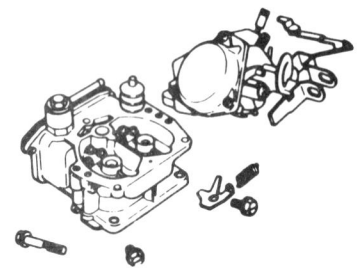

Fig. 3.19 Removal of throttle chamber from
main body (213282 type carburettor)

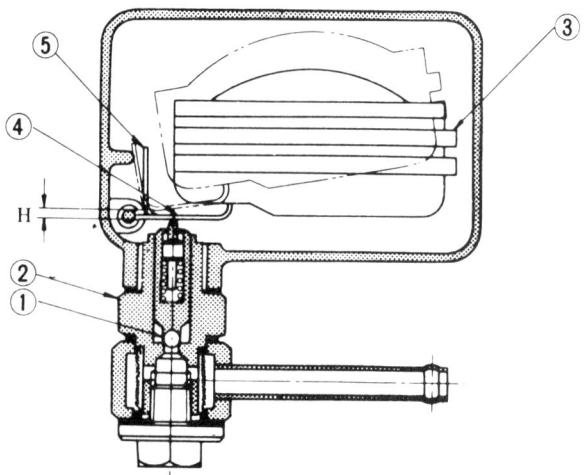

Fig. 3.21 Adjustment of fuel level (213282 type carburettor)

1 Ball valve	4 Float arm
2 Valve seat	5 Float stopper
3 Float	

Fig. 3.20 Removal of throttle valve
(213282 type carburettor)

17 Carburettor (213282–331 and 213282–341) – removal and refitting

1   Open the bonnet and remove the air cleaner assembly.
2   Slacken the clip and detach the feed pipe from the carburettor body. If a fuel return pipe is fitted this must be detached also.
3   Detach the distributor vacuum advance pipe from the carburettor.
4   Disconnect the throttle control rod from the carburettor throttle lever and then the choke control.
5   Undo and remove the four nuts and spring washers that secure the carburettor to the inlet manifold.
6   Carefully lift away the carburettor, discard the gaskets and recover any insulation packing used.
7   Refitting the carburettor is the reverse sequence to removal. Clean the mating faces free of any old gasket or jointing compound and always use new gaskets.

18 Carburettor (213282–331 and 213282–341) – dismantling and reassembly

1   Wash the exterior of the carburettor and wipe dry with a clean non-fluffy rag. As the unit is dismantled note the location of each part and place in order on clean newspaper.
2   Using a small screwdriver or pointed pliers remove the small E-clip and detach the accelerator pump operating lever from the top cover assembly.
3   Disconnect the throttle lever return spring and then the primary to secondary interlock mechanism return spring.
4   Undo and remove the four screws and spring washers and partially lift away the top cover assembly. Detach the choke linkage and completely remove the top cover.
5   Disconnect the throttle vacuum chamber diaphragm rod from the secondary throttle lever.
6   Undo and remove the four screws and spring washers that secure the carburettor flange to the main body.
7   Unscrew the primary and secondary bore main air bleeds and emulsion tubes from each side of the carburettor body.
8   Unscrew the two plugs which cover the main jets. Carefully remove both main jets.
9   Unscrew and remove the primary and secondary slow air bleeds and then the primary and secondary slow running jets.
10 Undo and remove the two screws from the accelerator pump bore cover and carefully withdraw the accelerator pump plunger assembly.
11 Turn the carburettor body upside down and recover the lower spring and ball valve.
12 Carefully withdraw the small pin from the plunger assembly and if necessary dismantle the components. Take extra care on noting their locations and which way round each part is fitted.
13 Unscrew the pump injector securing bolt and lift away the injector and sealing washers. Turn the carburettor body upside down and remove the small spring and ball from the injector bore.
14 Undo and remove the three screws securing the venturi to the secondary bore. Lift away the venturi and gasket.
15 On carburettors fitted with a fuel return assembly this should be removed next. This will give access to the needle valve and seat.
16 Using a box spanner unscrew and remove the needle valve and seat assembly.
17 Undo and remove the three float chamber securing screws and lift away the cover, glass and gasket. The spacer and float may now be removed from the chamber.
18 Undo and remove the three screws which secure the secondary throttle vacuum chamber assembly to the carburettor main body. Detach the assembly from the main body and recover the gasket.
19 Should it be necessary to dismantle the vacuum chamber, undo and remove the three screws on the outer cover. Carefully part the two halves of the assembly and lift away the diaphragm, spring and small check ball and spring.
20 For carburettors fitted to engines of cars with automatic transmission, remove the dashpot assembly and its mechanism.
21 On carburettors fitted with a fuel return system, if the unit was functioning correctly before dismantling, leave well alone. If not it should be dismantled for further investigation. It is important that the bi-metal portion is kept intact.
22 The carburettor top cover may be dismantled if the choke valve and shaft require attention. Mark the relative position of the choke

valve and cover to ensure correct reassembly.
23 Using a small file remove the peening from the ends of the choke valve retaining screws.
24 Disconnect the linkage from the end of the choke shaft.
25 Using a small screwdriver undo and remove the two choke valve securing screws. Withdraw the choke valve from the shaft.
26 Withdraw the choke valve shaft from the cover.
27 Should it be necessary to service the flange, first screw out and remove the idle mixture adjustment screw and spring.
28 Remove the throttle adjusting screw and spring.
29 Mark the relative positions of the primary and secondary throttle valves and their respective bores.
30 Using a small file remove the peening from the ends of the throttle plate securing screws.
31 Withdraw both throttle valves and then withdraw the throttle shafts from the flange.
32 Undo and remove the throttle lever and assembly retaining nut from the end of the primary throttle shaft.
33 The carburettor is now completely dismantled and, after cleaning, ready for inspection.
34 If a compressed air line is available carefully blow through all drillings. Do not use a wire probe to clean jets as it will only upset the calibration.
35 Lay a straight edge across the top cover, main body and flange to ensure that no part is warped causing either air or fuel leaks.
36 Inspect all castings for signs of cracking and gasket surfaces for unevenness.
37 Check the seating surfaces and the thread of the adjustment screw for damage.
38 Place the choke and throttle shafts back in their respective bores and check for an excessive clearance. If necessary obtain a new shaft or flange.
39 Reassembly of the carburettor is the reverse sequence to removal. Make sure that each part is clean for refitting and always use new gaskets. It will be necessary to check the fuel level in the float chamber as described in Section 19. The choke interlock adjustment will have to be set as described in Section 20. Also check the primary and secondary throttle interlock opening as described in Section 21. On models fitted with an automatic transmission the dashpot adjustment must be set as described in Section 23.

19 Carburettor (213282–331 and 213282–341), fuel level – check and adjustment

1   It will be observed that there is a horizontal line marked on the float chamber glass to indicate the correct fuel level. Should this level be correct before the carburettor was removed and overhauled and the original float and needle valve have been retained, it should not be necessary to re-adjust the fuel level.
2   This check and adjustment may be carried out with the carburettor either on or off the inlet manifold.
3   With the float chamber cover glass removed invert the carburettor and allow the float seat to rest against the needle valve.

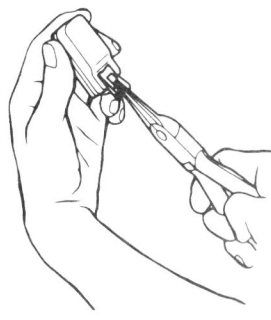

Fig. 3.22 Adjusting the float seat
(213282 type carburettor)

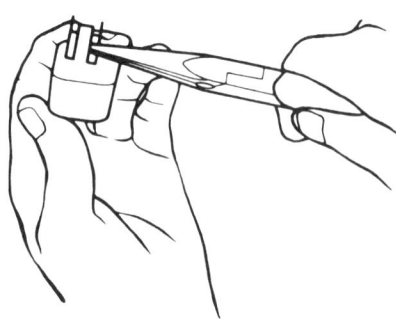

**Fig. 3.24 Adjusting the float stopper
(213282 type carburettor)**

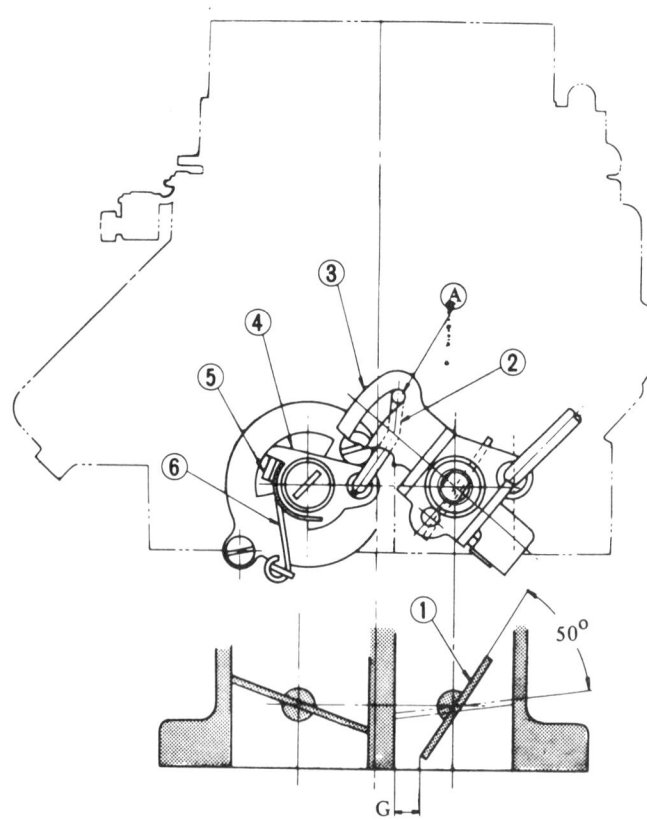

**Fig. 3.23 Adjustment of interlock opening
(213282 type carburettor)**

1 Throttle valve	4 Rocking arm
2 Connecting link	5 Secondary throttle arm
3 Throttle arm	6 Rocking arm return spring

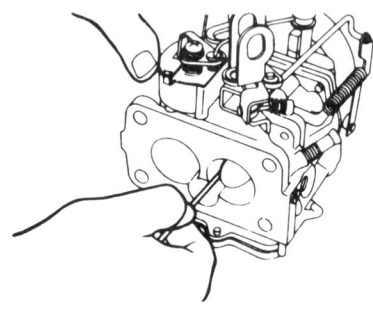

**Fig. 3.25 Measuring the interlock opening
(213282 type carburettor)**

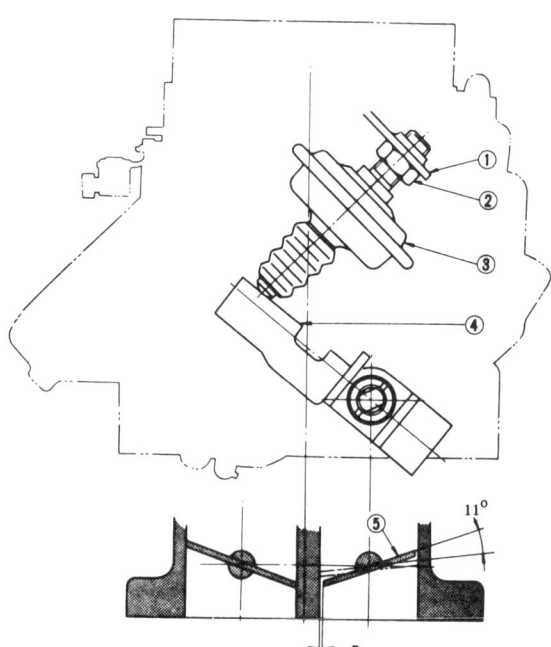

**Fig. 3.26 Measurement of dashpot operating clearance
(213282 type carburettor)**

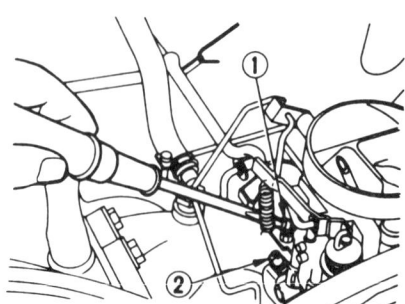

**Fig. 3.27 Engine idle adjustment
(213282 type carburettor)**

| 1 Throttle adjusting screw | 2 Idle adjusting screw |

1 Bracket	4 Throttle lever
2 Locknut	5 Throttle butterfly valve
3 Dashpot	

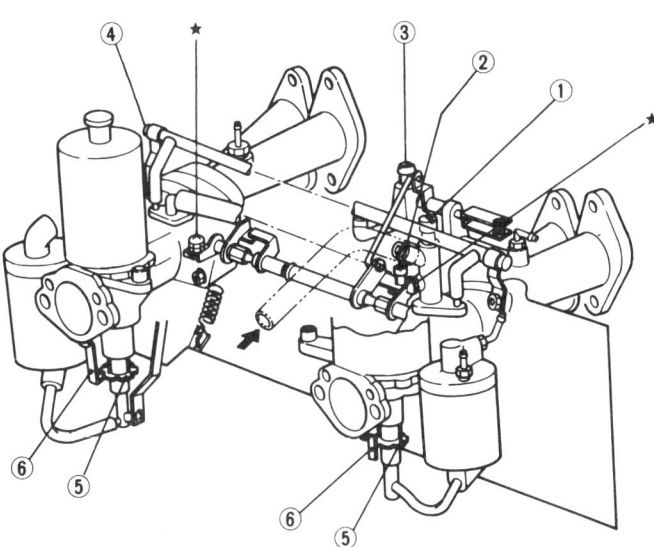

Fig. 3.28 Twin carburettor layout showing the principle adjustment controls (HJT38W-7 carburettor)

1 *Idle speed adjuster screw*   4 *Balance tube*
2 *Balance screw*   5 *Mixture adjustment nut*
3 *Idle mixture screw*   6 *Spring*

* *These throttle screws are preset and should not require attention*

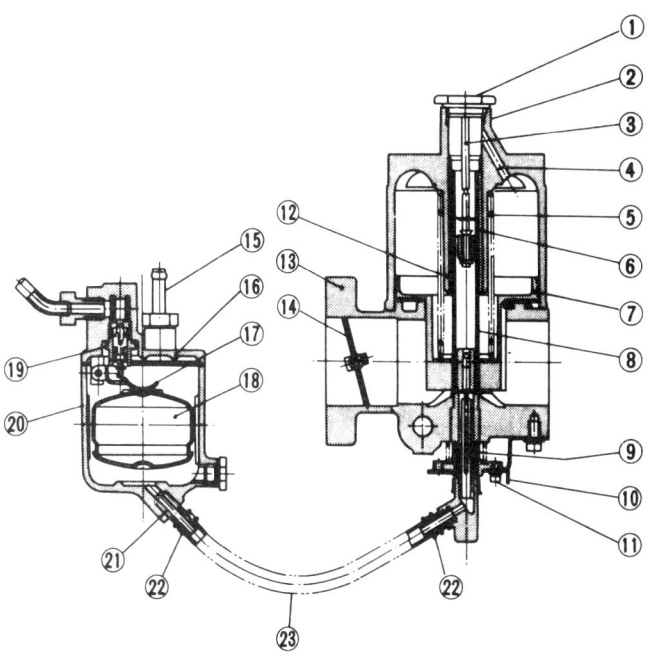

Fig. 3.29 Sectional view of HJT38W-7 carburettor showing

1 *Oil cap nut*   13 *Throttle chamber*
2 *Suction chamber*   14 *Throttle butterfly valve*
3 *Plunger rod*   15 *Nipple*
4 *Transverse hole*   16 *Float chamber cover*
5 *Spring*   17 *Float lever*
6 *Oil damper*   18 *Float*
7 *Piston*   19 *Needle valve*
8 *Piston rod*   20 *Float chamber*
9 *Nozzle*   21 *Sleeve*
10 *Leaf spring*   22 *Clip*
11 *Idle adjusting nut*   23 *Fuel hose*
12 *Suction guide*

4   If the carburettor is on the inlet manifold lift the float with the fingers until the needle valve is closed.
5   Bend the float tab gently using a pair of long nosed pliers until the upper face of the float is in a horizontal position.
6   With the carburettor in the normal fitted position, allow the float to settle into its down position.
7   Measure the effective stroke of the float. This is the distance the float seat travels from the fully down to the fully up position. The correct float stroke should be 0·039 in (1·0 mm).
8   If necessary bend the float stopper tab with a pair of long nosed pliers until the correct travel is obtained. Refit the float chamber gasket, glass and cover. Secure with the three retaining screws.

20 Carburettor (213282–331 and 213282–341) choke interlock – check and adjustment

1   When the choke valve is in the fully closed position the primary throttle valve should be opened by a specified amount which will give a set throttle valve opening angle from the fully closed position.
2   Refer to Section 17 and remove the carburettor from the inlet manifold.
3   Move the choke operating lever by hand until the choke valve is in the fully closed position.
4   Insert a rod of suitable diameter between the throttle valve and throttle chamber inner wall, then adjust the linkage until the rod is a good sliding fit. Adjustment is made by bending the connecting link with a pair of pliers until the gauge just slides between the choke valve and the bore. The correct clearance should be 0·2913 in (7·4 mm).

21 Carburettor (213282–341) primary and secondary throttle interlock opening – check and adjustment

1   Fig. 3.23 shows the primary valve open 50°. When the primary throttle valve opens 50°, the connecting link is contacted with the right-hand end of a groove on primary throttle arm (A).

2   When the throttle valve opens further, the locking arm is detached from the secondary throttle arm, permitting the start of the secondary system actuation.
3   The linkage between the primary and secondary throttles will operate properly if the distance 'G' between the throttle valve and the inner wall of the throttle chamber is 0.291 in (7.4 mm).
4   Adjust if necessary by bending the connecting link.

22 Carburettor (213282–331 and 213282–341) – adjustment

1   Before adjusting the carburettor run the engine up to its normal operating temperature and ensure that the fuel float level is as specified.
2   Commence adjustment by screwing in the idle screw fully and then unscrewing it about 2¼ turns.
3   Now adjust the throttle screw to obtain the correct idle speed.
4   Further adjust the idle screw to enable the engine to run smoothly. The throttle screw may need further adjustment to increase or reduce the engine speed to the specified speed.
5   If a vacuum gauge and tachometer are available a more accurate adjustment can be made. Insert the gauge into the plug hole in the inlet manifold and connect up the tachometer.
6   With the engine at its normal operating temperature, screw the throttle idle screw in or out as necessary until a steady engine speed of 600 rpm is attained.
7   Screw the idling mixture screw in or out until the highest vacuum reading on the gauge is obtained.
8   Recheck the engine idle speed.

23 Carburettor (213282–341) dashpot adjustment – automatic transmission

1   It is essential to maintain the correct relationship between the throttle lever and the dashpot stem for satisfactory throttle closing.
2   To obtain the correct setting between the throttle lever and the dashpot stem, loosen the locknut and rotate the dashpot, as necessary, so that the throttle lever touches the stem at 11° of throttle valve opening.
3   The clearance 'B' in Fig. 3.26 should be 0.023 in (0.586 mm).
4   Tighten the locknut on completion.

24 Carburettor (HJT38W–7) – general description

1   The variable choke SU-type carburettor is a relatively simple instrument. It differs from most carburettors in that instead of having a number of various sized fixed jets for different conditions, only one variable jet is fitted to deal with all possible conditions.
2   Air passing rapidly through the carburettor draws petrol from the jet so forming the petrol/air mixture. The amount of petrol drawn from the jet depends on the position of the tapered carburettor needle, which moves up and down the jet orifice according to the engine load and throttle opening, thus effectively altering the size of jet so that exactly the right amount of fuel is metered for the prevailing driving conditions.
3   The position of the tapered needle in the jet is determined by engine vacuum. The shank of the needle is held at its top end in a piston which slides up and down the dashpot in response to the degree of manifold vacuum.
4   With the throttle fully open, the full effect of inlet manifold vacuum is felt by the piston which has an air bleed into the choke tube on the outside of the throttle. This causes the piston to rise fully, bringing the needle with it. With the accelerator partially closed, only slight inlet manifold vacuum is felt by the piston (although, of course, on the engine side of the throttle the vacuum is greater), and the piston only rises a little, blocking most of the jet orifice with the metering needle.
5   To prevent the piston fluttering and giving a richer mixture when the accelerator pedal is suddenly depressed, an oil damper and light spring are fitted inside the dashpot.
6   The only portion of the piston assembly to come into contact with the piston chamber or dashpot is the actual piston rod. All the other parts of the piston assembly, including the lower choke portion, have sufficient clearance to prevent any direct metal to metal contact which is essential if the carburettor is to function correctly.

25 Carburettor (HJT38W–7) – removal and refitting

1   Disconnect and remove the complete air cleaner assembly from the carburettor air intake.
2   Slacken the clips and ease off the fuel feed pipes from the union on the float chamber cover. Plug the ends to prevent dirt ingress.
3   Slacken the clips and disconnect the float chamber breather hoses from their unions.
4   Disconnect the accelerator cable from the throttle linkage and the choke control cable from the choke levers.
5   Undo and remove the nuts and washers securing the carburettor body to the manifold studs. Lift away the complete carburettor installation.
6   Refitting the carburettors is the reverse sequence to removal. Always fit new gaskets to the inlet manifold flanges and one each side of the insulator block. Refer to the relevant Section and adjust the controls and carburettor settings.

26 Carburettors (HJT38W–7) – dismantling

The HJT38W–7 carburettor has only two moving parts – the throttle valve and the piston assembly – which makes it a straightforward instrument to service, but at the same time it is a delicate unit and clumsy handling can cause much damage. In particular it is easy to knock the finely tapered needle out of true, and the greatest care should be taken to keep all parts associated with the dashpot scrupulously clean.

1   Remove the oil dashpot plunger nut from the top of the dashpot.
2   Scribe marks on the suction chamber and carburettor body so that they may be refitted in their original positions. Undo and remove the four set screws and washers holding the suction chamber to the carburettor body, and lift away the suction chamber, light spring, piston and needle assembly.
3   To remove the metering needle from the choke portion of the piston unscrew the sunken retaining screw from the side of the piston choke and pull out the needle. When refitting the needle ensure that the shoulder is flush with the underside of the piston.
4   Note which way round the front chamber cover is fitted and then undo and remove the four set screws and washers holding the cover to the main body. Lift away the float chamber cover and recover the float.
5   Normally it is not necessary to dismantle the carburettor further, but if, because of wear or for some other reason it is wished to remove the jet, this is easily accomplished by first detaching the jet operating lever from the jet head and then removing the jet by extracting it from the underside of the carburettor. The jet adjustment nut can then be unscrewed together with the jet adjusting nut locking spring and shim.
6   If the larger jet locking screw above the jet adjusting screw is removed, then the jet will have to be recentred when the carburettor is reassembled. With the jet screw removed it is an easy matter to remove the jet bearing and sealing washer.
7   To remove the throttle and actuating spindle, release the two screws holding the throttle in position in the slot in the spindle, slide the throttle out of the spindle (note which way round it is fitted) and then remove the spindle.

27 Carburettor (HJT38W–7) float chamber – dismantling, examination and reassembly

1   To dismantle the float chamber, first disconnect the inlet pipe from the fuel pump at the top of the float chamber cover. Then disconnect the float chamber breather hose from the top of the float chamber cover.
2   Note the position of the float chamber cover and then undo and remove the four set screws. Lift away the float chamber cover.
3   Carefully insert a thin piece of bent wire under the float and lift it out. Check that the float is not cracked or leaking. If it is it must be repaired or renewed.
4   The float chamber cover contains the needle valve assembly which regulates the amount of fuel fed into the float chamber. One end of the float lever rests on top of the float, rising and falling with it, while the other pivots on a hinge pin which is held by two lugs. On the float chamber cover side of the float lever is a needle which rises and falls from its seating according to the movement of the lever. When the cover is in place the hinge pin is held in position by the walls of the float chamber. With the cover removed the pin is easily pushed out so freeing the float lever and the needle.
5   Examine the tip of the needle and the needle seating for wear. Wear is present when there is a discernible ridge in the chamfer of the needle. If this is evident then the needle and seating must be renewed. This is a simple operation and the hexagon head of the needle housing is easily screwed out. Never renew either the needle or the seating without renewing the other part, as otherwise it will not be possible to get a fuel tight joint.
6   Clean the float chamber thoroughly.
7   Reassembly is the reverse sequence to removal. Before refitting the float chamber cover check that the fuel level setting is correct.

28 Carburettor (HJT38W–7) – float chamber fuel level adjustment

1   It is essential that the fuel level in the float chamber is always correct as otherwise excessive fuel consumption may occur. On reassembly of the float chamber check the fuel level before refitting the float chamber cover.
2   Invert the float chamber so that the needle valve is closed. It should be just possible to slide a 0.4331 – 0.472 in (11 – 12 mm) bar between the curved portion of the float lever and the machined lip of the float chamber cover.
3   If the bar lifts the lever or if the lever stands proud of the bar then it is necessary to bend the lever at the point between the shank and

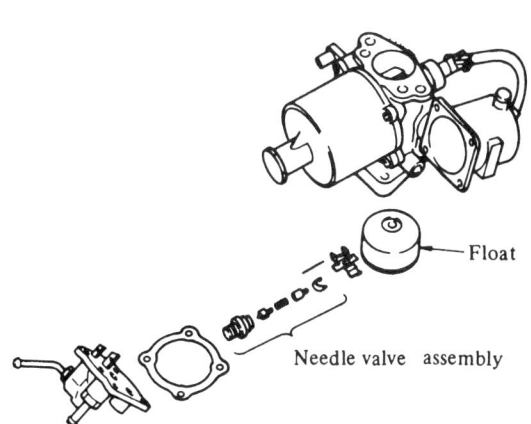

Fig. 3.30 The float chamber components (HJT38W-7 carburettor)

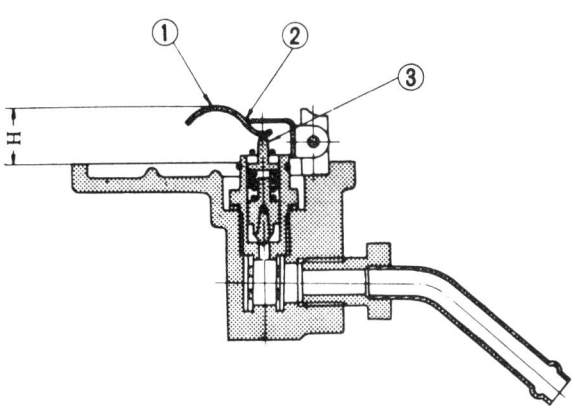

Fig. 3.31 Float level adjustment: Bend float lever (1) at point (2) and adjust to clearance H (0.433 to 0.472 in (11 to 12 mm). Ensure valve stem (3) is fully home (HJT38W-7 carburettor)

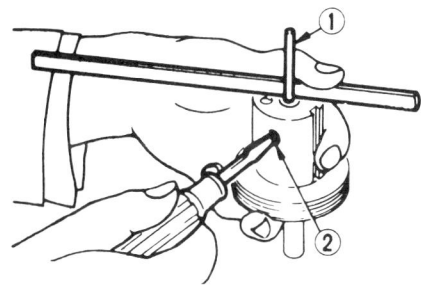

Fig. 3.32 Adjust the needle (1) so that its shoulder is flush to the piston-securing screw (2) (HJT38W-7 carburettor)

the curved portion until the clearance is correct. Never bend the flat portion of the lever.

29 Carburettor (HJT38W-7) – examination and repair

1   The HJT38W-7 carburettor generally speaking, is most reliable, but even so it may develop one of several faults which may not be readily apparent unless a careful inspection is carried out. The common faults which the carburettor is prone to are:

   (a)   Piston sticking
   (b)   Float needle sticking
   (c)   Float chamber flooding.
   (d)   Water and dirt in the carburettor.

2   In addition, the following parts are susceptible to wear after high mileages and as they virtually affect the economy of the engine should be checked and renewed where necessary every 24 000 miles (39 000 km).

The carburettor needle
3   If this has been incorrectly assembled at some time so that it is not centrally located in the jet orifice, then the metering needle will have a tiny ridge worn on it. If a ridge can be seen then the needle must be renewed. The carburettor needles are made to very fine tolerances and should a ridge be apparent no attempt should be made to rub the needle down with fine emery paper. If it is wished to clean the needle it can be polished lightly with metal polish.

The carburettor jet
4   If the needle is worn it is likely that the rim of the jet will be damaged where the needle has been striking it. It should be renewed as otherwise fuel consumption will suffer. The jet can also be badly worn or ridged on the outside from where it has been sliding up and down between the jet bearings every time the choke has been pulled out. Removal and renewal is the only answer here as well.
5   Check the edges of the throttle and the choke tube for wear. Renew if worn.
6   The washers fitted to the base of the jet and to the float chamber may all leak after a time and can cause much fuel wastage. It is wisest to renew them automatically when the carburettor is stripped down.
7   After high mileages the float chamber needle and seat are bound to be ridged. They are not an expensive item to renew and should be renewed as a set. They should never be renewed separately.

Piston sticking
8   The hardened piston rod which slides in the centre guide tube in the middle of the dashpot is the only part of the piston assembly (which comprises the jet needle, suction disc, and piston choke) that should make contact with the dashpot. The piston rim and the choke periphery are machined to very fine tolerances so that they will not touch the dashpot or the choke tube walls.
9   After high mileages, wear in the centre guide tube may allow the piston to touch the dashpot wall. This condition is known as sticking.
10   If piston sticking is suspected or it is wished to test for this condition, rotate the piston about the centre guide tube at the same time sliding it up and down inside the dashpot. If any portion of the piston makes contact with the dashpot wall then that portion of the wall must be polished with metal polish until clearance exists. In extreme cases, fine emery cloth can be used.
11   The greatest care should be taken to remove only the minimum amount of metal to provide the clearance, as too large a gap will cause air leakage and will upset the functioning of the carburettor. Clean down the walls of the dashpot and the piston rim and ensure that there is no oil on them. A trace of oil may be judiciously applied to the piston rod.
12   If the piston is sticking under no circumstances try to clear it by trying to alter the tension of the light return spring.

Water and dirt in carburettor
13   Because of the size of the jet orifice, water or dirt in the carburettor is normally easily cleared. If dirt in the carburettor is suspected lift the piston assembly and flood the float chamber. The normal level of fuel should be about $\frac{1}{16}$ in below the top of the jet and on flooding the carburettor fuel should well up out of the jet hole.
14   If very little or no petrol appears, start the engine (the jet is never

completely blocked) and with the throttle fully open, blank off the air intake. This will create a partial vacuum in the choke tube and help to suck out any foreign matter from the jet tube. Release the throttle as soon as the engine starts to race. Repeat this procedure several times, stop the engine, and then check the carburettor as described earlier in this Section. If this has failed to do the trick then there is no alternative but to remove and blow out the jet.

30 Carburettor (HJT38W–7) – jet centring

1   Remove the link between the jet head and lever. Remove the union holding the feed pipe to the base of the jet, together with the jet and jet adjusting nut securing spring.
2   Refit the jet and feed tube and press them up under the head of the large hexagonal jet locknut. Unscrew this nut slightly until the jet bearing can be turned.
3   Remove the damper securing nut and damper from the top of the dashpot and push the piston assembly right down so that the metering needle enters fully into the jet.
4   Tighten the jet locking nut and test the piston assembly to check that the needle is still quite free to slide in the jet orifice. On lifting the piston and then releasing it, the piston should hit the inside jet bridge with a soft metallic click, and the intensity of the click should be the same whether the jet is in its normal position or is fully lowered.
5   If the sound is different when the jet is fully lowered then the jet is not yet properly centralised and the process must be repeated.
6   When all is correct, remove the jet, refit the jet adjusting nut securing spring, the adjusting nut and jet, and the link between the jet head and the lever.

31 Carburettor (HJT38W–7) – reassembly

1   With all parts clean reassembly begins by inserting the jet bearing into the carburettor body. Then fit the washer and locking nut.
2   Provided that care was taken during dismantling, reassembly is now the reverse sequence to dismantling. It will be necessary to centre the jet assembly and check the float chamber fuel level. Full information will be found in earlier Sections.

32 Carburettor (HJT38W–7) – tuning

1   Start the engine and allow it to reach the normal operating temperature.
2   Check the carbon of the exhaust gas at idling speed with the choke fully in. If the exhaust tends to be black, and the tailpipe interior is also black it is a fair indication that the mixture is too rich. If the exhaust is colourless and the deposit in the exhaust pipe is very light grey it is likely that the mixture is too weak. This condition may also be accompanied by intermittent misfiring, while too rich a mixture will be associated with 'hunting'. Ideally the exhaust should be colourless with a medium grey exhaust pipe deposit.
3   Once the engine has reached its normal operating temperature remove the air cleaner installation and also disconnect the throttle linkage between the two instruments.
4   Only two adjustments are provided on the carburettor. Idling speed is governed by the throttle adjusting screw, and the mixture strength by the jet adjustment nut. The carburettor is correctly adjusted for the whole of its engine revolution range when the idling mixture strength is correct.
5   Idling speed adjusment is effected by the idling adjusting screw. To adjust the mixture set the engine to run around 1000 rpm by screwing in the idling screw for each carburettor.
6   Check the mixture strength by lifting the piston of the carburettor approximately 0.031 inch (0.8 mm) with a small screwdriver or using the small spring loaded pin located under the main body so as to disturb the air flow as little as possible, if:

    (a)   the speed of the engine increases appreciably, the mixture is too rich
    (b)   the engine speed immediately decreases, the mixture is too weak
    (c)   the engine speed increases very slightly, the mixture is correct

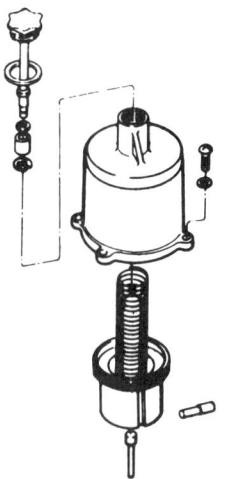

Fig. 3.33 The piston and damper assembly (HJT38W–7 carburettor)

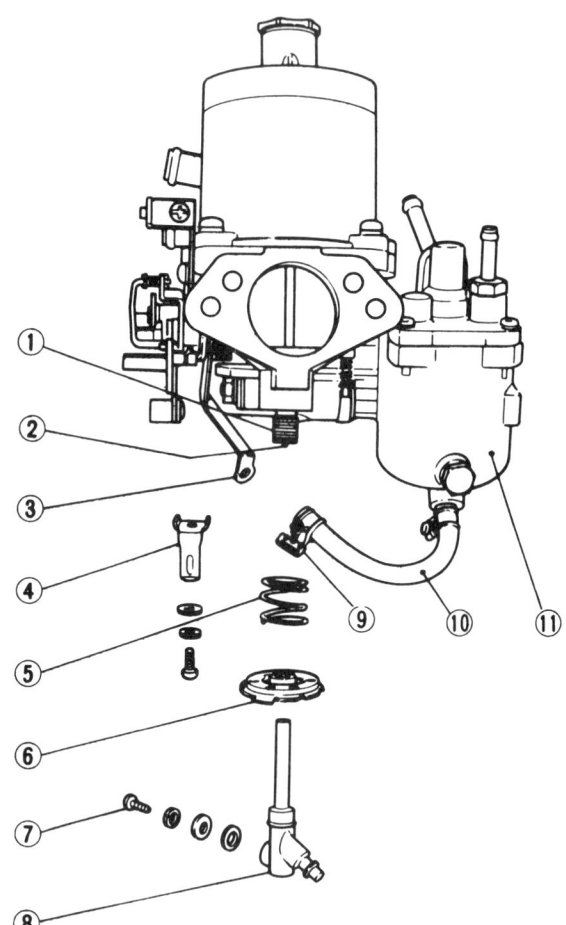

Fig. 3.34 The jet and mixture setting components (HJT38W–7 carburettor)

1	Nozzle sleeve	7	Screw
2	Jet needle	8	Nozzle
3	Connecting plate	9	Clip
4	Leaf spring	10	Fuel pipe
5	Idle adjusting screw spring	11	Float chamber
6	Idle adjusting screw nut		

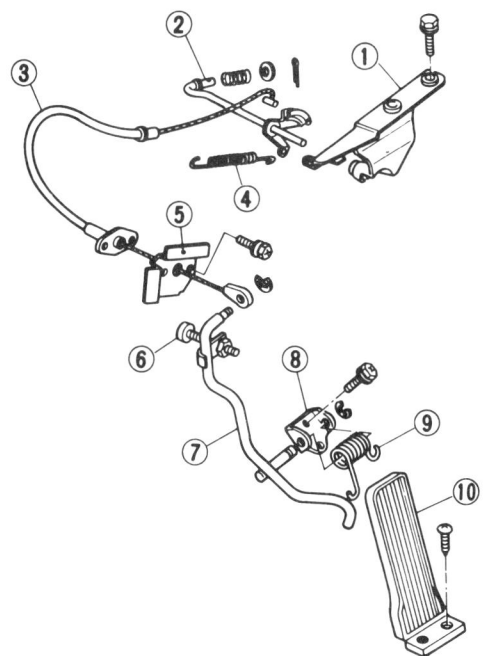

Fig. 3.35 The throttle control linkages on the HJT38W-7 carburettor

1 Throttle shaft
  support bracket
2 Throttle shaft
3 Throttle cable
4 Spring
5 Stopper bracket
6 Stopper bolt
7 Pedal cover
8 Pedal bracket
9 Return spring
10 Pedal

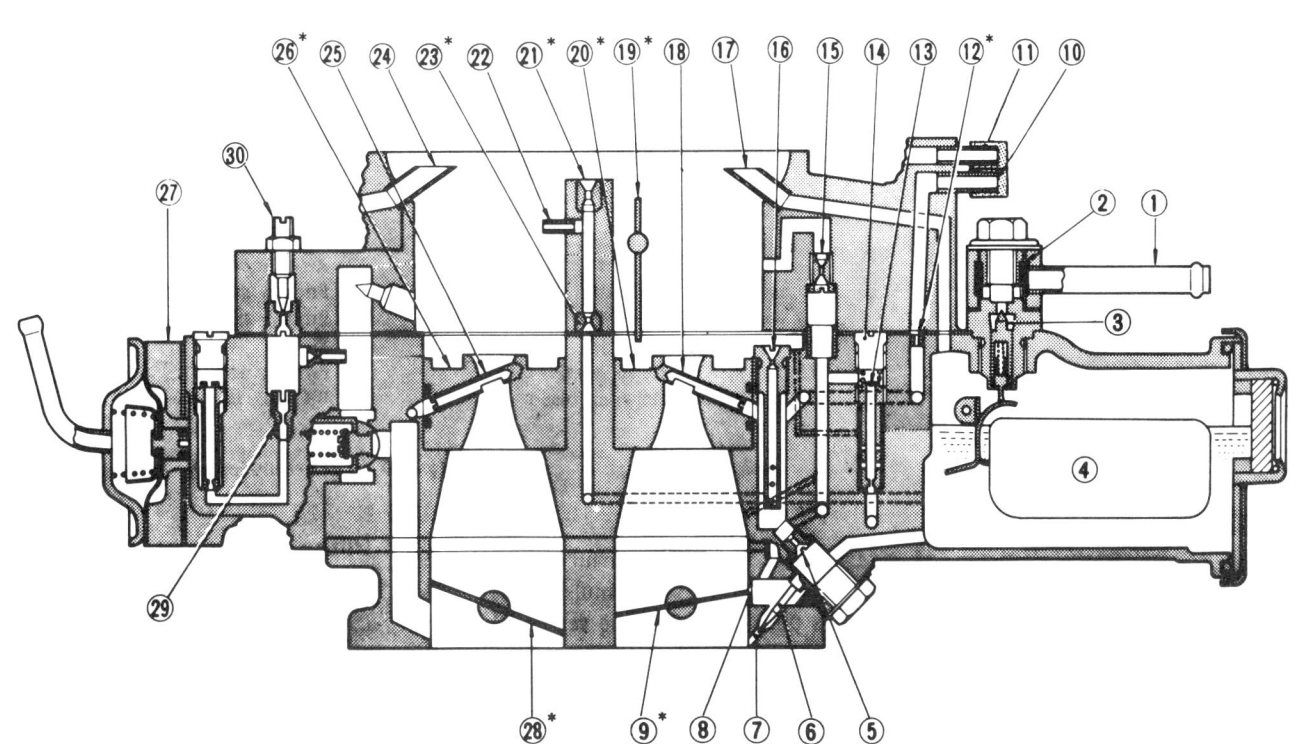

Fig. 3.36 Sectional view of DCH340 series carburettor

1 Fuel inlet	10 Primary altitude compensator pipe (California only)	15 Primary slow air bleed	23* Richer jet
2 Fuel filter		16 Primary main air bleed	24 Secondary air vent pipe
3 Needle		17 Primary air vent pipe	25 Secondary main nozzle
4 Float	11 Secondary altitude compensator pipe (California only)	18 Primary main nozzle	26* Secondary small venturi
5 Primary main jet		19 Choke valve	27 BCDD
6 Idle adjust screw		20* Primary small venturi	28* Secondary throttle valve
7 Idle hole	12* Safe orifice	21* High-speed enricher air bleed	29 BCDD coasting jet
8 Primary bypass hole	13 Primary slow jet		30 BCDD mixture adjusting screw
9* Primary throttle valve	14 Plug	22 Richer nozzle	

Do not remove or disturb these items

7   To enrich the mixture rotate the adjustment nut which is located at the bottom of the carburettor, downward. To weaken the mixture rotate the adjustment nut upward. Only turn the nut a little at a time and check the mixture strength between each turn.

8   It is likely that there will be a slight increase or decrease in rpm after the mixture adjustment has been made so the throttle idling adjusting screw should now be turned so that the engine idles at the recommended speed.

9   Once the two carburettors have been set it is now necessary to synchronize them. This means the idling suction must be equal on both.

10   It is best to use a vacuum synchronizing device but if one is not available it is possible to obtain fairly accurate synchronization by listening to the hiss made by the air flow into the inlet throats of each carburettor.

11   The aim is to adjust the throttle butterfly disc so that an equal amount of air enters each carburettor. With the two carburettors still disconnected from each other listen to the hiss from each carburettor and if a difference in intensity is noticed between them, then unscrew the throttle adjustment screw on the other carburettor until the hiss from both the carburettors is the same.

12   With a vacuum synchronizing device all that is necessary to do is place the instrument over the mouth of each carburettor in turn and adjust the adjusting screws until the reading on the gauge is identical for both carburettors.

13   Reconnect the two carburettors and refit the air cleaner assembly.

33 Carburettor (HJT38W–7) – controls

1   The accompanying illustration, Fig. 3.35, shows the respective accelerator and control cable components. Apart from the actual carburettor linkages, the control assembly is identical to that shown for other models in Section 38.

34 Carburettor (DCH340 Series) – general description

The carburettor is of the downdraught dual-barrel type. The primary throttle valve is mechanically operated while the secondary one is vacuum operated by a diaphragm unit which is actuated by the vacuum in the carburettor venturi.

An electrically assisted, bi-metal type automatic choke is incorporated. This incorporates a butterfly valve which closes one of the venturi tubes and is so synchronized with the primary valve plate that the latter opens sufficiently to provide a rich mixture and an increased slow-running speed for easy starting.

For idling and slow running the fuel passes through the slow running jet, the primary slow air bleed and the secondary slow air bleed. The fuel is finally ejected from the bypass and the idle holes. An anti-dieseling (run-on) solenoid valve is incorporated to ensure that the fuel supply is cut-off when the ignition is switched off, thus preventing the engine from running-on.

The accelerator pump is synchronized with the throttle valve. During periods of heavy acceleration, the pump which is of simple piston and valve construction, provides an additional metered quantity of fuel to enrich the normal mixture.

The secondary system provides a mixture for normal motoring conditions by means of a main jet and air bleed.

A high speed circuit is incorporated which consists of a richer jet, enricher air bleed and richer nozzle, and allows additional fuel to be drawn into the secondary bore as the air velocity through that bore increases.

A boost controlled deceleration device (BCDD) is incorporated to reduce the hydrocarbons emitted which tend to occur in excess during engine over-run, when the combustion chamber fuel/air mixture is too lean to permit complete combustion. The BCDD system comprises a vacuum control solenoid valve, and a speed detecting switch and amplifier (manual transmission) or inhibitor switch (automatic transmission).

35 Carburettor (DCH340 Series) – adjustments with carburettor fitted

Except where it is necessary for the engine to be running, the

adjustment given in this Section may also be carried out with the carburettor removed. It must be appreciated that any adjustments to the fuel (and emission control) systems may infringe federal or local laws, and should only be carried out when absolutely necessary. In all cases, adjustments should be checked by a suitably equipped Datsun agent or carburation specialist at the first possible opportunity.

Idle speed and mixture using a CO meter

1   Run the engine until the normal operating temperature is reached. Where applicable, disconnect the air hose between the 3-way connector and air check valve; plug the hose to prevent dust from entering.

2   Ensure that all carburettor and emission control pipes are satisfactorily connected then race the engine two or three times to 2000 rpm (approx). Allow the engine to idle for one minute then adjust the throttle speed screw to obtain the specified idle speed. Connect the CO meter to the vehicle exhaust.

3   Adjust the idle adjust (mixture) screw to obtain the specified CO percentage.

4   If necessary, repeat the procedure of paragraphs 2 and 3 to obtain the specified settings. If the idle mixture (CO percentage) cannot be adjusted within the limits of the idle limiter cap, the cap may be removed and the screw adjusted, provided that on completion of any adjustment it is fitted as shown in Fig. 3.39.

5   When applicable, reconnect the air check valve hose. If the engine speed increases, adjust the throttle speed screw as necessary.

Idle speed and mixture without using a CO meter

6   Repeat the procedure given in paragraph 1 and 2, but ignore the reference to the CO meter.

7   Rotate the idle adjust (mixture) screw until the most satisfactory idling is obtained, adjusting the idle speed screw, as necessary.

8   Rotate the idle adjust (mixture) screw clockwise until the engine speed drops by 60 to 70 rpm (manual transmission) or 15 to 25 rpm (automatic transmission) below the specified rpm. If the idle mixture cannot be adjusted within the limits of the idle limiter cap, the cap may be removed and the screw adjusted, provided that on completion it is refitted as shown in Fig. 3.39.

9   Where applicable, reconnect the air check valve hose. If the engine speed increases, adjust the throttle speed screw as necessary.

Fast idle

10   During normal tune-up operations it is possible to adjust the fast idle screw to obtain the specified rpm.

Vacuum break (air cleaner removed)

11   This arrangement opens the choke valve plate after the engine has been started to provide the correct fuel/air ratio of the mixture under the prevailing engine operating conditions.

12   The correct setting should be checked and any adjustment carried out in the following manner. Close the choke valve plate completely with the fingers and retain the valve plate in this position using a rubber band connected between the choke piston lever and carburettor body.

13   With a pair of pliers, grip the end of the vacuum diaphragm capsule operating rod and withdraw it as far as it will go without straining it. Now bend the connecting rod (if necessary) to provide a clearance between the edge of the choke valve plate and the carburettor body as given in the Specifications.

Choke unloader (air cleaner removed)

14   Close the choke valve plate completely with the fingers and retain the valve plate in this position using a rubber band connected between the choke piston lever and carburettor body.

15   Pull the throttle lever until it is fully open and bend the unloader tongue (if necessary) to provide a clearance between the choke valve and carburettor body as given in the Specifications.

Automatic choke

16   The normal position of the automatic choke bi-metal cover is for the mark on the cover to be opposite to the centre mark of the choke housing index. Where there is a tendency to overchoke on starting up, turn the cover in a clockwise direction by not more than one division.

Dashpot adjustment

17   Run the engine to normal operating temperature and check that

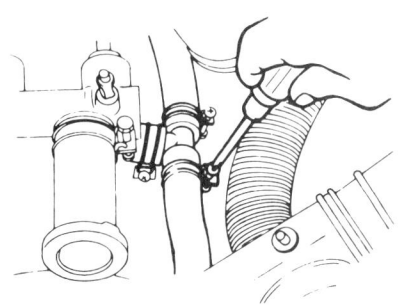

Fig. 3.37 Remove air check valve hose (DCH 340 series carburettor)

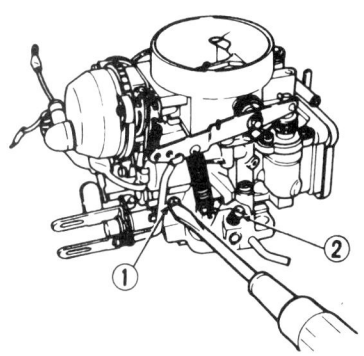

Fig. 3.38 Throttle idle speed (1) adjuster screw and idle mixture (2) adjusting screw – typical

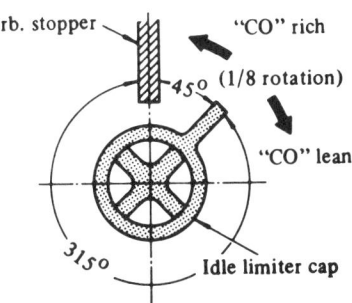

Fig. 3.39 Limiter cap correctly fitted (DCH340 series carburettor)

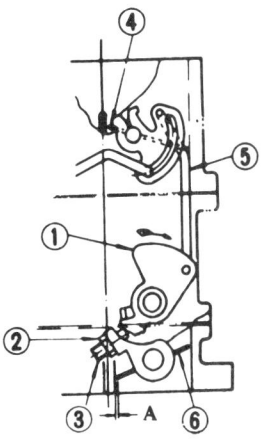

Fig. 3.40 Fast idle adjustment (DCH340 series carburettor)

1 Fast idle cam
2 Locknut
3 Fast idle adjuster screw
4 Choke valve
5 Choke connecting rod
6 Throttle valve

A – Fast idle gap (see Specifications)

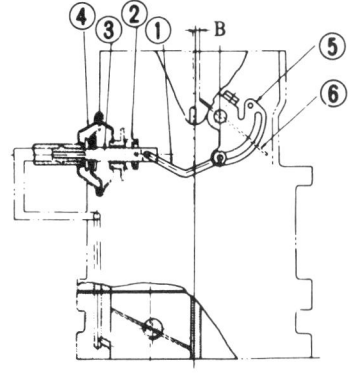

Fig. 3.41 Vacuum break adjustment (DCH 340 series carburettor)

1 Rod
2 Spring
3 Piston
4 Diaphragm unit cover
5 Piston lever
6 Choke valve

The clearance at B should be as follows:
Non-California – 0.0689 in (1.75 mm)
California models with manual transmission – 0.0638 in (1.62 mm)
California models with automatic transmission – 0.0591 in (1.50 mm)

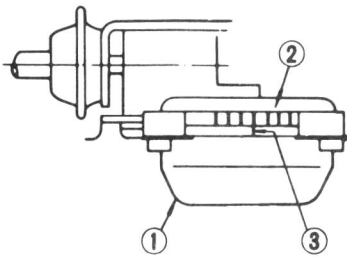

Fig. 3.42 Choke setting (DCH340 series carburettor)

1 Cover
2 Housing
3 Alignment mark

Fig. 3.43 Dashpot installation (DCH340 series carburettor)

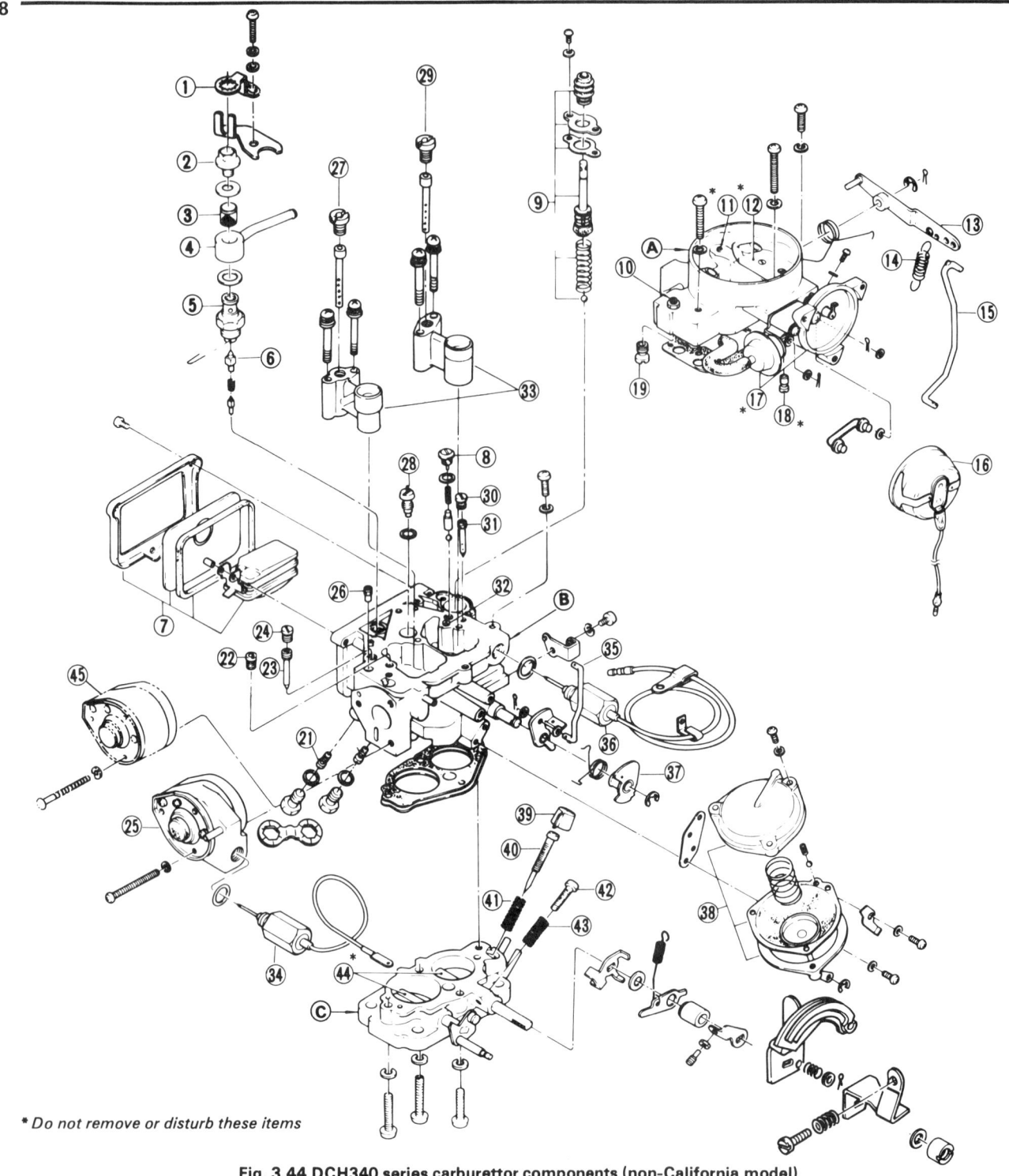

Fig. 3.44 DCH340 series carburettor components (non-California model)

1	Lever	12*	Choke valve
2	Filter set screw	13	Accelerating pump lever
3	Filter	14	Throttle return spring
4	Nipple	15	Pump rod
5	Needle valve body	16	Automatic choke cover
6	Needle valve	17	Automatic choke body and
7	Fuel chamber components		vacuum break diaphragm
8	Accelerating mechanism	18*	Enricher jet
	plug	19*	Coasting air bleed 1
9	Accelerating pump	20	Primary main jet
10	BCDD mixture adjusting	21	Secondary main jet
	screw	22	Secondary slow air bleed
11*	High speed enricher air	23	Secondary slow jet
	bleed	24	Plug

25	BCDD
26	Coast jet
27	Secondary main air bleed
28	Power valve
29	Primary main air bleed
30	Plug
31	Primary slow jet
32	Primary slow air bleed
33	Primary and secondary small venturi
34	BCDD solenoid
35	Choke connecting rod
36	Anti-dieseling solenoid valve

37	Fast idle cam
38	Diaphragm chamber components
39	Idle limiter cap
40	Idle adjusting screw
41	Spring
42	Throttle adjusting screw
43	Spring
44*	Primary and secondary throttle valve
45	BCDD (for Canada)
A	Choke chamber
B	Centre body
C	Throttle chamber

* Do not remove or disturb these items

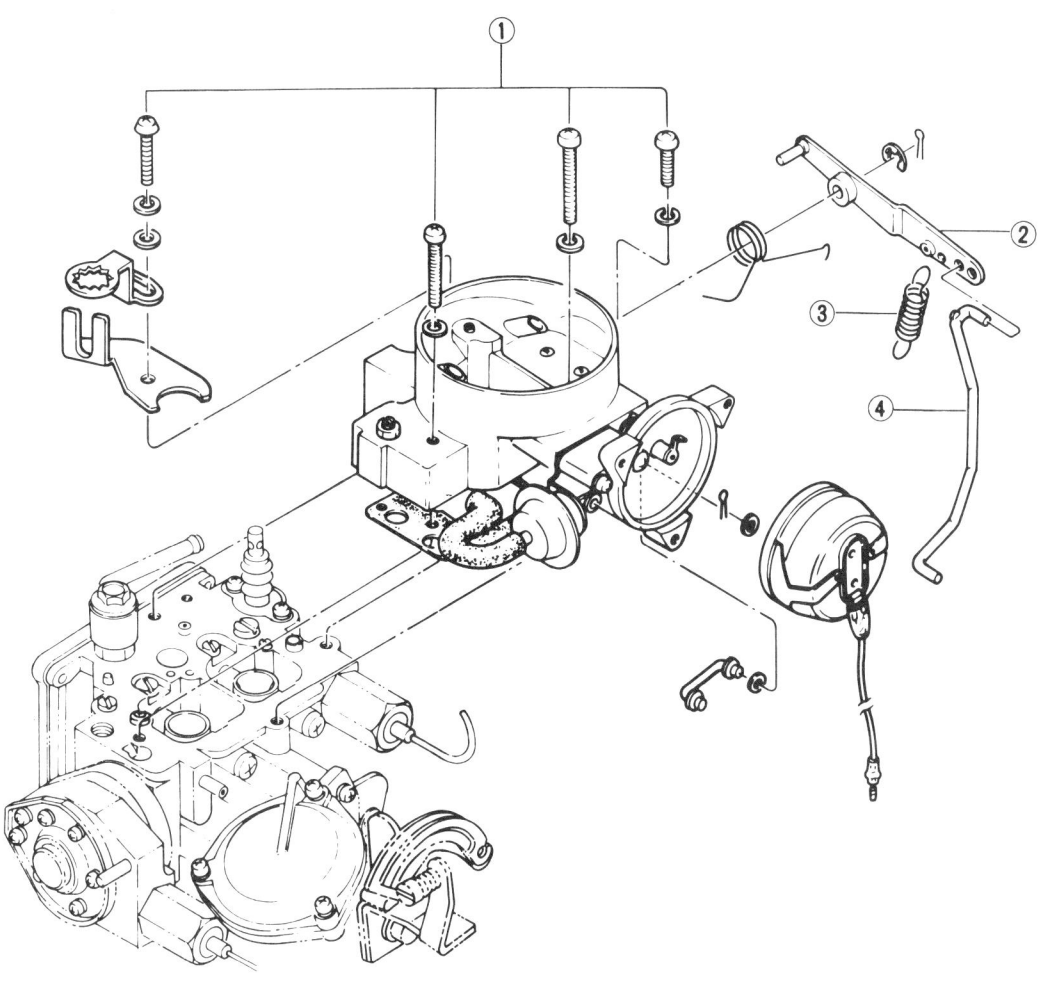

Fig. 3.45 Choke chamber components (DCH340 series carburettor)

1 Retaining screws   *3 Throttle return spring*
2 Pump lever   *4 Pump rod*

the slow-running adjustment is correct.

18 Release the dashpot locknut and then adjust the position of the dashpot so that it just touches the stop plate when the engine is running at the specified speed, with the throttle linkage held open with the hand.

19 Retighten the locknut without moving the dashpot.

20 Raise the engine speed to about 2000 rpm and suddenly release the accelerator. The engine speed should be reduced to 1000 rpm in approximately three seconds otherwise the adjustment has been incorrectly carried out or the dashpot is faulty.

Anti-dieseling solenoid valve

21 This cannot be adjusted, but in cases where the engine does not stop when the ignition is switched off a faulty solenoid is indicated and a new unit should be fitted.

Boost controlled deceleration device (BCDD) — adjustment

22 It is very unusual for this operation to be required but if new components have been fitted or performance is suspect proceed in the following manner.

23 A tachometer and Bourdon tube vacuum gauge will be required. Move automatic transmission lever to 'N' position.

24 Run the engine until normal operating temperature is reached and then connect the vacuum gauge directly to the intake manifold.

Connect the tachometer in accordance with the maker's instructions.

25 Disconnect the BCDD solenoid valve.

26 Raise the engine speed to between 3000 and 3500 rpm and then suddenly release the throttle. The manifold vacuum pressure will gradually decrease to indicate the BCDD operating pressure which should be as given in the Specifications.

27 If the pressure indicated on the gauge is higher than that specified, turn the adjusting screw on the valve in a clockwise direction; if lower, turn the screw anti-clockwise.

28 On California models there is an adjustment nut fitted. This should be turned clockwise if the pressure is lower than specified or anti-clockwise if pressure is higher. Repeat the testing procedure after any adjustment is made.

Float level

29 Although the fuel level can be seen with the carburettor fitted any adjustment requires its removal. Refer to Section 17, paragraph 24.

---

36 Carburettor (DCH340 Series)   removal, servicing and refitting

---

1   Remove the air cleaner (see Section 2 or 3 accordingly).

2   Disconnect the fuel and vacuum pipes from the carburettor, also

the leads to the automatic choke and anti-dieseling solenoid valve.

3   Disconnect the throttle linkage from the carburettor.

4   Unscrew the four securing nuts and remove the carburettor from the intake manifold.

5   Clean any dirt from the external surfaces of the unit with solvent or fuel.

6   Detach the accelerator pump rod and the choke rod.

7   Unhook the throttle return spring to remove.

8   Pull the vacuum hose from the diaphragm unit.

9   Unscrew the choke chamber securing screws and carefully lift the choke chamber unit from the centre body.

10   Remove the float chamber (4 screws).

11   Remove the lock lever, filter, fuel nipple and needle valve body.

12   Dismantle the accelerator pump and outlet valve taking care not to lose the ball and weight.

13   Remove the venturis, main air bleeds and emulsion tubes from the primary and secondary sides of the carburettor.

14   Remove the slow jet and slow air bleed, primary and secondary main jets.

15   If necessary, the fuel level gauge lever and float can be removed from the float chamber.

16   Remove the power valve.

17   Remove the return plate, sleeve, fast idle lever, spring hanger and throttle lever.

18   Unscrew the anti-dieseling valve by unscrewing it from the carburettor body.

19   The BCDD unit can be removed after unscrewing the securing screws (Fig. 3.46).

20   Clean and examine all components for wear. If the throttle plates or spindles or bushes are worn, it is recommended that the carburettor is renewed completely.

21   Obtain a repair kit which will contain all the necessary gaskets and other items requiring renewal.

22   Only clean jets by blowing through them with air from a tyre pump; never probe them with wire. It is worth checking their calibrations against those listed in Specifications in case a previous owner has substituted jets of incorrect size for the standard jets.

23   Reassembly is the reverse of the dismantling procedure, but the following special procedures and adjustments must be carried out.

Float level adjustment (also see Section 35)

24   The fuel level, when viewed through the sight glass of the float chamber should be 0·91 in (23 mm) below the chamber top flange. Where the level is incorrect, invert the float chamber and bend the float arm as necessary to provide the dimension H (Fig. 3.47). Now check that the stroke of the float arm h is also as given in the figure. If necessary, bend the stop to achieve this.

Fast idle adjustment

25   When the automatic choke is fully closed for cold starting, the fast idle cam opens the throttle by a predetermined amount to give the specified fast idle speed.

26   If the carburettor has been completely dismantled or new components have been fitted, set the fast idle screw on the second step of the cam and adjust the screw so that the gap A between the edge of the throttle valve plate and the carburettor is as given in the Specifications (see Fig. 3.40). Use a twist drill or rod of suitable diameter to carry out the measuring. A further minor adjustment can be made to the fast idle screw when the carburettor is fitted and the engine is running under cold start conditions.

Interlock opening of throttle valves

27   Check that when the primary throttle plate is opened 50°, the throttle valve adjust plate is contacting the return plate at point A (Fig. 3.48). Open the throttle plate further and check that the locking arm is detached from the secondary throttle arm, allowing the secondary system to function. Bend the connecting lever, if necessary, to obtain the specified throttle valve interlock opening, measured between the edge of the throttle valve and the throttle chamber inner wall, which is 0·2906 in (7·38 mm).

Vacuum break adjustment

28   Refer to the previous Section.

Choke unloader adjustment

29   Refer to the previous Section.

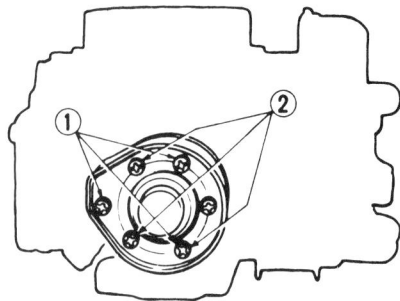

Fig. 3.46 BCDD screws (DCH340 series carburettor)

1 Securing screws

2 Assembly screws – do not remove

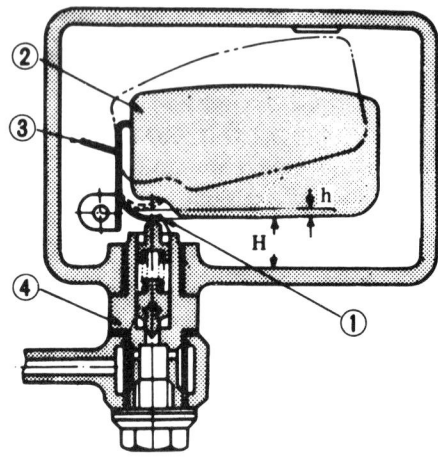

Fig. 3.47 Float level adjustment (DCH340 series carburettor)

1 Float seat   3 Float chamber
2 Float   4 Needle valve

$H = 0.283$ in $(7.2$ mm$)$
$h = 0.051$ to 0.067 in
$(1.3$ to 1.7 mm$)$

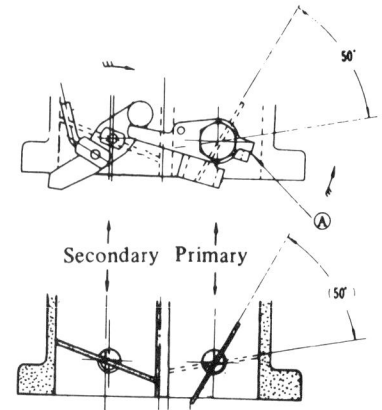

Secondary   Primary

Fig. 3.48 Interlock opening adjustment (DCH 340 series carburettor)

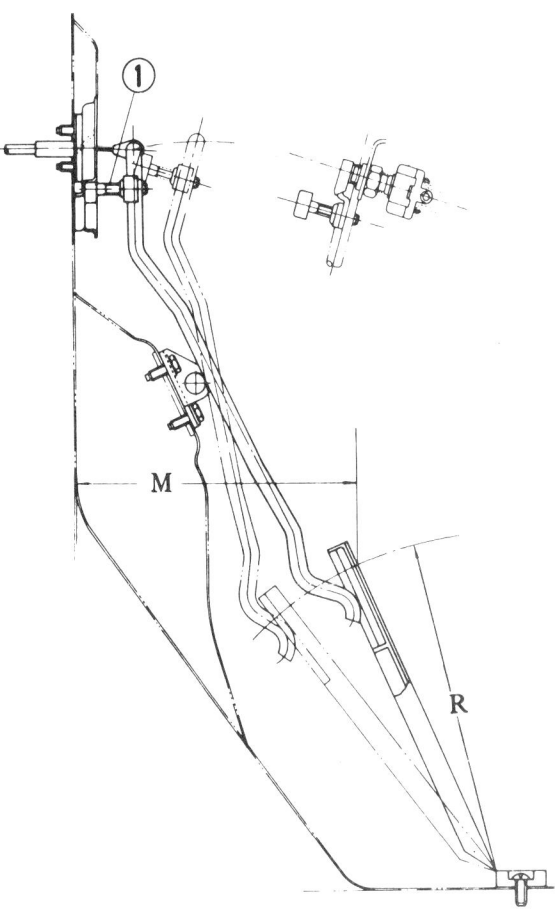

Fig. 3.49 The accelerator pedal linkage adjustment

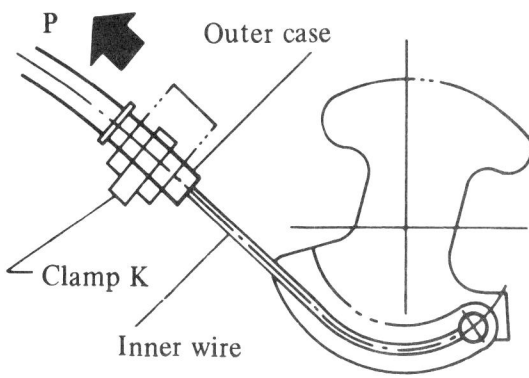

Fig. 3.50 Throttle cable adjustment

Refitting

30 Installation of the carburettor is the reverse of the removal procedure. Adjust the linkage, as described in Section 38.

37 Altitude compensator (California)

1 Any malfunction of the compensator can only be rectified by fitting a new unit. Ensure that the coloured hoses connect with the appropriate coloured port markings.

2 To check for a faulty unit, attach a length of tubing to the inlet and outlet hoses and suck and blow as appropriate. If there is no restriction during these operations then either the inlet, or outlet, valve will have failed.

38 Accelerator control linkages – removal and refitting

1 Remove the air cleaner; refer to Section 2 or 3 if necessary.

2 Disconnect the cable at the carburettor end. Open throttle to release nipple from its location.

3 Loosen the locknut and detach the outer case from the holder bracket.

4 Remove the spring clip and disconnect the cable from the accelerator pedal arm.

5 Remove the two screws attaching the outer case to the body and detach the cable.

6 Refitting is the reverse of the removal procedure. Lubricate the cable and linkages during assembly, and adjust the cable as follows:

7 Refer to Fig. 3.49 and rotate the stopper bolt (1) to give a clearance of 6·69 in (170 mm) between points marked M, and R should be 7·87 in (200 mm). Tighten the stopper bolt locknut to secure in the set position.

8 At the carburettor end the cable can be adjusted by pulling the cable casing away from the clamp as shown in Fig. 3.50, in direction P and check that the throttle lever is in the idle position. The outer case must be located to 0·04 in (1 mm) from where the throttle lever commences moving, then secure in this position with the clamp (K).

9 Ensure on completion that the throttle valve can fully open and that the cable and linkages are free to operate without binding or sticking. Check that the throttle lever returns fully when released.

10 On automatic transmission models the kickdown switch must also be checked for adjustment. Ensure that when operated, the stopper on the end of the pedal arm actuates the switch when the pedal is fully depressed. Loosen the locknut and adjust switch to suit if not. Tighten the locknut to secure.

39 Manual choke control – removal and refitting

1 Disconnect the choke control wire from the choke control lever at the carburettor.

2 Detach the choke knob by holding the inner wire with a pair of pliers and pushing on the knob. Rotate through 90° and pull off the knob.

3 Undo and remove the nut and spacer securing the choke control outer cable and sleeve to the dash panel.

4 Push the outer cable sleeve through the hole in the dash and draw out the cable assembly.

5 Refitting the choke control assembly is the reverse sequence to removal. Lubricate the inner cable with engine oil to ensure free operation.

6 The choke is correctly adjusted when the choke valve is fully closed and there is a small amount of cable slack when the knob is pushed in.

40 Fuel tank – removal and refitting

1 Disconnect the battery earth (ground) cable.

Saloon

2 Open the boot lid and unscrew the two retaining screws from the upright panel behind the rear seat.

3 Prise the four plastic panel clips free and remove the panel to gain

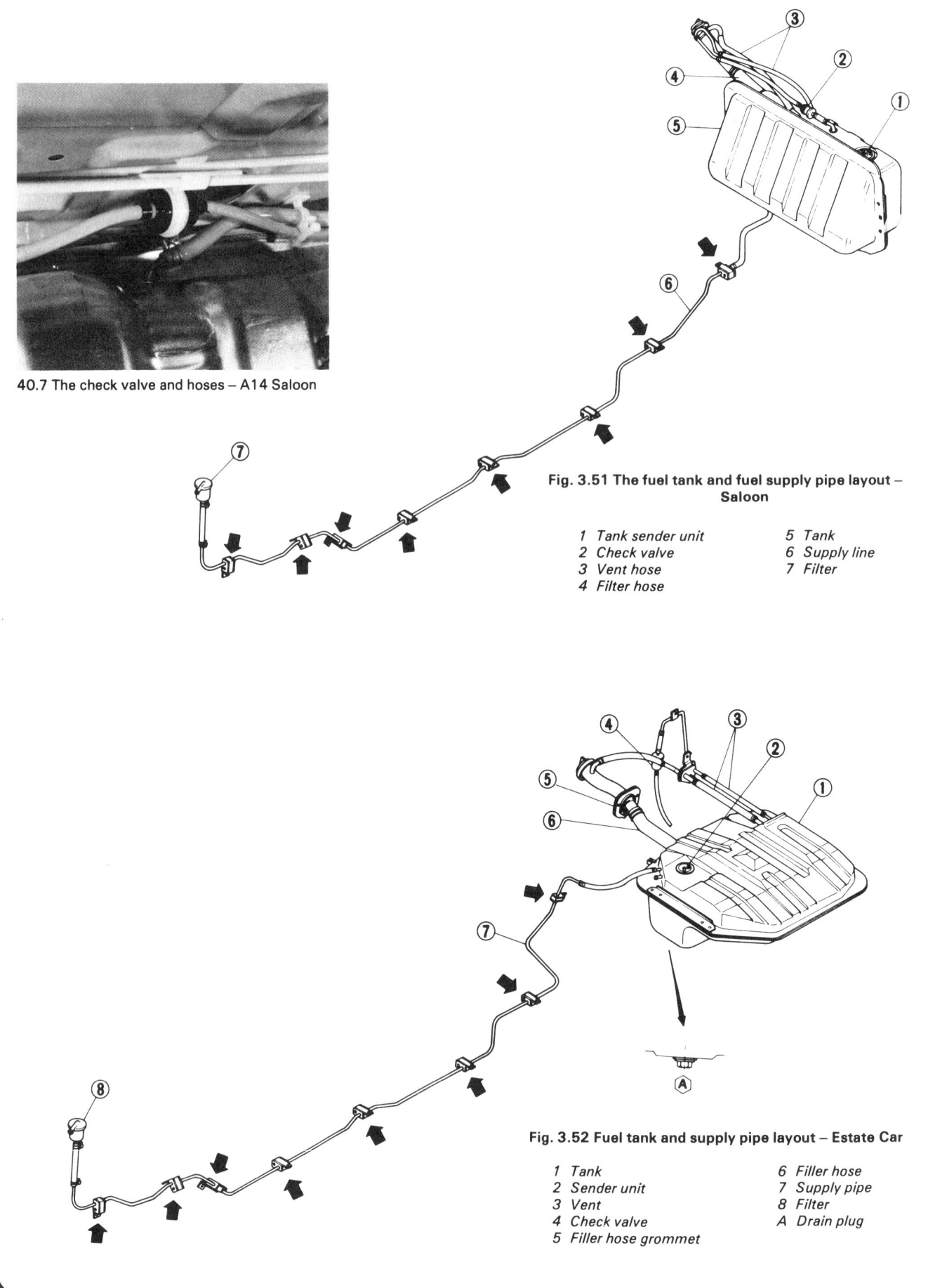

40.7 The check valve and hoses – A14 Saloon

**Fig. 3.51 The fuel tank and fuel supply pipe layout –
Saloon**

1 Tank sender unit
2 Check valve
3 Vent hose
4 Filter hose

5 Tank
6 Supply line
7 Filter

Fig. 3.52 Fuel tank and supply pipe layout – Estate Car

1 Tank
2 Sender unit
3 Vent
4 Check valve
5 Filler hose grommet

6 Filler hose
7 Supply pipe
8 Filter
A Drain plug

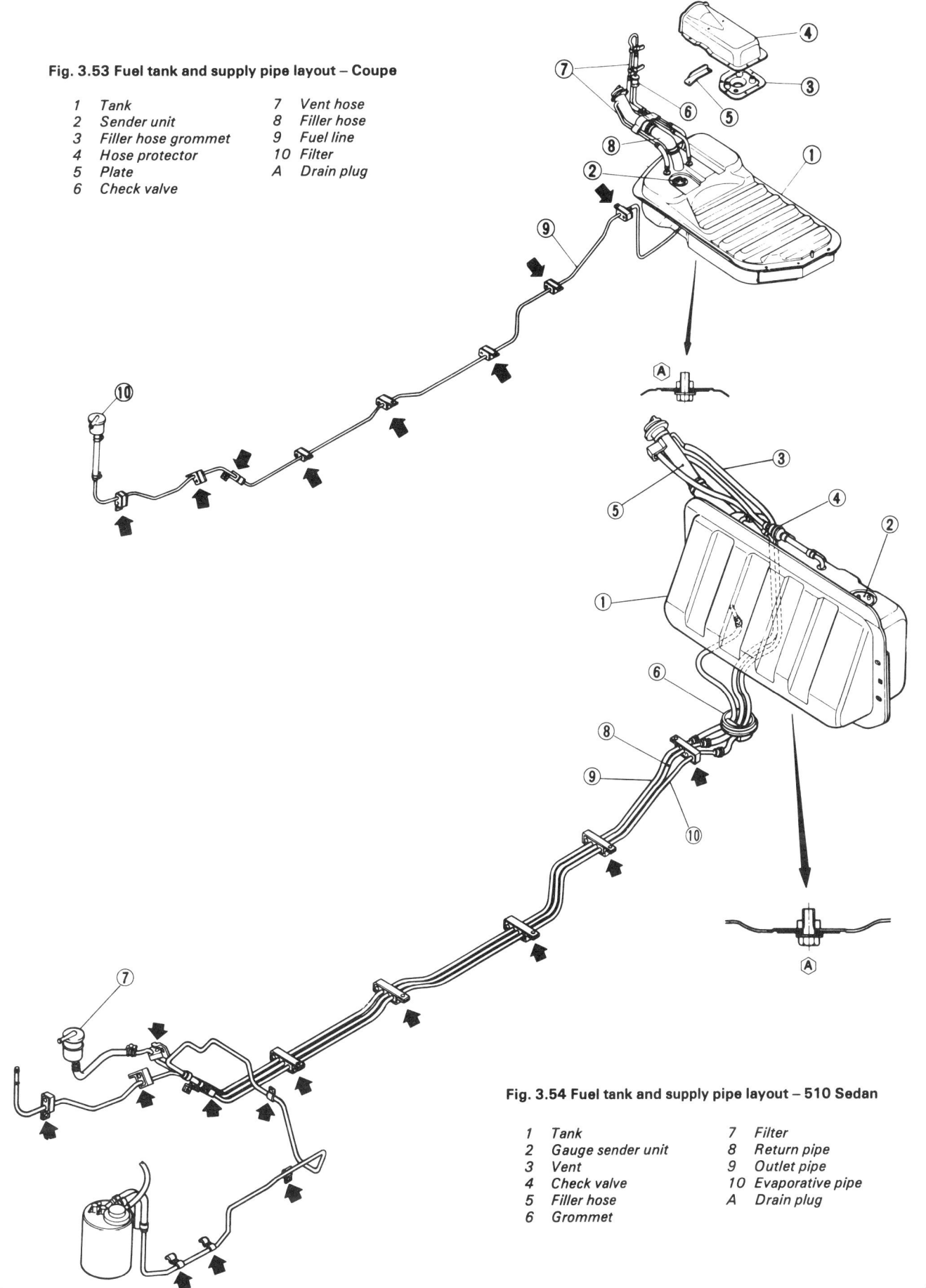

Fig. 3.53 Fuel tank and supply pipe layout – Coupe

1 Tank
2 Sender unit
3 Filler hose grommet
4 Hose protector
5 Plate
6 Check valve
7 Vent hose
8 Filler hose
9 Fuel line
10 Filter
A Drain plug

Fig. 3.54 Fuel tank and supply pipe layout – 510 Sedan

1 Tank
2 Gauge sender unit
3 Vent
4 Check valve
5 Filler hose
6 Grommet
7 Filter
8 Return pipe
9 Outlet pipe
10 Evaporative pipe
A Drain plug

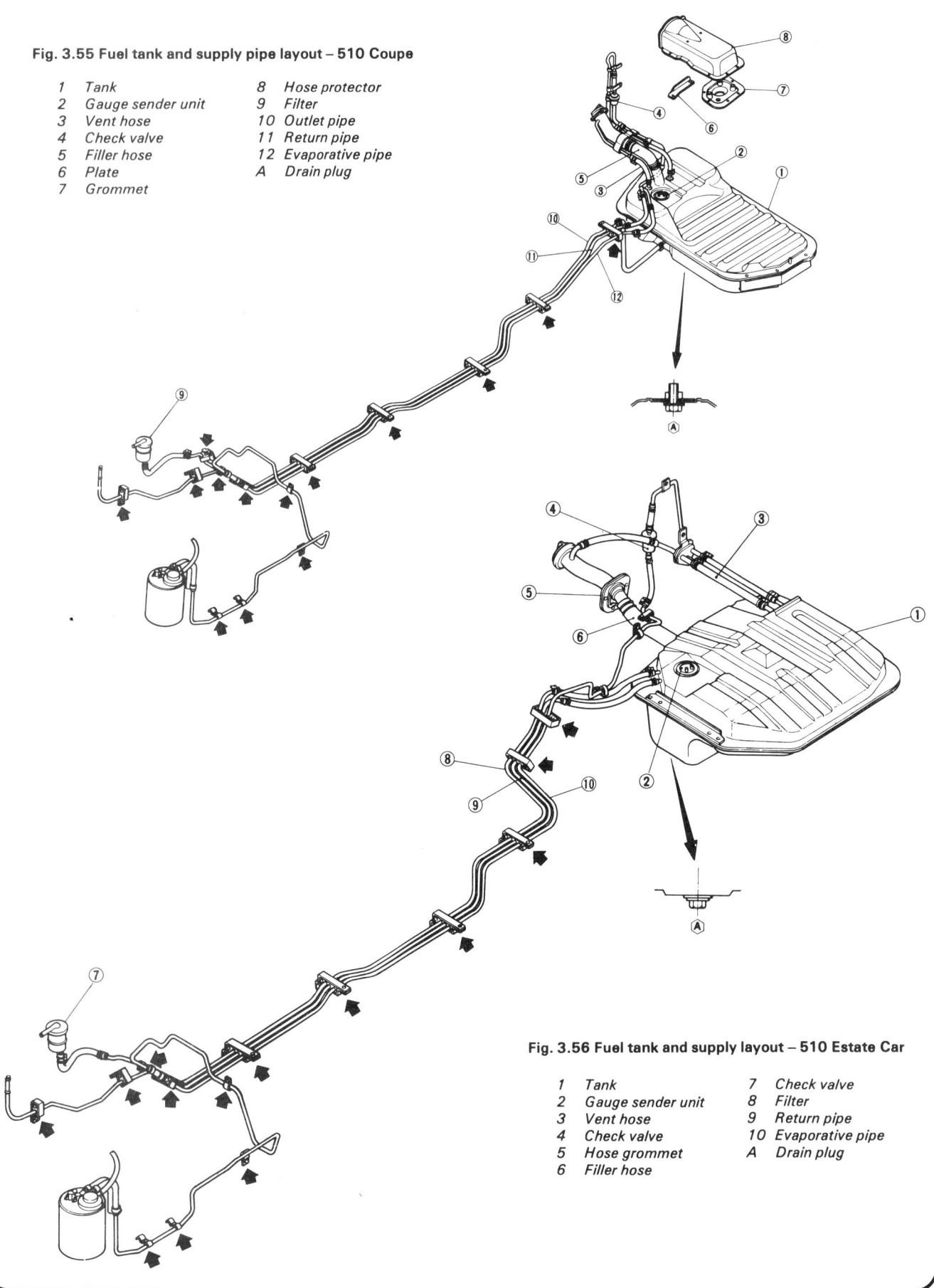

Fig. 3.55 Fuel tank and supply pipe layout – 510 Coupe

1	Tank	8	Hose protector
2	Gauge sender unit	9	Filter
3	Vent hose	10	Outlet pipe
4	Check valve	11	Return pipe
5	Filler hose	12	Evaporative pipe
6	Plate	A	Drain plug
7	Grommet		

Fig. 3.56 Fuel tank and supply layout – 510 Estate Car

1	Tank	7	Check valve
2	Gauge sender unit	8	Filter
3	Vent hose	9	Return pipe
4	Check valve	10	Evaporative pipe
5	Hose grommet	A	Drain plug
6	Filler hose		

access to the tank unit.

4   Unscrew the filler pipe dip and detach the pipe.

5   Disconnect the sender unit wiring.

6   Unscrew the drain plug and drain the fuel into a clean metal container of suitable capacity. Place a lid over the container and position it out of the way.

7   Disconnect the vent hose evaporative return hose and fuel supply hose as applicable (photo).

8   Unscrew the four retaining bolts and withdraw the tank unit.

Coupé

9   Access to the Coupé model fuel tank is made by carefully removing the luggage compartment carpet and board. The fuel filler hose cover must also be detached.

10 Detach the respective hoses, the plate and sender unit gauge wiring.

11 The tank can now be unbolted and removed from underneath.

Estate Car

12 Drain the fuel from the tank into a suitable container.

13 Detach the filler hose, vent hose and the supply hose from the front of the tank.

14 Remove the filler hose protector.

15 Lift out the spare wheel and then detach the fuel tank support.

16 Withdraw the tank and detach the sender unit wires.

Refitting

17 Refitting on all models is a direct reversal of removal but ensure that all hose connections are secure and not rubbing or being distorted against adjacent components. No attempt should be made to repair the fuel tank. This job must be done by your dealer.

---

41 Fuel gauge sender unit – removal and refitting

1   On Saloon models follow instructions 1 to 5 in Section 40.

2   On Coupé models follow instructions 1 and 9 in Section 40.

3   The fuel tank bolts must then be loosened and the tank lowered approximately $\frac{1}{2}$ in (10 to 15 mm) to gain access to the sender unit.

4   On Estate models, remove the fuel tank as described in Section 40.

5   Turn the sender unit anti-clockwise and remove from the tank.

6   Refitting is a direct reversal of removal but ensure that all hoses are securely connected – renew any that are defective. Reconnect the wires and refit the tank before refitting the panels and carpet.

---

42 Exhaust system – removal and refitting

Standard exhaust system

1   Unscrew and remove the nuts retaining the downpipe to the exhaust manifold (photo).

2   Remove the bolts securing the front and rear pipe flanges.

3   Detach the front pipe assembly from the car.

4   Unscrew and remove the rear pipe bracket retaining nut and washer, then carefully lower the rear pipe assembly.

5   The rear silencer can be detached from the pipe by twisting and tapping as shown (Fig. 3.60).

6   Refitting is the reverse of the removal procedure. It is recommended that a proprietary sealant is used at the muffler-to-front tube joint. Ensure that there is no strain on any of the mounting brackets or rubbers and that no part of the system contacts the vehicle floor or propeller shaft.

Exhaust system 510 model – Non-California

7   The procedure follows paragraphs 1 to 6 but the front pipe section to the manifold incorporates a tube shelter. This is retained by three clamps, secured by bolts from underneath.

8   On Estate Cars, the front pipe to rear section assembly pipe is secured by a U-clamp and not a flange. Renew this clamp when fitting a new system.

Exhaust system with Catalytic converter – California models

9   Remove the respective lower shelters (heat insulators).

10 Loosen the exhaust mounting insulator to body and detach the pipe from the mounting.

11 Disconnect the rear pipe from the catalytic converter and twist anti-clockwise and pull the pipe so that it clears the axle and remove it.

12 Detach the catalytic converter from the front exhaust pipe.

13 Loosen the manifold to front pipe nuts and disconnect the mounting bracket from the pipe and transmission.

14 Remove the bolts retaining the gusset and C-clamp and detach

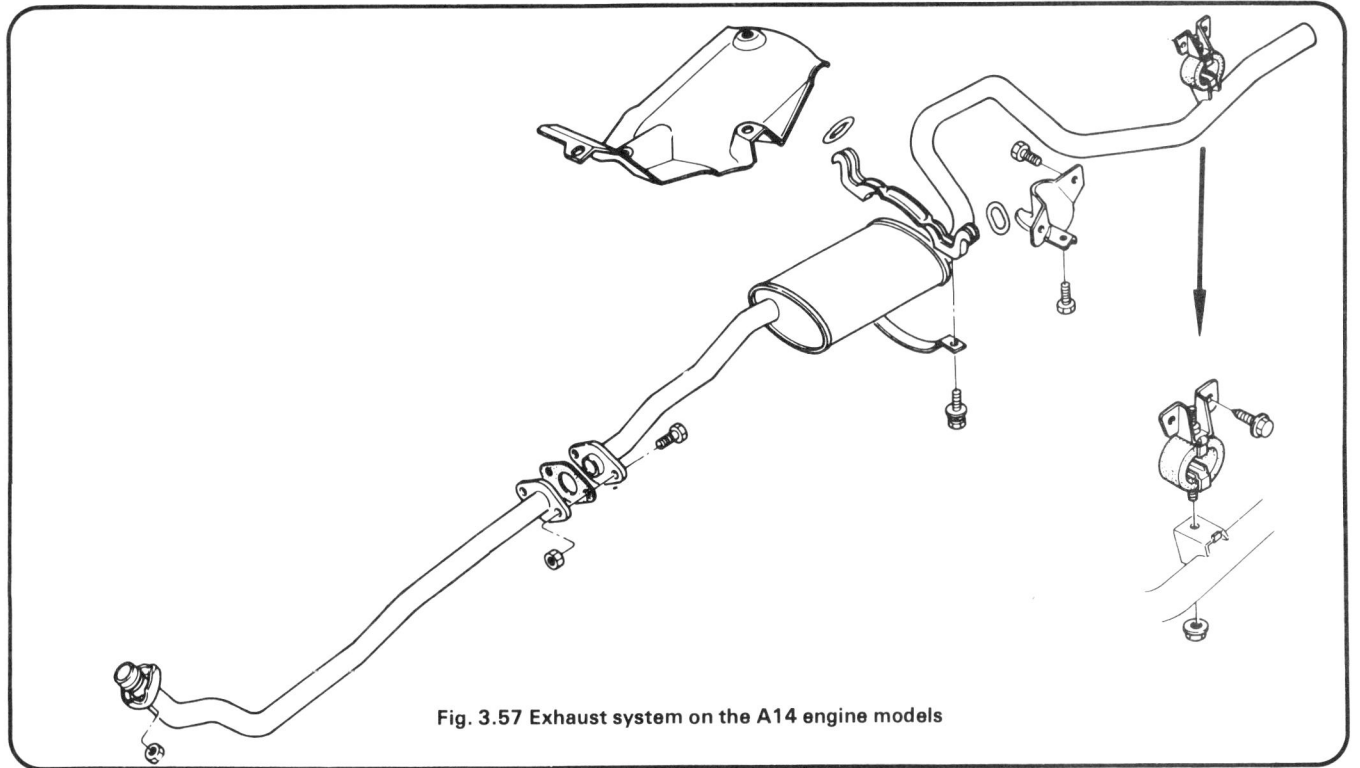

Fig. 3.57 Exhaust system on the A14 engine models

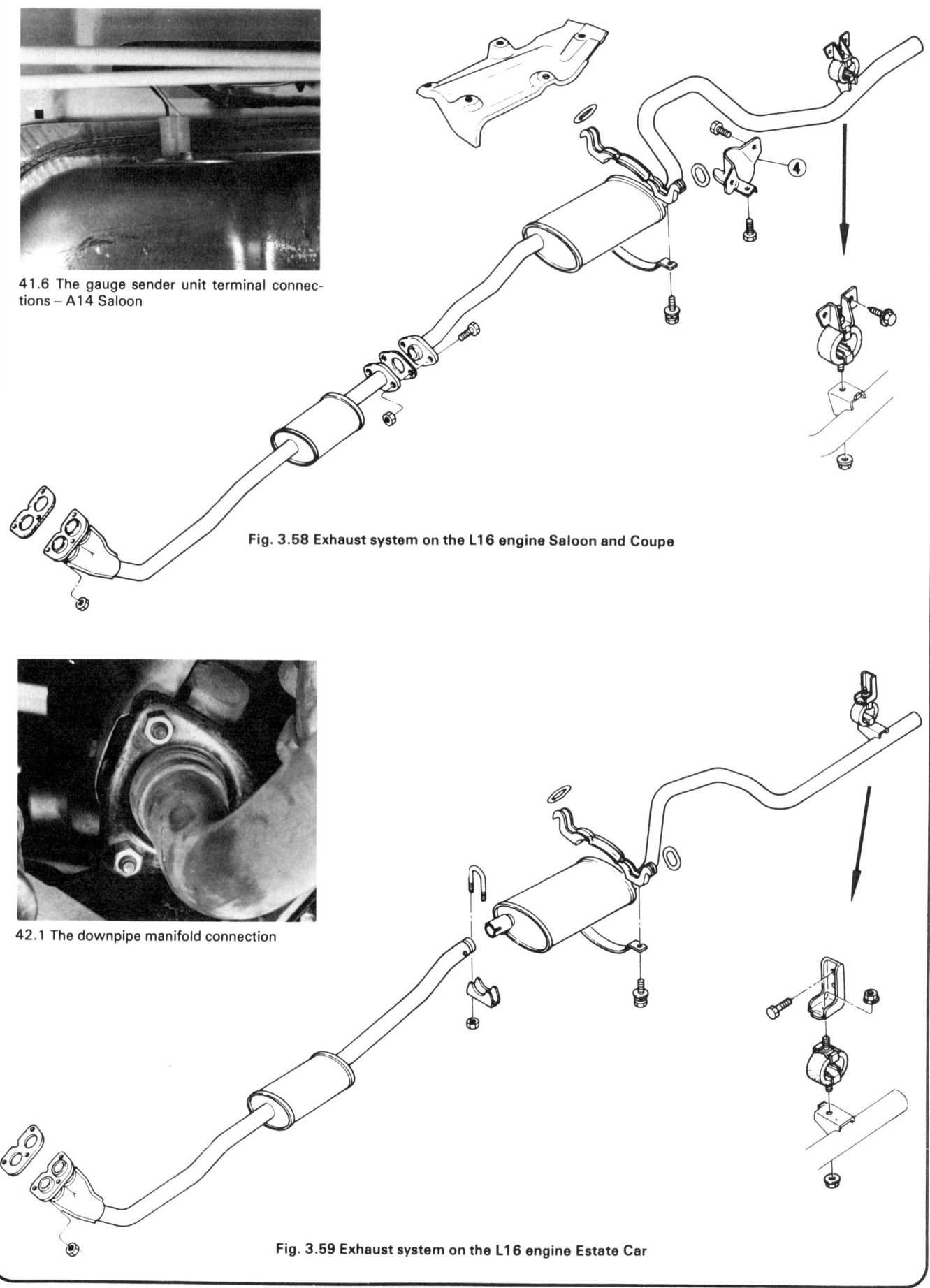

41.6 The gauge sender unit terminal connections – A14 Saloon

Fig. 3.58 Exhaust system on the L16 engine Saloon and Coupe

42.1 The downpipe manifold connection

Fig. 3.59 Exhaust system on the L16 engine Estate Car

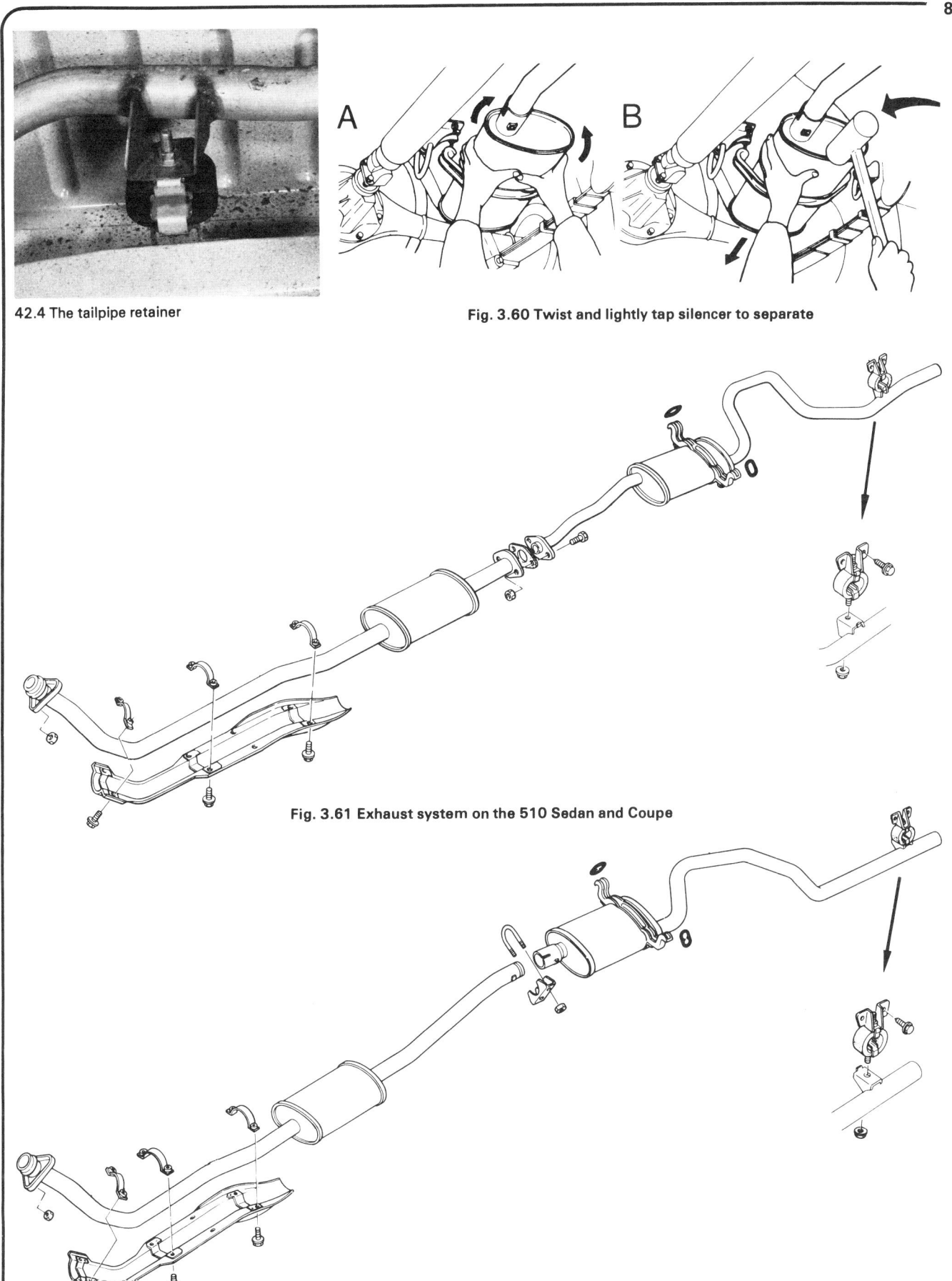

42.4 The tailpipe retainer

Fig. 3.60 Twist and lightly tap silencer to separate

A B

Fig. 3.61 Exhaust system on the 510 Sedan and Coupe

Fig. 3.62 Exhaust system on the 510 Estate Car

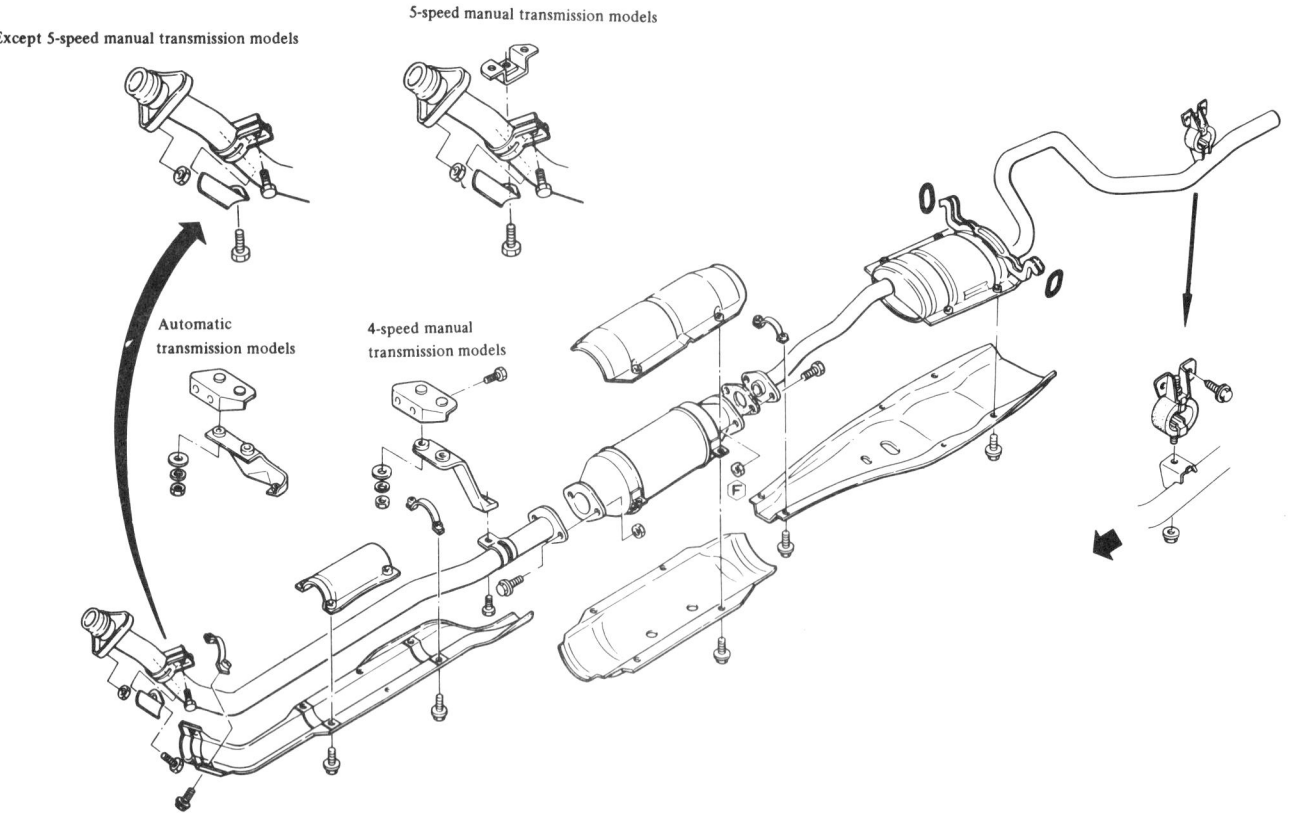

Except 5-speed manual transmission models

5-speed manual transmission models

Automatic
transmission models

4-speed manual
transmission models

**Fig. 3.63 Exhaust system on the 510 Sedan and Coupe –
California models**

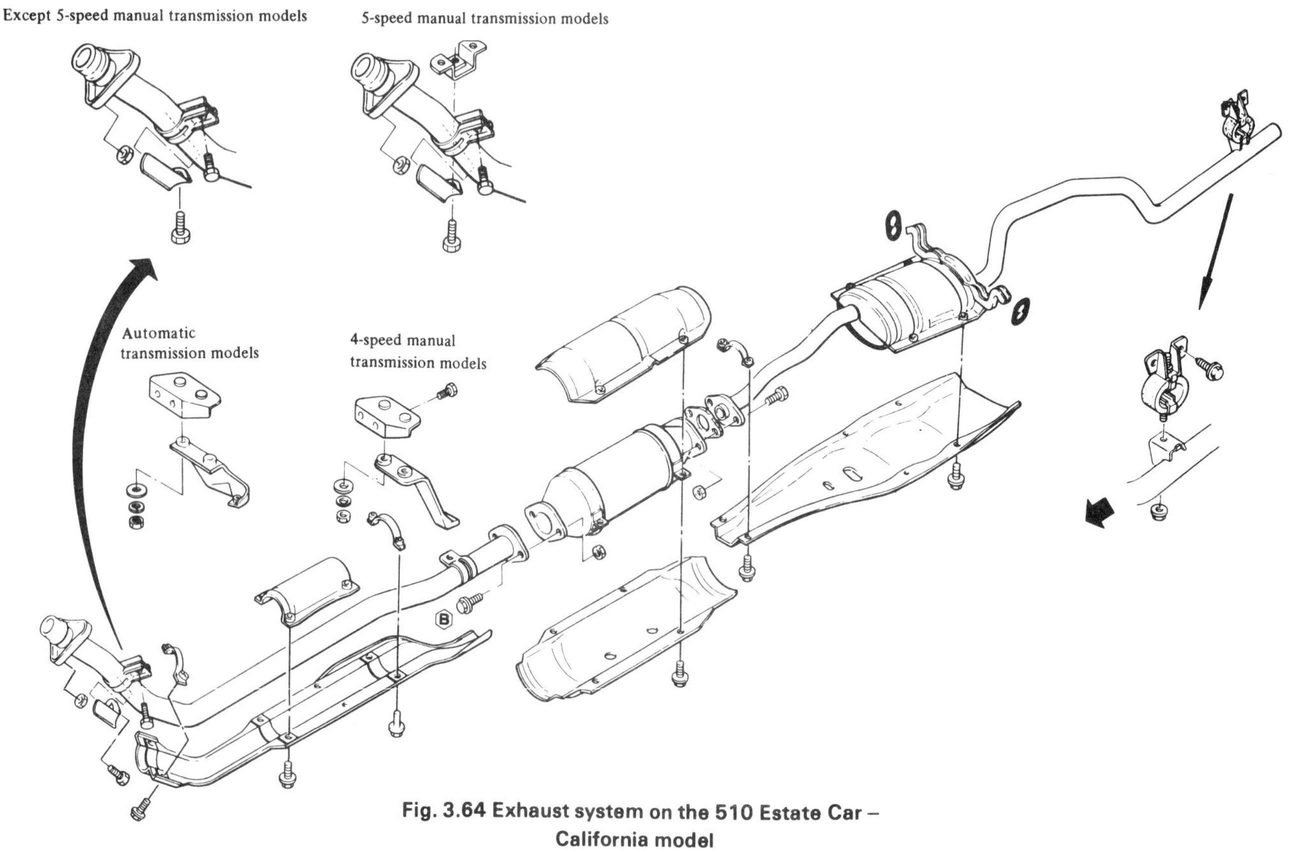

Except 5-speed manual transmission models

5-speed manual transmission models

Automatic
transmission models

4-speed manual
transmission models

**Fig. 3.64 Exhaust system on the 510 Estate Car –
California model**

the front exhaust system.

15 Refitting is a reversal of the removal procedure but it is recommended that a proprietary sealant is used on the system joints. Loosely assemble the system before tightening the respective retainers and ensure that there is no strain on mounting brackets or rubbers. Check that no part of the system contacts the vehicle floor or adjacent components.

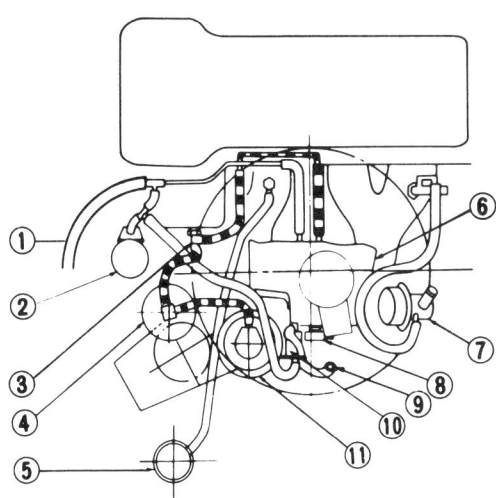

Fig. 3.65 The emission control – non-California models

1 Canister purge control line
2 Distributor
3 Thermal vacuum valve
4 BPT valve
5 Air control valve
6 Carburettor
7 AB valve
8 Inlet manifold vacuum outlet port
9 To air cleaner (manual transmission)
10 Vacuum switch valve (manual transmission)
11 EGR control valve

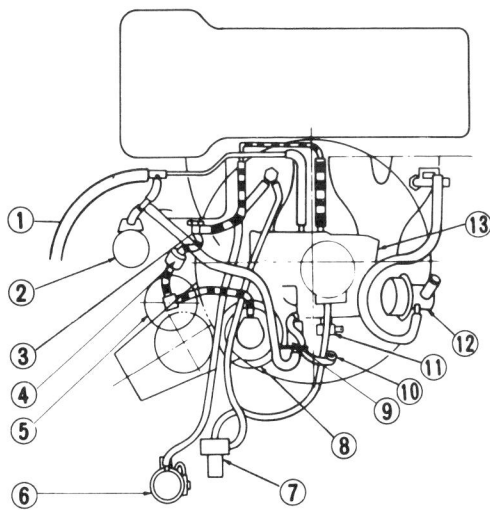

Fig. 3.66 The emission control layout – California models

1 Canister purge control line
2 Distributor
3 Thermal vacuum valve
4 Vacuum delay valve
5 BPT valve
6 CAC valve
7 BCDD vacuum control valve
8 EGR control valve
9 Vacuum switch valve (manual transmission)
10 To air cleaner (manual transmission)
11 Inlet manifold vacuum outlet
12 AB valve
13 Carburettor

43 Emission control system – description

The emission control system on USA models comprises three main sub systems, these being (a) crankcase emission control system, (b) exhaust emission control system and (c) an evaporative emission control system. On California models the emission control is more strict and therefore these have additional items incorporated into the system.

European models have a crankcase emission control system fitted only.

The complexity of the individual systems depends on the vehicle model and intended market.

The details and layout of the positive crankcase emission control system is shown in Chapter 1.

The exhaust emission control system and its components are shown in Figs. 1.10 and 1.11 in Chapter 1. The California models incorporate a catalytic converter and an altitude compensator.

The fuel evaporative loss system comprises a non-vented fuel tank, a separator, a vent line, carbon canister and a vacuum signal line.

Fuel vapour is emitted from the fuel tank and is stored in the canister (which is filled with activated carbon) during periods when the engine is not running.

As the throttle is opened, vacuum increases in the vacuum signal line and opens the purge control valve to admit vapour through the main valve port and thence to the inlet manifold.

Air injection system

This is a method of injecting air (generated in an external compressor) into the exhaust manifold in order to reduce hydrocarbons and carbon monoxide in the exhaust gas by providing conditions favourable for recombustion. The system comprises an air cleaner, engine driven air pump, relief valve, check valve, anti-backfire valve, air gallery and the associated hoses. Models for use in California also have an air control valve and emergency air relief valve to prevent excessive temperature rise in the catalytic converter.

Air is drawn through the air pump air cleaner, compressed, and directed through the check valve to the air gallery and injection nozzles. During high speed operation, excessive pump pressure is vented to ambient through the relief valve in the carburettor air cleaner.

The check valve is fitted in the delivery line at the injection gallery. The function of this valve is to prevent any exhaust gases passing into the air pump should the manifold pressure be greater than the pump injection pressure. It is designed to close against the exhaust manifold pressure should the air pump fail as a result, for example, of a broken drivebelt.

During deceleration, intake manifold vacuum opens the anti-backfire valve to allow fresh air to flow into the intake manifold. This ensures that the combustion cycle is more effective and reduces the amount of unburned gases exhausted.

On California models, the air control valve opens when the combined air pump pressure and intake manifold vacuum reach a predetermined level as happens during lightly loaded conditions. The air from the air pump is bled off to the air cleaner which means that the injection system is less effective, the exhaust gas temperature is lowered and the catalytic converter temperature can be maintained at the optimum operating temperature.

The emergency air relief valve bleeds air from the air pump when there is a prolonged condition of low manifold suction as happens during high continuous speed operation. This nullifies the air injection system, reduces the exhaust gas temperature and prevents the catalytic converter from overheating.

Exhaust gas recirculation

In this system, a small part of the exhaust gas is introduced into the combustion chamber to lower the spark flame temperature during combustion to reduce the nitrogen oxide content of the exhaust gases.

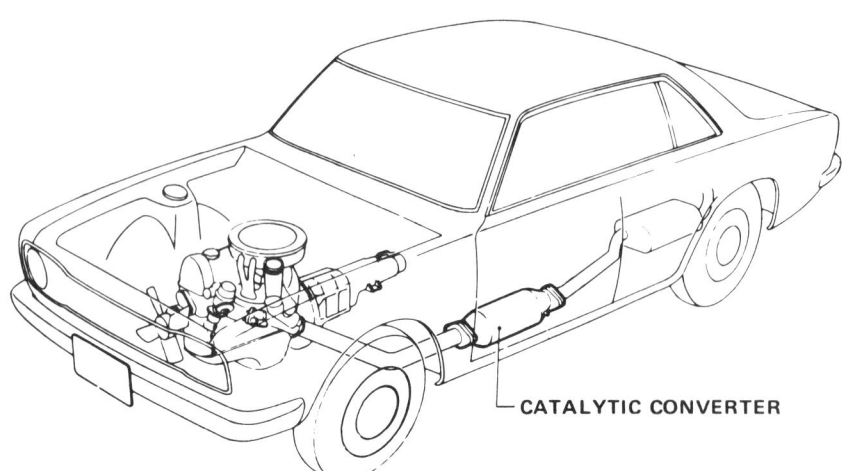

Fig. 3.67 California model showing catalytic converter

CATALYTIC CONVERTER

Fig. 3.68 The fuel evaporative control system. Note the different fuel tank arrangements for the Estate Car and Coupe models

ESTATE CAR

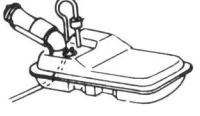

COUPE

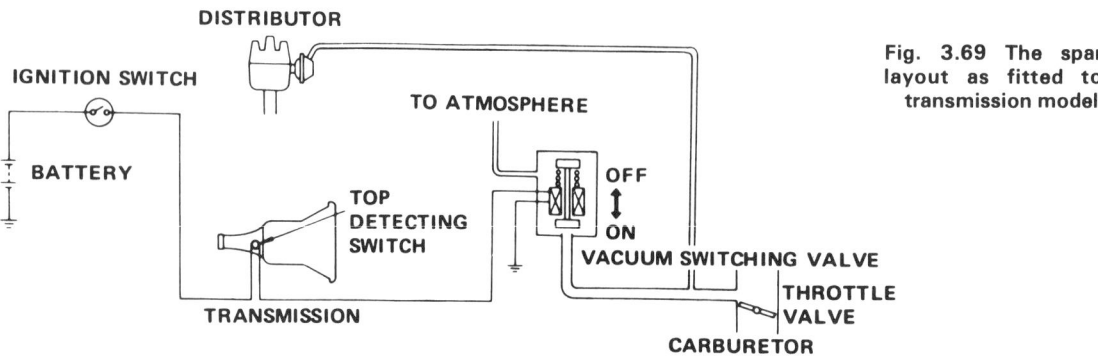

DISTRIBUTOR

IGNITION SWITCH

Fig. 3.69 The spark timing layout as fitted to manual transmission models (USA)

TO ATMOSPHERE

BATTERY

OFF

ON

TOP DETECTING SWITCH

VACUUM SWITCHING VALVE

THROTTLE VALVE

TRANSMISSION

CARBURETOR

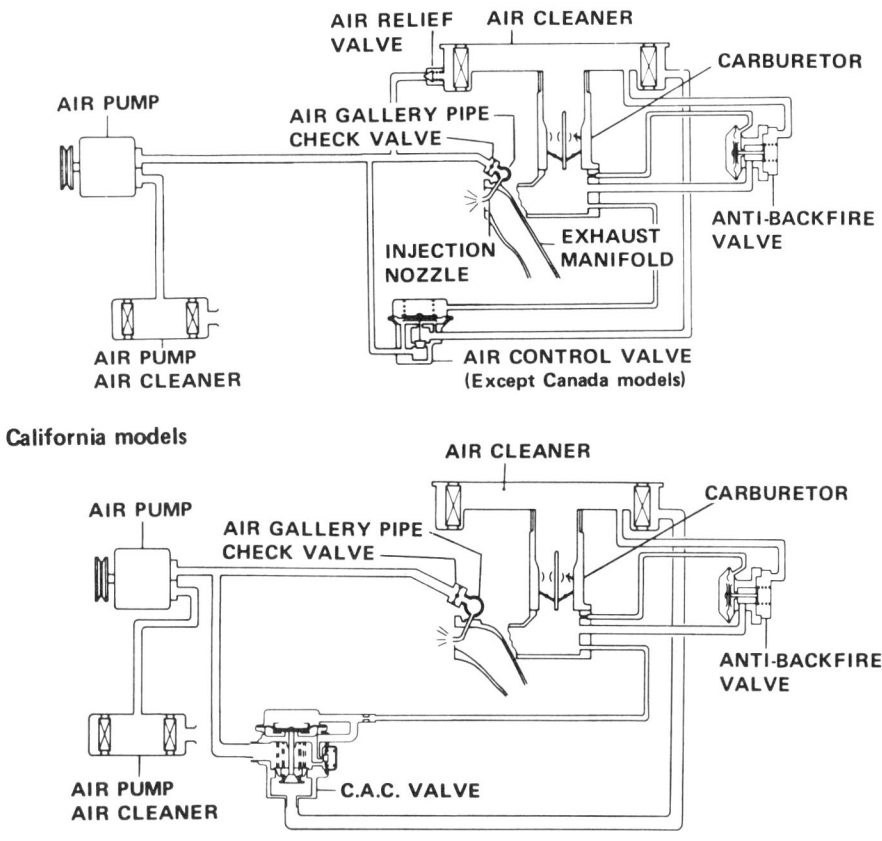

Fig. 3.70 The respective air injection systems of the non-California models (top) and the California models (lower)

The system used for 1974 models utilizes an EGR control valve, solenoid valve, water temperature switch, relay, EGR tube and vacuum tube. Later systems dispense with the solenoid valve, temperature switch and relay, and substitute a thermal vacuum valve.

When the EGR valve is open, a small amount of exhaust gas is fed from the exhaust manifold to the EGR passage in the intake manifold. On early systems the EGR valve was either open or closed, depending on whether the engine water temperature was above or below 31/41°C (88/106°F). On later systems, the EGR valve position is controlled by the manifold vacuum and temperature and is a modulating type.

A warning system is incorporated, except on vehicles operating in California and Canada, to warn that the system must be inspected after a pre-determined time.

Early fuel evaporative system

This system utilizes a thermostatically controlled heat control valve in the exhaust manifold to heat the intake manifold during the engine warm-up period. This improves the fuel atomization and results in lower hydrocarbon emissions from the exhaust.

Spark timing control

When top gear is selected a vacuum switching valve is energized and closes the vacuum valve between the carburettor and distributor. As a result the distributor advances the ignition timing.

When any other gear is selected the vacuum switching valve is de-energized allowing the distributor to return to its normal mode of operation.

Catalytic converter

Fitted in the exhaust system of vehicles destined for California, this device speeds up the chemical reaction of the hydrocarbons and carbon monoxide present in the exhaust gases so that they change into harmless carbon dioxide and water. Air for the chemical process is supplied by the air injection pump.

In the event of the system overheating, an increase in the vehicle floor temperature will result. This opens a temperature sensitive floor switch which illuminates a warning lamp through a relay becoming de-energized. During normal operating conditions, the warning lamp is illuminated during the engine start sequence as an indication of its serviceability. It is not unusual for the warning lamp to come on during periods of hard driving, or climbing gradients for long periods in low gears.

44 Emission control system – maintenance

1   The respective emission control components can only operate efficiently if the engine and its associate parts are in good condition and correctly adjusted. If the maintenance schedules given at the front of the book are closely adhered to then this should be the case but in particular check that the valve clearances are correct, the fuel lines are secure and the fuel line filter is changed at the specified mileage. The carburettor air filter and air pump filter must also be renewed regularly and the carburettors correctly adjusted. In the ignition circuit, check that the timing is in correct adjustment, also the distributor points and spark plug electrode clearances.
2   Check that all emission control vapour lines and their respective connections are secure and in good condition.
3   Check the condition of the air pump drivebelt and also its tension. Readjust if necessary.
4   Renew the positive crankcase ventilation valve (PCV) and filter at the prescribed mileage/time interval.
5   Remove the ventilation hoses occasionally and blow through with an air line. This is most essential whenever the PCV valve has been renewed. Check that the flame arrester is securely positioned in the air cleaner to rocker cover hose.
6   The fuel tank vacuum relief valve must be in good working condi-

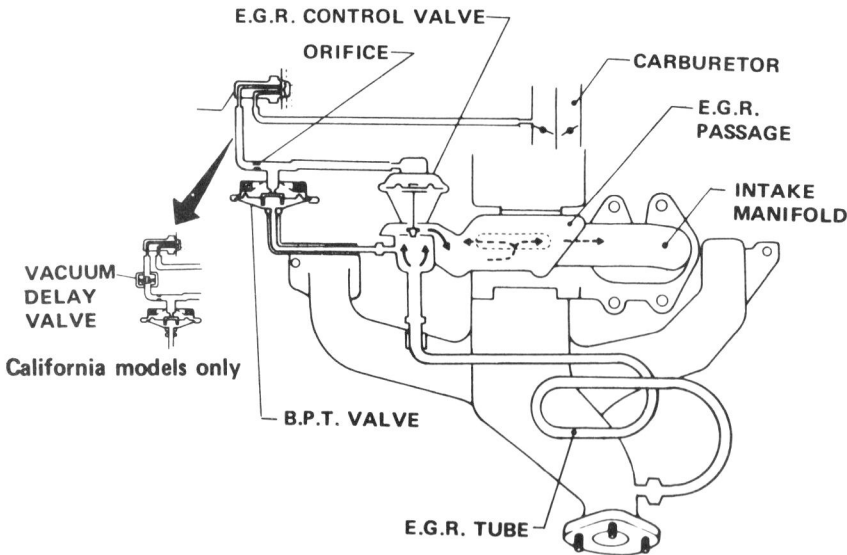

Fig. 3.71 The exhaust gas recirculation system (EGR). Note the vacuum delay valve which is fitted on the California models

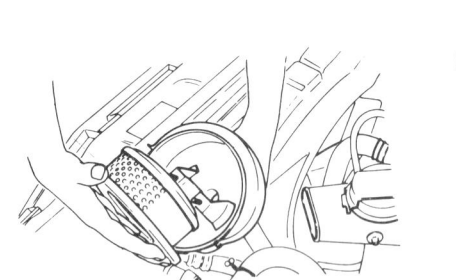

Fig. 3.72 Change the air pump filter at regular intervals as specified

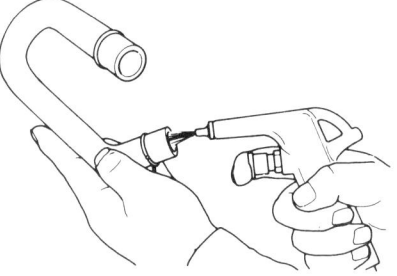

Fig. 3.73 Blow the ventilation hoses through to clear using an air gun

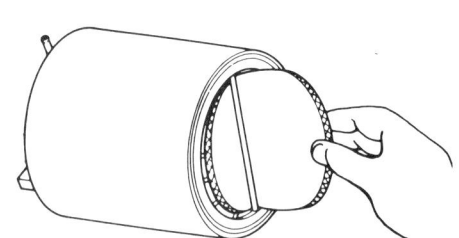

Fig. 3.74 Renew the carbon canister at the specified intervals

tion. If defective renew together with the fuel filler cap.

7   The carbon canister filter in the evaporative control system must be removed at regular intervals.

8   Specialized equipment is required to check the efficiency of the system and also to enable accurate adjustment of the carburettor idle and ignition timing to suit. Therefore apart from the above mentioned items and the following service sections, any more complex repair or overhauls of the emission control system components are best left to your Datsun dealer who has the specialised knowledge and equipment to deal with such problems.

45 Air injection system – maintenance and testing

1   Check all hoses, air gallery pipes and nozzles for security and condition.

2   Check and adjust the air pump drivebelt tension to obtain a deflection of 0·3 to 0·47 in (8 to 12 mm), when a load of 22 lb (10 kg) is applied at the midpoint of the longest run of the belt.

3   With the engine at normal operating temperature, disconnect the hose leading to the check valve.

4   Run the engine at approximately 2000 rpm and then let it return to idling speed, all the time watching for exhaust gas leaks from the valve. Where these are evident, renew the valve.

5   Check the operation of the air pump relief valve by first discon-

necting the hoses from the non-return valve and then removing the air control valve from the hose connector. Plug the connector.

6   Run the engine at a steady 3000 rpm and place the hand on the air outlet of the emergency relief valve (California models). A good air pressure should be felt but if it is not, renew the valve.

7   Now pull the vacuum hose from the air control valve. If air ejection ceases from the outlet nozzle, the valve is in good condition but if it persists, renew the valve which must be faulty.

8   The anti-backfire valve (flame-trap) can be checked, when the engine is at normal operating temperature, by disconnecting the hose from the air cleaner and placing a finger over the end of the hose. Run the engine at about 3000 rpm and then return it to idling. During this action, a strong suction effect should be felt on the finger which indicates that the valve is in good order.

9   Every 12 000 miles (19 000 km), renew the air pump air cleaner element. The assembly is located on the side of the engine compartment close to the air pump. The element and cleaner lower body are disposable, being an integral unit. A faulty or worn air pump should be renewed on an exchange basis.

46 Exhaust gas recirculation – maintenance and testing

1   Check the complete system for insecure or damaged hoses. Tighten or renew as appropriate.

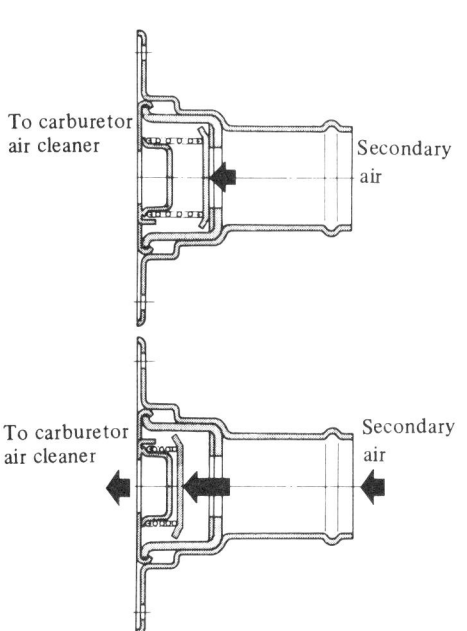

Fig. 3.75 The air pump relief valve showing closed and open positions

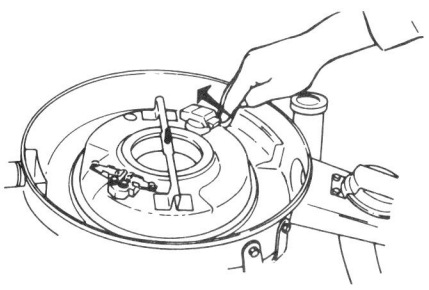

Fig. 3.76 Check the air pump relief valve (with filter removed)

2   Periodically, remove the EGR control valve and clean its seat with a wire brush.

3   The control valve can be checked for correct vacuum operation by connecting a piece of hose to it and sucking with the mouth. The valve should move into its fully extended position and retain this attitude for at least 30 seconds after the vacuum ceases.

4   Actuate the valve diaphragm by raising with finger as shown (Fig. 3.79) to ensure that it doesn't stick or bind.

5   To check the operation of the thermal type vacuum valve, unscrew it from its location in the cylinder head and to prevent water entering the valve, connect two lengths of suitable tube. Immerse the valve in a container of water and keeping the ends of the tube clear heat the water. Suck the end of the tube to supply vacuum to the valve and ensure that the vacuum passage only opens at a temperature of 104 to 127°F (40 to 53°C). The valve should then remain open as the temperature climbs. Renew the valve unit if it proves defective.

47 Early fuel evaporative system – maintenance and testing

1   Periodically inspect the operation of the heat control valve. On starting with the engine cold, the counterweight should be in its extreme anti-clockwise position.

2   During engine acceleration (engine still cold) the counterweight will rotate in a clockwise direction.

3   When the engine reaches normal operating temperature, the counterweight will have moved fully clockwise.

4   External components of the device can be renewed but as the internal valve plate is welded to the operating shaft, any fault or wear in these items will necessitate renewal of the complete manifold assembly.

48 Catalytic converter – maintenance and testing

1   Faults associated with the catalytic converter or floor temperature warning system, which cannot be rectified by tightening exhaust system clamps or reconnecting electrical leads, should be rectified by your Datsun dealer.

2   For information on removal of the catalytic converter, refer to Section 42.

49 Floor temperature sensing switch/relay unit – removal and refitting

1   A floor temperature sensing switch is fitted to models equipped witha catalytic converter, and its function is to activate a warning light should the floor temperature rise above a certain level.

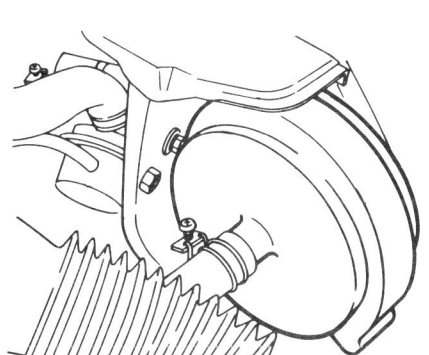

Fig. 3.77 The air pump air cleaner location

Fig. 3.78 Cleaning the EGR valve seat

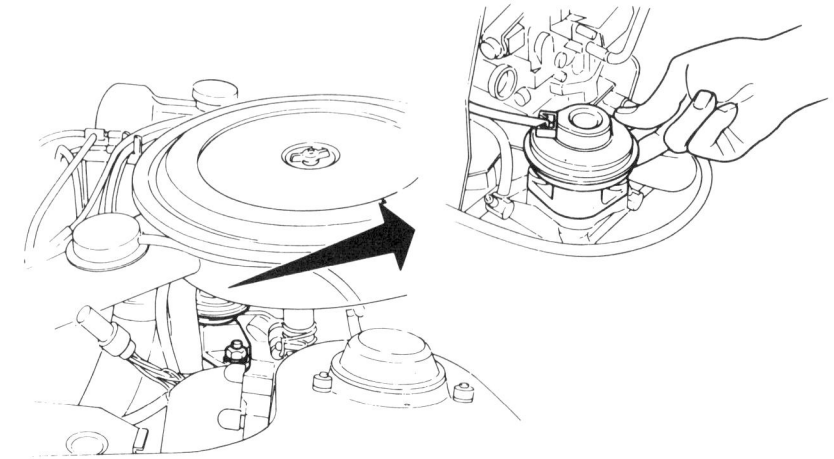

Fig. 3.79 Checking the EGR valve actuation

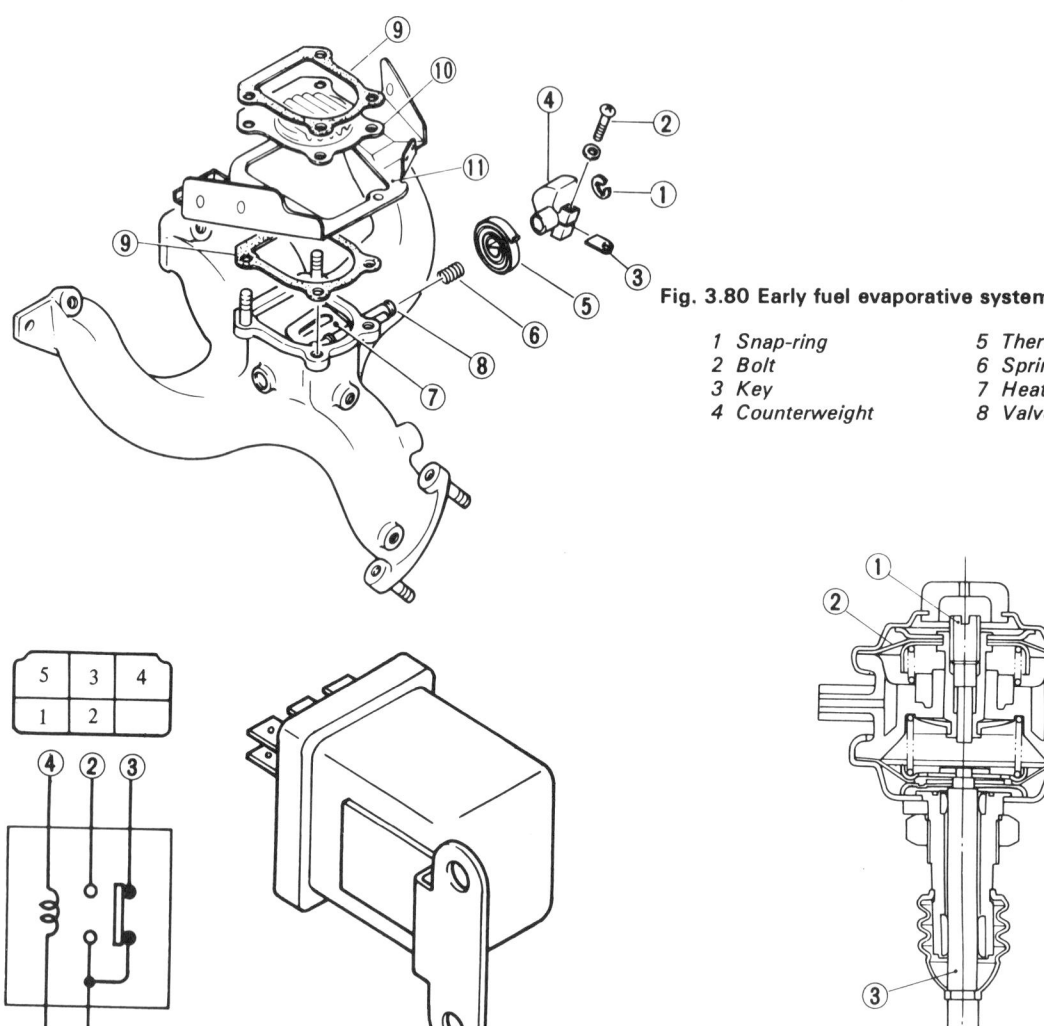

Fig. 3.80 Early fuel evaporative system – exploded view

1 Snap-ring
2 Bolt
3 Key
4 Counterweight

5 Thermostat spring
6 Spring
7 Heat control valve
8 Valve shaft

Fig. 3.81 The relay unit and connections

1 To warning lamp
2 From 'S' position
3 From 'IG' position

4 From the ignition switch
5 To the sensing switch

Fig. 3.82 The fast idle dashpot sectional view showing the adjuster screw (1) the diaphragm (2) and pushrod (3)

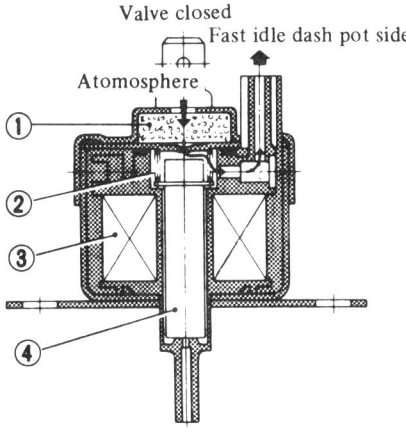

Fig. 3.83 Magnet valve in closed position

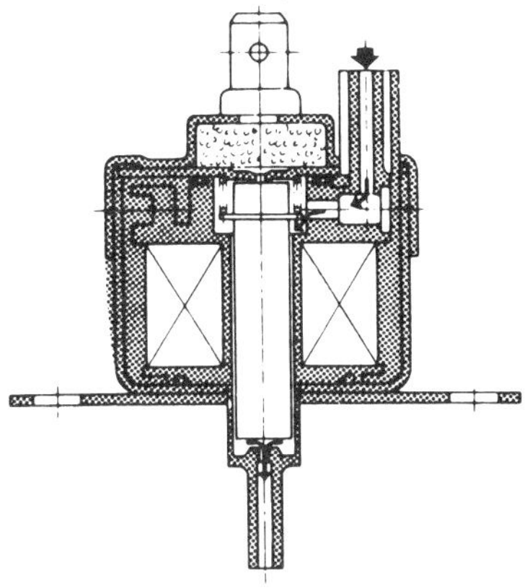

Fig. 3.84 Magnet valve in open position

1 *Filter* 3 *Coil*
2 *Spring* 4 *Valve*

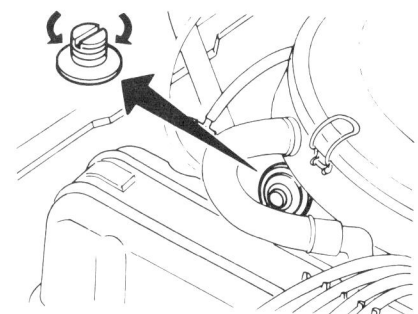

Fig. 3.85 The fast idle dashpot adjustment screw (with cap removed)

2   The rise in temperature may be caused by an engine malfunction or possibly severe driving conditions. When this occurs, the sensing switch goes off, the start line switch of the relay goes off and the ignition switch line turns on the floor temperature warning lamp.
3   Normally the light will be on while the starter motor is being operated but when the engine starts and the ignition key returns to the IG position the warning light should go out.
4   The location of the sensing switch differs according to model. In the Sedan it is under the fuel tank in the luggage compartment. In the Coupé it is under the luggage area floor board while in the Estate Car it is under the rear seat.
5   Removal is easy but first remove the battery ground lead.
6   Detach the switch wire from the connector, and loosen the cover screws.
7   Remove the screws and withdraw the sensor switch.
8   Refitting is a direct reversal of removal
9   Note that the relay unit for the sensor circuit is located on the right-hand side of the dash panel. Detach the dash panel to gain access to it. The relay unit is secured by a screw and the wiring can easily be detached at the connector if the unit is to be removed.
10 The warning lamp in the dash panel is accessible from the rear of the cluster lid.

50 Vacuum system (air conditioned models)

1   On models equipped with an air conditioning system a special fast idle control dashpot is incorporated into the carburation system. This device is designed to increase the idle speed of the engine to enable the conditioner unit to operate efficiently when the vehicle is stationary.

2   The fast idle dashpot operates in conjunction with a magnet valve which is located between the inlet manifold and the fast idle control device.
3   When the magnet valve is closed the inlet side vacuum port is closed and the fast idle dashpot side line is then open to the atmosphere.
4   When the valve is opened by the solenoid, the valve needle is lifted and allows the vacuum to be applied to the fast idle dashpot (from the inlet manifold).

Fast idle dashpot – removal and refitting
5   Detach the vacuum hose from the fast idle dashpot.
6   Refer to Section 3 and remove the air cleaner.
7   Unscrew the retaining nuts and withdraw the fast idle dashpot.
8   Refitting is the reversal of removal but on completion adjust the fast idle speed as follows.

Adjustment
9   Run the engine for a few minutes to warm it up to its normal operating temperature, and on automatic transmission models, select N position.
10 Check that the engine idle speed is as specified when the air conditioner is switched off. Adjust accordingly if necessary.
11 When the air conditioner is switched on the idle speed should increase to 800 rpm. To adjust the dashpot to achieve this figure, refer to Fig. 3.85, remove the protective cap from the dashpot and rotate the adjuster screw accordingly,. To increase the engine speed, turn the screw clockwise. To decrease the engine speed, turn the screw anti-clockwise.
12 Pump the accelerator a few times and check that when released the idle speed returns to the specified figure. Refit the cap on completion.

51 Fault diagnosis – fuel, exhaust and emission control systems

Symptom	Reason/s
Fuel consumption excessive	Air cleaner choked and dirty giving rich mixture
	Fuel leaking from carburettor, fuel pump, or fuel lines
	Float chamber flooding
	Generally worn carburettor
	Distributor condenser faulty
	Balance weights or vacuum advance mechanism in distributor faulty
	Carburettor incorrectly adjusted, mixture too rich
	Idling speed too high
	Contact breaker gap incorrect
	Valve clearances incorrect
	Choke valve incorrectly set
	Incorrectly set spark plugs
	Tyres under-inflated
	Wrong spark plugs fitted
	Brakes dragging
	If fitted emission control system faulty (see later in this Section)
Insufficient fuel delivery or weak mixture due to air leaks	Partially clogged filter in pump, carburettor or fuel line
	Incorrectly seating valves in fuel pump
	Fuel pump diaphragm leaking or damaged
	Gasket in fuel pump damaged
	Fuel pump valves sticking due to fuel gumming
	Too little fuel in fuel tank (prevalent when climbing steep hills)
	Union joints on pipe connections loose
	Split in fuel pipe on suction side of fuel pump
	Inlet manifold-to-block or inlet manifold-to-carburettor gaskets leaking
	Fuel tank relief valves stuck closed
Power reduced	Clogged main jets
	Accelerator linkage requires adjustment
	Fuel filter blocked
	Air cleaner blocked
	Power valve faulty
Erratic idling	Slow jet clogged
	Secondary throttle valve operating incorrectly
	Worn throttle valve shafts
	Broken carburettor flange gasket
	Incorrect adjusted BCDD
Flat spot or hesitation	Clogged jets
	Emulsion tube clogged
	Secondary throttle valve operating incorrectly
	Power valve faulty
Engine will not start	Fuel level incorrect
	Lack of fuel
	Incorrect setting of mixture screw
	Faulty anti-dieseling solenoid
	Incorrect fast idle adjustment

Emission control system faults

Erratic idling	Faulty anti-backfire valve
	Carbon canister purge line disconnected
	Exhaust gas heated valve stuck
	Faulty EGR valve
Power reduced	Faulty spark timing control valve
	Faulty altitude compensator (California)
	Faulty EGR valve
	Exhaust gas heated valve stuck

Chapter 4 Ignition system

Contents

Specifications

Distributor

Make	Hitachi
Type	
A14 engine models	D411–97 or T3T03574
L16 engine models	
Single carburettor	D411–58K
Twin carburettor	D409–54K
L20 engine	
All USA models with manual transmission	D4F5–06
Non-California with automatic transmission	D4F6–04
California with automatic transmission	D4F5–07
Rotation	Anti-clockwise
Contact points gap	0·018 to 0·022 in (0·45 to 0·55 mm)
Air gap (USA models)	0·008 to 0·016 in (0·2 to 0·4 mm)
Dwell angle (A14 and L16 engine)	49° to 55°
Condenser capacity	0·20 to 0·24 mfd

Firing order 1–3–4–2

Ignition timing*

A14 engine	7° BTDC @ 650 rpm
L16 engine	
D411–S8K distributor	10° BTDC @ 600 rpm
D409–54K distributor	14° BTDC @ 650 rpm
L20 engine with manual transmission	12° BTDC @ 600 rpm
L20 engine with automatic transmission	12° BTDC @ 600 rpm

Distributor vacuum advance feed pipe disconnected. Static timing figures are approximately the same as dynamic at idle speed.

Coil type

A14 engine	Hitachi C6R–206 or HP5–13E10
L16 engine	Hitachi 6R–200
L20 engine	Hitachi CIT–30 or STC–30

Spark plugs

A14 engine	Hitachi L46PW or NGK BP5ES or BPR5ES
L16 engine	
Single carburettor	NGK BP–5ES
Twin carburettor	NGK BP–6ES
L20 engine	
Cold plug	NGK BP7ES–11 or Hitachi L44PW–11
Hot plug	NGK BP4E–11 or BP5ES–11 or Hitachi L46PW–11 or L47PW–11
Standard plug	NGK BP6ES–11 or Hitachi L45PW–11

Plug gap
   A14 and L16 engines . . . . 0·031 to 0·035 in (0·8 to 0·9 mm)
   L20 engine . . . . 0·040 in (1·0 to 1·1 mm)

Torque wrench setting

	lbf ft	kgf m
Spark plug	11 to 18	1·5 to 2·5

1 General description

In order that the engine can run correctly, it is necessary for an electrical spark to ignite the fuel/air mixture in the combustion chamber at exactly the right moment in relation to engine speed and load. The ignition system is based on feeding low tension (LT) voltage from the battery to the coil where it is converted to high tension (HT) voltage. The high voltage tension is powerful enough to jump the spark plug gap in the cylinders many times a second under high compression pressures, providing that the system is in good condition and that all adjustments are correct.

The ignition system is divided into two circuits: the low tension circuit and the high tension circuit.

The low tension (sometimes known as the primary) circuit consists of the battery lead to the ignition switch, lead from the ignition switch to the low tension or primary coil windings (+ terminal) and the lead from the low tension coil windings (− terminal) to the contact breaker points and condenser in the distributor.

The high tension circuit consists of the high tension or secondary coil windings, the heavy ignition lead from the centre of the coil to the centre of the distributor cap, the rotor arm, and the spark plug leads and spark plugs.

The system functions in the following manner. Low tension voltage is changed in the coil into high tension voltage by the opening and closing of the contact breaker points in the low tension circuit. High tension voltage is then fed via the carbon brush in the centre of the distributor cap to the rotor arm of the distributor cap, and each time it comes in line with one of the four metal segments in the cap, which are connected to the spark plug leads, the opening and closing of the contact breaker points caused the high tension voltage to build up, jump the gap from the rotor arm to the appropriate metal segment and so via the spark plug lead to the spark plug, where it finally jumps the spark plug gap before going to earth.

The ignition is advanced and retarded automatically, to ensure the spark occurs at just the right instant for the particular load at the prevailing engine speed.

The ignition advance is controlled both mechanically and by a

vacuum operated system. The mechanical governor mechanism comprises two weights, which move out from the disposition by two light springs, and it is the tension of the springs which is largely responsible for correct spark advancement.

The vacuum control consists of a diaphragm, one side of which is connected via a small bore tube to the carburettor, and the other side to the contact breaker plate. Depression in the inlet manifold and carburettor, which varies with engine speed and throttle opening, causes the diaphragm to move, so moving the contact breaker plate and advancing or retarding the spark. A fine degree of control is achieved by a spring in the vacuum assembly. A resistor is incorporated in the ignition circuit for most models so that during starting, with the engine being cranked by the starter motor, full battery voltage is applied at the coil to maintain a good spark at the plug electrodes which would not be the case should a drop in voltage occur.

On some vehicles for the North American market equipped with a full emission control system a spark timing control system is employed. The system is designed to advance or retard the ignition timing in accordance with the prevailing engine operating conditions in order to reduce the emission of noxious exhaust fumes.

The system is governed by a vacuum switching valve which opens or closes the vacuum passage to advance or retard the ignition timing. The switching valve works in conjunction with a gear detecting switch on the transmission (manual). When top gear is selected the switch closes the vacuum passage to advance the ignition.

Vehicles built for use in the USA use a transistorized ignition system. The essential difference between this and the mechanical type is that the mechanical type 'make-and-break' contact points are replaced by a reluctor and coil which carry out the function electronically. As each of the projections of the reluctor passes the coil, the coil flux density changes and the resultant electrical signal is passed to transistorized circuit. The circuit cuts off the ignition coil primary feed which generates a high voltage in the coil secondary winding. After a pre-determined time the primary coil circuit is restored until the next reluctor projection passes the coil, when the cycle is repeated. The centrifugal vacuum advance and retard assemblies are of the same type as used in the mechanical type

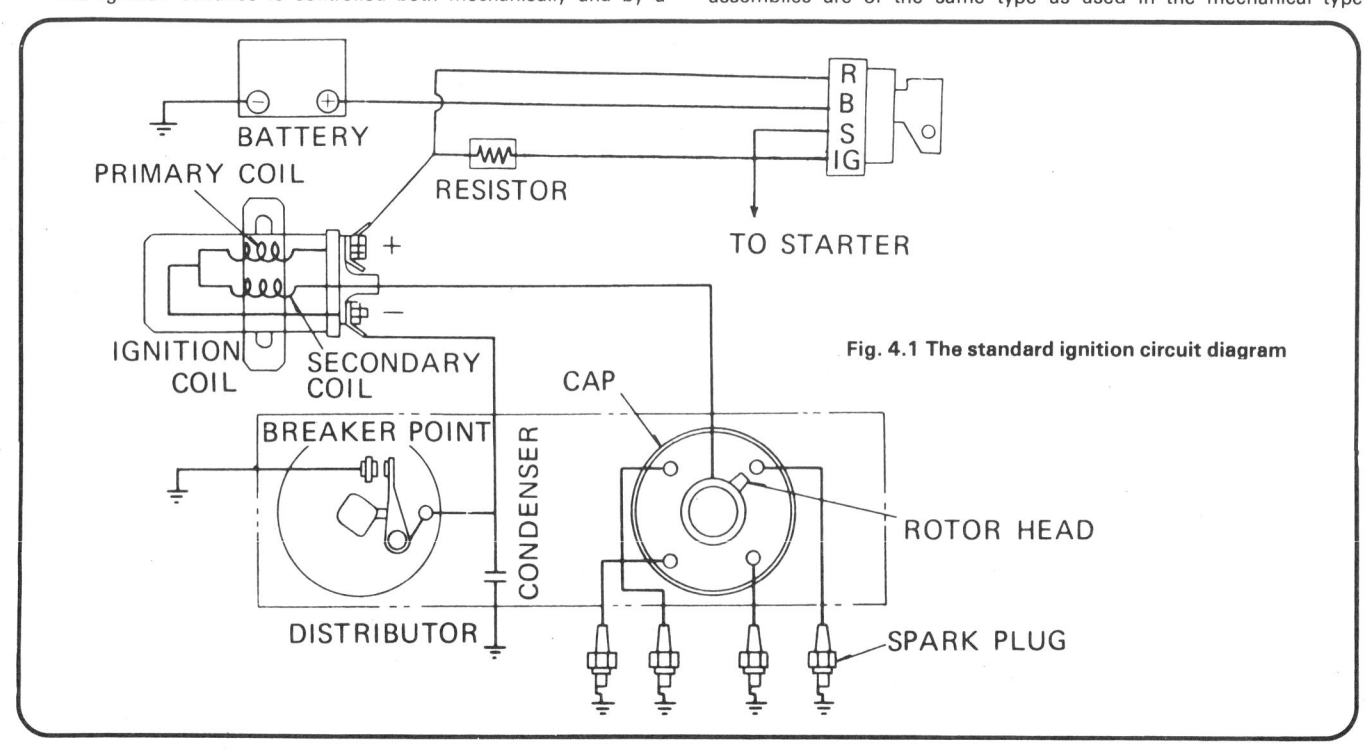

Fig. 4.1 The standard ignition circuit diagram

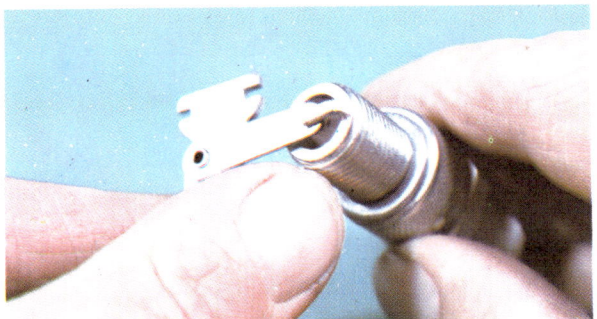

Measuring plug gap. A feeler gauge of the correct size (see ignition system specifications) should have a slight 'drag' when slid between the electrodes. Adjust gap if necessary

Adjusting plug gap. The plug gap is adjusted by bending the earth electrode inwards, or outwards, as necessary until the correct clearance is obtained. Note the use of the correct tool

Normal. Grey-brown deposits lightly coated core nose. Gap increasing by around 0.001 in (0.025 mm) per 1000 miles (1600 km). Plugs ideally suited to engine and engine in good condition

Carbon fouling. Dry, black, sooty deposits. Will cause weak spark and eventually misfire. Fault: over-rich fuel mixture. Check: carburettor mixture settings, float level and jet sizes; choke operation and cleanliness of air filter. Plugs can be re-used after cleaning

Oil fouling. Wet, oily deposits. Will cause weak spark and eventually misfire. Fault: worn bores/piston rings or valve guides; sometimes occurs (temporarily) during running-in period. Plugs can be re-used after thorough cleaning

Overheating. Electrodes have glazed appearance, core nose very white - few deposits. Fault: plug overheating. Check: plug value, ignition timing, fuel octane rating (too low) and fuel mixture (too weak). Discard plugs and cure fault immediately

Electrode damage. Electrodes burned away; core nose has burned, glazed appearance. Fault: initial pre-ignition. Check: as for 'Overheating' but may be more severe. Discard plugs and remedy fault before piston or valve damage occurs

Split core nose (may appear initially as a crack). Damage is self-evident, but cracks will only show after cleaning. Fault: pre-ignition or wrong gap-setting technique. Check: ignition timing, cooling system, fuel octane rating (too low) and fuel mixture (too weak). Discard plugs, rectify fault immediately

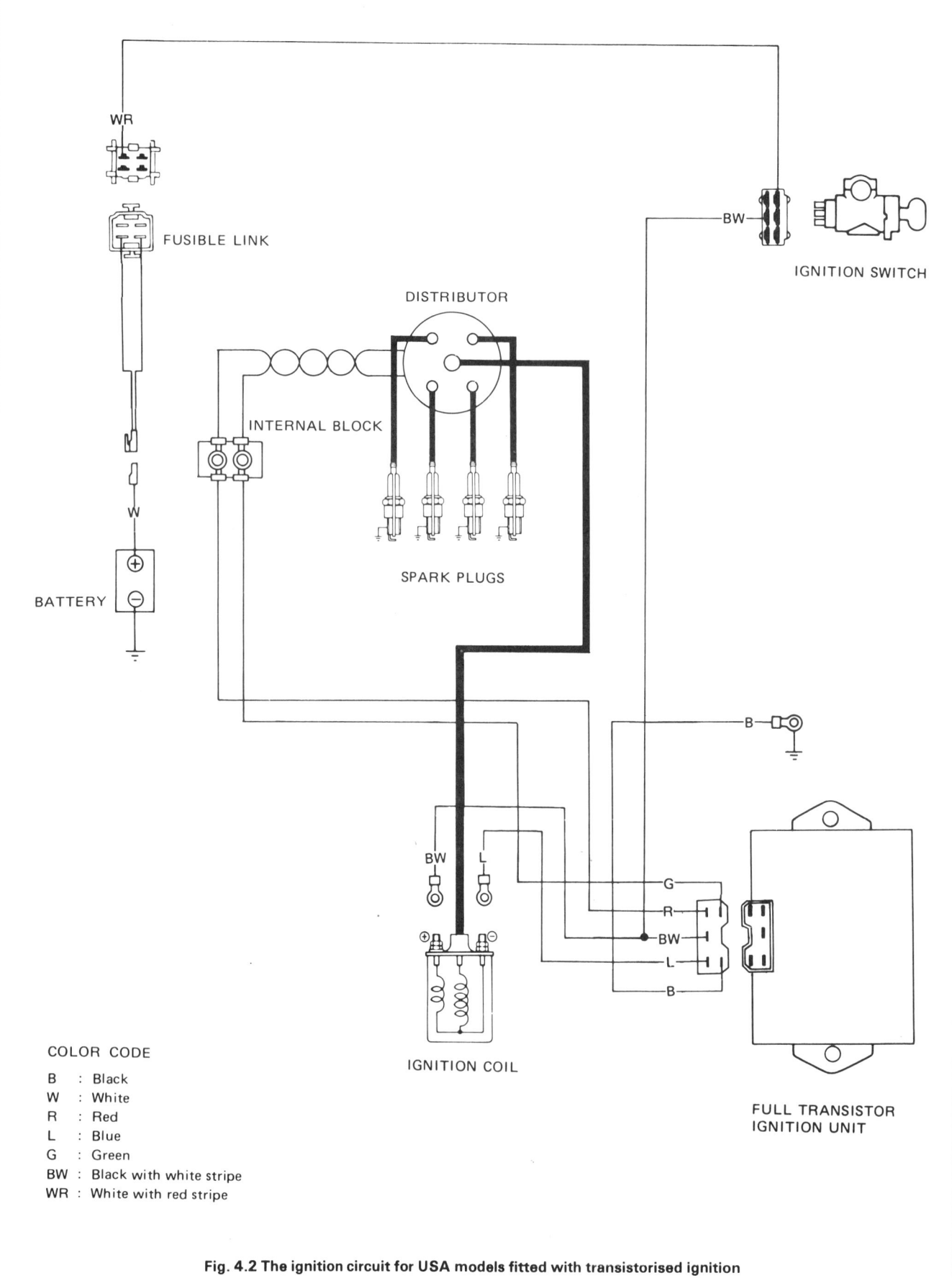

WR

FUSIBLE LINK

BATTERY

BW

IGNITION SWITCH

DISTRIBUTOR

INTERNAL BLOCK

SPARK PLUGS

B

BW   L

G
R
BW
L
B

IGNITION COIL

FULL TRANSISTOR
IGNITION UNIT

COLOR CODE

B : Black
W : White
R : Red
L : Blue
G : Green
BW : Black with white stripe
WR : White with red stripe

Fig. 4.2 The ignition circuit for USA models fitted with transistorised ignition

2.6 Insert feeler gauge to check clearance

2.7 Loosen contact plate screw to adjust

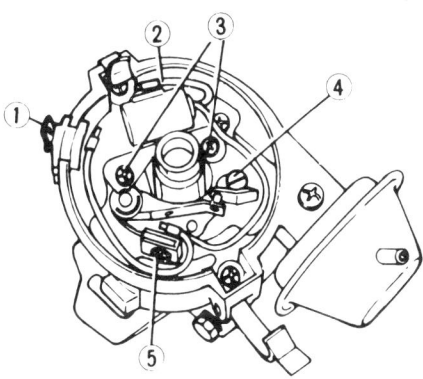

Fig. 4.3 The breaker assembly components

1 *Primary lead terminal*   4 *Adjuster*
2 *Earth lead wire*   5 *Screw*
3 *Set screw*

distributor.

Distributor models vary with the particular engine type and vehicle, and reference should be made to a main Datsun dealer when spare parts are required.

The description throughout this Chapter applies to all relevant model assemblies, but detail differences will be apparent in the particular components according to vehicle model and year of production. This is especially the case with distributors.

2 Contact breaker (mechanical type) – adjustment

1 To adjust the contact breaker points to the correct gap, first pull off the two clips securing the distributor cap to the distributor body, and lift away the cap. Clean the cap inside and out with a dry cloth. It is unlikely that the four segments will be badly burned or scored, but if they are the cap will have to be renewed. Light deposits on the segments can be carefully scraped off using a small penknife.
2 Inspect the carbon brush contact located in the top of the cap - see that it is unbroken and stands proud of the plastic surface.
3 Check the rotor arm. It must be clean and on the cam shoulder.
4 Gently pry the contact breaker points open to examine the condition of their faces. If they are rough, pitted or dirty, it will be necessary to remove them for resurfacing, or for new points to be fitted.
5 Presuming that the points are satisfactory, or that they have been cleaned or renewed, measure the gap between the points by turning the engine over until the heel of the breaker arm is on the highest point of the cam.
6 A feeler gauge of the specified thickness should now just fit between the points (photo).
7 If the gap varies from this amount, slacken the contact plate securing screw (photo).
8 Adjust the contact gap by inserting a screwdriver in the screw located in the cut-out of the breaker plate. Turn clockwise to increase and anti-clockwise to decrease the gap. When the gap is correct tighten the securing screw and check the gap again.
9 Ensure that the rotor is fully in position, locate the distributor cap and secure with spring blade retainers.

3 Contact breaker points – removal and refitting

1 Slip back the spring clips which secure the distributor cap in position. Remove the distributor cap and lay it on one side, removing one or two of the HT leads from the plugs if necessary to provide greater movement of the cap.
2 Pull the rotor from the distributor shaft.
3 Unscrew the setscrew, just enough to be able to slide out the primary (LT) lead terminal.
4 Unscrew and remove the contact breaker securing screws and detach the end of the earth lead. Pull the contact breaker assembly outward and upwards to remove it. Remove the pivot circlip to dismantle.
5 Inspect the faces of the contact points. If they are only lightly burned or pitted then they may be ground square on an oilstone or by rubbing a carborundum strip between them. Where the points are found to be severely burned or pitted, then they must be renewed and at the same time the cause of the erosion of the points established. This is most likely to be due to poor earth connections from the battery negative lead to body earth or the engine to earth strap. Remove the connecting bolts at these points, scrape the surfaces free from rust and corrosion and tighten the bolts using a star type lock washer. Other screws to check for security are: the baseplate to distributor body securing screws, the condenser securing screw and the distributor body to lockplate bolt. Looseness in any of these could contribute to a poor earth connection. Check the condenser (Section 4).
6 Refitting the contact breaker assembly is a reversal of removal and when fitted, adjust the points gap(s) as described in the preceeding Section, apply a smear of grease to the high points of the cam.

4 Condenser (capacitor) – removal, testing and refitting

1 The condenser ensures that with the contact breaker points open, the sparking between them is not excessive to cause severe pitting.

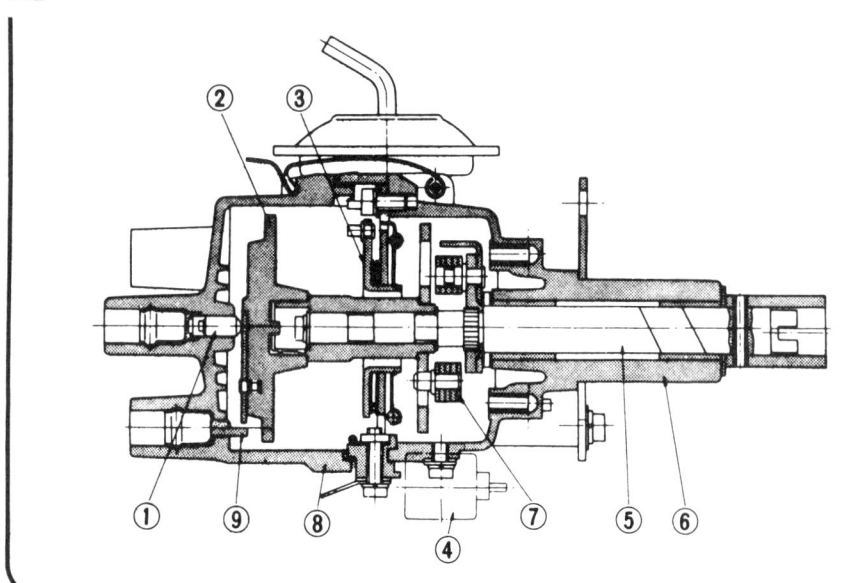

Fig. 4.4 Sectional view of the mechanical distributor

1 Carbon brush
2 Rotor arm
3 Contact breaker plate
4 Condenser
5 Shaft
6 Housing
7 Governor weight
8 Cap
9 Segment

5.5 Lift the distributor out – note the O-ring seal

6.3 The timing marks on the cover and alignment mark notch in the crankshaft pulley

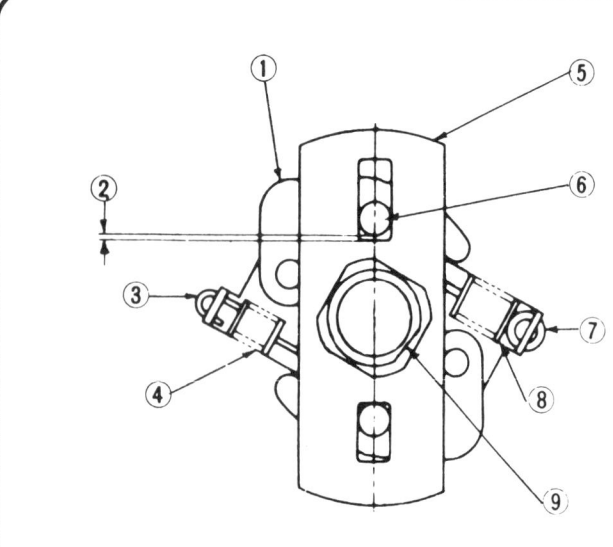

Fig. 4.5 Governor spring and cam setting

1 Governor weight
2 Clearance for start and end of advancing angle
3 Rectangular hook
4 Governor spring (B)
5 Cam plate
6 Pin
7 Circular hook
8 Governor spring (A)
9 Rotor positioning flat

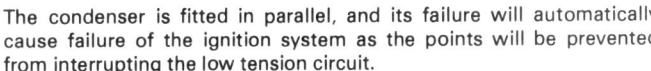

6.4 The distributor clamp plate showing the final adjustment marks to advance A or retard R the ignition timing

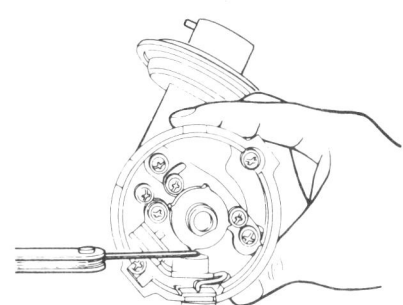

Fig. 4.6 Checking air gap – (transistor ignition)

The condenser is fitted in parallel, and its failure will automatically cause failure of the ignition system as the points will be prevented from interrupting the low tension circuit.

2 Testing for an unserviceable condenser may be effected by switching on the ignition and separating the contact points by hand. If this action is accompanied by a blue flash then condenser failure is indicated. Difficult starting, missing of the engine after several miles running or badly pitting points are other indications of the faulty condenser.

3 The surest test is by substitution of a new unit.

4 Removal of the condenser is by means of withdrawing the retaining screw and wire connector. Refit in the reverse sequence.

5 Distributor – removal and refitting

1 To remove the distributor complete with cap from the engine, begin by pulling the plug lead terminals off the spark plugs. Free the HT lead from the centre of the coil to the centre of the distributor by undoing the lead retaining cap from the coil.

2 Pull off the rubber pipe holding the vacuum tube to the distributor vacuum advance and retard take-off pipe.

3 Disconnect the low tension wire from the coil.

4 In order to simplify refitment of the distributor, rotate the crankshaft by means of the hexagon on the crankshaft pulley until the notch on the rim of the pulley aligns with the appropriate ignition timing mark (see Specifications) on the engine front cover. Index mark the position of the distributor body with respect to the fixing plate and cylinder block, and the rotor with respect to the distributor body.

5 Undo and remove the bolt which holds the distributor fixing plate to the block and lift the distributor out (photo).

6 Refitting is the reverse of the removal procedure, provided that the index marks are aligned correctly. If there is any doubt about the correct positioning of the distributor after it has been fitted, the ignition timing **must** be checked, as described in Section 6 or 9.

6 Ignition timing (mechanical type contact breaker)

1 Adjust the contact breaker points gap, as described in Section 2.

2 Turn the engine until No. 1 piston is rising on its compression stroke. This may be checked by removing No. 1 spark plug and placing a finger over the plug hole to feel the compression being generated or alternatively removing the distributor cap and observing that the rotor arm is coming up to align with the position of No. 1 contact segment in the distributor cap.

3 There is a notch on the rim of the crankshaft pulley and a scale on the timing cover (photo). Continue turning the crankshaft until the notch on the pulley is opposite the appropriate static ignition setting (initial advance) mark on the scale. Refer to the Specifications for this

setting as it varies between engine and model types.

4 Slacken the distributor clamp plate bolt.

5 Connect a 12 volt test lamp between the condenser flying lead terminal (on dual points distributors it is the advance condenser flying lead terminal) and the distributor body. Switch on the ignition.

6 Turn the distributor body to the position where even the slightest further movement will illuminate the test bulb.

7 Tighten the distributor clamp plate bolt and remove the test lamp. Switch off the ignition.

8 An alternative method of ignition timing is described in Section 9.

7 Distributor (mechanical type contact breaker) – dismantling and reassembly

1 Remove the cap and pull off the rotor.

2 Unscrew and remove the two screws which secure the vacuum capsule to the distributor body. Tilt the capsule slightly to disengage the actuating rod from the pivot of the movable baseplate. Withdraw the vacuum capsule.

3 Remove the contact breaker assembly.

4 Unscrew and remove the securing screws from the baseplate assembly and lift out the assembly.

5 If the movable and fixed baseplates are to be separated, remove the securing screws but take care not to lose the balls which are sandwiched betweem the two components.

6 Knock out the pin from the collar at the base of the distributor shaft using a suitable drift.

7 The shaft and counterweight assembly may now be withdrawn through the upper end of the distributor body.

8 Where it is necessary to remove the cam from the top of the distributor shaft, first mark the relative position of the cam to the shaft, then unscrew and remove the screw from the cam recess.

9 Where the counterweights and their springs are to be dismantled, take care not to stretch the springs.

10 Check all components for wear and renew as appropriate.

11 Grease the counterweight pivots and reassemble by reversing the dismantling procedure but ensure that the rotor positioning flat on the cam is towards the circular hook and also that the circular and rectangular ended springs are correctly located (see Fig. 4.5).

8 Distributor (transistorized ignition type) – air-gap adjustment

1 On this type of distributor the only adjustment is to ensure that the air gap, measured between the reluctor (rotor) projections and the pole piece of the pick-up coil, is as specified.

2 If adjustment is required, loosen the pick-up coil screws and move the coil until the correct gap is measured using a feeler guage.

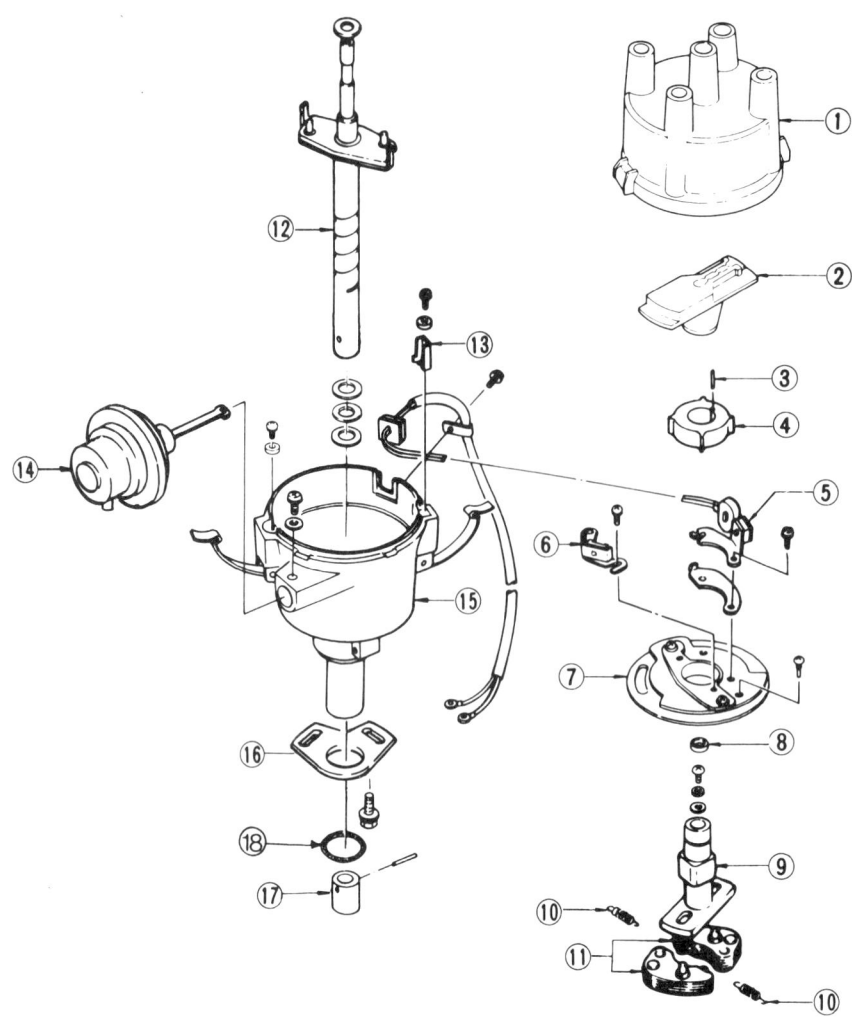

Fig. 4.7 The transistor ignition distributor components

1	Cap	6	Contactor	11	Weight (governor)	15	Housing
2	Rotor head	7	Breaker plate unit	12	Shaft unit	16	Plate
3	Roll pin	8	Packing	13	Cap setter	17	Collar
4	Reluctor	9	Shaft	14	Vacuum controller	18	O-ring
5	Pick-up coil	10	Spring (governor)				

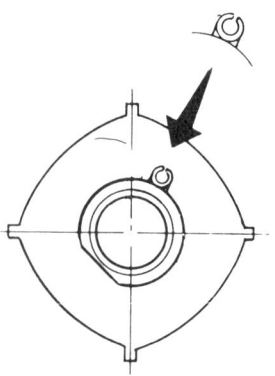

Fig. 4.8 The reluctor tension pin position

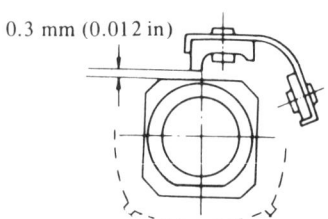

0.3 mm (0.012 in)

Fig. 4.9 Cam to contact clearance

9 Ignition timing using a stroboscopic lamp

1   This method of ignition timing is essential for the transistorized ignition system. It is generally accepted as being a preferable method of setting the timing where a mechanical type contact breaker is fitted although for most practical purposes the method given in Section 6 is satisfactory. First run the engine up to its normal operating temperature.
2   Initially check the contact breaker points gap (Section 2) or air gap (Section 8).
3   Mark the notch on the crankshaft pulley with chalk or white paint.
4   Mark in a similar manner, the appropriate line on the timing cover scale (see Specifications for static timing figure according to engine and vehicle type).
5   Disconnect the vacuum pipe (which runs from the vacuum capsule on the distributor to the carburettor). Disconnect the pipe from the distributor end and plug the pipe.
6   Connect a stroboscope in accordance with the makers instructions (usually interposed between No. 1 spark plug and HT lead).
7   Start the engine (which should previously have been run to normal operating temperature) and let it idle (see recommended speeds in the Specifications) otherwise the mechanical advance mechanism will operate and give a false ignition timing.
8   Point the stroboscope at the ignition timing marks when they will appear stationary, and if the ignition timing is correct, in alignment. If the marks are not in alignment, loosen the distributor clamp plate screw and turn the distributor.
9   Switch off ignition, tighten the clamp plate and remove the stroboscope.
10 Reconnect the vacuum pipe to the distributor.

10 Distributor (transistor type) – dismantling and reassembly

1   Remove the distributor cap and rotor.
2   Remove the two screws which secure the vacuum capsule, tilt it slightly to disengage the operating rod from the baseplate pivot.
3   Unscrew and remove the screws which hold the pick-up coils and remove it.
4   Using two bars as levers, pry the reluctor from the distributor shaft and then remove the tension pin.
5   Unscrew and remove the screws which secure the baseplate and lift off the baseplate.
6   Drive out the pin from the lower end of the shaft, remove the collar and then withdraw the upper counterweight assembly and shaft from the top of the distributor.
7   Unscrew and remove the screw from the recess at the end of the shaft then remove the camplate and weight assembly.
8   Where the weights and springs are dismantled, take care not to stretch the springs.

9   Renew any worn components.
10 Reassembly is a reversal of dismantling but ensure that the following conditions are met:

(a)   *The reluctor is correctly located on the distributor shaft with regard to the positions of the flat and the tension pin. Note that the slot in the tension pin must face outwards (Fig.4.8).*

(b)   *If the contactor has been disturbed, adjust the cam to contactor clearance to 0.012 in (0.3 mm) on reassembly (Fig. 4.9)*

(c)   *Grease the counterweight pivots and the top of the rotor shaft sparingly with a general purpose grease*

11 Transistorized ignition unit

1   The unit is located below the left-hand side of the facia panel within the vehicle.
2   It performs the following functions:

(a)   *It 'makes' and 'breaks' the current in the primary circuit of the ignition coil*

(b)   *Sets and maintains the make-and-break cycle according to engine speed*

(c)   *Incorporates a delayed cut-out to disconnect the primary current within a period not exceeding ten seconds if the ignition is left switched on with the engine not running*

3   A fault in the transistorized ignition system can only be checked and traced using an oscilloscope and this work should therefore be left to an auto-electrician.
4   Any fault occuring in the unit itself will require a new unit as the original cannot be repaired.
5   To renew a unit, disconnect the lead from the battery negative terminal.
6   Disconnect the wiring harness from the unit.
7   Unscrew and remove the securing setscrews and lift the unit from its location.
8   Refitting is a reversal of removal but take great care to connect the wiring harness correctly.
9   Where a transistorized ignition unit is fitted, do not disconnect the spark plug or coil wires when the engine is running.

12 Spark plugs and high tension (HT) leads

1   The correct functioning of the spark plugs is vital for the correct running and efficiency of the engine. The plugs fitted as standard together with hot or cold alternatives are listed on the Specifications page.
2   At intervals of 3000 miles (4800 km) the plugs should be

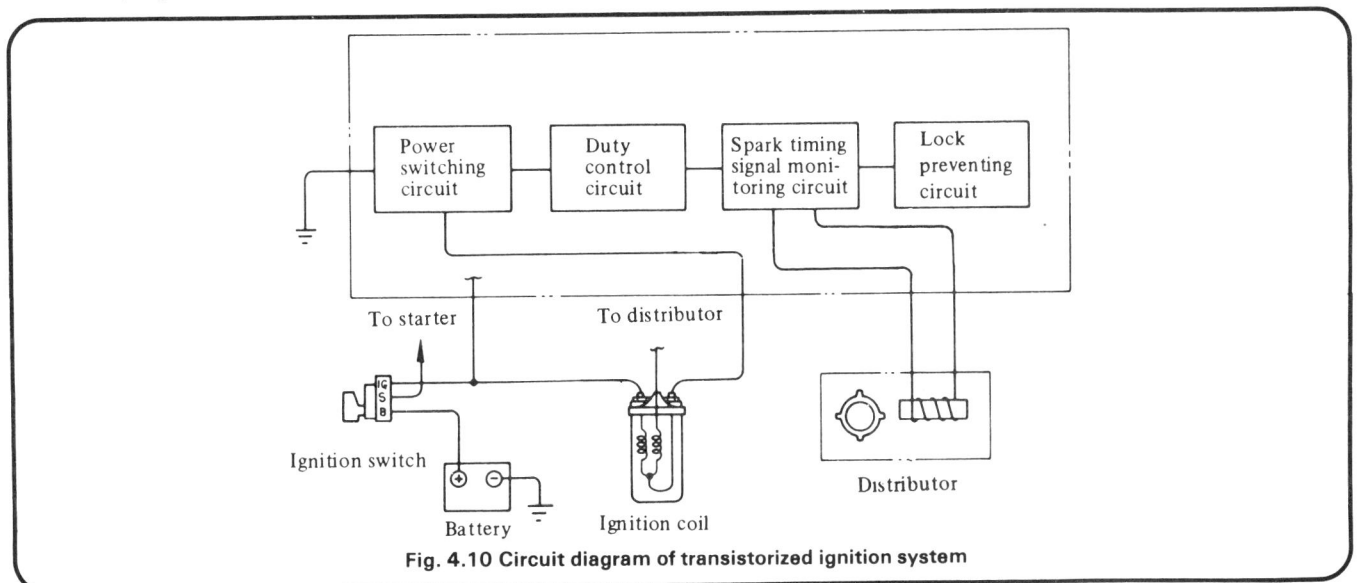

Fig. 4.10 Circuit diagram of transistorized ignition system

removed, examined, cleaned and, if worn excessively, renewed. The condition of the spark plug will also tell much about the overall condition of the engine.

3　If the insulator nose of the spark plug is clean and white, with no deposits, this is indicative of a weak mixture, or too hot a plug. (A hot plug transfers heat away from the electrode slowly – a cold plug transfers it away quickly).

4　If the top and insulator nose is covered with hard black looking deposits, then this is indicative that the mixture is too rich. Should the plug be black and oily, then it is likely that the engine is fairly worn, as well as the mixture being too rich.

5　If the insulator nose is covered with light tan to greyish brown deposits, then the mixture is correct and it is likely that the engine is in good condition.

6　If there are any traces of long brown tapering stains on the outside of the white portion of the plug, then the plug will have to be renewed, as this shows that there is a faulty joint between the plug body and the insulator, and compression is being allowed to leak away.

7　Plugs should be cleaned by a sand blasting machine, which will free them from carbon more thoroughly than cleaning by hand. The machine will also test the condition of the plugs under compression. Any plug that fails to spark at the recommended pressure should be renewed.

8　The spark plug gap is of considerable importance, as, if it is too large or too small the size of the spark and its efficiency will be seriously impaired. The spark plug gap should be set to the specified gap for the best results.

9　To set it, measure the gap with a feeler gauge, and then bend open, or closed, the outer plug electrode until the correct gap is achieved. The centre electrode should never be bent as this may crack the insulation and cause plug failure, if nothing worse.

10　When refitting the plugs, remember to use new plug washers and install the leads from the distributor in the correct firing order 1-3-4-2, number 1 cylinder being the one nearest the radiator.

11　The plug leads require no attention other than being kept clean and wiped over regularly.

13　Ignition system (mechanical contact breaker) – fault diagnosis

Engine fails to start

1　If the engine fails to start and the car was running normally when it was last used, first check there is fuel in the fuel tank. If the engine turns over normally on the starter motor and the battery is evidently well charged, then the fault may be in either the high or low tension circuits. First check the HT circuit. If the battery is known to be fully charged; the ignition light comes on, and the starter motor fails to turn the engine, check the tightness of the leads on the battery terminals and also the secureness of the earth lead to its connection to the body. It is quite common for the leads to have worked loose, even if they look and feel secure. If one of the battery terminal posts gets very hot when trying to work the starter motor this is a sure indication of a faulty connection to that terminal.

2　One of the commonest reasons for bad starting is wet or damp spark plug leads and distributor. Remove the distributor cap. If condensation is visible internally, dry the cap with a rag and also wipe over the leads. Refit the cap.

3　If the engine still fails to start, check that current is reaching the plugs by disconnecting each plug lead in turn at the spark plug end, and hold the end of the cable about $\frac{3}{16}$ (5 mm) away from the cylinder block. Spin the engine on the starter motor.

4　Sparking between the end of the cable and the block should be fairly strong with a regular blue spark. (Hold the lead with rubber to avoid electric shock). If current is reaching the plugs, then remove them and clean, and regap them. The engine should now start.

5　If there is no spark at the plug leads take off the HT lead from the centre of the distributor cap and hold it to the block as before. Spin the engine on the starter once more. A rapid succession of blue sparks between the end of the lead and the block indicate that the coil is in order and that the distributor cap is cracked, the rotor arm faulty, or the carbon brush in the top of the distributor cap is not making good contact with the spring on the rotor arm. Possibly the points are in bad condition. Clean and reset them as described in this Chapter.

6　If there are no sparks from the end of the lead from the coil check the connections at the coil end of the lead. If it is in order start checking the low tension circuit.

7　Use a 12v voltmeter or a 12v bulb and two lengths of wire. With the ignition switch on and the points open test between the low tension wire to the coil (it is marked SW or +) and earth. No reading indicates a break in the supply from the ignition switch. Check the connections at the switch and resistor to see if any are loose. Refit them and the engine should run. A reading shows a faulty coil or condenser, or broken lead between the coil and the distributor.

8　Take the condenser wire off the points assembly and with the point open, test between the moving points and earth. If there now is a reading, then the fault is in the condenser. Fit a new one and the fault is cleared.

9　With no reading from the moving point to earth take a reading between earth and the negative terminal of the coil. A reading here shows a broken wire which needs to be renewed between the coil and distributor. No reading confirms that the coil has failed and must be renewed, after which the engine will run once more. Remember to refit the condenser wire to the points assembly. For these tests it is sufficient to separate the points with a piece of dry paper while testing with the points open.

Engine misfires

10　If the engine misfires regularly, run it at a fast idling speed. Pull off each of the plug caps in turn and listen to the note of the engine. Hold the plug cap in a dry cloth or with a rubber glove as additional protection against a shock from the HT supply.

11　No difference in engine running will be noticed when the lead from the defective circuit is removed. Removing the lead from one of the good cylinders will accentuate the misfire.

12　Remove the plug lead from the end of the defective plug and hold it about $\frac{3}{16}$ inch (5 mm) away from the block. Restart the engine. If the sparking is fairly strong and regular the fault must lie in the spark plug.

13　The plug may be loose, the insulation may be cracked, or the points may have burnt away giving too wide a gap for the spark to jump. Worse still, one of the points may have broken off. Either renew the plug, or clean it, reset the gap, and then test it.

14　If there is no spark at the end of the plug lead, or if it is weak and intermittent, check the ignition lead from the distributor to the plug. If the insulation is cracked or perished, renew the lead. Check the connections at the distributor cap.

15　If there is still no spark, examine the distributor cap carefully for tracking. This can be recognised by a very thin black line running between two or more electrodes, or between an electrode and some other part of the distributor. These lines are paths which now conduct electricity across the cap thus letting it run to earth. The only answer is a new distributor cap.

16　Apart from the ignition timing being incorrect, other causes of misfiring have already been dealt with under the Section dealing with the failure of the engine to start. To recap - these are that:

(a)　The coil may be faulty giving an intermittent misfire
(b)　There may be a damaged wire or loose connection in the low tension circuit
(c)　The condenser may be short circuiting
(d)　There may be a mechanical fault in the distributor (broken driving spindle or contact breaker spring)

17　If the ignition timing is too far retarded, it should be noted that the engine will tend to overheat, and there will be quite a noticeable drop in power. If the engine is overheating and the power is down, and the ignition timing is correct, then the carburettor should be checked, as it is likely that this is where the fault lies.

14　Ignition system (transistorized type) – testing and fault diagnosis

1　Expensive and special equipment is required to test the transistor unit. It is therefore recommended that the unit, which is located on the facia panel within the car interior, should be removed and tested by a competent automobile electrician.

2　Apart from this, check the security of all HT and LT leads and examine the distributor cap for cracks.

3　The testing procedure described in the preceding Section will apply except in respect of the contact breaker which of course should be ignored. The air gap between the reluctor and the pick-up coil should however be checked as described earlier in this Chapter (Section 8).

Chapter 5 Clutch

Contents

Specifications

Type	Single dry plate	

Clutch disc

	A14 engine	L16 and L20 engines
Lining outside diameter	7.09 in (180 mm)	7.87 in (200 mm)
Lining inside diameter	4.92 in (125 mm)	5.12 in (130 mm)
Lining thickness	0.138 in (3.5 mm)	0.138 in (3.5 mm)
Torsion springs	6	6
Minimum depth of rivet head from surface	0.012 in (0.3 mm)	0.012 in (0.3 mm)
Allowable face remount	0.039 in (1.0 mm)	0.039 in (1.0 mm)
Allowable spline free play (Measured at outer edge of disc)	0.016 in (0.4 mm)	0.016 in (0.4 mm)

Clutch pedal

	LH drive	RH drive
Pedal height		
A14 engine	5.87 to 6.10 in (149 to 155 mm)	5.31 to 5.55 in (135 to 141 mm)
L16 and L20 engines	6.34 to 6.57 in (161 to 167 mm)	5.59 to 5.83 in (142 to 148 mm)
Pedal free play	0.04 to 0.20 in (1 to 5 mm)	0.04 to 0.20 in (1 to 5 mm)
Withdrawal lever play (A14 engine)	0.039 to 0.079 in (1.0 to 2.0 mm)	0.118 to 0.157 in (3.0 to 4.0 mm)
Pedal free travel (A14 engine)	0.63 to 1.30 in (16 to 33 mm)	0.51 to 0.67 in (13 to 17 mm)

Master cylinder

Cylinder diameter	$\frac{5}{8}$ (15.87)
Cylinder bore to piston clearance – maximum	0.0059 in (0.15 mm)

Slave cylinder

Cylinder bore to piston clearance – maximum	0.0059 in (0.15 mm)

Torque wrench settings

	lbf ft	kgf m
Clutch cover bolts	12 to 15	1.6 to 2.1
Master cylinder retaining nuts	5.8 to 8.7	0.8 to 1.2
Master cylinder pushrod locknut	5.8 to 8.7	0.8 to 1.2
Pedal stop locknut	5.8 to 8.7	0.8 to 1.2
Clutch tube flare nut	11 to 13	1.5 to 1.8
Slave cylinder to housing bolt	22 to 30	3.1 to 4.1
Hose to slave cylinder	12 to 14	1.7 to 2.0
Slave cylinder pushrod locknut	5.8 to 8.7	0.8 to 1.2
Slave cylinder bleed screw	5.1 to 6.5	0.7 to 0.9
Pedal fulcrum pin-nut	14 to 17	1.9 to 2.4

1   General description

A diaphragm spring clutch is fitted to all manual transmission models but the method of actuation differs according to model. On the L16 and L20 engine variants and all A14 engine models fitted with left-hand drive, the clutch actuation is by a normal hydraulic method. On A14 engine versions fitted with right-hand drive, the clutch is operated by mechanical means.

The hydraulic system comprises a master cylinder which is mounted to the bulkhead and is operated by the pushrod connected to the clutch pedal. A hydraulic line connects the master and slave cylinders. The slave cylinder which is mounted on the outside of the clutch housing, operates the clutch withdrawal lever which in turn actuates the clutch.

The mechanical system dispenses with the hydraulic circuit and uses a control cable between the pedal and the clutch unit withdrawal lever.

2   Clutch pedal – adjustment

Hydraulic clutch (L16 and L20 engines)
1   Measure the height of the clutch pedal pad upper surface from the floor and check the reading against the relevant figure quoted in the Specifications.
2   If necessary, adjustment can be made by loosening the locknut and turning the adjuster bolt accordingly. Retighten the locknut to secure.
3   The pedal free play must now be checked and if necessary adjusted. To do this depress the pedal with the fingers and check the amount of free movement. If adjustment is required, loosen the push-rod locknut and adjust accordingly. Retighten the locknut and check the clutch operation.

Hydraulic clutch (A14 engine)
4   Check the free play of the withdrawal lever on the slave cylinder pushrod. The free play should be 0.039 to 0.079 in (1.0 to 2.0 mm) between lever and the push-nut (Fig. 5.2). To adjust, loosen the locknut and push-nut. The push-rod is then adjusted by tightening it so that the release bearing just touches the diaphragm spring. Unscrew the pushrod about 1¼ turns to give the specified clearance of the withdrawal lever. Retighten the locknut to secure. Operate the clutch a few times and recheck the clearances.

Cable operated clutch
5   Measure the height of the clutch pedal pad upper surface from the floor and check the reading against the Specifications.
6   To adjust the pedal, loosen the locknut and turn the pedal stopper adjustment nut accordingly. Retighten the locknut to secure.
7   To adjust the clutch pedal free travel, raise the bonnet and support it. Withdraw the E-ring from the clutch control cable at its junction to the bulkhead. The cable can then be adjusted at this point to give the correct pedal clearance. Refit the E-ring to secure the cable in the desired position.
8   Operate the clutch pedal a few times after adjustment and check the play at the withdrawal lever (Fig. 5.5). The correct withdrawal lever push nut to lever free play should be 0.118 to 0.157 in (3.0 to 4.0 mm). If necessary, readjust.

3   Hydraulic system – bleeding

1   The hydraulic system should be bled when it has air in the system, which is usually the case after overhauling a part of the system or a joint or seal has a leak. Bleeding is simply the method of removing air from the system, and this is achieved as follows.
2   Gather together a clean glass jar, a length of rubber tubing which fits tightly over the bleed nipple on the slave cylinder, a tin of hydraulic brake fluid and someone to help. Clean the outside of the master cylinder before removing cap.
3   Check that the master cylinder is full. If it is not, fill it and cover the bottom two inches of the jar with hydraulic fluid.
4   Remove the rubber dust cap from the bleed nipple on the slave cylinder, and with a suitable spanner open the bleed nipple approximately three quarters of a turn.

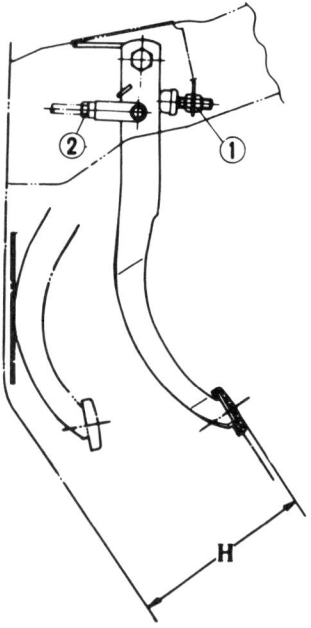

Fig. 5.1 Measure the clutch pedal height at H

1 and 2 are the adjustment locknuts

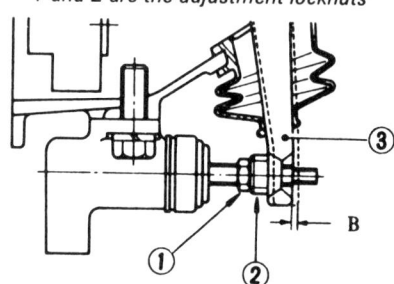

Fig. 5.2 Clutch pedal adjustment on the LH drive A14 model

1 Locknut   3 Withdrawal lever
2 Adjuster nut   B Free play

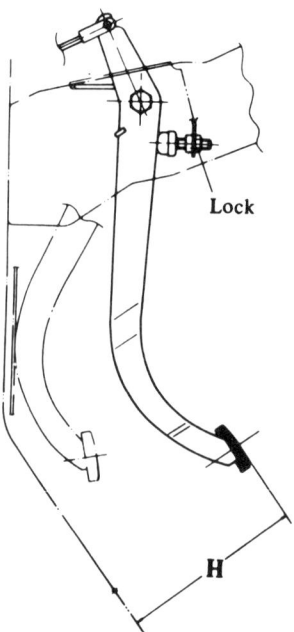

Fig. 5.3 Cable operated clutch (A14 models – RH drive only)

Check the pedal height at H

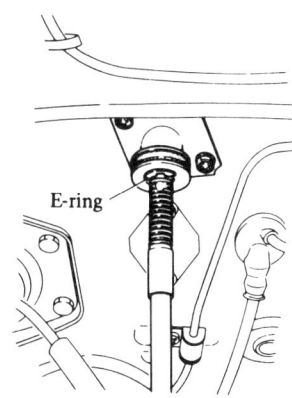

Fig. 5.4 Clutch cable adjuster ring

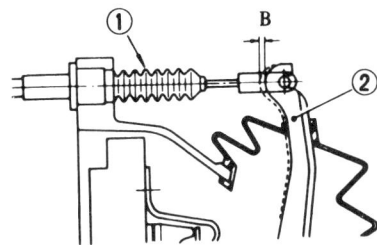

Fig. 5.5 Clutch pedal free travel adjustment

1 *Control cable*   *B Free travel*
2 *Withdrawal lever*

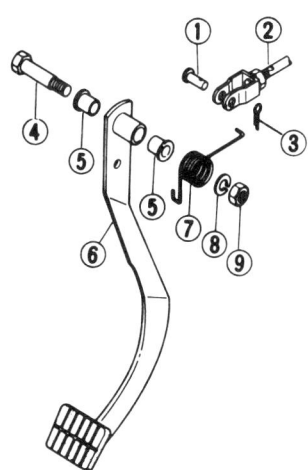

Fig. 5.6 Clutch pedal components

1 *Clevis pin*   6 *Clutch pedal*
2 *Master cylinder pushrod* 7 *Return spring*
3 *Split pin*   8 *Lock washer*
4 *Fulcrum pin*   9 *Nut*
5 *Bush*

5   Place one end of the tube over the nipple and insert the other end in the jar so that the tube orifice is below the level of the fluid.

6   The assistant should now depress the pedal and hold it down at the end of its stroke. Close the bleed screw and allow the pedal to return to its normal position.

7   Continue this series of operations until clear hydraulic fluid without any traces of air bubbles emerges from the end of the tubing. Be sure that the reservoir is checked frequently to ensure that the hydraulic fluid does not drop too far, thus letting air into the system.

8   When no more air bubbles appear tighten the bleed nipple on the downstroke.

9   Refit the rubber dust cap over the bleed nipple.

10 Check that the hydraulic fluid level is up to the mark in the reservoir and refit cap. Do not allow dirt into the system.

4   Clutch pedal – removal and refitting

Hydraulic clutch

1   From inside the car carefully withdraw the clutch pedal to pushrod clevis pin spring pin. The cotter pin can now be withdrawn.

2   Detach the pedal return spring, then undo and remove the fulcrum bolt securing nut and spring washer. Extract the fulcrum bolt.

Cable clutch

3   Raise the bonnet and remove the E-ring from the clutch cable at the bulkhead. Slacken the adjustment and then unhook the cable from the pedal. Proceed as in paragraphs 1 and 2 above.

All models

4   Refitting the pedal is the reverse sequence to removal but lubricate the pedal bushes and shaft and also the spring coils to prevent squeaking. Recheck the pedal height and adjust as described in Section 2.

5   Clutch – removal and refitting

1   To gain access to the clutch the transmission unit or engine must be removed and the respective details on these operations are given in Chapter 1 or 6 accordingly. The transmission is the easier of the two to remove but the car will have to be suitably raised to enable the work to be carried out. A pair of ramps are ideal but if blocks are used make certain they are secure!

2   The clutch assembly is easily removed from the flywheel by unscrewing the retaining bolts. Unscrew them progressively and diagonally which will prevent any possible distortion of the cover flange, and also prevent the cover flange from suddenly flying off its location dowels. These dowels are not equidistant and the cover flange to flywheel position does not need to be marked - their relative positions cannot be mixed.

3   With the bolts and spring washers removed, lift the clutch assembly off the locating dowels. The driven plate or clutch disc will fall out at this stage, as it is not attached to either the clutch cover assembly or the flywheel. Carefully make a note of which way round it is fitted.

4   It is important that no oil or grease gets on the clutch disc friction linings, or the pressure plate and flywheel faces. It is advisable to handle the parts with clean hands and to wipe down the pressure plate and flywheel faces with a clean dry rag before inspection or refitting commences.

5   To refit the clutch plate place the clutch disc against the flywheel with the larger end of the hub away from the flywheel. On no account should the clutch disc be refitted the wrong way round as it will be found impossible to operate the clutch.

6   Refit the clutch cover assembly loosely on the dowels. Refit the six bolts and spring washers and tighten them finger tight so that the clutch disc is gripped but can still be moved.

7   The clutch disc must now be centralised so that when the engine and gearbox are mated, the gearbox input shaft splines pass through the splines in the centre of the hub.

8   Centralisation can be carried out quite easily by inserting a round bar or long screwdriver through the hole in the centre of the clutch, so that the end of the bar rests in the small hole in the end of the crankshaft containing the input shaft bearing bush. Moving the bar sideways or up and down will move the clutch disc in whichever direction is

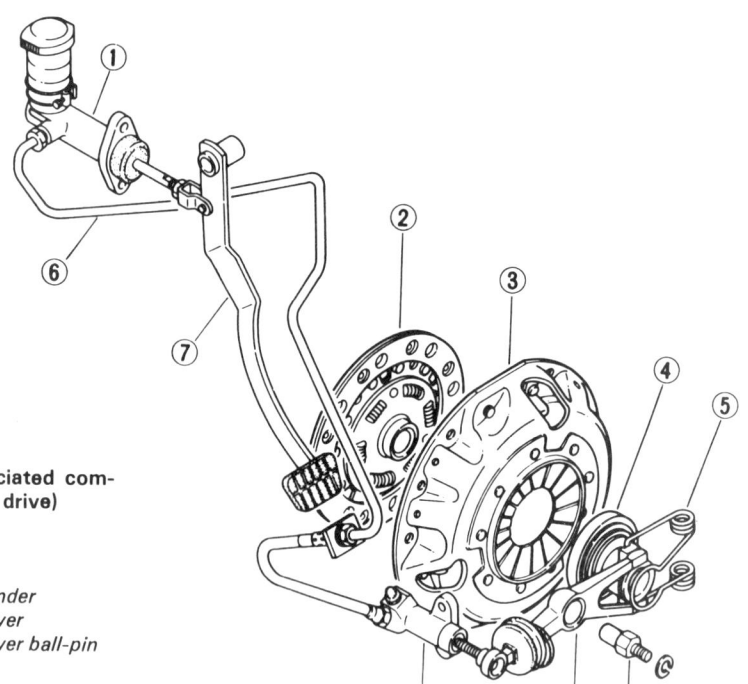

Fig. 5.7 The hydraulically operated clutch and associated components as fitted to the A14 engine models – (LH drive)

1 Master cylinder	6 Hydraulic line
2 Clutch disc	7 Clutch pedal
3 Clutch cover	8 Operating cylinder
4 Release bearing and sleeve	9 Withdrawal lever
5 Return spring	10 Withdrawal lever ball-pin

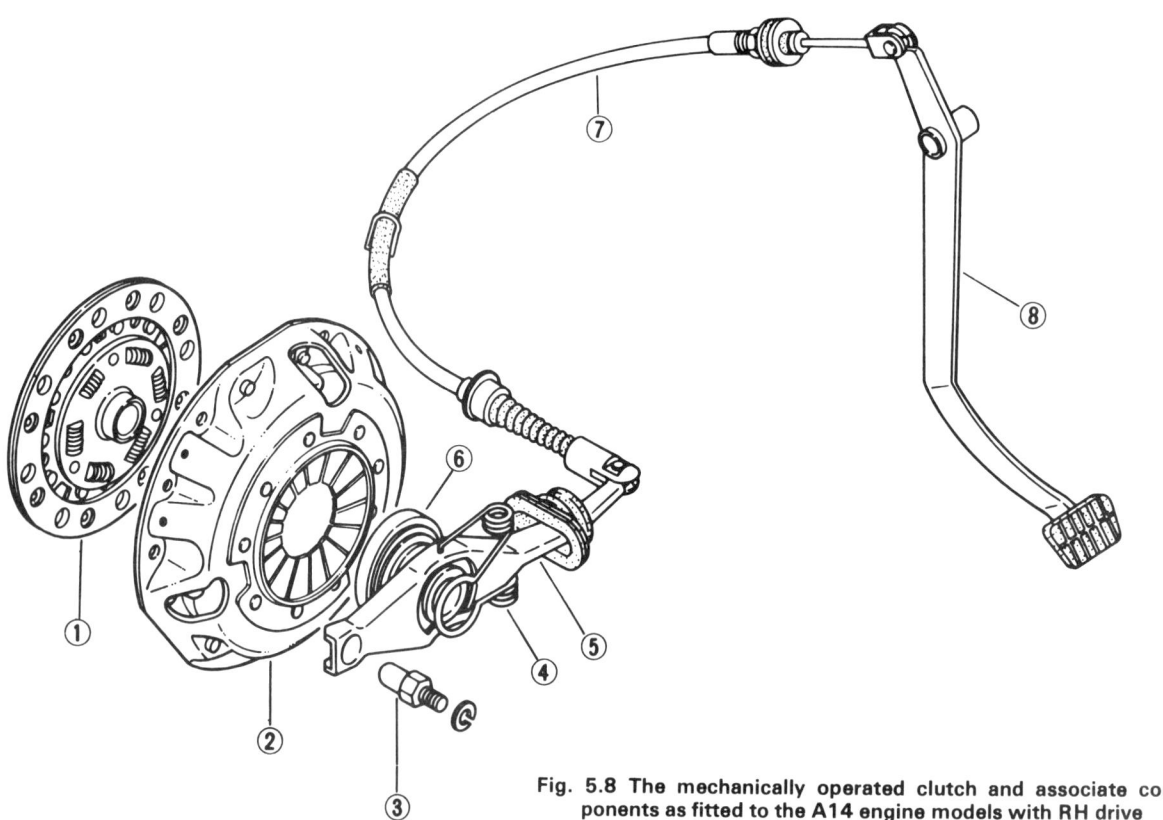

Fig. 5.8 The mechanically operated clutch and associate components as fitted to the A14 engine models with RH drive

1 Clutch disc	5 Withdrawal lever
2 Clutch cover	6 Release bearing and sleeve
3 Withdrawal lever ball-pin	7 Clutch control cable
4 Return spring	8 Clutch pedal

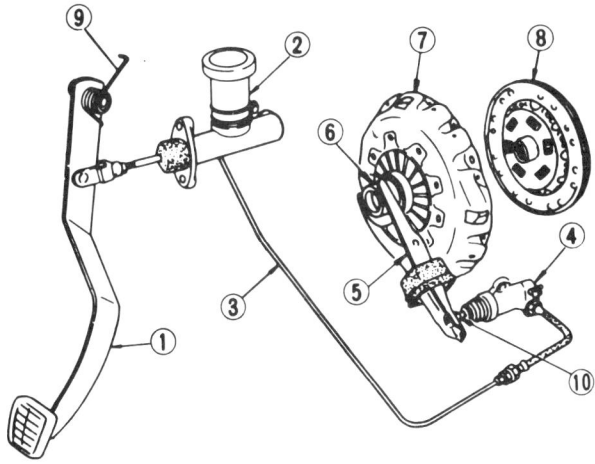

Fig. 5.9 The hydraulically operated clutch and associate components as fitted to all L16 and L20 engine models

1 Clutch pedal	6 Release bearing
2 Clutch master cylinder	7 Cover assembly
3 Hydraulic hose	8 Disc assembly
4 Slave cylinder	9 Return spring
5 Withdrawal lever	10 Pushrod

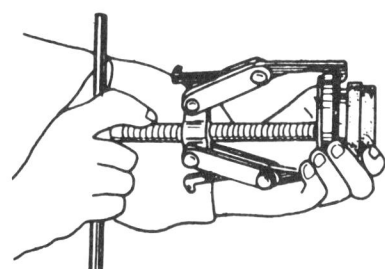

Fig. 5.10 Use a suitable puller to withdraw the bearing

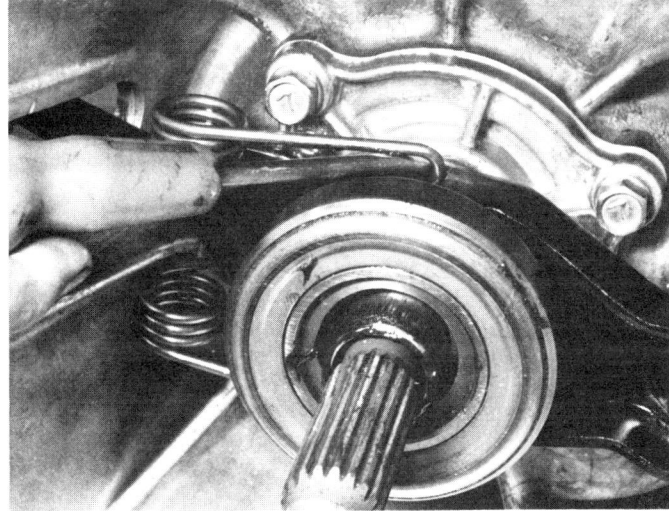

7.3 Prise the spring free using a screwdriver blade

necessary to achieve centralisation.

9 Centralisation is easily judged by removing the bar or screwdriver and viewing the driven plate hub in relation to the hole in the centre of the diaphragm spring. When the hub is exactly in the centre of the release bearing hole, all is correct. Alternatively, if an old input shaft can be borrowed this will eliminate all guesswork as it will fit the bush and centre of the clutch hub exactly, obviating the need for visual alignment.

10 Tighten the clutch bolts firmly in a diagonal sequence to ensure the cover plate is pulled evenly, and without distortion of the flange. Tighten the bolts to the recommended torque wrench setting.

11 Mate the engine and gearbox, bleed the slave cylinder if the pipe was disconnected and check the clutch for correct operation and adjustment (Section 2).

6 Clutch inspection

1 In the normal course of events clutch dismantling and reassembly is the term used for simply fitting a new clutch pressure plate and friction disc. Under no circumstances should the pressure plate assembly be dismantled. If a fault develops in the assembly an exchange unit must be fitted.

2 If a new clutch is being fitted it is false economy not to renew the release bearing at the same time. This will preclude having to fit it at a later date when wear on the clutch linings is very small.

3 Examine the clutch disc friction linings for wear or loose rivets and the disc rim for distortion, cracks and worn splines.

4 It is always best to renew the clutch driven plate as an assembly to preclude further trouble, but, if it is wished to merely renew the linings, the rivets should be drilled out, and not knocked out with a centre punch. The manufacturers do not advise that the linings only are renewed and personal experience dictates that it is far more satisfactory to renew the driven plate complete than to try to economise by fitting only new friction linings.

5 Check the machined faces of the flywheel and the pressure plate. If either is badly grooved it should be machined until smooth, or a new component fitted. If the pressure plate is cracked or split it must be renewed.

6 Examine the hub splines for wear and make sure that the centre hub is not loose.

7 If on examination the clutch assembly is bathed in oil, then either the engine crankshaft rear main oil seal or transmission input shaft seal are defective and must therefore be renewed. Wash the respective clutch components in a suitable grease solvent and renew the clutch disc as it will be impossible to fully extract the impregnated oil from the linings.

7 Clutch release bearing – removal and refitting

1 To gain access it is necessary to remove the transmission as described in Chapter 6. If preferred the engine can be removed instead.

2 Remove the rubber dust cover from the housing, noting which way round it is fitted.

3 Use a screwdriver blade and prise the return spring from the bearing sleeve (photo).

4 Withdraw the release bearing and sleeve from the housing.

5 To separate the bearing and sleeve use a suitable puller.

6 The bearing should be checked for signs of overheating, excessive wear or roughness. If any of these conditions are apparent, the bearing must be renewed.

7 To refit the bearing, use a bench vice with suitable packing and press the bearing into position on the sleeve. Smear some high melting point grease onto the respective contact surface areas (bearing sleeve, ball-pin and release lever).

8 Refitting is the reverse of the removal procedure.

8 Clutch cable – removal and refitting

1 Raise the bonnet and support it.

2 Withdraw the E-clip from the clutch cable at the bulkhead.

3 Detach the cable from the pedal in the car.

4 Unhook the cable from the clutch withdrawal lever at the clutch

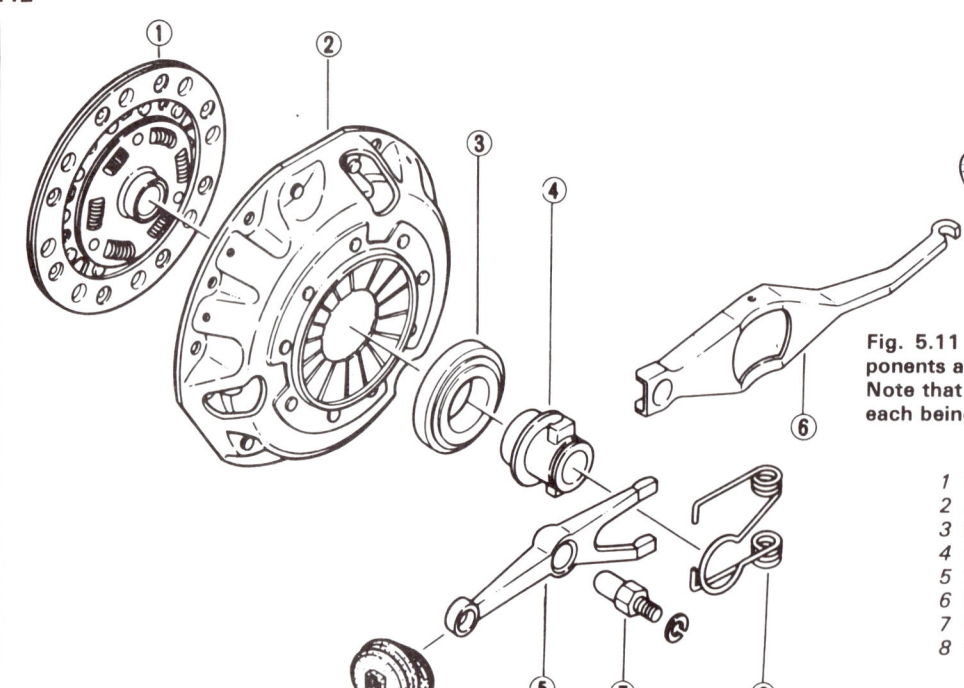

Fig. 5.11 The clutch release bearing components as fitted to the A14 engine models. Note that two withdrawal levers are shown each being for either right or left-hand drive accordingly

1 Clutch disc
2 Clutch cover
3 Release bearing
4 Bearing sleeve
5 Withdrawal lever (LH drive)
6 Withdrawal lever (RH drive)
7 Withdrawal lever ball pin
8 Return spring

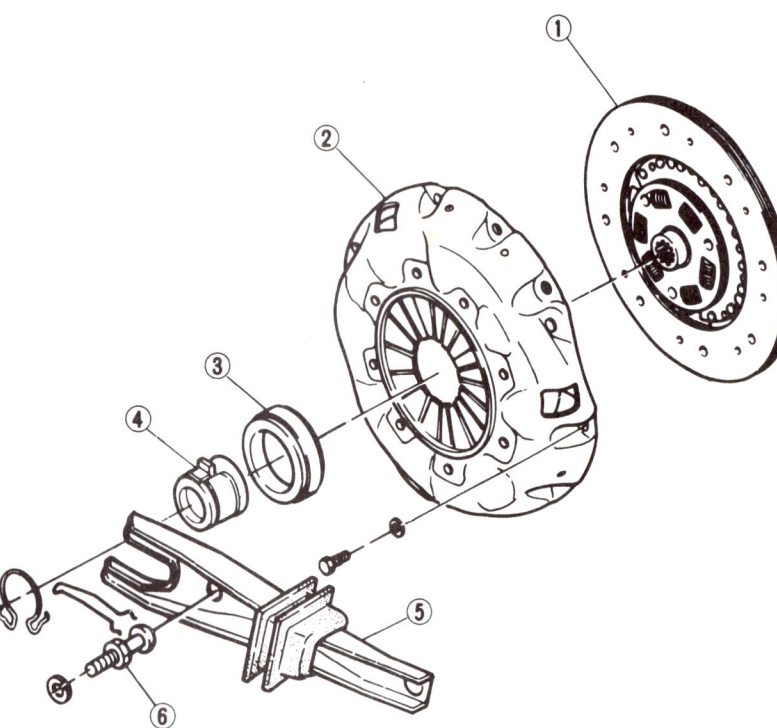

Fig. 5.12 The clutch release bearing components as fitted to all A16 engine models

1 Clutch disc		5 Withdrawal lever and dust cover	
2 Clutch cover			
3 Release bearing		6 Withdrawal lever ball pin	
4 Sleeve			

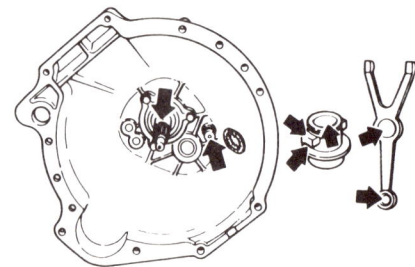

Fig. 5.13 The release mechanism lubrication points. Smear points indicated with a light coating of multi-purpose grease

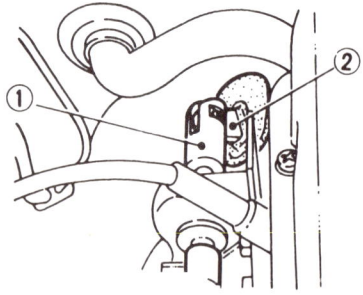

Fig. 5.14 Detach the control cable (1) from the withdrawal lever (2)

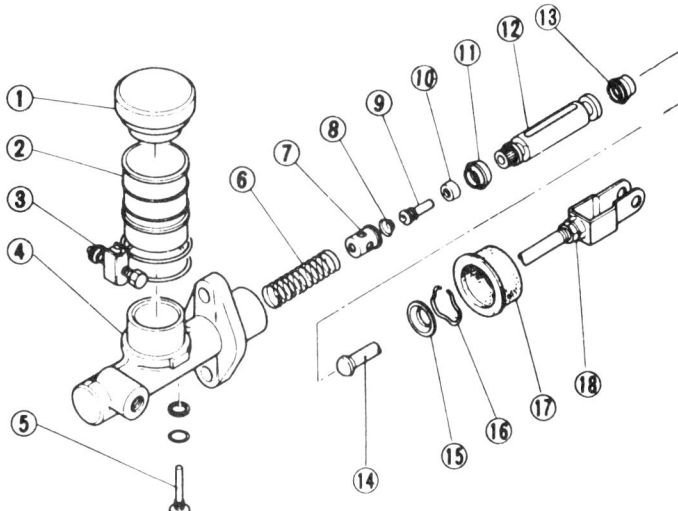

Fig. 5.15 The clutch master cylinder components

1	Reservoir cap	10	Supply valve
2	Reservoir	11	Primary cup
3	Reservoir clip	12	Piston
4	Body	13	Secondary cup
5	Supply valve stopper	14	Pushrod
6	Return spring	15	Stopper
7	Spring seat	16	Stopper ring
8	Valve spring	17	Dust cover
9	Valve rod	18	Locknut

housing end and extract the cable assembly. Do not stretch or bend the cable beyond its normal radius.

5   Reassemble in the reverse sequence to removal but lubricate the cable and connections. Make sure that the cable will not rub or interfere with any adjacent components and finally, check the clutch pedal height adjustment and pedal free travel (see Section 2). **Note:** *The clutch cable is pre lubricated during manufacture and does not therefore require any further applications of oil or grease.*

9   Clutch flexible hydraulic hose – removal and refitting

1   Wipe clean the slave cylinder and main line unions to prevent dirt ingress. Obtain a clean and dry jar and keep it handy to catch the hydraulic fluid in during the following operation.
2   Carefully detach the hose from the metal pipe and catch the hydraulic fluid as it drains out from the ends.
3   Detach the hose from the slave cylinder.
4   Refitting the flexible hose is the reverse sequence to removal. It will be necessary to bleed the hydraulic system as described in Section 3 of this Chapter.

10 Clutch master cylinder – removal and refitting

1   Drain the fluid from the clutch master cylinder reservoir by attaching a rubber tube to the slave cylinder bleed nipple. Undo the nipple approximately three quarters of a turn and then pump the fluid into a suitable container by operating the clutch pedal. Note that the pedal must be held in against the floor at the completion of each stroke and the bleed nipple tightened before the pedal is allowed to return. When the pedal has returned to its normal position loosen the bleed nipple and repeat the process, until the reservoir is empty.
2   Place a rag under the master cylinder to catch any hydraulic fluid that may be spilt. Unscrew the union nut from the end of the metal pipe where it enters the clutch master cylinder and gently pull the pipe clear.
3   Withdraw the spring clip retaining the pushrod yoke to pedal clevis and remove the clevis pin.
4   Undo and remove the two bolts and spring washers that secure the master cylinder to the bulkhead. Lift away the master cylinder taking care not to allow hydraulic fluid to come into contact with the paintwork, as it acts as a solvent.
5   Refitting the master cylinder is the reverse sequence to removal. Bleed the system as described in Section 2 of this Chapter.

11 Clutch master cylinder – dismantling, examination and reassembly

1   Ease back the rubber dust cover from the pushrod end.
2   Using a pair of circlip pliers release the circlip retaining the pushrod assembly. Lift away the pushrod complete with rubber boot and shaped washer.
3   By shaking hard, the piston assembly may be removed from the cylinder bore.
4   Carefully straighten the lip on the spring seat and separate the spring seat, spring and valve assembly from the piston.
5   Slide the valve end spring seat down the valve rod and carefully remove the seal. Also remove the piston cup from the piston noting which way round it is fitted.
6   Thoroughly clean the parts in brake fluid or methylated spirits. After drying the items inspect the seals for signs of distortion, swelling, splitting or hardening although it is recommended new rubber parts be fitted after dismantling as a matter of course.
7   Inspect the bore and piston for signs of deep scoring. If scoring is evident, fit a new cylinder. Make sure the port at the bottom of the bore is clear by poking gently with a piece of wire.
8   As the parts are refitted to the cylinder bore make sure that they are thoroughly wetted with clean hydraulic fluid, and keep all parts perfectly clean during reassembly.

12 Clutch slave cylinder – removal and refitting

1   Wipe the top of the master cylinder reservoir and unscrew the cap. Place a piece of polythene sheet over the top of the reservoir and refit the cap. This will stop hydraulic fluid syphoning out during subsequent operations.
2   Wipe the area around the flexible pipe to metal pipe union and disconnect the flexible pipe.
3   Undo and remove the two bolts and spring washers securing the slave cylinder to the clutch housing. Lift away the slave cylinder.
4   Refitting the slave cylinder is the reverse sequence to removal. It will be necessary to bleed the hydraulic system as described in Section 3 of this Chapter.

13 Clutch slave cylinder – dismantling, examination and reassembly

1   Clean the outside of the slave cylinder before dismantling.
2   Pull off the rubber dust cover and by shaking hard, the piston, seal

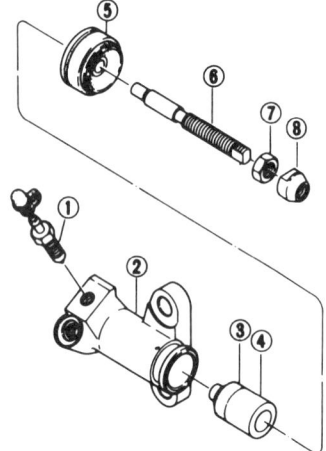

Fig. 5.16 Slave cylinder as fitted to the LH drive A14 engine models

1 *Bleed nipple*	5 *Dust cover*
2 *Body*	6 *Pushrod*
3 *Piston cup*	7 *Locknut*
4 *Piston*	8 *Push-nut*

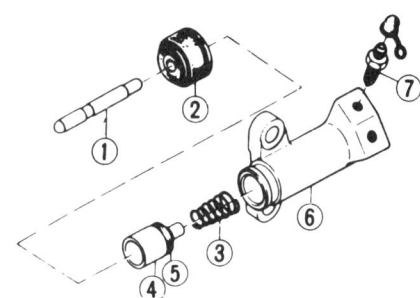

Fig. 5.17 Slave cylinder as fitted to the L16 engine models

1 *Pushrod*	5 *Piston cup*
2 *Dust cover*	6 *Operating cylinder*
3 *Piston spring*	7 *Bleed nipple*
4 *Piston*	

and spring should come out of the cylinder bore.

3   If they prove stubborn carefully use a foot pump air jet on the hydraulic hose connection and this should remove the internal parts, but do take care as they will fly out. It is recommended that a plastic bag be placed over the dust cover end to catch the parts.

4   Remove the seal from the piston noting which way round it is fitted.

5   Wash all internal parts with either brake fluid or methylated spirits and dry using a non-fluffy rag.

6   Inspect the bore and piston for signs of deep scoring. Fit a new cylinder.

7   Carefully examine the rubber components for signs of swelling, distortion, splitting, hardening or other wear. Should any such condi-

tion exist it is recommended that new parts be fitted.

8   All parts should be reassembled wetted with clean hydraulic fluid.

9   Fit the new seal to the piston. On L16 and L20 engined models, the slave cylinder assembly incorporates a tapered spring. Place the smaller diameter end of the spring onto the piston projection.

10 Insert the spring and piston into the bore taking care not to roll the lip of the seal.

11 Apply a little grease to the correct specification, to either end of the pushrod and pack the dust cover.

12 Fit the dust cover over the end of the slave cylinder engaging the lips over the groove in the body.

13 Fit the pushrod to the slave cylinder by pushing through the hole in the dust cover.

---

14 Fault diagnosis – clutch

Symptom	Reason/s
Judder when taking up drive	Loose engine transmission mountings Badly worn friction surfaces or contaminated with oil Worn splines on transmission input shaft or driven plate hub Worn input shaft spigot bush (pilot bearing) in flywheel
Clutch spin (failure to disengage) so that gears cannot be meshed	Incorrect release bearing to diaphragm spring finger clearance Driven plate sticking on input shaft splines due to rust. May occur after vehicle standing idle for long period Damaged or misaligned pressure plate assembly
Clutch slip (increase in engine speed does not result in increase in vehicle road speed – particularly on gradients)	Incorrect release bearing to diaphragm spring finger clearance Friction surfaces worn out or oil contaminated
Noise evident on depressing clutch pedal	Dry, worn or damaged release bearing Insufficient pedal free travel Weak or broken pedal return spring Weak or broken clutch release lever return spring Excessive play between driven plate hub splines and input shaft splines
Noise evident as clutch pedal released	Distorted driven plate Broken or weak driven plate cushion coil springs Insufficient pedal free play Weak or broken clutch pedal return spring Weak or broken release lever return spring Distorted or worn input shaft Release bearing loose on retainer hub

Chapter 6 Part A Manual gearbox

Contents

Specifications

| Type . . . . | 4-speed F4W60 or F4W63L and 5-speed FS5W63A all with synchromesh on all forward gears |

Gear ratios
F4W60

1st	3.513 : 1
2nd	2.170 : 1
3rd	1.378 : 1
4th	1.000 : 1
Reverse	3.764 : 1

F4W63L

	DX Saloon	Other Saloons and all Estate Car
1st	3.382 : 1	3.657 : 1
2nd	2.013 : 1	2.177 : 1
3rd	1.312 : 1	1.419 : 1
4th	1.000 : 1	1.000 : 1
Reverse	3.365 : 1	3.638 : 1

FS5W63A

	Coupe (standard)	Coupe (alternative)
1st	3.382 : 1	3.657 : 1
2nd	2.013 : 1	2.177 : 1
3rd	1.312 : 1	1.419 : 1
4th	1.000 : 1	1.000 : 1
5th	0.854 : 1	0.852 : 1
Reverse	3.570 : 1	3.860 : 1

Gearbox component tolerances (F4W60)
Gear endplay

1st	0.0059 to 0.0098 in (0.15 to 0.25 mm)
2nd	0.0118 to 0.0157 in (0.30 to 0.40 mm)
3rd	0.0059 to 0.0118 in (0.15 to 0.30 mm)
Counter gear	0.0039 to 0.0079 in (0.10 to 0.20 mm)
Reverse idler gear	0.0039 to 0.0106 in (0.10 to 0.27 mm)
Baulk ring to gear clearance	0.0315 to 0.0650 in (0.80 to 1.65 mm)
Gear backlash	0.0020 to 0.0071 in (0.05 to 0.18 mm)

Gearbox component tolerances (F4W63L)
Gear endplay

1st	0.0102 to 0.0142 in (0.26 to 0.36 mm)
2nd	0.0079 to 0.0118 in (0.20 to 0.30 mm)
3rd	0.0020 to 0.0079 in (0.05 to 0.20 mm)

Counter gear .... 0.0020 to 0.0059 in (0.05 to 0.15 mm)
Reverse idler gear .... 0.0039 to 0.0118 in (0.10 to 0.30 mm)
Baulk ring to gear clearance .... 0.0472 to 0.0591 in (1.20 to 1.50 mm)
Gear backlash .... 0.0020 to 0.0079 in (0.05 to 0.20 mm)

Gearbox component tolerances (FS5W63A)
Gear endplay
1st .... 0.0106 to 0.0146 in (0.27 to 0.37 mm)
2nd .... 0.0079 to 0.0118 in (0.20 to 0.30 mm)
3rd .... 0.0020 to 0.0059 in (0.05 to 0.15 mm)
5th .... 0.0020 to 0.0079 in (0.05 to 0.20 mm)
Reverse idler gear .... 0.0059 to 0.0157 in (0.15 to 0.40 mm)
Baulk ring to gear clearance .... 0.0472 to 0.0591 in (1.20 to 1.50 mm)
Gear backlash .... 0.0020 to 0.0079 in (0.05 to 0.20 mm)

Lubricant capacity
F4 W60 .... 2¼ Imp pints (2¾ US pints, 1.3 litres)
F4 W63L and FS5 W63A .... 3 Imp pints (3⅝ US pints, 1.7 litres)

Torque wrench settings

	lbf ft	kgf m
F4W60 type transmission		
Engine to transmission bolt	12 to 16	1.6 to 2.2
Engine/transmission rear plate bolt	12 to 16	1.6 to 2.2
Transmission to gusset bolt	33 to 44	4.6 to 6.1
Transmission rear mounting bolt	6.5 to 8.7	0.9 to 1.2
Crossmember mounting bolt	23 to 31	3.2 to 4.3
Rear engine mounting bolt	6.5 to 8.7	0.9 to 1.2
Control lever pin-nut (clutch)	9 to 12	1.3 to 1.7
Clutch slave cylinder bolt	22 to 30	3.1 to 4.1
Starter motor bolt	22 to 29	3.0 to 4.0
Transmission drain plug	18 to 29	2.5 to 4.0
Lubricant filler plug	18 to 29	2.5 to 4.0
Reverse light switch	14 to 22	2.0 to 3.5
Return spring plug	3.6 to 7.2	0.5 to 1.0
Speedometer lock plate bolt	2.2 to 3.6	0.3 to 0.5
Front cover bolt	7 to 12	1.0 to 1.6
Stopper pin-bolt	3.6 to 5.8	0.5 to 0.8
Rear extension attachment bolt	12 to 16	1.6 to 2.2
Check ball plug	5.1 to 7.2	0.7 to 1.0
Main shaft bearing retainer screw	5.1 to 7.2	0.7 to 1.0
Striker lever locking nut	6.5 to 8.7	0.9 to 1.2
Ball-pin	14 to 22	2.0 to 3.0
F4W 63L type transmission		
Torque wrench settings are the same as the F4W60 type transmission except for the following:		
Engine/transmission rear plate bolt	2.2 to 2.9	0.3 to 0.4
Engine to transmission bolt	29 to 35	4.0 to 4.8
Transmission drain plug	18 to 25	2.5 to 3.5
Filler plug	18 to 25	2.5 to 3.5
Reversing light switch	14 to 22	2.0 to 3.0
Change lever installation nut	14 to 16	1.9 to 2.2
Speedometer locking plate bolt	2.2 to 2.9	0.3 to 0.4
Bottom cover bolt	5.8 to 7.2	0.8 to 1.0
Front cover bolt	5.8 to 7.2	0.8 to 1.0
Rear extension bolt	10 to 13	1.4 to 1.8
Check ball plug	12 to 15	1.7 to 2.1
Mainshaft locking nut	65 to 80	9.0 to 11.0
Mainshaft bearing retainer screw	5.8 to 7.2	0.8 to 1.0
Ball-pin	22 to 36	3.0 to 5.0
FS5 W63A type transmission		
Torque wrench settings are the same as the F4W 63L type transmission except for the following:		
Transmission to engine bolt	27 to 36	3.7 to 5.0
Return spring plug	5.8 to 7.2	0.8 to 1.0
Front cover bolt	9 to 13	1.3 to 1.8
Rear extension installation bolt	9 to 13	1.3 to 1.8
Check ball plug	12 to 16	1.6 to 2.2
Mainshaft locking nut	101 to 123	14.0 to 17.0
Mainshaft bearing retainer screw	5.8 to 9.4	0.8 to 1.3
Shift arm bracket	59 to 72	8.2 to 10.0
Striking lever locknut	6.5 to 8.7	0.9 to 1.2

1 General description

There are three types of manual gearbox fitted to the cars within the range covered. There are two four-speed gearboxes, these being the F4W60 as fitted to all L14 engine models, or the F4W63L gearbox fitted to the L16 and L20 engine versions, (with the exception of the Coupe). The Coupe has a five-speed gearbox and this is designated the FS5W63A type.

All models have synchromesh fitted to all forward gears. The gears are helical and the mainshaft and countershaft forward gears are in constant mesh.

When the gearchange lever is operated the relevant coupling sleeve is made to slide on the synchronizer hub and engages its inner teeth with the outer teeth formed on the mainshaft gear. The synchronizer hub is splined to the mainshaft so enabling them to rotate in unison.

Reverse gear selection is made by the reverse gear on the mainshaft and the reverse idler gear being engaged in mesh. The movement of the lever is transferred via a striking rod to the selector rods and forks. The selector forks are constantly engaged with the grooves of the synchro coupling sleeves.

The gearbox types differ mainly in their method of construction. The F4W63L gearbox comprises a gearcase, rear extension and of course the respective gear assemblies being the mainshaft, countershaft and input shaft.

With the F4W60 and FS5W63A gearboxes, the principle components are the gearcase, adaptor plate and rear extension. The gear assemblies are initially mounted at the rear in the adaptor plate and this combined assembly is then fitted to the gearcase, the shafts at the forward end being located in bearings in the gearcase front face. The rear extension is fitted to the rear face of the adaptor plate.

With this type of gearbox the gears are only accessible for inspection on removal of the rear extension and adaptor plate assembly, which necessitates removal of the gearbox from the car.

2 Gearbox – removal and refitting

1 On all manual gearbox models, the gearbox can be removed from the vehicle either as a complete unit with the engine as described in Chapter 1, or as a separate unit leaving the engine in place.

2 The removal operations of the three specific types of manual gearbox are basically the same and where differences occur the respective procedures are given individually.

3 Preferably place the vehicle over an inspection pit but if one is not available, raise the vehicle and support on axle-stands making sure that there is sufficient clearance below the bodyframe to enable the largest diameter of the clutch bellhousing to pass through during the removal operations.

4 Disconnect the battery earth lead and drain the gearbox oil.

5 Unscrew the centre console retaining screws and remove the console (see Chapter 12).

6 The gear lever must now be removed. On the F4W60 type transmission this is best achieved by removing the retaining bolt and nut from underneath the vehicle (photo). On the F4W63L gearbox, place the lever in neutral and remove the rubber boot from the aperture in the gearbox tunnel. Now using open ended spanners as shown in Fig. 6.1, unscrew and remove the lever from the top. On the FS5W63A gearbox, the lever is located by a pin and E-clip. Remove the rubber grommet and then prise the E-clip free and withdraw the pin to free the lever.

7 Working from underneath the vehicle, disconnect the exhaust pipe at the front from the exhaust manifold flange. When free, tie the pipe to one side out of the way.

8 Unscrew and disconnect the speedometer cable connection from the gearbox extension (photo).

9 Carefully disconnect the reversing light switch wires from the connector.

10 On models fitted with a hydraulic clutch control, refer to Chapter 5 and disconnect the operating (slave) cylinder from the clutch housing.

2.6 Extract the gear lever retaining bolt from underneath on the F4W60 transmission models

2.8 Disconnect the speedometer cable

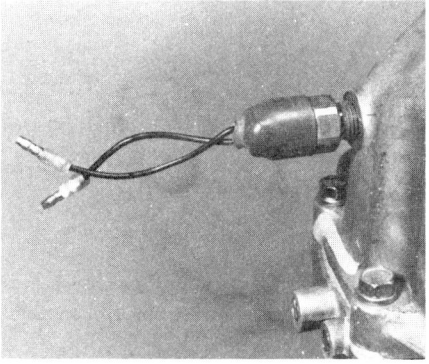

3.5 Remove the reversing light switch

Fig. 6.1 Method of disconnecting the gear lever on the F4W63L type gearbox

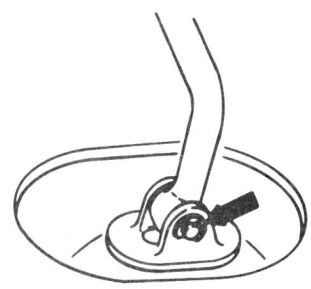

Fig. 6.2 The E-clip retainer on the FS5W63A type gearbox

Fig. 6.3 Remove the stopper pin bolt

3.6 Remove the speedometer pinion unit

3.8 Unscrew the return spring plug and extract the springs and plunger

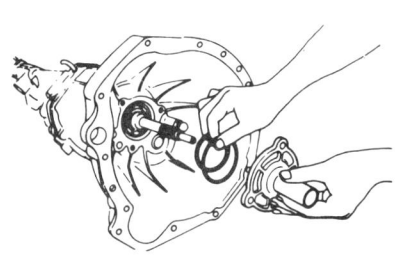

Fig. 6.4 Withdraw the front cover, O-ring and shim

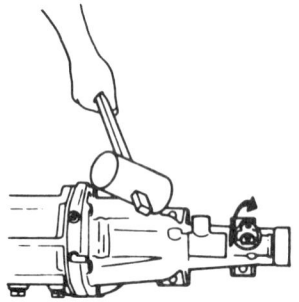

Fig. 6.5 Remove the rear extension – turn striker rod as shown by arrow

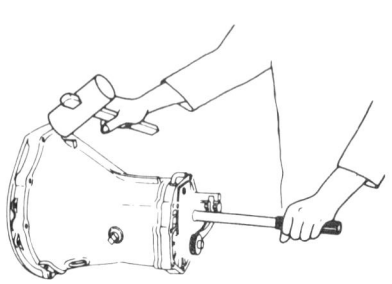

Fig. 6.6 Withdrawing the adaptor plate assembly

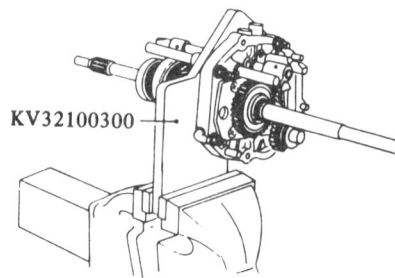

KV32100300

Fig. 6.7 Method of securing the adaptor plate using special tool KV32100300

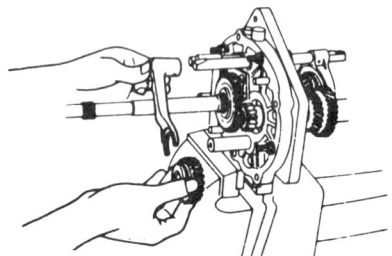

Fig. 6.8 Remove reverse shift fork and idler gear

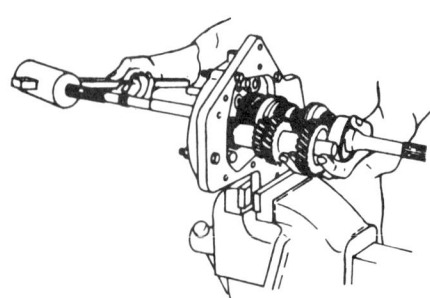

Fig. 6.9 Removing the gear assemblies from the adaptor plate

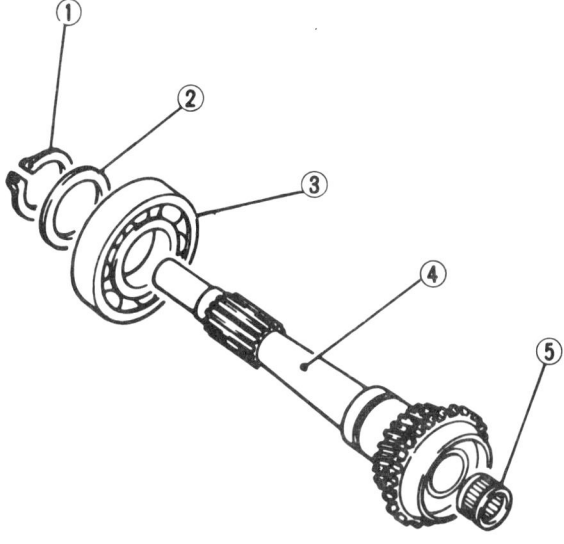

Fig. 6.10 The main drivegear (input shaft) components

1 Circlip
2 Spacer
3 Bearing
4 Shaft
5 Roller bearing

11 On models fitted with a cable operated clutch, detach the cable from the operating lever, as described in Chapter 5.

12 Refer to Chapter 7 and remove the propeller shaft.

13 To support the engine when the gearbox is removed, position a jack or axle-stand underneath. Employ a piece of wood between the jack or stand and the sump to prevent damage. Never place a support under the sump drain plug.

14 Place a jack under the gearbox and raise it so that it just supports it.

15 Disconnect and withdraw the starter motor from its housing.

16 The supporting crossmember under the gearbox extension must now be removed. Slacken the two bolts locating the crossmember to the gearbox extension and then unscrew and remove the four bolts (two each side) securing the crossmember to the underbody.

17 The engine to gearbox securing bolts can now be unscrewed and removed.

18 If a trolley jack has been used to support the gearbox it can be lowered just sufficiently to allow the gearbox to be withdrawn rearwards from the engine. Under no circumstances allow the full weight of the gearbox to hang on the input shaft during removal as this could distort or damage it. If a trolley jack isn't available for this operation, then an assistant will be required to help support the gearbox during withdrawal from the engine.

19 Refitting is a reversal of the removal procedure but apply a smear of high melting point grease to the input shaft splines. Check that the clutch shaft pilot bearing in the rear end of the crankshaft is in good order before refitting the gearbox.

20 When the gearbox is fitted, check the clutch adjustment as described in Chapter 5, and refill the gearbox with the correct grade and quantity of oil. Finally check that all connections and fittings are secure.

3 Gearbox (F4W60) – dismantling into major assemblies

1 Before commencing work on the gearbox, clean off it's external surfaces using a water soluble solvent or paraffin.

2 If not already done on removal, drain the transmission lubricant.

3 Refer to Chapter 5 and remove the clutch release mechanism.

4 If still attached, remove the crossmember mounting support bracket from the extension housing.

5 Unscrew and withdraw the reverse light switch (photo).

6 Unscrew and remove the retaining bolt from the speedometer drivegear retaining housing flange and withdraw the unit (photo).

7 Unscrew and remove the nut and stopper pin-bolt from the rear extension (Fig. 6.3).

8 The return spring plug, spring, reverse check spring and plunger can now be carefully removed from the rear extension unit (photo).

9 Unscrew the retaining bolts from the front cover and withdraw it together with the O-ring and adjustment shim over the input shaft. Keep the shim with the O-ring and cover.

10 Using a suitable pair of circlip pliers, extract the front main drive bearing retaining circlip from the bearing orifice.

11 Unscrew and remove the rear extension unit retaining bolts, and note the position of the cable retainer clip.

12 Check that the gearbox is in neutral and rotate the striker rod (selector rail) in a clockwise direction and simultaneously drive the extension rearwards from the main housing. Lightly tap around the housing using a soft head mallet. Do not use a screwdriver to prise the two housings apart. If the extension housing is reluctant to part company with the main housing check that the striker rod is fully positioned to release it from the shift rod/fork.

13 Support the mainshaft and tap the gearbox housing with a soft head mallet as shown (Fig. 6.6) to enable the housing and adaptor plate assembly to be disconnected.

14 Now that the gear assembly is removed an initial inspection can be made of the components. If it is decided to dismantle the complete assembly, it is a good system to devise a method of supporting the adaptor plate assembly. An adaptor plate retainer can easily be fabricated and bolted to the adaptor plate so that it can be securely held in a vice for convenience when working. Figure 6.7 shows the special adaptor setting plate tool manufactured by Datsun (Tool No. KV32100300).

15 Remove the thrust washer from the counter gear (laygear) taking note which way round it is fitted (slot to front).

Shift forks and rods – dismantling

16 Using a suitable pin punch, drive out the respective roll pins retaining the shift forks to the rods.

17 Withdraw the reverse idler gear and shift fork.

18 Unscrew and remove the three check ball plugs and extract the springs and balls.

19 Lightly tap the selector rods on the front end and extract them together with their shift forks. Note which way round the shift forks are fitted and refit them to their respective shafts on removal to avoid confusion during assembly.

Gear assemblies – dismantling

20 Using a suitable pair of circlip pliers, remove the circlip at the rear of the mainshaft. Then withdraw the thrust washer and reverse gear from the mainshaft, but note which way round the gear is facing.

21 The bearing retainer plate can now be removed by unscrewing the four cross-head screws. We found them to be extremely tight and had to use a large cross-head screwdriver and gripped the screwdriver shaft with a pair of molegrips to provide the additional effort required to loosen the screws.

22 Using circlip pliers, extract the circlip locating the mainshaft rear bearing.

23 The mainshaft gear assembly can now be driven from the adaptor together with the counter gear unit. Support both gear assemblies and tap them free with a soft head mallet hitting their rear end faces (Fig. 6.9). Take care not to drop or damage the gears during removal.

24 The gearbox major components are now removed and can be inspected and if necessary dismantled further for repair or renewal, but note that further operations should not be undertaken unless the facilities of a press and/or a bearing puller are available. With this in mind, read the further dismantling procedures through and decide whether or not you have suitable facilities to undertake further work.

Mainshaft – dismantling

25 Extract the circlip from the mainshaft at the front using suitable pliers. Withdraw the 3rd and 4th synchronizer unit, complete with baulk rings, 3rd gear and the needle roller bearing. Using a suitable bearing puller withdraw the mainshaft bearing. If available use special Datsun bearing puller No. ST30031000, and press the bearing free as in Fig. 6.11. Withdraw the thrust washer, 1st gear together with its bush and needle roller bearing. Remove the 1st/2nd synchronizer unit together with baulk rings and needle roller bearing.

Main drivegear (input shaft) – dismantling

26 Using suitable circlip pliers, remove the circlip and withdraw the spacer. A bearing puller or if available Datsun special tool No. ST 22730000 and a press are needed to remove the bearing from the shaft. Do not drop the shaft and gear.

Counter gear (laygear) – dismantling

27 Remove the circlip from the counter shaft and using a suitable puller or Datsun special puller No. ST22730000 withdraw the countershaft reverse gear. Use the same puller and remove the counter gear rear bearing. Alternatively use a suitable pulley.

4 Synchromesh hubs (F4W60) – dismantling and inspection

1 The synchro hubs are only too easy to dismantle – just push the centre out and the whole assembly flies apart. The point is to prevent this happening, before you are ready. Do not dismantle the hubs without reason and do not mix up the parts of the two hubs.

2 It is most important to check backlash in the splines between the outer sleeve and inner hub. If any is noticeable the whole assembly must be renewed.

3 Mark the hubs and sleeve so that you may reassemble them on the same splines. With the hub and sleeve separated, the teeth at the end of the splines which engage with corresponding teeth of the gear wheels, must be checked for damage and wear.

4 Do not confuse the keystone shape at the ends of the teeth. This shape matches the gear teeth shape and it is a design characteristic to minimise jump-out tendencies.

5 If the synchronizing cones are being renewed it is sensible also to renew the sliding keys and springs which hold them in position.

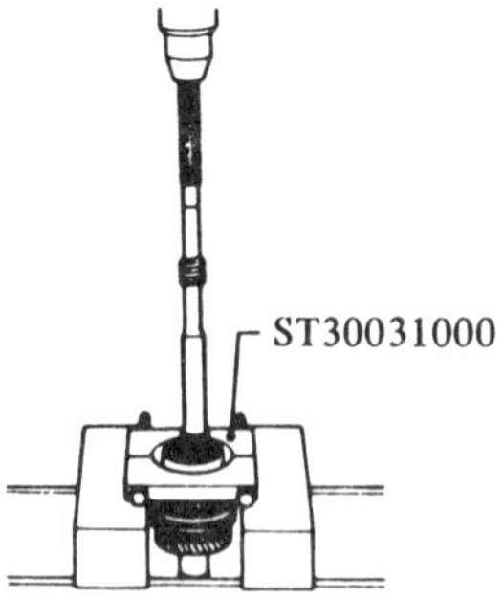

ST30031000

Fig. 6.11 Removing the bearing using special tool

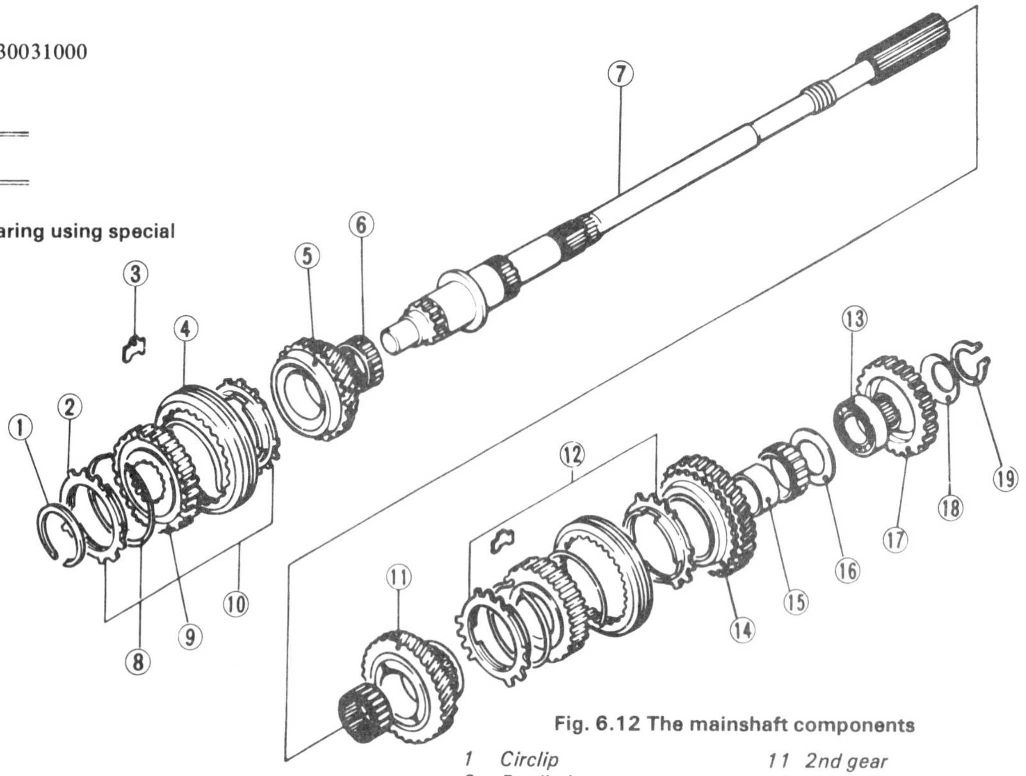

Fig. 6.12 The mainshaft components

1	Circlip	11	2nd gear
2	Baulk ring	12	1st and 2nd synchro assembly
3	Shift insert		
4	Coupling sleeve	13	Mainshaft bearing
5	3rd gear	14	1st gear
6	Needle roller bearing	15	Bush – 1st speed gear
7	Mainshaft	16	Thrust washer
8	Spread spring	17	Reverse gear
9	Synchro hub	18	Thrust washer
10	3rd and 4th synchro assembly	19	Circlip

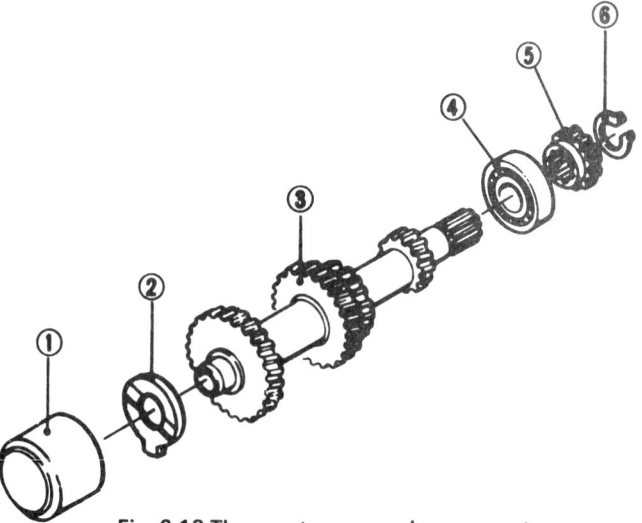

Fig. 6.13 The counter gear and components

1	Needle roller bearing	4	Bearing
2	Thrust washer	5	Reverse gear
3	Counter gear	6	Circlip

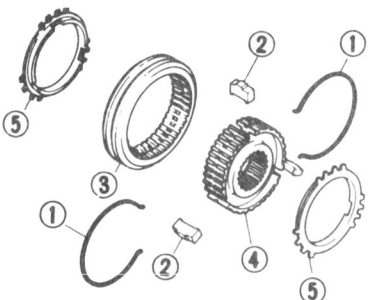

Fig. 6.14 The synchromesh hub assembly components

1	Spread spring	4	Hub
2	Shifter insert	5	Baulk ring
3	Sleeve coupling		

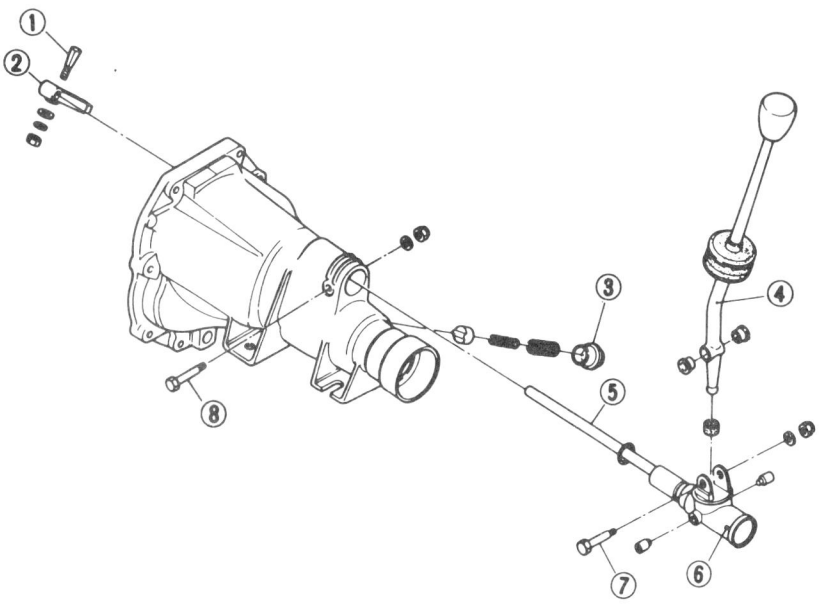

Fig. 6.15 Gear lever and rear extension components

1 Locking pin
2 Striker lever
3 Plug and plunger with springs
4 Control lever
5 Striker rod
6 Striker rod guide
7 Lever pin
8 Stopper pin bolt

6.5 Method of checking the baulk ring to cone clearance, using feeler gauges. Apply pressure to baulk ring when checking

6.6 Check the gear endplay

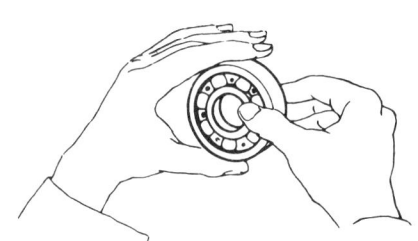

Fig. 6.16 Check the ball bearings for wear

5 Rear extension (F4W60) – dismantling, inspection and assembly

1 To remove the striking lever from the striking rod, unscrew the lockpin nut and remove with washers. Extract the pin and withdraw the lever.

2 Withdraw the striker rod and guide from the rear extension housing.

3 The oilseal can be prised out of its housing, and should normally be renewed during an overhaul of the gearbox.

4 Do not remove the bush from the rear extension.

5 Clean and check the housing for signs of cracks or damage. In particular look for any damage or distortion to the mating face to the adaptor plate. Clean off any small protrusions or sealant taking care not to damage or score the surface. Should the rear extension bush be damaged or show any signs of wear, then the housing and bush must be renewed as they are a combined assembly.

6 To reassemble the rear extension housing, first check that it is perfectly clean, in particular the seal housing. Lubricate the seal housing with clean gear oil and press a new seal into position using a tube drift. Check that the seal is correctly located and lubricate the sealing lip with gear oil to assist assembly when fitting over the shaft, and the cavity between the seal lips should be packed with a multi-purpose grease.

7 Lubricate the striker rod guide in the extension, also the O-ring groove. With a new O-ring fitted, carefully fit the striker rod and when fully home relocate the striking lever. Insert the lockpin and secure with washers and the nut, tightening to the torque settings given in the specifications.

8 If a new welch plug is to be fitted, smear its aperture with sealant prior to fitting.

6 Gearbox components – inspection

1 It is assumed that the gearbox has been dismantled for reasons of excessive noise, lack of synchromesh action on certain gears or for failure to stay in gear. If anything more drastic than this (total failure, seizure or main casing cracked) it would be better to leave it alone and look for a replacement, either secondhand or an exchange.

2 With the exception of oilseals, clean all components using a suitable solvent, ready for inspection.

3 All oilseals and O-rings should be renewed as a matter of course.

4 Examine all gears for excessively worn, chipped or damaged teeth, and renew any defective gears.

5 Use feeler gauges and check the baulk ring to cone clearance. Apply hand pressure to the baulk ring and insert the feeler gauge. The clearance must be at least 0.020 in (0.5 mm), if not renew the baulk ring.

6 Check the gear endplay as shown in the photo using feeler gauges. The gear endplay is given in the Specifications.

7 All ball race bearings should be checked for chatter and roughness

after they have been flushed out. It is advisable to renew these anyway even though they may not appear too badly worn. Circlips which are all important in locating bearings, gears and hubs, should be checked to ensure that they are undistorted and undamaged. In any case a selection of new circlips of varying thicknesses should be obtained to compensate for variations in new components fitted, and wear in old ones. The specifications given in the respective reassembly sequences (Section 7) indicate what shims are available.

8   The thrust washers at the ends of the counter gear cluster should be renewed, as they will almost certainly have worn if the gearbox is of any age.

9   Needle roller bearings are usually found in good order, but if in any doubt renew the needle rollers as necessary.

10   Further details regarding the inspection of the synchro hub assemblies is given in Section 4.

11   If renewing the counter shaft needle roller bearing in the gearbox case, refer to Fig. 6.17 and ensure that it projects 0.08 in (2 mm) from the front face of the gearbox case. Never refit a bearing once removed, always renew it.

12   Any wear or damage found in the counter gear assembly will necessitate renewal of the complete assembly. The needle roller bearings and thrust washers can be renewed separately. When renewing a counter shaft, it is normal to renew the corresponding mainshaft gears as matched sets.

13   Examine reverse gears for wear or damage and renew as appropriate.

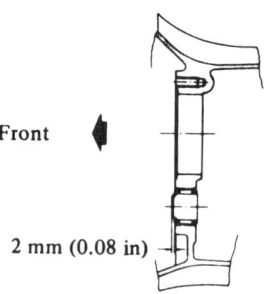

Fig. 6.17 The countershaft needle roller bearing location – leave the correct clearance indicated when fitting

---

7   Gearbox (F4W60) – reassembly

1   Clean and lubricate with gear oil all components prior to assembly. Commence by reassembling the synchromesh hubs.

Synchromesh hubs – reassembly

2   Insert a synchro hub into its respective coupling sleeve and then locate the three shift inserts into their grooves.

3   Refit the spread spring with its protrusion located in the groove to retain the insert on the inside of the coupling sleeve. Fit the second spread spring to the opposing side of the hub. When fitting the synchromesh springs they must be located so that their respective opposing positions are offset to each other (Fig. 6.18).

4   Operate the hub and sleeve by hand to ensure that they function correctly.

Fig. 6.18 The synchromnesh hub spring positions – offset to each other

Mainshaft – reassembly

5   Grease and locate the 2nd gear needle roller bearing onto the mainshaft, then fit the 2nd gear (photo).

6   Locate the baulk ring onto the 2nd gear and refit the 1st/2nd synchromesh hub unit (photo).

7   Slide the 1st gear needle bearing bush onto the shaft (photo), and then locate the bearing (photo).

8   Fit the baulk ring and 1st gear (photo).

9   Locate the thrust washer against the 1st gear and then fit the ball bearing with its circlip groove in the outer race offset away from 1st gear as shown (photo), and press into position.

10   To the front end of the mainshaft, grease and locate the 3rd gear needle roller bearing against the distance piece and then fit the 3rd gear and its baulk ring (photo).

11   Fit the 3rd/4th synchromesh unit (photo), then select a suitable circlip to locate the synchro hub unit. The circlips are available in varying thicknesses to suit so that when fully located in the shaft groove there is the minimum clearance possible between the synchro hub and circlip. Circlips are available in the following thicknesses:

    (a) 0.0610 to 0.0630 in (1.55 to 1.60 mm)
    (b) 0.0630 to 0.0650 in (1.60 to 1.65 mm)
    (c) 0.0650 to 0.0669 in (1.65 to 1.70 mm).

Main drivegear – assembly

12   Press the main drivegear ball bearing into position over the shaft with the groove in the outer race offset to the front.

13   Locate the spacer against the bearing and then select and fit a circlip of a suitable thickness to take up any clearance. The following circlip sizes are available:

    (a) 0.0528 to 0.0551 in (1.34 to 1.40 mm)
    (b) 0.0551 to 0.0575 in (1.40 to 1.46 mm)

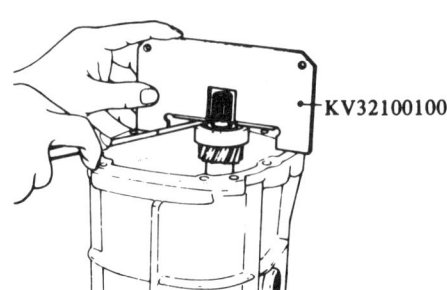

Fig. 6.19 Using special tool to gauge the counter gear endfloat

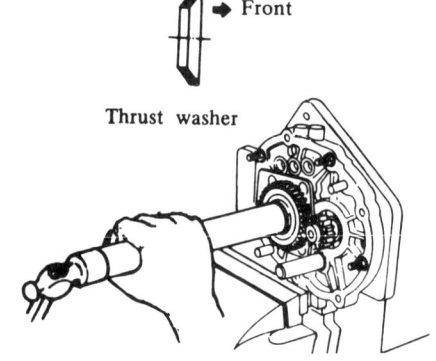

Fig. 6.20 Fitting the reverse gear, washer and circlip using a tube drift

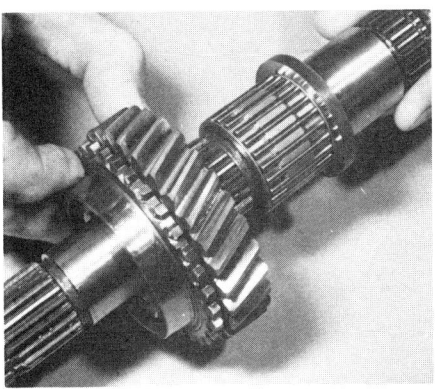

7.5 Locate 2nd gear over the needle roller bearing

7.6 Refit the baulk ring and 1st/2nd synchro hub

7.7a Slide 1st gear bearing bush into position ...

7.7b ... followed by the bearing

7.8 Fit 1st gear and baulk ring

7.9 Locate thrust washer and refit bearing

7.10 Fit roller bearing, 3rd gear and baulk ring

7.11a Fit synchro unit and then ...

7.11b ... check the circlip thickness required

7.11c Fit the circlip to complete

7.14 Fit the needle roller bearing into the main drivegear

7.18 Reverse gear and circlip fitted

7.19 The mainshaft, countershaft and main drivegear gear assemblies realigned

7.20 Locate the gear assemblies to the adaptor plate

7.21 Fit the mainshaft rear bearing circlip

7.22 The retainer plate refitted

7.23 Reverse gear, thrust washer and circlip

7.24 Reverse gear shift rod, and idle gear. Note rod position

7.25a Fitting an interlock plunger using a magnetic rod

7.25b The plunger in position

7.26 Insert the 3rd/4th selector (shift) rod and fork

7.28a Refitting the 1st gear selector (shift) rod and fork

7.28b Tap home the roll pin using a suitable drift

7.32 Thrust washer correctly positioned

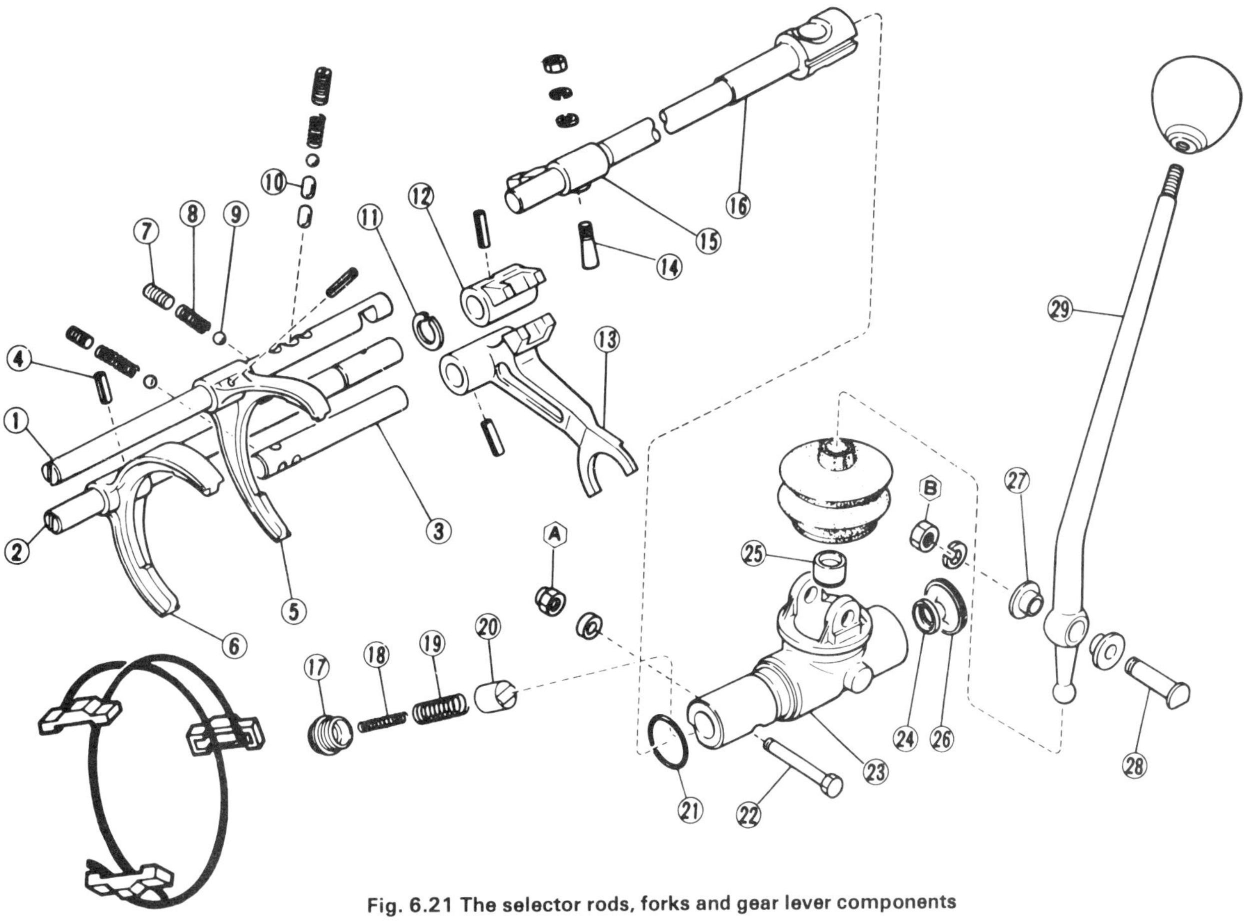

Fig. 6.21 The selector rods, forks and gear lever components

1	1st/2nd fork rod	9	Steel ball
2	3rd/top fork rod	10	Interlock plunger
3	Reverse fork rod	11	Stopper ring
4	Retaining pin	12	Shift rod A bracket
5	1st/2nd shift fork	13	Reverse shift fork
6	3rd/top shift fork	14	Lock pin
7	Check ball plug	15	Striking lever
8	Check ball spring		

16	Striker rod	23	Striker guide assembly
17	Return spring plug	24	Striker guide oil seal
18	Reverse check spring	25	Control lever bushing
19	Return spring	26	Expansion plug
20	Plunger	27	Control pin bushing
21	O-ring	28	Control arm pin
22	Stopper pin bolt	29	Control lever

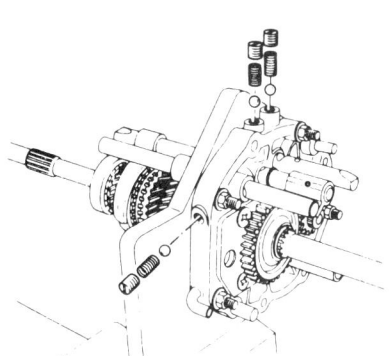

Fig. 6.22 The check ball and spring position

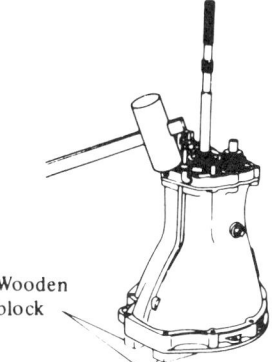

Wooden block

Fig. 6.23 Lightly tap the adaptor assembly home. Note casing wooden block supports

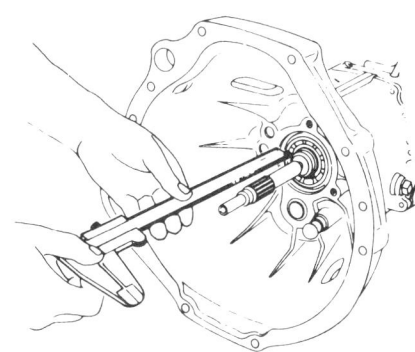

Fig. 6.24 Measure the front cover adjustment shim requirement

7.33 The adapter plate assembly and gearbox reunited. Note dowel position for correct alignment

7.36 Refit the circlips to the main bearing housing

7.37 The striking lever showing nut and washers

7.40 Fit the stopper pin bolt

7.41 Checking the gear engagement

7.42 Fit a new rear seal into the extension

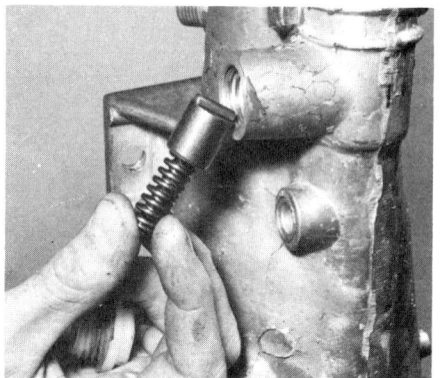

7.43 Fit the plunger and springs

7.47 Refit the front cover followed by ...

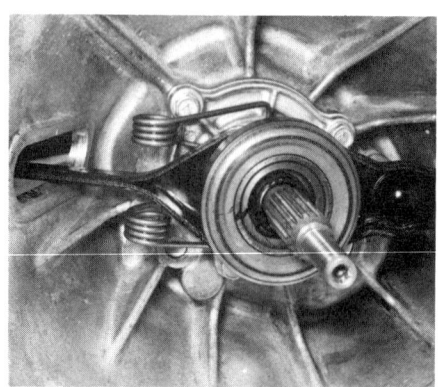

7.48 ... the clutch release mechanism

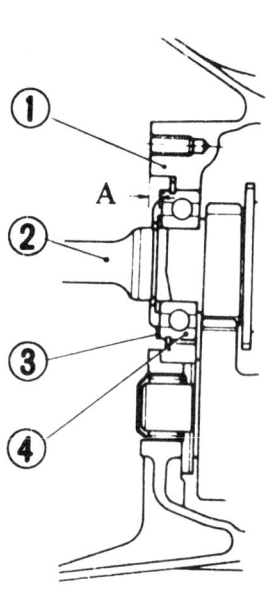

Fig. 6.25 The shim requirement is measured at 'A'

1 Gearcase
2 Main drivegear shaft
3 Adjustment shim position
4 Ball bearing

(c) 0.0575 to 0.0598 in (1.46 to 1.52 mm)
(d) 0.0598 to 0.0622 in (1.52 to 1.58 mm)
(e) 0.0622 to 0.0646 in (1.58 to 1.64 mm)
(f) 0.0646 to 0.0669 in (1.64 to 1.70 mm)
(g) 0.0669 to 0.0693 in (1.70 to 1.76 mm)

When fitted the circlip must be fully located in its groove.
14 Lubricate the caged roller bearing with a medium grease and locate in the main drivegear (photo). Mate the main drivegear to the mainshaft and check for correct engagement.

Counter gear (layshaft) – reassembly
15 Press the ball bearing onto the countershaft.
16 Fit the countershaft thrust washer and gear and locate in the gearbox casing. Now using a clock gauge or special Datsun height gauge, tool No. KV 32100100 as shown in Fig. 6.19, check the end-float of the counter gear. Thrust washers are available in varying thicknesses to provide the necessary endplay which should be 0.0039 to 0.0079 in (0.10 to 0.20 mm). The available thrust washer thicknesses are:

(a) 0.0866 to 0.0886 in (2.20 to 2.25 mm)
(b) 0.0866 to 0.0906 in (2.25 to 2.30 mm)
(c) 0.0906 to 0.0925 in (2.30 to 2.35 mm)
(d) 0.0925 to 0.945 in (2.35 to 2.40 mm)
(e) 0.0945 to 0.0965 in (2.40 to 2.45 mm)
(f) 0.0965 to 0.0984 in (2.45 to 2.50 mm)
(g) 0.0984 to 0.1004 in (2.50 to 2.55 mm)
(h) 0.1004 to 0.1024 in (2.55 to 2.60 mm)

17 Having decided on the correct washer thickness required, withdraw the counter gear from the gearbox case.
18 The reverse gear can now be pressed onto the countershaft and when fully positioned fit the circlip into the shaft groove against the gear (photo).

Main components – assembly
19 Align the corresponding gears of the mainshaft, countershaft and input shaft assemblies as shown (photo).
20 Locate them as a unit into the adaptor plate (photo). To do this the adaptor plate will have to be firmly supported whilst the mainshaft and countershaft are pressed and/or tapped carefully into position.
21 Fit the circlip to the mainshaft rear bearing groove as shown (photo) and ensure that the circlip is fully located.
22 Refit the bearing retainer plate and secure with setscrews. Tighten them to the specified torque (see Specifications). Punch mark the screw edges to lock them.
23 Now fit the reverse gear to the mainshaft, followed by the thrust washer and circlip. Ensure that the circlip is fully located in its groove, and the washer whish is dished must have its concave face to the front (Fig. 6.20). When fitting, locate the washer and circlip and tap home using a tube drift as shown.

Selector rods and forks
24 Engage neutral when reassembling the selector rod and forks. Insert the reverse shift rod through the adaptor plate and locate the reverse shift fork and idler gear as shown (photo). Align the roll pin hole in the rod and fork and drift home a new roll pin to secure.
25 Lubricate and insert an interlock plunger (photo).
26 Insert the 3rd and 4th gear shift rod (aligning the notches with the interlock ball holes) and locate the shift fork (photo). Refit the shift rod 'A' bracket on the rear end of the rod if it has been removed and secure both bracket and fork using roll pins.
27 Lubricate and insert an interlock plunger.
28 Insert 1st gear shift rod and fork (photo). Secure the two using a roll pin (photo), but ensure that the rod interlock plunger detent is aligned correctly.
29 Refit the respective check balls, springs and plugs. Apply a locking solution to each plug to prevent them working loose, but make sure the threads are clean when applying. Screw the plugs down so that their heads are flush with the adaptor plate outside edge. Note that the check ball plug for the 1st/2nd fork rod is longer than the others.
30 On completion of assembling the shift fork/rod assemblies check that the shift rods and gears operate in the correct manner. The gears must engage smoothly.

Adaptor plate assembly to gearbox
31 Before fitting the adaptor plate and gears to the gearbox, check

that the mating surfaces of both are perfectly clean and then apply an even amount of sealant to them.
32 Position the previously selected thrust washer as shown in the photo with the oil groove face towards the roller bearing. Smear the faces of the thrust washer with grease before fitting.
33 The adaptor plate assembly and gearbox housing can now be carefully reassembled. Check that the dowel pin and location hole are in line before lightly tapping home.
34 If they have been removed and not yet refitted, refit the main drive ball bearing and the counter gear needle roller bearing into their respective housings. Press or drive them in using a suitable tube drift but ensure that they are exactly in line before pressing or driving home.
35 Refit the circlip to the mainshaft groove. Check that the mainshaft assembly rotates freely.
36 Insert the circlip to the main bearing housing.

Rear extension – refitting
37 If it has been removed, refit the striking rod through the extension housing and relocate the striking lever. Secure with the lockpin, washers and nut (photo).
38 Check that the mating surfaces of both the rear extension and adaptor plate are clean and smear them with some sealant.
39 Ensure that the fork rods are in neutral and rotate the strike rod in the extension in a clockwise direction. Carefully refit the extension to the gearbox and check that the striker rod lever fully engages with the selector fork brackets. Locate the retaining bolts and washers (don't forget the wire location clip fitted to the top right-hand bolt), but do not fully tighten just yet.
40 The stopper pin-bolt must now be fitted and the guide unit may have to be manoeuvred to allow the bolt to pass through fully (photo). Smear the bolt with sealant before refitting.
41 Before tightening the bolts retaining the extension, use a long handled screwdriver and pass it through the guide unit, engage with the striking rod and check the gear selection action (photo). If satisfactory tighten the bolts to the specified torque.
42 Carefully tap or press the rear extension oil seal into position (photo).
43 Smear the plunger assembly with grease and refit it into the extension housing (photo) with springs and plug. Apply some locking sealant to the threads of the plug prior to fitting.
44 Refit the speedometer pinion unit and tighten the retaining bolt to the specified torque.
45 Refit the reversing light switch. Apply locking sealant to the switch threads prior to refitting.
46 Before refitting the front cover the adjustment shim thickness must be checked using a vernier/depth gauge as shown in Fig. 6.24. The depth is measured between the front face of the transmission case and the main drive bearing outer race, 'A' in Fig. 6.25, with the shim in place. According to the depth calculation, the shim should be selected as given on the table below:

If 'A' equals:	Use shim thickness
0.2382 to 0.2398 in (6.05 to 6.09 mm)	0.0197 in (0.50 mm)
0.2402 to 0.2417 in (6.10 to 6.14 mm)	0.0217 in (0.55 mm)
0.2421 to 0.2437 in (6.15 to 6.19 mm)	0.0236 in (0.60 mm)
0.2441 to 0.2457 in (6.20 to 6.24 mm)	0.0256 in (0.65 mm)
0.2461 to 0.2476 in (6.25 to 6.29 mm)	0.0276 in (0.70 mm)
0.2480 to 0.2496 in (6.30 to 6.34 mm)	0.0295 in (0.75 mm)
0.2500 to 0.2516 in (6.35 to 6.39 mm)	0.0315 in (0.80 mm)

47 Having selected a suitable shim the front cover can now be refitted, together with the new O-ring. Tighten the cover bolts to the specified torque.
48 Refit the clutch release lever and bearing assembly (Chapter 5) to complete the gearbox assembly.
49 The gearbox unit is now ready for reassembly to the engine and/or car. The fitting procedure is basically a reversal of the removal sequence but refer to Section 2, paragraphs 19 and 20 for further details.

8 Gearbox (F4W63L) – dismantling into major assemblies

1 Before work commences, clean the external surfaces with paraffin or a water soluble solvent.
2 Drain the oil (unless this was done before removal).

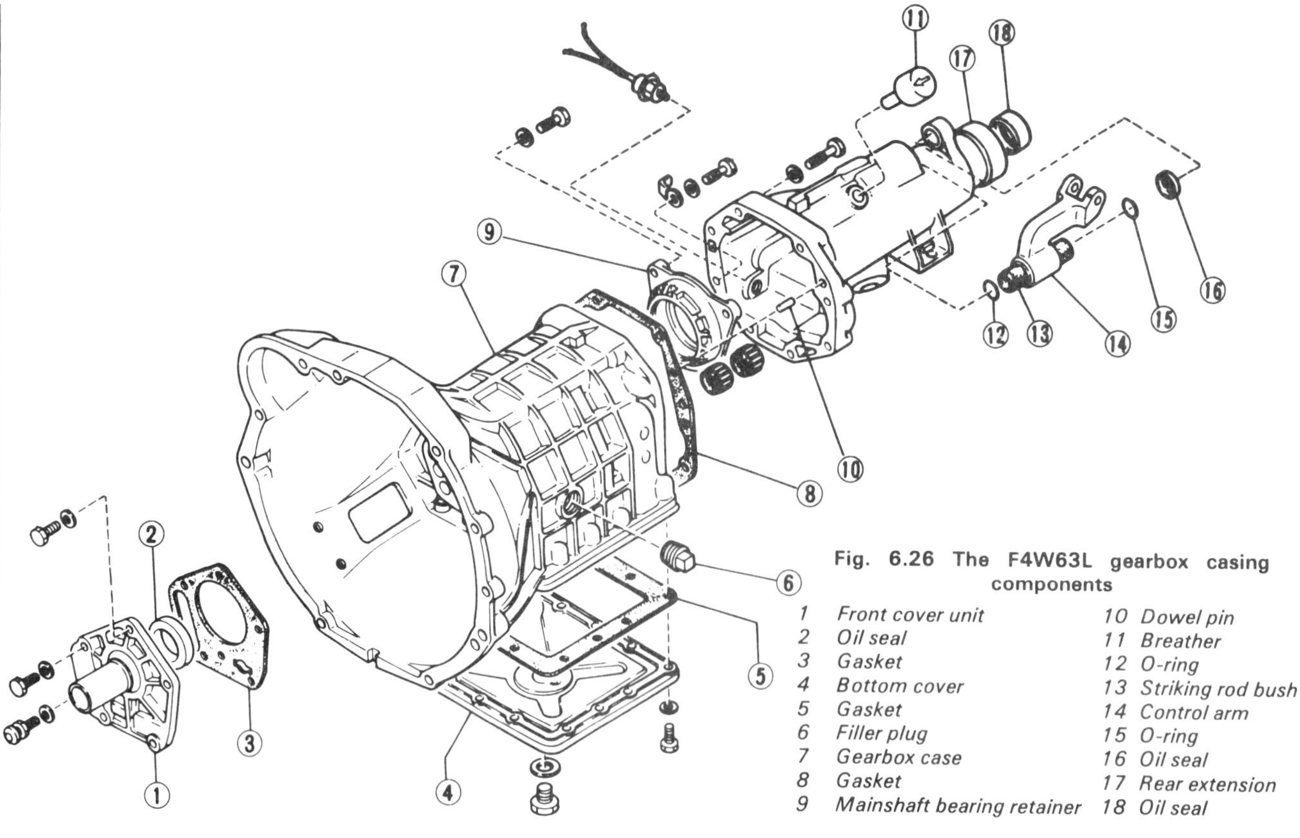

Fig. 6.26 The F4W63L gearbox casing components

1 Front cover unit	10 Dowel pin
2 Oil seal	11 Breather
3 Gasket	12 O-ring
4 Bottom cover	13 Striking rod bush
5 Gasket	14 Control arm
6 Filler plug	15 O-ring
7 Gearbox case	16 Oil seal
8 Gasket	17 Rear extension
9 Mainshaft bearing retainer	18 Oil seal

8.3a Speedometer gear and retainer

8.3b Withdrawing the speedometer gear

8.6 Magnetic plug in gearbox cover plate

8.7 Removing the reverse lamp switch

8.8 Remote control rod pin and circlip

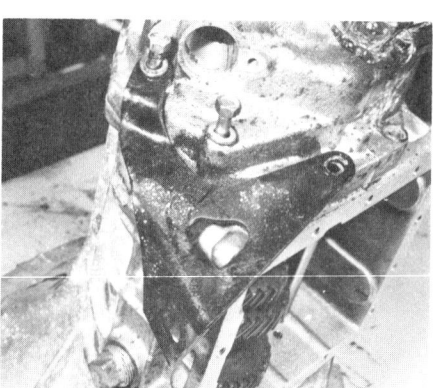

8.9 Removing extension housing bolts

8.14a Remove reverse selector rod and fork ...   8.14b ... the 3rd/4th selector rod and fork ...   8.14c ... and the 1st/2nd selector rod and fork

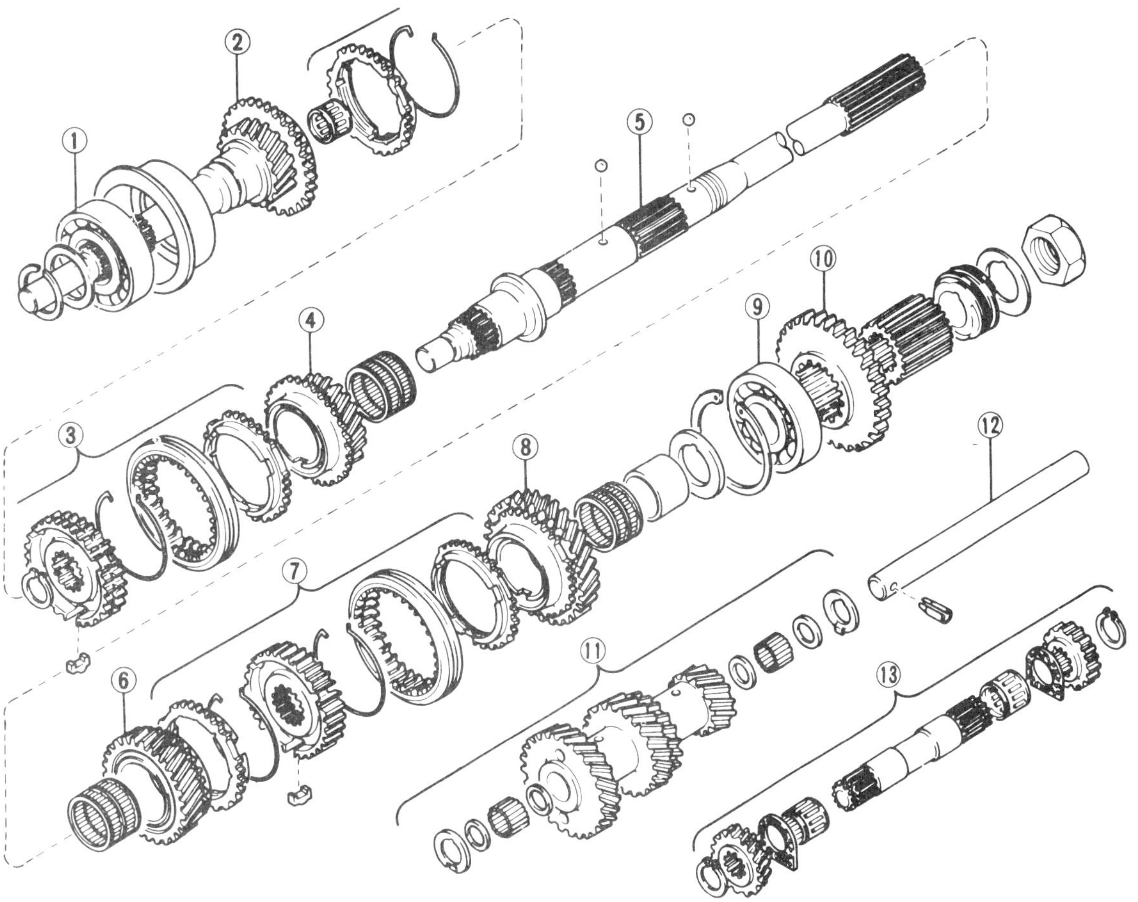

Fig. 6.27 The F4W63L gearbox gear assemblies

1	Main drive (input shaft) bearing	8	1st gear
2	Main drive (input shaft) gear	9	Mainshaft bearing
3	3rd/4th synchro assembly	10	Reverse gear
4	3rd gear	11	Counter gear assembly
5	Mainshaft	12	Countershaft
6	2nd gear	13	Idler gear assembly
7	1st/2nd synchro assembly		

Fig. 6.28 The F4W63L gearbox gear selector components

1 to 3　Check plug, spring and ball
4 to 8　Interlock plunger assembly
9　Reverse fork pin
10　Reverse pin return spring
11　Roll pin
12　Retainer pin
13　Control arm pin
14　Striking rod pin
15　Thrust washer
16　Control bush
17　Control lever bracket
18　Control spring
19　Striking pin C-ring
20　Control lever
21　Upper washer
22　Lower washer
23　Control lever washer
24　1st/2nd fork rod
25　3rd/4th fork rod
26　Reverse fork rod
27　Reverse selector fork
28　1st/2nd shift fork
29　3rd/4th fork rod
30　Control arm

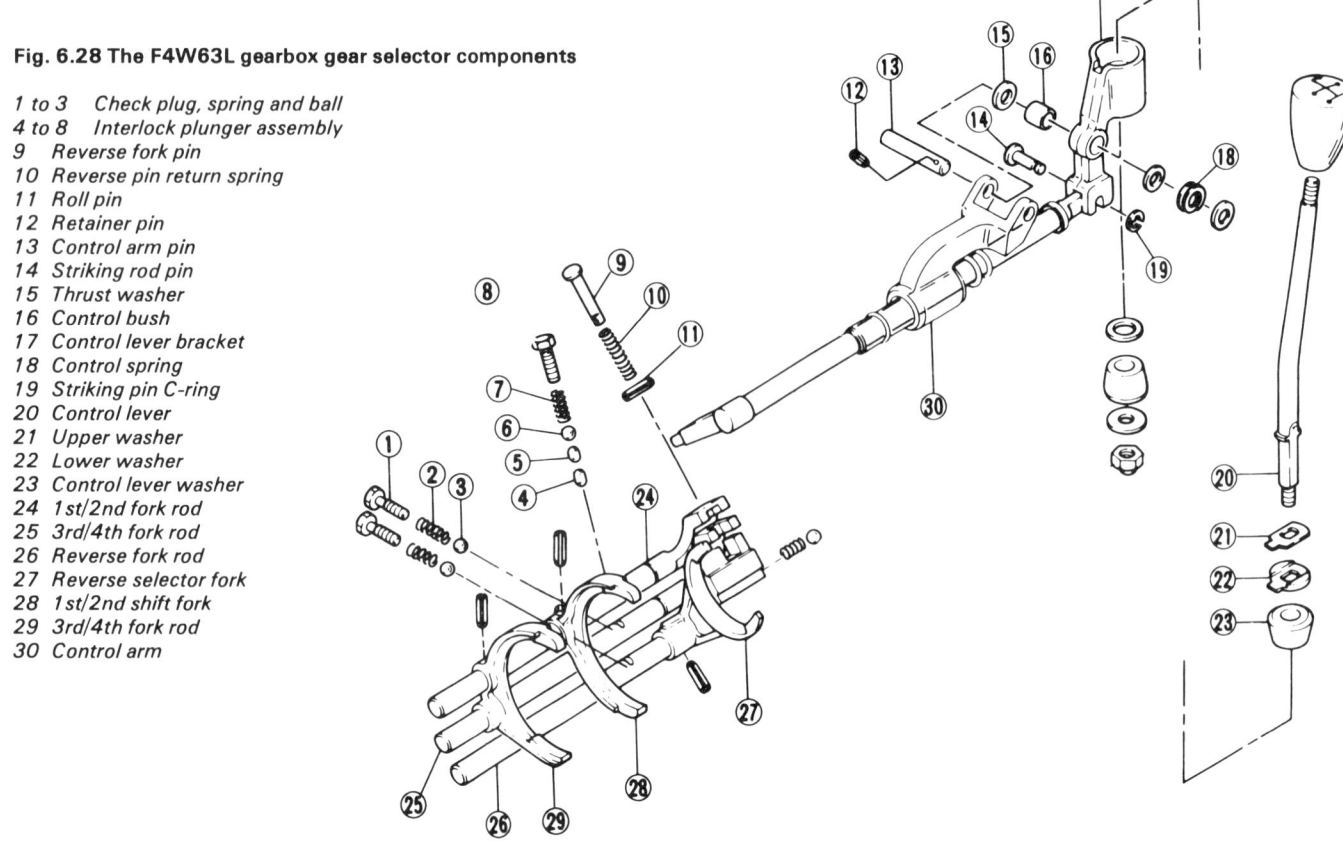

3　With the unit on the bench, unscrew and remove the speedometer pinion and housing assembly (photos).
4　Remove the dust excluding bolt from the clutch bellhousing, then extract the clutch withdrawal lever and release bearing.
5　Unbolt and remove the front cover.
6　Unbolt and remove the gearbox lower cover plate, noting the internal magnet which should be wiped clean (photo).
7　Unscrew and remove the reverse lamp (back-up lamp) switch (photo).
8　Make sure that the gears are set in the neutral position and then withdraw the pin from the remote control rod (photo).
9　Unscrew and remove the six bolts which secure the rear extension housing to the gearbox casing (photo).
10　Tap off the extension housing using a soft-faced or wooden mallet.
11　Remove the remote control rod.
12　Unscrew the detent ball plugs, and extract the springs and balls.
13　Drive out the tension pins which secure the shift forks to the selector rods.
14　Withdraw each of the selector rods and remove the shift forks (taking care to retrieve the interlock plugs (photo).
15　Using a screwdriver, move the synchronizer sleeves so that the gears engage and lock up the mainshaft.
16　Straighten the lockwasher tab and release the mainshaft end nut. Return the synchronizer sleeves to their neutral positions.
17　Using a piece of rod of suitable diameter, tap out the countershaft towards the front of the gearbox. Lift out the counter gear together with thrust washers and needle bearings.
18　Pry off the circlip which retains the reverse idler gear in position. The circlip is located at the front end of the shaft.
19　Withdraw the idler gear shaft from the rear of the gearbox casing.
20　Unscrew and remove the bolts which secure the mainshaft rear bearing retainer.
21　Withdraw the mainshaft assembly from the rear of the casing.
22　Extract the pilot bearing which is located between the mainshaft and the input shaft (main drivegear).
23　Using the wooden handle of a hammer as a drift, tap out the input

shaft from the front of the gearbox.
24　The gearbox is now completely dismantled into its major components, further operations should not be undertaken unless the facilities of a press or extractors are available.

9　Mainshaft (F4W63L) – dismantling, servicing and reassembly

1　Extract the circlip from the front end of the mainshaft.
2　Withdraw 3rd/4th synchro unit and 3rd gear.
3　The mainshaft end nut will have to be released (see paragraphs 15 and 16, of Section 8). Now unscrew and remove it, and withdraw reverse gear, reverse gear hub and the speedometer drivegear. Make sure that the speedometer gear locking ball is retained.
4　Draw off 1st gear, ball bearing and retainer from the rear end of the mainshaft. This may be carried out by using a puller having its legs engaged behind the front face of 1st gear or otherwise supporting 1st gear and pressing the mainshaft from the gear, bearing and retainer. Do not use 2nd gear front face as a pressure area during these operations or the mainshaft 1st gear spacer may collapse. Extract the thrust washer and locking ball located between the bearing and 1st gear.
5　In a similar manner to that just described in the preceding paragraph, either draw off 1st/2nd gear synchro, and 2nd gear, or press the mainshaft from them.
6　Extract the circlip and drive the mainshaft rear bearing from its retainer (photo).
7　The synchro hubs can be dismantled and serviced as described in Section 4, but do not dismantle them without reason and do not mix up the parts of the two hubs. When checking the baulk ring to cone clearances, the minimum allowable clearance is 0.0315 in (0.80 mm).
8　Examine the respective components as described in Section 6 and check the gear endplay with the figures given in the Specifications.
9　Note that paragraph 11 of Section 6 does not apply to this type of gearbox.
10　Commence reassembly by fitting 2nd gear needle roller bearing, 2nd gear and 2nd gear baulk ring (photo).

9.6 Mainshaft rear bearing and circlip

9.10 Refitting the needle roller bearing, 2nd and baulk ring to mainshaft

9.11 Fitting 1st/2nd synchro unit

9.12 Refitting 1st gear spacer

9.13a Fitting 1st gear baulk ring and needle roller bearing

9.13b Fitting 1st gear and thrust washer locking ball to mainshaft

9.13c 1st gear thrust washer retained by locking ball

9.14 Bearing ready for pressing onto mainshaft

9.15 Refitting 3rd gear, baulk ring and needle roller bearing

9.16 Fitting 3rd/4th synchro unit

9.17 Fit the selected circlip to front end of mainshaft

9.18a Fitting reverse gear

11 Refit 1st/2nd synchro unit checking that it is fitted the correct way round (photo).
12 Drive on 1st gear spacer using a piece of brass tubing (photo).
13 Refit 1st gear baulk ring, the needle bearing, 1st gear, locking ball and the thrust washer (photos).
14 Press on the mainshaft bearing (photo).
15 Refit 3rd gear needle roller bearing, 3rd gear and baulk ring (photo).
16 Refit 3rd/4th synchro unit checking that it is fitted the correct way round (photo).
17 Fit a circlip of the correct size to provide the minimum clearance between the endface of the syncho-hub and the circlip groove. Synchro hub circlip sizes:

> *0.0551 to 0.0571 in (1.40 to 1.45)*
> *0.0571 to 0.0591 in (1.45 to 1.50)*
> *0.0591 to 0.0610 in (1.50 to 1.55)*
> *0.0610 to 0.0630 in (1.55 to 1.60)*
> *0.0630 to 0.0650 in (1.60 to 1.65)*

18 To the rear end of the mainshaft, fit the reverse gear, locking ball and speedometer drivegear, lockplate and mainshaft nut. Do not tighten the nut fully at this stage (see Section 11) (photos).

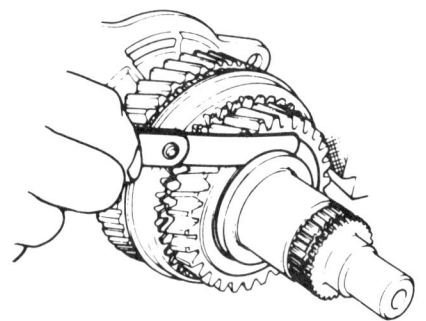

Fig. 6.29 Measure the gear endplay using feeler gauges

10 Main drivegear (F4W63L) – dismantling and reassembly

1 From the front end of the shaft extract the circlip and thrust washer.
2 Using a suitable puller or press, remove the bearing from the shaft.
3 Examine the gearteeth and splines for wear or damage, and check the bearing. Renew components as necessary.
4 Reassembly is a reversal of dismantling, but select a circlip from those listed which will provide the minimum endfloat between the face of the spacer and the circlip groove (photo). The circlips available are:

> *0.0587 to 0.0610 in (1.49 to 1.55 mm)*
> *0.0614 to 0.0638 in (1.56 to 1.62 mm)*
> *0.0638 to 0.0661 in (1.62 to 1.68 mm)*
> *0.0661 to 0.0685 in (1.68 to 1.74 mm)*
> *0.0685 to 0:0709 in (1.74 to 1.80 mm)*
> *0.0709 to 0.0732 in (1.80 to 1.86 mm)*
> *0.0732 to 0.0756 in (1.86 to 1.92 mm)*

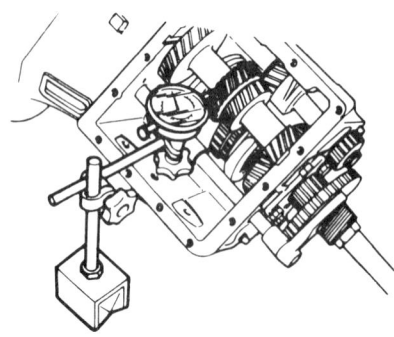

Fig. 6.30 A method of checking the gear backlash using a dial gauge

11 Gearbox (F4W63L) – reassembly

1 Using a soft faced mallet, tap the input shaft into the front of the gearbox casing (photo).
2 Refit the pilot bearing and then insert the mainshaft assembly from the rear of the casing (photo).
3 Insert and tighten the mainshaft rear bearing retainer bolts.
4 Refit the reverse idler shaft so that the identification mark is towards the rear of the gearbox. (Fig. 6.35).
5 Assemble the thrust washer and the helical-type idler gear and secure it with the circlip at the front end of the shaft (photo).
6 Now insert a 0.004 in (0.1 mm) feeler gauge between the helical-type gear and its thrust washer. Push the idler shaft fully rearwards and fit the thrust washer and spur-type gear to the rear end of the idler shaft. Secure the gear with a suitable circlip so that when the feeler gauge is withdrawn from between the helical gear and its thrust washer, the correct endfloat of between 0.004 and 0.012 in (0.10 and 0.30 mm) will be established. Note that the reverse idler shaft thrust washers must be fitted so that the sides with the oil grooves are towards the gears (photo). Circlips are available in the following thicknesses:

> *0.0413 to 0.0453 in (1.05 to 1.15 mm)*
> *0.0453 to 0.0492 in (1.15 to 1.25 mm)*
> *0.0492 to 0.0531 in (1.25 to 1.35 mm)*
> *0.0531 to 0.0571 in (1.35 to 1.45 mm)*
> *0.0571 to 0.0610 in (1.45 to 1.55 mm)*

7 Stick the countershaft thrust washers into position in the interior of the gearbox casing using a dab of thick grease. Make sure that they are securely held by their lock tabs and that the smaller washer is at the rear (photo).

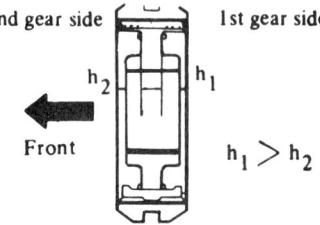

2nd gear side   1st gear side

h_2 h_1

Front $h_1 > h_2$

Fig. 6.31 Fit the 1st/2nd synchro hub facing as shown

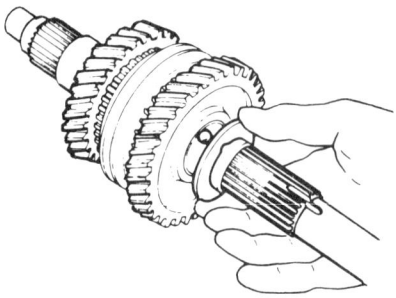

Fig. 6.32 Fit the thrust washer and ball

9.18b Lockplate and mainshaft nut fitted

10.4 Input shaft bearing thrust washer and circlip

11.1a Fitting input shaft

11.1b Mainshaft/input shaft needle roller pilot bearing

11.2 Fitting mainshaft assembly from rear of casing

11.4 Reverse idler shaft and thrust washer

11.5 Reverse idler gear and circlip at front end of shaft

11.6 Reverse idler gear and circlip at rear end of shaft

11.7 Countershaft thrust washer showing locating tap

11.8 Countershaft needle rollers

11.9 Fitting counter gear

11.11 Countershaft tension pin fitted

11.12 Tightening the mainshaft nut

11.14 Fit shift forks to synchro sleeve grooves
1 – 3rd/4th 2 – 1st/2nd

11.15 Securing 1st/2nd selector shift fork to selector rod

11.16 Inserting an interlock plunger between 1st/2nd and 3rd/4th selector rods

11.18a Fitting reverse selector fork

11.18b Correct alignment of reverse selector rod

11.19a Inserting a detent ball

11.19b Inserting detent springs

11.19c Fitting detent plugs

11.22 Remote control rod correctly engaged

11.24a Front cover gasket and countershaft tension pin correctly aligned

11.24b Front cover installation. Note the position of the clutch release lever pivot bolt

8 Using a dummy countershaft or rod, inserted through the counter gear, fit the needle rollers and washers at both ends of the counter gear, again using thick grease to retain them (21 needle rollers at each end) (photo).

9 Place the counter gear assembly into position and then insert the countershaft so that it displaces the dummy shaft or rod without dislodging the needler rollers or thrust washers (photo).

10 Now check the countergear endfloat. This should be between 0.002 and 0.004 in (0.05 and 0.15 mm) and, if otherwise, change the rear thrust washer for one of different thickness. Rear thrust washers are available as follows:

0.0925 to 0.945 in (2.35 to 2.40 mm)
0.0945 to 0.0965 in (2.40 to 2.45 mm)
0.0965 to 0.0984 in (2.45 to 2.50 mm)
0.0984 to 0.1004 in (2.50 to 2.55 mm)
0.1004 to 0.1024 in (2.55 to 2.60 mm)

11 Drive in the new retaining pin (if removed at dismantling) (photo).

12 Move the synchro sleeves to mesh the gears and lock the mainshaft. Tighten the mainshaft nut to the specified torque and bend up the lockplate (photo).

13 Return the synchro sleeves to the neutral position.

14 Engage the 1st/2nd and 3rd/4th shift forks with the sleeve grooves of the respective synchro units (photo).

15 Fit the 1st/2nd selector rod so that it passes through the shift fork and then secure the fork to the rod with a new tension pin (photo).

16 With the 1st/2nd selector rod in the neutral mode, insert the interlock plunger and then fit the 3rd/4th selector rod and secure the 3rd/4th shift fork to it using a new tension pin (photo).

17 Set the 3rd/4th selector rod in the neutral mode and insert the second interlock plunger.

18 Refit the reverse selector rod and shift fork. The slot in the reverse selector rod must be positioned as shown (photos).

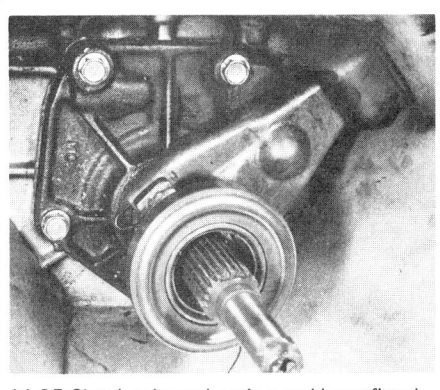

11.25 Clutch release bearing and lever fitted

11.26 Fitting gearbox lower cover plate

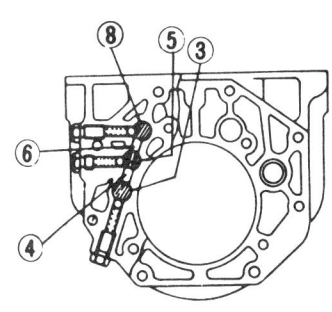

Fig. 6.33 Sectional view of the interlocking mechanism

3 1st/2nd shift rod   6 Interlock plunger
4 Interlock plunger   8 Reverse shift rod
5 3rd/4th shift rod

Fig. 6.34 The FS5W63A type gearbox case and associate components

1 Front cover
2 Oil seal
3 Ball pin bolt
4 Gearbox case
5 Breather tube
6 Reverse light switch
7 Sleeve yoke dust cover
8 Oil seal
9 Speedometer pinion
10 Speedometer sleeve
11 Rear extension
12 Adapter plate

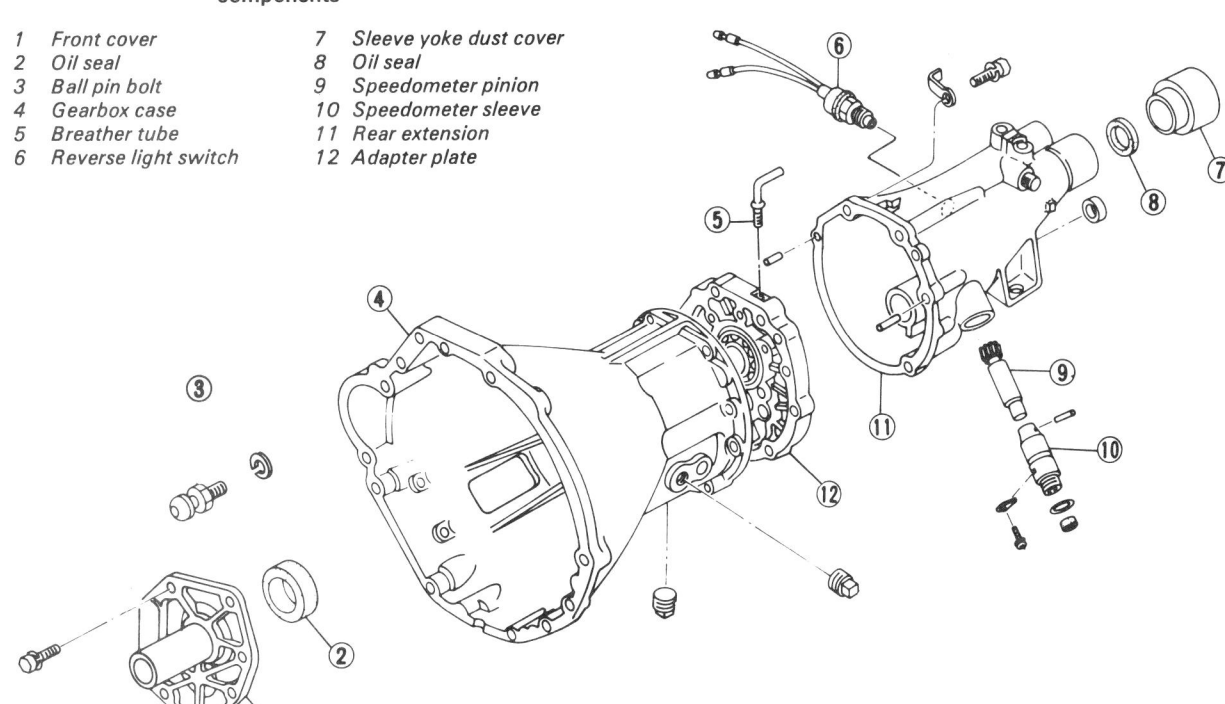

19 Insert the detent balls, springs and plugs. Apply a non-setting gasket sealant to the threads of the plugs before fitting them (photos).
20 Check the operation of the selectors and gear engagement making sure it is smooth and positive.
21 Set the gears in neutral, and then position a new gasket on the rear face of the gearbox.
22 Refit the rear extension housing making sure that before it is pushed fully home, the remote control rod engages correctly with the selector shaft dogs (photo).
23 Insert and tighten the extension housing bolts to the specified torque.
24 Refit the front cover, making sure that the gasket and countershaft roll pins are correctly aligned, and that the oil seal is not damaged as it passes over the splines of the input shaft. Tighten the securing bolts to the specified torque (photos).
25 Refit the release bearing, withdrawal lever and dust excluder (photo). (Now is the time to renew the release bearing and the clutch components if they are worn – see Chapter 5).
26 Invert the gearbox and refit the bottom cover plate using a new gasket (photo).

---

12 Gearbox (FS5W63A) – dismantling into major assemblies

1 Refer to Section 3 and follow paragraphs 1 to 11 inclusive with the exception of paragraph 7 which does not apply.
2 Using a soft head hammer, lightly tap the rear extension away from the main housing.
3 The adaptor plate and gear assemblies can now be separated from the housing. Grip and pull the mainshaft with one hand and lightly tap the main housing away from the adaptor plate as shown in Fig. 6.36 using a soft head hammer.
4 Refer to paragraph 4 of Section 3 which now applies but note that the special adaptor setting plate manufactured by Datsun is Tool No. ST22490000.

Shift forks and rods – dismantling
5 Use a suitable pin punch and drive the selector fork retaining pins from the respective fork rods.
6 Unscrew and remove the check ball plugs, and extract the springs and balls from each housing. The selector fork rods can now be driven out of the adaptor plate and the respective interlock plungers and forks removed.
Note: *It is not necessary to remove the selector rods in order to withdraw the gears and shafts.*

Mainshaft and countershaft – dismantling and removal
7 Using suitable circlip pliers, remove the circlip from the rear end of the mainshaft. The bearing must now be withdrawn and this can be achieved using a suitable puller.
8 Remove the second circlip from its position on the shaft behind the bearing.
9 Position the 1st and 2nd gears so that they are both in engagement to lock the shaft. Now relieve the staking on the nut on the mainshaft and unscrew and remove it.
10 The respective components can now be withdrawn from the mainshaft. As they are removed note their location, position and sequence of removal so that they can be refitted in the correct order.
11 Remove the speedometer drivegear and steel ball.
12 The following items can be removed separately or simultaneously as a unit as shown in Fig. 6.40.

(a) Synchro hub assembly and reverse gear
(b) 1st gear, needle roller bearing assembly and thrust washer
(c) Idler gear and needle roller bearing assembly

13 Remove the circlip and thrust washer from the rear end of the countershaft, followed by 1st counter gear. The gear will have to be withdrawn using a puller taking care not to damage the gear teeth.
14 The mainshaft can now be removed in the following manner. Support the adaptor plate and shaft assembly and lightly tap the mainshaft through the adaptor plate sufficient to allow the main drivegear and counter gear to be removed. Withdraw the mainshaft and gear assembly.
15 The gearbox major components are now removed and can be further inspected and if necessary further dismantled for repair and/or

renewal. Note that further operations should not be undertaken without the aid of a press or bearing puller. A micrometer or similar fine measuring instrument will also be required.

Mainshaft
16 Withdraw the thrust washer and steel ball followed by 2nd gear and its needle roller bearing.
17 Using a suitable puller, withdraw the bearing bush, the 3rd speed gear together with the 2nd/3rd synchromesh hub.
18 Unclip and withdraw the circlip at the front of the mainshaft, then remove the 4th/5th gear synchromesh hub assembly.
19 Withdraw 5th gear.

Main drivegear (input shaft assembly)
20 Unclip and remove the circlip using suitable pliers and then withdraw the spacer and washer.
21 The main drive bearing can now be removed using a suitable puller or press.

Counter gear (layshaft) assembly
22 Withdraw the bearing at the front using a suitable puller or press.
23 Withdraw the rear bearing in a similar manner.

---

13 Synchromesh hubs (FS5W63A) – dismantling and inspection

1 Refer to Section 4.

---

14 Rear extension (FS5W63A) – dismantling, inspection and assembly

1 Unscrew the nut and remove with washers from the striking lever. Extract the lever from the rod.
2 Withdraw the rod stopper pin and reverse selector plug, spring and plunger.
3 The striking rod and guide can now be withdrawn from the rear extension.
4 Refer to Section 5, paragraphs 3, 4 and 5 which are also applicable to this instance.
5 To reassemble the extension, use a drift tube and drive or press the new oilseal into position in the rear cover. The seal must be smeared into gear oil before fitting, including the seal lip. Smear some medium multi-purpose grease into the cavity between the seal lips, as shown in Fig. 6.43.
6 Smear the O-ring and plunger grooves in the striker rod with some general purpose grease and fit the O-ring.
7 Refit the striker rod carefully into the extension housing.
8 Relocate the striker lever assembly and retain with nut and washers. Refit the stopper pin.
9 Refit the reverse plunger, spring and plug.

---

15 Gearbox components (FS5W63A) – inspection

1 In general the gearbox inspection procedures should follow those details given in Section 6, paragraphs 1 to 5 but note that the baulk ring to cone clearance must be at least 0.031 in (0.8 mm) otherwise renew the ring.
2 If the adaptor plate bearing is to be removed, unscrew the retainer plate screws. These will probably be tight and will require the use of a good size cross-head screwdriver and possible a mole grip wrench around its shaft to give assistance. The bearing can be driven or pressed out. Reassemble in the reverse order but torque tighten the retaining screws to 5.8 to 9.4 lbf ft (0.8 to 1.3 kgf m). Stake each screw edge as shown using a punch (Fig. 6.44) to prevent them working loose.
3 Measure the endplay of the gears as shown in Fig. 6.46 using feeler gauges. The normal gear endplay is as given in the Specifications.
4 Check all bearings for wear or signs of damage after they have been cleaned. Renew any suspect or defective parts.
5 Check the condition of the circlips but don't get them mixed up as they are of selected thicknesses. The circlips should generally be renewed as a matter of practise and if other corresponding com-

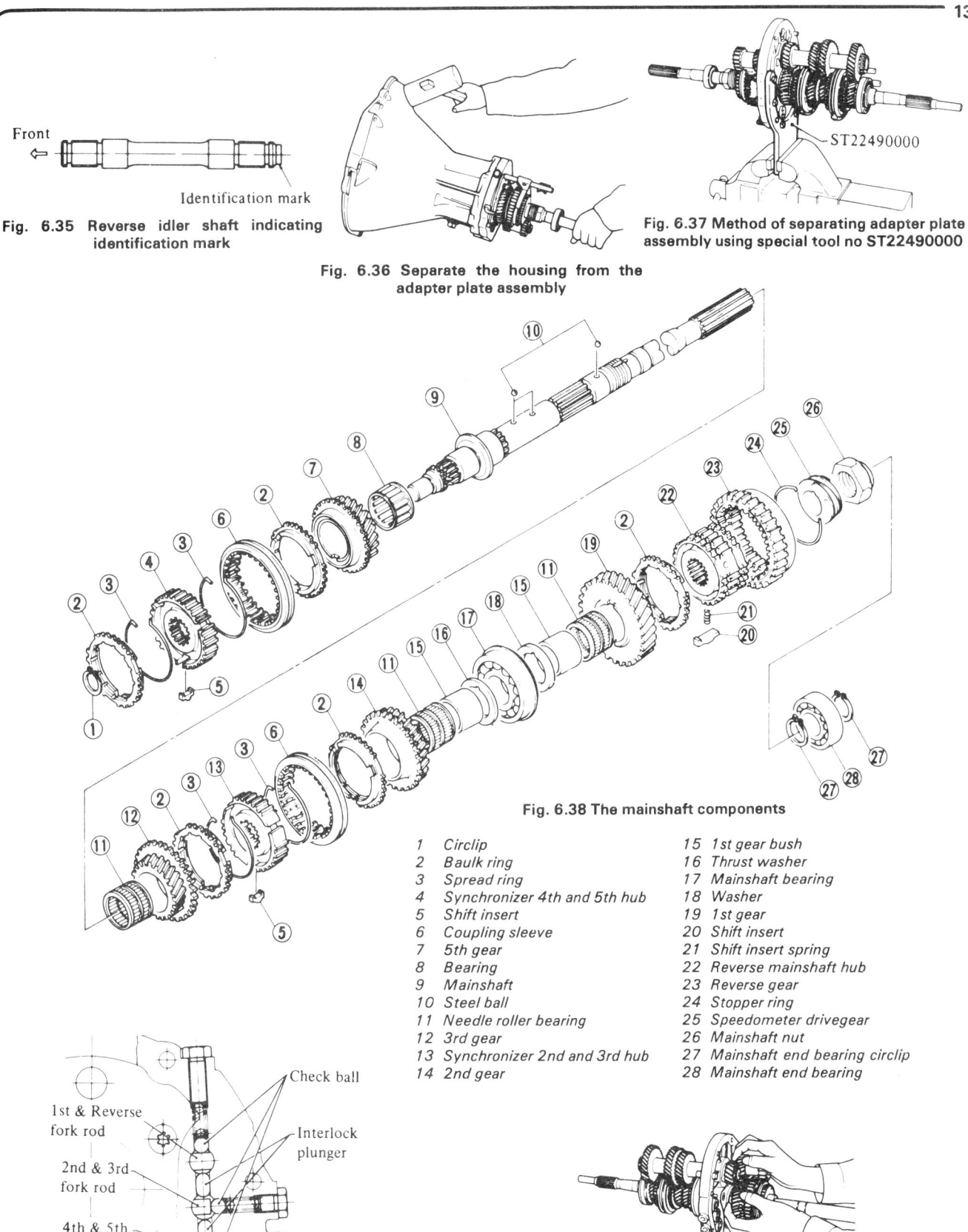

Front ⇐

Identification mark

Fig. 6.35 Reverse idler shaft indicating identification mark

Fig. 6.36 Separate the housing from the adapter plate assembly

ST22490000

Fig. 6.37 Method of separating adapter plate assembly using special tool no ST22490000

Fig. 6.38 The mainshaft components

1 Circlip	15 1st gear bush
2 Baulk ring	16 Thrust washer
3 Spread ring	17 Mainshaft bearing
4 Synchronizer 4th and 5th hub	18 Washer
5 Shift insert	19 1st gear
6 Coupling sleeve	20 Shift insert
7 5th gear	21 Shift insert spring
8 Bearing	22 Reverse mainshaft hub
9 Mainshaft	23 Reverse gear
10 Steel ball	24 Stopper ring
11 Needle roller bearing	25 Speedometer drivegear
12 3rd gear	26 Mainshaft nut
13 Synchronizer 2nd and 3rd hub	27 Mainshaft end bearing circlip
14 2nd gear	28 Mainshaft end bearing

Check ball

1st & Reverse fork rod

Interlock plunger

2nd & 3rd fork rod

4th & 5th fork rod

Fig. 6.39 The check ball and interlock plunger positions

Fig. 6.40 Method of removing 1st gear, reverse idler and the reverse main gear assemblies

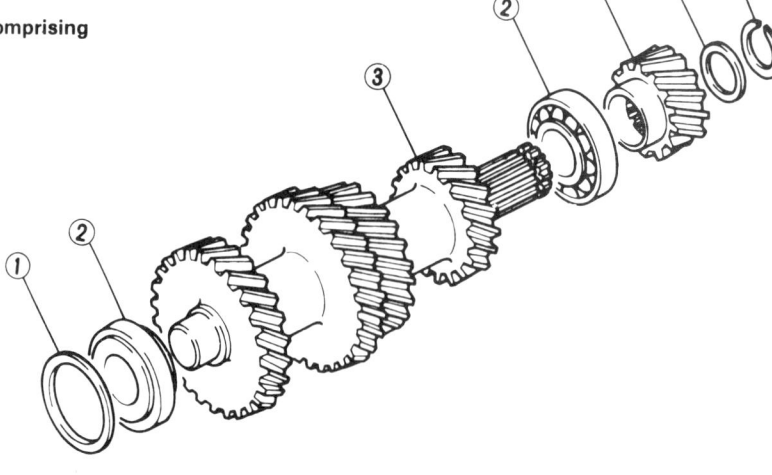

Fig. 6.41 The countershaft gear assembly comprising

1 *Shim*
2 *Bearing*
3 *Countershaft gear unit*
4 *Main drivegear shaft*
5 *Pilot roller bearing*

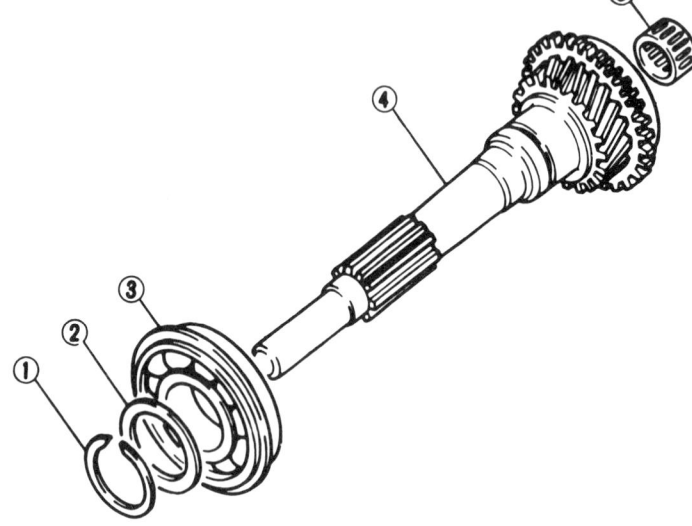

Fig. 6.42 The main drive gear (input shaft)

1 *Circlip*
2 *Spacer*
3 *Bearing*
4 *Main drive gear (input shaft)*
5 *Pilot roller bearing*

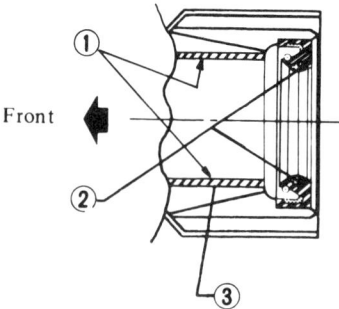

Fig. 6.43 Lubricate the rear extension oil seal as shown

1 *Gear oil*
2 *Medium general purpose grease*
3 *Bush*

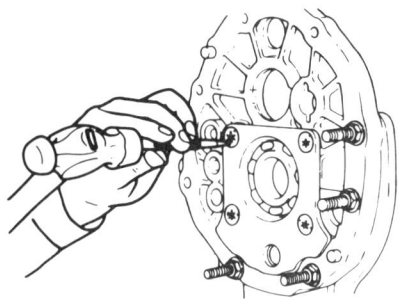

Fig. 6.44 Stake punch the screw heads to secure

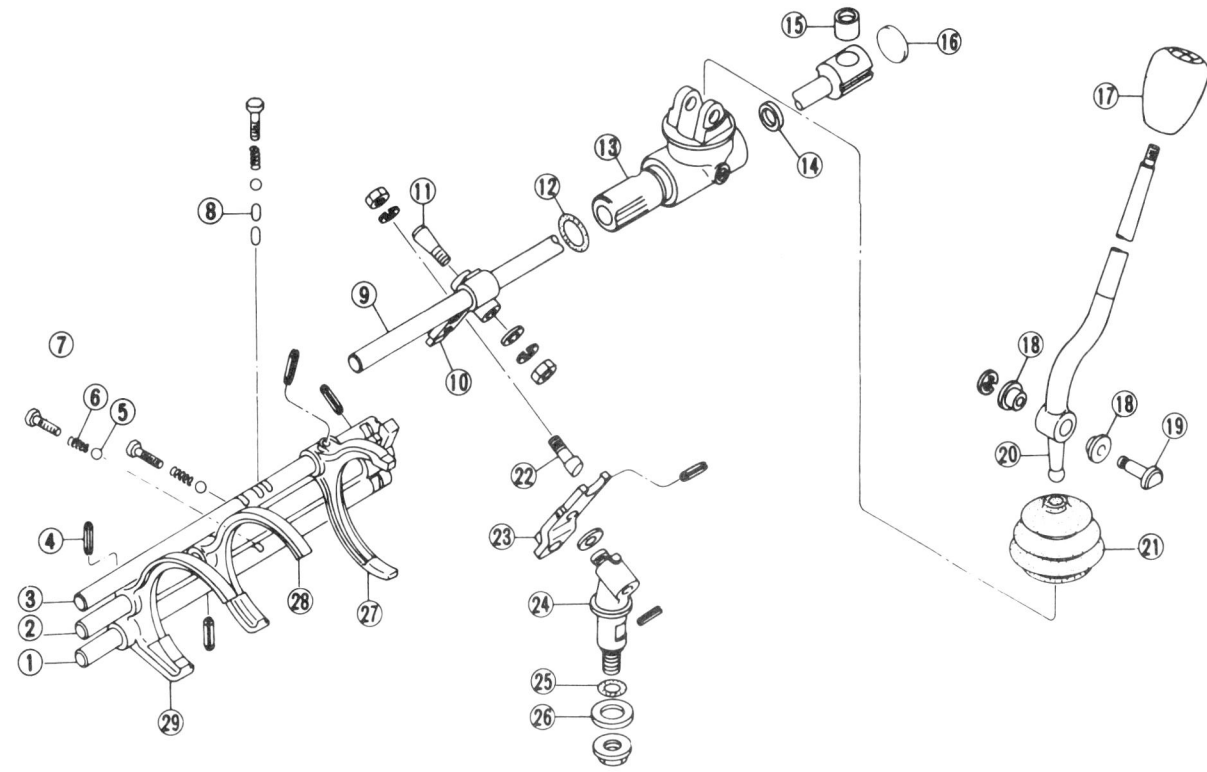

Fig. 6.45 The selector components

1	4th/5th fork rod	6	Spring
2	2nd/3rd fork rod	7	Plug
3	1st/Reverse fork rod	8	Plunger
4	Securing pin	9	Striker rod
5	Check ball	10	Striker lever

11	Lock pin	16	Plug
12	O-ring	17	Knob
13	Striker guide	18	Bush (control pin)
14	Oil seal	19	Control arm pin
15	Bush	20	Lever

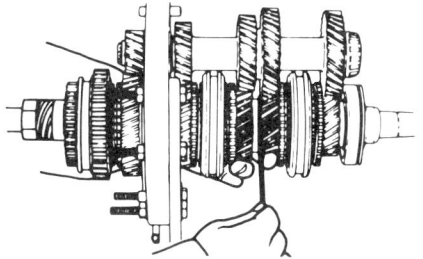

Fig. 6.46 Check the gear endplay using a feeler gauge as shown

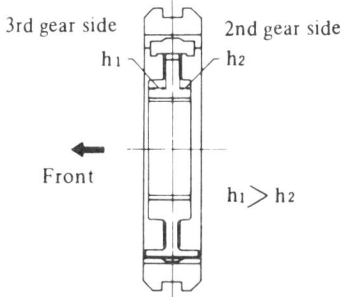

Fig. 6.47 This shows the offset position of the 2nd/3rd gear synchronizer and it's directional location

3rd gear side   2nd gear side

h_1 h_2

Front

$h_1 > h_2$

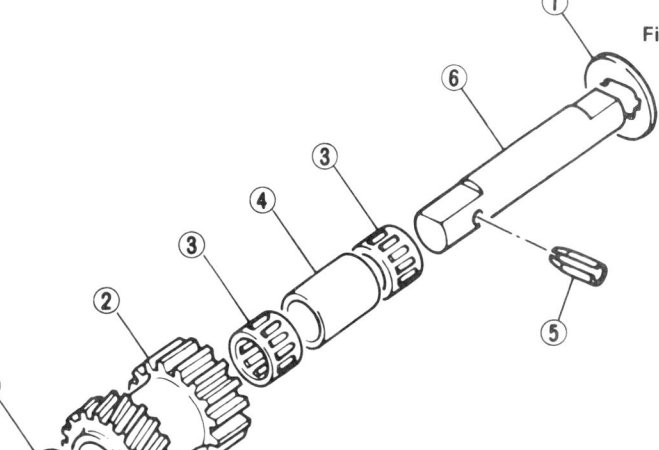

Fig. 6.48 The reverse idler gear and components

1	Thrust washer	4	Spacer
2	Idler gear	5	Securing pin
3	Bearing (roller)	6	Shaft

ponents are being renewed then it will be advisable to get an assortment of thicknesses to compensate for any variation in fitting tolerances (sizes are given in the assembly instructions).

6   Thrust washers are almost certainly fairly worn if the gearbox is of any age, and should therefore be renewed as a matter of course.

7   Any wear or damage of the counter gear assembly will necessitate the renewal of the complete assembly. When renewing the countershaft assembly it is advisable to also renew the corresponding mainshaft gears so that they wear in equally.

8   Examine the reverse gears and renew if badly worn or damaged.

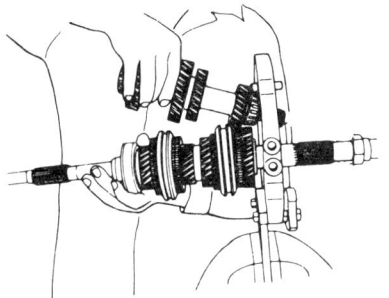

Fig. 6.49 Refitting the counter gear

16 Gearbox (FS5W63A) – reassembly

1   Refer to Section 7, paragraphs 1 to 4 inclusive.

Mainshaft assembly

2   Lubricate and fit the 5th gear needle roller bearing into position on the mainshaft. Slide the 5th gear into place over the bearing and then locate the baulk ring onto the gear.

3   Refit the 5th gear synchromesh hub unit, and then select a circlip of the correct thickness to secure and give the smallest posible clearance between the circlip and the hub endface. Circlip thicknesses available are as follows:

0.0551 to 0.0571 in (1.40 to 1.45 mm)
0.0571 to 0.0591 in (1.45 to 1.50 mm)
0.0591 to 0.0610 in (1.50 to 1.55 mm)
0.0610 to 0.0630 in (1.55 to 1.60 mm)
0.0630 to 0.0650 in (1.60 to 1.65 mm)

Check that the circlip is fully located in its groove.

4   Onto the rear of the mainshaft fit the 3rd gear and its needle roller bearing. Lubricate the bearing well before fitting.

5   Position the 3rd gear baulk ring against the gear and slide the 2nd/3rd synchromesh hub over the shaft. Refer to Fig. 6.47 which indicates the correct hub position.

6   The 2nd gear bush and thrust washer can now be fitted by tapping into position using a soft head hammer.

7   Lubricate and fit the needle roller bearing over the bush together with 2nd gear and its baulk ring. Locate the steel ball and thrust washer.

8   The mainshaft is now ready for assembly to the adaptor plate.

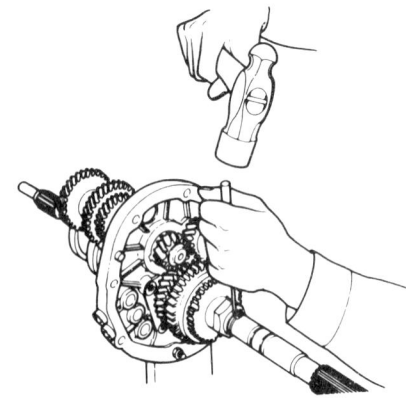

Fig. 6.50 Using a punch stake the nut in line with shaft groove to secure

Main drivegear (input shaft)

9   Press or drive the new bearing onto the mainshaft using a suitable tube drift. The bearing must be fully located to enable the circlip groove in the shaft to be fully clear when the spacer washer is assembled.

10   Fit the spacer washer and select a circlip of the required thickness to eliminate any end clearance. The available circlip thicknesses are:

0.0587 to 0.0610 in (1.49 to 1.55 mm)
0.0614 to 0.0638 in (1.56 to 1.62 mm)
0.0638 to 0.0661 in (1.62 to 1.68 mm)
0.0661 to 0.0685 in (1.68 to 1.74 mm)
0.0685 to 0.0709 in (1.74 to 1.80 mm)
0.0709 to 0.0732 in (1.80 to 1.86 mm)
0.0732 to 0.0756 in (1.86 to 1.92 mm)

Check that the circlip is fully located in it's groove.

Counter gear and reverse idler gear

11   Press or drift the respective front and rear counter gear bearings into position using suitable tube drifts.

12   Lubricate the reverse idler shaft and locate the needle bearing spacer, and a needle roller bearing on each side of it. Fit the reverse idler gear over the bearings and locate the thrust washers on each end noting the side face of each washer that is coloured brown must be positioned towards the gears.

Gear assemblies to adaptor plate

13   With the adaptor plate securely held, fit the mainshaft into position, tapping lightly with a soft head hammer, but allow for a thrust washer to bearing clearance of 0.39 in (10 mm).

14   If not already fitted, locate the baulk ring to the main drivegear

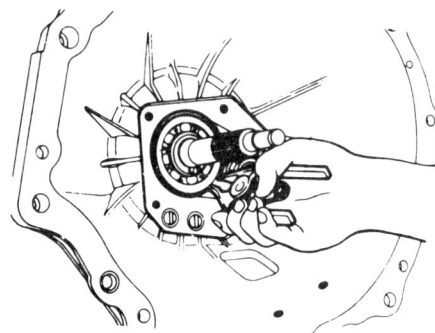

Fig. 6.51 Fitting the bearing circlip

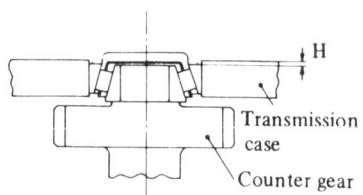

Fig. 6.52 Check depth of bearing front face to gearbox case to calculate correct shim requirement

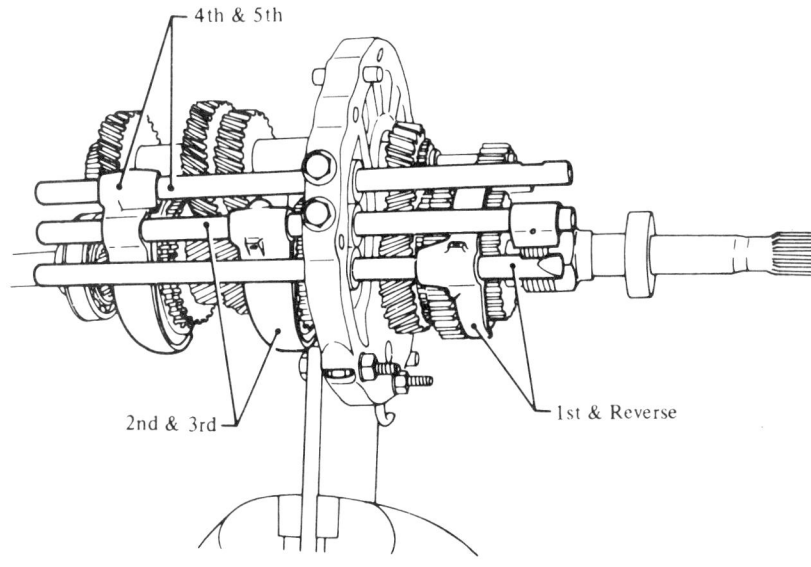

4th & 5th

2nd & 3rd

1st & Reverse

Fig. 6.53 The shift fork and rod positions

cone surface.

15 Lubricate the mainshaft pilot roller bearing and insert it into position in the main drivegear shaft.

16 Fit the main drivegear into position on the mainshaft and support with one hand.

17 Now refit the counter gear unit into position so that it meshes with corresponding mainshaft and drivegears. This can be a fiddly operation and care must be taken not to force or damage the gears or bearings during assembly.

18 When the respective gear assemblies are in position, support them by hand and get an assistant to drive the mainshaft fully home into the adaptor plate, together with the main drivegear and counter gear. Special care must be taken during this operation to keep the respective assemblies in line with each other and again, do not use excessive force to achieve full assembly to the adaptor plate.

19 Press or drift the 1st counter gear onto the counter shaft using a suitable drift tube. Secure in position with spacer washer and circlip. Fit the steel ball and thick thrust washer onto the rear of the mainshaft.

20 Slide the needle bearing bush and bearing into position followed by 1st gear. The synchromesh hub (incorporating reverse gear) can now be fitted together with the baulk ring.

21 Refit the idler gear assembly.

22 Fit and initially tighten the mainshaft nut. Position 1st and 2nd gears so that they are simultaneously locked to prevent the mainshaft from turning then tighten the nut to the specified torque as given in the Specifications. Stake punch the nut in line with the shaft groove to secure.

23 Disengage the 1st and 2nd gears and then check the respective gear endfloats as given in Section 15.

24 Measure and select a circlip that is 0.043 in (1.1 mm) thick and fit it in the mainshaft groove at the front of the end bearing.

25 Fit the mainshaft end bearing using a tube drift to press or drive into position and a circlip is then fitted to its rear side groove in the mainshaft. Select a circlip of suitable thickness that will eliminate any endfloat. Circlips for this application are available as follows:

0.043 in (1.1 mm)
0.047 in (1.2 mm)
0.051 in (1.3 mm)
0.055 in (1.4 mm)

Selector forks and rods – reassembly

26 Commence the reassembly of the selector forks and rods by refitting the 1st/reverse fork rod through the adaptor plate and fork and locate in the neutral position. Insert the interlock plunger into position in the adaptor plate.

27 Refit the 2nd/3rd selector rod and engage with the 2nd/3rd shift fork and in the second hole of the 4th/5th selector fork as shown. With

the rod located in its neutral position the interlock plunger can be fitted.

28 The 4th/5th selector rod can now be fitted and located through the first hole of the 4th/5th selector fork.

29 With the holes of the selector forks and rods in exact alignment, locate and drive the new roll retaining pins into position so that they are flush with the outside surface of the forks.

30 The check balls, springs and plugs can now be fitted, but to prevent them from working loose, apply some locking sealant to the threads of the plugs. Note that the plug for the 1st/reverse rod is longer than the other two.

31 On completion, check the operation of the selectors. Assuming that the components have been well lubricated during assembly, the gears should engage smoothly and precisely.

---

17 Gearbox (FS5W63A) – major components assembly

1   Check that the respective mating surfaces of the adaptor plate and the transmission case are perfectly clean and then smear them both with an even application of sealant.

2   The adaptor plate assembly and gearbox casing can now be reunited. Support the adaptor plate and lightly tap the gearbox case into position aligning the dowel pin with its hole in the casing.

3   If removed, refit the new counter gear and main drive bearings into the front of the casing. Press or drive them into position using a suitable tube drift.

4   Check that the main drive shaft rotates freely and then fit the circlip to the main drive bearing to secure in position.

Rear extension

5   Ensure that the mating surfaces of the rear extension and the adaptor plate are perfectly clean and smooth, then apply an even layer of sealant to both surfaces.

6   Select 5th gear, and then carefully refit the rear extension, but take care not to dislodge the shaft arm from the striking pin. The shift arm must engage with the 4th/5th selector fork rod. The striking lever pin is then fitted into the other selector fork rods.

7   When the rear extension is fully positioned and located over the adaptor plate dowel pin, refit the retaining through bolts and tighten progressively to the specified torque. Don't forget to refit the cable clip under the head of the top right-hand bolt.

8   Grease the plunger and refit it into the extension case, followed by the springs and plug. Smear the threads of the plug with a locking sealer to prevent it working loose. Tighten the plug to the specified torque.

9   Refit the speedometer pinion unit and the reversing light switch and secure.

Front cover

10 Stand the gearbox on its rear end and support it in this position while rotating the main drive shaft. This will ensure that the tapered roller bearing of the counter gear is fully positioned so that an accurate measurement can be taken to calculate the shim requirement.
11   The shim requirement can be measured using a suitable depth gauge to find the height difference between the front face of the bearing cup (outer race) and the front face of the gearbox case. Select shims from those available so that the top face of the shim and the gearbox case front face are flush. Shims are available in thicknesses from a minimum size of 0.0531 in (1.350 mm), increasing in increments of 0.0010 in (0.025 mm) to a maximum thickness of 0.0699 in (1.775 mm).

12 Smear the selected shim/s with a medium general purpose grease and locate it onto the bearing front face.
13 Check that the mating surfaces of the front cover and gearcase are perfectly clean, apply some sealant solution evenly to both surfaces, and carefully fit the front cover into position. The lips of the oilseal in the cover should be lubricated with oil to assist in the fitting of the cover, and prevent distortion of the rubber when being fitted.
14 Smear the threads of the cover through bolts with some sealant and then fit and tighten them to the specified torque.
15 Refit the clutch withdrawal lever assembly (see Chapter 5), and refit the rubber dust cover.
16 Before fitting into the car, check the operation of the gear selectors and ensure that all gears can be selected smoothly.

18 Fault diagnosis – manual transmission

Symptom	Reason/s
Weak or ineffective synchromesh	Synchro cones worn or damaged
	Baulk rings worn
	Defective synchro unit
Jumps out of gear	Worn interlock plunger
	Worn detent ball
	Weak or broken detent spring
	Worn shift fork or synchro sleeve groove
	Worn gear
Excessive noise	Incorrect oil grade
	Oil level too low
	Worn gear teeth
	Worn mainshaft bearings
	Worn thrust washers
	Worn input or mainshaft splines
Difficult gear changing or selection	Incorrect clutch free movement

Chapter 6 Part B Automatic transmission

Contents

Specifications

Type	. . . .	JATCO 3N71B, three forward speeds and reverse, three element torque converter with planetary geartrain

Ratios

1st	. . . .	2.458 : 1
2nd	. . . .	1.458 : 1
3rd	. . . .	1.000 : 1
Reverse	. . . .	2.182 : 1

Engine idling speed . . . . 600 rpm in 'D' (800 rpm with air-conditioning system)

Stall speed . . . . 1900 to 2200 rpm

Fluid capacity . . . . 9.5 Imp.pt (5.5 litres, 11.6 US pt)

Fluid type . . . . Dexron

Torque wrench settings	lbf ft	kgf m
Driveplate to crankshaft bolts	100 to 116	13.8 to 16.0
Driveplate to torque converter	35	4.8
Torque converter housing to engine	35	4.8
Transmission casing to converter housing	40	5.5
Transmission casing to rear extension	20	2.8
Fluid cooler connection to transmission	35	4.8
Selector range lever nut	25	3.5

19 General description

The automatic transmission unit fitted in some models is the JATCO 3N71B.

The unit provides three forward ratios and one reverse. Changing of the forward gear ratios is completely automatic in relation to the vehicle speed and engine torque input and is dependent upon the vacuum pressure in the manifold and the vehicle road speed to actuate the gear change mechanism at the precise time.

The transmission has six selector positions:

P – parking position which locks the output shaft to the interior wall of the transmission housing. This is a safety device for use when the vehicle is parked on an incline. The engine may be started with 'P' selected and this position should always be selected when adjusting the engine while it is running. Never attempt to select 'P' when the vehicle is in motion.

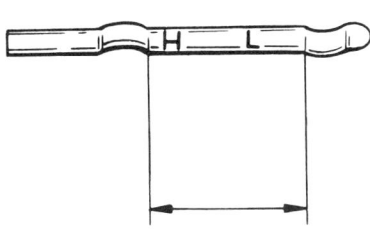

Fig. 6.54 Maintain the level in the range indicated

R – reverse gear.

N – neutral. Select this position to start the engine or when idling in traffic for long periods.

D – drive, for all normal motoring conditions.

2 – locks the transmission in second gear for wet road conditions or steep hill climbing or descents. The engine can be over revved in this position. The maximum speed in this gear should not exceed 66 mph (105 kph) or for USA models 70 mph (110 kph). Never change down into this gear at speeds above those given.

1 – The selection of this ratio above road speeds of approximately 37 mph (60 kph) or 40 mph (65 kph) for USA models will engage 2nd gear but as the speed drops below these speeds the transmission will engage first gear. This position gives maximum retardation on steep gradients.

Due to the complexity of the automatic transmission unit, any internal adjustment or servicing should be left to a Datsun agent or automatic transmission specialist. The information given in this Chapter is therefore confined to those operations which are considered within the scope of the home mechanic. An automatic transmission should give many ten of thousands of miles service provided normal maintenance and adjustment is carried out. When the unit finally requires major overhaul, consideration should be given to exchanging the old transmission for a factory reconditioned one, the removal and refitting being well within the capabilities of the home mechanic as described later in this Chapter. The hydraulic fluid does not require periodic draining or refilling, but the fluid level must be regularly checked (see next Section).

Periodically clean the outside of the transmission housing as the accumulation of dirt and oil is liable to cause overheating of the unit under extreme conditions.

Adjust the engine idling speed as specified, (see Chapter 3 for further details).

20 Fluid level – checking

1   Run the vehicle on the road until normal operating temperature is attained.

2   With the engine idling, select each gear position in turn and then place the speed selector lever in 'P'.

3   Allow the engine to continue to idle and after a period of two minutes, withdraw the dipstick, wipe it on a piece of clean lint-free cloth; re-insert it, quickly withdrawing it and reading off the oil level.

4   Top-up as necessary but do not overfill.

5   Switch off the engine.

6   The need for frequent topping-up indicates a leak either in the transmission unit itself, or from the fluid cooler or connecting pipes.

21 Automatic transmission – removal and refitting

1   Removal of the engine and automatic transmission as a combined unit is described in Chapter 1 of this manual. Where it is decided to remove the transmission leaving the engine in position in the vehicle, proceed as follows.

2   Disconnect the battery earth lead.

3   Jack the vehicle to an adequate working height and support on stands or blocks. Alternatively position the vehicle over a pit.

4   Disconnect the exhaust downpipe from the manifold.

5   Disconnect the leads from the starter inhibitor switch.

6   Disconnect the wire from the downshift solenoid.

7   Disconnect the vacuum pipe from the vacuum capsule which is located just forward of the downshift solenoid.

8   Separate the selector lever from the selector linkage.

9   Disconnect the speedometer drive cable from the rear extension housing.

10   Disconnect the fluid filler tubes. Plug the opening.

11   Disconnect the fluid cooler tubes from the transmission casing and plug the openings.

12   Remove the propeller shaft; for further information see Chapter 7.

13   Support the engine sump with a jack; use a block of wood to prevent damage to the surface of the sump.

14   Remove the rubber plug from the lower part of the engine rear plate. Mark the torque converter housing and driveplate in relation to each other for exact alignment.

15   Unscrew and remove the four bolts which secure the torque converter to the driveplate. Access to each of these bolts, in turn is obtained by rotating the engine slowly, using a wrench on the crankshaft pulley bolt.

16   Unbolt and withdraw the starter motor.

17   Support the transmission with a jack (preferably a trolley type).

18   Detach the rear transmission mounting from the transmission housing and the vehicle body.

19   Unscrew and remove the transmission to engine securing bolts.

20   Lower the two jacks sufficiently to allow the transmission unit to be withdrawn from below and to the rear of the vehicle. The help of an

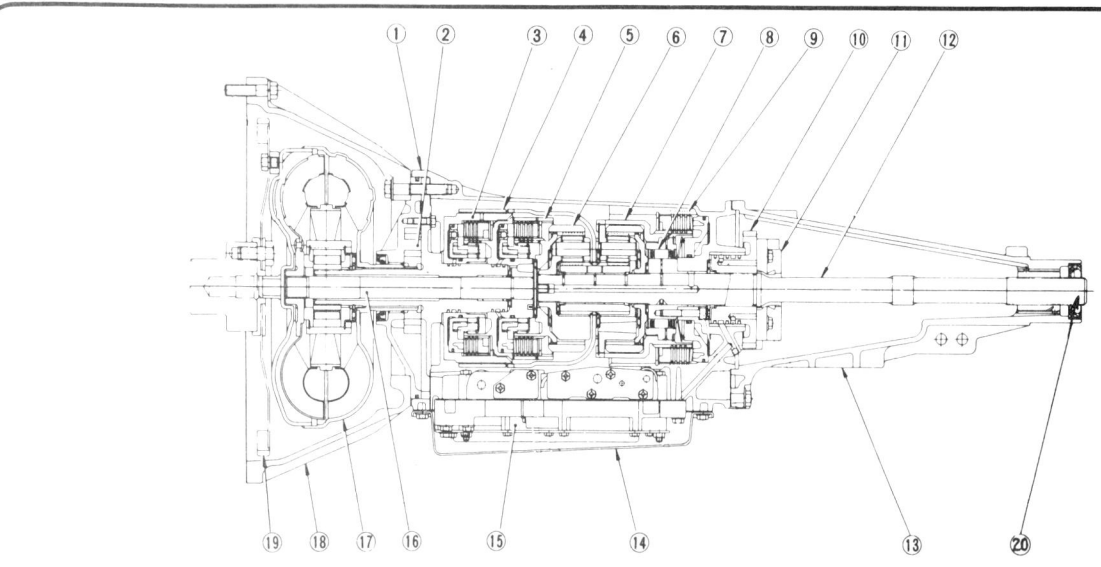

Fig. 6.55 Sectional view of the automatic transmission unit

1	Transmission housing	6	Front planetary gear	11	Governor	16	Input shaft
2	Oil pump	7	Rear planetary gear	12	Output shaft	17	Torque converter
3	Front clutch	8	One way clutch	13	Rear extension	18	Converter housing
4	Brake band	9	Low/reverse brake	14	Sump	19	Driveplate
5	Rear clutch	10	Oil distributor	15	Control valve	20	Rear extension oil seal

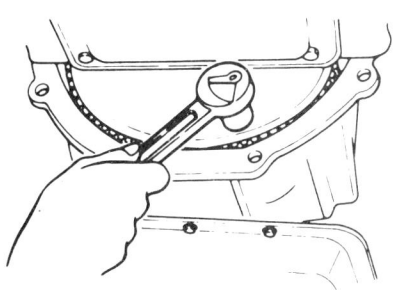

Fig. 6.56 Removing driveplate/converter bolt

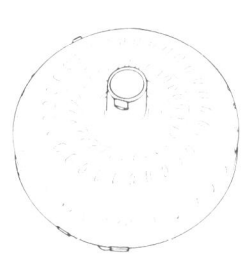

Fig. 6.57 Torque converter alignment notch

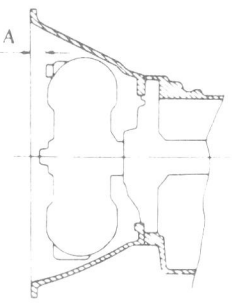

Fig. 6.58 Torque converter fitted dimension measured at 'A'

Fig. 6.59 Automatic transmission selector linkage

1 Control lever knob
2 Pusher
3 Control lever
D Retainer
E Pivot
F Range lever nut
G Bracket nuts
H Trunnion nuts

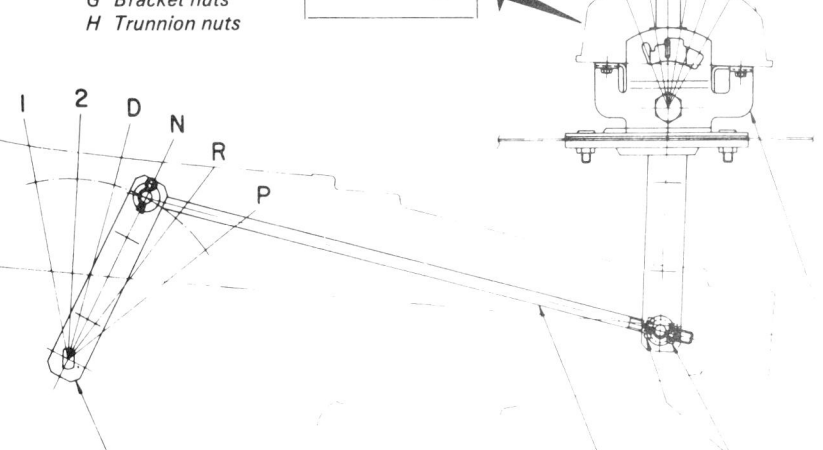

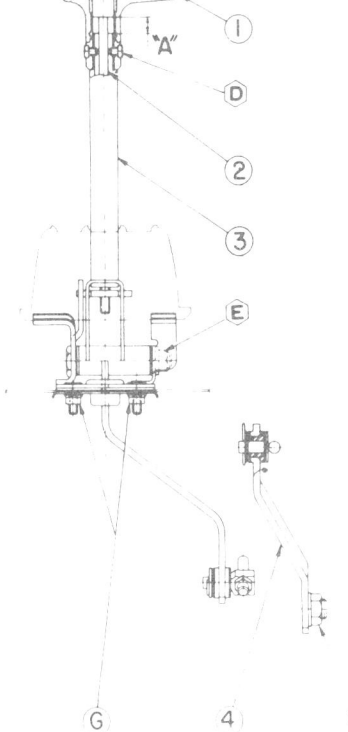

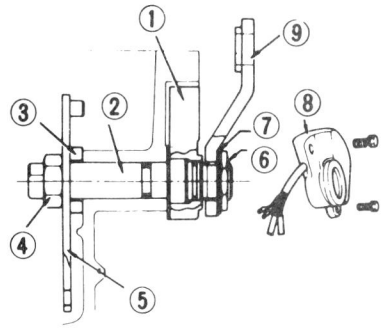

Fig. 6.60 Starter inhibitor and reverse lamp switch

1 Switch	6 Washer
2 Shaft	7 Nut
3 Washer	8 Switch (detached)
4 Nut	9 Range select lever
5 Plate	

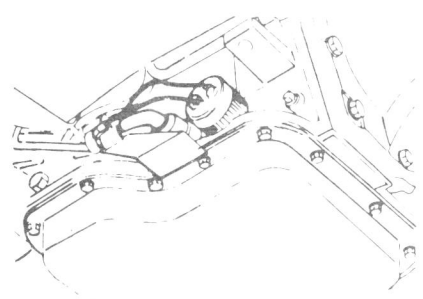

Fig. 6.61 The downshift solenoid location

assistant will probably be required due to the weight of the unit. Do not forget that the transmission is still filled with fluid. If necessary, this can be drained by removing the sump or standing the unit on end to allow the fluid to drain from the extension housing.

21 Refitting is basically the reverse of the removal procedure but should the torque converter have been separated from the main assembly, ensure that the notch on the converter is correctly aligned with the corresponding one on the oil pump. To check that the torque converter has been correctly fitted, the dimension 'A' should exceed 0.846 in (21.5 mm). See Fig. 6.58.

22 Tighten all bolts to the specified torque settings. Refill the unit with the correct grade and quantity of fluid if any was spilled or drained.

23 Check the operation of the inhibitor switch and the selector linkage and adjust, if necessary, as described later in this Chapter.

22 Selector linkage – removal and refitting

1 Remove the two small screws which secure the knob to the speed selector lever. Remove the knob.

2 Remove the console from the transmission tunnel.

3 Unbolt the selector lever bracket and the lever on the side of the transmission, and withdraw the complete selector linkage.

4 Refitting is the reverse of the removal procedure but adjust the linkage as described in the following Section before fitting the control knob.

23 Selector linkage – adjustment

1 Set dimension 'A' (Fig. 6.59) with the control knob removed, then fit the control knob again. Dimension 'A' = 0.43 to 0.47in (11 to 12 mm).

2 Check dimension 'B' (Fig. 6.59) and adjust, if necessary, by rotating the pusher. Dimension 'B' = 0.004 to 0.020 in (0.1 to 0.5 mm).

3 Loosen trunnion nuts 'H' (Fig. 6.59), set the control lever and selector lever at 'N' and obtain clearance 'C' by adjustment of the nuts as necessary. Dimension 'C' = 0.04 in (1 mm).

4 Ensure that the linkage operates satisfactorily throughout the selection range.

24 Kick-down switch and downshift solenoid – checking

1 If the kick-down facility fails to operate or operates at an incorrect change point, first check the security of the switch on the accelerator pedal arm and the wiring between the switch and the solenoid.

2 Turn the ignition key so that the ignition and oil pressure lamps illuminate but without operating the starter motor. Depress the accelerator pedal fully and as the switch actuates, a distinct click should be heard from the solenoid. Where this is absent a new switch or solenoid must be installed. **Note:** *when the solenoid is removed,*

fluid will drain out. This can be re-used if collected in a clean container, do not forget to refill with fluid on completion.

25 Starter inhibitor and reverse lamp switch – testing and adjustment

1 Check that the starter motor operates only in 'N' and 'P' and the reversing lamps illuminate only with the selector lever in 'R'.

2 Any deviation from this arrangement should be rectified by adjustment, first having checked the correct setting of the selector linkage (Fig. 6.59).

3 Refer to Fig. 6.61 and detach the range selector lever (9) from the selector rod which connects it to the hand control. Now move the range selector lever to the 'N' position, (slot in shaft vertical).

4 Connect an ohmmeter (or a test lamp) to the black and yellow wires of the inhibitor switch. With the ignition switch on, the meter should indicate continuity of circuit when the range selector lever is within 3 degrees (either side) of the 'N' and 'P' positions.

5 Repeat the test with the meter connected to the red and black wires and the range lever in 'R'.

6 Where the switch requires adjusting to provide the correct moment of contact in the three selector positions, move the range level to 'N' and then remove the retaining nut (6), the two inhibitor switch securing bolts and the screw located below the switch.

7 Align the hole, from which the screw was removed, with the pinhole in the manual shaft (2). A thin rod or piece of wire may be used to do this. Holding this alignment, fit the inhibitor switch securing bolts and tighten them. Remove the alignment rod and fit the screw.

8 Refit the remaining switch components and test for correct operation as previously described. If the test procedure does not prove positive, renew the switch.

26 Rear extension oil seal – renewal

1 After a considerable mileage, leakage may occur from the seal which surrounds the shaft at the rear end of the automatic transmission extension housing. This leakage will be evident from the state of the underbody and from the reduction in the level of the hydraulic fluid.

2 Remove the propeller shaft as described in Chapter 7.

3 Taking care not to damage the splined output shaft and the alloy housing, pry the old oil seal from its location. Drive in the new one using a tubular drift.

4 Should the seal be very tight in its recess, then support the transmission on a jack and remove the rear mounting. Unbolt the rear extension housing from the transmission casing.

5 Pull the extension housing straight off over the output shaft and governor assembly.

6 Using a suitable drift applied form the interior of the rear extension housing, remove the old oil seal. At the same time check the bush and renew it if it is scored or worn.

7 Refitting is the reverse of the removal procedure, but always use a new gasket between the rear extension and main housing.

27 Fault diagnosis – automatic transmission

In addition to the information given in this Chapter, reference should be made to Chapter 3 for the servicing and maintenance of the emission control equipment (where applicable) used on models equipped with automatic transmission

Symptom	Reason/s
Engine will not start in 'N' or 'P'	Faulty starter or ignition circuit Incorrect linkage adjustment Incorrectly installed inhibitor switch
Engine starts in selector positions other than 'N' or 'P'	Incorrect linkage adjustment Incorrectly installed inhibitor switch
Severe bump when selecting 'D' or 'R' and excessive creep when idling	Idling speed too high Vacuum circuit leaking
Poor acceleration and low maximum speed	Incorrect oil level Incorrect linkage adjustment

The most likely causes of faulty operation are incorrect oil level and linkage adjustment. Any other faults or mal-operation of the automatic transmission unit must be due to internal faults and should be rectified by your Datsun dealer. An indication of a major internal fault may be gained from the colour of the oil which under normal conditions should be transparent red. If it becomes discoloured or black then burned clutch or brake bands must be suspected

Chapter 7 Propeller shaft

Contents

Specifications

Type . . . .   Tubular steel, one or two-piece with centre bearing depending on model

Universal joint axial play

140J	Nil
160J and 510	Less than 0.0008 in (0.02 mm)

Torque wrench settings

	lbf ft	kgf m
Propeller shaft pinion flange bolts	17 to 24	2.4 to 3.3
Centre bearing bracket/body bolts	26 to 35	3.6 to 4.8
Central companion flange nut	145 to 174	20 to 24
Rear shaft yoke flange to front shaft flange bolts	17 to 24˙	2.4 to 3.3
Centre bearing bracket retaining nuts	5.8 to 8.0	0.8 to 1.1

1 General description

The tubular propeller shaft transmits the drive from the gearbox to the rear axle. Universal joints are incorporated into the shaft assembly and are necessary to allow the axle unit to move at the constantly varying angles caused by the corresponding movements of the suspension to which the axle is attached.

The fore-and-aft movements between the gearbox and the rear axle are balanced by a sliding joint.

Each universal joint comprises a centre spider, needle roller bearings and two yokes. The roller bearings are lubricated and sealed for life during manufacture.

One-piece and two-piece propeller shaft assemblies are fitted according to model. The two-piece propeller shaft has an additional universal joint assembly which is centrally situated and the forward shaft is additionally supported by a centre bearing and support bracket assembly.

2 Propeller shaft – testing for wear whilst on car

1   To check for wear, grasp each unit of the universal joint, and with a twisting action, determine whether there is any play or slackness in the joint. This will indicate any wear in the bearings. Do not be confused by backlash between the crownwheel and pinion in the differential.

2   Try an up and down rocking movement which will indicate wear of the thrust faces on the spiders and those inside the cups.

3   On centre bearing type propeller shafts, check the resilience of the rubber by grasping either side of the bearing and lifting up and down.

An easy action indicates the rubber has probably been contaminated by oil or tired through age.

4   Wear in the needle roller bearings is characterised by vibration in the transmission, 'clonks' on taking up the drive, and, in extreme cases of lack of lubrication, metallic squeaking and ultimately grating and shrieking sounds as the bearings break up.

3 Propeller shaft – removal and refitting

1   Raise the rear of the vehicle and make secure with axle-stands. Alternatively (and preferably) this job can be better achieved if positioned over a pit and jack the rear wheels clear of the ground.

2   Place the vehicle in gear and fully apply the handbrake to ensure that the propeller shaft does not rotate when loosening the companion flange to the axle bolts.

3   Scribe an alignment mark across the outer faces of the propeller shaft and companion flanges. It is important that they are refitted in the same relative position to each other on assembly.

4   Unscrew and remove the respective pinion/companion flange nuts/bolts.

5   On models with a two-piece propeller shaft, support it centrally and unscrew the centre bearing support retaining bolts.

6   Place a suitable container under the rear of the gearbox to catch any oil which may be spilt on removing the propeller shaft.

7   Carefully lower the rear end of the propeller shaft and when clear of the axle housing, withdraw it to the rear of the car.

8   Refitting the propeller shaft is a direct reversal of the removal procedure but ensure that the companion flange marks are in alignment. Tighten the respective bolts to the specified torque wrench settings.

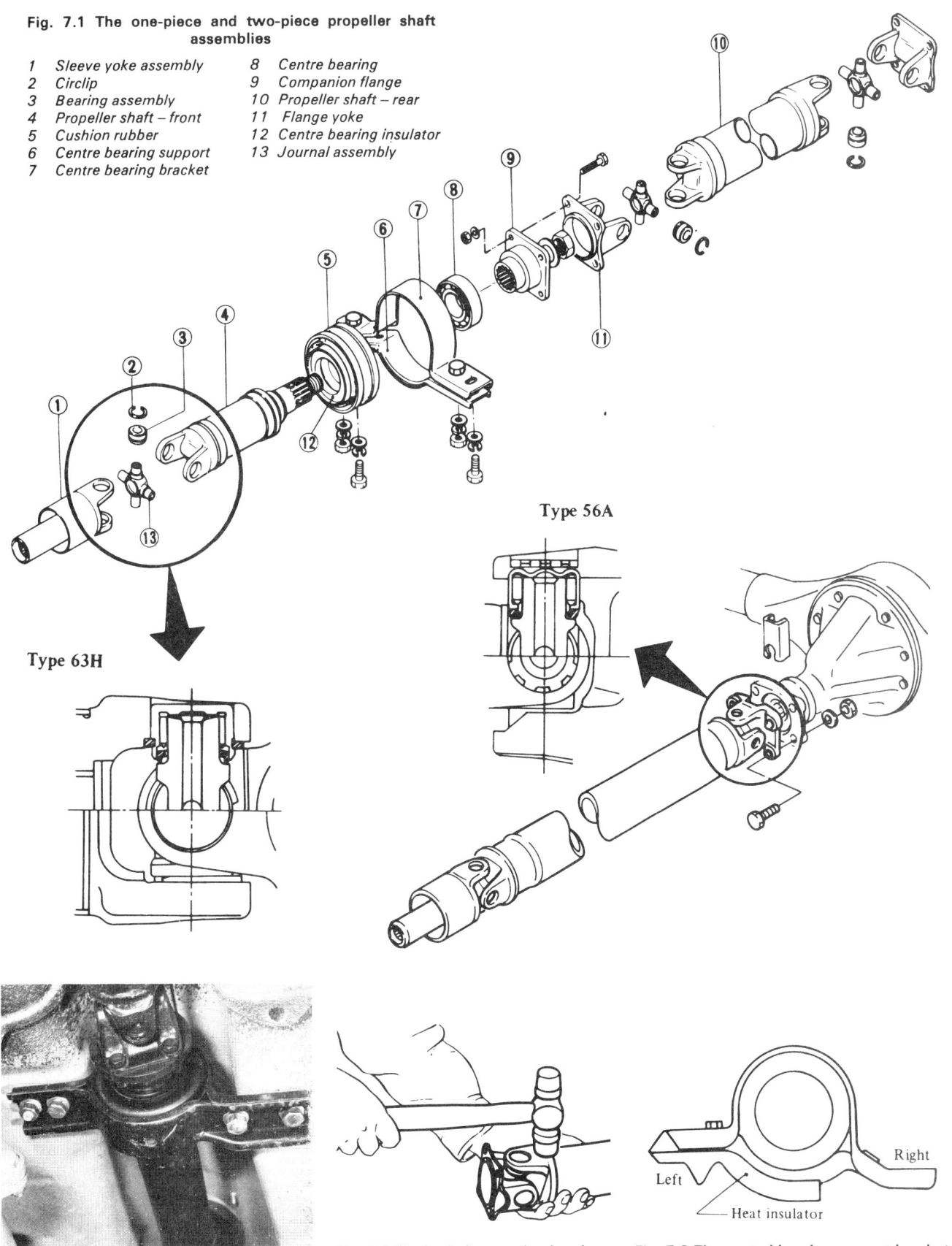

Fig. 7.1 The one-piece and two-piece propeller shaft assemblies

1 Sleeve yoke assembly
2 Circlip
3 Bearing assembly
4 Propeller shaft – front
5 Cushion rubber
6 Centre bearing support
7 Centre bearing bracket
8 Centre bearing
9 Companion flange
10 Propeller shaft – rear
11 Flange yoke
12 Centre bearing insulator
13 Journal assembly

Type 63H

Type 56A

3.5 The centre bearing assembly in position showing support bracket retaining bolts and their respective positions

Fig. 7.2 Method of extracting bearings

Fig. 7.3 The central bearing support bracket showing position of the heat insulator

4   Universal joints – inspection and repair (one-piece)

1   Before dismantling make sure that a repair kit is available otherwise an exchange unit must be obtained.
2   Mark all parts to ensure that, if they are refitted they are in their original positions.
3   Clean away all traces of dirt and grease from the area around the universal joint.
4   Remove the four circlips from the journal assembly using a screwdriver.
5   Hold the propeller shaft using a soft faced hammer tap the universal joint yoke so as to remove the bearing cups by 'shock' action.
6   Remove all four bearing cups in the manner described and then free the propeller shaft from the spider.
7   Thoroughly clean out the yokes and journals.
8   Check to see if the journal diameter has worn. If it has it must be renewed.
9   Renew the spider seal rings if there is evidence of damage.
10 Inspect the sleeve yoke spline to gearbox main shaft splines for wear. The sleeve yoke must be renewed if backlash is evident.
11 If vibrations from the propeller shaft have been experienced check the run out at the centre by rotating on V-shaped blocks and a dial indicator gauge at the centre. The run-out must not exceed 0.0236 in (0.6 mm).
12 To reassemble fit new oil seals and retainers on the spider journals, place the spider on the propeller shaft yoke and assemble the needle rollers into the bearing cups retaining them with some thick grease.
13 Fill each bearing cup about 1/3 full with high melting point grease. Also fill the grease holes in the journal spider with grease taking care that all air bubbles are eliminated.
14 Refit the bearing cups on the spider and tap the bearings home so that they lie squarely in position. Secure with the circlips. Seven different thickness circlips are available to give an axial play as given in the Specifications.

5   Universal joints – inspection and repair (two-piece)

The sequence is basically identical with that for the one-piece type. To overhaul the middle universal joint it will be necessary to part the two halves. This is done by marking the two flanges and then removing the four nuts, bolts and spring washers.

6   Centre bearing – removal and refitting (two-piece)

1   Remove the propeller shaft assembly as outlined in Section 3.
2   Part the two halves as described in Section 5.
3   With a scriber or file mark the relationship of the companion flange to the propeller shaft.
4   It will now be necessary to hold the companion flange in a vice or wrench. Using a socket wrench undo and remove the retaining nut and plain washer. This nut will be very tight and is staked in position on its upper face in the shaft groove.
5   Using a soft metal drift or a puller remove the centre bearing assembly.
6   Check the centre bearing by rotating the race. If it feels rough or noisy it must be discarded. Also check the inner track for 'rock' which ideally should not be evident.
7   Before fitting a rear bearing assembly check that it compares exactly with the old one removed. It is not necessary to lubricate the bearing as it is sealed during manufacture.
8   Reassembly and refitting is the reverse sequence to removal but the following additional points should be noted:

(a)   Tighten the centre bearing locknut to a torque wrench setting of 145-174 lbf ft (20-24 kgf m), and using a suitable punch, indent the upper part of the nut into the shaft groove
(b)   Tighten the companion flange securing nuts and bolts to a torque wrench setting of 17-24 lbf ft (2.4-3.3 kgf m)
(c)   Note that the centre bearing bracket and support is positioned with the exhaust heat insulator to the left side

7   Fault diagnosis – propeller shaft

Symptom	Reason/s
Vibration at medium or high speed	Worn or damaged universal joint needle bearing
	Unbalance due to bent or dented propeller shaft
	Loose propeller shaft installation
	Worn gearbox rear extension bushing
	Damaged centre bearing or insulator
	Tight universal joints
	Undercoating or mud on the shaft causing unbalance
	Tyre unbalance
	Balance weights missing
Knocking sound during starting or noise during coasting on propeller shaft	Worn damaged universal joint
	Worn sleeve yoke and main shaft spline
	Loose propeller shaft installation
	Loose joint installation
	Damaged centre bearing or insulator
	Loose or missing bolts at centre bearing bracket to body
Scraping noise	Dust cover on sleeve yoke rubbing on gearbox rear extension
	Dust cover on companion flange rubbing on differential carrier
Whine or whistle	Damaged centre bearing

Chapter 8 Rear axle

Contents

Specifications

Type . . . .   Hypoid final drive and differential unit of the semi-floating type

Designation type
140J . . . .   H150 A
160J and 510 . . . .   H165 B

Gear ratios

	Manual	Automatic
140J	3.889 : 1	—
160J	3.700 : 1 or 3.889 : 1	3.889 : 1
510	3.545 : 1	3.545 : 1

Crownwheel to pinion backlash . . . .   0.0039 to 0.0059 in (0.10 to 0.15 mm)

Side gear to thrust washer clearance . . . .   0.0039 to 0.0079 in (0.10 to 0.20 mm)
Lubricant capacity
H150 A . . . . $1\frac{5}{8}$ Imp pint ($1\frac{7}{8}$ US pint, 0.9 litre)
H165 B . . . .   2 Imp pint ($2\frac{3}{8}$ US pint, 1.1 litres)

Torque wrench settings

	lbf ft	kgf m
Oil drain plug and filler plug	43 to 72	6 to 10
Drive pinion nut	101 to 217	14 to 30
Side bearing cap bolt	36 to 43	5.0 to 6.0
Ring gear bolt		
H150 A	43 to 51	6.0 to 7.0
H165 B	51 to 58	7.0 to 8.0
Companion flange bolts	17 to 24	2.4 to 3.3
Gear carrier/axle case bolts, nuts		
H150 A	12 to 17	1.6 to 2.4
H165 B	14 to 18	2.0 to 2.5

1 General description

The rear axle is a semi-floating type and the method employed to locate it depends on the particular model. For the Saloon and Coupe models a link suspension with coil springs is used. On the Estate car version a normal leaf spring suspension is fitted.

The banjo type casing carries the differential assembly which comprises a hypoid crownwheel and pinion. Although basically the same in design and layout there are two types of differential unit currently in use. For the 140J models the differential unit is designated the H150 A whilst the 160J and 510 versions have the H165 B differential.

It is possible to carry out any repairs to the axle without removing the complete axle casing from the car. Removing the differential unit is a relatively simple matter, but if found to be worn or damaged it is generally advisable and of course much simpler to buy a reconditioned exchange unit instead of repairing the existing one, which requires specialised knowledge and equipment.

2 Axleshaft (halfshaft) bearing and oil seal – removal and refitting

Refer to Chapter 9 and 11 for additional information and illustrations of the axle associate components

1   Jack-up the rear of the vehicle and support the rear axle and body frame with stands.
2   Remove the rear roadwheel and brake drum.

3   Disconnect the handbrake cable by withdrawing the clevis pin.

4   The brake pipe must now be disconnected from the backplate. Before undoing the union nut, remove the hydraulic reservoir cap at the master cylinder, and place a piece of polythene or plastic over the hole and then refit the cap. This seals the system causing a vacuum and prevents the fluid running freely from the brake pipe when it is disconnected.

5   Clean around the brake pipe union and then unscrew it to free the pipe. Plug it to prevent fluid leakage and the ingress of dirt.

6   Unscrew and remove the backplate retaining nuts.

7   A slide hammer (special tool ST36230000 if available) must now be attached to the wheel studs and the axleshaft withdrawn complete with brake assembly and backplate. If a slide hammer is not available, an old road wheel can be fitted to the axle-flange and the inner rim of the wheel struck at two opposing points.

8   Remove the bearing collar by splitting with a chisel, but make sure that a new collar is available first!

9   If a new bearing is to be fitted, this is a job best left to your Datsun dealer as a press will be required.

10   Reassembling and refitting the axleshaft assembly is the reverse sequence to removal, but note the following:

   (a) *Pack the bearing with wheel bearing grease before refitting*
   (b) *Lubricate the oilseal lip with a smear of grease*
   (c) *Refer to Fig. 8.5 and adjust gap 'C' using shims accordingly*
   (d) *Take care when inserting the shaft not to damage the oil seal lip*

11   Top-up the rear axle oil level on completion and bleed the brakes – see Chapter 9.

3   Rear axle unit (link type) – removal and refitting

Refer to Fig. 11.20 in Chapter 11.

1   The rear end of the car must be raised so that the wheels are clear of the ground, use axle-stands or blocks to support as shown (Fig. 8.1) and block each side of the front wheels to prevent them rolling.

2   Place a jack under the differential carrier and just support it.

3   Remove the rear roadwheels.

4   Mark the companion flanges and unscrew the propeller shaft bolts to disconnect.

5   Disconnect the handbrake cable adjuster.

6   Unscrew the master cylinder filler cap, place a piece of plastic over the orifice to seal it and refit the cap. This will prevent excessive leakage when the brake pipe is detached.

7   Detach the brake pipe from the hose and plug the ends to prevent leakage of fluid and the ingress of dirt.

8   Unscrew and remove the lower end bolts from the shock absorbers. Compress the shock absorber to clear the bracket.

9   Slowly lower the jack under the differential carrier and when the coil springs are fully extended they can be extracted.

10   Raise the jack again and when back at its original height unscrew and remove the upper and lower link bolts at the axle casing side (Fig. 8.7).

11   Check that all fittings and attachments are disconnected then slowly lower the jack and remove the axle assembly.

12   Refitting of the axle assembly is a direct reversal of the removal sequence but do not fully tighten the upper and lower link bolts until the vehicle has been lowered to the ground.

4   Rear axle unit (leaf spring type) – removal and refitting

Refer to Fig. 11.23 in Chapter 11.

1   The removal and refitting instructions are identical to those of the link type axle except after the shock absorbers have been disconnected at their lower ends, the jack is slowly lowered and the U-bolt nuts are progressively removed in a diagonal sequence. Remove the U-bolts and with the aid of an assistant the axle unit can be withdrawn at the side between the leaf spring and wheel arch. Alternatively the springs can be disconnected at their rear shackles and lowered to allow the axle to be removed at the rear.

2   On reassembly do not fully tighten the shock absorber bolts until the car has been lowered to the ground.

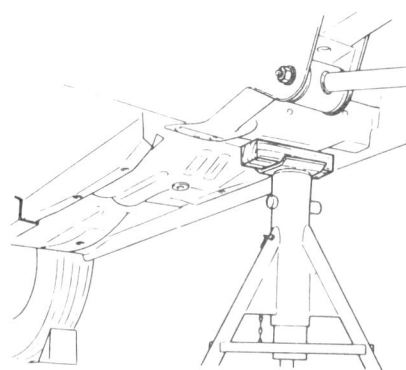

Fig. 8.1 Support the vehicle at the point shown

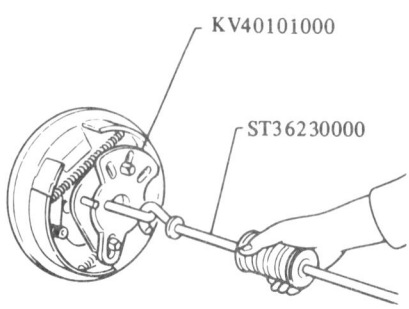

Fig. 8.2 Withdraw the axleshaft and hub assembly using special tools KV40101000 and ST36230000

Fig. 8.3 Split the bearing collar using a cold chisel

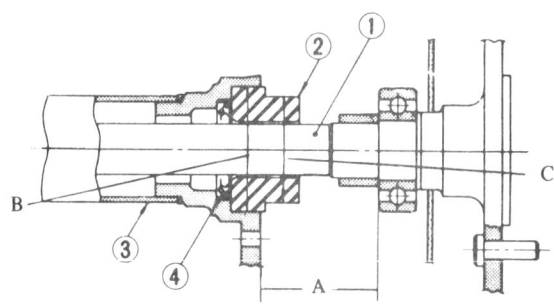

Fig. 8.4 Sectional view of axleshaft unit

1 Rear axleshaft   *A 2.76 to 3.54 in (70 to 90 mm)*
2 Axleshaft guide   *B 2.83 in diameter (72 mm)*
3 Axle casing   *C 2.44 in diameter (62 mm)*
4 Oil seal

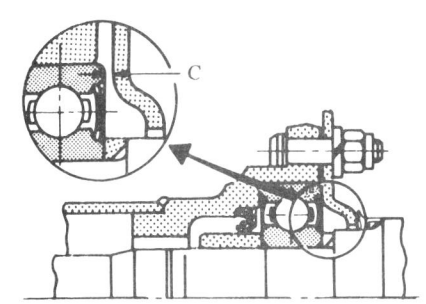

Fig. 8.5 Check that gap 'C' is within 0.004 in (0.1 mm). Adjust using shims between the axle tube end and the wheel bearing if necessary to achieve this tolerance

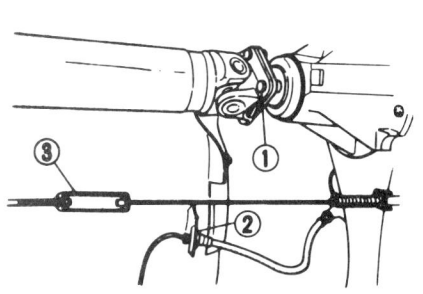

Fig. 8.6 Disconnect 1 the propeller shaft flange 2 the brake pipe and 3 the handbrake cable adjuster

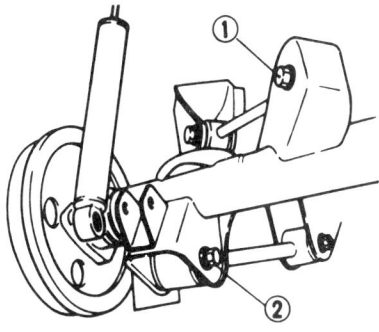

Fig. 8.7 Disconnect upper and lower links at 1 and 2

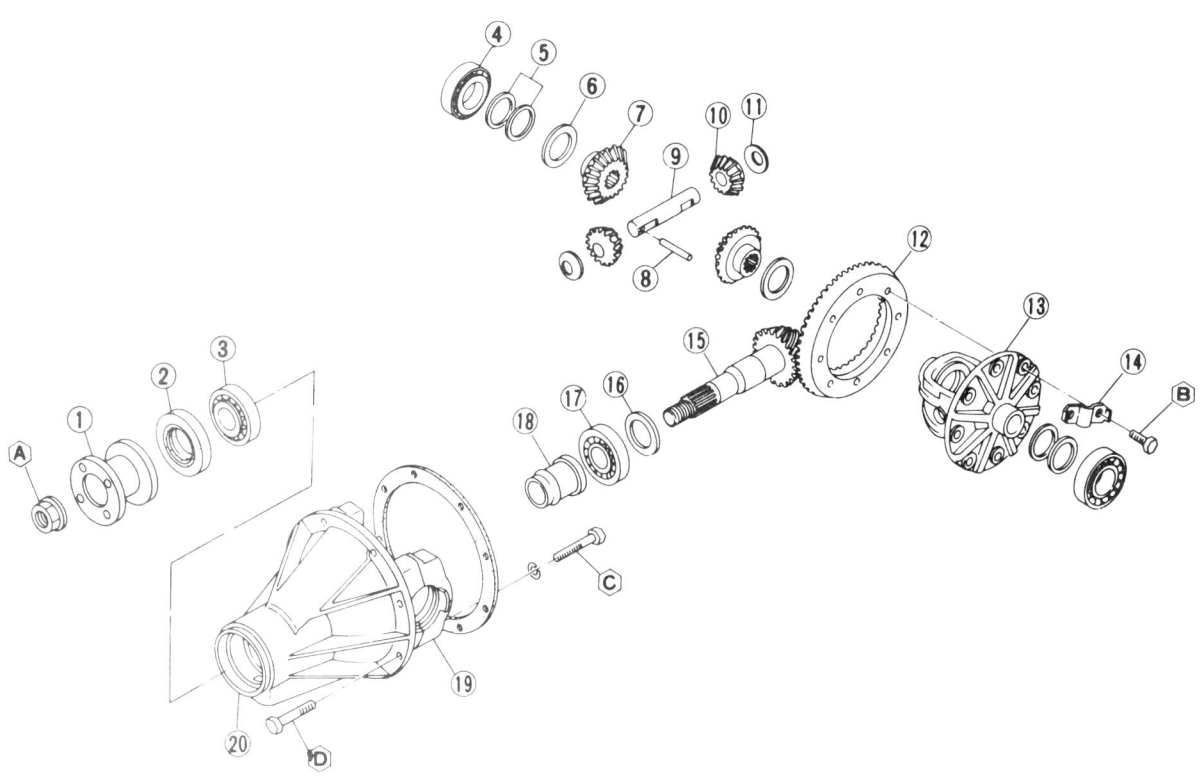

Fig. 8.8 The H150A type differential unit component parts

1	Propeller shaft companion flange	6 Thrust washer	12 Ring gear	17 Pinion rear bearing

1   Propeller shaft companion flange
2   Oil seal
3   Pinion front bearing
4   Side bearing
5   Side bearing adjustment shim

6   Thrust washer
7   Side gear
8   Lock pin
9   Pinion mate shaft
10 Pinion
11 Thrust washer

12 Ring gear
13 Differential gear housing
14 Lock strap
15 Drive pinion
16 Pinion height adjustment washer

17 Pinion rear bearing
18 Collapsible spacer
19 Side bearing cap
20 Differential housing

The retaining nut/bolts tightening torque are:
A 101 to 217 lbf ft (14 to 30 kgf m)
B   43 to   51 lbf ft (6.0 to 7.0 kgf m)
C   36 to   43 lbf ft (5.0 to 6.0 kgf m)
D   12 to   17 lbf ft (1.6 to 2.4 kgf m)

Fig. 8.9 The H165B type differential unit component parts

1 Propeller shaft companion flange	11 Thrust washer
2 Oil seal	12 Ring gear
3 Pinion front bearing	13 Differential gear housing
4 Side bearing	14 Lock strap
5 Side bearing adjustment shim	15 Drive pinion
6 Thrust washer	16 Pinion height adjustment washer
7 Side gear	17 Pinion rear bearing
8 Lock pin	18 Collapsible spacer
9 Pinion mate shaft	19 Side bearing cap
10 Pinion	20 Differential housing

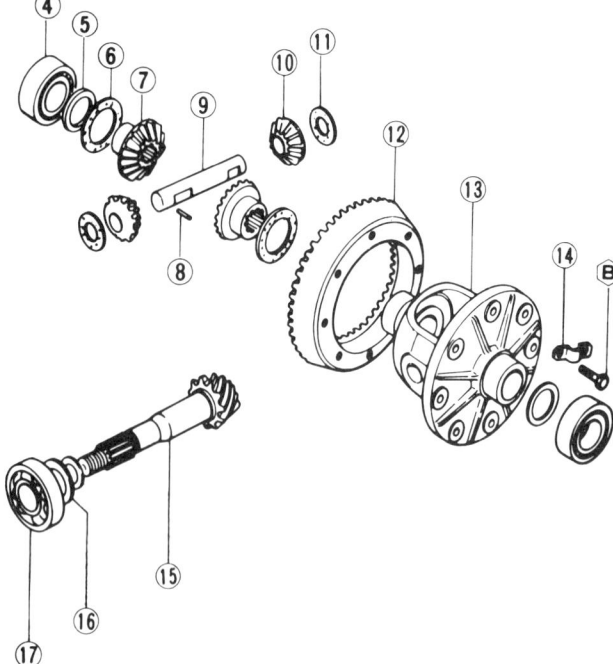

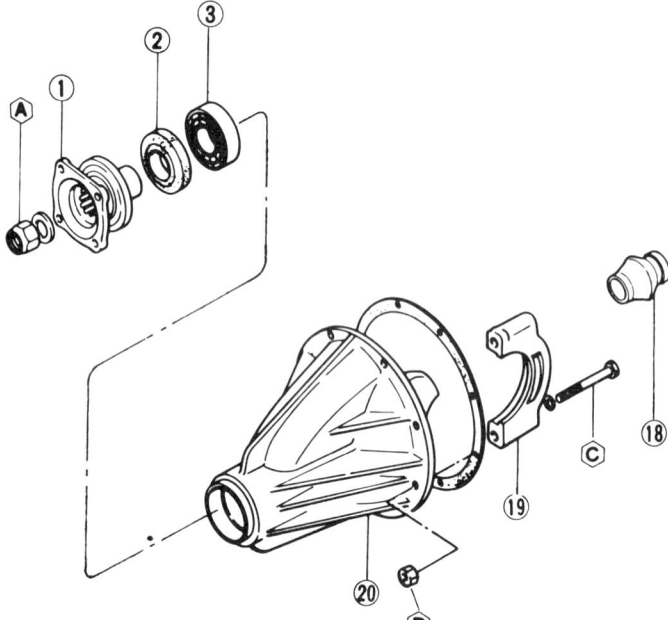

The retaining nut/bolt tightening torques are:

A   101 to 217 lbf ft   C   36 to 43 lbf ft
    (14.0 to 30.0 kgf m)   (5.0 to 6.0 kgf m)
B   51 to 58 lbf ft   D   14 to 18 lbf ft
    (7.0 to 8.0 kgf m)   (2.0 to 2.5 kgf m)

the differential unit to the correct level with oil of the specified grade.

5   Differential unit and carrier – removal and refitting

1   The overhaul of the rear axle differential unit is not within the scope of the home mechanic due to the specialized gauges and tools which are required. Where the unit requires servicing or repair due to wear or excessive noise, it is most economical to exchange it for a factory reconditioned assembly and this Section is limited to a description of the removal and refitting procedure.

2   Drain the oil from the rear axle.

3   Jack-up the axle, remove the roadwheels and partially withdraw the axleshafts as described in Section 2.

4   Mark the propeller shaft to companion flange to ensure correct relative realignment on assembly, then unscrew and remove the retaining bolts/nuts to disconnect the propeller shaft.

5   Progressively loosen and remove the respective differential unit securing nuts. Withdraw the differential unit from the axle casing.

6   Do not dismantle the differential unit for inspection. Wash the respective components in petrol and blow or wipe clean. Support the carrier and rotate the gears, look for broken teeth or signs of excessive wear or heat. Check the crownwheel to pinion backlash using a dial gauge or feeler gauges. The correct backlash and side gear to thrust washer clearances are given in the Specifications. If excessive wear or damage is apparent, exchange the unit.

7   Before refitting, scrape all signs of the old gasket from the mating surface of the axle casing. Do not apply sealant to the new gasket.

8   Fit the differential carrier so that the pinion assembly is at the lowest point. Refit and tighten the retaining bolts to the specified torque (apply sealant to bolt threads).

9   Refit the axleshaft and relocate the propeller shaft (align the marks).

10   Top up the master cylinder and bleed the brakes (see Chapter 9).

11   Refit the roadwheels, lower and remove the jack and then top-up

6   Pinion oil seal – renewal

1   The pinion oil seal cannot be renewed with the differential carrier still in position in the vehicle. This is due to the use of a collapsible type spacer, between the pinion bearings, which must be renewed if the pinion adjustment is disturbed by removal of the pinion nut.

2   Remove the differential carrier, as described in Section 5.

3   Unbolt and remove the side bearing caps.

4   Withdraw the differential case assembly.

5   Unscrew and remove the drive pinion nut and coupling. Extract the pinion oil seal.

6   Withdraw the pinion to the rear and the front pinion bearing race to the front.

7   Extract the collapsible spacer.

8   Insert a new collapsible spacer onto the pinion and fit the front bearing race.

9   Tap a new oil seal into position and apply some grease to the seal lips.

10   Refit the pinion coupling and screw on the pinion nut finger-tight.

11   Now tighten the pinion nut (coupling flange held quite still until any endfloat in drive pinion is just eliminated).

12   The pinion nut should now be tightened a fraction at a time until, with a spring balance attached to one of the coupling flange bolt holes, the force required to turn it (preload) is as follows:

H 150 A   5.2 to 6.9 lbf in (6.0 to 8.0 kgf cm)
H 165 B   6.1 to 8.7 lbf in (7.0 to 10.0 kgf cm)

13   Turn the pinion in both directions during the tightening process to settle the bearings.

14   Fit the differential case assembly and side bearing caps, and refit the carrier to the axle casing, as described in Section 5.

7 Fault diagnosis – rear axle

Symptom	Reason/s
Noise on drive, coasting or overrun	Shortage of oil Incorrect crownwheel to pinion mesh Worn pinion bearings Worn side bearings Loose bearing cap bolts
Noise on turn	Differential side gears worn, damaged or tight
Knock on taking up drive or during gearchange	Excessive crownwheel to pinion backlash Worn gears Worn axleshaft splines Pinion bearing preload too low Loose drive coupling nut Loose securing bolts or nuts within unit Loose roadwheel nuts or elongated wheel nut holes
Oil leakage	Defective gaskets or oil seals possibly caused by clogged breather or oil level too high

Chapter 9 Braking system

Contents

Specifications

System type .... Disc brakes front and drum brakes rear hydraulically operated with servo assistance. Mechanical handbrake to rear wheels only

Front brakes
Pad thickness .... 0.39 in (10 mm)
Disc pad wear limit .... 0.08 in (2 mm)
Disc outside diameter .... 9.65 in (245 mm)
Wheel cylinder inner diameter .... 2.0 in (51.1 mm)
Maximum disc run-out .... 0.0047 in (0.12 mm)

Rear brakes
Drum inside diameter
    A14 models .... 8 in (203.2 mm)
    L16 and L20 models .... 9 in (228.6 mm)
Wheel cylinder diameter .... 0.8125 in (20.64 mm)
Lining wear limit .... 0.059 in (1.5 mm)
Maximum drum wear limit
    8 in drum .... 8.05 in (204.5 mm)
    9 in drum .... 9.06 in (230.0 mm)

Master cylinder diameter
A14 engine
    RH drive .... 0.750 in (19.05 mm)
    LH drive .... 0.812 in (20.64 mm)
L16 engine
    RH drive .... 0.750 in (19.05 mm)
    LH drive .... 0.812 in (20.64 mm)
L20 engine .... 0.812 in (20.64 mm)

Master cylinder to piston clearance (Max) .... 0.0059 in (0.15 mm)

Brake pedal free play .... 0.04 to 0.20 in (1 to 5 mm)

Torque wrench settings

	lbf ft	kgf m
Caliper bolt	53 to 72	7.3 to 9.9

Disc bolts	28 to 38	3.9 to 5.3
Rear wheel brake cylinder bolts	4.3 to 5.8	0.6 to 0.8
Front disc plate bolts	20 to 27	2.7 to 3.7
Brake warning lamp switch locknut	9 to 11	1.2 to 1.5
Pedal fulcrum pin	14 to 17	1.9 to 2.4
Air bleeder valve	5.1 to 6.5	0.7 to 0.9
Master cylinder to Master-Vac	5.8 to 8.0	0.8 to 1.1
Brake tube flare nut	11 to 13	1.5 to 1.8
Brake hose connector	12 to 14	1.7 to 2.0
Master-Vac rod locknut	12 to 16	1.6 to 2.2
Master-Vac pushrod adjuster nut	12 to 16	1.6 to 2.2
Master-Vac flange to steel cover	5.8 to 8.0	0.8 to 1.1
Master-Vac to body	5.8 to 8.0	0.8 to 1.1

1 General description

The brake system fitted to models covered by this manual have disc brakes at the front and drum brakes at the rear, and these are operated hydraulically with power assistance by a Master-Vac servo unit.

The hydraulic system is of the dual line type whereby the front brakes and rear brakes are operated by individual hydraulic circuits so that if a line should fail, braking action will still be available on two wheels.

The rear drum brakes are of the internal expanding type, the shoes and linings moving outwards and into frictional contact with the rotating brake drum. The brake shoes are actuated by a single wheel cylinder on each wheel.

The front disc brakes are of the rotating disc and semi rigid mounted caliper design. The disc is secured to the flange of the hub and the caliper mounted on the steering swivel.

Each caliper contains two piston operated friction pads, which on application of the footbrake pinch the disc between them.

Application of the footbrake creates hydraulic pressure in the master cylinder and fluid from the cylinder travels via steel and flexible pipes to the cylinder in each caliper, thus pushing the pistons, to which are attached the friction pads, into contact with either side of the disc.

Two seals are fitted to the operating cylinder; the outer seal prevents moisture and dirt entering the cylinder, while the inner seal which is retained in a groove inside the cylinder, prevents fluid leakage.

As the friction pads wear so the pistons move further out of the cylinder due to the elasticity of the seals and the level of the fluid in the hydraulic reservoir drops. Disc pads wear is therefore taken up automatically and eliminates the need for periodic adjustment by the owner.

A Nissen Proportioning (NP) valve is incorporated into the hydraulic circuit and this regulates the fluid flow to prevent the rear brakes locking before the front brakes.

The twin master cylinder reservoirs have level indicators fitted to the caps and should the level fall below the specified level then a warning light is actuated to inform the driver.

The handbrake is either a central lever type or a stick type. The stick type is mounted under the dashboard panel and both types operate the rear wheel brakes only via cables which are adjustable.

When the handbrake is applied a switch is actuated and when the ignition is on a warning light on the dashboard will indicate to show that the handbrake is in the 'On' position.

2 Brake adjustments

Front disc brake adjustment

1   The front disc brakes do not require adjustment as they automatically compensate for wear to the pads.

Rear drum brakes

2   The rear drum brakes on some models are automatically adjusted when the handbrake (parkbrake) is applied. It is therefore important to check that the handbrake is correctly adjusted as detailed in Section 3.

3   On those models fitted with manually adjustable rear brakes proceed as follows. First raise the rear of the vehicle and support with axle-stands or similar to secure. Wedge the front wheels with suitable blocks.

4   Apply the footbrake several times to centralize the brake shoes. Check that the handbrake is fully released.

5   Prise the rubber boot from the inside of the backplate to expose the adjuster wheel, then using a screwdriver, turn the adjuster nut downwards to take up the adjustment (Fig. 9.1).

6   Rotate the adjuster nut downwards until the wheel is binding on turning and then unscrew the adjuster nut just sufficiently to enable the roadwheel to spin freely and without binding.

7   Refit the rubber boot and adjust the opposing brake.

3 Handbrake adjustment

1   Where applicable, adjust the rear brakes as detailed previously.

2   There are two types of handbrake mechanism these being the centre lever type and the stick type.

Centre lever type

3   Chock the front wheels and raise the rear of the vehicle so that the wheels are clear of the ground and fit axle-stands.

4   Loosen the locknut against the turn buckle and rotate the turn buckle to adjust (photo). The adjustment is correct when the lever is applied using average pressure (44 lb) the full stroke should be 4.17 to 4.69 in (106 to 119 mm). This can be felt during application and is about 6 to 7 notches.

5   Retighten the locknut on completion and check that when the control lever is fully released, the wheels are able to spin freely without the brakes binding or sticking.

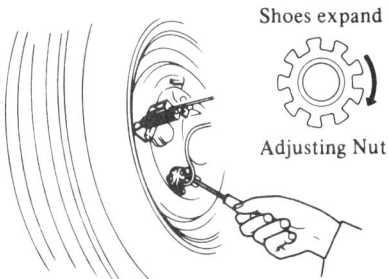

Fig. 9.1 Adjusting the rear drum brakes

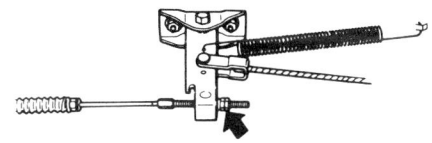

Fig. 9.2 The handbrake adjuster and locknut on the stick type system

3.4 The turnbuckle adjuster of the centre lever handbrake system

Stick type

6   Refer to paragraph three and raise the car.

7   Refering to Fig. 9.3 loosen the locknut and rotate the adjustment nut at the mediation lever to enable the handbrake lever to be applied 11 to 13 notches, at an average pressure (44 lb) and giving a lever stroke of 4.1 to 4.5 in (105 to 115 mm).

8   Tighten the locknut on completion and then check that when the handbrake lever is released that the rear wheels are free to spin without binding. Ensure that the respective toggle levers fully return to their normal 'off' positions.

4   Handbrake warning light switch adjustment

1   Bend the warning lamp switch bracket as necessary so that when the lever is pulled on by one notch, the light comes on and when the lever is fully released, the light goes out.

5   Bleeding the hydraulic system

1   Removal of all air from the hydraulic system is essential to the correct working of the braking system. Before undertaking this, examine the fluid reservoir cap to ensure that the vent hole is clear. Check the level of fluid in the reservoir(s) and top-up if required.

2   Check all brake line unions and connections for seepage, and at the same time check the condition of the rubber hoses which may be perished.

3   If the condition of the wheel cylinder is in doubt, check for signs of fluid leakage.

4   If there is any possibility that incorrect fluid has been used in the system, drain the fluid out and flush through with isopropyl alcohol or methylated spirits. Renew all piston seals and cups since they will be affected and could fail under pressure.

5   Gather together a clean glass jar, a 12 inch (300 mm) length of tubing which fits tightly over the bleed valve and a tin of the correct brake fluid.

6   To bleed the system, clean the area around the bleed valves and start at the rear left-hand wheel by removing the rubber or plastic cover from the end of the bleed valve.

7   Place the end of the tube in the clean jar which should contain sufficient fluid to keep the end of the tube underneath during the operation.

8   Open the bleed valve $\frac{1}{4}$ turn with a wrench, depress the brake pedal and close the bleed valve again just before full travel of the brake pedal is reached. This will expel brake fluid and air from the end of the tube.

9   Repeat this operation until no more air is expelled from that particular bleed valve then tighten the valve to the specified torque. During the bleeding operation ensure that the master cylinder reservoir is topped-up as necessary or more air will be introduced into the system.

10   Repeat this operation on the second rear brake, and then the front brakes, starting with the left-hand brake unit.

11   When completed, check the level of the fluid in the reservoir and then check the feel of the brake pedal, which should be firm and free from any 'spongy' action, which is normally associated with air in the system.

12   It will be noticed that during the bleeding operation, the effort required to depress the pedal the full stroke will increase because of loss of the vacuum assistance as it is destroyed by repeated operation of the servo unit. Although the servo unit will be inoperative as far as assistance is concerned it does not affect the brake bleeding operation.

6   Brake hoses – inspection, removal and refitting

1   Inspect the condition of the flexible hydraulic hoses. If they are swollen, damaged or chafed they must be renewed.

2   Wipe the top of the brake master cylinder reservoir and unscrew the cap. Place a piece of polythene sheet over the top of the reservoir and refit the cap. This is to stop hydraulic fluid syphoning out during subsequent operations. Note that tandem master cylinders have two reservoirs but it is not necessary to cover both cylinders unless both front and rear hoses are being removed.

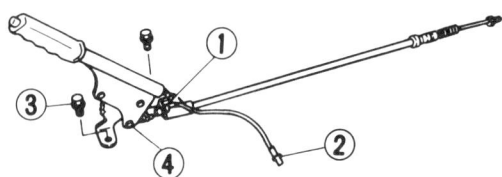

Fig. 9.3 The handbrake (centre lever type) showing the warning switch (1), the terminal (2) and the bolt (3) and pin (4)

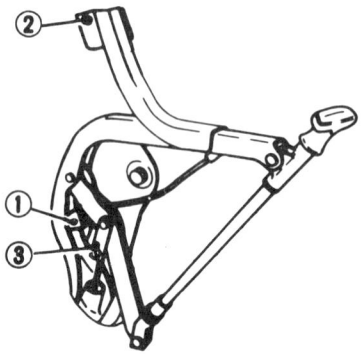

Fig. 9.4 The stick type handbrake lever showing the warning switch (1), the nut (2), and the clevis pin (3)

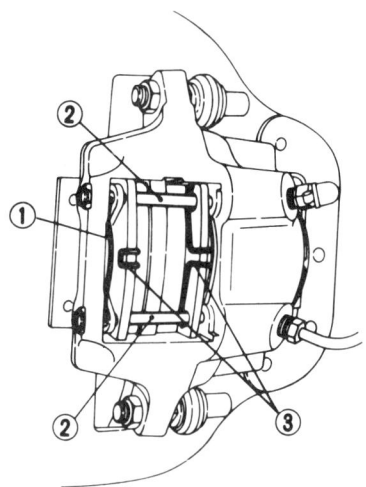

Fig. 9.5 The disc caliper showing pad retaining clip (1), pad retaining pins (2) and the anti-squeal springs (3)

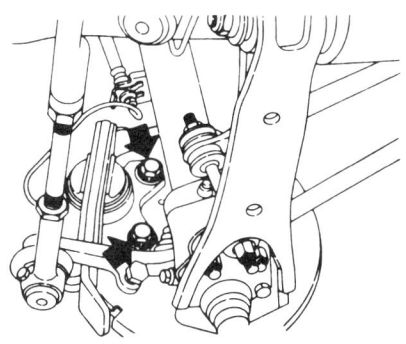

Fig. 9.6 Caliper retaining bolts

5.10 The disc brake bleed nipple

6.8 Rear axle showing brake line retaining clips

7.3 Remove the retaining clip

7.4 Remove anti-squeal springs and retaining pins

7.5 Withdraw the pads for inspection

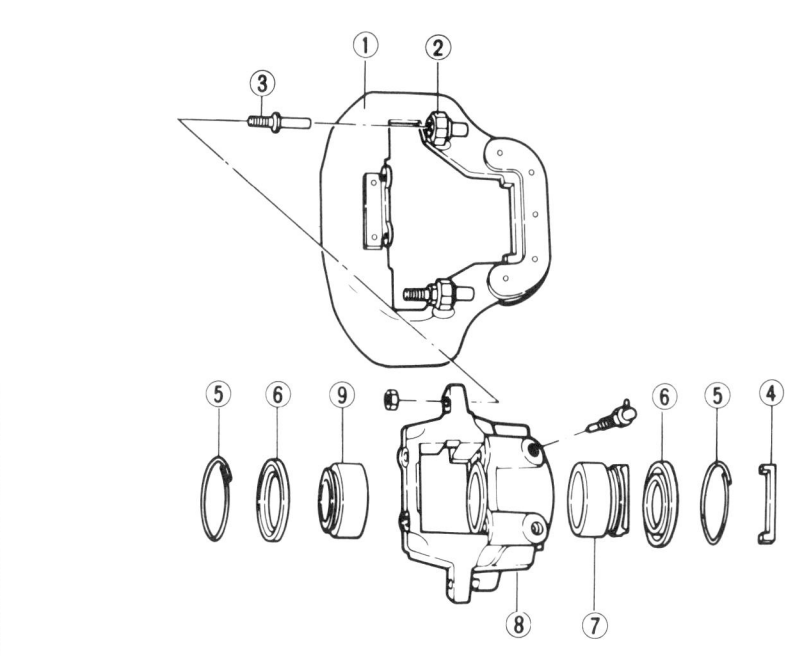

Fig. 9.7 The caliper components

1 Yoke	8 Cylinder body
2 Gripper	9 Piston
3 Pin	10 Brake pad
4 Holder	11 Anti-squeal spring
5 Retaining ring	12 Pad retaining pin
6 Dust seal	13 Clip
7 Piston	

Front brake hose

3   First jack-up the vehicle to take the weight off the suspension. To remove the hose, wipe the unions and bracket free of dust, and undo the union nut from the metal pipe end.

4   Withdraw the metal clip securing the hose to the bracket and detach the hose from the bracket. Unscrew the hose from the wheel cylinder.

5   Refitting is the reverse of the removal procedure but ensure that the hose is connected at the wheel cylinder end first, with the wheels in the 'straight-ahead' position. On completion, the front brakes must be bled of air, as described in the previous Section.

Rear brake hose

6   To remove a rear flexible hose, wipe the unions, bracket and three way adaptor free of dust, and undo the union nut from the metal pipe end.

7   Withdraw the metal clip securing the hose to the bracket and detach the hose from the bracket. Unscrew the hose from the three-way adaptor.

8   Refitting is a direct reversal of the removal procedure. Ensure that the hose is connected at the three-way adaptor end first. The brake lines must be secured in position against the axle housing by fastening the retaining clips as shown in photo.

9   On completion bleed the rear brakes as described previously.

---

7 Front disc brake pad – inspection, removal and refitting

1   Due to the design of the caliper the pad to disc clearance is automatically adjusted.

2   To check the pad lining thickness, chock the rear wheels, jack-up the front of the car and support on firmly based stands. Remove the roadwheels.

3   Use a pair of needle nose pliers or similar and withdraw the retaining clip (photo).

4   Extract the pad pins (photo) and anti-squeal springs.

5   The pads can now be withdrawn (photo).

6   Carefully clean all traces of dirt or rust from the recesses in the caliper in which the pads lie, and the exposed face of the piston.

7   Use a piece of wood or screwdriver to fully retract the piston with the caliper cylinder, but don't push the cylinder in too far as the internal seal may be damaged.

8   Pads must always be renewed in sets of four and not singly. Also pads must not be interchanged side to side.

9   Fit new pads into position and retain with anti-squeal spring and pad pin, followed by the clip.

10   Refit the roadwheels and lower the car. Tighten the wheel nuts securely and refit the wheel trim.

11   To correctly seat the pads pump the brake pedal several times and finally top-up the hydraulic fluid level in the master cylinder reservoir as necessary.

---

8 Front disc brake caliper – removal and refitting

1   Chock the rear wheels, apply the handbrake, jack-up the front of the car and support on firmly based stands. Remove the roadwheel.

2   Refer to Section 6 and detach the flexible hose.

3   Refer to Section 7 and remove the pads.

4   Undo and remove the two bolts and spring washers that secure the caliper to the steering knuckle. Lift away the caliper.

5   Refitting is the reverse sequence to removal. The securing bolts must be tightened to the torque wrench setting given in the Specifications. It will be necessary to bleed the hydraulic system as described in Section 5.

---

9 Front disc brake caliper – dismantling and reassembly

1   Remove the pads and caliper assembly to a clean workbench where the respective components can be dismantled and laid out for inspection.

2   Drain out any fluid that may still be left in the caliper cylinder.

3   Unscrew and remove the gripper pin nuts, and separate the yoke and cylinder body.

4   Remove the yoke holder, the retaining rings and seals from the respective pistons.

5   To remove the piston, the air jet from an air line or front pump should be used. Tighten the bleed screw and apply the jet to the hydraulic pipe aperture in the cylinder body. The piston assembly should now be ejected.

6   Carefully remove the rubber seals from the grooves in the cylinder bore.

7   Unscrew and remove the bleed screw. Further dismantling should not be necessary unless it is obvious that a part has worn. If damage exists the assembly must be renewed as a whole.

8   Thoroughly clean all parts and wipe with a clean non-fluffy rag. The seals must be renewed. Always use clean brake fluid to clean the cylinder components, never use a mineral oil!

9   Check the cylinder bore and pistons for signs of deep scoring or damage and renew if evident.

10   Commence reassembly by inserting the piston seals into position.

11   Lubricate the pistons with brake fluid and also the cylinder bores. Fit the respective pistons in the directions indicated in Fig. 9.8, ensuring that they are correctly positioned and not inserted too far which could damage the seals, see Fig. 9.9.

12   Carefully refit the dust seal and secure with the retaining ring. The sealing surface of the seal should be smeared with some disc brake grease prior to assembly and any excess grease wiped clean on assembly.

13   Reassemble the yoke and tighten the gripper pin nuts to secure.

14   Refit the caliper to the steering knuckle and tighten the mounting bolts to the specified torque.

15   When the pads have been refitted and the brakes bled (Sections 7 and 5), apply pressure to the brakes to ensure that there is no leakage of fluid from the caliper assemblies. Check that the disc is free to rotate on releasing the brake.

---

10 Disc brake – removal and refitting

1   Chock the rear wheels, apply the handbrake, jack-up the front of the car and support on firmly based stands. Remove the roadwheel.

2   Refer to Section 7 and remove the brake pads.

3   Undo and remove the caliper securing bolts and spring washers. Lift the caliper from the disc and suspend on a piece of wire so that the flexible hose is not strained.

4   Using a screwdriver remove the grease cap from the hub.

5   Straighten the ears and withdraw the split pin locking the castellated nut to the stub axle.

6   Tighten the castellated nut and with a dial indicator gauge on the outer circumference or feeler gauges and suitable packing measure the run-out. This must not exceed 0.0047 in (0.12 mm). If this figure is exceeded the surface must be refaced or a new disc obtained. The minimum allowable disc thickness is 0.331 in (8.4 mm).

7   Undo and remove the castellated nut, washer and outer hub bearing.

8   The hub and disc assembly may now be drawn from the stub axle. Should it be necessary to renew the hub bearings further information will be found in Chapter 11.

9   Mark the relative positions of the disc and hub so that they may be refitted in their original positions.

10   Undo and remove the four bolts and separate the hub from the disc.

11   Thoroughly clean the disc and inspect for signs of deep scoring or excessive corrosion. If these are evident the disc may be reground, but do not make the disc thinner than the minimum allowance.

12   Refitting the disc is the reverse sequence to removal. Tighten the disc retaining bolts to the torque wrench setting given in the Specifications.

13   Refer to Chapter 11 and adjust the hub bearings.

14   Recheck the disc run-out. If a new disc was fitted and the run-out is excessive check the hub flange for run-out and for dirt trapped between the mating surfaces, rectify by either cleaning or fitting a new hub.

---

11 Rear drum brakes – inspection, removal and replacement

1   After high mileages it will be necessary to fit new shoes and linings. Refitting new linings to shoes s not considered economic or

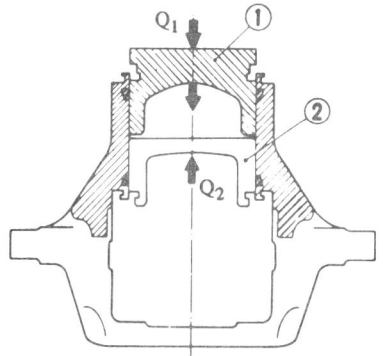

Fig. 9.8 Insert piston 1 in direction Q1 and insert piston 2 in direction Q2

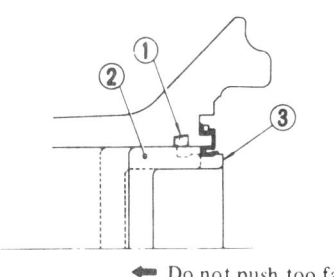

← Do not push too far

Fig. 9.9 Ensure that piston is not inserted beyond seal

1 Seal
2 Piston B
3 Correct position

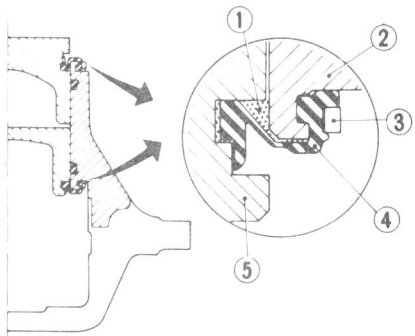

Fig. 9.10 Dust seal installed showing position of grease (1) between cylinder body (2) and seal (4). Also shown are the securing ring (3) and piston (5)

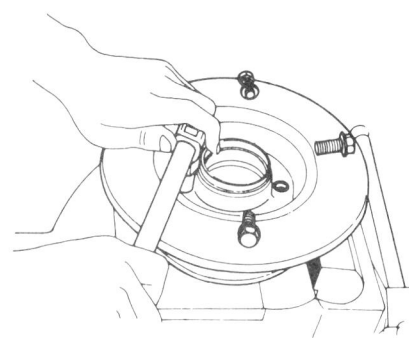

Fig. 9.11 Separating the disc from the hub

Fig. 9.12 The rear drum brake components

1	Backplate	7	Stopper pin
2	Wheel cylinder components	8	Anti-rattle pin
3	Brake shoe	9	Spring seat
4	Return spring	10	Spring
5	Adjuster unit	11	Retainer
6	Stopper		

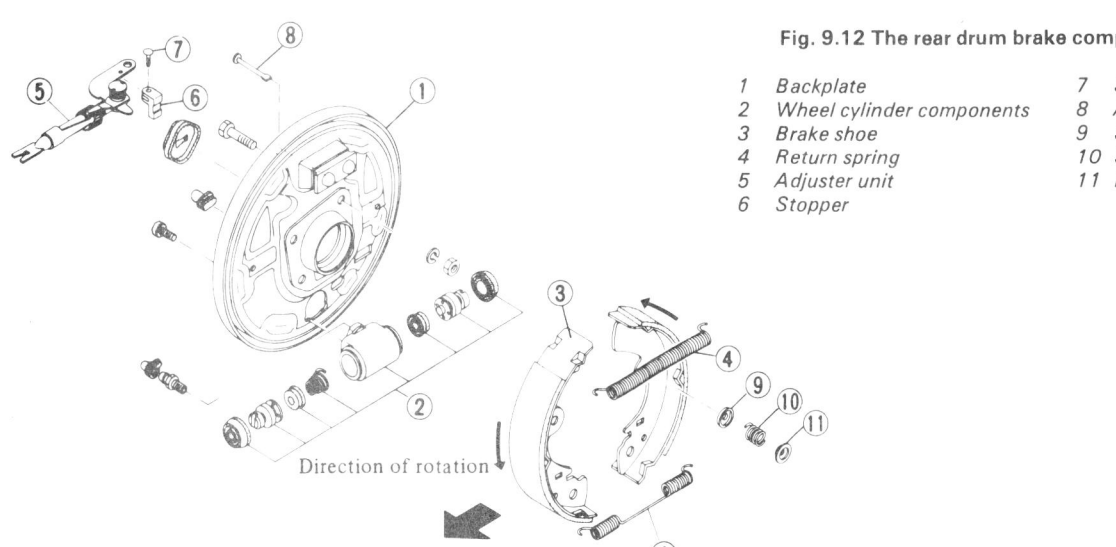

Direction of rotation

Front of car

11.4 Method of removing brake drum

11.6 Twist retainer to release

11.11 Check the cylinder for signs of leakage

11.14 The shoes correctly reassembled, note also the spring position

11.15a The adjuster

11.15b The completed assembly prior to refitting the drum

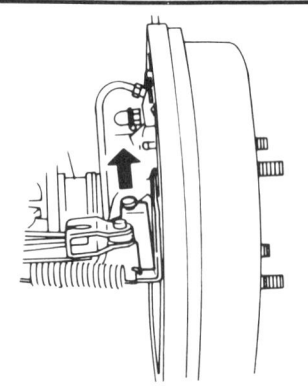
Fig. 9.13 Remove the pin and stopper

Fig. 9.14 Lubricate the adjusters as indicated

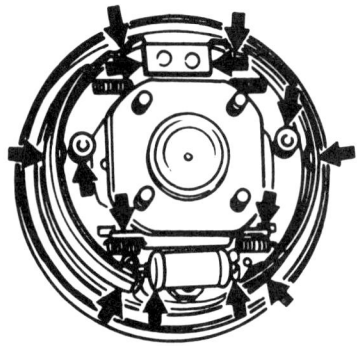
Fig. 9.15 Lubrication points (arrowed)

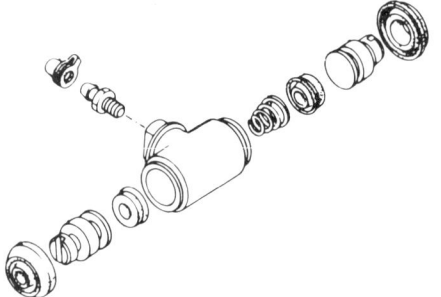
Fig. 9.16 The wheel cylinder components

possible, without the use of special equipment. However, if the services of a local garage or workshop having brake re-lining equipment are available, then there is no reason why the original shoes should not be successfully relined. Ensure that the correct specification linings are fitted to the shoes.

2 Chock the front wheels, jack-up the rear of the car and support on firmly based stands, remove the roadwheel.

3 On 510 models, engage the handbrake and extract the split pin from the stopper. Remove stopper from toggle lever. Release the handbrake lever.

4 The drum can now be removed but mark its relative position to the hub before withdrawal. If it proves reluctant to move, screw in two suitable bolts into the holes in the drum to draw it from the studs (photo). Alternatively try tapping the outside rim of the drum using a soft face hammer and rotate the drum to free it.

5 Check the lining thickness (see Specifications), and inspect the drum friction surface for wear or scoring.

6 Use a pair of pliers to rotate the brake shoe antirattle spring retainer through 90° and lift away the retainer cup, spring and spring seat (photo).

7 Make a note of the locations of the shoe return springs and the way round they are fitted. Carefully ease the shoes from the slots in the wheel cylinder and adjuster.

8 Lift the shoes and return springs from the backplate.

9 If the shoes are to be left off for a while, do not depress the brake pedal otherwise the pistons will be ejected from the cylinders causing unnecessary work.

10 Thoroughly clean all traces of dust from the shoes, backplate and brake drums using a stiff brush. It is recommended that compressed air is not used as it blows up dust which should not be inhaled. Brake dust can cause judder or squeal and, therefore, it is important to clean out as described.

11 Check that the pistons are free to move in the cylinders, that the rubber dust covers are undamaged and in position, and that there are no hydraulic fluid leaks.

12 Apply a drop of oil to the adjuster threads.

13 Prior to reassembly, smear a trace of brake grease to the steady platforms and shoe locations on the cylinders. Do not allow any grease to come into contact with the linings or rubber parts.

14 Refit the shoes in the reverse sequence to removal. The pull off springs should preferably be renewed every time new shoes are fitted, and must be refitted in their original web holes. Position them between the web and backplate.

15 Back off the adjuster and refit the brake drum. Refit the roadwheel.

16 Note that the right-hand brake adjuster has a right-hand thread whilst the left-hand adjuster has a left-hand thread. Lubricate the adjuster as shown in Fig. 9.14 using brake grease. Also apply brake grease to those items arrowed in Fig. 9.15, being the principle brake pivot and contact areas.

12 Rear brake backplate – removal and refitting

The backplate is removed during the axleshaft (halfshaft) removal procedure, therefore refer to Chapter 8 Section 2 for further details.

13 Rear brake wheel cylinder – removal, servicing and refitting

If hydraulic fluid is leaking from the brake wheel cylinder, it may be necessary to dismantle it and renew the seal. Should brake fluid be found running down the side of the wheel or a pool of liquid forms alongside one wheel and the level in the master cylinder has dropped, it is indicative that the seals have failed.

1 Remove the brake drum and shoes as described in Section 11.

2 Clean down the rear of the backplate to catch any hydraulic fluid which may issue from the open pipe or wheel cylinder.

3 Wipe the top of the brake master cylinder reservoir and unscrew the caps. Place a piece of thick polythene over the top of the reservoirs and refit the caps. This is to stop hydraulic fluid syphoning out. On models with a fluid level indicator it will be necessary to plug the open ends of the pipe to prevent loss of hydraulic fluid.

4 Disconnect the brake line to wheel cylinder cup nut and plug the pipe when detached to prevent any possible leakage or ingress of dirt (photo).

5 Unscrew and remove the wheel cylinder retaining bolts and withdraw the cylinder unit.

6 To dismantle the cylinder unit prise the dust covers from each end of the cylinder body and withdraw the pistons, cups and spring, noting the position of each as they are extracted. Do not use any hard or sharp objects to extract the piston assemblies as the boss must not be scored or damaged in any way.

7 Inspect the inside of the cylinder for score marks caused by impurities in the hydraulic fluid. **Note:** *if the wheel cylinder requires renewal always ensure that the replacement is identical to the one removed.*

8 If the cylinder is sound, thoroughly clean it out with fresh hydraulic fluid.

9 If a new kit is obtained, ensure that it is suitable for your cylinder as there are two types fitted, Nabco or Tokico, and their respective components are not interchangeable. It is therefore important to quote which type you require when ordering replacements, better still take the cylinder along for comparison.

10 Smear new seals with clean hydraulic fluid to assist assembly to pistons, and make certain they are facing the correct way.

11 Lubricate the cylinder bore with clean hydraulic fluid and reassemble the spring and piston assemblies and fit new rubber dust seals onto each end of the cylinder to complete.

12 Relocate the cylinder unit into the backplate and loosely fit the retaining bolts.

13 Remove the plug from the hydraulic pipe, and carefully screw the pipe retaining nut back into the cylinder.

14 When the hydraulic pipe is located, tighten the wheel cylinder retaining bolts to the specified torque and then tighten the pipe nut – but don't overtighten.

15 Reassembly of the brake shoes, springs and drum is a reversal of the removal procedure as given in Section 11.

16 Bleed the rear brakes on completion (Section 5) and check the cylinder for signs of possible fluid leakage and efficient operation.

14 Master cylinder – removal and refitting

1 Wipe clean the master cylinder and caps to prevent the ingress of dirt to components during the following operations (photo).

2 Unscrew the hydraulic unions from the master cylinder and drain the fluid into a suitable container.

3 Unscrew the master cylinder securing nuts at the flange to the servo unit and carefully withdraw the cylinder unit.

4 Refitting is the reversal of the removal procedure. After topping-up the reservoirs, bleed the master cylinder at the bleed nipples and then bleed the hydraulic system as described in Section 5.

15 Master cylinder – dismantling and reassembly

1 Assuming that the cylinder has been removed (see previous Section) and drained out, commence dismantling by extracting the stopper ring from end of the bore.

2 Extract the stopper using a small screwdriver.

3 Unscrew and remove the stopper screw from underneath the cylinder body.

4 The primary and secondary piston assemblies may now be withdrawn from the cylinder bore. Make a special note of the assembly order as the parts are removed.

5 Carefully remove the seals making a note of which way round they are fitted.

6 Unscrew the plugs located on the underside of the cylinder body and withdraw the check valve parts. These must be kept in their respective sets.

7 Thoroughly clean the parts in brake fluid, isopropyl alcohol or methylated spirits. After drying the items, inspect the seals for signs of distortion, swelling, splitting or hardening although it is recommended new rubber parts are always fitted after dismantling as a matter of course.

8 Inspect the bore and piston for signs of deep scoring marks which, if evident, means a new cylinder should be fitted. Make sure that the ports in the bore are clean by poking gently with a piece of wire.

9 If for any reason the reservoir tanks have to be removed, they must be renewed on assembly. Do *not* refit the old ones.

10 The fluid level gauge assemblies are not repairable and they

should not therefore be interfered with. If they are defective then they must be renewed as a unit.

11 Before assembly check that you have the correct seal kit or exchange parts/unit, as there are two types of master cylinder fitted. Although basically similar in design one is manufactured by Tokico and the other by Nabco. As the components of each are not interchangeable it is most important to specify which type you have when ordering spare parts or replacements, better still take the old parts along to the dealer for direct comparison.

12 As the parts are refitted to the cylinder bore make sure that they are thoroughly wetted with clean hydraulic fluid.

13 Fit new seals to the pistons making sure they are the correct way round as noted during removal.

14 With the cylinder bore well lubricated, insert the secondary return spring, secondary piston, primary return spring and primary piston into the bore. Take care not to roll the seal lips whilst inserting into the bore.

15 Refit the stopper and stopper ring to secure.
16 Insert the check valve assemblies and secure with plugs.
17 Don't forget to insert the stopper screw and use a new washer.

16 Master-Vac servo unit – description

A Master-Vac vacuum servo unit is fitted and operates in series with the master cylinder to provide assistance to the driver when the brake pedal is depressed. This reduces the effort required by the driver to operate the brake under all braking conditions.

The unit operates by vacuum obtained from the intake manifold and comprises basically a booster diaphragm and control valve assembly.

The servo unit and hydraulic master cylinder are connected together so that the servo unit piston rod (valve rod) acts as the master

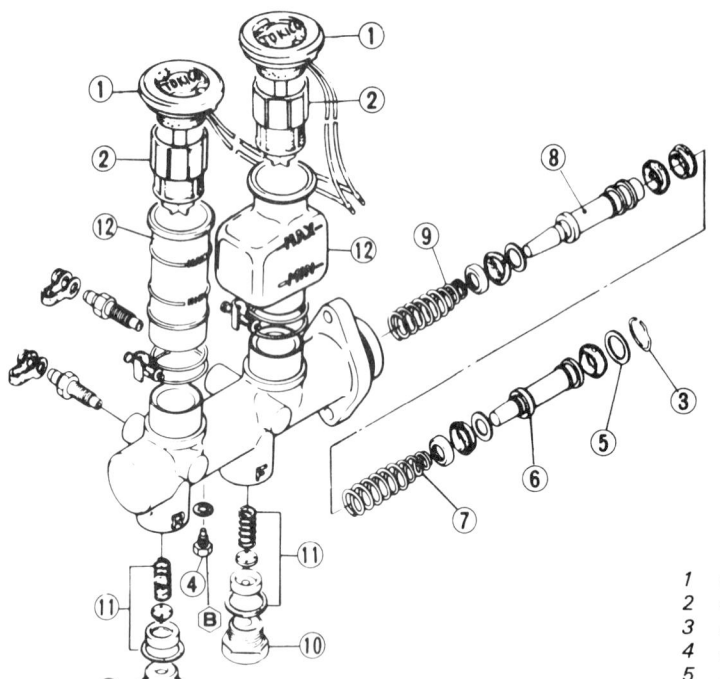

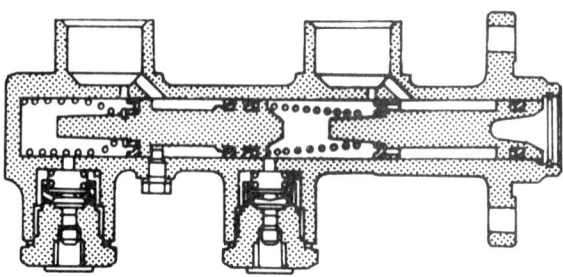

Fig. 9.17 The Tikico type master cylinder components

1	Cap	7	Primary piston return spring
2	Filter	8	Secondary piston
3	Stopper ring	9	Return spring – secondary piston
4	Stopper screw	10	Plugs
5	Stopper	11	Check valves
6	Primary piston	12	Reservoirs

13.4 View showing brake line connection (1), cylinder retaining bolts (2) and bleeder, (3). Note rubber plug to left of bleeder nipple which is removed to adjust brakes, (4)

14.1 Wipe the cylinder body and reservoir caps clean before starting removal

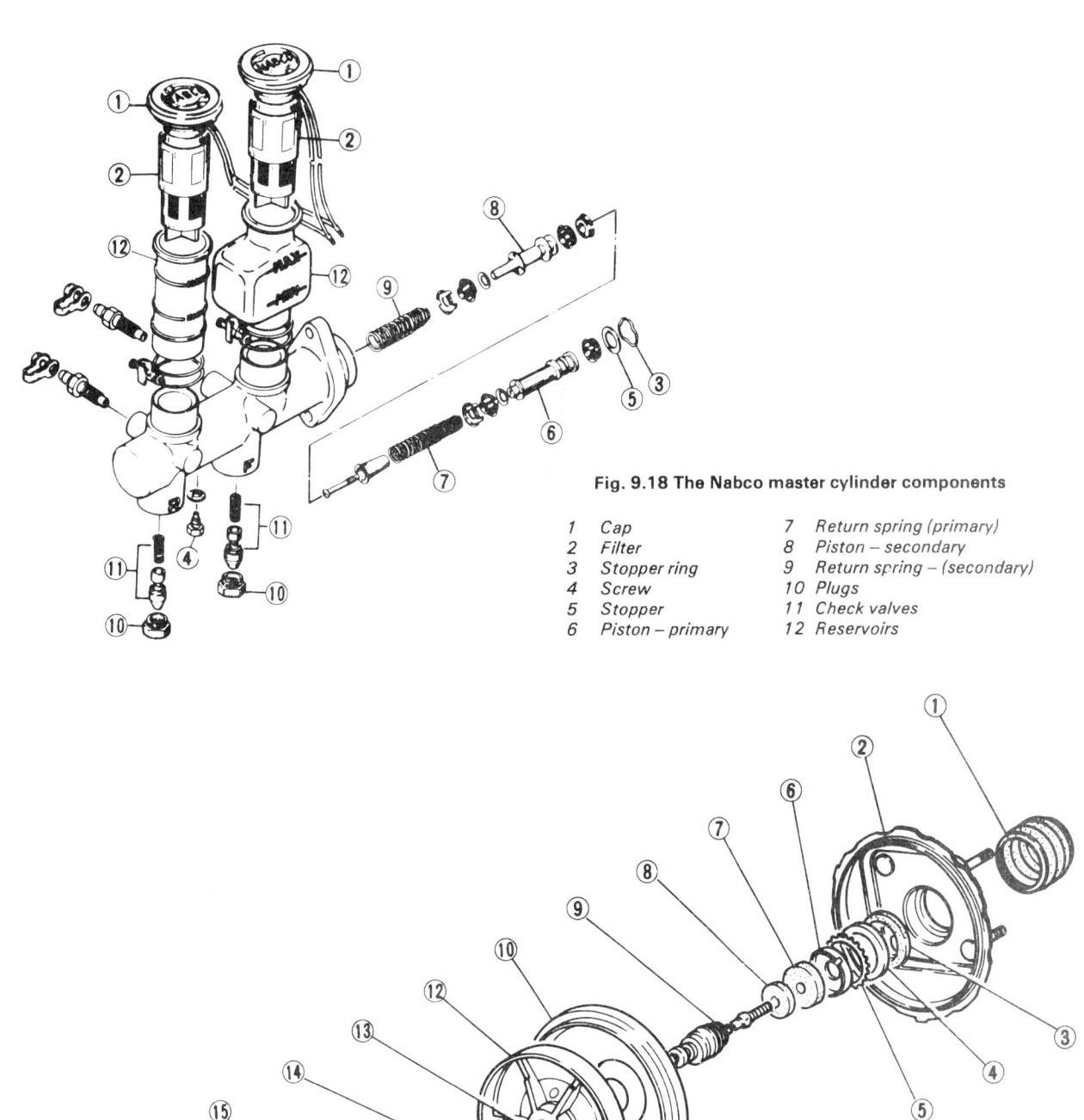

Fig. 9.18 The Nabco master cylinder components

1	Cap	7	Return spring (primary)
2	Filter	8	Piston – secondary
3	Stopper ring	9	Return spring – (secondary)
4	Screw	10	Plugs
5	Stopper	11	Check valves
6	Piston – primary	12	Reservoirs

Fig. 9.19 The Master-Vac vacuum servo unit components

1	Valve guard	8	Filter silencer	13	Reaction disc
2	Rear shell and stud unit	9	Valve operating rod and plunger unit	14	Pushrod assembly
3	Seal	10	Diaphragm	15	Diaphragm return spring
4	Bearing			16	Front shell and stud unit
5	Retainer	11	Key	17	Plate and seal assembly
6	Air silencer retainer	12	Diaphragm plate	18	Flange
7	Silencer				

cylinder pushrod. The driver's braking effort is transmitted through another pushrod to the servo unit piston and its built-in control system. The servo unit piston is attached to a rolling diaphragm which ensures an airtight seal between the two major parts of the servo unit casing. The forward chamber is held under vacuum conditions created in the intake manifold of the engine and, during periods when the brake pedal is not in use, the controls open a passage to the rear chamber so placing it under vacuum conditions as well. When the brake pedal is depressed, the vacuum passage to the rear chamber is cut off and the chamber opened to atmospheric pressure. The consequent pressure difference across the servo piston pushes the piston forward in the vacuum chamber and operates the main pushrod to the master cylinder.

The controls are designed so that assistance is given under all conditions and, when the brakes are not required, vacuum in the rear chamber is established when the brake pedal is released.

Under normal operating conditions the vacuum servo unit is very reliable and does not require overhaul except at very high mileage. In this case it is far better to obtain a service exchange unit, rather than repair the original unit. If overhaul is to be carried out make sure that the necessary kit is available.

17 Master-Vac servo unit – removal and refitting

1　Remove the suction hose from the connection on the servo unit.
2　Remove the master cylinder; refer to Section 14 if necessary.
3　Using a pair of pliers, extract the split pin in the end of the brake pedal to pushrod clevis pin. Withdraw the clevis pin. To assist this it may be necessary to release the pedal return spring.
4　Undo and remove the four nuts and spring washers that secure the unit to the bulkhead. Lift the unit away from the engine bulkhead.
5　Refitting of the servo unit is the reverse sequence to removal.

18 Master-Vac servo unit – dismantling, inspection and reassembly

Thoroughly clean the outside of the unit using a stiff brush and wipe with a lint-free rag. It cannot be too strongly emphasised that cleanliness is important when working on the servo unit. Before any attempt is made to dismantle, refer to Fig. 9.20 where it will be seen that two items of equipment are required. Firstly, a base plate must be made to enable the unit to be safely held in the vice. Secondly, a lever must be made similar to the form shown. Without these items it is impossible to dismantle satisfactorily.

1　Using a file or scriber, mark a line across the two halves of the unit to act as a datum for alignment.
2　Fit the previously made base-plate into a firm vice and attach the unit to the plate using the master cylinder studs.
3　Fit the lever to the four studs on the rear shell.
4　Use a piece of long rubber hose and connect one end to the adaptor on the engine inlet manifold and the other end to the servo unit. Start the engine and this will create a vacuum in the unit so drawing the two halves together.
5　Rotate the lever in an anti-clockwise direction until the front shell indentations are in line with the recesses in the rim of the rear shell. Then press the lever assembly down firmly whilst an assistant stops the engine and quickly removes the vacuum pipe from the inlet manifold connector. Depress the operating rod so as to release the vacuum, whereupon the front and rear halves should part. If necessary, use a soft faced hammer and slightly tap the front half to break the bond.
6　Unscrew the locknut and yoke from the pushrod and then remove the valve body rubber gaiter. Separate the diaphragm assembly from the rear shell.
7　Using a screwdriver, carefully pry out the retainer and then remove the bearing and seal from the shell. This operation should only be done if it is absolutely necessary to renew the seal or bearing.
8　Carefully detach the diaphragm from the diaphragm plate.
9　Using a screwdriver, carefully and evenly remove the air silencer retainer from the diaphragm plate.
10　Withdraw the valve plunger stop key by lightly pushing on the valve operating rod and sliding it from its location.
11　Withdraw the silencer and plunger assembly.

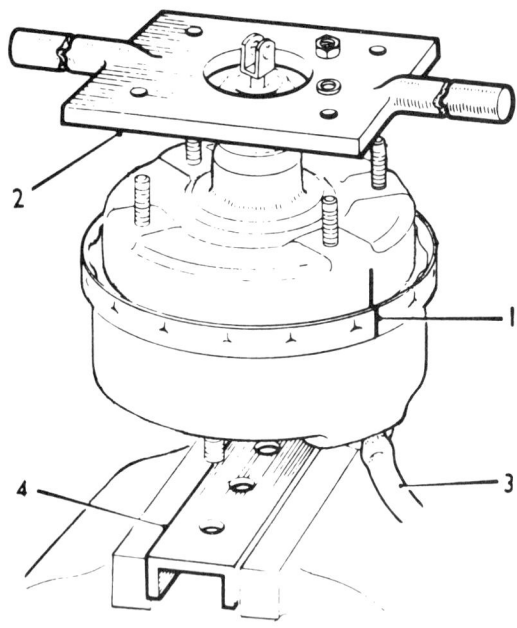

Fig. 9.20 Special tools required to dismantle servo unit

1 Scribe marks　　　*3 Vacuum applied*
2 Lever　　　　　　*4 Base plate*

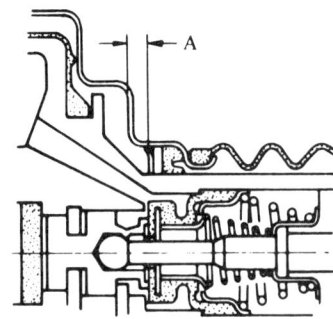

Fig. 9.21 Fitting dimension for the seal

A 0.264 to 0.276 in (6.7 to 7.0 mm)

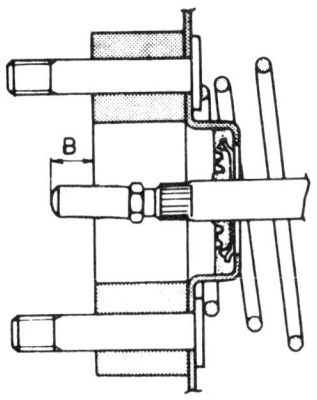

Fig. 9.22 Master-Vac pushrod setting dimension

B = 0.384 to 0.393 (9.75 to 10.00 mm)

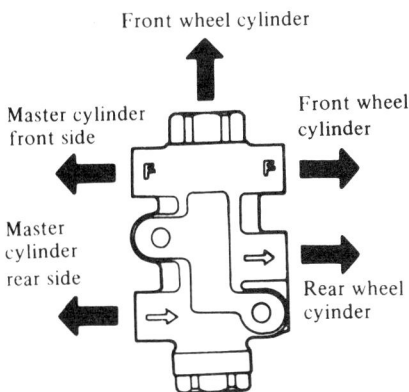

Fig. 9.23 The NP valve connections (RH drive models)

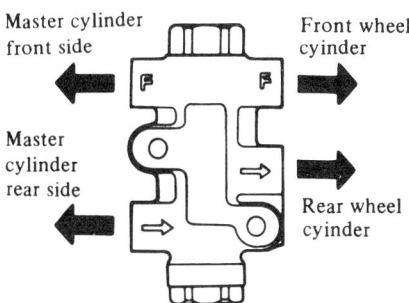

Fig. 9.24 The NP valve connections (LH drive models)

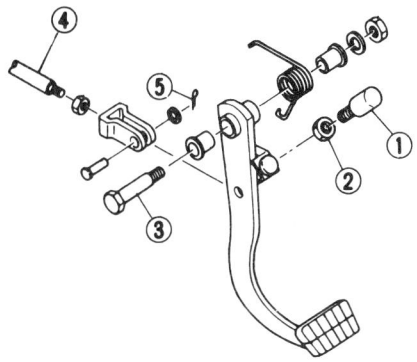

Fig. 9.25 The brake pedal components

1　*Brake light switch*	4　*Operating rod*
2　*Locknut*	5　*Split pin*
3　*Fulcrum pin*	

12 Next remove the reaction disc.

13 Remove the two nuts and spring washers, and withdraw the front seal assembly from the front cover. It is recommended that unless the seal is to be renewed it should be left in its housing.

14 Thoroughly clean all parts and wipe with a clean lint-free rag. Inspect for signs of damage, stripped threads etc, and obtain new parts as necessary. All seals must be renewed and for this a 'Major Repair Kit' should be purchased. This will also contain the special grease required during reassembly.

15 To reassemble, first apply a little of the special grease to the sealing surface and lip of the seal. Fit the seal to the rear shell using a drift of suitable diameter. Ensure that dimension A (Fig. 9.21) is maintained.

16 Apply a little special grease to the sliding contact portions on the circumference of the plunger assembly.

17 Fit the plunger assembly and silencer into the diaphragm plate and retain in position with the stop key. As the plate is made of bakelite take care not to damage it during this operation.

18 Refit the diaphragm into the cover and then smear a little special grease on the diaphragm plate. Refit the reaction disc.

19 Smear a little special grease onto the inner wall of the seal and front shell with which the seal comes into contact. Refit the front seal assembly.

20 Refit the front shell to the base plate, and the lever to the rear shell. Reconnect the vacuum hose. Position the diaphragm return spring in the front shell. Lightly smear the outer head of the diaphragm with special grease and locate the diaphragm assembly in the rear shell. Position the rear shell assembly on the return spring and align the previously made scribed marks.

21 Adjust the end of the pushrod to obtain dimension 'B' as in Fig. 9.22.

22 An assistant should start the engine. Watching one's fingers very carefully, press the two halves of the unit together and, using the lever tool, turn clockwise to lock the two halves together. Stop the engine and disconnect the hose.

23 Refit the servo unit and check for correct operation after overhaul, first start the engine and run for a minimum period of two minutes and then switch off. Wait for ten minutes and apply the footbrake very carefully, listening to hear the rush of air into the servo unit. This will indicate that vacuum was retained and the unit is operating correctly.

19 Nissan Proportioning (NP) valve

The NP valve is fitted between the front and rear brake lines and enables the front brakes to operate normally even when the rear brake line has developed a serious leak. Also should there be a leak in the front brake line the rear brake will still function.

It is recommended that every 24 000 miles (40 000 km) valve operation be checked for correct operation. Remove all luggage and then drive the car to a dry road. With the car travelling at 30 mph (50 km/h) apply the brakes suddenly.

The valve is functioning normally when the rear wheels lock simultaneously with the front wheels or when the front wheels lock before the rear wheels.

Should the rear wheels lock before the front wheels then it is probable that the NP valve has developed an internal fault and it should be renewed.

20 Brake fluid level gauge

1 A brake fluid level gauge is fitted into the reservoir on some models and is designed to light the brake warning light on the instrument panel when the level of fluid falls below a certain level in the reservoir.

2 The float rides on the surface of the hydraulic fluid and when the level drops to the danger point a magnet in the float operates a switch so completing the circuit.

3 To check the operation of the switch; with the ignition switched on, but the engine not running, slowly raise the cap and ascertain that the brake warning light is extinguished when the float is raised up to the cap (photo).

21 Brake pedal – removal and refitting

1 Extract the split pin from the clevis to pedal pin. Withdraw the pin

20.3 Lift the cap to check the warning light — the float is seen in its lowest position (warning light on)

22.9 Cable located in lockplate

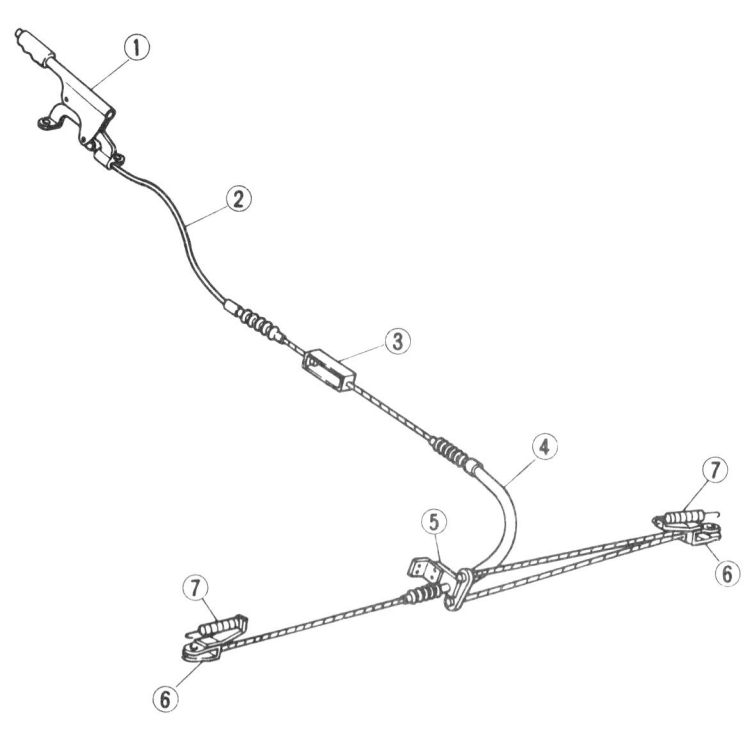

Fig. 9.26 The centre lever handbrake layout

1 Lever	3 Adjuster	5 Strap
2 Cable (front)	4 Cable (rear)	6 Return spring

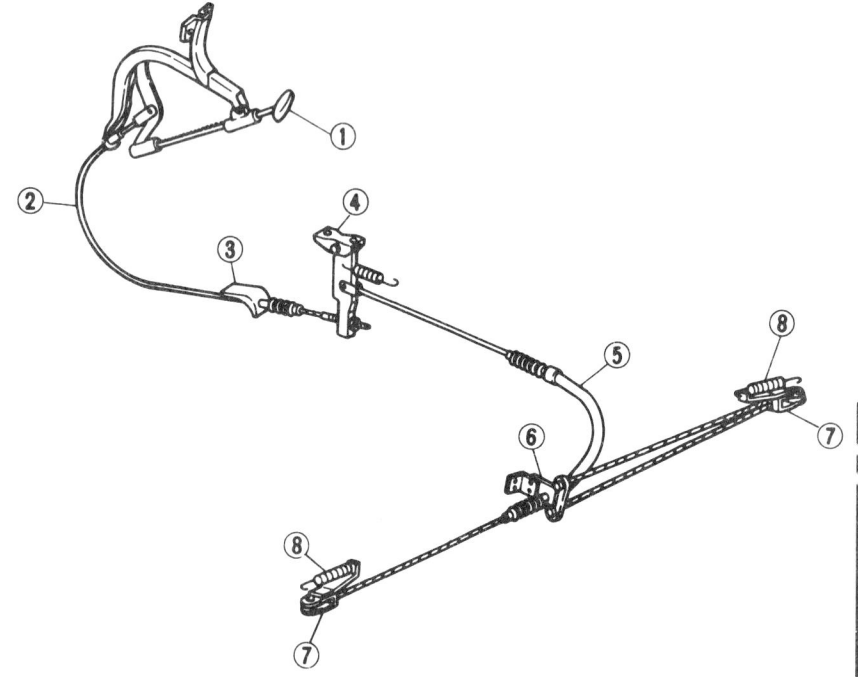

Fig. 9.27 The stick type handbrake layout

1 Control stem	4 Mediation lever	7 Clevis
2 Cable (front)	5 Cable rear	8 Return spring
3 Cable bracket	6 Strap	

22.11 The cable clevis and pin in position also showing return spring

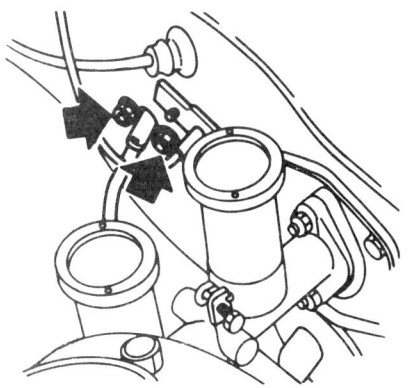

Fig. 9.28 The cable to dashpanel nuts

from the clevis and pedal to separate.

2 Unscrew and remove the fulcrum pin nut and washer, withdraw the fulcrum pin.

3 The pedal and spring can be removed together but note the way round that the spring is attached. If necessary, drift out the bushes.

4 Refitting is a direct reversal of removal but smear the bushes and return spring with a general purpose grease. Use a new split pin to secure the clevis pin.

5 Check the pedal height and fully depressed positions and adjust as necessary at the pushrod yoke or switch until correct movement is obtained.

22 Handbrake (centre lever type) – lever and cables – removal and refitting

Control lever and front cable

1 Disconnect the battery earth cable.

2 Remove the central console box where applicable to gain access to the handbrake lever and warning switch.

3 Detach the handbrake warning switch wire at the terminal connector.

4 Unscrew and remove the handbrake lever bolts and detach the grommet rubber.

5 Working underneath the car remove the locking plate and disconnect the cable adjuster, then carefully withdraw the cable together with the control lever unit through the interior.

6 To detach the cable, remove the split pin and extract the clevis pin.

7 Refitting is a direct reversal of the removal procedure but ensure that a new split pin is used to secure the clevis pin when reassembling the cable. Check that the cable is clear of surrounding components and is able to operate without binding. Readjust the handbrake as described in Section 3. Check that the warning light switch operates correctly before refitting the central console.

Rear cable

8 Working underneath the car, detach the adjuster from the front cable.

9 Prise the lockplate free (photo) at the cables rear axle location.

10 Unscrew the securing set screws and disconnect the strap retainer unit on the rear axle casing.

11 Disconnect the return spring and detach the cable from the operating lever in the backplate (photo). The cable is retained to the lever by a clevis and pin. Extract the split-pin and withdraw the clevis pin to separate.

12 Refitting is a reversal of the removal procedure but use a new split-pin to retain the clevis pin. Smear the clevis pin/s and adjuster with grease during assembly and to other sliding contact surfaces. Check that the cables are clear of surrounding components and do not bind when operated. Adjust the handbrake as described in Section 3.

23 Handbrake (stick type) lever and cables – removal and refitting

Control lever

1 Disconnect the battery earth cable.

2 Unscrew and remove the control bracket retaining nuts under the dashboard panel.

3 Withdraw the split-pin from the clevis pin of the control stem to bracket and remove the clevis pin.

4 Now remove the cable from the control stem clevis and withdraw the control assembly.

5 Refitting is a reversal of the removal but smear the clevis pins with grease to lubricate and check brake cable adjustment. Also check that the warning light and switch are fully operational.

Front cable

6 To remove the front cable, disconnect it from the control lever clevis under the dashboard panel.

7 Unscrew and remove the nuts retaining the cable to the dashpanel withdraw the cable through the engine compartment (Fig. 9.28).

8 Working underneath the car, unclip the return spring from the mediation lever and then loosen the front cable adjuster locknut and detach the front cable to remove.

9 Refitting is a reversal of removal but readjust the cable adjuster on completion and check that the cable does not bind on other components.

Rear cable

10 Working underneath the car, extract the split-pin from the clevis pin, withdraw it and detach the cable from the mediation lever.

11 Refer to Section 22 and follow instructions 9 to 12.

Fault diagnosis overleaf

24 Fault diagnosis – braking system

Symptom	Reason/s
Pedal travels almost to floor before brakes operate	Brake fluid level too low Wheel cylinder leaking Master cylinder leaking (bubbles in master cylinder fluid) Brake flexible hose leaking Brake line fractured Brake system unions loose Shoe linings excessively worn
Brake pedal feel 'springy'	New linings not yet bedded-in Brake drums badly worn or cracked Master cylinder securing nuts loose
Brake pedal feels 'spongy' and 'soggy'	Wheel cylinder leaking Master cylinder leaking (bubbles in master cylinder reservoir) Brake pipe line or flexible hose leaking Unions in brake system loose Blocked reservoir cap vent hole
Excessive effort required to brake vehicle	Shoe linings badly worn New shoes recently fitted – not yet bedded-in Harder linings fitted than standard resulting in increase in pedal pressure Linings and brake drums contaminated with oil, grease or hydraulic fluid Servo unit inoperative or faulty Scored drums
Brakes uneven and pulling to one side	Linings and drums contaminated with oil, grease or hydraulic fluid Tyre pressure unequal Radial ply tyres fitted at one end of the vehicle only Brake shoes fitted incorrectly Different type of linings fitted at each wheel Anchorages for front or rear suspension loose Brake drums badly worn, cracked or distorted Incorrect front wheel alignment Incorrectly adjusted front wheel bearings
Brakes tend to bind, drag or lock-on	Air in hydraulic system Wheel cylinders seized Handbrake cables too tight Weak shoe return springs Incorrectly set foot pedal or pushrod Master cylinder seized Brakes over-adjusted

Chapter 10 Electrical system

Contents

Specifications

System type . . . . 12V, negative ground (earth)

Battery
Type . . . . Lead acid
Rating . . . . Varies according to market, consult your Datsun dealer or battery
                                                                              specialist for a replacement

Alternator – 140J and 160J models
Type . . . . Hitachi LT 135-13B (LT 135-19B or LT 150-05 option)
Rating:
   LT135 series . . . . 35 amps at 12 volts
   LT150 series . . . . 50 amps at 12 volts
Output current (hot) at rpm:
   LT135 series . . . . 28 amps at 2500 rpm
   LT150 series . . . . 37.5 amps at 2500 rpm
Pulley ratio . . . . 2.25 : 1
Brush length (minimum) . . . . 0.276 in (7 mm)
Slip ring outer diameter (minimum) . . . . 1.22 in (31 mm)

Alternator – 510 model
Type . . . . Hitachi LR150-35 or LR160-47 (optional)
Rating:
   LR 150 series . . . . 50 amps at 12 volts
   LR 160 series . . . . 60 amps at 12 volts
Output current (hot) at rpm:
   LR 150 series . . . . 40 amps at 2500 rpm
   LR 160 series . . . . 41 to 49 amps at 2500 rpm

Pulley ratio 2.90
Brush length (minimum) . . . .   0.295 in (7.5 mm)
Slip ring outside diameter . . . .   1.18 in (30 mm)

Voltage regulator

A 14 engine . . . .   TLIZ-57B or RQB 2220B
L 16 engine . . . .   TLIZ-57 or TLIZ-58
L 20 engine . . . .   TRIZ-27 (Transistorized)

	TL 1Z-57 and 58	**RQB2220B**
Regulating voltage (with fully charged battery)	14.3 to 15.3V at 68°F (20°C)	14.3 to 15.3V at 68°F (20°C)
Voltage coil resistance	10.5 ohms at 68°F (20°C)	23.6 ohms at 68°F (20°C)
Core gap	0.024 to 0.039 in (0.6 to 1.0 mm)	0.028 to 0.051 in (0.7 to 1.3 mm)
Points gap	0.012 to 0.016 in (0.3 to 0.4 mm)	0.012 to 0.016 in (0.3 to 0.4 mm)

Charge relay

Release voltage . . . .   4.2 to 5.2 at 'N' terminal
Voltage coil resistance
   TL1Z-57 and 58 . . . .   37.8 ohms at 68°F (20°C)
   RQB2220B . . . .   23.6 ohms at 68°F (20°C)
Core gap
   TL12-57 and 58 . . . .   0.031 to 0.039 in (0.8 to 1.0 mm)
   RQB2220B . . . .   0.035 to 0.055 in (0.9 to 1.4 mm)
Point gap
   TL12-57 and 58 . . . .   0.016 to 0.024 in (0.4 to 0.6 mm)
   RQB2220B . . . .   0.028 to 0.043 in (0.7 to 1.1 mm)

Starter motor

Manufacturer . . . .   Hitachi
Type
   A 14 engine . . . .   S114-160 or MCA02-0
   L 16 engine S114-103P
   L20 engine (automatic transmission) S114-180F
   L20 engine (manual transmission) S114-170E

	S114-160	**MC A02-0**	**S114-103P**	**S114-180F**	**S114-170E**
No load current	60 amp	60 amp	less than 60 amp	less than 60 amp	less than 60 amp
No load speed	7200 rpm-plus	7200 rpm-plus	7000 rpm-plus	6000 rpm-plus	7000 rpm-plus
Minimum brush length	0.472 in (12 mm)	0.453 in (11.5 mm)	0.492 in (12.5 mm)	0.47 in (12 mm)	0.47 in (12 mm)

Fuses

Fusebox location . . . .   Beneath instrument panel, between steering column and driver's side door
Fuse rating and protected circuits . . . .   Stated on fusebox cover

Fusible link

Colour . . . .   Green
Location . . . .   In battery positive lead
Rating . . . .   20 amp continuous
                                                                                              200 amp for 5 seconds

Bulbs

	USA and Canada (watts)	**General areas including UK (watts)**
Headlamp:		
Inner – high beam	37.5	37.5
Outer – low beam/high beam	37.5/50	37.5/50
Front combination lamp:		
Turn signal	27	21
Parking lamp	8	5
Side flasher	–	5
Side marker	8	–
License plate:		
Estate car	7.5	5
Saloon and Coupe	10	5
Rear combination lamp:		
Turn signal	27	21
Turn signal/stop lamp	23	–
Tail/stop lamp	8/27	5/21
Tail/turn signal and stop lamp	8/23	–
Tail lamp	8	5
Back-up lamp (reverse lamp)	27	21
Interior light	10	5

Engine compartment light	6	6
Wiper/washer illimination lamp	3.4	–
Heater control illumination lamp	3.4	3.4
Instrument panel and warning lamps (except tachometer)	1.7	1.7
Tachometer illumination lamp	3.4	3.4
Boot light:		
Saloon	3.4	–
Coupe	5	–
Estate Car	10	–
Floor temperature warning light	3.4	–
Fuel level warning light	3.4	–
Automatic transmission selection lever light	3.4	3.4
Seat belt warning light	3.4	–
Heated rear window switch light	1.4	1.5
Clock light	3.4	3.4
Brake warning light	3.4	3.4 (or 1.7, SSS models)
Oil pressure warning light	3.4	3.4
Charge warning light	3.4	3.4 (or 1.7, SSS models)
Main beam pilot light	3.4	3.4 (or 1.7, SSS models)

1 General description

The electrical system is 12 volt negative earth and the major components comprise a 12 volt battery, an alternator which is driven from the crankshaft pulley and a starter motor.

The battery supplies a steady current for the ignition, lighting, and other electrical circuits and provides a reserve of electricity when the current consumed by the electrical equipment exceeds that being produced by the alternator.

The alternator has a regulator which ensures a high output if the battery is in a low state of charge or the demand from the electrical equipment is high, and a low output if the battery is fully charged and there is little demand for the electrical equipment.

When fitting electrical accessories to cars with a negative earth system it is important, if they contain silicone diodes or transistors, that they are connected correctly, otherwise serious damage may result to the components concerned. Items such as radios, tape players, electric ignition systems, automatic headlight dipping etc, should all be checked for correct polarity.

It is important that the battery positive lead is always disconnected if the battery is to be boost charged. Also if body repairs are to be carried out using electric arc welding equipment, the alternator must be disconnected otherwise serious damage can be caused to the more delicate instruments. Whenever the battery has to be disconnected it must always be reconnected with the negative terminal earthed.

2 Battery – removal and refitting

1   The battery is situated in the engine compartment on the right-hand side at the front.
2   When removing the battery, always disconnect the negative cable first, followed by the positive cable. Then remove the nuts from the battery clamps and lift out the battery.
3   Refitting is the reverse of the removal procedure but before fitting the terminals smear them with a little petroleum jelly.

3 Battery – maintenance and inspection

1   Keep the top of the battery clean by wiping away dirt and moisture.
2   Remove the plugs or lid from the cells and check that the electrolyte level is just above the separator plates. If the level has fallen, add only distilled water until the electrolyte level is just above the separator plates.
3   As well as keeping the terminals clean and covered with petroleum jelly, the top of the battery, and especially the top of the cells, should be kept clean and dry. This helps prevent corosion and ensures that the battery does not become partially discharged by leakage through dampness and dirt.
4   Once every three months, remove the battery and inspect the battery securing bolts, the battery clamp plate, tray and battery leads

for corrosion (white fluffy deposits on the metal which are brittle to touch). If any corrosion is found, clean off the deposits with an ammonia or soda solution and paint over the clean metal with a fine base primer and/or underbody paint.
5   At the same time inspect the battery case for cracks. If a crack is found, clean and plug it with one of the proprietary compounds marketed for this purpose. If leakage through the crack has been excessive then it will be necessary to refill the appropriate cell with fresh electrolyte as detailed later. Cracks are frequently caused to the top of the battery cases by pouring in distilled water in the middle of winter *after* instead of *before* a run. This gives the water no chance to mix with the electrolyte and so the former freezes and splits the battery case.
6   If topping-up the battery becomes excessive and the case has been inspected for cracks that could cause leakage, but none are found, the battery is being over-charged and the voltage regulator will have to be checked and reset.
7   With the battery on the bench at the three monthly interval check, measure its specific gravity with a hydrometer to determine the state of charge and condition of the electrolyte. There should be very little variation between the different cells and if a variation in excess of 0.025 is present it will be due to either:

(a) *Loss of electrolyte from the battery at some time caused by spillage or a leak, resulting in a drop in the specific gravity of electrolyte when the deficiency was replaced with distilled water instead of fresh electrolyte.*
(b) *An internal short circuit caused by buckling of the plates or a similar malady pointing to the likelihood of total battery failure in the near future.*

8   The specific gravity of the electrolyte for fully charged conditions at the electrolyte temperature indicated, is listed in Table A. The specific gravity of a fully discharged battery at different temperatures of the electrolyte is given in Table B.

Table A
Specific Gravity – Battery Fully Charged
1.268 at 100°F or 38°C electrolyte temperature
1.272 at 90°F or 32°C electrolyte temperature
1.276 at 80°F or 27°C electrolyte temperature
1.280 at 70°F or 21°C electrolyte temperature
1.284 at 60°F or 16°C electrolyte temperature
1.288 at 50°F or 10°C electrolyte temperature
1.292 at 40°F or 4°C electrolyte temperature
1.296 at 30°F or –1.5°C electrolyte temperature

Table B
Specific Gravity – Battery Fully Discharged
1.098 at 100°F or 38°C electrolyte temperature
1.102 at 90°F or 32°C electrolyte temperature
1.106 at 80°F or 27°C electrolyte temperature
1.110 at 70°F or 21°C electrolyte temperature
1.114 at 60°F or 16°C electrolyte temperature
1.118 at 50°F or 10°C electrolyte temperature
1.112 at 40°F or 4°C electrolyte temperature
1.126 at 30°F or –1.5°C electrolyte temperature

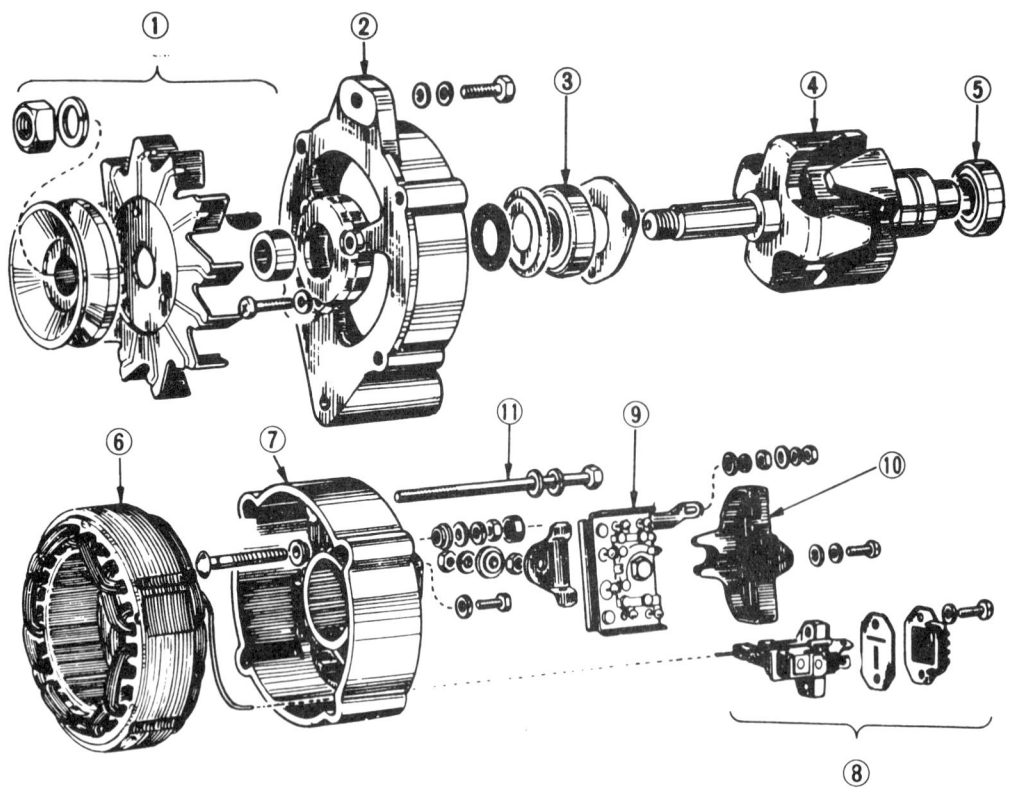

Fig. 10.1 Alternator as fitted to 140J and 160J models

1 Pulley group	4 Rotor	7 Rear cover	10 Diode cover
2 Front cover	5 Rear bearing	8 Brush assembly	11 Through bolts
3 Front bearing	6 Stator	9 Diode set	

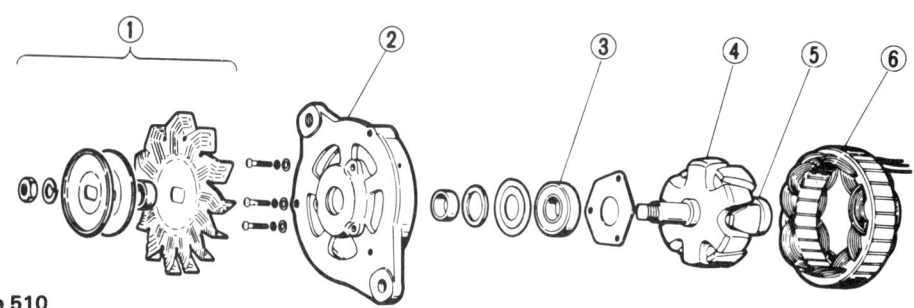

Fig. 10.2 Alternator as fitted to the 510 Series (USA)

1 Pulley unit
2 Front cover
3 Bearing (front)
4 Rotor
5 Bearing (rear)
6 Stator
7 Diode set
8 Brush assembly
9 IC voltage regulator
10 Cover (rear)
11 Through bolts

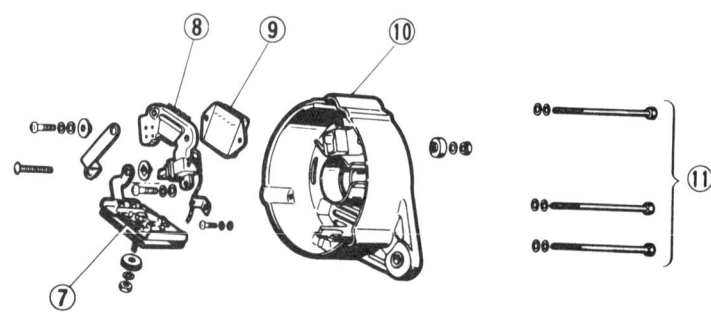

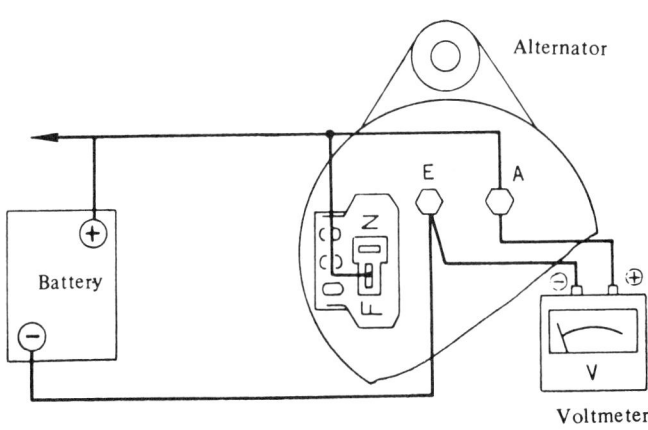

Fig. 10.3 Test the alternator using a voltmeter

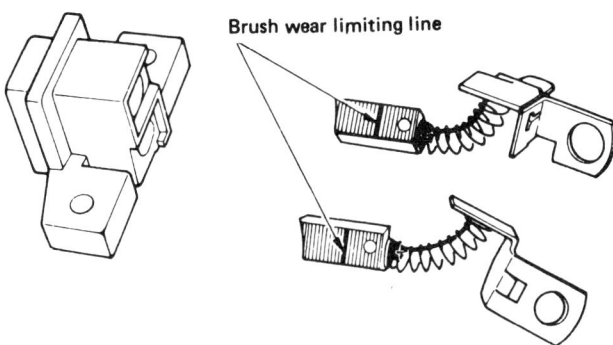

Fig. 10.4 Brushes removed showing the wear limit lines

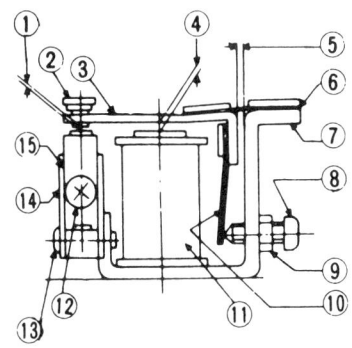

Fig. 10.5 Voltage regulator unit

1 Points clearance	*9 Locking nut*
2 Lower contact	*10 Spring*
3 Armature	*11 Coil*
4 Core gap	*12 Screw (3 mm)*
5 Yoke gap	*13 Screw (4 mm)*
6 Spring	*14 Contact set*
7 Yoke	*15 Contact (upper)*
8 Adjuster screw	

4 Electrolyte replenishment

1   If the battery is in a fully charged state and one of the cells maintains a specific gravity reading which is 0.025 or more lower than the others, and a check of each cell has been made with a battery testing meter to check for short circuits (a four to seven second test should give a steady reading of between 1.2 to 1.8 volts), then it is likely that the electrolyte has been lost from the cell with the low reading at some time.

2   Top-up the cell with a solution of 1 part of sulphuric acid to 2.5 parts water. If the cell is already fully topped up draw some electrolyte out of it with a pipette.

3   When mixing the sulphuric acid and water *never add water to sulphuric acid* – always pour the acid slowly onto the water in a glass container. *If water is added to sulphuric acid it will explode.*

4   Continue to top-up the cell with the freshly made electrolyte and then recharge the battery and check the hydrometer readings.

Note: *If the battery is not removed from the vehicle when being charged it is essential that the cables are disconnected as described in Section 2.*

5 Battery charging

1   Under normal operating conditions there should be no need to charge a battery from an external source, and if it is found to be necessary either the battery, alternator or voltage regulator are at fault.

2   When a vehicle has not been used for a period of time (particularly in very cold conditions) and it is found that the battery condition will not allow the engine to start, it is a good idea to charge the battery for about five hours at an initial charging current of about five amps. (The amount of charge and charging time will obviously depend on the battery condition, but the charging current will fall as the battery charge builds up). Alternatively a trickle charge at an initial current of about 1.5 amps can safely be used overnight.

3   The use of rapid boost chargers, which are claimed to restore the full charge of a battery in a very short time, should be avoided if at all possible as the battery plates are likely to suffer damage.

6 Alternator – general description, maintenance and precautions

1   Briefly, the alternator comprises a rotor and stator. Current is generated in the coils of the stator as soon as the rotor revolves. This current is three-phase alternating, which is then rectified by positive and negative silicon diodes; the charging current required to maintain the battery charge is controlled by a regulator unit.

2   Maintenance consists of occasionally wiping away any oil or dirt which may have accumulated on the outside of the unit.

3   No lubrication is required as the bearings are grease-sealed for life.

4   Check the drivebelt tension periodically to ensure that its specified deflection is correctly maintained (see Chapter 2).

5   Take extreme care when making circuit connections to a vehicle fitted with an alternator and observe the following. When making connections to the alternator from a battery, always match correct polarity. Before using electric-arc welding equipment to repair any part of the vehicle, disconnect the connector from the alternator and disconnect the battery cables. Always disconnect both battery cables before using a mains charger. If boosting from another battery, always connect in parallel using heavy cable.

7 Alternator – testing in the vehicle

1   Where a faulty alternator is suspected, first ensure that the battery is fully charged; if necessary charge from an outside source.

2   Obtain a 0 to 30 voltmeter.

3   Disconnect the leads from the alternator terminals.

4   Connect a test probe from the voltmeter positive terminal to the 'N' or 'BAT' terminal of the alternator. Connect the voltmeter negative terminal to earth and check that the voltmeter indicates battery voltage (12 volts).

5   Switch the headlights to main beam.

6   Start the engine and gradually increase its speed to approximately 1100rpm and check the reading on the voltmeter. If it registers over

8.2 The lead wires and connector

8.3 Alternator pivot mounting bolts and link arm adjuster bolt at the top (fan belt removed)

11.1 The voltage regulator

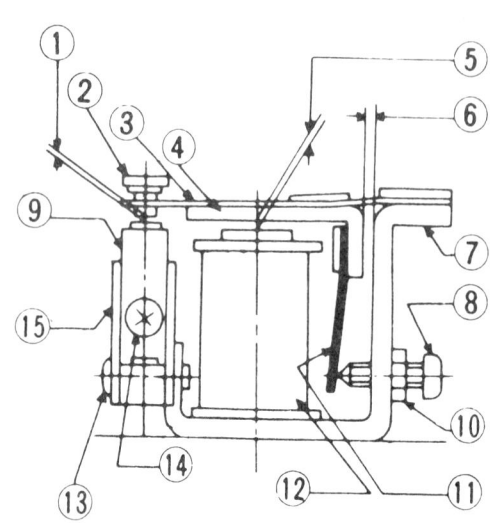

Fig. 10.6 The charge relay unit

1   Points gap
2   Relay contact
3   Spring
4   Armature
5   Core gap
6   Yoke gap
7   Yoke
8   Screw (adjuster)
9   Regulator contact
10 Locking nut
11 Spring
12 Coil
13 Screw (3 mm)
14 Screw (4 mm)
15 Contact set

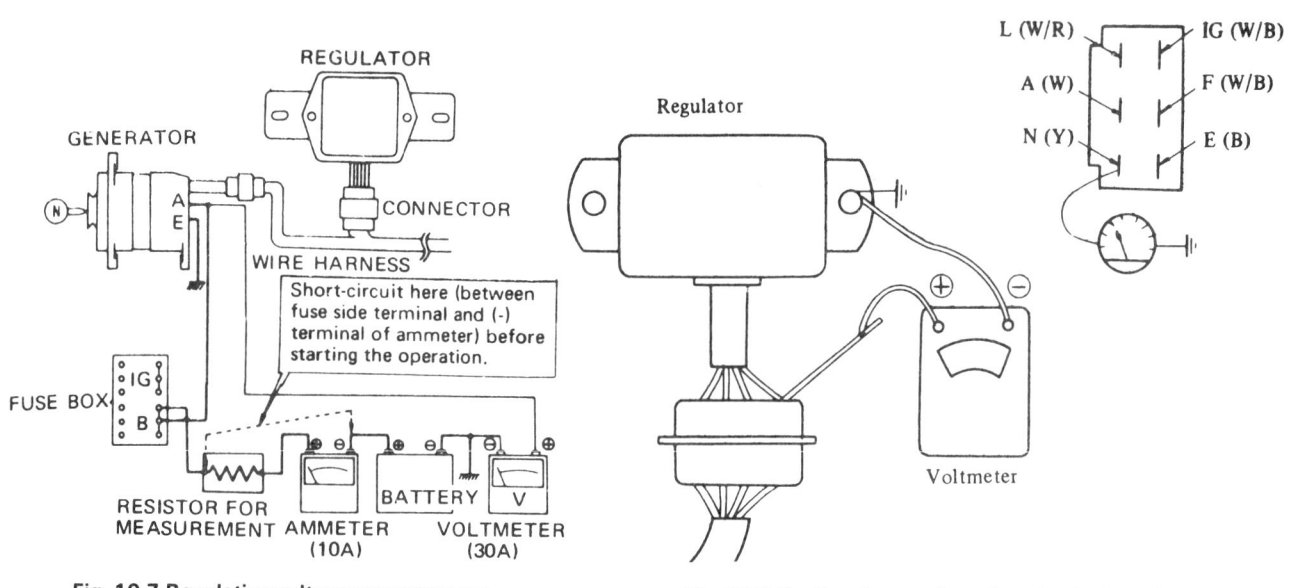

Short-circuit here (between fuse side terminal and (-) terminal of ammeter) before starting the operation.

Fig. 10.7 Regulating voltage measurement

Fig. 10.8 Testing the regulator (mechanical type)

12.5 volts then the alternator is in good condition; if it registers below 12.5 volts then the alternator is faulty, amd must be removed and repaired. Do not exceed 1100rpm during the test.

8 Alternator – removal and installation

1 Detach the battery earth cable.
2 Disconnect the lead wires and connector (photo), from the rear of the alternator.
3 Slacken the alternator pivot mounting bolts and also the adjustment link bolt (photo) sufficiently to allow the alternator to be hinged inwards towards the engine.
4 Disconnect the fan belt from the alternator pulley and then remove the pivot and adjusting link bolts whilst supporting the alternator, and lift it clear.
5 Refitting is a reversal of the removal procedure but ensure that the fan belt tension is correctly adjusted as described in Chapter 2.

9 Alternator – brush renewal

1 These are the most likely components to require renewal, and their wear should be checked at 50 000 mile (80 000 km) intervals or whenever the alternator is suspected of being faulty (indicated by a discharged battery).
2 On the LR150–35 and LR160–47 alternators (USA models), the brush removal necessitates the removal of the rear cover. It is therefore recommended that unless you are familiar with the circuitry and components of alternators, renewal of the brushes is best left to your local Datsun dealer or auto electrician.
3 On those alternators where brushes can be renewed externally proceed as follows.
4 Remove the brush holder securing screws and withdraw the cover.
5 Remove the brush holder complete with brushes. Do not disconnect the 'N' terminal from the stator coil lead.
6 If the brushes have worn down to the limit marked on them, renew them.
7 Check that the brushes move smoothly in their holders; otherwise clean the holders free from any dust or dirt.
8 Refitting of the brushes is the reverse of the removal procedure.

10 Alternator – fault finding and repair

1 Due to the specialist knowledge and equipment required to test and service an alternator it is recommended that if the performance is suspect, the car be taken to an automobile electrician who will have the facilities for such work. Because of this recommendation no further detailed service information is given.

11 Regulator – description, testing and adjustment

140 and 160J models
1 The regulator is located on the right side of the engine compartment, and incorporates a separate voltage regulator and cut-out (photo).
2 The voltage regulator controls the output from the alternator depending upon the state of the battery and the demands of the vehicle electrical equipment, and it ensures that the battery is not overcharged. The cut-out is virtually an automatic switch which completes the charging circuit as soon as the alternator starts to rotate and isolates it when the engine stops so that the battery cannot be discharged through the alternator. One visual indication of the correct functioning of the cut-out is the ignition warning lamp. When the lamp is out, the system is charging.
3 Before testing, check that the alternator drivebelt is not broken or slack, and that all electrical leads are secure.
4 Test the regulator voltage with the unit still fitted in the vehicle. If it has been removed make sure that it is positioned with the connector plug hanging downward. Carry out the testing with the engine compartment cold, and complete the test within one minute to prevent the regulator heating up and affecting the specified voltage readings.

5 Establish the ambient temperature within the engine compartment, turn off all vehicle electrical equipment and ensure that the battery is in a fully charged state. Connect a dc (15 to 30v) voltmeter, adc (5 to 30 A) ammeter and a 0.25 ohm 25 watt resistor, as shown (Fig. 10.7).
6 Start the engine and immediately detach the short circuit wire. Increase the engine speed to 2500 rpm and check the voltmeter reading according to the pre-determined ambient temperature table below.
7 If the voltage does not conform to that specified, continue to run the engine at 2500 rpm for several minutes and then with the engine idling check that the ammeter reads below 5 amps. If the reading is above this, the battery is not fully charged and must be removed for charging as otherwise accurate testing cannot be carried out.

Ambient temperature		Rated regulating voltage
°C	(°F)	(V)
–10	(14)	14.75 to 15.25
0	(32)	14.60 to 15.20
10	(50)	14.45 to 14.95
20	(68)	14.30 to 14.80
30	(86)	14.15 to 14.65
40	(104)	14.00 to 14.50

8 Switch off the engine, remove the cover from the voltage regulator and inspect the surfaces of the contacts. If these are rough or pitted, clean them by drawing a strip of very fine emery cloth between them.
9 Using feeler gauges, check and adjust the core gap, if necessary, to between 0.0315 to 0.0394 in (0.8 to 1.0 mm).
10 Check and adjust the contact points gap if necessary, to between 0.0157 to 0.0236 in (0.4 to 0.6 mm).
11 By now the voltage regulator will have cooled down so that the previous test may be repeated. If the voltage/temperature are still not correct, switch off the engine and adjust the regulator screw. Do this by loosening the locknut and turning the screw clockwise to increase the voltage reading and anti-clockwise to reduce it.
12 Turn the adjuster screw only fractionally before retesting the voltage charging rate again with the unit cold. Finally tighten the locknut.
13 If the cut-out is operating incorrectly, first check the fan belt and the ignition warning lamp bulb. Connect the positive terminal of a dc voltmeter to the 'N' socket of the regulator connector plug, and the voltmeter negative terminal to ground as shown (Fig. 10.8).
14 Start the engine and let it idle. Check the voltmeter reading. If the reading is zero volts, check for continuity between the 'N' terminals of the regulator unit and the alternator. If the reading is below 5.2 volts and the ignition warning lamp remains on, check and adjust the core gap and points gap to the specified respective clearances. Remember that this time the adjustments are carried out to the cut-out not the voltage regulator although the procedure is similar.
15 If the reading is over 5.2 volts with the ignition warning lamp on, and the core and points gap are correctly set, the complete regulator unit must be renewed.
16 The cut-out is operating correctly if the voltmeter shows a reading of more than 5.2 volts (ignition lamp out).

510 models
17 On 510 models the voltage regulator is a fully transistorized integrated circuit type. This unit is fully sealed and therefore requires no maintenance or adjustments.
18 In the unlikely event of it becoming defective, it is not repairable and must therefore be replaced by a new unit.
19 To test the regulator, specialized knowledge and equipment is required and this should therefore be entrusted to your Datsun dealer or local automotive electrician.

12 Starter motor – general description

1 The starter motor incorporates a solenoid mounted on top of the starter motor body. When the ignition switch is operated, the solenoid moves the starter drive pinion, through the medium of the shift lever, into engagement with the flywheel or driveplate starter ring gear. As the solenoid reaches the end of its stroke and with the pinion by now partially engaged with the flywheel ring gear, the main fixed and

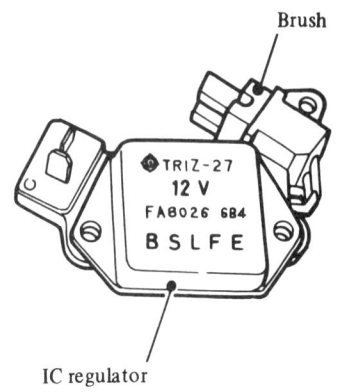
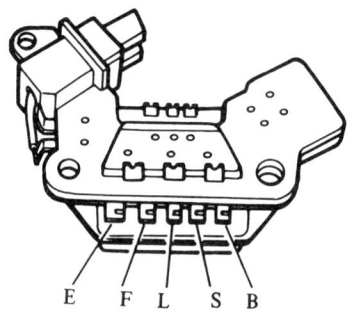

Brush

TRIZ-27
12 V
FA8026 684
B S L F E

IC regulator

E F L S B

Fig. 10.9 The transistorized regulator incorporated in the alternator in 510 models

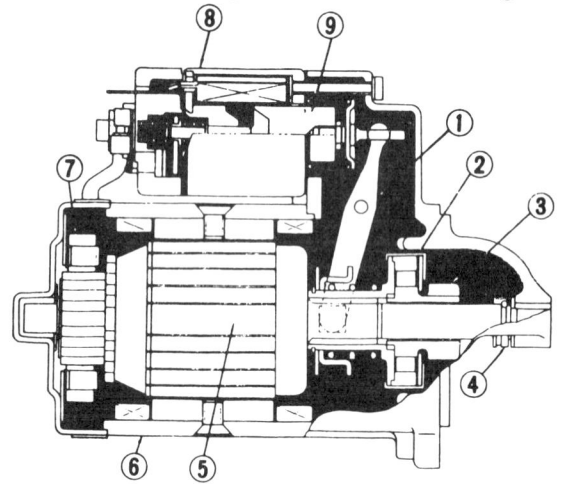

Fig. 10.10 Sectional view of starter motor (non-reduction gear type)

1	Shift lever	6	Yoke
2	Overrun clutch	7	Brush
3	Pinion	8	Solenoid
4	Pinion stop	9	Plunger
5	Armature		

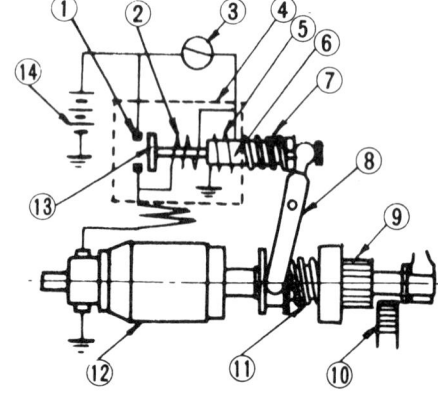

Fig. 10.11 Starter motor circuit (non-reduction gear type)

1	Stationary contact	8	Shifter lever
2	Series coil	9	Pinion
3	Switch (ignition)	10	Ring gear
4	Solenoid	11	Sleeve spring (pinion)
5	Coil (shunt)	12	Armature
6	Plunger	13	Moving contact
7	Return spring	14	Battery

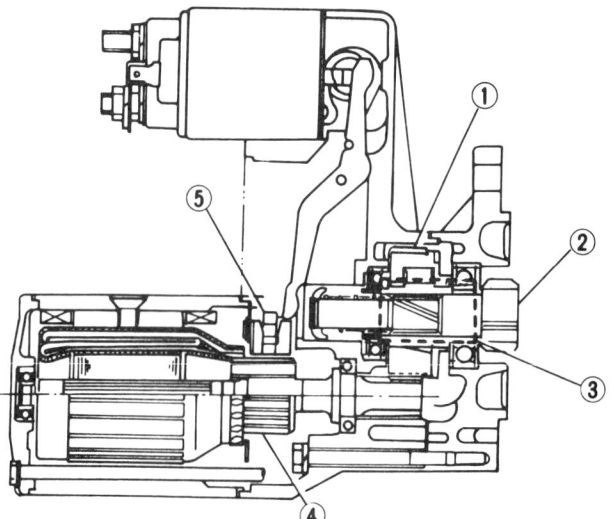

Fig. 10.12 Sectional view of starter – (reduction gear type)

1	Reduction gear	4	Commutator
2	Pinion	5	Brush
3	Overrun clutch		

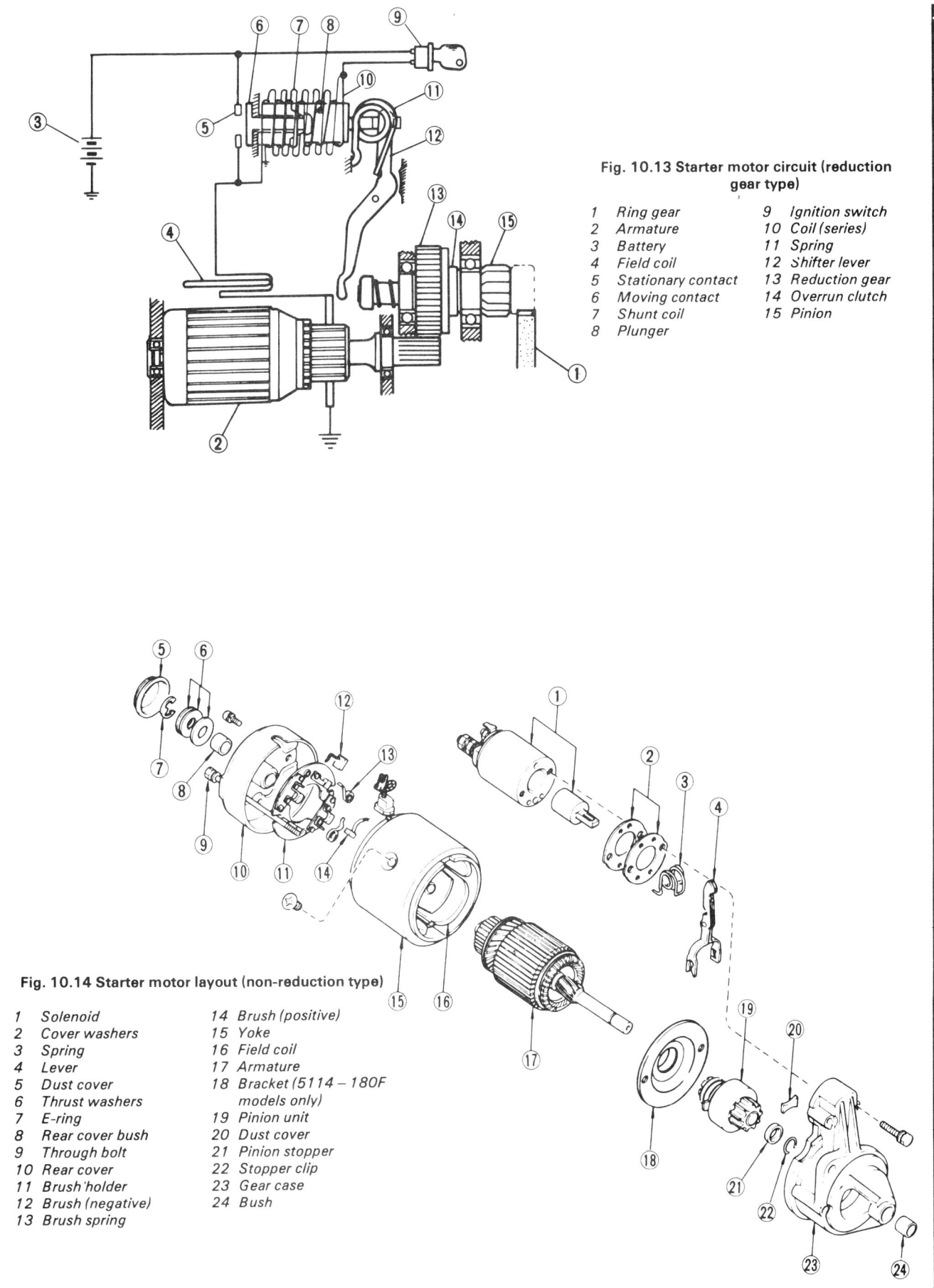

Fig. 10.13 Starter motor circuit (reduction gear type)

1	Ring gear	9	Ignition switch
2	Armature	10	Coil (series)
3	Battery	11	Spring
4	Field coil	12	Shifter lever
5	Stationary contact	13	Reduction gear
6	Moving contact	14	Overrun clutch
7	Shunt coil	15	Pinion
8	Plunger		

Fig. 10.14 Starter motor layout (non-reduction type)

1	Solenoid	14	Brush (positive)
2	Cover washers	15	Yoke
3	Spring	16	Field coil
4	Lever	17	Armature
5	Dust cover	18	Bracket (5114 – 180F models only)
6	Thrust washers		
7	E-ring	19	Pinion unit
8	Rear cover bush	20	Dust cover
9	Through bolt	21	Pinion stopper
10	Rear cover	22	Stopper clip
11	Brush holder	23	Gear case
12	Brush (negative)	24	Bush
13	Brush spring		

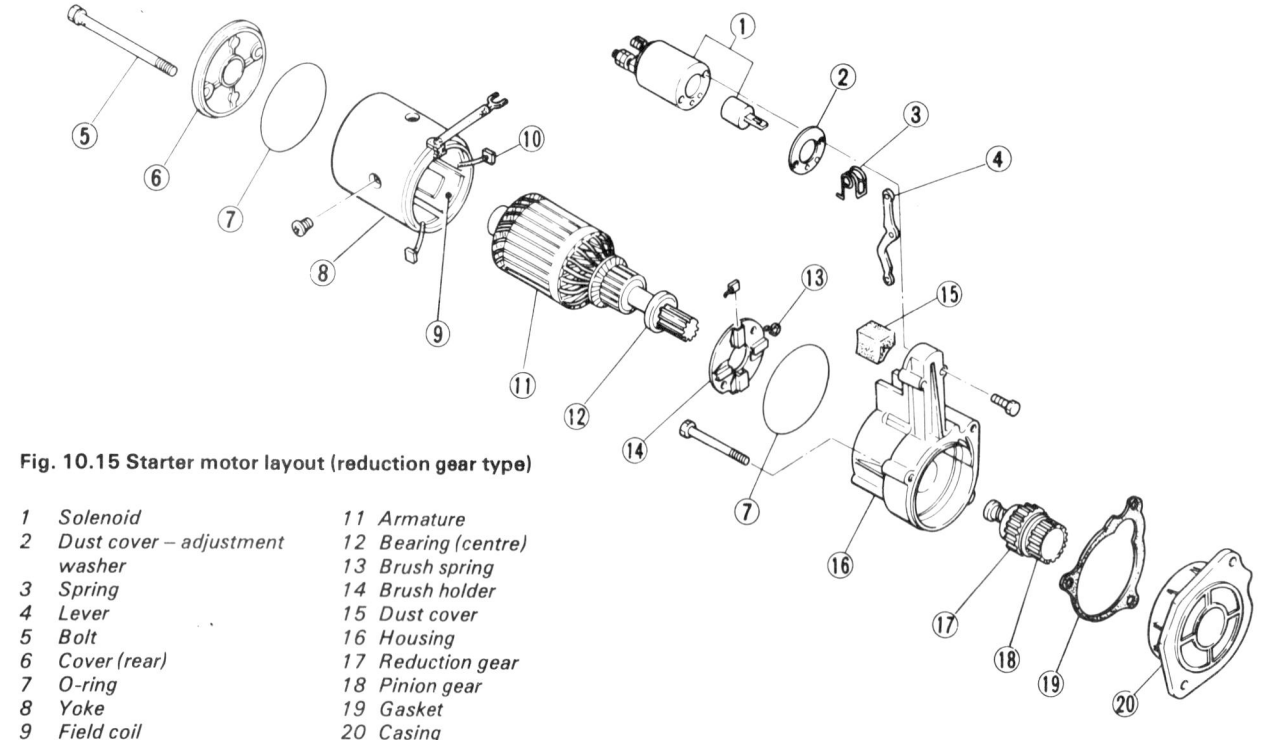

Fig. 10.15 Starter motor layout (reduction gear type)

1	Solenoid	11	Armature
2	Dust cover – adjustment	12	Bearing (centre)
	washer	13	Brush spring
3	Spring	14	Brush holder
4	Lever	15	Dust cover
5	Bolt	16	Housing
6	Cover (rear)	17	Reduction gear
7	O-ring	18	Pinion gear
8	Yoke	19	Gasket
9	Field coil	20	Casing
10	Brush		

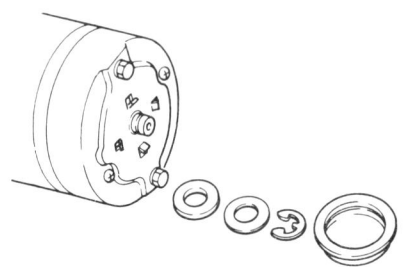

Fig. 10.16 Dust cover, E-ring and thrust washers

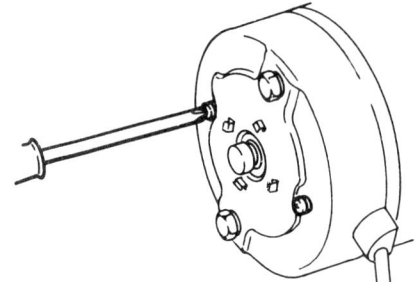

Fig. 10.17 Remove brush holder set screws

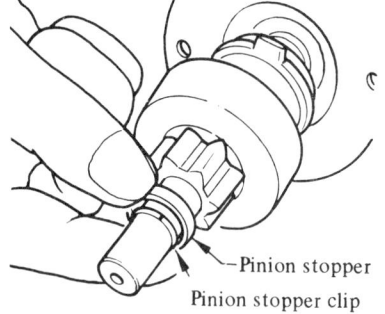

—Pinion stopper

Pinion stopper clip

Fig. 10.18 Pinion stopper and clip

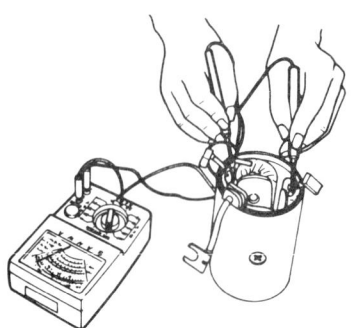

Fig. 10.19 Testing field coil circuit

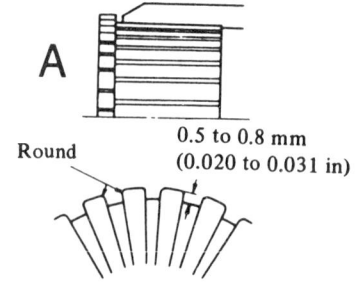

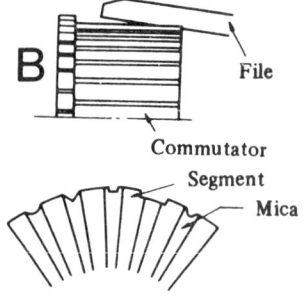

A

Round

0.5 to 0.8 mm
(0.020 to 0.031 in)

Correct

B

File

Commutator

Segment

Mica

Incorrect

Fig. 10.20 The correct 'A' and incorrect 'B' method of undercutting the commutator segment separators

moving contacts close and energize the starter motor to rotate the engine. This fractional pre-engagement of the starter drive does much to reduce the wear on the flywheel ring gear associated with inertia type starter motors.

2 On some models the starter motor is fitted with a reduction gear, which is situated between the armature and pinion gear, and is designed to reduce the armature speed and increase the rotational torque.

3 An overrun clutch transmits drive torque from the armature or when fitted, reduction gear, to the ring gear on the flywheel (or driveplate on automatic models).

4 This system enables the mesh between the flywheel and pinion to be more positive and once the engine has started the clutch prevents the armature continuing to rotate, reducing wear and possible damage.

13 Starter motor – removal and refitting

1 Disconnect the battery earth lead.

2 Disconnect the black and yellow wire from the 'S' terminal on the solenoid, and the black cable from the 'B' terminal (also on the end cover of the solenoid).

3 Unscrew and remove the two starter motor securing bolts, pull the starter forward, tilt it slightly to clear the motor shaft support from the flywheel ring gear and withdraw it.

4 Refitting is the reverse of the removal procedure.

14 Starter motor (non-reduction gear type) – dismantling, servicing and reassembly

1 Disconnect the lead from the 'M' terminal of the solenoid.

2 Remove the solenoid securing screws and withdraw the solenoid from the starter motor.

3 Remove the dust cover, the E-ring and the two thrust washers from the rear cover where applicable.

4 Unscrew and remove the two screws which secure the brush holder.

5 Unscrew and remove the two tie-bolts and the rear cover.

6 Using a length of wire with a hook at its end, remove the brushes by pulling the brush springs aside.

7 Remove the brush holder.

8 Withdraw the yoke assembly and extract the armature assembly and shift lever. Push the pinion stop towards the pinion to expose the circlip. Extract the circlip and then withdraw the stop and clutch assembly.

9 Check the brushes for wear. If their length is less than that specified, renew them.

10 If an ohmmeter is available, test the field coil for continuity. To do this, connect one probe of the meter to the field coil positive terminal and the other to the positive brush holder. If no reading is indicated then the field coil circuit has a break in it.

11 Connect one probe of the meter to the field coil positive lead and

the other one to the yoke. If there is a low resistance, then the field coil is earthed due to a breakdown in insulation. When this fault is discovered, the field coils should be renewed by an automotive electrician as it is very difficult to remove the field coil securing screws without special equipment. In any event, it will probably be more economical to exchange the complete starter motor for a reconditioned unit.

12 Undercut the separators of the commutator using an old hacksaw blade ground to suit to a depth of 0.02 to 0.03 in (0.5 to 0.8 mm). The commutator may be polished with a piece of very fine glass paper – never use emery cloth as the carborundum particles will become embedded in the copper surfaces.

13 The armature may be tested for insulation breakdown again using the ohmmeter. To do this, place one probe on the armature shaft and the other on each of the commutator segments in turn. If there is a reading indicated at any time during the test then the armature must be renewed.

14 Wash the components of the drivegear in paraffin, inspect for wear or damage, particularly to the pinion teeth and renew as appropriate. Refitting is a reversal of dismantling but stake a new stop washer in position and lubricate the sliding surfaces of the pinion assembly with a light oil, applied sparingly.

15 Reassembly of the remaining components of the starter motor is the reverse of the dismantling procedure.

16 When the starter motor has been fully reassembled, actuate the solenoid which will throw the drivegear forward into its normal flywheel engagement position. Do this by connecting jumper leads between the battery terminal and the solenoid 'M' terminal and between the battery positive terminal and the solenoid 'S' terminal. Now check the gap between the end face of the drive pinion and the mating face of the thrust washer. This should be between 0.012 and 0.059 in (0.3 to 1.5 mm) measured either with a vernier or feeler gauge. Adjusting washers are available in different thicknesses.

15 Starter motor (reduction gear types) – dismantling, servicing and reassembly

1 Detach the connection plate from the 'M' terminal on the solenoid unit.

2 Unscrew and remove the solenoid retaining screws and withdraw the solenoid unit. The torsion spring can be removed at this stage but note how it is located.

3 Unscrew the through bolts and carefully remove the rear cover, by prising it free using a screwdriver or similar but take care not to damage the packing.

4 Withdraw the yoke assembly and extract the armature unit.

5 The brushes and holders can now be removed but note that the positive brush differs in that the brush is isolated from its holder and the connecting wire is attached to the fluid coil.

6 To extract the brushes hook back the retaining spring and pull the brushes from their respective holders but keep them in order noting

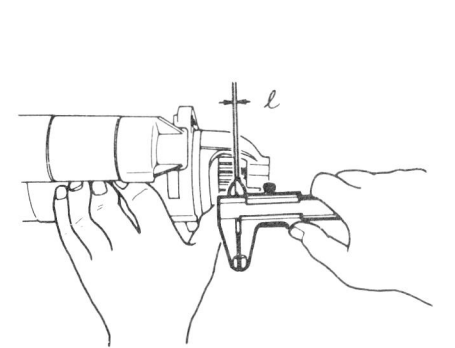

Fig. 10.21 Measure drive pinion endface to thrust washer clearance (L)

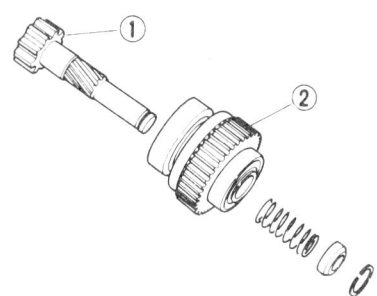

Fig. 10.22 Pinion/reduction gear overrun clutch

1   Pinion   2   Reduction gear

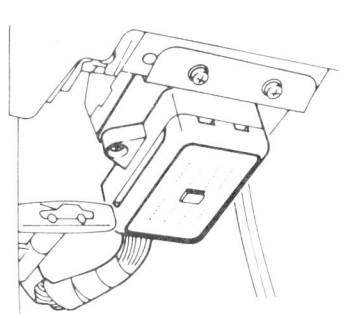

Fig. 10.23 The fuse box

Fig. 10.24 The fusible link

16.32 The fuse box with cover removed

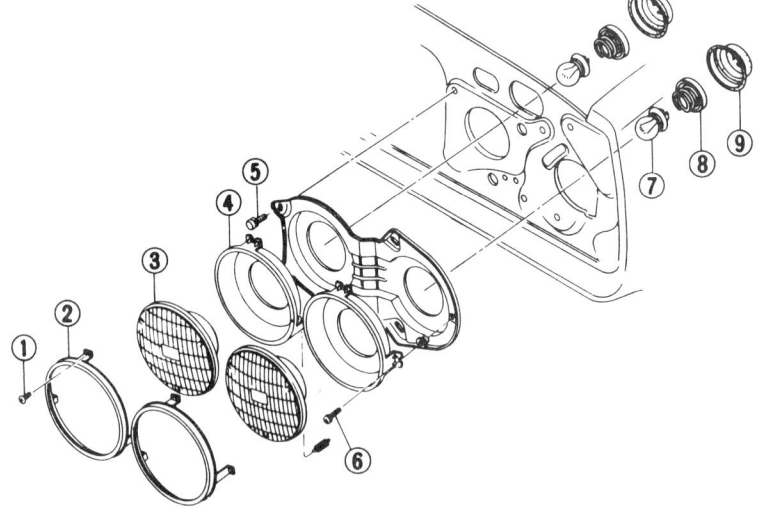

Fig. 10.25 Bulb type headlamp units

1	Screw	4	Mounting ring	7	Bulb
2	Retaining screw	5	Screw	8	Retainer
3	Headlight unit	6	Adjuster screw	9	Cover

19.1 Front combination lamp lens removal

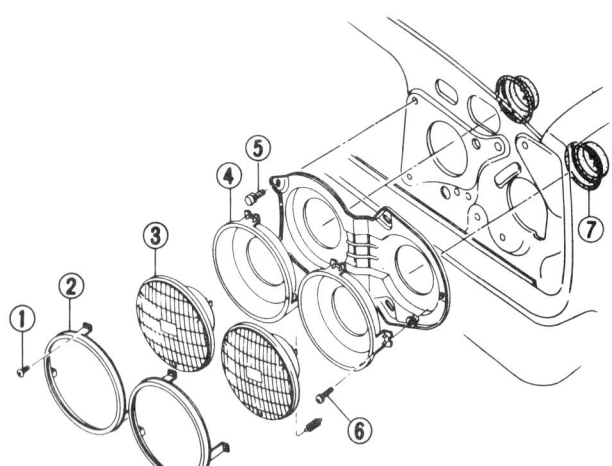

Fig. 10.26 Sealed beam headlight units

1	Screw	4	Mounting ring	6	Adjuster screw
2	Securing ring	5	Screw	7	Cover
3	Sealed beam unit				

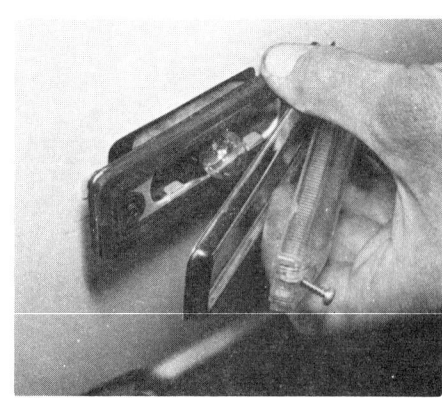

20.1 Side marker light lens/unit removal

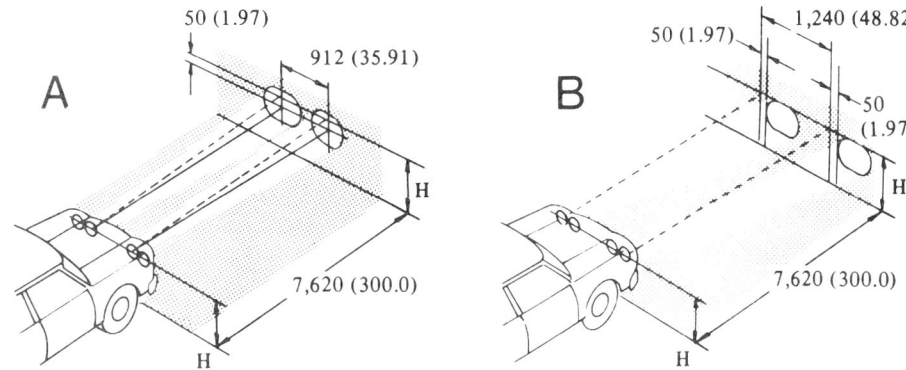

Fig. 10.27 The high (A) and low beam (B) adjustment positions. H Horizontal centre line of headlights

their positions in case they do not require renewal.

7   To detach the centre housing from the gearcase simply unscrew and remove the retaining bolts. The reduction/pinion gears can then be removed for examination.

8   The examination of the respective components closely follows that of the non-reduction gear type in Section 14, paragraphs 9 to 16, but in addition check the condition of the pinion and reduction gear with overrun clutch components.

9   Any damage or signs of excessive wear in these parts will necessitate renewal. Check also that the sleeve slides freely on the shaft.

16 Fuses and fusible link

1   The fusebox is located beneath the instrument panel between the steering column and the driver's door. Fuse ratings and the circuits protected are marked on the fusebox (photos).

2   A fusible link is incorporated in the battery-to-alternator wiring harness within the engine compartment. It provides an additional protection for the starting, charging, lighting and accessory circuits (photo).

3   In the event of a fuse or fusible link blowing, always establish the cause before fitting a new one. This is most likely to be due to faulty insulation somewhere in the wiring circuit. Always carry a spare fuse for each rating, and never be tempted to substitute a piece of wire or a nail for the correct fuse as a fire may be caused or, at least, the electrical component ruined.

17 Headlight unit – removal and refitting

Headlight bulb – removal

1   The bulbs can be removed for renewal without removing the complete headlight unit.

2   Raise and support the bonnet and from inside the front panel, peel back the rubber cover and detach the headlight wire connector and rubber surround.

3   Rotate the retaining ring to remove it and withdraw the bulb and holder.

4   Refitting of the bulb is a direct reversal of the removal procedure but check operation on completion.

Headlight unit removal

5   Remove the radiator grille referring to Chapter 12 if necessary.

6   Unscrew and remove the three headlight unit retaining screws (photo). Do not disturb the beam alignment screws or the lights will have to be readjusted.

7   Withdraw the headlight unit and disconnect the lead wire connectors and rubber cover to remove it completely.

8   Refit in the reverse order but ensure that the headlight unit is the correct way up and if necessary, realign the beam adjustment before refitting the grille.

18 Headlamp aiming (beam alignment)

1   The only entirely satisfactory way of checking headlamp beam alignment is by the use of special optical testers.

2   However, where this equipment is not available, the following beam aiming procedure may be used.

3   Ensure that the tyres are correctly inflated and that the vehicle is on a flat level surface facing a flat wall. Ensure that the fuel tank, radiator and oil sump are full or topped-up to the recommended levels.

4   Referring to Fig. 10.27 position the vehicle at the prescribed distance from a wall and mark the wall to show the correresponding alignment indicator marks for your model. High and low beam adjustment settings are shown but check whether you have sealed or bulb type headlight units before marking for alignment. Note that the illustrations shown are for right-hand drive vehicles. For left-hand drive models the aiming pattern is simply reversed.

5   With the car positioned correctly, adjust the beam alignment screws to obtain the correct adjustment.

19 Front combination light

Bulb renewal

1   Remove the retaining screws and take off the lens (photo).

2   Press in the bulb and rotate is anti-clockwise to remove it from its socket.

3   Fit the new bulb, ensuring that it is locked in the socket and check operation.

4   Position the gasket to the lamp body and fit the lens (and lamp body) using the two screws.

Lamp removal and refitting

5   Disconnect the lamp wires at the connector, and remove the grommet from the body panel.

6   Remove the lens as described in paragraph 1 then withdraw the lamp body.

7   Refitting is the reverse of the removal procedure.

20 Side marker light (front and rear)

Bulb renewal

1   Remove the retaining screws and take off the lens and rim (photo).

2   According to the particular type, either press in the bulb and rotate it anti-clockwise to remove it, or pull the bulb and socket forward and take the bulb out.

3   Fit the new bulb (and socket where applicable).

4   Position the gasket to the lamp body and refit the lens and rim.

Lamp removal and refitting

5   Disconnect the two lamp wires at the connectors, and remove the

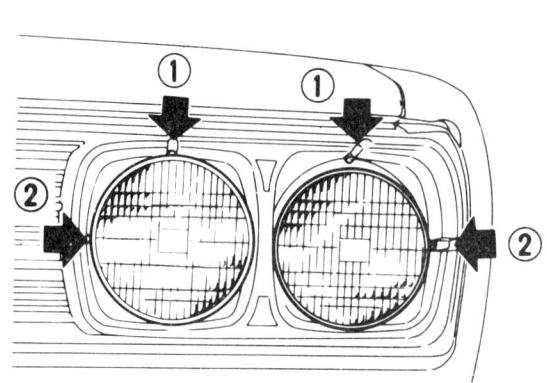

Fig. 10.28 Headlight adjustment screws

1   Vertical plane adjustment
2   Horizontal plane adjustment

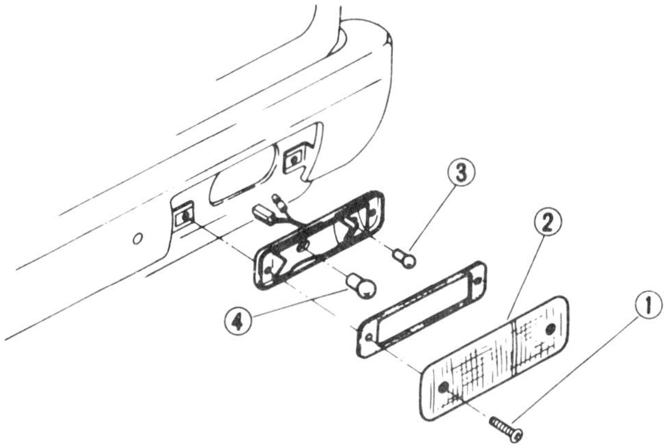

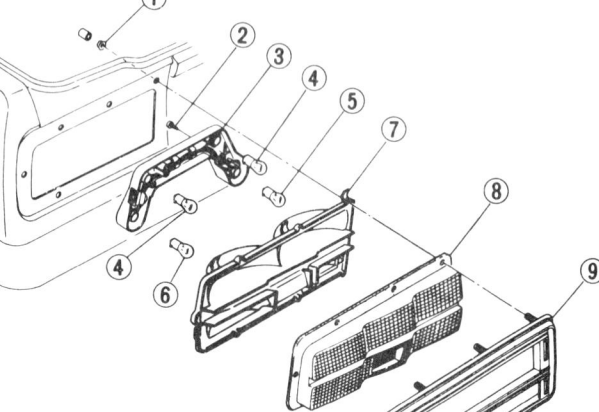

Fig. 10.29 Front combination light assembly

1   Screw   3   Bulb (park)
2   Lens   4   Bulb (indicator)

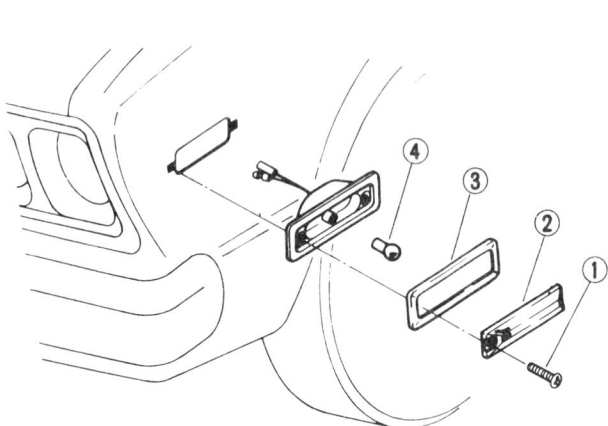

Fig. 10.30 Side marker light assembly

1   Screw   3   Seal
2   Lens   4   Bulb

Fig. 10.31 Rear combination light assembly – Saloon

1   Retaining nut   6   Indicator bulb
2   Screw   7   Housing
3   Rear cover   8   Lens
4   Stop/tail bulb   9   Rim
5   Reversing bulb

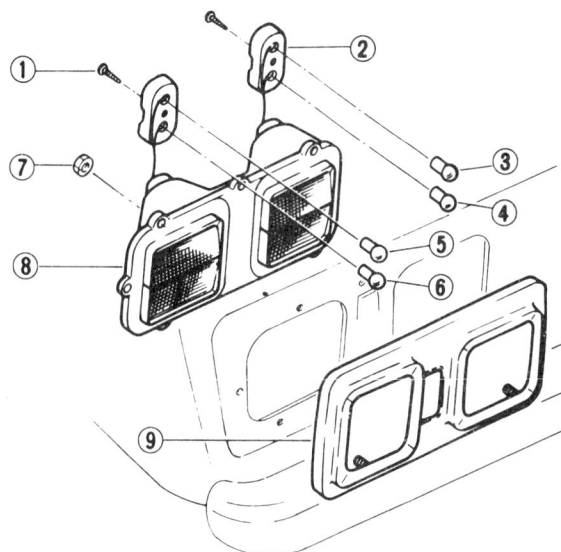

Fig. 10.32 Rear combination light assembly – Coupe

1   Screw   6   Indicator bulb
2   Rear cover   7   Nut
3   Stop light bulb   8   Lens
4   Reverse bulb   9   Rim
5   Tail light bulb

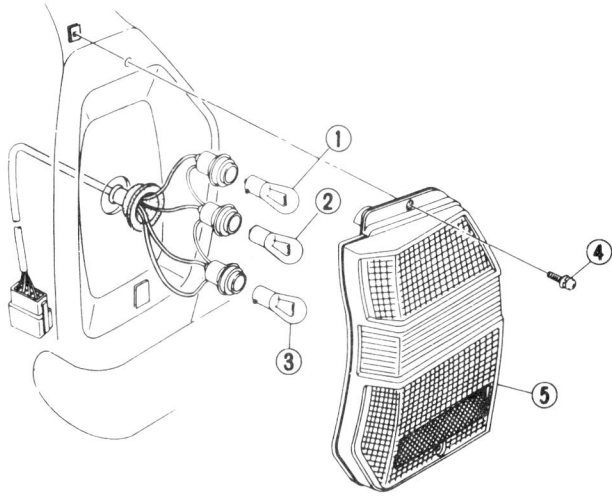

Fig. 10.33 Rear combination light assembly – Estate Car

1	Indicator bulb	4	Screw
2	Reverse bulb	5	Lens
3	Tail/stop light bulb		

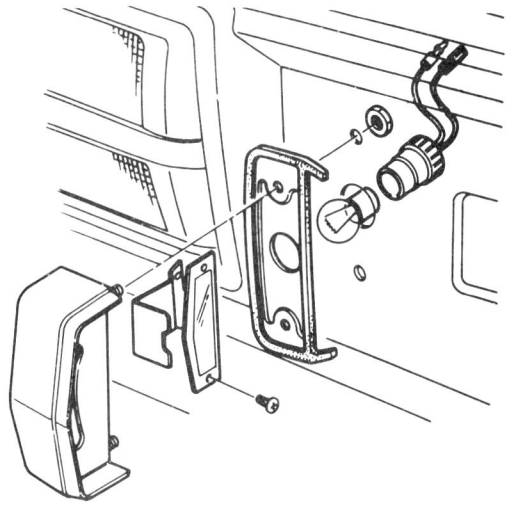

Fig. 10.34 Licence plate light for Saloon and Coupe 510 models

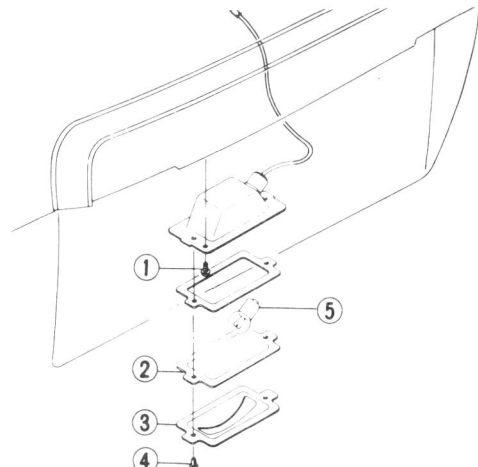

Fig. 10.35 Licence plate light – Estate Car

1	Screw	4	Screw
2	Lens	5	Bulb
3	Rim		

grommet (where applicable) from the body panel.

6 Remove the two retaining screws, the lens and the rim, and withdraw the lamp from the vehicle.

7 Refitting is the reverse of the removal procedure.

21 Rear combination lights

Bulb renewal – Saloon

1 Unclip the rear panel cover in the boot to gain access to the bulb holder units.

2 Remove the retaining screws and withdraw the combination bulb holder unit (photo).

3 Twist and remove the offending bulb/s. Refit in the reverse order and check the operation.

Bulb renewal – Coupe

4 Unclip the rear luggage finisher to gain access to the bulb holders.

5 Unscrew the central retaining screw and withdraw the bulb holder/s. Twist the bulb to remove it.

6 Refitting is a direct reversal of the removal process. Check operation on completion.

Bulb renewal – Estate Car

7 Remove the lens retaining screws and withdraw the lens.

8 Pull bulb holder from lens socket.

9 Press, twist and remove the bulb to be renewed.

10 Refit in the reverse order and check operation.

Lamp removal and refitting

11 On Saloon and Coupe models remove the bulb holder unit, then unscrew the lens retaining nuts on the inside. Remove the lens retainer nuts and light unit.

12 Refit in the reverse order but check that the seals are in good condition and are not distorted during assembly.

22 License plate light

Saloon and Coupe (European models)

1 Unscrew and remove the lens retaining screws to gain access to the bulb. Refit in the reverse order.

Saloon and Hatchback (USA - 510 models)

2 Unclip and fold down the rear panel cover. Unscrew the unit retaining nuts, remove the lens and extract the bulb. Refit in the reverse order and check operation.

Estate Car (all markets)

3 Unscrew the lens retaining screws and remove the lens.

4 Renew the bulb and reassemble in the reverse order to removal. Check operation on completion.

23 Interior light

1 To remove the lens, rotate it anti-clockwise. The festoon bulb can then be prised from the holder for renewal (photo).

2 To remove the light unit, detach the lens, unscrew the securing screws and then carefully pulling the light unit downwards, disconnect the wires.

3 Refit in the reverse order and check operation.

Luggage compartment light – Coupe

4 Unscrew and remove the lens retaining screws. Remove the lens and extract the bulb for renewal if necessary.

5 To remove the unit, pull it from the cavity (having removed the lens) and detach the wires.

6 Refit in the reverse order and check operation.

Rear interior light – Estate Car

7 To remove the lens press the retaining clip tab upwards and detach the lens. Prise the festoon bulb free.

8 To remove the unit, unscrew the retaining screws and detach the wiring.

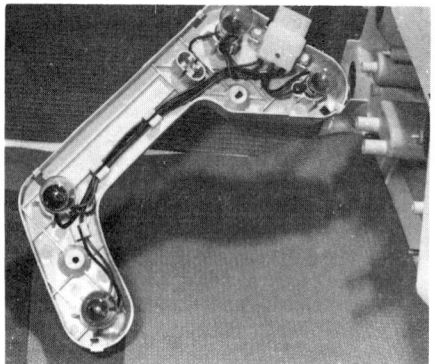

21.2 Rear combination light bulb holder

23.1 Remove the lens to replace bulb – Saloon

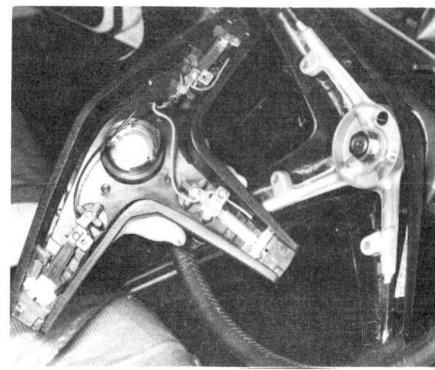

25.2 Remove the horn ring

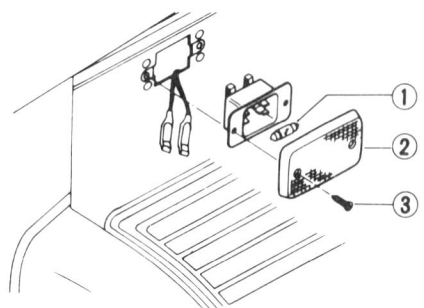

Fig. 10.36 Luggage compartment light –
Coupe

1   Bulb   3   Screw
2   Lens

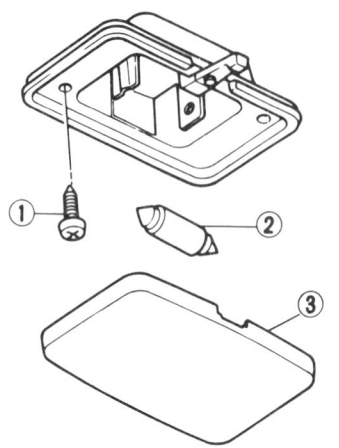

Fig. 10.37 Interior light (rear) in Estate Car

1   Screw   3   Lens
2   Bulb

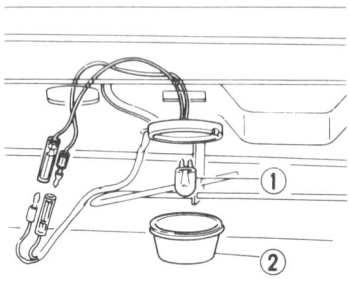

Fig. 10.38 Boot light – Saloon

1   Bulb   2   Lens

9   Refitting is a reversal of removal but check operation on completion.

24 Luggage compartment light

1   Twist the lens to remove it. Pull the bulb from its holder to remove.
2   Refit in the reverse order and check operation.

25 Combination light and indicator switch – removal and refitting

1   Disconnect the battery earth cable.
2   Unscrew and remove the horn pad ring from the steering wheel (photo).
3   Unscrew the steering wheel retaining nut and withdraw the steering wheel.
4   Remove the steering column cover retaining screws and detach the cover.
5   Detach the combination switch wires at the connector and then loosen the switch retaining screw to remove the switch unit.
6   Refit the combination switch in the reverse sequence to removal but ensure that the respective circuits are fully operational before refitting the column cover. Tighten the steering wheel nut to the specified torque wrench setting given in Chapter 11.

26 Ignition switch – removal and refitting

1   Disconnect the battery earth cable.
2   Unscrew and remove the steering column cover, and then detach the wiring harness connector.

3   Unscrew the small switch body to steering lock retaining screw and remove the switch.
4   Reverse the above procedure to refit the ignition switch.

27 Light relay unit – removal and refitting

1   Disconnect the battery earth cable.
2   Detach the wiring harness at the connector.
3   Unscrew and remove the relay securing screws and remove the relay unit.
4   Refit in the reverse order and check operation.

28 Stop light switch – removal and refitting

1   The stop light switch is located above the brake pedal and can be removed as follows.
2   Detach the battery earth cable.
3   Detach the lead wires at the switch connections, slacken the locknut and then unscrew the switch unit and remove it.
4   Refit in the reverse order and retighten the locknut. Check operation on completion.

29 Reversing light switch – removal and refitting

1   This is located in the gearbox unit and can easily be removed from underneath the car. Disconnect the wires at the connector near the switch and then using a suitable spanner unscrew the switch to remove.
2   Refit in the reverse order.

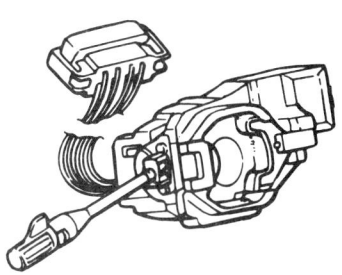

Fig. 10.39 Combination light and indicator switch

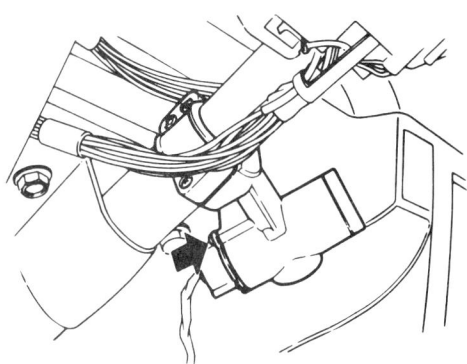

Fig. 10.40 The ignition switch – arrow indicates retaining screw position

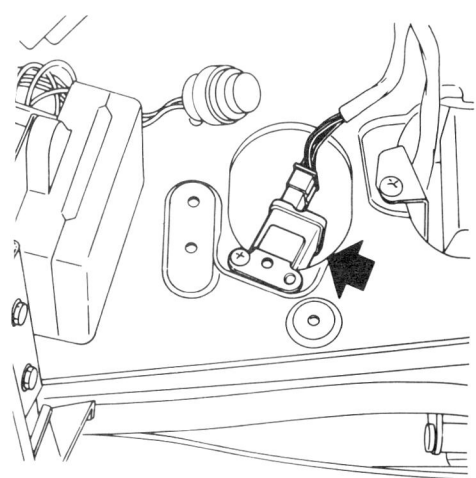

Fig. 10.41 The ignition relay unit

30 Interior light door switch – removal and refitting

1 Disconnect the earth cable from the battery.
2 Carefully pull the switch unit from the lower door pillar and disconnect the wires at the connector.
3 On Coupe models it is necessary to detach the side box from the rear armrest and then peel back the tape retaining harness to body from within the side box.
4 Refitting is a direct reversal of removal.

31 Ignition relay (510 models) – removal and refitting

1 Detach the battery earth cable.
2 Detach the left-hand side dash finisher and then disconnect the wiring harness at the connector.
3 Unscrew the relay unit retaining screw and withdraw the unit.
4 Refit in the reverse order to removal.

32 Illumination control switch – removal and refitting

1 The switch incorporates a 35 ohm variable resistance to control the brightness of the heater control illumination lamp, wiper switch illumination lamp and lighting switch illumination lamp.
2 Detach the battery earth cable.
3 Detach the wiring harness connector from the rear of the control unit.
4 To remove the control knob, push and twist it, and withdraw with washer.
5 Use a suitable spanner and remove the control unit retaining nut, and withdraw the unit from underneath.
6 Refit in the reverse sequence.

33 Hazard warning light switch – removal and refitting

1 Detach the battery earth cable.
2 Unscrew the securing screws and remove the upper steering column cover, then detach the wiring harness connector to the switch.
3 Unscrew the retaining screw to remove the switch unit.
4 Refit in the reverse order to removal.

34 Tailgate door light switch (Estate Car) – removal and refitting

1 Detach the battery earth cable.
2 The switch is located on the right-hand tailgate hinge. First remove the hinge cover to gain access to the switch.
3 The switch can then be carefully pulled from its retaining bracket and the wiring disconnected.
4 Reverse the above procedure to refit the switch assembly.

35 Luggage compartment light switch (Coupe) – removal and refitting

1 Detach the battery earth cable.
2 The switch is located on the side of the rear door lock. To remove the switch carefully pull it free from its bracket and disconnect the wire at the connector.
3 Refitting is a direct reversal of removal.

36 Handbrake warning switch – removal and refitting

Refer to Chapter 9, Section 22.

37 Combination instrument panel – removal and refitting

1 Disconnect the battery earth cable and remove the instrument panel as described in Chapter 12, Section 30.
2 With the speedometer cable disconnected, detach the wire ter-

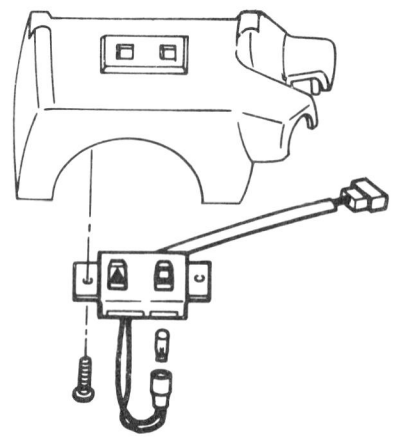

Fig. 10.42 The hazard warning light switch

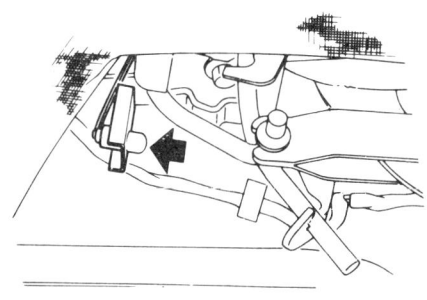

Fig. 10.43 The tailgate door switch in the Estate Car

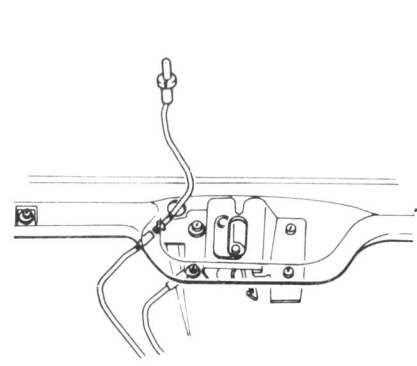

Fig. 10.44 Luggage compartment light switch position in the Coupe

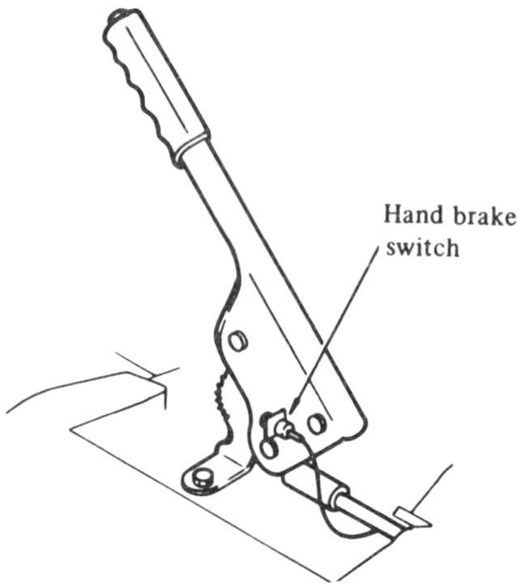

Fig. 10.45 The handbrake warning switch position (centre lever type)

Hand brake switch

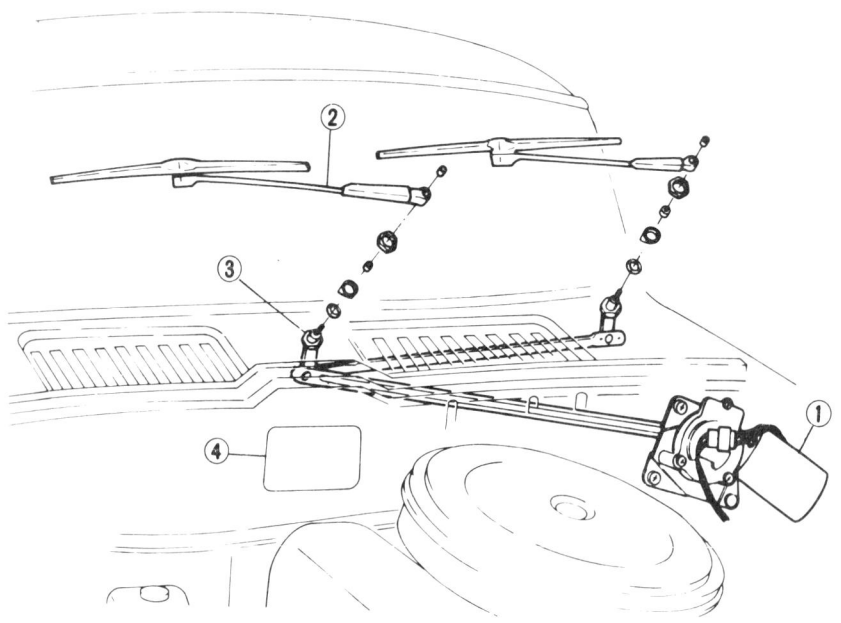

Fig. 10.46 The wiper linkage assembly

1	Motor	3	Pivot
2	Wiper arm	4	Inspecting cover

minal connector and remove the panel retaining screws to withdraw the panel.

3   Refit in the reverse order of removal.

Speedometer – removal and refitting

4   Remove the combination meter as described previously.
5   Detach the reset knob of the odometer (mileage recorder).
6   Remove the screws retaining the printed circuit board.
7   Loosen the speedometer retaining screws and withdraw the speedometer.
8   Refitting is a reversal of the removal procedure.

Fuel level and water temperature gauges

9   Proceed as described in paragraphs 1 and 2.
10 Remove the retaining screws and remove the gauge.
11 Refitting is the reversal of removal.

Tachometer – removal and refitting

12 Proceed as described in paragraphs 1 and 2.
13 Detach the speedometer mileage reset knob and then the tachometer from the printed circuit board terminal.
14 Unscrew the circuit board retaining screws and loosen the tachometer securing screws to remove the tachometer.
15 Refitting is a direct reversal of the removal procedure.

---

38 Windscreen wiper and washer assembly – removal and refitting

Wiper motor

1   Disconnect the battery earth cable.
2   Pull the wire connector from the wiper motor.
3   Unscrew and remove the wiper motor securing bolts.
4   Pull the motor unit carefully from the bulkhead to gain access to the wiper arm interconnecting rod securing nut. Unscrew the nut and detach the motor unit from the rod.

5   Assemble in the reverse order but ensure that the electrical connections are secure.

Windscreen wiper linkage

6   Remove the wiper motor as described previously.
7   Unscrew the central inspection cover screws (in the middle of the bulkhead), and remove the cover.
8   Detach the wiper arm from the pivot shaft. To do this lift the wiper arm from the windshield and loosen the attachment bolt.
9   Slacken the pivot retaining nut and withdraw the link assembly.
10 Refit in the reverse order and ensure that the wiper arm is refitted at the correct operational angle on the pivot.

Wiper and washer switch

11 Detach the battery earth cable.
12 Unscrew and remove the steering column cover.
13 Unscrew the retaining screws securing the wiper switch to the combination switch and separate the two assemblies.
14 Refit in the reverse order.

Intermittent wiper amplifier

15 Detach the battery earth cable.
16 Remove the windscreen washer tank from its bracket.
17 Loosen the screw and remove the relay bracket and then detach the wiring connector to the amplifier.
18 The amplifier can be removed after unscrewing the retaining screw.
19 Refit in the reverse order.

Windscreen washer assembly

20 The reservoir and motor (pump) are retained on a bracket on the inner wing panel as shown, Fig. 10.51.
21 If the pipe or nozzles are to be removed, detach the pipe from the

38.2 The wiper motor

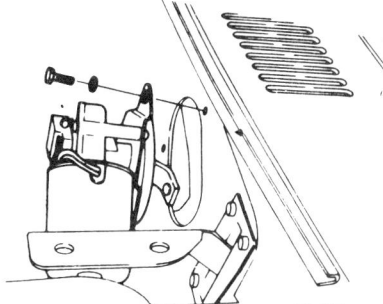

Fig. 10.47 Remove the wiper motor retaining bolts

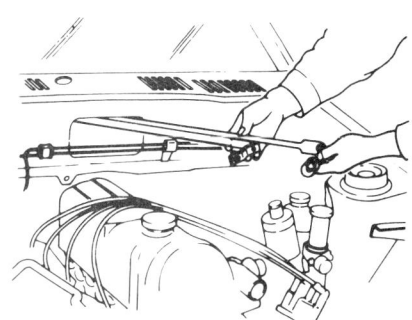

Fig. 10.48 Remove link assembly through inspection cover aperture

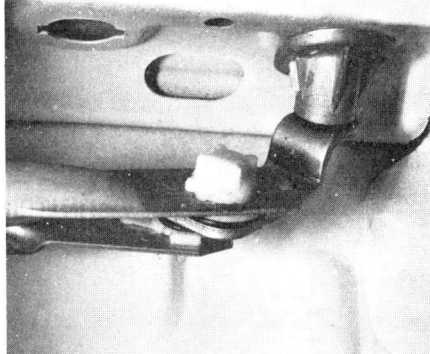

38.8 The windscreen wiper linkage

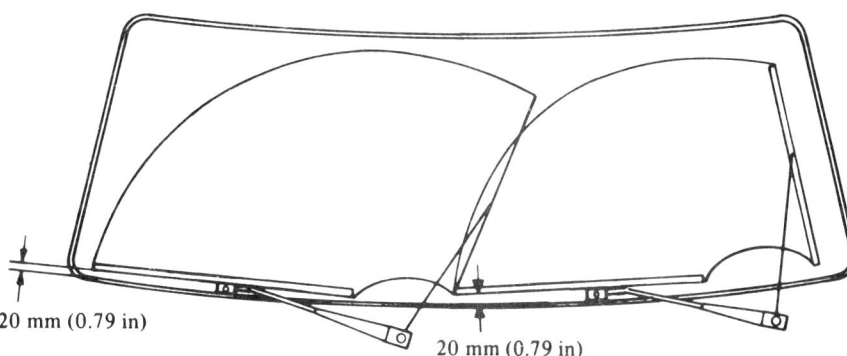

20 mm (0.79 in)

20 mm (0.79 in)

Fig. 10.49 The correct wiper arm setting adjustment

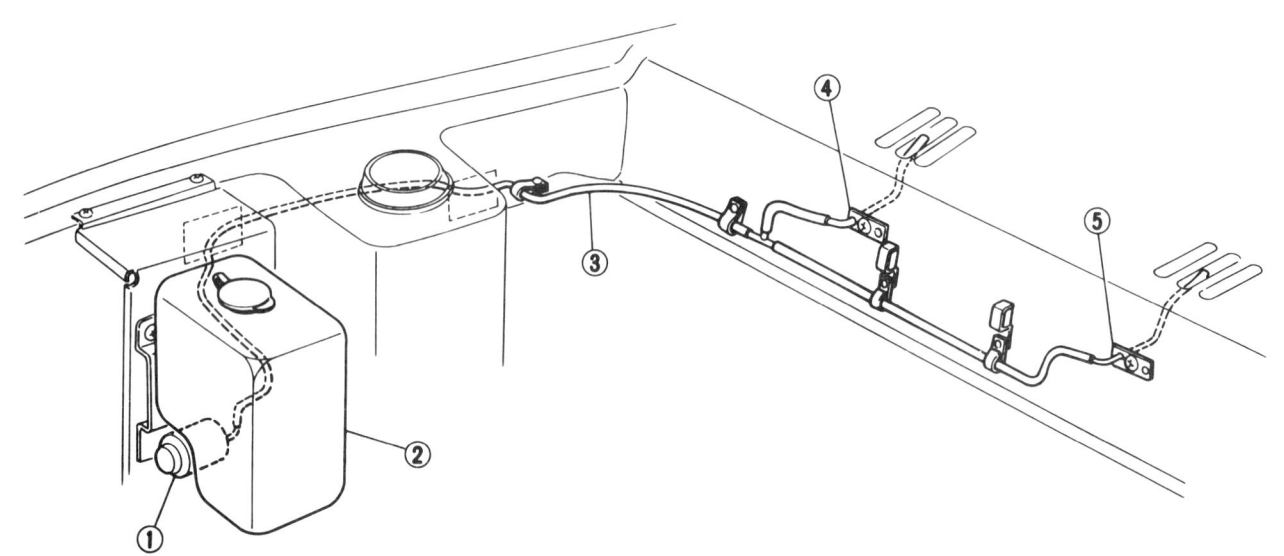

Fig. 10.50 The windscreen washer assembly

1	Pump unit	4 and 5	Right-hand and left-
2	Reservoir tank		hand nozzles
3	Tubing		

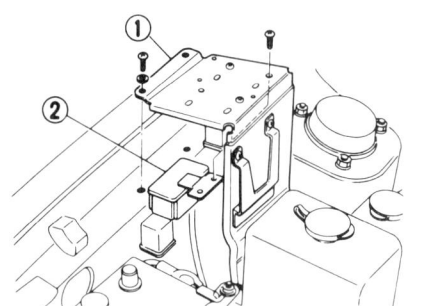

Fig. 10.51 The wiper amplifier (2) and the relay bracket (1)

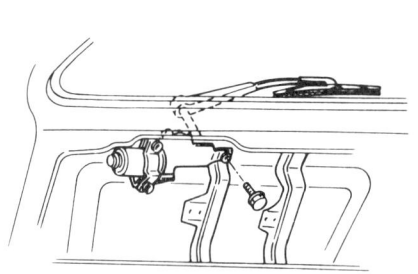

Fig. 10.52 Rear window wiper motor location (Estate car)

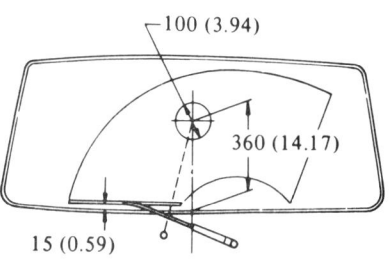

Unit: mm (in)·

Fig. 10.53 Rear window wiper adjustment and washer nozzle setting

100 (3.94)
360 (14.17)
15 (0.59)

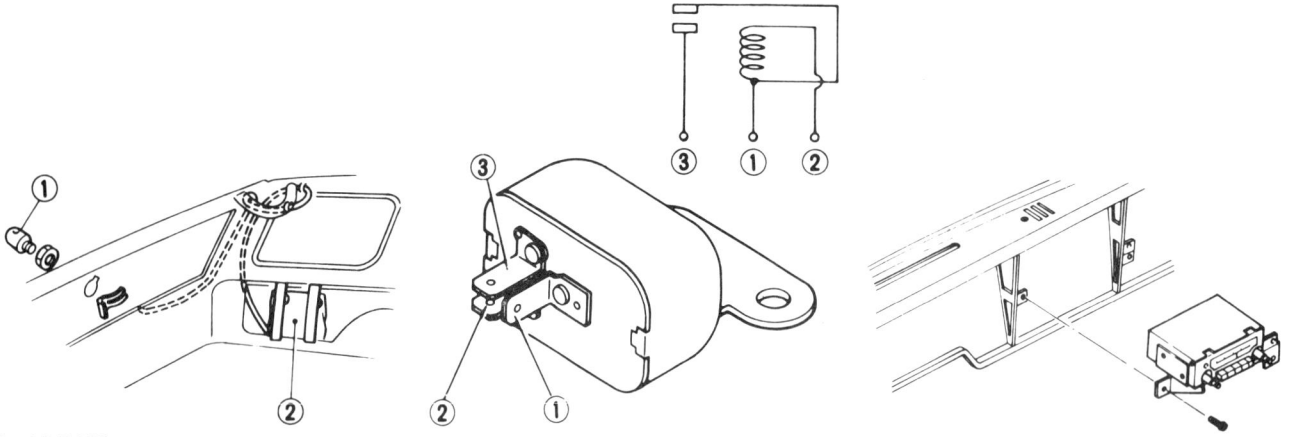

Fig. 10.54 The rear window washer position

1   Nozzle   2   Reservoir

Fig. 10.55 The horn relay unit and circuit

Fig. 10.56 Radio attachment bracket position

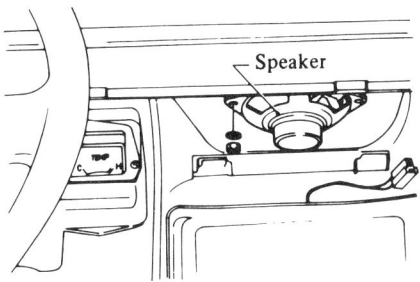

Fig. 10.57 The speaker location and attachment nuts

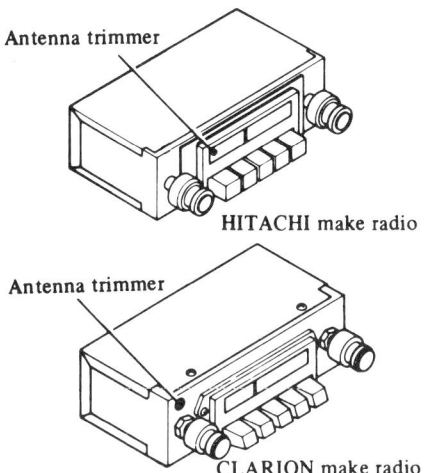

Fig. 10.58 The Hitachi and Clarion radios showing respective trimmer locations

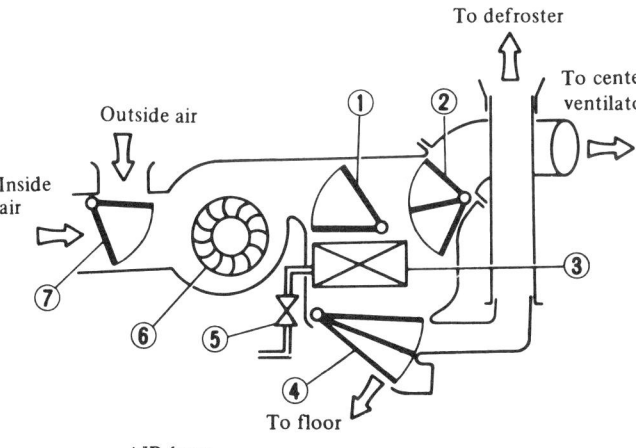

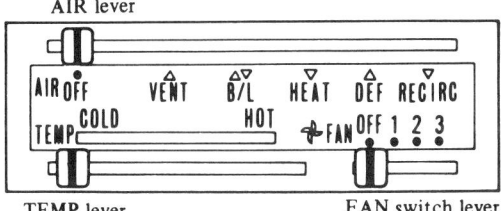

Fig. 10.59 The heater and control layout

1	Air mix vent	5	Water cock
2	Ventilation door	6	Blower unit
3	Core (radiator)	7	Air intake
4	Floor door		

pump outlet, release the pipe from the body guide clips (bend them up) and then detach the pipe from the nozzles or T-piece connector as required.

22 The nozzles are retained by a screw which secures the bracket. If new nozzles are fitted, adjust the nozzle pipe by bending accordingly through the top grille vents to obtain the desired spray pattern.

39 Rear window wiper (Estate Car)

1 Disconnect the earth cable from the battery.
2 Lift the wiper arm and loosen the retaining bolt, then withdraw the arm and blade assembly.
3 Detach the inner panel and sealer screen from the tailgate.
4 Detach the wire from the wiper motor connection and then unscrew the retaining bolts to remove the motor unit.
5 Refitting is a reversal of the removal procedure but check that the wiper arm is correctly positioned on the pivot shaft.

Rear windscreen washer

6 This is located in the rear side panel (left-hand side) and the inner panel must therefore be removed for access.
7 The washer nozzle is secured by a slotted clip and locknut. To remove or disconnect the nozzle the rear tailgate inner panel must be detached. The connecting pipe can then be detached and the retaining clip prised free to release the nozzle on the outside.
8 Refit in the reverse order.

Rear windscreen wiper switch

9 Detach the battery earth cable.
10 Separate the harness to switch connector and then push the switch knob and twist it to remove.
11 Unscrew the securing nut and remove the switch.
12 Refit in the reverse sequence.

40 Horns and horn relay

1 Detach the battery earth cable.
2 Detach the horn wire at the connector and then unscrew the horn retaining bolt to remove.
3 Refit in the reverse order.

Horn relay

4 Detach the battery earth cable.
5 Detach the relay wire at the terminal connector of horn ·relay. Unscrew and remove the relay retaining screws to remove.
6 Refitting is a reversal of the removal procedure.

41 Radio – removal and refitting

1 Disconnect the battery earth cable.
2 Remove the facia panel as described in Chapter 12, Section 29.
3 Unscrew and remove the radio bracket retaining screws. Carefully lift the radio clear complete with bracket.
4 Detach the wire connector and aerial cable.
5 Refitting is a direct reversal of the removal procedure, but check the operation before refitting the facia ɲanel.

Radio speaker

6 Detach the battery earth cable.
7 Remove the radio.
8 Unscrew and remove the speaker unit attachment nuts and carefully remove the speaker unit.
9 Refitting is a direct reversal of removal.

Aerial and cable

10 To remove the aerial unscrew the upper and lower supports to the front pillar.
11 The feeder cable is accessible on removal of the front pillar moulding, then detach the facia (Chapter 12, Section 29) to disconnect the feeder cable from the receiver unit.
12 Carefully extract the cable through the front pillar.
13 Refitting is a direct reversal of the removal procedure.

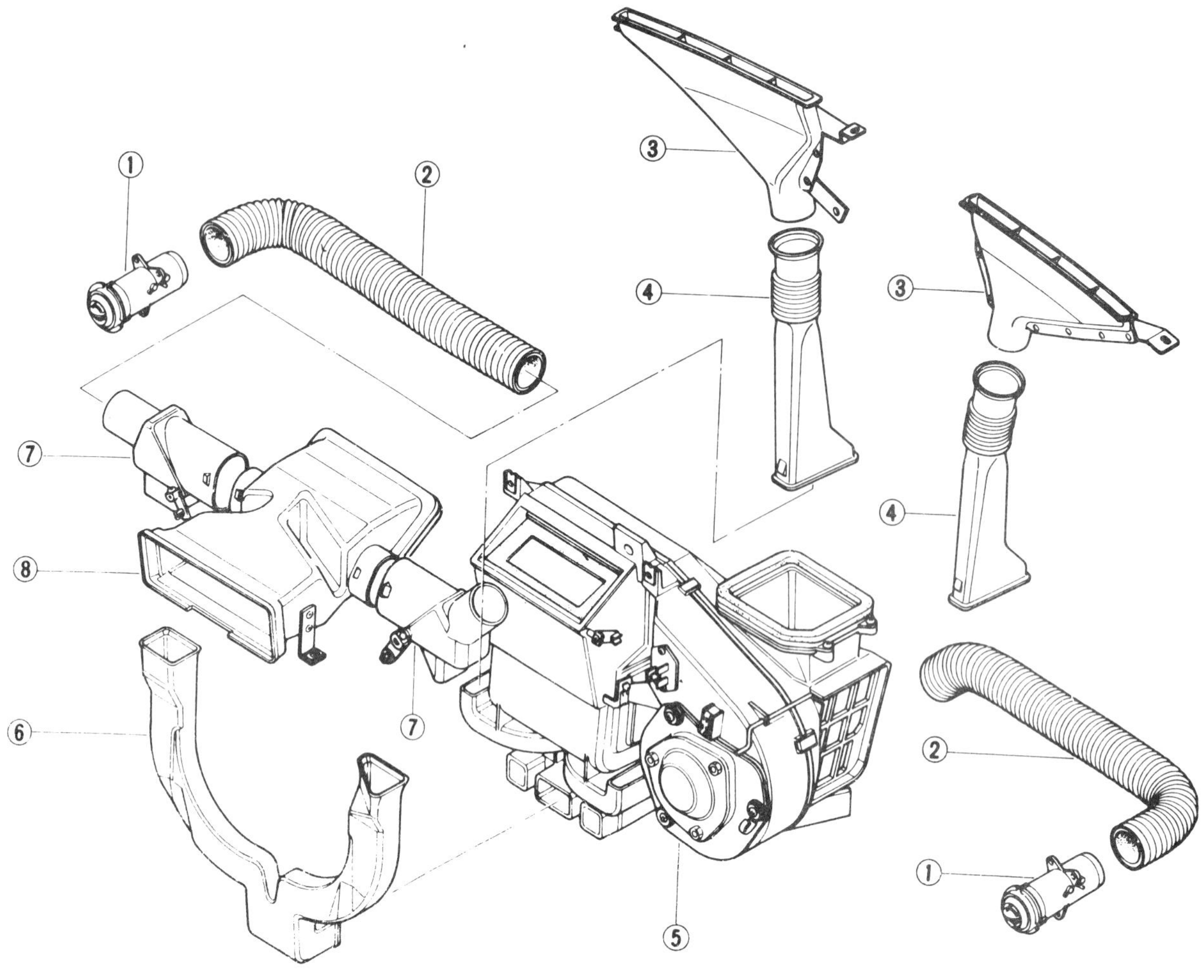

Fig. 10.60 The heater unit components

1	Side outlet	4	Ducting	6	Side defroster ducting (centre)	7	Connector
2	Cooler duct	5	Heater unit			8	Vent ducting - centre
3	Defroster nozzle						

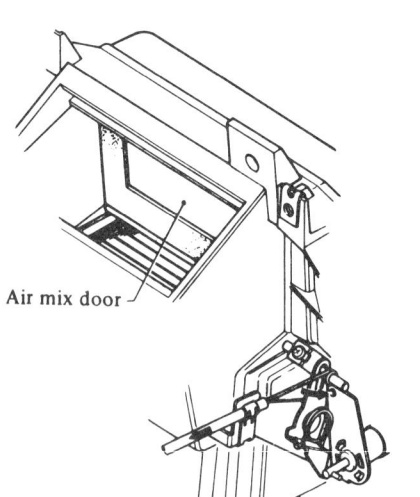

Air mix door

Fig. 10.61 Temperature control cable adjustment

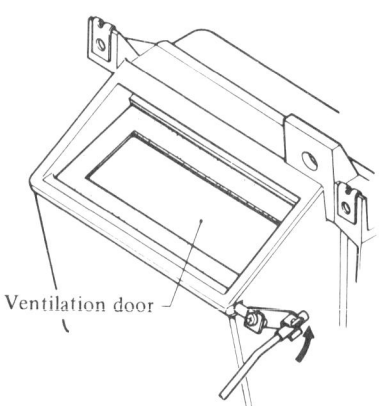

Ventilation door

Fig. 10.62 Ventilation door adjustment

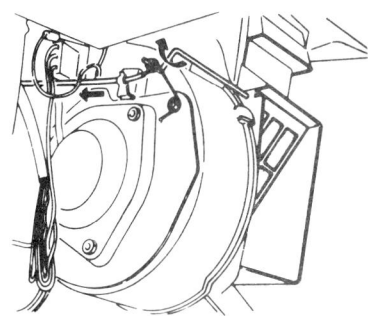

Fig. 10.63 Air intake door adjustment

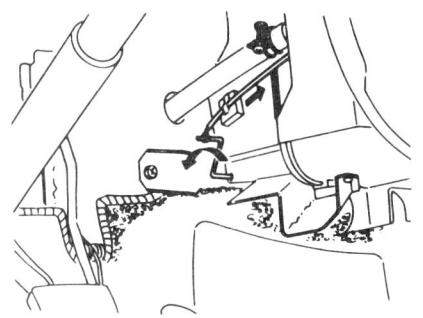

Fig. 10.64 Floor door adjustment (left-hand drive shown)

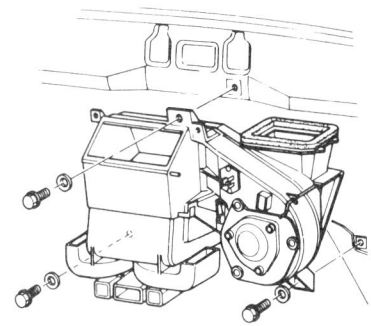

Fig. 10.65 Heater unit retaining bolts

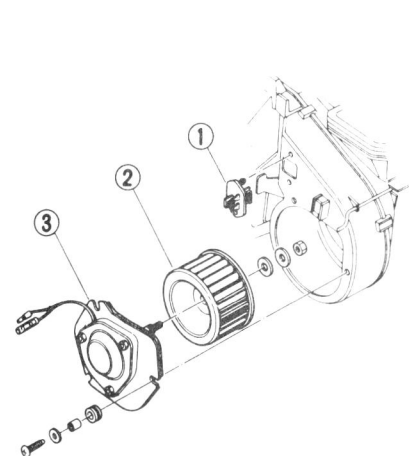

Fig. 10.66 Blower motor (3), blower (2) and resistor (1)

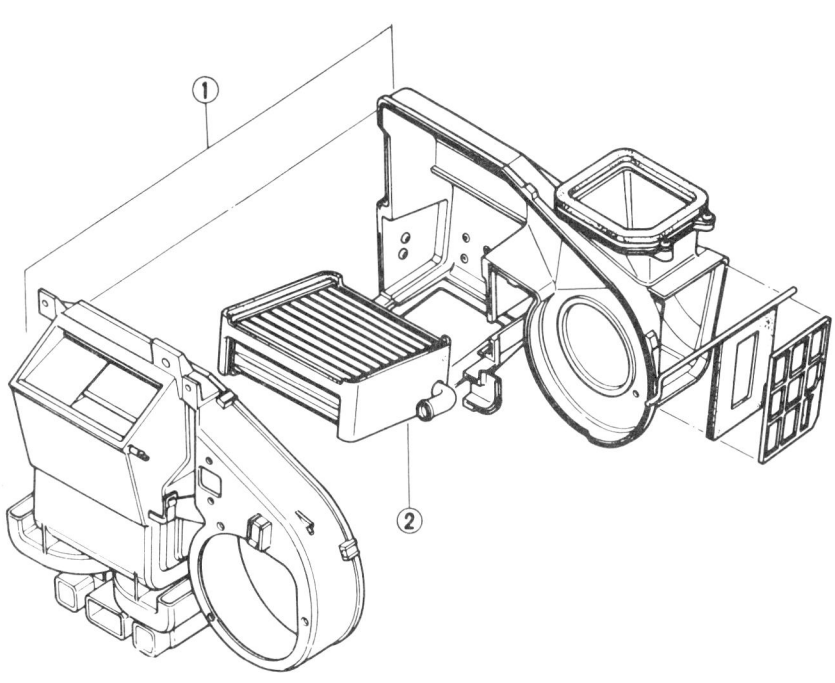

Fig. 10.67 Separate the case (1) to remove the core (2)

Aerial adjustment

14 If a new radio receiver or aerial has been fitted it may be necessary to adjust the receiver or aerial trimmer to suit locality. This is accomplished by first raising the aerial fully.

15 Tune the radio receiver into the weakest station between 1200 to 1600 Hz. Now slowly turn the trimmer screw in each direction to adjust it to the most sensitive receiving level.

42 Heater unit

Heater control – removal, refitting and adjustments

1 Detach the battery earth cable.
2 Remove the facia panel as described in Chapter 12, Section 30.
3 Remove the defroster ducts.
4 Detach the door control cables and rods.
5 Detach the wiring harness connector.
6 Loosen the attachment screws and withdraw the heater control unit (and bracket).
7 Refitting is a reversal of the removal procedure but adjust the control cables and rods as follows.

Air mix door adjustment

8 With the temperature control set in the maximum position, press the air mix door lever as indicated by the arrows in Fig. 10.61. Press the temperature control cable casing (outer) towards the temperature lever and simultaneously retain the casing with the clip. Ensure that the coolant cock is fully shut when engaging the 'Temp' control lever at its maximum 'cold' position.

Ventilation door adjustment

9 Position the air lever in the 'Recirc' location and press the ventilation door as shown by the arrow in Fig. 10.62, to close the flow to the central outlet.
10 Press the ventilation door control rod to locate in the relay lever clamp. The ventilation door must be fully open whilst the air lever is positioned at the vent location.

Air intake door

11 Position the air lever to 'off' and then press the air intake door as shown in Fig. 10.63 to close the outside air flow. The air intake door cable casing is now pushed towards the air lever and simultaneously retained in the clip. Ensure that the air intake door is opened fully when the air lever is in the Vent position (enabling outside air to flow through the intake).

Floor door

12 With the air lever set in the 'off' position refer to Fig. 10.64 and push the door in the direction shown to close the air flow. Press the control cable casing towards the air lever and retain in the clip.

Fig. 10.68 Kickdown switch location

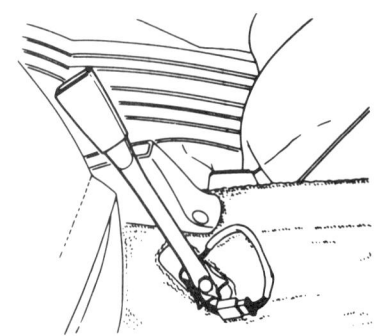

Fig. 10.69 Seat belt warning light wiring connector

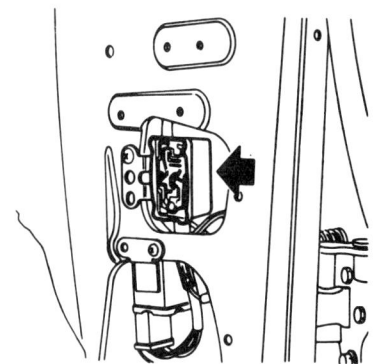

Fig. 10.70 Timer unit (seat belt warning)

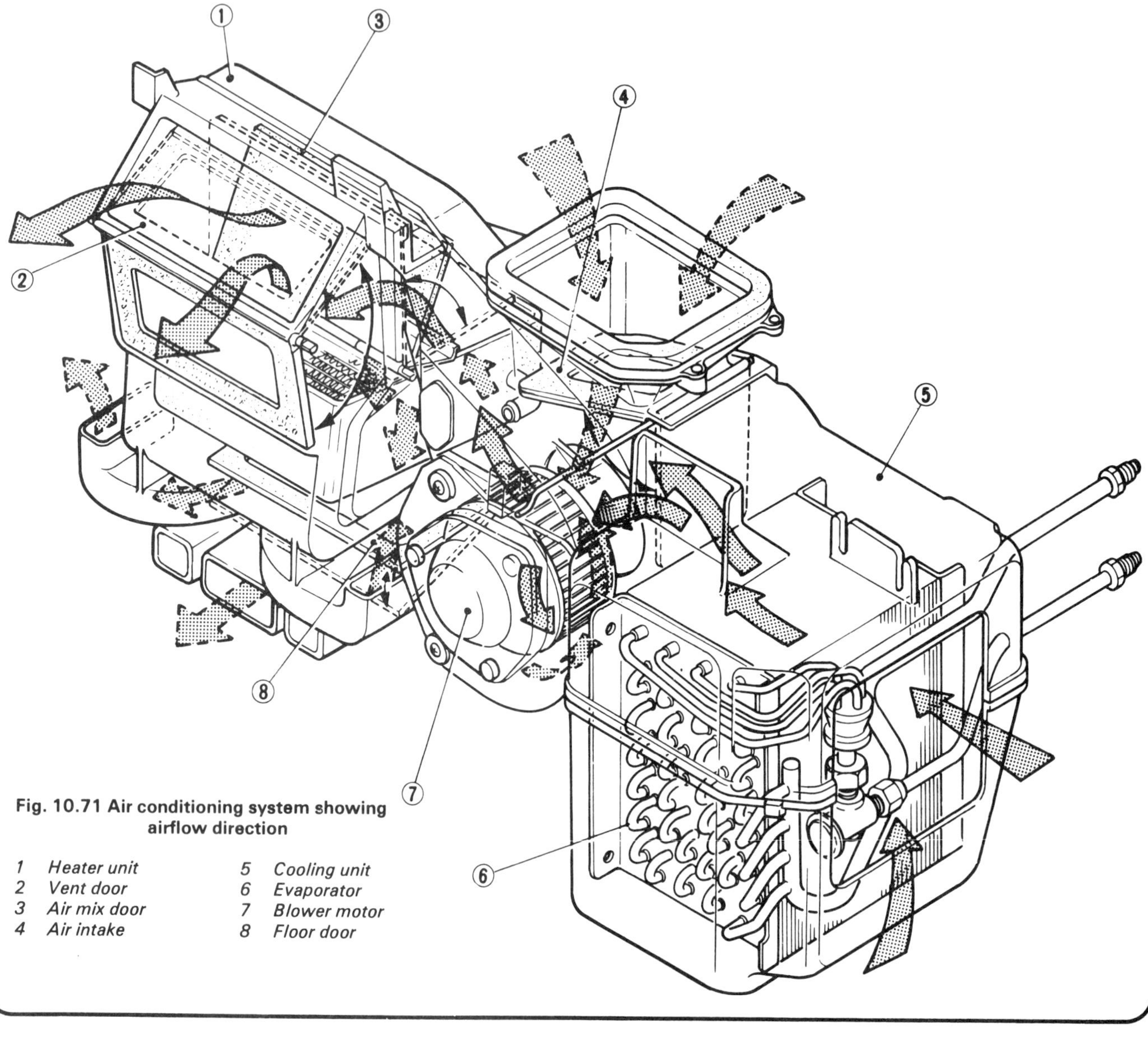

Fig. 10.71 Air conditioning system showing airflow direction

1	Heater unit	5	Cooling unit
2	Vent door	6	Evaporator
3	Air mix door	7	Blower motor
4	Air intake	8	Floor door

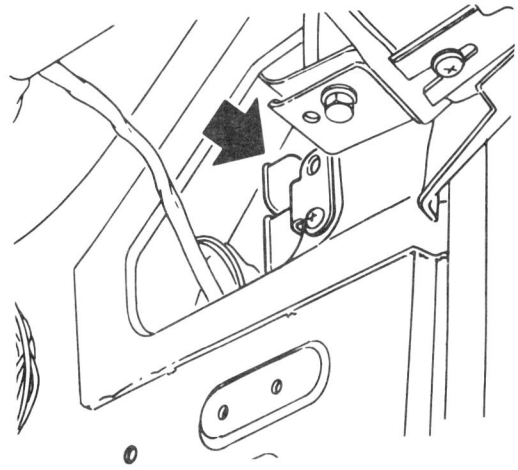

Fig. 10.72 Warning buzzer location

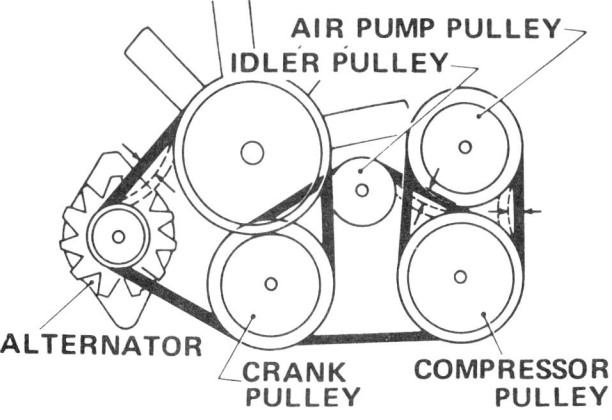

Fig. 10.73 Drivebelt layout showing tension check points (arrowed)

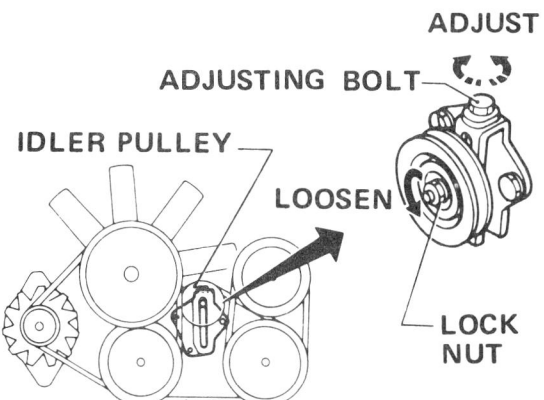

Fig. 10.74 Idler pulley adjuster

Heater unit – removal and refitting
13 Refer to Chapter 2 and drain the engine coolant.
14 Disconnect the battery earth cable and remove the centre console.
15 Remove the heater control unit, radio and heater ducts.
16 Unscrew and remove the defroster nozzle.
17 Detach the wiring harness from the blower motor connector.
18 Slacken the securing clips and detach the inlet and outlet coolant hoses.
19 Unscrew the retaining nuts and carefully withdraw the heater unit.
20 Refitting of the heater unit is a direct reversal of the removal procedure but readjust the controls as described in this Section.

Heater unit – dismantling and assembly
21 With the unit removed, unscrew and remove the resistor plug.
22 Unscrew and remove the blower unit retaining screws and withdraw the blower unit from the casing.
23 To remove the core unit, unclip the heater unit casing clips and split the casing. Withdraw the core.
24 Refitting is a direct reversal of the removal procedure but on completion readjust the heater controls and check for satisfactory operation.

---

43 Automatic transmission kickdown switch – removal and refitting

1 Disconnect the battery earth cable.
2 Detach the lead wires from the switch connector.
3 Slacken the locknut and then unscrew the switch unit to remove.
4 Refitting is a direct reversal of the removal procedure.

---

44 Seat belt warning system (510 models)

Belt switch – removal and refitting
1 If the seat belt switch is faulty it will have to be replaced as a unit with a new inner belt as they are a combined assembly.
2 Detach the battery earth cable.
3 With the seat adjusted in the forward position, separate the wiring harness at the connector (Fig. 10.69).
4 Unscrew the retaining bolt and remove the inner seat belt.
5 Refitting is a direct reversal of removal, but tighten the anchor bolt to a torque wrench setting of 14 to 27 lbf ft (2.0 to 3.8 kgf m).

Timer unit – removal and refitting
6 With the battery earth cable detached, remove the side finisher from the right dash panel.
7 Separate the wiring harness at the connector and unscrew the timing unit retaining screw to remove the timer.
8 Reverse the removal procedure to refit the timer unit.

Warning buzzer – removal and refitting
9 With the battery earth cable disconnected, separate the wire harness connector and remove the buzzer unit after unscrewing the retaining screw.
10 Refitting is a direct reversal of the removal procedure.

---

45 Air conditioning system – description and maintenance

1 An air conditioning system is available as an optional extra on the '510' range. The system combines heater, refrigeration and blower unit assemblies.
2 The heater system works on the normal principle in conjunction with the engine cooling system and incorporating its own booster (blower) motor.
3 The refrigeration system is shown in Fig. 10.71 and comprises five principle components these being an evaporator, a compressor, a condenser, a receiver drier and an expansion valve.
4 Due to the nature of the refrigeration gases used in the system, no servicing other than a few basic maintenance tasks can be undertaken by the home mechanic.
5 If it is necessary to disconnect any part of the refrigeration system in order to undertake work on other components, it is most important that the circuit be discharged prior to commencing work by a Datsun

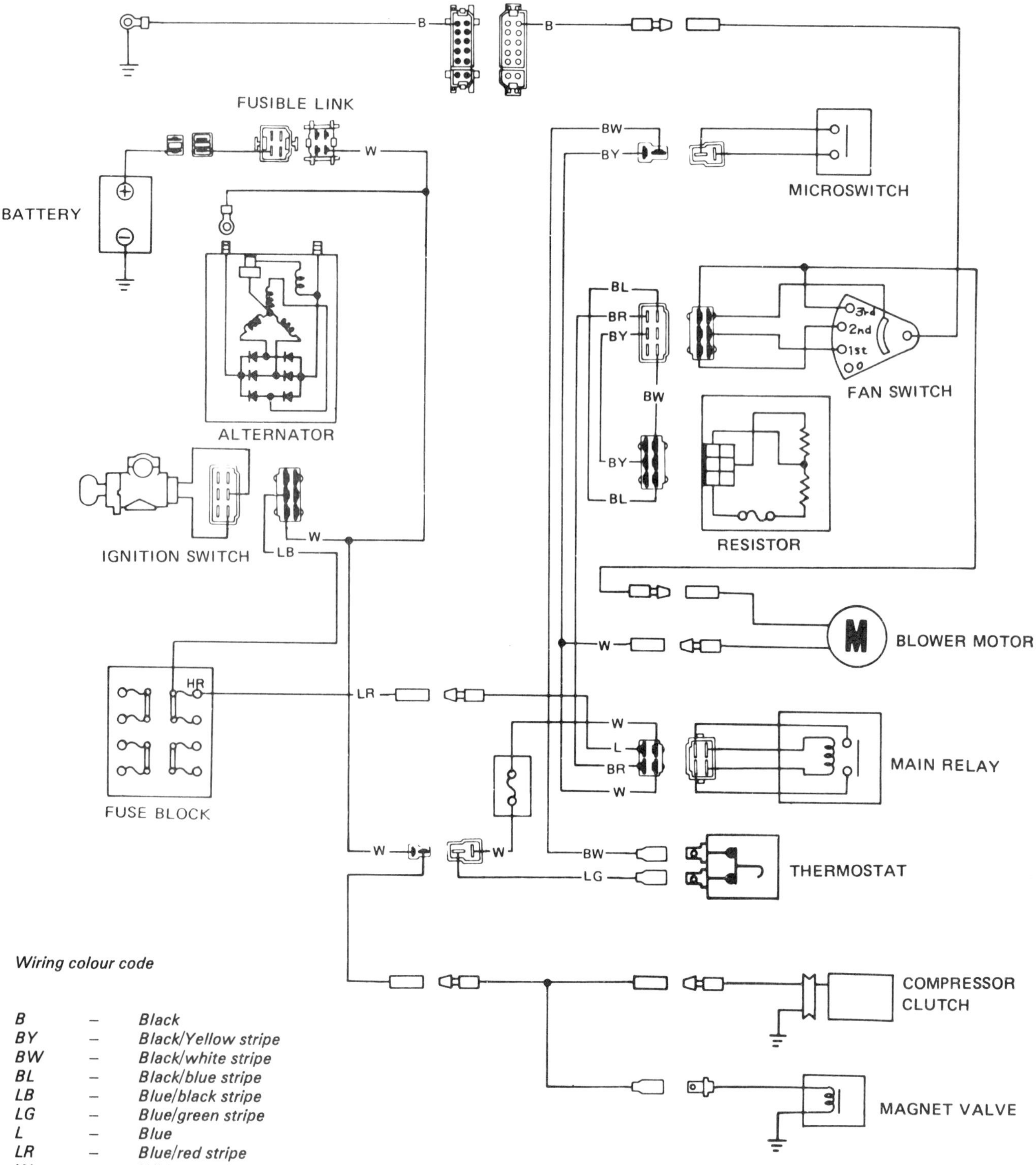
B
B
FUSIBLE LINK
W
BATTERY
ALTERNATOR
IGNITION SWITCH
W
LB
HR
FUSE BLOCK
LR
BW
BY
MICROSWITCH
BL
BR
BY
BW
BY
BL
3rd
2nd
1st
FAN SWITCH
RESISTOR
M
BLOWER MOTOR
W
W
L
BR
W
MAIN RELAY
BW
LG
THERMOSTAT
W
W
COMPRESSOR CLUTCH
MAGNET VALVE

Wiring colour code

B	–	*Black*
BY	–	*Black/Yellow stripe*
BW	–	*Black/white stripe*
BL	–	*Black/blue stripe*
LB	–	*Blue/black stripe*
LG	–	*Blue/green stripe*
L	–	*Blue*
LR	–	*Blue/red stripe*
W	–	*White*

Fig. 10.75 The air conditioning system electrical circuit diagram

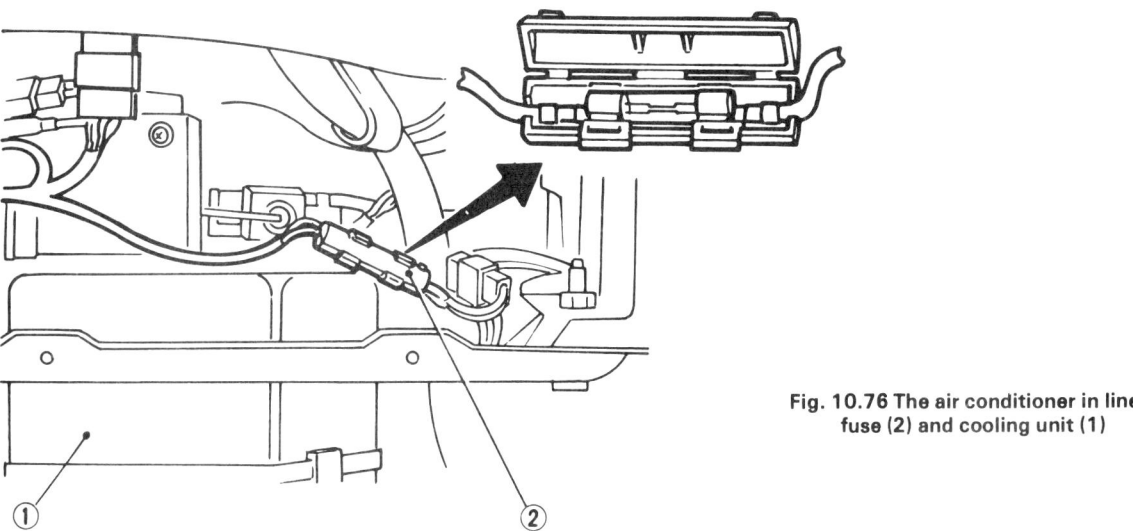

Fig. 10.76 The air conditioner in line
fuse (2) and cooling unit (1)

dealer or refrigeration engineer having the necessary knowledge and equipment. On completion of the particular service or overhaul the refrigeration system must be recharged again requiring specialized equipment and knowledge.

6   The maintenance tasks which can be carried out safely include checking the compressor belt tension. The driving belt layout is shown in Fig. 10.73 and the tension check points are arrowed. There should be a total deflection of 0.31 to 0.47 in (8 to 12 mm) under an average finger pressure.

7   The tension may be adjusted by moving the position of the idler pulley bolt in the desired direction. Further adjustment is obtainable by loosening the air pump mounting bolts and pivoting the unit in the direction required to tighten or loosen the pressure (in the same manner as the alternator).

8   Examine the system hoses and their connections for signs of leakage or deterioration. If evident the connection clips must be tightened or if necessary have the hose renewed by your Datsun agent or refrigeration mechanic.

9   Should the vehicle not be used regularly, the engine must be run for a period of about ten minutes once monthly at about 1500 rpm, to keep it in good condition.

10   If it is suspected that the amount of refrigerant in the system is incorrect, start the engine and hold it at a steady speed of 1500 rpm. Set the AIR lever in the A/C position and switch on the blower to maximum speed. Check the sight glass after an interval of about five minutes. The sight glass is located on the receiver drier. If a continuous stream of bubbles or mist is observed, then there is very little refrigerant left in the system. Where some bubbles are seen at intervals of 1 or 2 seconds then there is sufficient refrigerant in the system. The system is correctly charged when conditions within the sight glass are almost transparent with a few bubbles appearing if the engine speed is raised or lowered. If the system requires recharging, this must be carried out professionally.

11   The air conditioning electrical circuit is shown in the accompanying diagrams (Fig. 10.75). No maintenance is required for this part of the system apart from the occasional check to ensure that the wiring and connections are in good condition and securely located. A line fuse is incorporated into the circuit and in the event of this 'blowing' the cause should be located and rectified before fitting a new fuse.

12   To change the fuse, detach the battery earth cable and refer to Chapter 12 to remove the facia panel as given in Section 30. Withdraw the fuse holder from the harness and open it as shown in Fig. 10.76 to remove the old fuse. Always replace with a fuse of the correct value which is 20 amp.

46 Fault finding chart – electrical system

Symptom	Reason/s
Starter motor fails to turn engine	Battery discharged
	Battery defective internally
	Battery terminal leads loose or earth lead not securely attached to body
	Loose or broken connections in starter motor circuit
	Starter motor switch or solenoid faulty
	Starter motor pinion jammed in mesh with flywheel gear ring
	Starter brushes badly worn, sticking, or brush wires loose
	Commutator dirty, worn or burnt
	Starter motor armature faulty
	Field coils earthed
Starter motor turns engine very slowly	Battery in discharged condition
	Starter brushes badly worn, sticking, or brush wires loose
	Loose wires in starter motor circuit
Starter motor operates without turning engine	Starter motor pinion sticking on the screwed sleeve
	Pinion or flywheel gear teeth broken or worn

Starter motor noisy or excessively rough	Pinion or flywheel gear teeth broken or worn Starter drive main spring broken Starter motor retaining bolts loose
Battery will not hold charge for more than a few days	Battery defective internally Electrolyte level too low or electrolyte too weak due to leakage Plate separators no longer fully effective Battery plates severely sulphated Fan/alternator belt slipping Battery terminal connections loose or corroded Alternator not charging properly Short in lighting circuit causing continual battery drain Regulator unit not working correctly
Ignition light fails to go out, battery runs flat in a few days	Fan belt loose and slipping or broken Alternator faulty

Failure of individual electrical equipment to function correctly is dealt with alphabetically, item by item, under the headings listed below

Fuel gauge gives no reading	Fuel tank empty! Electric cable between tank sender unit and gauge earthed or loose Fuel gauge case not earthed Fuel gauge supply cable interrupted Fuel gauge unit broken
Fuel gauge registers full all the time	Electric cable between tank unit and gauge broken or disconnected
Horn operates all the time	Horn push either earthed or stuck down Horn cable to horn push earthed
Horn fails to operate	Blown fuse Cable or cable connection loose, broken or disconnected Horn has an internal fault
Horn emits intermittent or unsatisfactory noise	Cable connections loose Horn incorrectly adjusted
Lights do not come on	If engine not running, battery discharged Light bulb filament burnt out or bulbs broken Wire connections loose, disconnected or broken Light switch shorting or otherwise faulty
Lights come on but fade out	If engine not running battery discharged
Lights gives very poor illumination	Lamp glasses dirty Reflector tarnished or dirty Lamps badly out of adjustment Incorrect bulb with too low wattage fitted Existing bulbs old and badly discoloured Electrical wiring too thin not allowing full current to pass
Lights work erratically – flashing on and off, especially over bumps	Battery terminals or earth connections loose Lights not earthing properly Contacts in light switch faulty
Wiper motor fails to work	Blown fuse Wire connections loose, disconnected or broken Brushes badly worn Armature worn or faulty Field coils faulty
Wiper motor works very slowly and takes excessive current	Commutator dirty, greasy or burnt Drive to wheelboxes bent or unlubricated Wheelbox spindle binding or damaged Armature bearings dry or unaligned Armature badly worn or faulty
Wiper motor works slowly and takes little current	Brushes badly worn Commutator dirty, greasy or burnt Armature badly worn or faulty
Wiper motor works but wiper blades remain static	Driving cable rack disengaged or faulty Wheelbox gear and spindle damaged or worn Wiper motor gearbox parts badly worn

Fig. 10.77 Wiring diagram for 140J and 160J models

Key

A	Automatic transmission models
M	Manual transmission models
AE	A14 engine models
LE	L16 engine models
L	Left-hand drive models
R	Right-hand drive models
SW	Sweden
L*	Left-hand drive models except Sweden
*	Except Sweden
S	Saloon
K	Coupe

Switch and relay positions

1	Ignition switch in lock position
2	Lighting switch, wiper switch in Off position
3	Doors closed
4	Gearbox in neutral
5	Handbrake applied

Wiring colour code

W	White
B	Black
R	Red
G	Green
L	Blue
Y	Yellow
Br	Brown

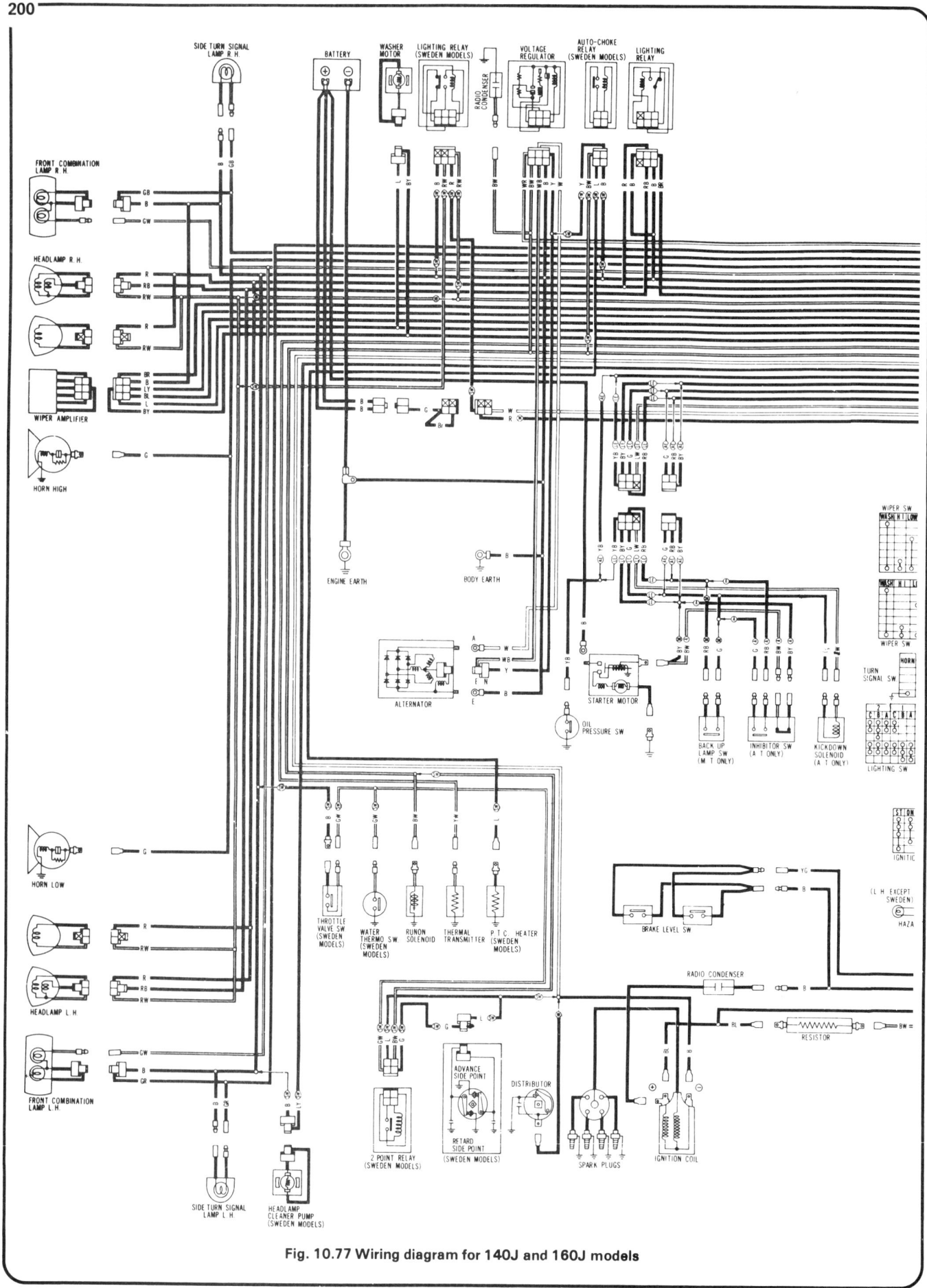

Fig. 10.77 Wiring diagram for 140J and 160J models

Fig. 10.77 Wiring diagram for 140J and 160J models – continued

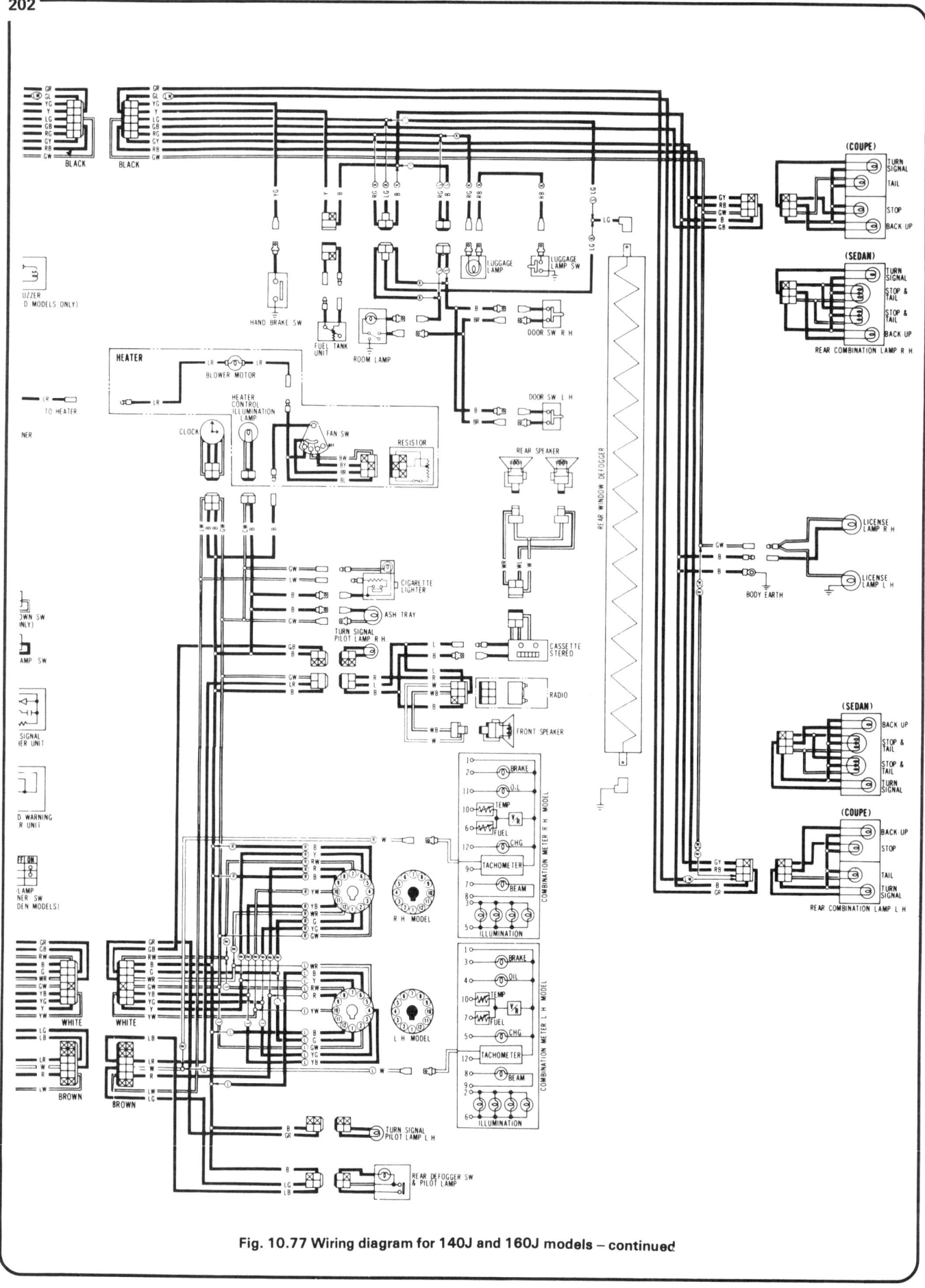

Fig. 10.77 Wiring diagram for 140J and 160J models – continued

Fig. 10.78 Wiring diagram for 510 models

Key

A	Automatic transmission models
M	Manual transmission models
C	California models
V	Non-California models for USA
N	Non-California models for Canada
S	Saloon
H	Coupe
W	Estate car
K	Air conditioner

Switch and relay positions

1	Ignition switch in Lock position
2	Lighting switch, wiper switch in Off position
3	Door closed
4	Gearbox in neutral
5	Handbrake applied
6	Drivers seat belt unoccupied

Wiring colour code

B	Black
W	White
R	Red
G	Green
L	Blue
Y	Yellow
Lg	Light green
Br	Brown

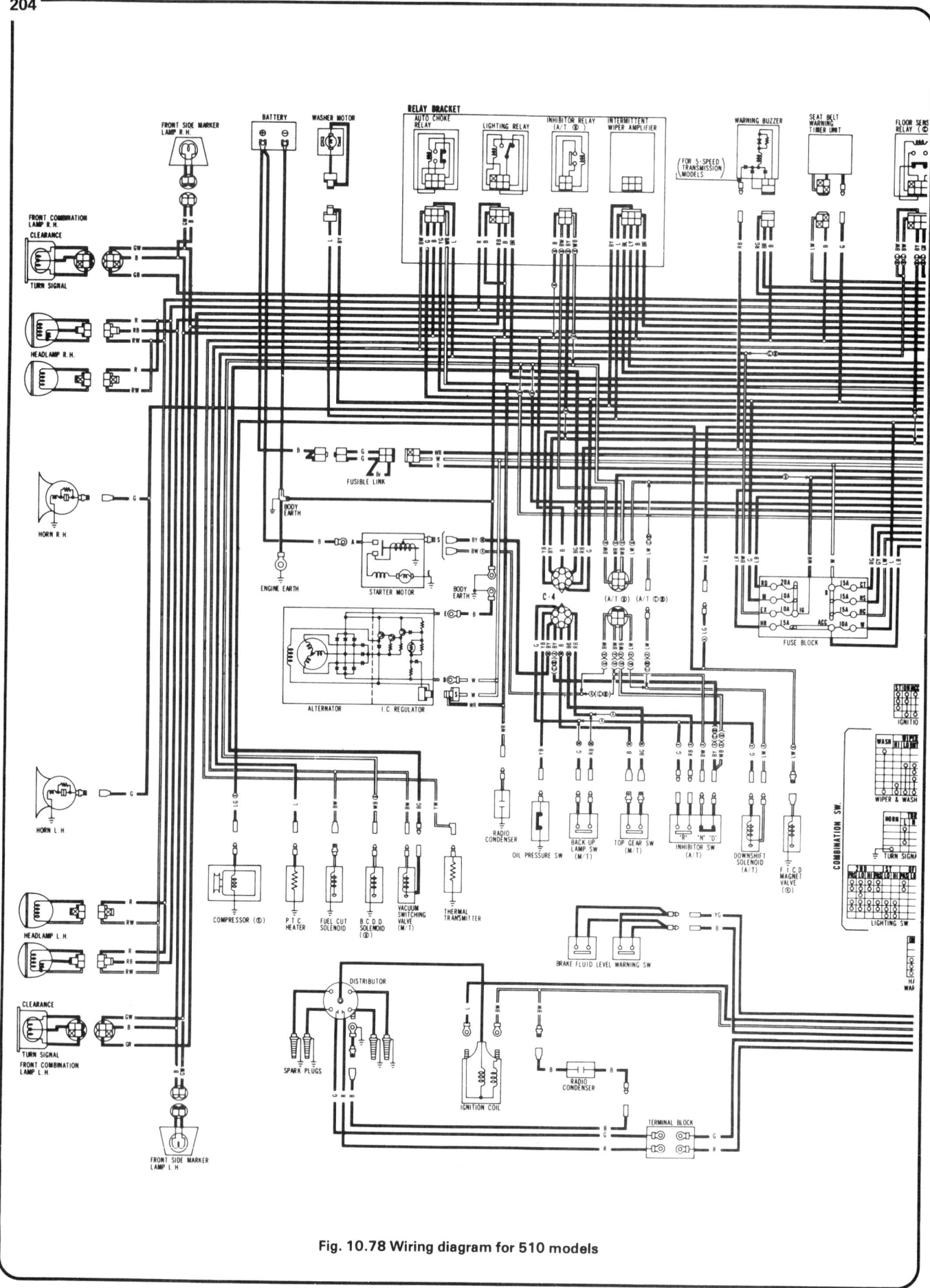

Fig. 10.78 Wiring diagram for 510 models

Fig. 10.78 Wiring diagram for 510 models – continued

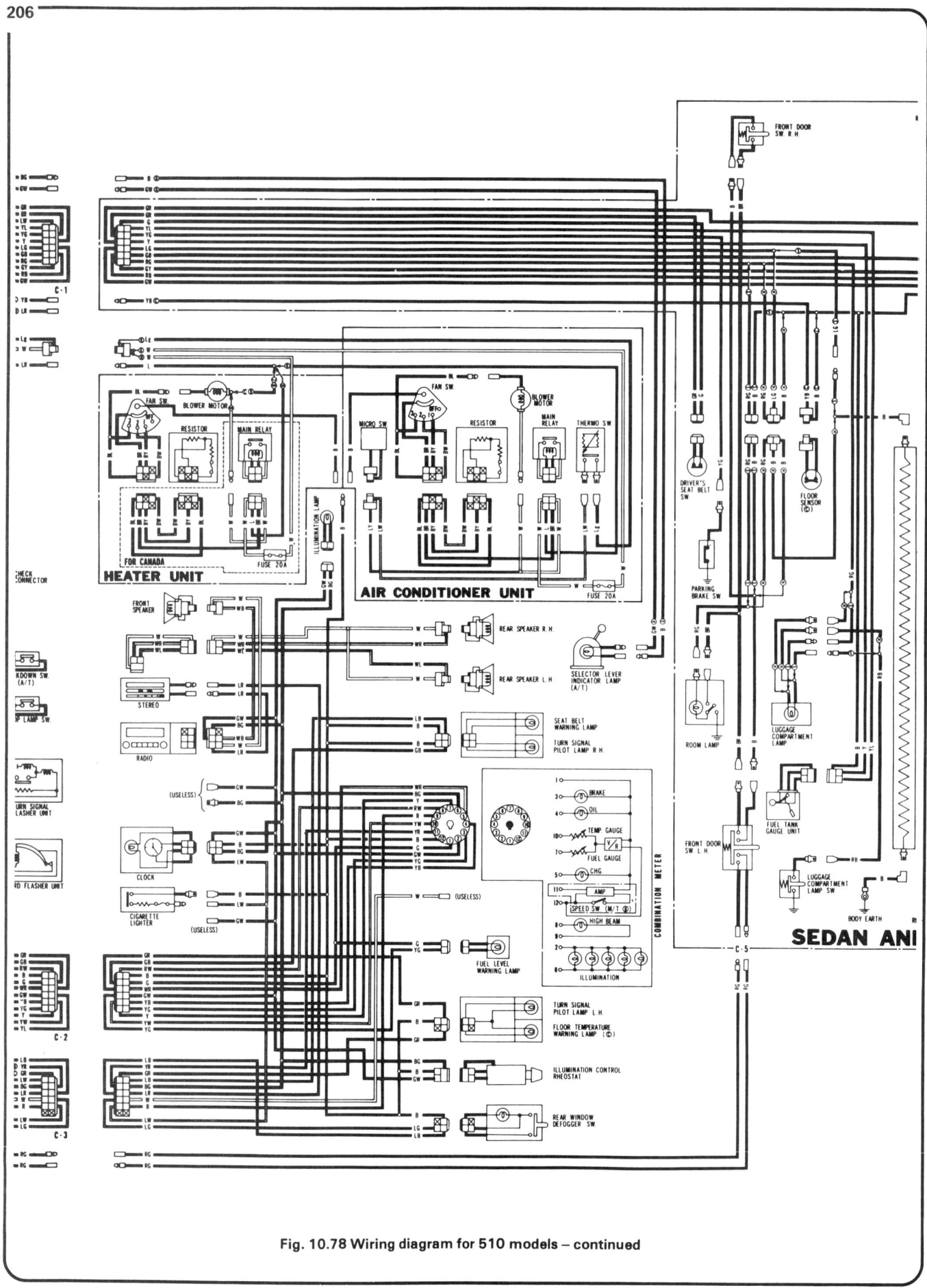

Fig. 10.78 Wiring diagram for 510 models – continued

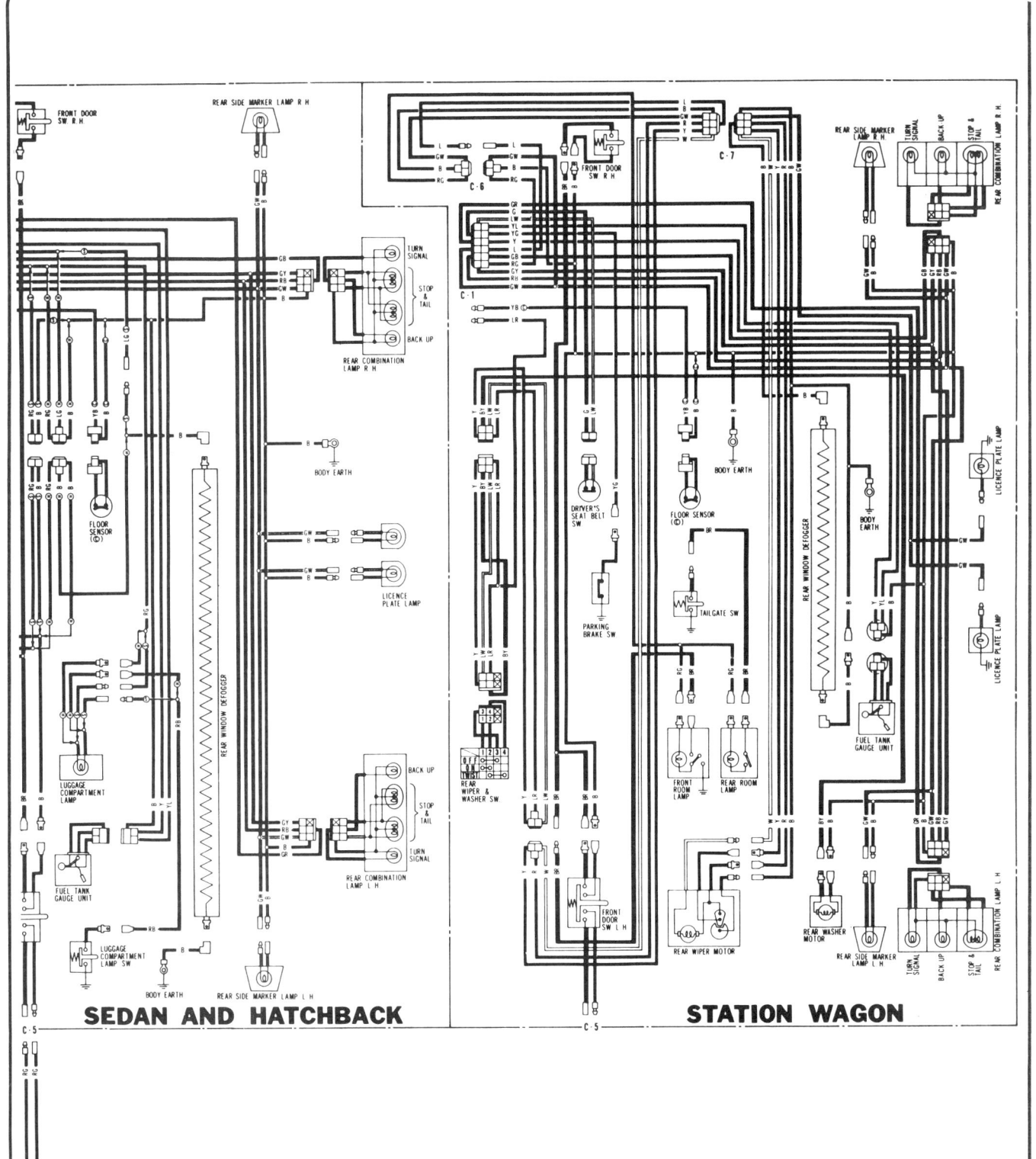

SEDAN AND HATCHBACK

STATION WAGON

Fig. 10.78 Wiring diagram for 510 models – continued

Chapter 11 Suspension and steering

Contents

Specifications

Front suspension
Type . . . .   Independent strut and coil springs, with double acting shock absorbers and stabilizer bar

Coil spring diameter . . . .   3.94 in (100 mm)

Coil gauge . . . .   0.43 in (11 mm)

Stabilizer bar diameter
Saloon and Coupe . . . .   0.75 in (19 mm)
Estate car . . . .   0.83 in (21 mm)

Wheel alignment – unladen
Toe-in . . . .   0.04 to 0.12 in (1 to 3 mm)
Camber angle
    Saloon and Coupe . . . .   −0° 15' to 1° 15'
    Estate Car . . . .   1° 05' to 1° 35'
Caster angle
    Saloon and Coupe (140J and 160J) . . . .   45' to 2° 15'
    Saloon and Coupe (510) . . . .   1° 05' to 2° 35'
    Estate Car . . . .   55' to 2° 25'
Kingpin inclination
    Saloon and Coupe . . . .   8° 05' to 9° 35'
    Estate Car . . . .   7° 45' to 9° 15'

Rear suspension
Type . . . .   Live axle with four link location, helical springs and double acting shock absorbers for Saloon and Coupe models or leaf spring and double acting shock absorbers for Estate Car models

Coil spring diameter . . . .   3.54 in (90 mm)

Coil gauge . . . .   0.413 in (10.5 mm)

Camber (unladen) . . . .   5.04 in (128 mm)

Steering system
Type . . . .   Recirculating ball nut and worm

Gear ratio	16.5 : 1	
Steering worm turning torque	3.5 to 6.9 lbf in (4.0 to 8.0 kgf cm)	
Sector shaft adjusting screw endplay	0.0004 to 0.0012 in (0.01 to 0.03 mm)	
Gear arm backlash (top end)	0.004 in (0.1 mm)	
Steering gear oil capacity	$\frac{1}{2}$ Imp pt ($\frac{5}{8}$ US pint)-(0.28 litre)	
Steering gear oil type	SAE90EP Gear oil	
Steering linkage balljoint turning torque	4.3 to 21.7 in lb (5 to 25 kg cm)	

Wheels and tyres
Wheel size

Steel	$4\frac{1}{2}$J – 13	
Aluminium	5J - 13	

Tyre pressures (measured when cold)
140 and 160J models

Saloon/Coupe with 5.60-13-4PR tyres	24 lbf/in² (1.6 kgf/cm²)	
Estate Car with 5.60-13-4PR tyres	26 lbf/in² (1.8 kgf/cm²)	
All 140/160 models with 6.45(S)-13-4PR tyres	24 lbf/in² (1.6 kgf/cm²)	
All 140/160 models with 165SR-13 tyres	26 lbf/in² (1.8 kgf/cm²)	

510 models

Saloon 2 door with 165-13/6.45-13-4PR tyres	26 lbf/in² (1.8 kgf/cm²)	
Other models with 165 SR13 tyres	26 lbf/in² (1.8 kgf/cm²)	

Torque wrench settings

	lbf ft	kgf m
Wheel nut (steel)	58 to 65	8.0 to 9.0
Wheel nut (aluminium)	58 to 72	8.0 to 10.0
Disc brake hub nut	22 to 25	3.0 to 3.5
Strut to wing inner panel	18 to 25	2.5 to 3.5
Steering knuckle arm to strut nut	53 to 72	7.3 to 9.9
Gland packing (suspension strut)	72 to 94	10.0 to 13.0
Strut piston self locking nut	43 to 54	6.0 to 7.5
Suspension balljoint	35 to 87 (in lb)	40 to 100 (kg cm)
Transverse link balljoint	37 to 44	5.1 to 6.1
Transverse link/tension rod	37 to 44	5.1 to 6.1
Balljoint/knuckle arm	40 to 72	5.5 to 10.0
Transverse link bolt/nut	28 to 36	3.9 to 5.0
Side rod balljoint/knuckle arm	22 to 51	3.0 to 7.0
Knuckle arm/strut	53 to 72	7.3 to 9.9
Crossmember to bodyframe	23 to 31	3.2 to 4.3
Engine mounting insulator to suspension member		
A14 engine	12 to 15	1.6 to 2.1
L16 and L20 engine	23 to 30	3.2 to 4.1
Tension rod bracket/body	23 to 31	3.2 to 4.3
Stabilizer bar bracket	23 to 31	3.2 to 4.3
Stabilizer bar connecting rod	12 to 15	1.6 to 2.1
Tension rod bush installation nut	33 to 40	4.5 to 5.5
Rear shock absorber (link type suspension) retaining nut – upper	11 to 14	1.5 to 2.0
Rear shock absorber (link type suspension) retaining nut – lower	51 to 58	7.0 to 8.0
Rear shock absorber (leaf spring suspension) –		
upper/lower nuts	26 to 33	3.6 to 4.5
Rear leaf spring front bracket nuts	43 to 47	6.0 to 6.5
Rear leaf spring pin nut (front)	43 to 47	6.0 to 6.5
Rear leaf spring shackle pin nuts	43 to 47	6.0 to 6.5
Rear leaf spring U-bolt nuts	33 to 40	4.5 to 5.5
Idler nut	40 to 51	5.5 to 7.0
Idler to body bolts	51 to 58	7.0 to 8.0
Column tube bracket nuts	2.5 to 3.3	0.35 to 0.45
Column clamp bolts	9 to 13	1.3 to 1.8
Wormshaft clamp bolt	29 to 36	4.0 to 5.0
Steering wheel nut	27 to 38	3.8 to 5.2
Steering gear housing to body	51 to 58	7.0 to 8.0
Rubber coupling to worm shaft	29 to 36	4.0 to 5.0
Sector shaft/gear arm nut	94 to 108	13 to 15
Steering box rear cover bolts	11 to 18	1.5 to 2.5
Sector shaft cover bolts	11 to 18	1.5 to 2.5
Adjuster screw locknut	12 to 18	1.7 to 2.5

1 General description

The independent front suspension comprises a vertical strut

(telescopic shock absorber) which is located in and works in conjunction with the coil spring. The top of the coil spring and strut are located in the inner wing panel, whilst the lower end of the strut is attached to

2.3 Remove the dust cover ...

2.4 ... and withdraw the split pin

2.5 Fitting outer bearing cone

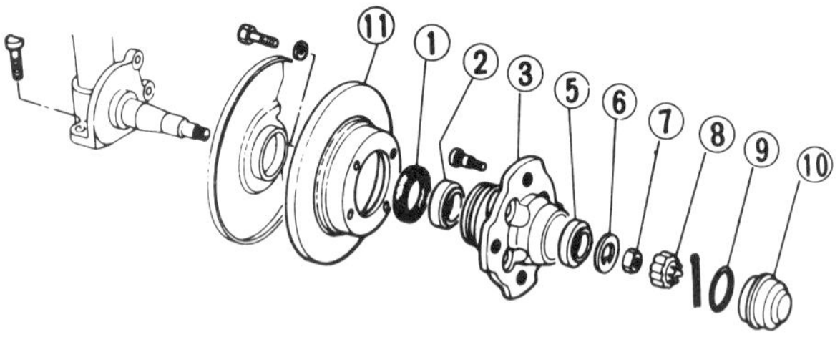

Fig. 11.1 The front wheel hub assembly

1	Seal	7	Nut
2	Inner bearing	8	Adjuster cap
3	Hub	9	O-ring
5	Outer wheel bearing	10	Hub cap
6	Bearing washer	11	Disc rotor

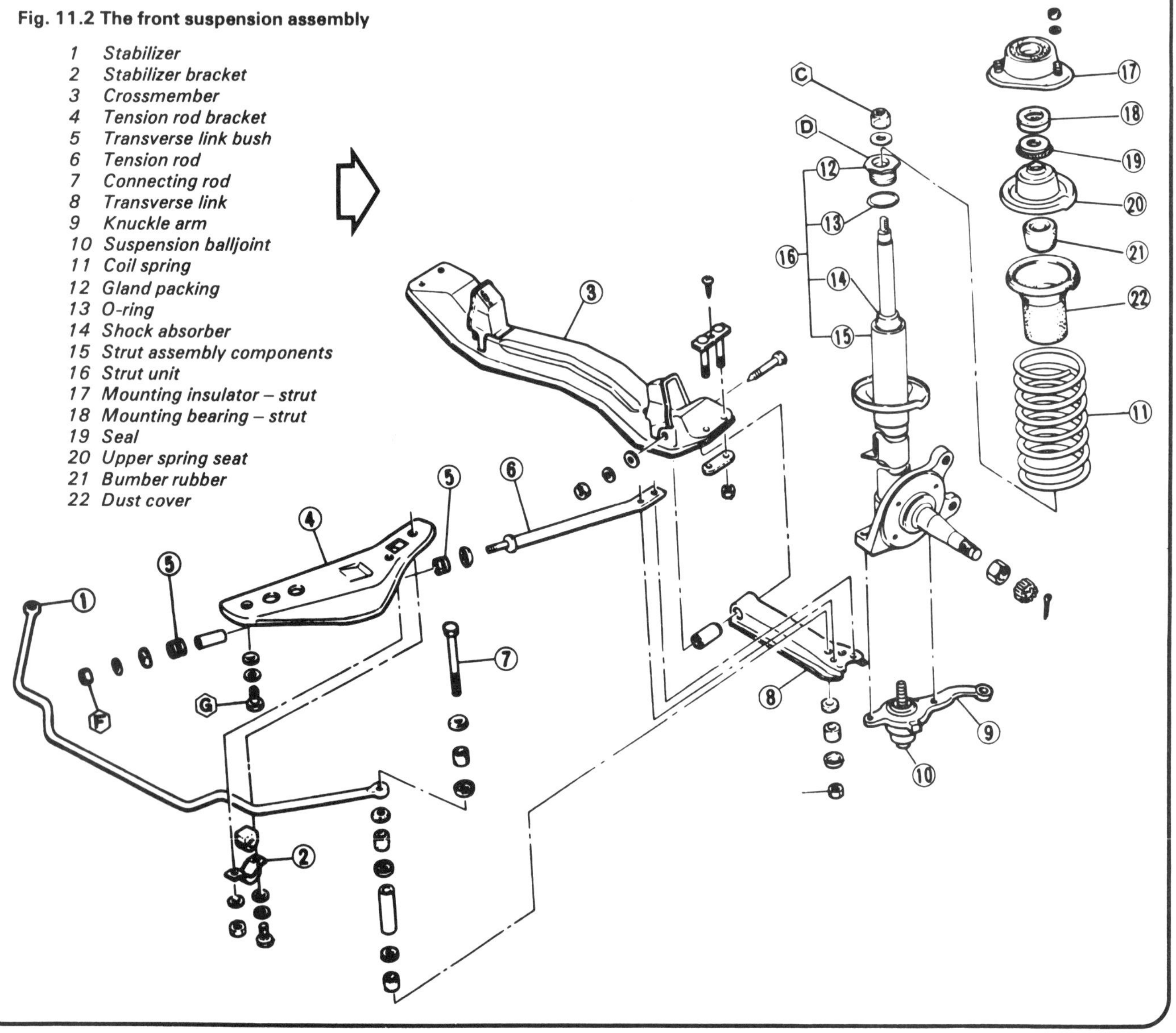

Fig. 11.2 The front suspension assembly

1 Stabilizer
2 Stabilizer bracket
3 Crossmember
4 Tension rod bracket
5 Transverse link bush
6 Tension rod
7 Connecting rod
8 Transverse link
9 Knuckle arm
10 Suspension balljoint
11 Coil spring
12 Gland packing
13 O-ring
14 Shock absorber
15 Strut assembly components
16 Strut unit
17 Mounting insulator – strut
18 Mounting bearing – strut
19 Seal
20 Upper spring seat
21 Bumber rubber
22 Dust cover

the steering knuckle arm. This in turn is attached to the transverse link which pivots from the suspension crossmember. A stabilizer bar is also fitted.

The steering system comprises a steering wheel and collapsible type column, recirculating ball-nut steering gear, idler arm assembly, cross rod, side rods (tie-rods), steering knuckle arms and kingpins. The steering gear is adjustable for worn bearing preload by the use of the shims, and for sector shaft endplay by means of an adjusting screw.

The front wheel hubs are supported on opposed taper roller bearings on the steering knuckle spindle (stub axle). The rear hubs are supported at their outer ends in single roller bearings; details of removal procedures etc, will be found in Chapter 8.

The type of rear suspension depends on the model. On Estate Car versions a semi elliptic leaf spring suspension is fitted to uprate the carrying capacity. Double acting telescopic shock absorbers are fitted and are located to the underside of the body at the top and the spring to axle U-bolt location plate at the bottom. The spring location and shackle pins and bushes are removable for renewal when necessary.

The rear suspension on all other models is the four link and coil spring type. The coil spring is located vertically between the axle casing and body underframe. The link assemblies have renewable bush bolts and bushes. Double acting telescopic shock absorbers are fitted.

2 Front wheel hub – removal, refitting and adjustment

1 Check that the handbrake is fully applied, chock the rear wheels and jack-up the front of the car and support on firmly based axle-stands. Remove the roadwheel.
2 Refer to Chapter 9 and remove the disc brake caliper unit.
3 Use a screwdriver and carefully prise the dust cover from the hub centre (photo).
4 Straighten the split pin and extract it from the wheel bearing locking nut (photo). Unscrew and remove the nut and washer.
5 The wheel hub and disc can now be withdrawn.
6 To dismantle the hub place the assembly in a vice and with a suitable drift, remove the grease seal.

7 Lift away the inner bearing cone and then using a drift remove the inner and outer tracks from the interior of the hub assembly. Note which way round the tapers face.
8 Wash the bearings, cups and hub assembly in paraffin and wipe dry with a non-fluffy rag.
9 Inspect the bearing outer tracks and cones for signs of overheating, scoring, corrosion or damage. Assemble each race and check for roughness of movement. If any of these signs are evident new races must be fitted.
10 To reassemble the front hub first fit the bearing outer tracks making sure that the tapers face outwards. Use a suitable diameter tubular drift and drive fully home.
11 Pack the two bearing cone assemblies with a recommended grease.
12 Insert the inner bearing cone assembly and then refit the seal, lip innermost, using the tubular drift. Take care that it is not distorted as it is being driven home.
13 Smear a little grease on the seal lip to provide initial lubrication.
14 Pack the hub with grease and refit to the stub axle.
15 Refit the outer bearing cone (photo) and refit the washer and nut to secure. Tighten the nut to the specified torque wrench setting, and rotate the hub to check for any sign of binding or stiffness. Recheck the torque wrench setting and then unscrew the nut approximately 90° to the nearest split pin hole alignment.
16 Locate the adjusting cap over the nut and insert the split pin to secure. Use a new split pin and bend over the ears to secure.
17 Fit a new O-ring to the dust cover and refit the cover onto the hub.
18 Refit the caliper unit and bleed the brakes as described in Chapter 9.
19 Refit the roadwheel and trim to complete.

3 Front suspension spring and strut unit – removal and refitting

1 With the handbrake fully applied, chock the rear wheels and jack-up the front of the car. Support with axle-stands and remove the roadwheel/s.

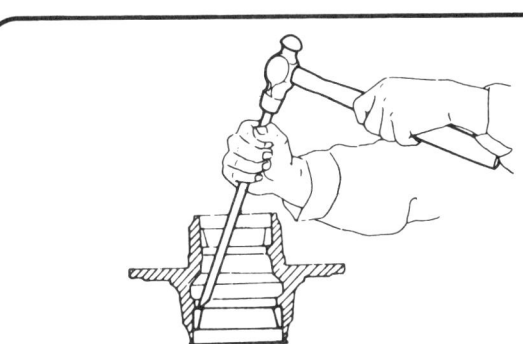

Fig. 11.3 Drive out the bearing cups

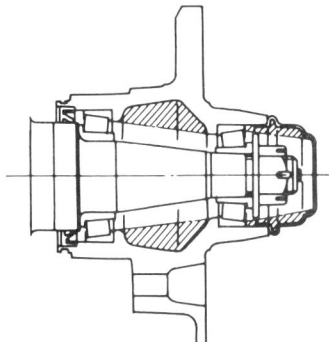

Fig. 11.4 Pack central shaded area with lubricant

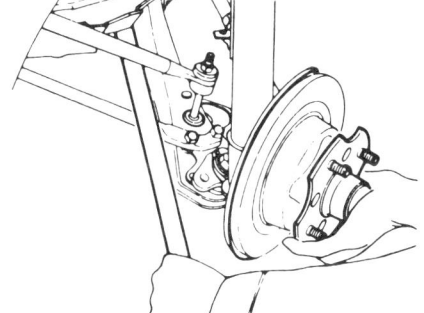

Fig. 11.5 Method of separating the strut and knuckle arm

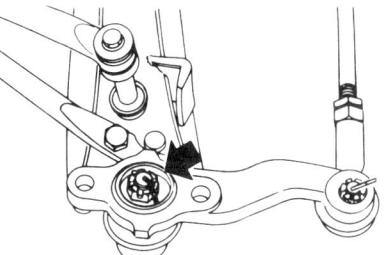
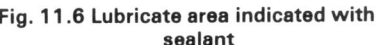

Fig. 11.6 Lubricate area indicated with sealant

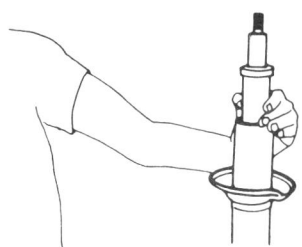

Fig. 11.7 Withdraw piston rod and cylinder slowly

2   Refer to Chapter 9 and remove the disc brake caliper unit.
3   Unscrew and remove the nut that retains the strut to the knuckle arm underneath and separate the two components. It will probably be necessary to prise them apart using a bar in the manner shown in Fig. 11.5.
4   Place a jack or suitable support under the strut to take its weight during the following operation.
5   Raise and secure the bonnet. Unscrew and remove the three nuts retaining the top of the strut to the inner wing panel.
6   Now carefully lower the jack or support under the strut, and lift away the strut unit and spring.
7   If the strut assembly is in need of an overhaul or a new coil spring is to be fitted, it is recommended that this be left to your Datsun dealer who has the necessary equipment to undertake this task. The overhaul procedure is given in the next Section but read it through carefully first to ensure that you have the correct tools for the job.
8   Refitting of the suspension strut and spring unit is the reverse of the removal procedure but note the following points:

   (a) *Ensure that the brake hose assembly is secure and not twisted or rubbing against adjacent steering or suspension components*
   (b) *Smear the area around the joint of the steering knuckle arm and the strut with a suitable sealant (Fig. 11.6)*
   (c) *Tighten the strut to wing panel attachment bolts and lower strut to knuckle nut to the specified torque wrench settings*

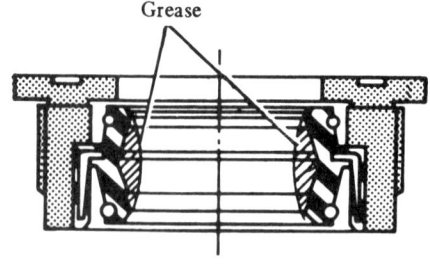

Fig. 11.8 Lubricate the grease points indicated

4   Front suspension spring and strut assembly – overhaul

It is recommended that, if the strut assembly is in need of overhaul or it is necessary for new coil springs to be fitted, this job be left to the local Datsun garage. The reason for this is that special tools are necessary to compress the spring, keep the spring in a compressed state and to dismantle the strut assembly.

The following instructions are given for those who wish to attempt the job. Before removing the strut assembly from the car it is necessary to fit clips to the coil spring to keep it in the compressed condition. These should be either borrowed from the local Datsun garage or made up using some high tensile steel rod at least 0.5 inch (12.70 mm) in diameter with the ends bent over. The length should accommodate as many coils as possible. Refer to Section 3 and follow the instructions given in paragraph 1. Then place a jack under the strut and compress the road spring by raising the jack. Fit the spring clips and tie firmly in place with strong wire or cord. Now follow the instructions given in paragraph 2 to 6 inclusive.

1   Thoroughly clean the unit by working in paraffin and then wiping dry with a clean non-fluffy rag.
2   Fit the coil spring compressor to the suspension unit, make sure that it is correctly positioned and then compress the spring. This is not applicable if the spring clips are in position.
3   Unscrew the self locking nut on the top of the strut and remove with washer and the mounting insulator.
4   Withdraw the strut bearing, dust seal, spring seating the spring and bump stop rubber.
5   Compress the piston rod fully until it bottoms and then unscrew the gland packing using a suitable spanner.
6   Extract the O-ring from the top of the piston rod guide.
7   Withdraw the piston and cylinder slowly to prevent the loss of oil.
8   The piston and piston rod guide must not be dismantled from the cylinder as they are pre-set at the factory and are a matching assembly.
9   Tilt the inner cylinder and allow the hydraulic fluid to drain out into a container. Also drain out any fluid inside the outer casing. Fresh fluid will be required during reassembly.
10   Wash all parts in petrol and wipe dry. Make quite sure no dirt is allowed to contact any internal parts.
11   Inspect the outer casing for signs of distortion, cracking or accident damage and obtain new if any such condition is apparent.
12   Inspect the spindle for hair line cracks on the base or damaged threads. If evident the complete strut assembly should be renewed.
13   Inspect the rubber and metal joint for signs of damage or deterioration. Obtain new parts if evident.
14   If noise originated from the strut when driving over rough road sur-

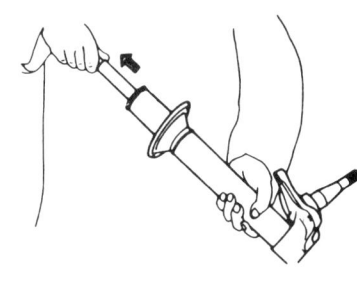

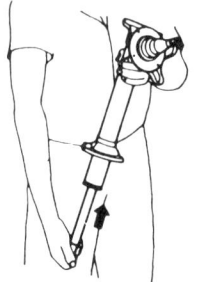

Fig. 11.9 Method of bleeding the shock absorber unit

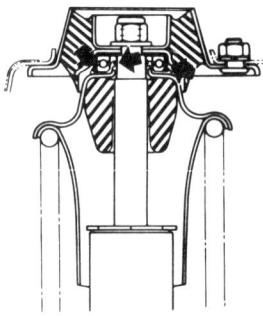

Fig. 11.10 Lubrication area. Note position of bearing

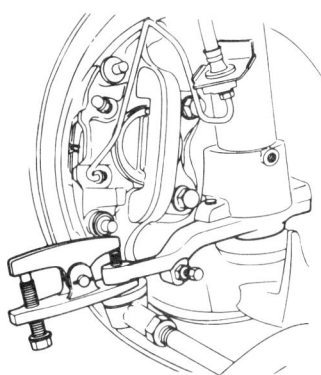

Fig. 11.11 Separating the side rod joint using a balljoint separator

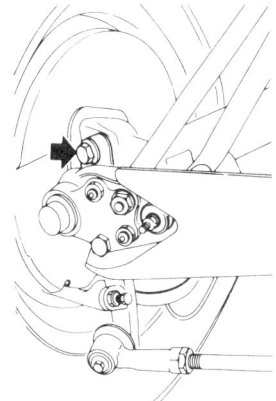

Fig. 11.12 Knuckle arm bolts indicated

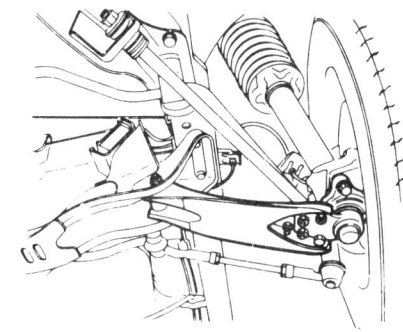

Fig. 11.13 Transverse link assembly

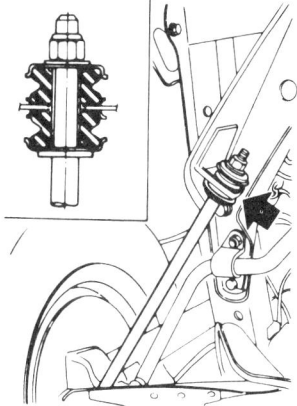

Fig.11.14 Correct location for tension rod bushes

faces the cause is probably due to the strut mounting bearing having worn. Obtain a new bearing assembly.

15 Before reassembly commences make sure that every part is really clean and free from dust.

16 The gland packing and O-ring must automatically be renewed whenever the strut is dismantled.

17 Commence reassembly by ensuring that all components are spotlessly clean.

18 Fit the piston rod and cylinder into position in the outer casing.

19 Fill the assembly with the recommended grade of hydraulic fluid. For AMPCO (ATSUGI) units use 325 cc of KYB (KAYABA) units use 394 cc. Do not deviate from the quoted amounts otherwise the operating efficiency of the unit will be altered.

20 Refit the piston rod guide into the cylinder, taking care not to scratch or damage the guide.

21 Fit a new O-ring onto the rod guide.

22 Before fitting the gland packing, smear the lips with a molybdenum disulphide grease. Insert the gland packing and guide, then tighten to the specified torque. This will have to be estimated if the special tool is not available. It is important that, when tightening the gland packing, the piston rod must be extended approximately 4·72 in (120 mm) from the end of the outer casing to allow the spring to be fitted.

23 It is now necessary to bleed the shock absorber system by holding the strut with the spindle end down and pulling the piston rod out completely.

24 Now invert the strut so that the spindle end is uppermost and push the piston rod inward as far as it will go.

25 Repeat the procedure described in paragraph 23 several times until an equal pressure is felt during both strokes.

26 Pull the piston rod out fully and fit the rebound rubber, to prevent the piston rod falling by its own weight.

27 Locate the spring on the lower spring seat with the end fitted into the recess and compress the spring with the special tool if spring clips are not fitted.

28 Refer to Fig. 11.10 and lubricate the dust seal with a general purpose grease.

29 Refit the dust cover, upper spring seat, mounting bearing and insulator.

30 Refit and tighten the piston rod self locking nut to the specified torque wrench setting.

31 With the spring correctly located release the spring compressor. If clips have been used leave in position until the strut has been reassembled to the car.

32 Raise the rebound rubber until it is seated under the upper spring seat.

33 The strut assembly is now ready for refitting to the car.

5 Transverse link and lower balljoint – removal and refitting

1 Chock the rear wheels, apply the handbrake, jack-up the front of the car and support on firmly based axle-stands. Remove the relevant roadwheel.

2 Detach the splashboard.

3 Undo and remove the bolts which secure the knuckle arm in position.

4 Straighten the ears and withdraw the split pin from the side rod socket balljoint castellated nut. Undo and remove the nut and separate the side rod socket from the knuckle arm.

5 The tension rod and stabilizer should now be detached from the transverse link.

6 Unscrew and remove the bolt securing the transverse link and suspension crossmember (photo).

7 Undo and remove the balljoint securing nut and lift the balljoint from the transverse link.

8 Wash all parts and wipe dry. Carefully inspect the transverse link for signs of cracks, distortion or accident damage. Should the rubber and inner tube joints be sticky or show signs of cracking the transverse link should be renewed as a complete assembled unit.

9 Inspect the balljoint for endplay and damage. Check the dust cover for cracks and deterioration. Should there be endplay or damage to the balljoint a new one must be fitted. Generally a new balljoint assembly is supplied complete with a dust cover. It is not possible to dismantle and overhaul the balljoint assembly.

10 Inspect the transverse link bushing and if it is worn or the rubber

5.6 Transverse link to crossmember connection

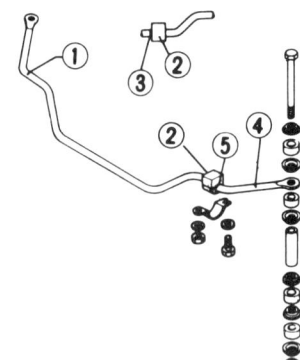

Fig. 11.15 Stabilizer bar components showing identification mark positions

1   Identification mark position
2   Bush
3   Identification mark
4   White paint
5   Identification mark

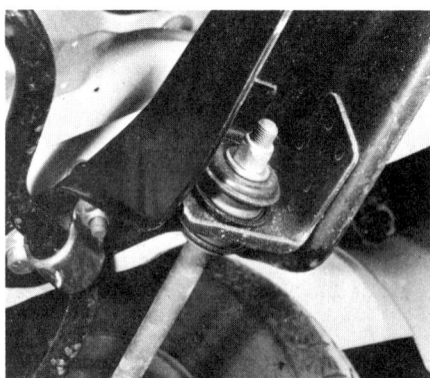

6.4 Tension rod to bracket connection

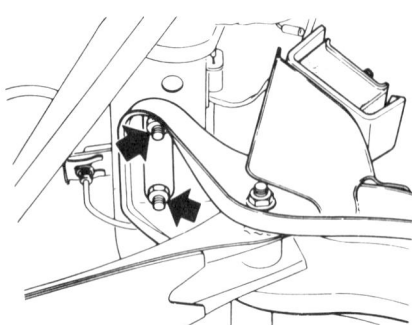

Fig. 11.16 Engine mounting nut positions

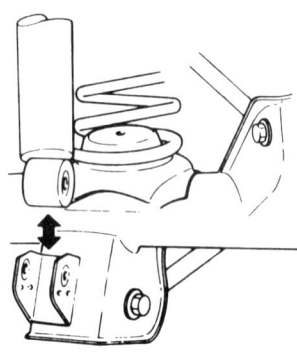

Fig. 11.17 Shock absorber lower end mounting (Saloon and Coupe)

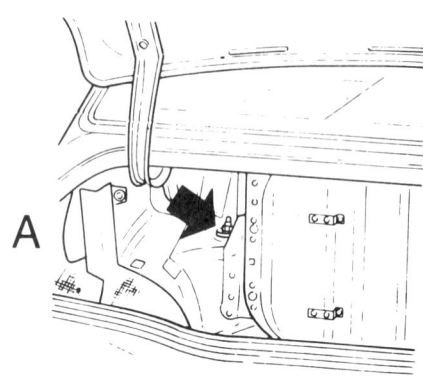

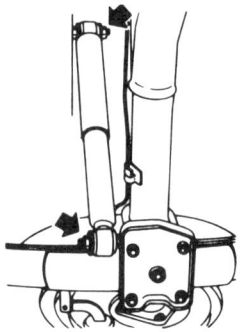

Fig. 11.19 Shock absorber mounting positions – Estate Car

Fig. 11.18 Upper shock absorber connections

A – Saloon   B – Coupe

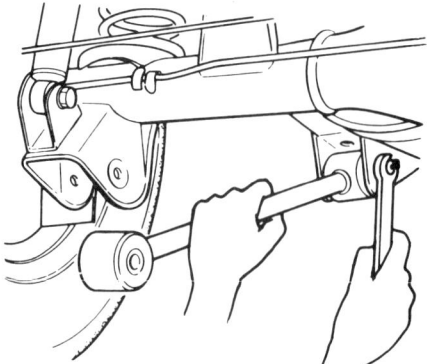

Fig. 11.21 Detach lower link

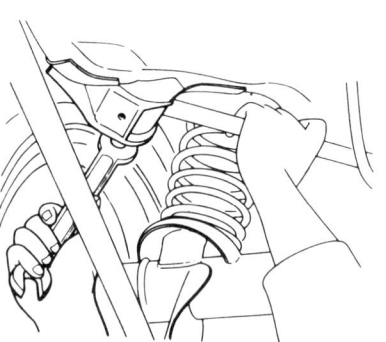

Fig. 11.20 Detach upper link

contaminated it must be renewed. The old bush may be drifted out and a new one fitted. Take care to ensure that the bush is fitted the correct way round.

11 Refitting the transverse link and lower balljoint is the reverse sequence to removal, but the following additional points should be noted.

(a) *Do not fully tighten the transverse link mounting bolts until the car has been lowered to the ground*

(b) *Tighten the balljoint nut to the specified torque wrench setting*

(c) *Tighten the transverse link mounting bolts to the specified torque*

(d) *Always lubricate a new balljoint by removing the plug and fitting a grease nipple. Use a grease gun and lubricate with a general purpose grease until old grease is expelled. Remove the nipple and refit the plug*

6 Stabilizer bar and tension rod – removal and refitting

1 Apply the handbrake and jack-up the front of the vehicle and support on firmly based axle-stands.

2 Remove the roadwheel.

3 Where applicable, remove the splashboard.

4 Loosen the tension rod to bracket retaining nut (photo). Remove the two bolts retaining the tension rod to transverse link to release the tension rod.

5 Using a pair of spanners, unscrew the nuts retaining the stabilizer bar to the connection rod.

6 Unscrew and remove the bolts and nuts retaining the stabilizer bar

bracket and then remove the stabilizer bar.

7 Inspect the components for signs of wear damage or distortion. In particular check the rubber bushes and renew as necessary.

8 Refit in the reverse order but note the following:

(a) *Ensure that the stabilizer bar is centrally located. If new, position the arm with the white identification mark on the left side of the vehicle and position the stabilizer bar mounting bushes to enable the outer side of the bush to be drawn in to the inner side of the mark*

(b) *Ensure that the tension rod bush is seated correctly*

(c) *Tighten the tension rod bolt to the specified torque wrench setting*

(d) *Ensure that the tension rod to stabilizer bar clearance is equal on each side*

(e) *When fitting the tension rod tighten to the specified torque on the bracket side first, then fit the other end to the transverse link*

7 Front suspension crossmember – removal and refitting

1 Refer to Section 7 and remove the transverse link.

2 Take the weight from the engine mountings by lifting the engine using a hoist and sling.

3 Unscrew the engine mounting nuts and remove the crossmember bar.

4 Refit in the reverse order but tighten the mounting nuts and suspension member to body nuts to the specified torque wrench setting.

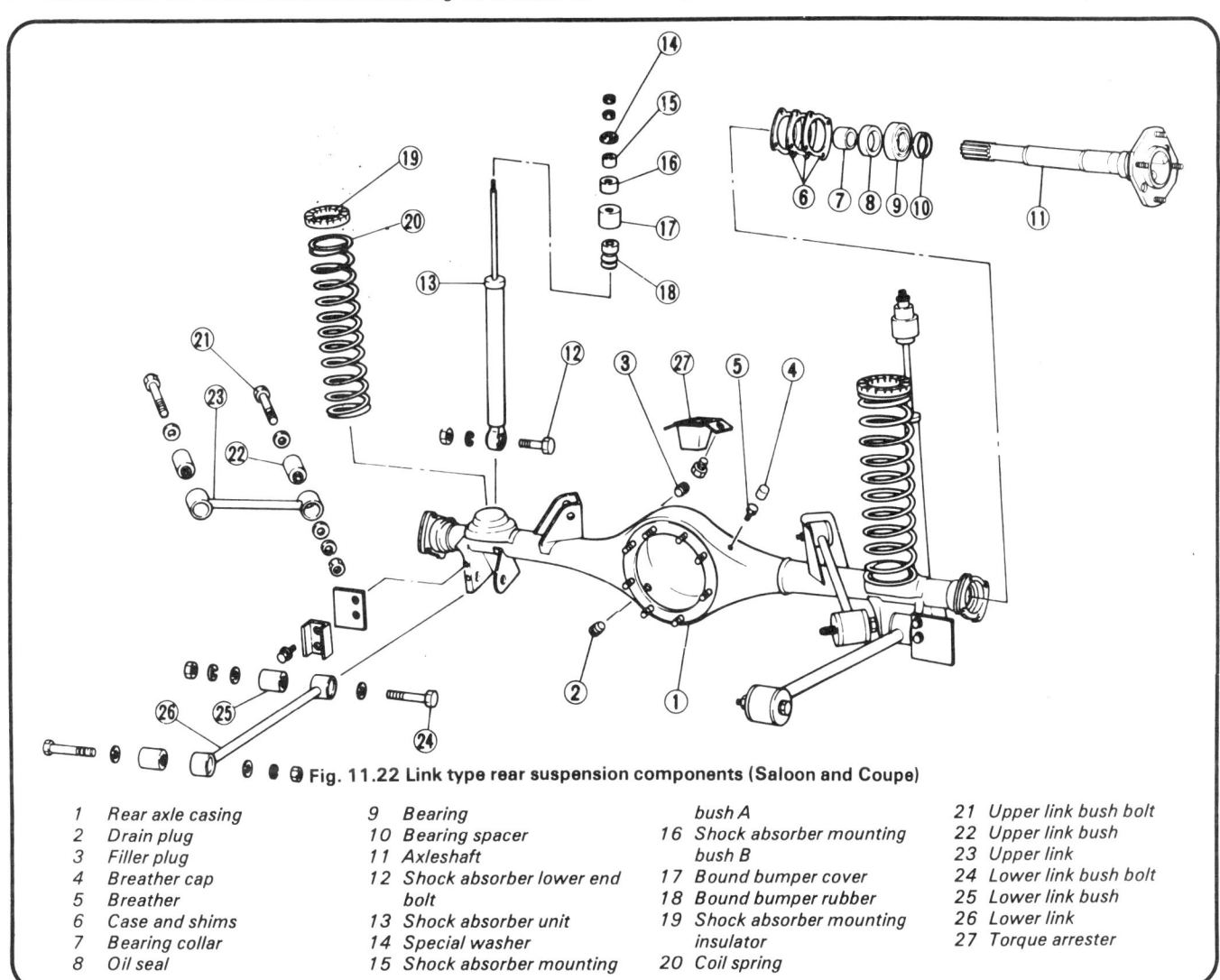

Fig. 11.22 Link type rear suspension components (Saloon and Coupe)

1	Rear axle casing	9	Bearing
2	Drain plug	10	Bearing spacer
3	Filler plug	11	Axleshaft
4	Breather cap	12	Shock absorber lower end bolt
5	Breather	13	Shock absorber unit
6	Case and shims	14	Special washer
7	Bearing collar	15	Shock absorber mounting
8	Oil seal		

bush A
16 Shock absorber mounting bush B
17 Bound bumper cover
18 Bound bumper rubber
19 Shock absorber mounting insulator
20 Coil spring

21 Upper link bush bolt
22 Upper link bush
23 Upper link
24 Lower link bush bolt
25 Lower link bush
26 Lower link
27 Torque arrester

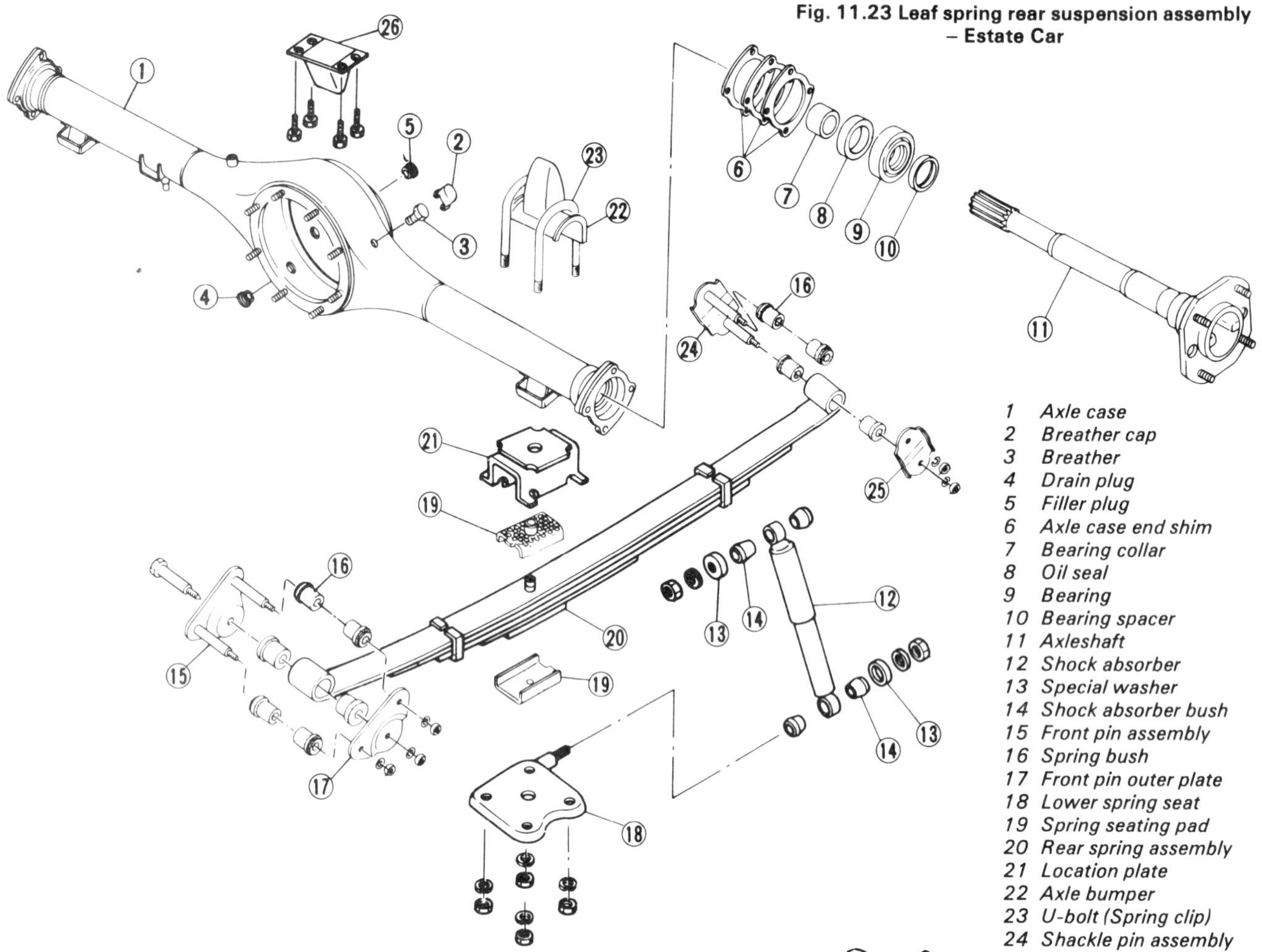

Fig. 11.23 Leaf spring rear suspension assembly – Estate Car

1 Axle case
2 Breather cap
3 Breather
4 Drain plug
5 Filler plug
6 Axle case end shim
7 Bearing collar
8 Oil seal
9 Bearing
10 Bearing spacer
11 Axleshaft
12 Shock absorber
13 Special washer
14 Shock absorber bush
15 Front pin assembly
16 Spring bush
17 Front pin outer plate
18 Lower spring seat
19 Spring seating pad
20 Rear spring assembly
21 Location plate
22 Axle bumper
23 U-bolt (Spring clip)
24 Shackle pin assembly
25 Shackle
26 Torque arrester

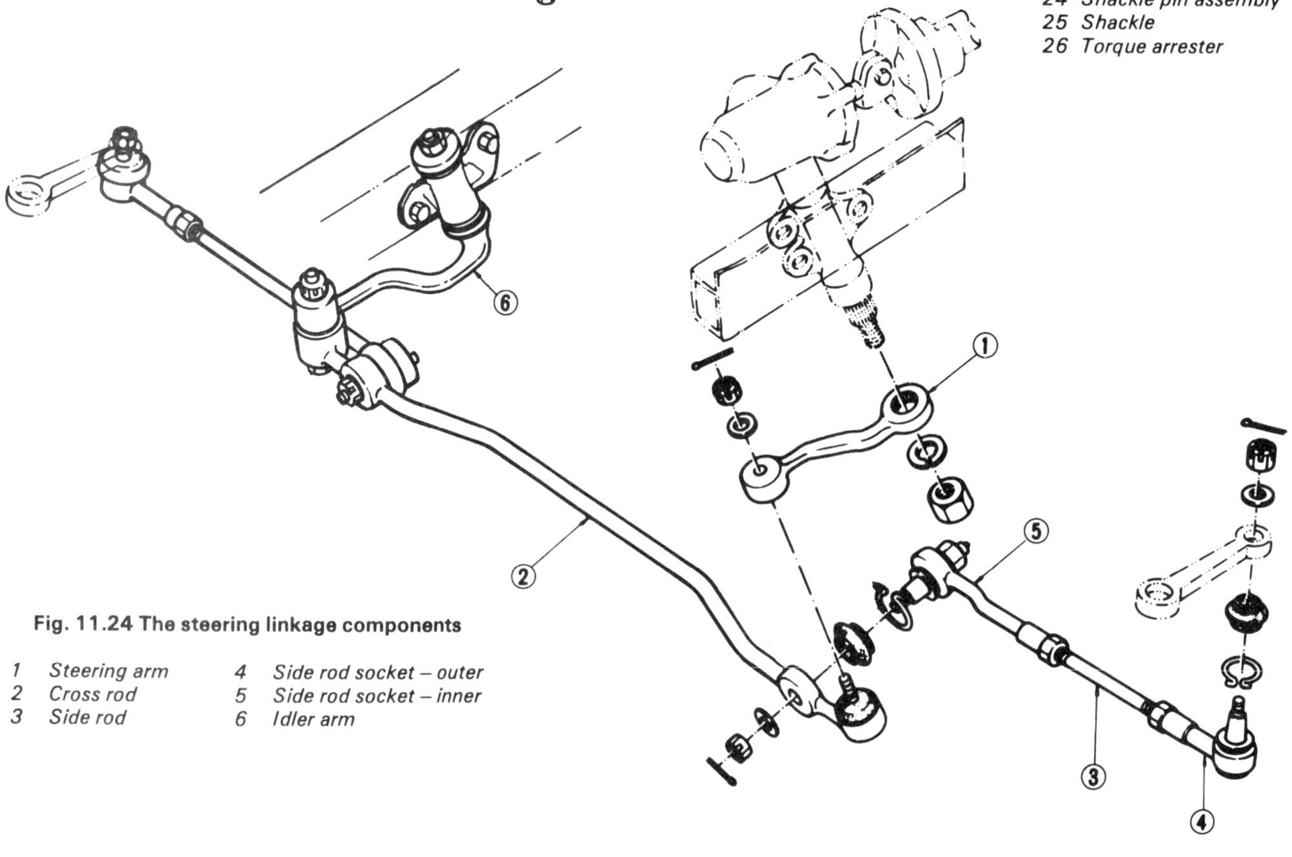

Fig. 11.24 The steering linkage components

1 Steering arm
2 Cross rod
3 Side rod
4 Side rod socket – outer
5 Side rod socket – inner
6 Idler arm

8 Rear suspension shock absorber

Link type rear suspension

1   Refer to Fig. 11.18 and unscrew the rear shock absorber upper retaining nuts.
2   Chock the front wheels and raise the rear of the vehicle and support with stands on the axle tube. Check for security before commencing work underneath.
3   Unscrew the nut and remove with spring washer from the lower shock absorber location bolt. Withdraw the bolt.
4   Compress and remove the shock absorber.
5   Clean and inspect for leaks and/or general wear. The rear shock absorbers are not repairable and no attempt should be made to effect repairs.
6   Refit in the reverse order and tighten the retaining nuts to the specified torque wrench settings after the car has been lowered to the ground.

Leaf spring type rear suspension

7   The shock absorber on the leaf spring type rear suspension is also a double acting telescopic type but the upper retaining bolt and nut is accessible from underneath the car (Fig. 11.19).
8   Refer to paragraph 2 and raise the rear of the vehicle.
9   Unscrew and remove the upper and lower shock absorber retaining nuts and withdraw the unit.
10   Clean and inspect the shock absorber/s. If they show any signs of leakage then they must be renewed as they are not repairable. Check the bushes for wear or deterioration and renew if necessary.
11   Refitting of the shock absorbers is a direct reversal of the removal procedure but note the following:

   (a)   When the shock absorber is relocated, do not fully tighten the retaining nuts until the car is lowered and has its weight on the wheels. By doing this the rubber bushes will be in their normal position and will not be distorted
   (b)   Tighten the retaining nuts to the specified torque wrench setting

9 Rear coil springs – removal and refitting

1   Chock the front wheels on each side and then raise the rear of the vehicle as high as possible and make secure with axle-stands placed firmly under the body member.
2   Place a jack under the differential casing and raise it for support.
3   Remove the roadwheel.
4   Disconnect the lower end of the shock absorber and then slowly lower the jack under the axle allowing the coil spring to be fully extended for removal.
5   Coil spring installation is a direct reversal of the removal procedure but ensure that the spring is correctly located before raising the jack under the differential case to compress the spring. Tighten the shock absorber retaining bolt/nut to the specified torque wrench setting.

10 Rear axle upper and lower links – removal and refitting

1   If just one link is to be removed then follow the procedure given in this Section. Should it be necessary to remove more than one then the axle unit will have to be removed and this is described in Chapter 8.
2   If the upper and lower links are to be removed note the difference in the retaining bolt length and ensure that on reassembly they are refitted correctly.
3   Chock the front wheels and raise the rear of the vehicle high enough to work under, and support with firmly based axle-stands.
4   The upper or lower link can now be disconnected at each end by removing the retaining bolts and nuts.
5   If the rubber bushes are to be renewed, support the link securely in a vice with the 'eye' as close as possible to the jaws. Drive or cut the old bushes out and clean out the aperture. Press or drift in the new bushes and to assist, lubricate with a little soap prior to inserting the bushes. Do not deform or damage the bush during assembly.

6   Refitting of the link is the reverse of removal but ensure that the retaining nuts are tightened to the specified torque wrench setting.

11 Rear wheel bearings

Rear wheel bearing inspection and renewal is covered in Chapter 8, Sections 2 and 3 accordingly.

12 Leaf spring unit – removal

1   Chock the front wheels, then raise the rear of the vehicle with the jack head on the body sidemember.
2   Place an axle-stand beneath the sidemember, remove the jack then position the jack to just take the weight of the axle.
3   Detach the shock absorber lower mounting from the spring plate.
4   Remove the U-bolt nuts then raise the jack beneath the axle to separate the axle from the spring.
5   Remove the nuts from the rear spring shackle. Carefully drive out the bolts to free the rear end of the spring.
6   Remove the pin at the front end of the spring to permit the spring to be removed.
7   Examine the spring for broken or distorted leaves; if any are found a new spring must be obtained. If the rubber bushes are damaged they can be pressed out using a suitable diameter drift and spacer between the jaws of a vise. Coat new ones with a soap and water solution to ease their installation.
8   Refitting of the spring is the reverse of the removal procedure, but ensure that the weight of the vehicle is on the roadwheel before the front pin nut, shackle nuts, U-bolts nuts and shock absorber mounting are torque tightened.

13 Steering linkage – inspection for wear

1   Wear in the steering gear and linkage is indicated when there is considerable movement in the steering wheel without corresponding movement at the roadwheels. Wear is also indicated when the vehicle tends to 'wander' off the line one is trying to steer. There are three main steering 'groups' to examine in such circumstances. These are the wheel bearings, the linkage joints and bushes, and the steering gear itself.
2   First jack-up the front of the vehicle and support it on stands under the side frame members so that both front wheels are clear of the ground.
3   Grip the top and bottom of the wheel and try to rock it. It will not take any great effort to be able to feel any play in the wheel bearing. If this play is very noticeable it would be as well to adjust it straight away as it could confuse further examinations. It is also possible that during this check play may be found in the steering king-pin which must be rectified accordingly.
4   Next grip each side of the wheel and try rocking it laterally. Steady pressure will, of course, turn the steering but an alternated back and forth pressure will reveal any loose joint. If some play is felt it would be easier to get assistance from someone so that while one person rocks the wheel from side to side, the other can look at the joints and bushes on the track rods and connections. Excluding the steering gear itself there are eight places where the play may occur. The two outer balljoints on the side rods are the most likely, followed by the two inner joints on the same rods where they join the cross rod. Any play in these means renewal of the side rod(s). Next are the two balljoints, one at each end of the cross rod. Finally check the steering gear arm balljoint, and the one on the idler arm which supports the cross rod on the side opposite the steering gear. This unit is bolted to the side frame member and any play calls for renewal of the bushes.
5   Finally, the steering gear itself is checked. First make sure that the bolts holding the steering gear to the side frame member are tight, then get another person to help examine the mechanism. One should look at, or get hold of, the gear arm at the bottom of the steering gear while the other turns the steering wheel a little way from side to side. The amount of lost motion between the steering wheel and the gear arm indicates the degree of wear somewhere in the steering mechanism. This check should be carried out with the wheel first of all in the straight ahead position and then at nearly full lock on each side.

If the play only occurs noticeably in the straight ahead position then the wear is most probably in the worm and/or nut. If it occurs at all positions of the steering, then the wear is probably in the rocker shaft bush. An oil leak at this point is another indication of such wear. In either case the steering gear will need removal for closer examination and repair.

14 Steering linkage – removal and refitting

1   Raise the front of the car and make secure with axle-stands. Chock the rear wheels and ensure that the handbrake is fully applied.
2   Using a wire brush clean off the respective balljoint nuts and stud threads to ease removal. Apply penetrating oil to any that look rusty or corroded.
3   Extract the split pins from the side rod balljoint studs and unscrew the retaining nuts.
4   Use a ball-joint separator or hammer and split wedges and detach the ball-studs from the knuckle arms.
5   If the cross rod is not to be removed, detach the side rod inner ends in a similar manner.
6   To remove the cross rod and side rods as an assembly, detach the cross rod to gear arm and idler arm balljoints as described in paragraph 4. If the idler unit is to be removed also unscrew the bolts retaining it to the body member.
7   With the steering linkage assembly removed either as a complete or sub-assembly, the respective components can be dismantled cleaned and inspected as required.
8   Check the balljoints in particular. If the ball-studs are worn or the axial play is excessive, it will be necessary to renew a side rod or the cross rod ball-and-socket assemblies.
9   Refitting of the steering linkage is basically the reverse of the removal procedure. However, the following points must be noted:

   (a) Always renew perished or broken balljoint dust covers
   (b) Adjust the side rod lengths to that shown in Fig. 11.28 between the outer and inner ball-stud centres (photo). This should give the correct toe-in adjustment when fitted, although this must be checked and any further adjustments made on completion
   (c) Check that the adjusting bar on the rod assembly is screwed into each socket by at least 0.87 in (22 mm)
   (d) All joints should be lubricated with a general purpose grease during assembly. The idler arm assembly is fitted with a grease plug which must be removed and a grease nipple fitted to lubricate. When grease is forced from the dust seal/joint socket remove the nipple and refit the plug
   (e) Tighten all nuts to the specified torque and always use new split (cotter) pins to retain

15 Steering wheel and column – removal and refitting

1   Disconnect the battery earth cable.
2   Three types of steering wheel have been fitted depending on model and market and only the method of removing the centre pad differs. On the 'T' section horn pad (photo), unscrew the pad retaining screws from underneath, and lift the pad clear.
   On the 'Sport' models fitted with a round horn pad (Fig. 11.26), pull the pad out and remove. On the two spoke steering wheel pull the pad out so that the spring touches the plate (Fig. 11.27) and then slide the pad forwards to disengage at the top and then the bottom.
3   Use a suitable socket and unscrew the steering wheel nut. Index mark the relative positions of the steering wheel and column to ensure correct reassembly position.
4   Use a steering wheel puller to withdraw the wheel from the column. If a puller is not available use a soft head mallet and lightly tap the wheel from behind whilst pulling from the shaft. Do not use heavy blows or excessive force. Do not strike the end of the steering column shaft as this could damage the collapsible shaft and/or bearing.
5   To remove the column, remove the upper and lower steering column shell covers.
6   Remove the turn signal switch assembly; refer to Chapter 10, if necessary.
7   Unscrew and remove the jacket tube to dash panel retaining nuts.
8   Unscrew and remove the steering column clamp bolts.

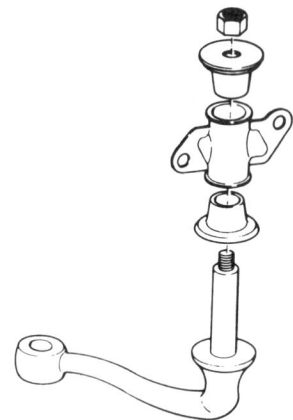

Fig. 11.25 The idler arm assembly components

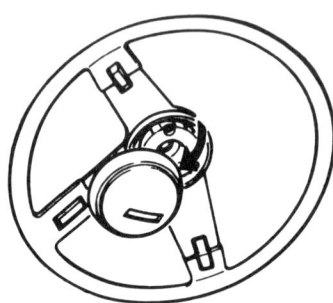

Fig. 11.26 Removing horn pad – 'Sport' type steering wheel

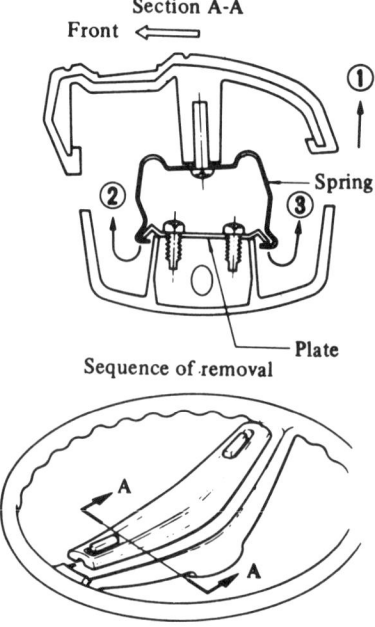

Fig. 11.27 Removing horn pad – two spoke steering wheel

14.9 Steering linkage rod

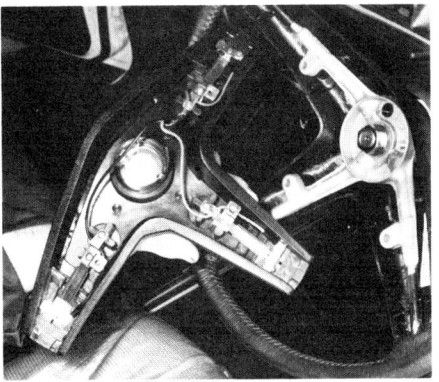
15.2 Remove steering wheel centre pad – three spoke standard type wheel

15.9 Steering column coupling to steering box connection showing coupling retaining clamp bolt (centre)

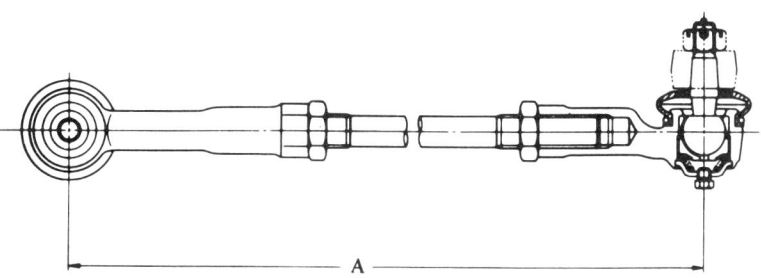
Fig. 11.28 Adjust to make dimension A = 12.40 in (315 mm)

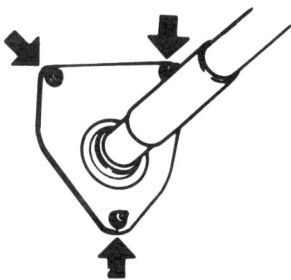
Fig. 11.29 Jacket tube nuts

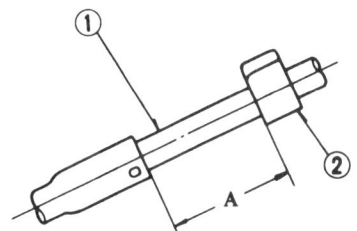
Fig. 11.30 Jacket tube to clamp dimension (A) = 7.24 in (184 mm)

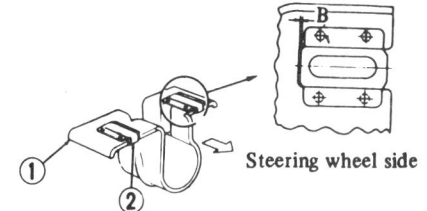
Fig. 11.31 Column clamp dimension (B) = 0 in (0 mm)

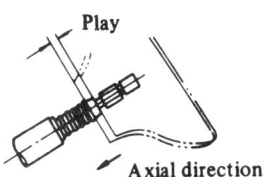
Fig. 11.32 Steering axial play

Fig. 11.33 Check sector shaft serrations for damage

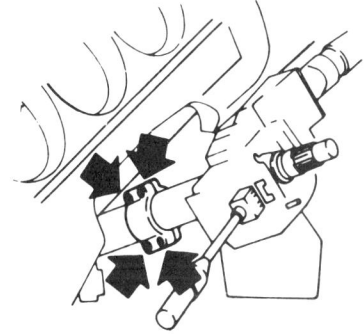
Fig. 11.34 Steering lock retaining screws

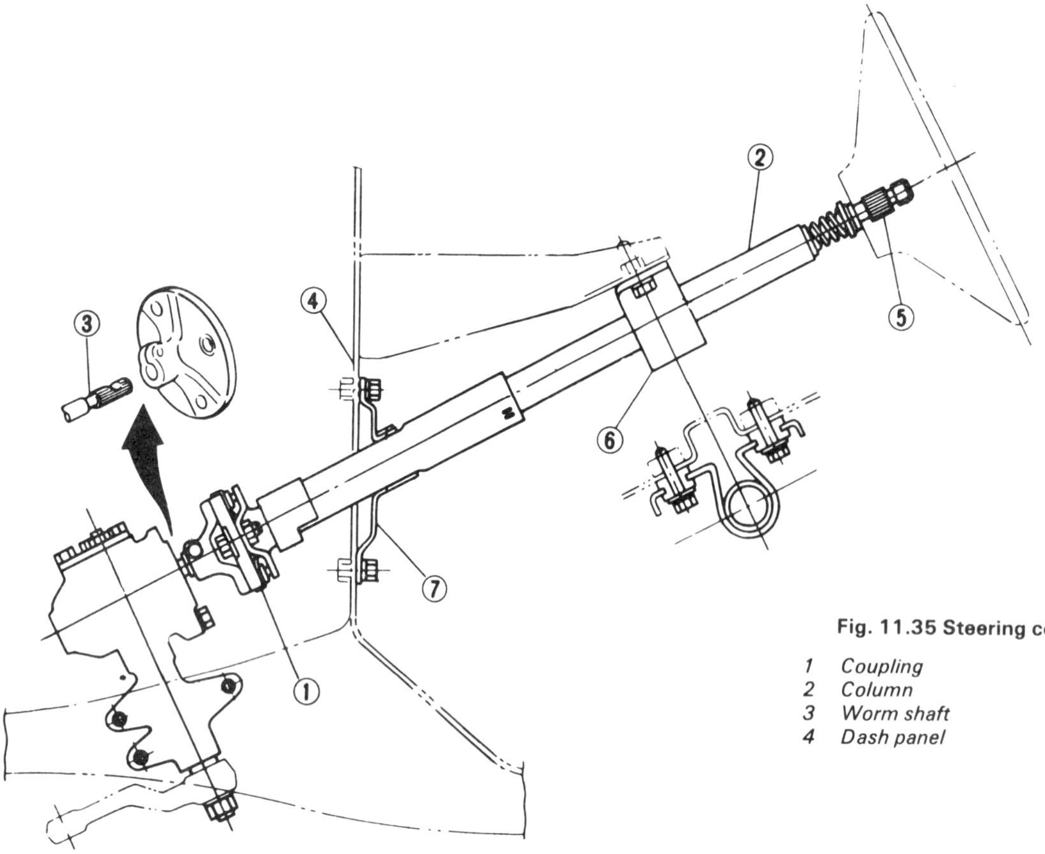

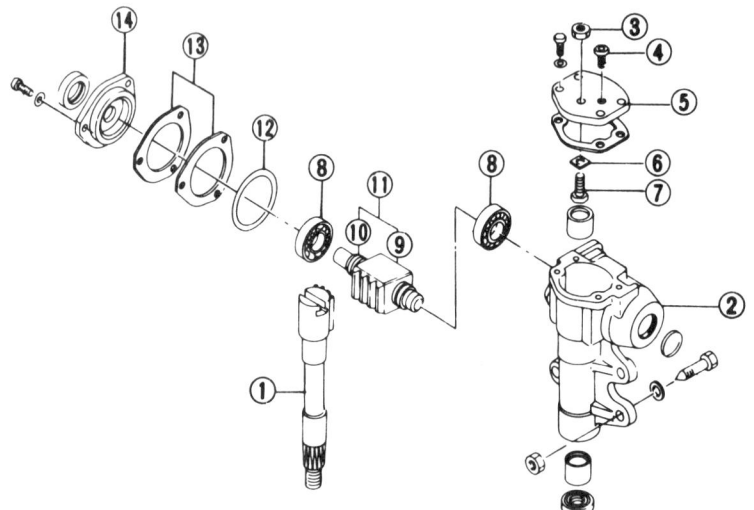

Fig. 11.35 Steering column connections

1	Coupling	5	Steering shaft
2	Column	6	Clamp
3	Worm shaft	7	Jacket tube flange
4	Dash panel		

Fig. 11.36 Steering box components

1	Sector shaft	8	Bearing
2	Gear housing	9	Ballnut
3	Locknut	10	Worm shaft
4	Filler plug	11	Steering worm unit
5	Cover	12	O-ring
6	Adjustment shim	13	Bearing shim
7	Adjustment screw	14	Cover (rear)

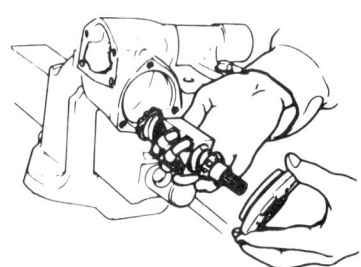

Fig. 11.37 Withdraw the steering worm

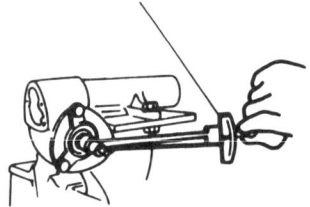

Fig. 11.38 Checking initial turning torque using torque gauge

9   Now unscrew and extract the worm shaft to rubber coupling retaining bolt, (photo) and then carefully withdraw the steering column through the interior.

10   The collapsible type steering column must not be dismantled and is non-repairable so if damaged or faulty in any way it must be renewed as a unit.

11   If you car has suffered accident damage at the front check the following:

(a) *Jacket tube to clamp dimension (Fig. 11.30)*
(b) *Column clamp dimension as in Fig. 11.31*
(c) *Steering wheel axial play as in Fig. 11.32*
(d) *Steering sector shaft serration for distortion*

12   If any of these items are suspect or damaged renew them and arrange for your Datsun dealer to carry out a thorough check for any further damage.

13   Refitting of the column and wheel assembly is a direct reversal of the removal process, but note the following:

(a) *Check that the roadwheels are set in the straight ahead position during assembly*
(b) *When the respective components are assembled do not fully tighten the bolts until the column is fully located*
(c) *The punch mark on the top of the column must face upwards*
(d) *Tighten the bolts and nuts to the specified torque in the following order:*
    (i) Jacket tube bracket nuts
    (ii) Worm shaft clamp bolt
    (iii) Column clamp bolts
    (iv) Steering wheel nut
(e) *On completion check the steering movement before testing on road. Check horn for correct operation*

16   Steering lock – removal and refitting

1   The steering lock self shearing type screws must be broken using a drill or similar suitable tool.

2   Withdraw the screws and remove the lock assembly.

3   Relocate the steering lock with its hole in alignment with the corresponding hole in the jacket tube and then insert the self shear screws. Tighten and cut their heads off.

17   Steering box – removal and refitting

1   Unscrew and extract the worm shaft to column coupling bolt.

2   Unscrew the gear arm to sector shaft retaining nut and remove with lock washer. Index mark the arm and shaft as an aid for alignment during assembly.

3   Separate the arm from the sector shaft using a hammer and wedges or balljoint separator.

4   On those vehicles with left-hand drive, detach the front exhaust tube and manifold, and rest the exhaust tube on the cross rod.

5   Remove the bolts securing the gear housing to the vehicle frame.

6   Support and remove the steering box through the engine compartment.

7   Refit in the reverse order to removal but be sure to align the gear arm and sector shaft correctly. Torque tighten the retaining bolts to that specified.

18   Steering box – dismantling, inspection and reassembly

1   Unscrew the steering box filler plug and drain the oil into a suitable container.

2   Secure the steering box in a vice and then slacken off the adjustment screw locknut.

3   Remove the cover retaining bolts and prise the cover and gasket free.

4   Remove the bolts retaining the rear cover and prise the cover free. Withdraw the bearing adjuster shims and then the steering worm unit.

Note: *Take care not to allow the ball nut to roll to either end of the worm or the ball guides will get damaged when nut is rotated. It is important that the ball nut is not detached from the worm shaft unit. If*

damaged or badly worn, renew as a unit.

5   If the sector shaft needle bearings are worn or defective the gear housing must be renewed – do not remove the bearings from the housing.

6   Wash all components in paraffin and dry them carefully with a lint free cloth.

7   Commence inspection by checking the sector shaft gear teeth surfaces for signs of excessive wear or damage, and if present renew. Check the shaft splines for wear and damage and renew if necessary. Should the splines be found to be damaged then check the gear housing for any signs of deformation.

8   Inspect the steering column shaft assembly. Examine the gear teeth surfaces for wear and damage, and if found renew. Check the ball nut for smooth operation; the ball nut should move under its own weight over the full length of the worm gear when holding the shaft assembly vertical, but take care that the ball guide is not damaged during this operation.

9   The bearings and bushings must be carefully examined for signs of excessive wear and/or damage and renewed as necessary.

10   Renew oilseal and O-ring as a matter of course.

11   Acquire a selection of the respective adjusting shims prior to commencing the reassembly of the steering box.

12   Make sure all parts are clean before commencing assembly.

13   Commence reassembly by lubricating the respective internal components of the steering box with clean gear oil.

14   Fill the cavity between the seal lips of the new oil seal with a multi-purpose grease and press it carefully into the gear housing rear cover with the lettered side facing outwards.

15   Refit the steering worm unit into the housing, together with the worm bearings.

16   Refit the rear cover complete with O-ring and bearing shims. Fit the thickest shim towards the gear housing, and tighten the cover retaining bolts to the specified torque.

17   Now check the initial turning torque of the steering gear which should be between 3·5 to 6·9 lbf in (4·0 to 8·0 kgf cm).

18   Rotate the shaft a few times to ensure that the worm bearings are fully seated. Recheck the turning torque and if necessary readjust by adding or removing shims accordingly. Shims are available in the following thicknesses.

0·030 in (0·762 mm)
0·010 in (0·254 mm)
0·005 in (0·127 mm)
0·002 in (0·050 mm)

19   Refit the adjusting screw with shim into the T-shape groove of the sector shaft head. Adjust the shaft to screw endplay, which should be 0·0004 to 0·0012 in (0·01 to 0·03 mm), by selecting shims to suit. Shims are available in the following thicknesses:

0·0620 to 0·0630 in (1·575 to 1·600 mm)
0·0610 to 0·0620 in (1·550 to 1·575 mm)
0·0600 to 0·0610 in (1·525 to 1·550 mm)
0·0591 to 0·0600 in (1·500 to 1·525 mm)
0·0581 to 0·0591 in (1·475 to 1·500 mm)
0·0571 to 0·0581 in (1·450 to 1·475 mm)

When fitting the selected shim note which face is upper (Fig. 11.39).

20   Rotate the ball nut until it is in the mid-position of its travel, then refit the sector shaft and adjusting screw together into the gear housing. Ensure that the sector shaft centre gear engages with that of the ball nut.

21   Refit the sector shaft cover using a non-setting gasket sealant on the gasket surfaces.

22   Rotate the adjusting screw anti-clockwise and fit the shaft cover and fixing bolts. Lightly tighten the cover bolts.

23   Pull the sector shaft towards the cover approximately 0·079 to 0·118 in (2 to 3 mm) by turning the adjusting screw anti-clockwise. Tighten the sector shaft cover bolts to the specified torque.

24   Press the sector shaft up to the ball nut gear, turning the adjustment screw in a clockwise direction. When the shaft gear is lightly in mesh with the ball nut gear temporarily retain the adjusting screw in this position by tightening the locknut.

25   Fit the gear arm, and ensure that the sector shaft moves smoothly throughout its range of travel.

26   Adjust the steering gear backlash at the mid-position of its travel (by means of the adjusting screw) to obtain the specified backlash of

18.29 General view of steering box (fitted) showing filler plug and adjuster screw and locknut

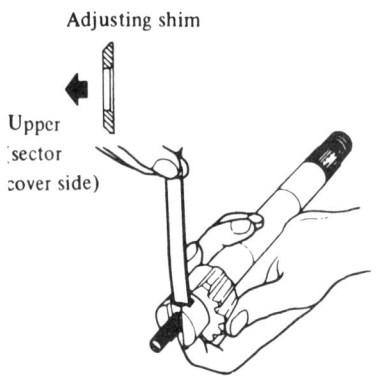

Fig. 11.39 Measuring the endplay. Note adjuster shim position

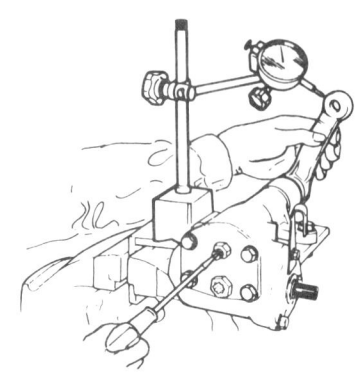

Fig. 11.40 Measuring the backlash using a dial gauge

0·004 in (0·1 mm), when measured at the outer end of the gear arm.

27 Turn the adjusting screw 1/8 to 1/6 of a turn (45 to 60°) then tighten the locknut to the specified torque.

28 The worm shaft turning torque should now be checked and should be between 4·3 to 21·7 lbf in (5 to 27 kgf cm) measured centrally. Readjust the screw to suit if necessary.

29 Fill the steering gearbox with the specified type and quantity of gear oil and refit the filler plug to complete (photo).

19 Front wheel alignment and steering geometry

1 Accurate front wheel alignment is essential for good steering and satisfactory tyre wear. Before considering the steering geometry, check that the tyres are correctly inflated, that the front wheels are not buckled, the hub bearings are not worn or incorrectly adjusted, and that the steering linkage is in good order, without slackness or wear at the joints.

2 Wheel alignment consists of five factors:

Camber is the angle at which the front wheels are set from the vertical when viewed from the front of the vehicle. Positive camber is the amount (in degrees) that the wheels are tilted outwards at the top from the vertical, and is adjusted by means of shims between the suspension upper arm spindle and the arm mounting bracket at the front and rear.

Castor is the angle between the steering axis and a vertical line when viewed from each side of the vehicle. Positive castor is when the steering axis is inclined rearward; the angle is adjusted by means of shims between the suspension upper arm spindle and the arm mounting bracket at the front or rear.

Steering axis inclination is the angle, when viewed from the front of the vehicle, between the vertical and an imaginary line drawn through the kingpin. The angle is not adjustable. *Steering angle* is the angle through which the front wheels swivel from lock-to-lock, and is adjustable by means of stopper bolts on the steering knuckles.

Toe-in is the amount by which the distance between the front inside edges of the roadwheels (measured at hub height) is less than the diametrically opposite distance measured between the rear inside edges of the front roadwheels.

3 Due to the need for special gap gauges and correct weighting of the car suspension it is not within the scope of the home mechanic to check steering geometry other than checking the toe-in and the steering angle. This should be checked however by a properly equipped garage after any part of the steering or the front end of the vehicle has been damaged in an accident. Front wheel tracking (toe-in) checks are best carried out with modern setting equipment but a reasonably accurate alternative and adjustment procedure may be carried out as follows.

Toe-in

4 Place the vehicle on level ground with the wheels in the straight ahead position.

5 Obtain or make a toe-in gauge. One may be easily made from tubing, cranked to clear the sump having an adjustable nut and setscrew at one end.

6 Using the gauge, measure the distance between the two inner wheel rims at hub height at the rear of the wheels.

7 Rotate the wheels (by pushing the car backwards or forwards) through 180° (half a turn) and again using the gauge, measure the distance of hub height between the two inner wheel rims at the front of the wheels. This measurement should be less than that previously taken at the rear of the wheel by the amount given in the Specifications, and represents the correct toe-in.

8 Where the toe-in is found to be incorrect, slacken the locknuts on each end of the cross rod, and rotate the rod until the correct toe-in is obtained. Tighten the locknuts, ensuring that the balljoints are held in the centre of their arc of travel during tightening. Ensure that dimension 'A' (Fig. 11.28) is as specified. **Note**: *Toe-in is reduced by rotating the cross rod forwards (ie; clockwise when viewed from the right side of the vehicle), and vice versa.*

Steering angles

9 The steering angles differ between the inner and outer roadwheels during a turn on full steering lock (see Specifications). These angles can only be satisfactorily measured on turn-tables at a garage but in an emergency in order to prevent a tyre rubbing against the inside of a wheel arch, the stopper bolts can be adjusted.

10 Remove the caps from the bolt heads (where applicable), and loosen the locknuts.

11 Turn one or both bolts in or out as necessary to reduce or increase one or both steering angles. Tighten the locknuts after any adjustment.

20 Roadwheels and tyres

1 Whenever the roadwheels are removed it is a good idea to clean the insides to remove accumulations of mud.

2 Check the condition of the wheel for rust, and repaint if necessary.

3 Examine the wheel stud holes. If these are tending to become elongated or the dished recesses in which the nuts seat have worn or become overcompressed, then the wheel will have to be renewed.

4 With a roadwheel removed, pick out any embedded flints from the tyre tread, and check for splits in the sidewalls or damage to the tyre carcass generally.

5 Where the depth of tread pattern is 1 mm or less, the tyre must be renewed. The tyres fitted as original equipment have tread markers at six points around the circumference. These markings give warning of 1·6 mm of tread remaining.

6 Rotation of the roadwheels to even out wear is a worthwhile idea if the wheels have been balanced off the car.

7 If the wheels have been balanced on the car then they cannot be moved round the car as the balance of the wheel, tyre and hub will be upset.

8 It is recommended that wheels are balanced whenever new tyres are fitted, and rebalanced halfway through the life of the tyre to compensate for the loss of tread rubber due to wear.

9 Finally, always keep the tyres (including the spare) inflated to the recommended pressures, and always refit the dust caps on the tyre valves. Tyre pressures are best checked first thing in the morning when the tyres are cold.

21 Fault diagnosis – suspension and steering

Symptom	Reason/s
Steering feels vague, car wanders and floats at speed	Tyre pressures uneven Shock absorbers worn Spring broken Steering gear balljoints badly worn Suspension geometry incorrect Steering mechanism free play excessive Front suspension and rear axle pick-up point out of alignment
Stiff and heavy steering	Tyre pressures too low No grease in king-pin joints Front wheel toe-in incorrect Suspension geometry incorrect Steering gear incorrectly adjusted too tightly Steering column badly misaligned
Wheel wobble and vibration	Wheel nuts loose Front wheels and tyres out of balance Steering king-pins badly worn Hub bearings badly worn Steering gear free play excessive Front springs weak or broken

Chapter 12 Bodywork and fittings

Contents

1 General description

The body on all models is of a combined body and underframe integral construction. Apart from the front wings which are secured by bolts, the various panel sections are welded together making a strong, rigid body structure.

There are basically three body styles available these being a four door Saloon, a two door Coupe or a four door Estate Car. The 510 model Saloon (USA models) is also available in a two door version.

All major components are insulated from the body to minimise the road and engine noises within the body shell.

The car year and chassis number must be quoted when ordering body parts. The chassis number is located at the top of the engine compartment on the cowl (Fig. 12.3).

2 Maintenance – bodywork and underframe

1 The condition of your car's bodywork is of considerable importance as it is upon this that the second-hand value of the car will mainly depend. It is much more difficult to repair neglected bodywork than to renew mechanical assemblies. The hidden portions of the body, such as the wheel arches, the underframe and the engine compartment are equally important, although obviously not requiring such frequent attention as the immediately visible paintwork.

2 Once a year or every 12 000 miles (20 000 km) it is a sound scheme to visit your local main agent and have the underside of the body steam-cleaned. All traces of dirt and oil will be removed and the underside can then be inspected carefully for rust, damaged hydraulic pipes, frayed electrical wiring and similar maladies.

3 At the same time, the engine compartment should be cleaned in a similar manner. If steam-cleaning facilities are not available then brush a water-soluble cleanser over the whole engine and engine compart-ment with a stiff paint brush, working it well in where there is an accumulation of oil and dirt. Do not paint the ignition system, and protect it with oily rags when the cleanser is washed off. As the cleanser is washed away it will take with it all traces of oil and dirt leaving the engine looking clean and bright.

4 The wheel arches should be given particular attention as undersealing can easily come away here and stones and dirt thrown up from the roadwheels can soon cause the paint to chip and flake, and so allow rust to set in. If rust is found, clean down to the bare metal with wet-and-dry paper, apply an anti-corrosive coating such as zinc primer or red lead, and renew the paintwork and undercoating.

5 The bodywork should be washed once a week or when dirty. Thoroughly wet the car to soften the dirt and then wash the car down with a soft sponge and plenty of clean water. If the surplus dirt is not washed off very gently, in time it will wear paint down as surely as wet-and-dry paper. It is best to use a hose if this is available. Give the car a final wash down and then dry with a soft chamois leather to prevent the formation of spots.

6 Spots of tar and grease thrown up from the road can be removed by a rag dampened with petrol.

7 Once every six months, or more frequently if wished, give the bodywork and chromium trim a thoroughly good wax polish. If a chromium cleaner is used to remove rust on any of the car's plated parts remember that the cleaner also removes part of the chromium, so use sparingly.

3 Maintenance – upholstery and carpets

1 Remove the carpets or mats and thoroughly vacuum-clean the interior of the car every three months or more frequently, if necessary.

2 Beat out the carpets and vacuum-clean them if they are very dirty. If the upholstery is soiled, apply an upholstery cleaner with a damp sponge and wipe off with a clean dry cloth.

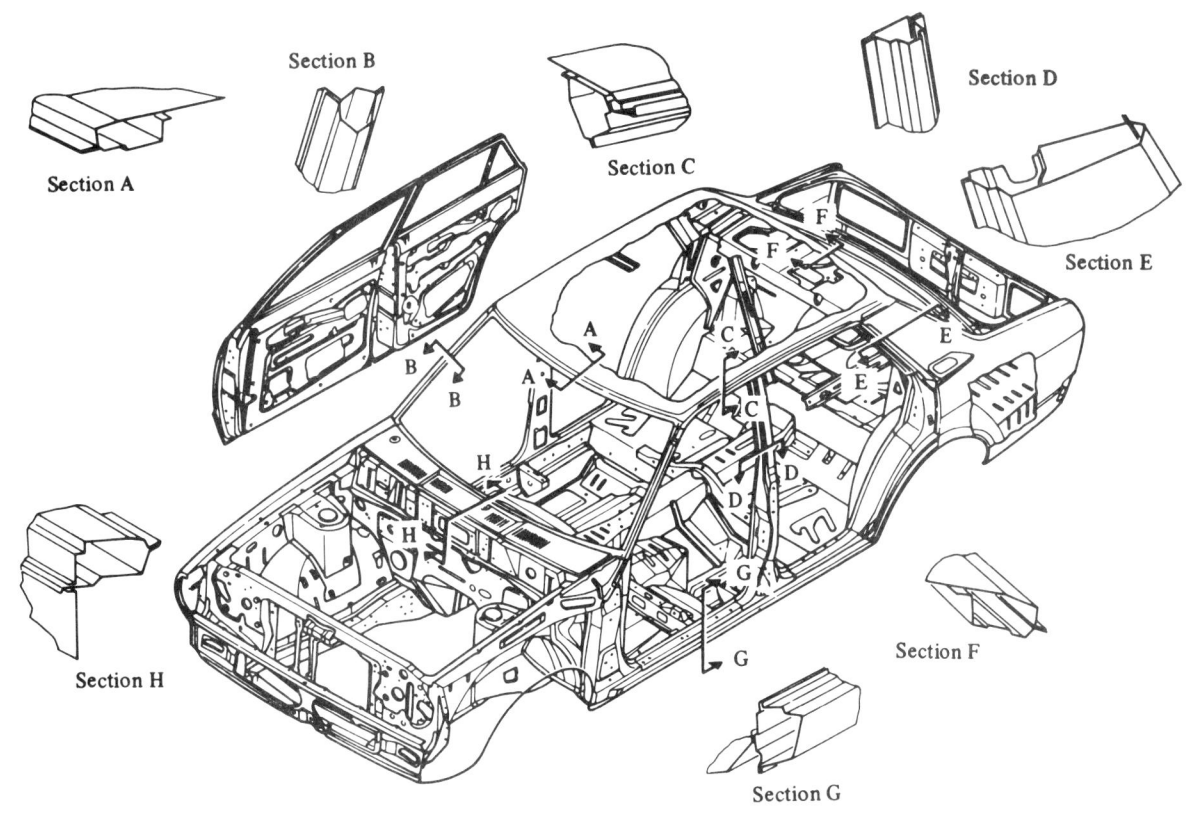

Fig. 12.1 Main body panels – Saloon

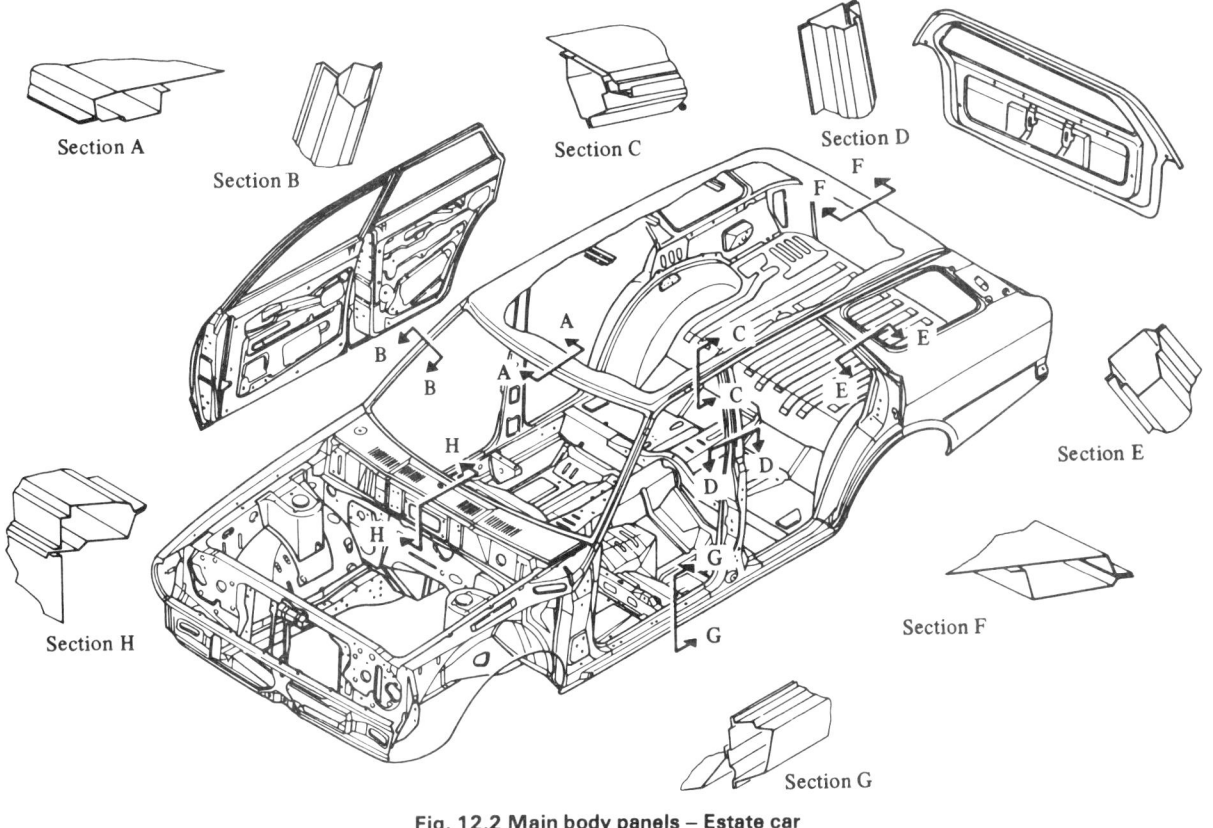

Fig. 12.2 Main body panels – Estate car

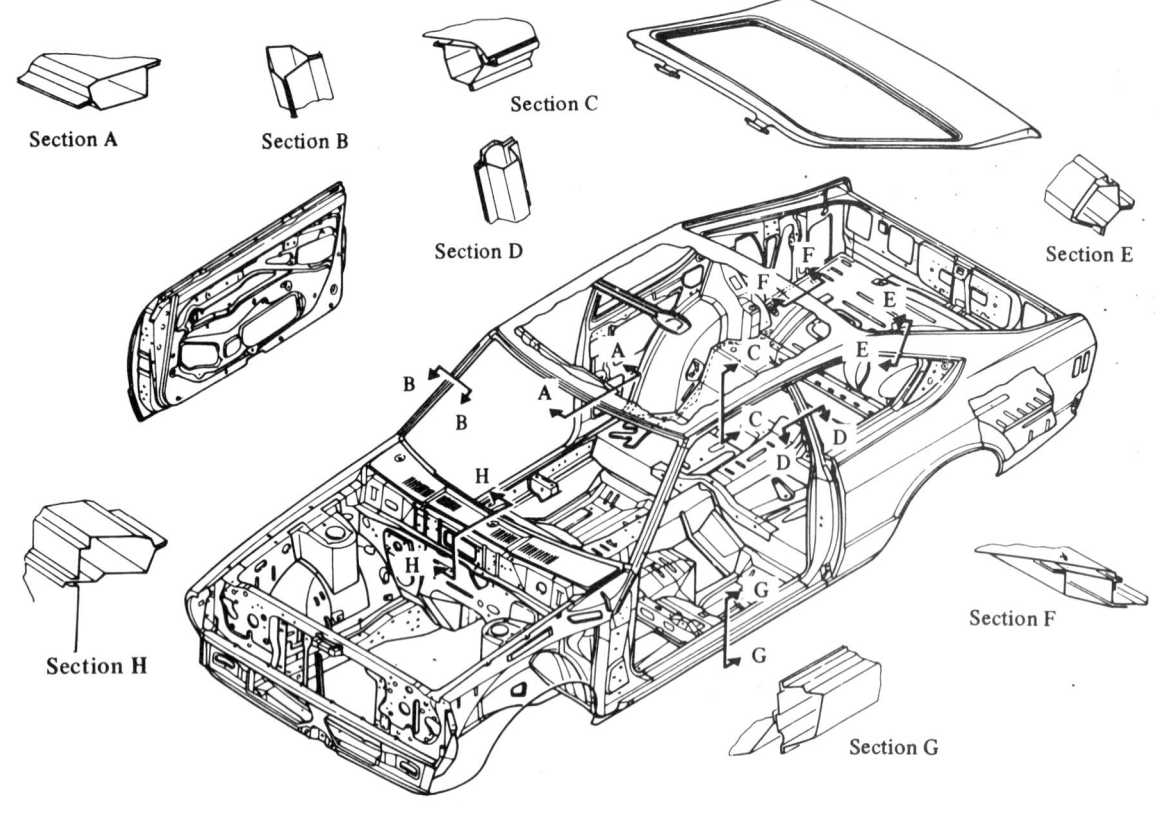

Fig. 12.3 Main body panels – Coupe

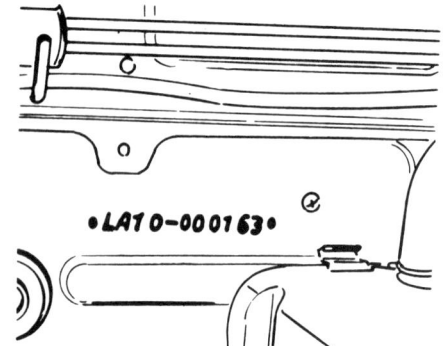

Fig. 12.4 Chassis number position

4   Minor body damage – repair

The photo sequences on pages 230 and 231 illustrate the operations detailed in the following sub-sections.

Repair of minor scratches in the car's bodywork

If the scratch is very superficial, and does not penetrate to the metal of the bodywork, repair is very simple. Lightly rub the area of the scratch with a paintwork renovator, or a very fine cutting paste, to remove loose paint from the scratch and to clear the surrounding bodywork of wax polish. Rinse the area with clean water.

Apply touch-up paint to the scratch using a thin paint brush; continue to apply thin layers of paint until the surface of the paint in the scratch is level with the surrounding paintwork. Allow the new paint at least two weeks to harden: then blend it into the surrounding paintwork by rubbing the paintwork, in the scratch area, with a paintwork renovator or a very fine cutting paste. Finally, apply wax polish.

An alternative to painting over the scratch is to use a paint transfer. Use the same preparation for the affected area, then simply pick a patch of a suitable size to cover the scratch completely. Hold the patch against the scratch and burnish its backing paper; the paper will adhere to the paintwork, freeing itself from the backing paper at the same time. Polish the affected area to blend the patch into the surrounding paintwork.

Where the scratch has penetrated right through to the metal of the bodywork, causing the metal to rust, a different repair technique is required. Remove any loose rust from the bottom of the scratch with a penknife, then apply rust inhibiting paint to prevent the formation of rust in the future. Using a rubber or nylon applicator fill the scratch with bodystopper paste. If required, this paste can be mixed with cellulose thinners to provide a very thin paste which is ideal for filling narrow scratches. Before the stopper-paste in the scratch hardens, wrap a piece of smooth cotton rag around the top of a finger. Dip the finger in cellulose thinners and then quickly sweep it across the surface of the stopper-paste in the scratch; this will ensure that the surface of the stopper-paste is slightly hollowed. The scratch can now be painted over as described earlier in this Section.

Repair of dents in the car's bodywork

When deep denting of the car's bodywork has taken place, the first task is to pull the dent out, until the affected bodywork almost attains its original shape. There is little point in trying to restore the original shape completely, as the metal in the damaged area will have stretched on impact and cannot be reshaped fully to its original contour. It is better to bring the level of the dent up to a point which is about $\frac{1}{8}$ in (3 mm) below the level of the surrounding bodywork. In cases where the dent is very shallow anyway, it is not worth trying to pull it out at all.

If the underside of the dent is accessible, it can be hammered out gently from behind, using a mallet with a wooden or plastic head. Whilst doing this, hold a suitable block of wood firmly against the impact from the hammer blows and thus prevent a large area of the bodywork from being 'belled-out'.

Should the dent be in a section of the bodywork which has double skin or some other factor making it inaccessible from behind, a different technique is called for. Drill several small holes through the metal inside the area – particularly in the deeper section. Then screw long self-tapping screws into the holes just sufficiently for them to gain a good purchase in the metal. Now the dent can be pulled out by pulling on the protruding heads of the screws with a pair of pliers.

The next stage of the repair is the removal of the paint from the damaged area, and from an inch or so of the surrounding 'sound' bodywork. This is accomplished most easily by using a wire brush or abrasive pad on a power drill, although it can be done just as effectively by hand using sheets of abrasive paper. To complete the preparation for filling, score the surface of the bare metal with a screwdriver or the tang of a file, or alternatively, drill small holes in the affected area. This will provide a really good 'key' for the filler paste.

To complete the repair see the Section on filling and respraying.

Repair of rust holes or gashes in the car's bodywork

Remove all paint from the affected area and from an inch or so of the surrounding 'sound' bodywork, using an abrasive pad or a wire brush on a power drill. If these are not available a few sheets of abrasive paper will do the job just as effectively. With the paint removed you will be able to gauge the severity of the corrosion and therefore decide whether to renew the whole panel (if this is possible) or to repair the affected area. New body panels are not as expensive as most people think and it is often quicker and more satisfactory to fit a new panel than to attempt to repair large areas of corrosion.

Remove all fittings from the affected area except those which will act as a guide to the original shape of the damaged bodywork (eg headlamp shells etc). Then, using tin snips or a hacksaw blade, remove all loose metal and any other metal badly affected by corrosion. Hammer the edges of the hole inwards in order to create a slight depression for the filler paste.

Wire brush the affected area to remove the powdery rust from the surface of the remaining metal. Paint the affected area with rust inhibiting paint; if the back of the rusted area is accessible treat this also.

Before filling can take place it will be necessary to block the hole in some way. This can be achieved by the use of one of the following materials: Zinc gauze, Aluminium tape or Polyurethane foam.

Zinc gauze is probably the best material to use for a large hole. Cut a piece to the approximate size and shape of the hole to be filled, then position it in the hole so that its edges are below the level of the surrounding bodywork. It can be retained in position by several blobs of filler paste around its periphery.

Aluminium tape should be used for small or very narrow holes. Pull a piece off the roll and trim it to the approximate size and shape required, then pull off the backing paper (if used) and stick the tape over the hole; it can be overlapped if the thickness of one piece is insufficient. Burnish down the edges of the tape with the handle of a screwdriver or similar, to ensure that the tape is securely attached to the metal underneath.

Polyurethane foam is best used where the hole is situated in a section of bodywork of complex shape, backed by a small box section (eg where the sill panel meets the rear wheel arch on most cars). The usual mixing procedure for this foam is as follows: put equal amounts of fluid from each of the two cans provided in the kit, into one container. Stir until the mixture begins to thicken, then quickly pour this mixture into the hole, and hold a piece of cardboard over the larger apertures. Almost immediately the polyurethane will begin to expand, gushing out of any small holes left unblocked. When the foam hardens it can be cut back to just below the level of the surrounding bodywork with a hacksaw blade.

Bodywork repairs – filling and respraying

Before using this Section, see the Sections on dent, deep scratch, rust holes and gash repairs.

Many types of bodyfiller are available, but generally speaking those proprietary kits which contain a tin of filler paste and a tube of resin hardener are best for this type of repair. A wide, flexible plastic or nylon applicator will be found invaluable for imparting a smooth and well contoured finish to the surface of the filler.

Mix up a little filler on a clean piece of card or board – use the hardener sparingly (follow the maker's instructions on the pack) otherwise the filler will set very rapidly.

Using the applicator apply the filler paste to the prepared area: draw the applicator across the surface of the filler to achieve the correct contour and to level the filler surface. As soon as a contour that approximates the correct one is achieved, stop working the paste – if you carry on too long the paste will become sticky and begin to 'pick up' on the applicator. Continue to add thin layers of filler paste at twenty-minute intervals until the level of the filler is just proud of the surrounding bodywork.

Once the filler has hardened, excess can be removed using a Surform plane or Dreadnought file. From then on, progressively finer grades of abrasive paper should be used, starting with a 40 grade production paper and finishing with 400 grade wet-and-dry paper. Always wrap the abrasive paper around a flat rubber, cork, or wooden block – otherwise the surface of the filler will not be completely flat. During the smoothing of the filler surface the wet-and-dry paper should be periodically rinsed in water. This will ensure that a very smooth finish is imparted to the filler at the final stage.

At this stage the 'dent' should be surrounded by a ring of bare metal, which in turn should be encircled by the finely 'feathered' edge of the good paintwork. Rinse the repair area with clean water, until all of the dust produced by the rubbing-down operation has gone.

Spray the whole repair area with a light coat of primer – this will show up any imperfections in the surface of the filler. Repair these imperfections with fresh filler paste or bodystopper, and once more smooth the surface with abrasive paper. If bodystopper is used, it can be mixed with cellulose thinners to form a really thin paste which is ideal for filling small holes. Repeat this spray and repair procedure until you are satisfied that the surface of the filler, and the feathered edge of the paintwork are perfect. Clean the repair area with clean water and allow to dry fully.

The repair area is now ready for final spraying. Paint spraying must be carried out in a warm, dry, windless and dust free atmosphere. This condition can be created artificially if you have access to a large indoor working area, but if you are forced to work in the open, you will have to pick your day very carefully. If you are working indoors, dousing the floor in the work area with water will 'lay' the dust which would otherwise be in the atmosphere. If the repair area is confined to one body panel, mask off the surrounding panels; this will help to minimise the effects of a slight mis-match in paint colours. Bodywork fittings (eg chrome strips, door handles etc) will also need to be removed or masked off. Use genuine masking tape and several thicknesses of newspaper for the masking operations.

Before commencing to spray, agitate the aerosol can thoroughly, then spray a test area (an old tin, or similar) until the technique is mastered. Cover the repair area with a thick coat of primer; the thickness should be built up using several thin layers of paint rather than one thick one. Using 400 grade wet-and-dry paper, rub down the surface of the primer until it is really smooth. While doing this, the work area should be thoroughly doused with water, and the wet-and-dry paper periodically rinsed in water. Allow to dry before spraying on more paint.

Spray on the top coat, again building up the thickness by using several thin layers of paint. Start spraying in the centre of the repair area and then using a circular motion, work outwards until the whole repair area and about 2 inches of the surrounding original paintwork is covered. Remove all masking material 10 to 15 minutes after spraying on the final coat of paint.

Allow the new paint at least two weeks to harden, then, using a paintwork renovator or a very fine cutting paste, blend the edges of the paint into the existing paintwork. Finally, apply wax polish.

5 Major body damage – repair

1 Because the car is built without a separate chassis frame and the body is therefore integral with the underframe, major damage must be repaired by competent mechanics with the necessary welding and hydraulic straightening equipment.

2 If the damage has been serious it is vital that the body is checked for correct alignment as otherwise the handling of the car will suffer

and many other faults such as excessive tyre wear and wear in the transmission and steering may occur.

3   There is a special body jig which most large body repair shops have, and to ensure that all is correct it is important that the jig be used for all major repair work.

6   Front bumper – removal and refitting

European models
1   For safety reasons disconnect the battery positive terminal.
2   Disconnect the front direction indicator light cable connectors.
3   Undo and remove the bolts and washers securing the front bumper side bracket to the lower side of the front wing.
4   Undo and remove the bolts that secure the front bumper stay to body side member and draw the front bumper forward from the body. Take care not to scratch the paintwork.
5   Refitting the front bumper is the reverse sequence to removal, but align the bumper correctly prior to tightening the securing bolts.

USA models
6   The bumper assembly on these models incorporate shock absorbers and side bumper units to assist in the event of a sudden impact – see Fig. 12.6.
7   The removal procedure follows that of the European model bumper given previously. Under no circumstances should the shock absorber units be dismantled if they are removed, but if faulty renew them.
8   Refitting is a reversal of the removal procedure but check the bumpers for correct alignment on completion. The ground clearance from the lower edge of the bumpers should be 14.17 to 16.34 in (360 to 415 mm).

7   Rear bumper – removal and refitting

European models
1   If your model incorporates the number plate light into the rear bumper, detach the battery earth cable and then disconnect the rear number plate light cable connections.
2   Unscrew and remove the bolts securing the bumper stay to the body side member.
3   Unscrew and remove the bolts securing the rear bumper side bracket to the rear lower wing section.
4   Carefully withdraw the bumper from the car taking care not to scratch the paintwork.
5   Refit the bumper in the reverse sequence but ensure that the bumper is correctly aligned before fully tightening the securing bolts.

USA models
6   The bumper assemblies on these models incorporate shock absorbers and side bumpers to assist in the event of a sudden impact – see Fig. 12.9.
7   The removal procedure is similar to that of the European models given previously but note the following. Under no circumstances should the shock absorber units be dismantled if they are removed. If they are defective, renew them.
8   Refitting is the reversal of the removal procedure but check the bumpers for correct alignment on completion. The ground clearance from the lower edge of the bumpers should be 14.80 to 17.00 in (376 to 431 mm) for Saloon and Coupe models and 14.76 to 16.73 in (375 to 425 mm) for Estate Car models.

8   Windscreen – removal and refiting

If you are unfortunate enough to have a windscreen shatter fitting a new windscreen is one of the few jobs that the average owner is advised to leave to a body repair specialist. The reason for this is that the glass is not located in the body in the normal manner but uses a special sealer and clips. Body specialists are fimiliar with the special procedures involved and the equipment necessary so in this case leave it to the specialist.

9   Radiator grille – removal and refitting

1   Open and secure the bonnet in the raised position with the stay.
2   Unscrew and remove the radiator grille screws at the top (to front body crossmember).
3   To remove the clips at the bottom, use a screwdriver and insert the blade between the clips and grille and twist. Lift the grille clear.
4   Refitting is the reverse of the removal procedure.

10   Front apron – removal and refitting

1   Refer to Sections 6 and 9 and remove the front bumper and the radiator grille.
2   Unscrew and remove the front apron attachment screws from the positions arrowed in Fig. 12.10 and lift the panel clear.
3   Refit in the reverse order.

11   Front wing – removal and refitting

1   Disconnect the battery earth terminal.

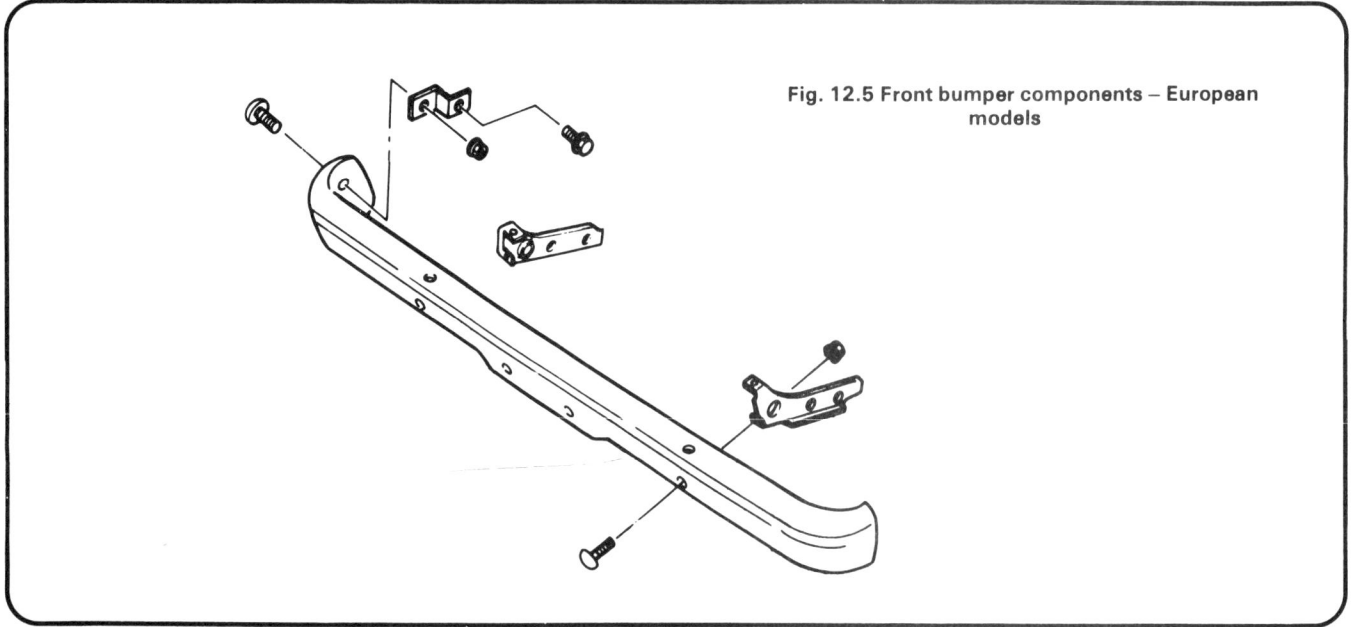

Fig. 12.5 Front bumper components – European models

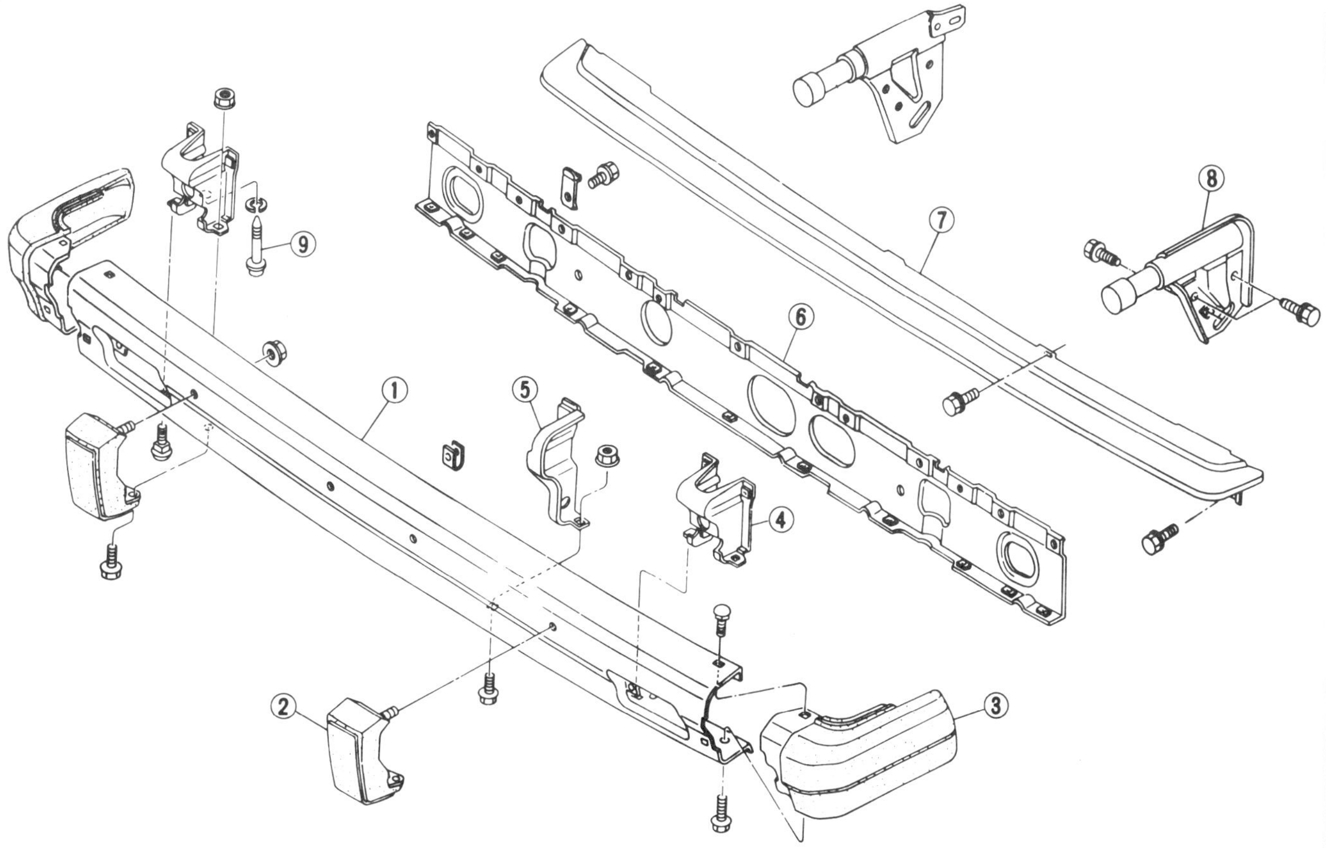

Fig. 12.6 Front bumper components – 510 models (USA)

1	Centre bumper – front	4	Mounting bracket	6	Reinforcement
2	Overrider	5	Baffle plate	7	Sight shield
3	Side bumper			8	Shock absorber
				9	Retaining bolts

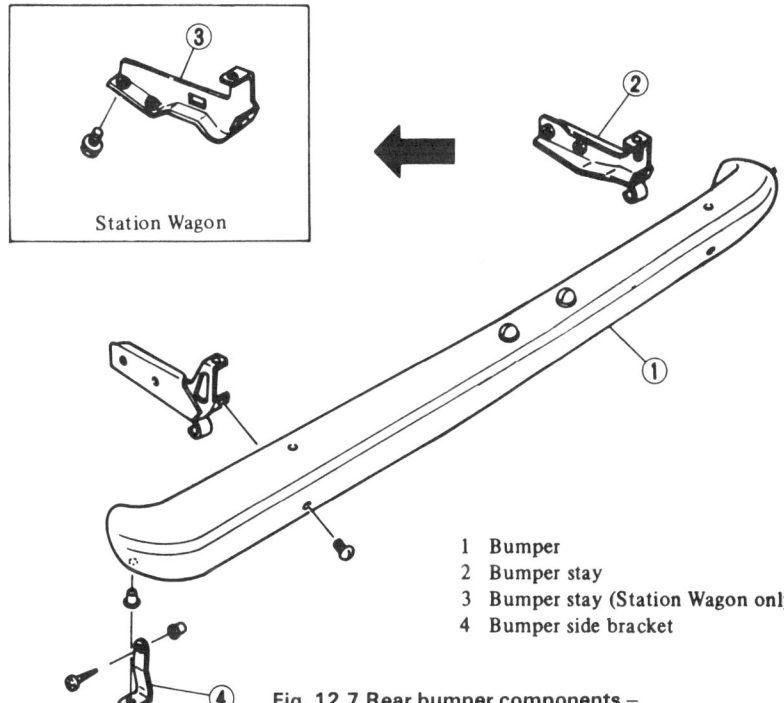

Station Wagon

1 Bumper
2 Bumper stay
3 Bumper stay (Station Wagon only)
4 Bumper side bracket

Fig. 12.7 Rear bumper components – European models

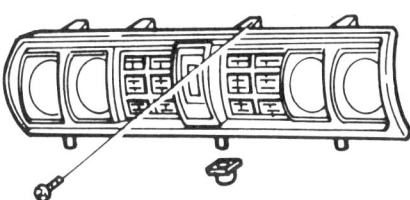

Fig. 12.8 The radiator grille

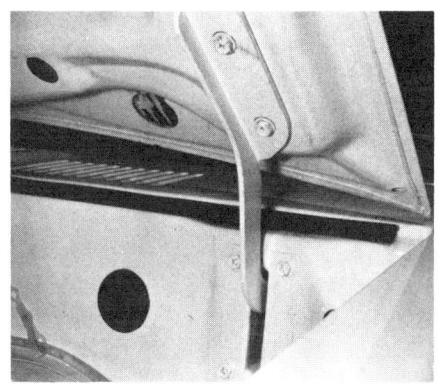

12.1 Mark the outline of the hinge location before removing bolts

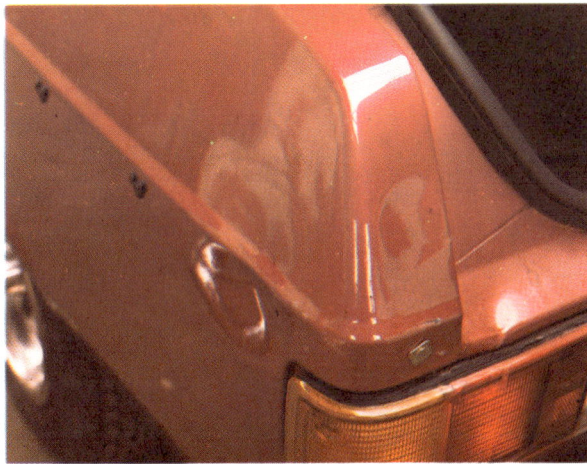

This sequence of photographs deals with the repair of the dent and scratch (above rear lamp) shown in this photo. The procedure will be similar for the repair of a hole. It should be noted that the procedures given here are simplified - more explicit instructions will be found in the text

In the case of a dent the first job - after removing surrounding trim - is to hammer out the dent where access is possible. This will minimise filling. Here, the large dent having been hammered out, the damaged area is being made slightly concave

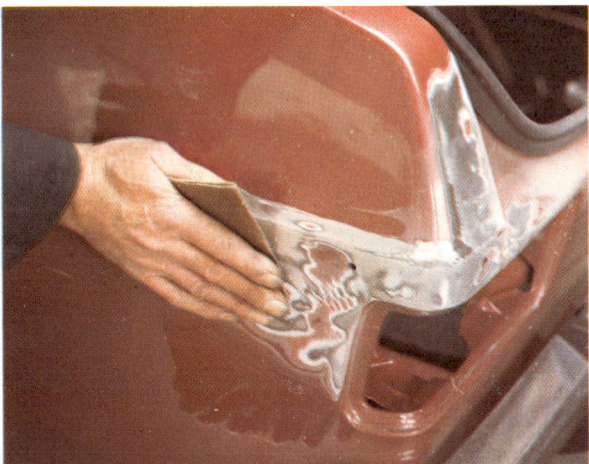

Now all paint must be removed from the damaged area, by rubbing with coarse abrasive paper. Alternatively, a wire brush or abrasive pad can be used in a power drill. Where the repair area meets good paintwork, the edge pf the paintwork should be 'feathered', using a finer grade of abrasive paper

In the case of a hole caused by rusting, all damaged sheet-metal should be cut away before proceeding to this stage. Here, the damaged area is being treated with rust remover and inhibitor before being filled

Mix the body filler according to its manufacturer's instructions. In the case of corrosion damage, it will be necessary to block off any large holes before filling - this can be done with zinc gauze or aluminium tape. Make sure the area is absolutely clean before ...

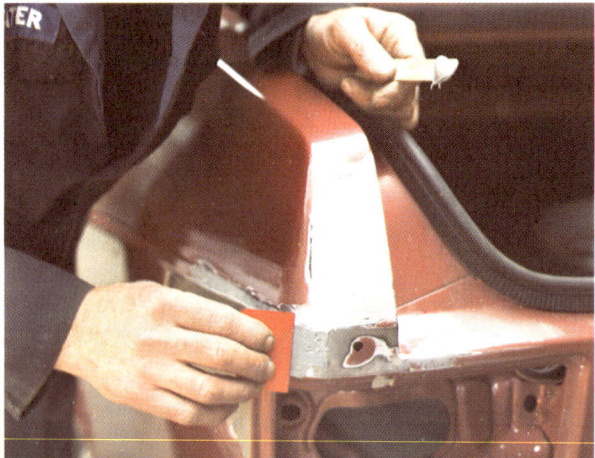

... applying the filler. Filler should be applied with a flexible applicator, as shown, for best results: the wooden spatula being used for confined areas. Apply thin layers of filler at 20-minute intervals, until the surface of the filler is slightly proud of the surrounding bodywork

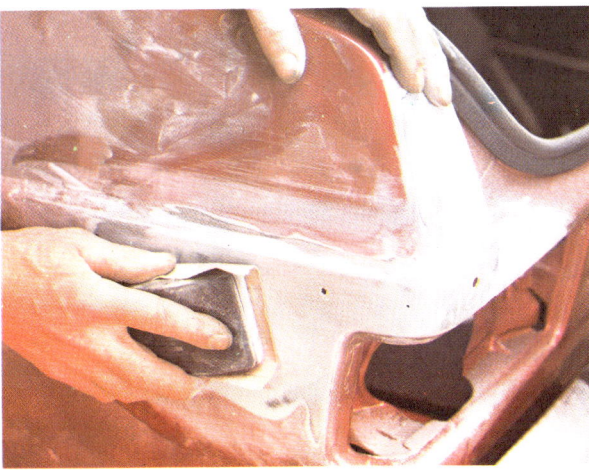

Initial shaping can be done with a Surform plane or Dreadnought file. Then, using progressively finer grades of wet-and-dry paper, wrapped around a sanding block, and copious amounts of clean water, rub-down the filler until really smooth and flat. Again, feather the edges of adjoining paintwork

The whole repair area can now be sprayed or brush-painted with primer. If spraying, ensure adjoining areas are protected from over-spray. Note that at least one-inch of the surrounding sound paintwork should be coated with primer. Primer has a 'thick' consistency, so will fill small imperfections

Again, using plenty of water, rub down the primer with a fine grade of wet-and-dry paper (400 grade is probably best) until it is really smooth and well blended into the surrounding paint-work. Any remaining imperfections can now be filled by carefully applied knifing stopper paste

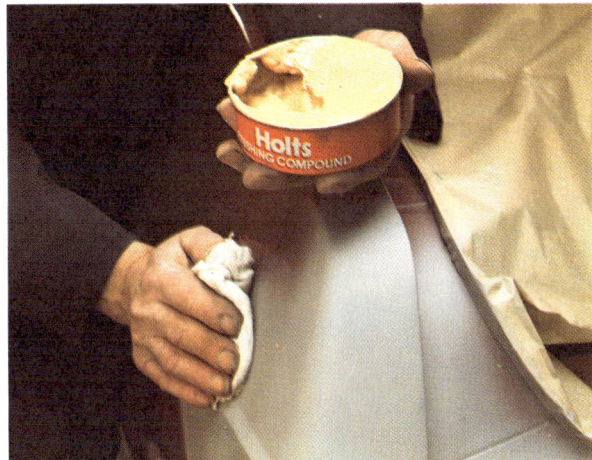

When the stopper has hardened, rub-down the repair area again before applying the final coat of primer. Before rubbing-down this last coat of primer, ensure the repair area is blemish-free - use more stopper if necessary. To ensure that the surface of the primer is really smooth use some finishing compound

The top coat can now be applied. When working out of doors, pick a dry, warm and wind-free day. Ensure surrounding areas are protected from over-spray. Agitate the aerosol thoroughly, then spray the centre of the repair area, working outwards with a circular motion. Apply the paint as several thin coats.

After a period of about two-weeks, which the paint needs to harden fully, the surface of the repaired area can be 'cut' with a mild cutting compound prior to wax polishing. When carrying out bodywork repairs, remember that the quality of the finished job is proportional to the time and effort expended

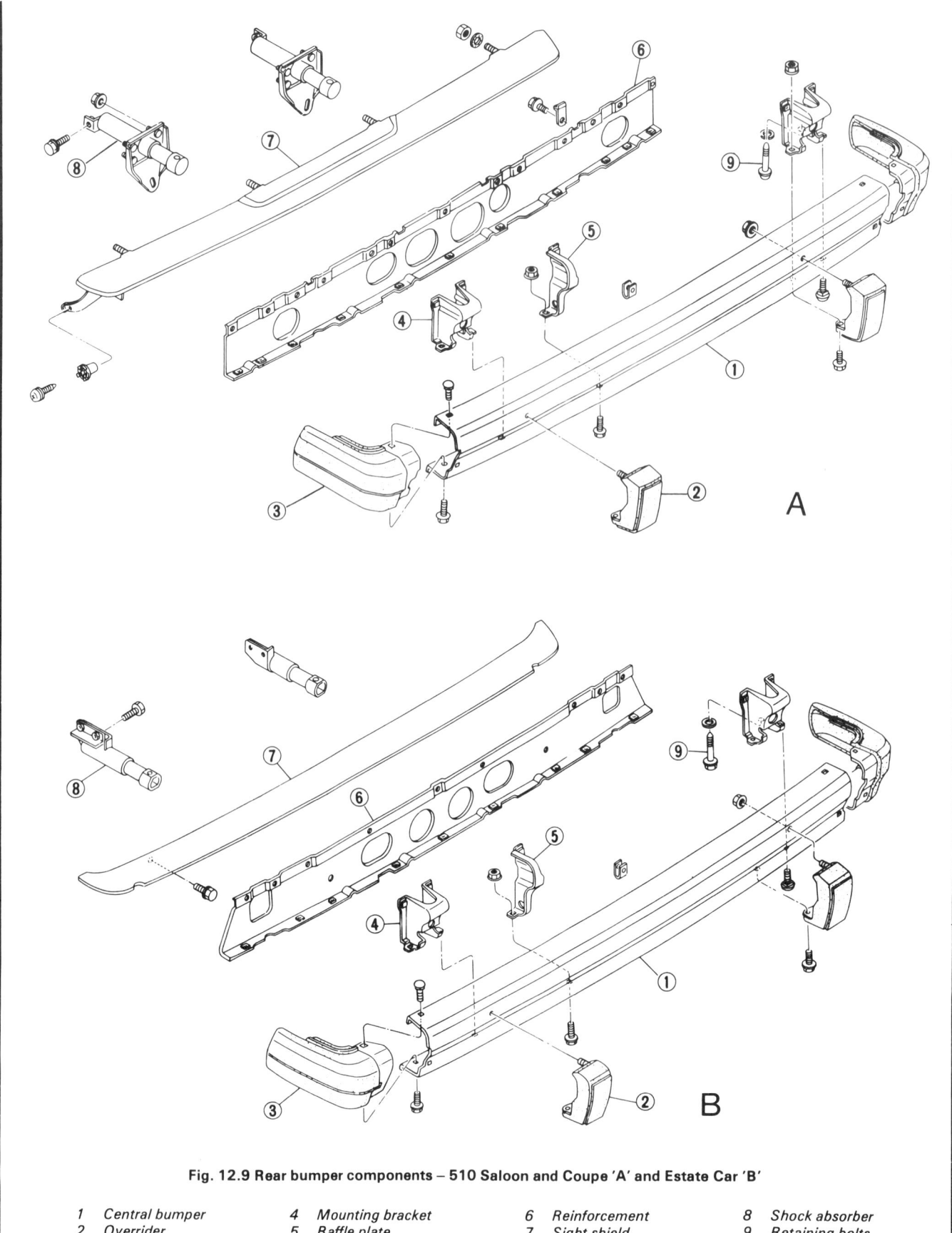

Fig. 12.9 Rear bumper components – 510 Saloon and Coupe 'A' and Estate Car 'B'

1 Central bumper	4 Mounting bracket	6 Reinforcement	8 Shock absorber
2 Overrider	5 Baffle plate	7 Sight shield	9 Retaining bolts
3 Side bumper			

2   Refer to Sections 6 and 9 and remove the front bumper and radiator grille.
3   Disconnect and remove the side turn indicator light from the wing panel (see Chapter 10).
4   Unscrew the wing to inner panel retaining bolts, also the front apron, inner sill and moulding and front pillar bolts to wing panel – see Fig. 12.11.
5   Prior to removing the wing, check that there are no other fittings still attached, then lift the panel away.
6   Refit the wing panel in the reverse sequence but apply some suitable body sealant between the wing and inner panel.

12 Bonnet – removal and refitting

1   Open the bonnet and, to act as a datum for refitting, mark the position of the hinges on the bonnet using a soft pencil.
2   With the assistance of a second person hold the bonnet in the open position, undo and remove the bolts, spring and plain washers that hold each hinge to the bonnet. Lift away the bonnet taking care not to scratch the top of the wing.
3   Whilst the bonnet is being lifted away take care when detaching the bonnet support rod.
4   Refitting the bonnet is the reverse sequence to removal. Any adjustments necessary may be made at the hinge, catch or rubber bump pads on the front panel. Lubricate the hinge pivots and lock with a little engine oil.

13 Bonnet lock and control cable – removal and refitting

1   Raise and secure the bonnet.
2   Compress the catch and detach the cable nipple from its location slot. Prise the outer cable clip free at the catch.
3   If the cable is to be removed, unclip the cable from the location clip and from inside the vehicle, detach the cable bracket by removing the retaining bolts. Withdraw the cable through the interior.
4   To remove the bonnet catch simply unscrew and remove the securing bolts.
5   To refit, reverse the removal instructions but note the following:

   (a) Lubricate the safety catch lever, spring and pivot on assembly
   (b) Do not refit any defective parts – always renew them
   (c) Check the operation of the catch before closing the bonnet
   (d) Check the operation of the catch when the bonnet is closed and adjust if necessary (Fig. 12.16).

14 Boot lid (Saloons) – removal and refitting

1   Open the boot lid and, using a soft pencil, mark the outline of the hinges on the lid to act as a datum for refitting.
2   With the assistance of a second person hold the boot lid in the open position and then remove the two bolts, spring and plain washers to each hinge.

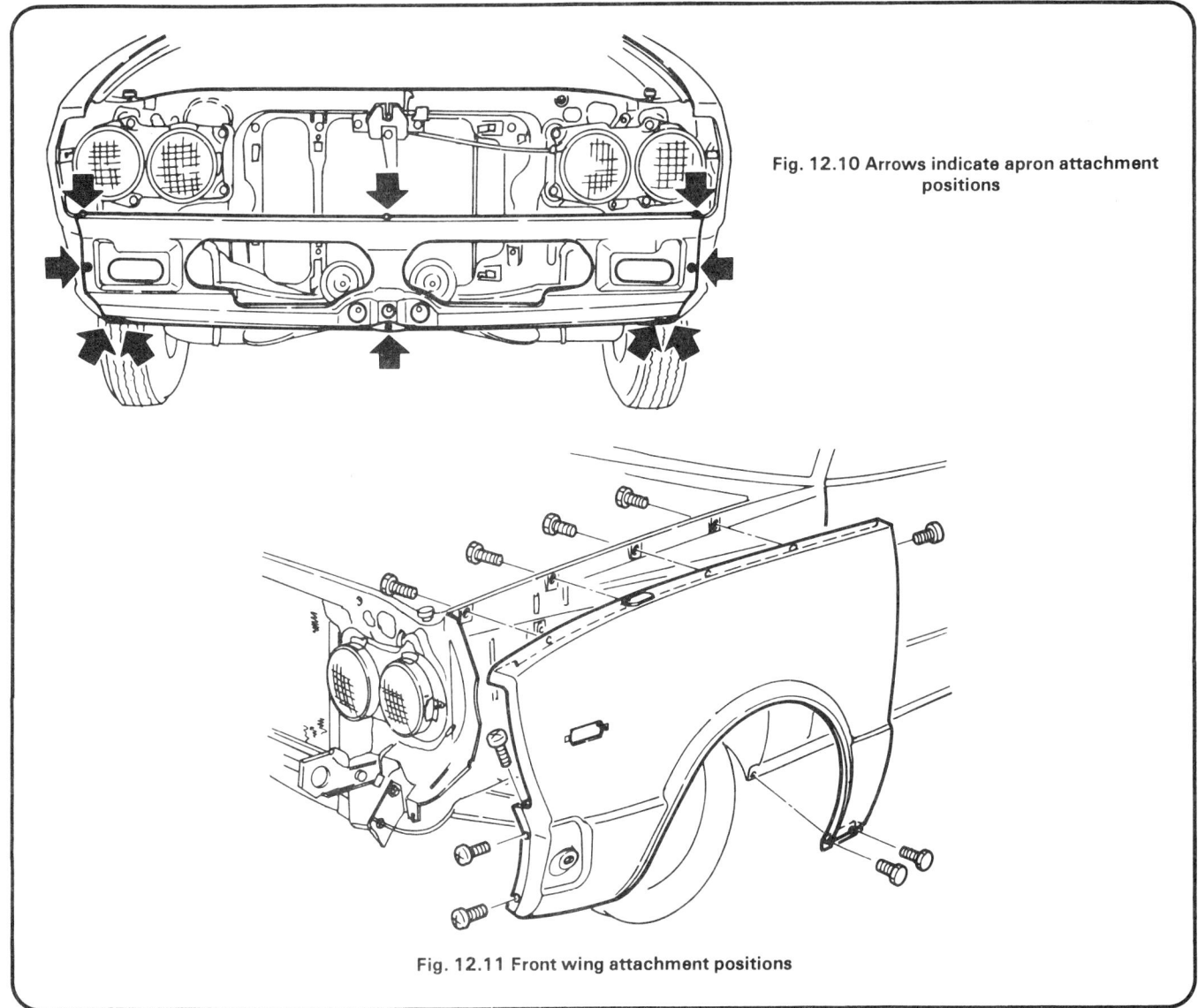

Fig. 12.10 Arrows indicate apron attachment positions

Fig. 12.11 Front wing attachment positions

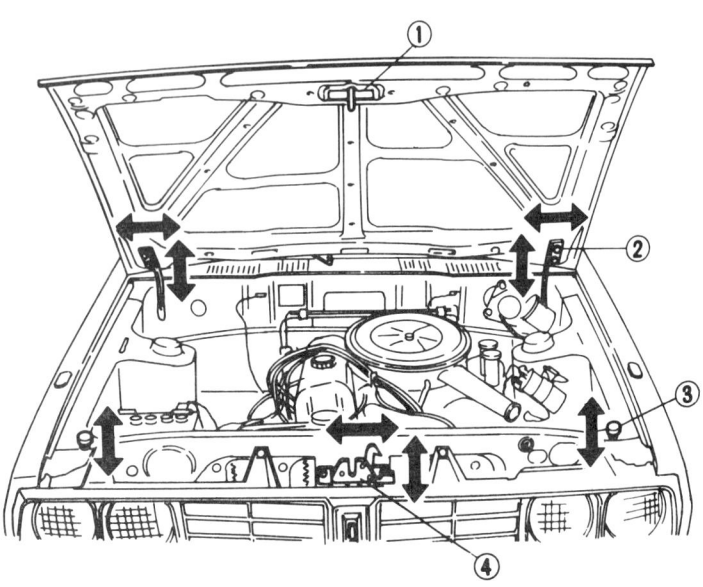

13.1 The bonnet catch with cable still attached

Fig. 12.12 Bonnet adjustment and location positions

1	Striker	3	Bumper stop
2	Hinge	4	Lock

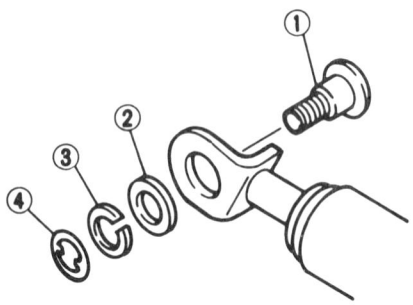

Fig. 12.13 Stay bolt washer locations

1	Bolt	3	Spring washer
2	Rubber spacer	4	Stopper ring

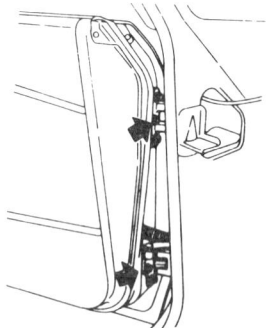

Fig. 12.14 The front door hinge bolt positions

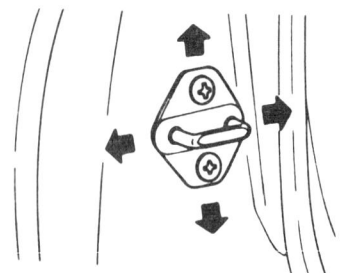

Fig. 12.15 Door lock striker is fully adjustable to suit

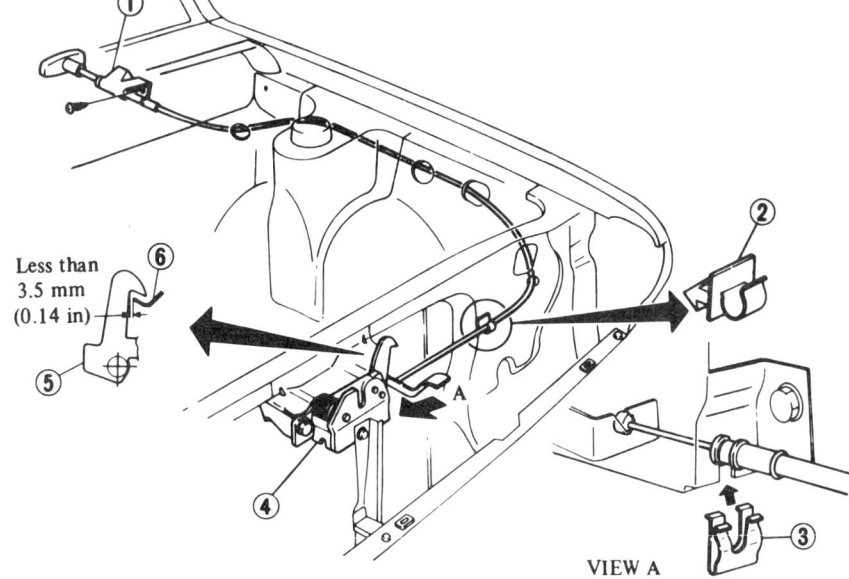

Less than 3.5 mm (0.14 in)

VIEW A

Fig. 12.16 The bonnet catch and release cable assembly

1	Bracket	4	Lock
2	Clamp	5	Safety catch lever
3	Clip	6	Bonnet (hood)

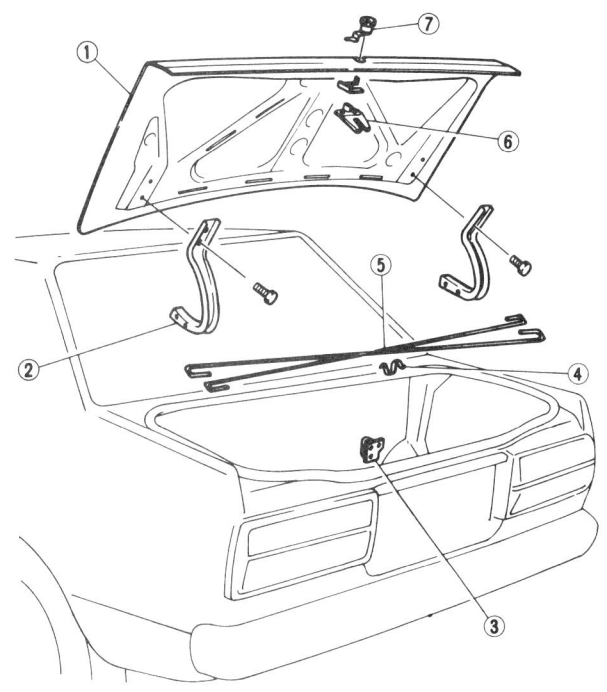

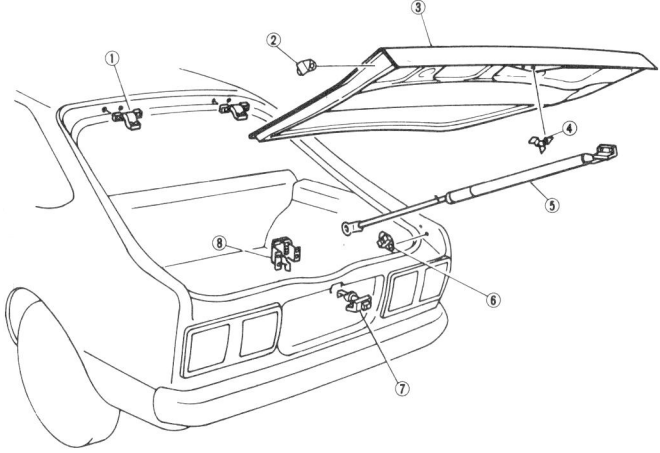

Fig. 12.17 Boot lid and components

1	Lid	5	Torsion bar
2	Hinge	6	Lock
3	Striker	7	Lock cylinder
4	Torsion bar clip		

Fig. 12.18 The Coupe rear door assembly

1	Hinge	5	Stay
2	Side stop striker	6	Side stopper
3	Rear door	7	Lock cylinder
4	Striker	8	Back door lock

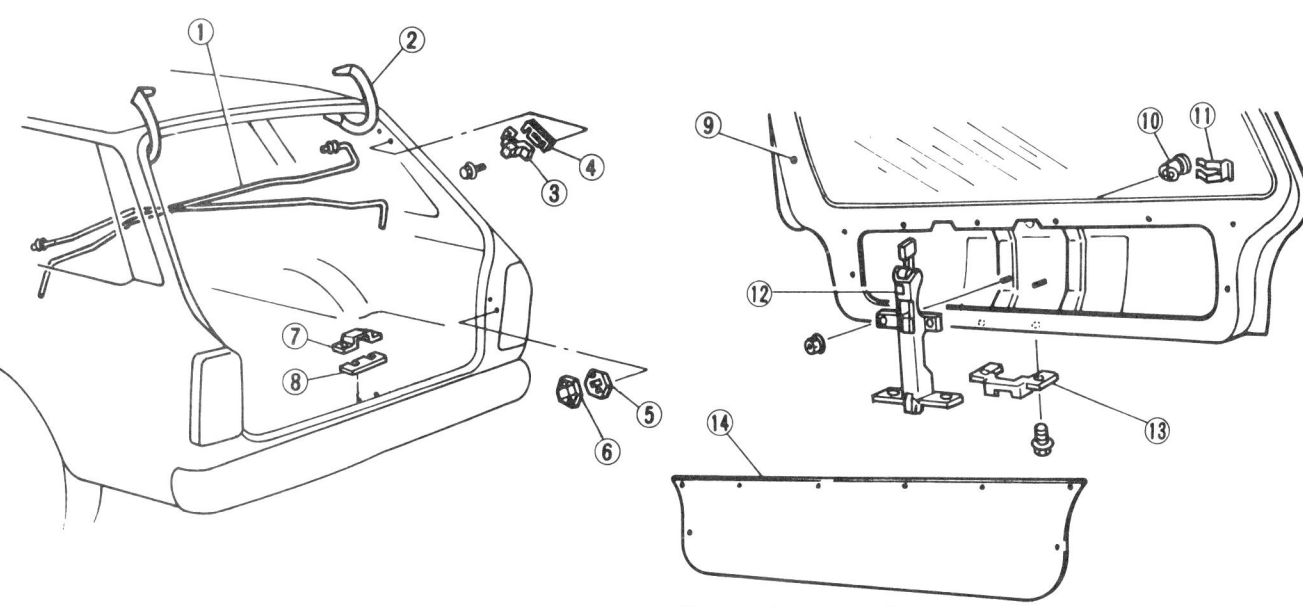

Fig. 12.19 The Estate Car tailgate and components

1	Torsion bar	5	Wedge bumper shim	9	Tailgate	12	Lock
2	Hinge	6	Wedge bumper	10	Lock cylinder	13	Striker catch
3	Bumper rubber	7	Striker	11	Retainer clip	14	Tailgate trim panel
4	Bumper rubber shim	8	Striker shim				

3   Lift away the boot lid.

4   Refiting the boot lid is the reverse sequence to removal. If necessary adjust the position of the hinges relative to the lid until the lid is centralised in the aperture.

5   To obtain a watertight fit between the boot lid and weatherstrip move the striker up and down or side to side as necessary.

15 Boot lid torsion bar assembly (Saloon) – removal and refitting

1   Open the boot lid and then remove the luggage compartment finisher panel securing screws. Lift away the finisher panel.

2   Support the boot lid with a piece of wood and carefully draw the end of the left torsion bar out of the hole drilled in the side panel – Watch your fingers!

3   Detach the torsion bar from the bracket and hinge.

4   The right-hand torsion bar is now removed in a similar manner to the left-hand torsion bar.

5   To refit the assembly first position the end of the right-hand torsion bar onto the right boot lid hinge.

6   Twist the torsion bar rearward and engage the bar in the torsion bar bracket.

7   Fit the left-hand torsion bar in a similar manner to the right.

16 Tailgate (Estate) – removal and refiting

1   Open the tailgate and support it in the open position with a piece of wood. The assistance of a second person is required to hold the tailgate as it is detached from the hinges.

2   Using a soft pencil, mark the outline of the hinge on the tailgate to act as a datum for refitting.

3   Detach the rear screen demister wires.

4   Undo and remove the three bolts and washers securing each hinge to the tailgate and carefully lift away the tailgate. Refitting the tailgate is the reverse sequence to removal.

5   Should it be necessary to adjust the position of the tailgate in the aperture, it may be moved up or down and side to side at the tailgate to hinge securing bolts. The fore and aft movement adjustment is obtained by slackening the bolts securing the tailgate hinges to the body.

17 Tailgate torsion bar assembly (Estate) – removal and refitting

1   Open the tailgate and support it in the open position with a piece of wood.

2   Undo and remove the fixing that secures the tailgate hinge cover to body, lift away the cover.

3   Undo and remove the screws fixing the head-lining rear end to the tailgate aperture rail panel (clean hands). Detach the head-lining.

4   Using a suitable pry bar detach the left torsion bar from the bracket.

5   Remove the right-hand torsion bar (painted yellow) from the bracket in a similar manner to the left-hand torsion bar.

6   Refitting the assembly is the reverse sequence to removal, but always refit the yellow bar first.

7   To adjust the tailgate, loosen the tailgate/hinge bolts and adjust the tailgate accordingly, then retighten the bolts. If the tailgate needs to be adjusted in the fore and aft direction, first remove the hinge cover, then the rear welt. Detach the rear end of the headlining and slacken the tailgate hinge bolts to the body. The tailgate can now be adjusted to enable it to fit evenly with equal clearances between it and the roof on each side. Retighten the bolts when the correct position has been located. Reverse the dismantling instructions to complete but check the tailgate action and security when closed.

18 Coupe rear door – removal and refitting

1   Raise the door and using a soft lead pencil, mark the outline of the hinge on the rear door to act as a guide when refitting.

2   With the aid of an assistant, support the door and unscrew the stay bolts.

3   Unscrew and remove the door to hinge bolts and lift the door

clear.

4   Refit in the reverse order but check the door adjustment before fully tightening the hinge bolts. Note the respective positions of the stay bolt components and refit as shown in Fig. 12.13.

5   To adjust the catch, loosen the bolts and move the catch in the desired direction, then retighten the bolts.

19 Front and rear doors – removal, refitting and adjustment

1   Open the door to be removed and position a support under it to take its weight. An assistant should be enlisted to hold the door.

2   Unscrew and remove the respective bolts that secure the door hinges to the body.

3   Carefully lift the door clear from the side of the car.

4   Refit in the reverse order and if necessary adjust as follows.

Adjustment

5   Any adjustment to be made to either the front or rear doors can be made by slackening the hinge bolts and repositioning the hinges on the body mounting locations. The door should be adjusted to give an even clearance from its periphery to the body aperture on all faces.

6   Further adjustment will probably be needed to the door lock striker plate and this can be moved in the direction required by simply loosening the two retaining screws. Make sure that both the hinge bolts and lock striker plate screws are securely tightened on completion.

20 Door trim – removal and refitting

1   Unscrew the lock knob and door pull (photo).

2   Unscrew and remove the inner door catch backing strip. Remove the strip (photo).

3   To remove the window winder handle, prise the handle and trim apart, and with a suitable wire hook reach down inside the handle and pull free the release spring from the winder pivot. Pull the handle free (photos).

4   Prise the trim carefully away from the door around the edges which is retained by plastic clips. The trim can now be lifted clear of the door.

5   Refitment of the trim is a direct reversal of the removal sequence but ensure that the spring clip is correctly located to retain the window winder handle.

21 Front door lock and control unit – removal, refitting and adjustment

1   First remove the inner door trim panel as described and peel back the dust sheet (photo).

2   Refer to Fig. 12.21 and turn the lock cylinder clip in the direction indicated by the arrow, and detach the rod.

3   Unscrew and remove the inside door handle and lock screws. Remove the lock unit (photo).

4   The outer door handle can be removed by unscrewing the securing nuts.

5   The lock cylinder can be removed by prising free the retaining clip.

6   Refit in the reverse order but note the following:

(a)   *Lubricate the springs and levers with grease prior to final assembly*

(b)   *If adjustment is necessary, refer to the adjustment clearance shown in Fig. 12.20 which shows the free play necessary. Adjustment can be made by turning the adjuster nut to obtain the specified clearance of 0 to 0.04 in (0. to 1 mm)*

22 Rear door lock and control unit – removal, refitting and adjustment

1   Remove the inner trim panel as given in Section 21.

2   Unscrew the inner door handle retaining screws. Detach the bell crank and remove the door lock unit through the inner door.

3   The outer handle can now be removed by unscrewing the retaining nuts.

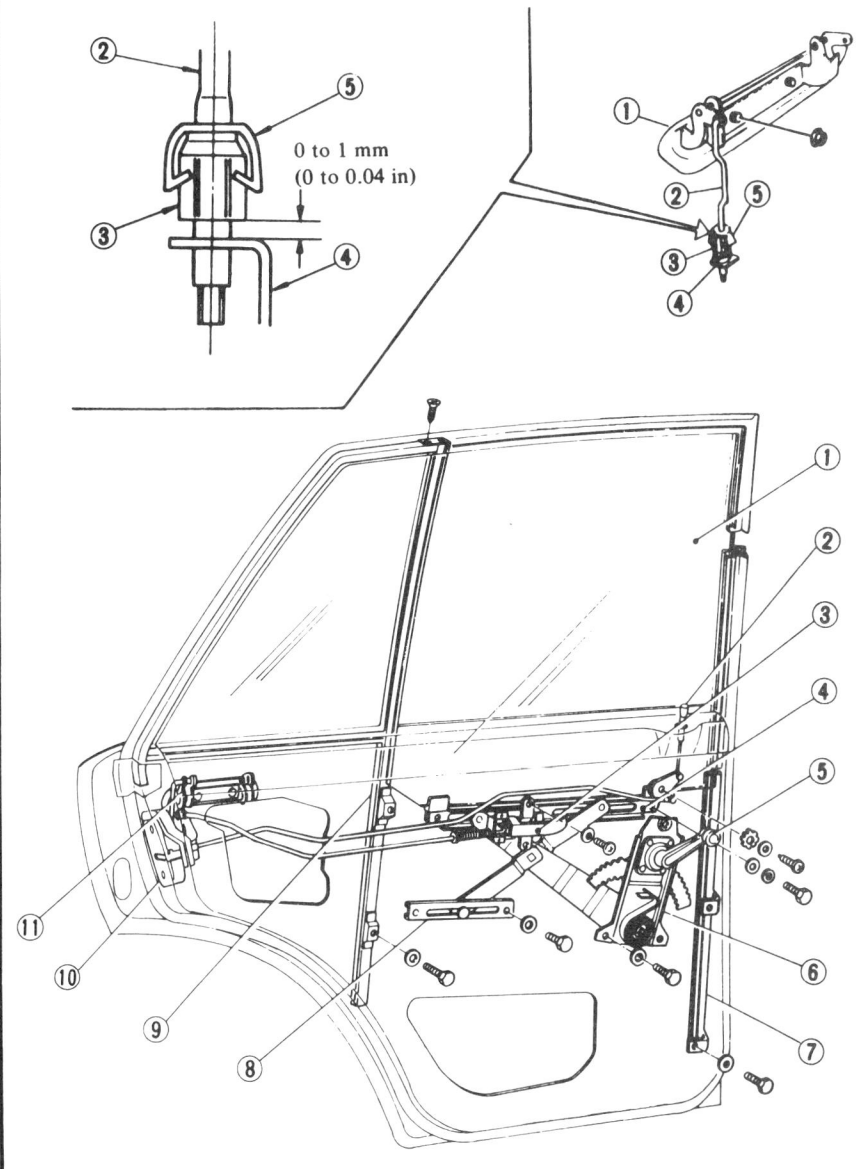

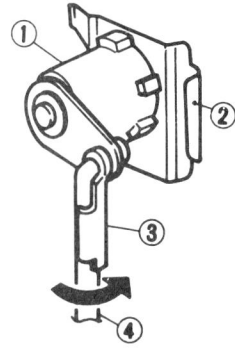

Fig. 12.20 Lock adjustment

1 Exterior handle
2 Exterior handle rod
3 Nylon adjustment nut
4 Lock lever
5 Clip

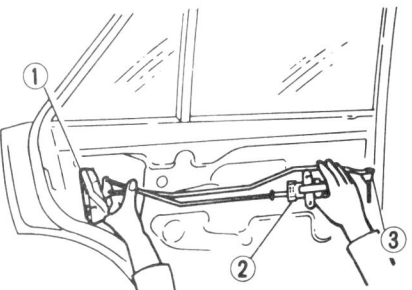

Fig. 12.21 Lock cylinder and rod assembly

1 Cylinder   3 Clip
2 Securing clip   4 Rod

Fig. 12.22 Rear door (Saloon and Estate Car) components

1 Glass
2 Inner lock knob
3 Inner handle
4 Guide channel 'A'
5 Regulator handle
6 Regulator
7 Lower sash
8 Guide channel 'B'
9 Centre sash
10 Lock unit
11 Exterior handle

Fig.12.23 Door lock removal

1 Lock
2 Inner door handle
3 Bell crank

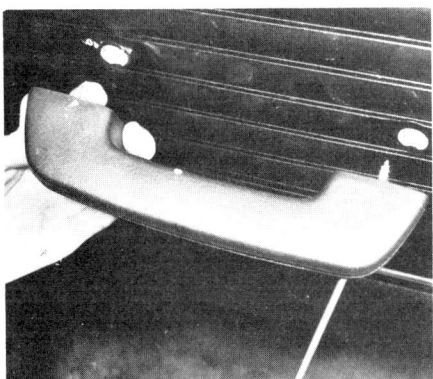

20.1 Withdraw the door pull/arm rest

20.2 Remove the inner catch backing strip

20.3a Using a wire hook ...

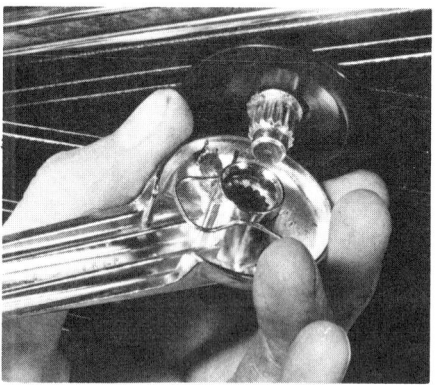
20.30b ... pull back the release spring to remove the window winder

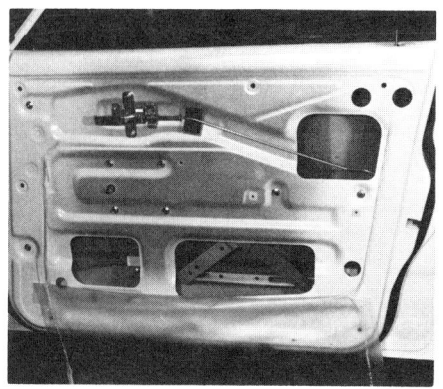
21.1 Front door trim removed (Saloon)

21.3 Door handle and retaining screws (inner)

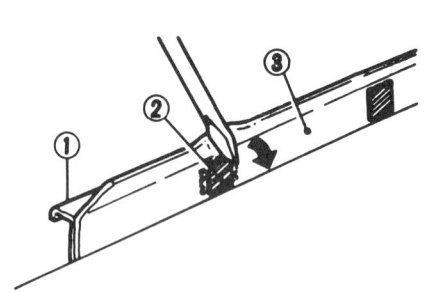
Fig. 12.24 Turn moulding clips (2) 90° to remove

1   Outside moulding
3   Rubber seal

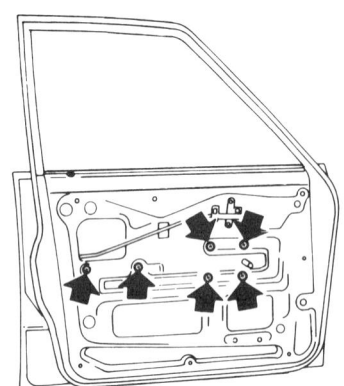
Fig. 12.25 Regulator retaining screw positions

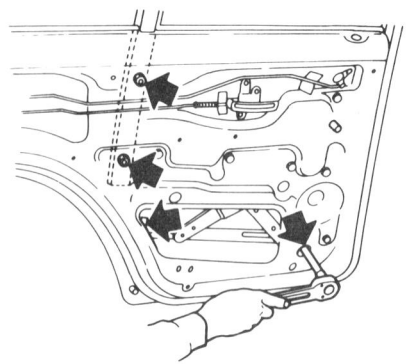
Fig. 12.26 The rear door glass/regulator and sash retaining bolt positions

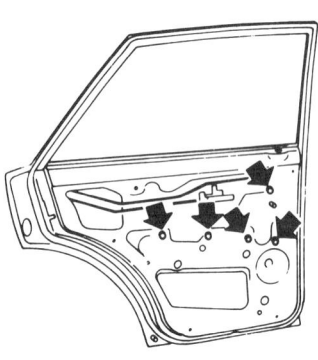
Fig. 12.27 Rear door regulator attachment screw positions

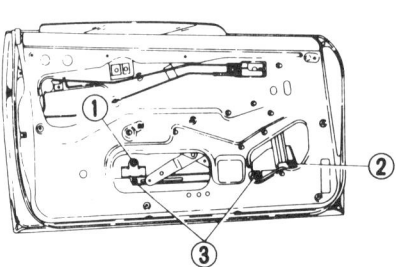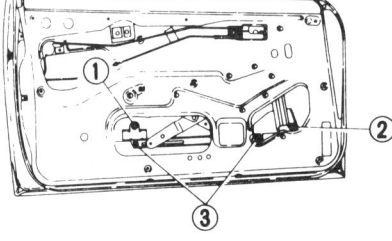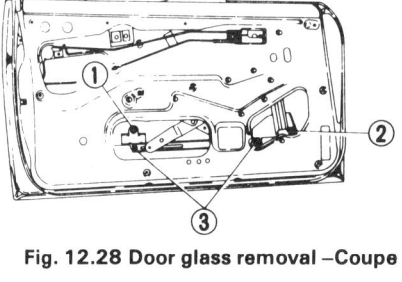
Fig. 12.28 Door glass removal –Coupe

1   Rear stop 'A'
2   Front stop
3   Regulator/glass adjuster bolts

Fig. 12.29 Guide rail adjuster bolts (Coupe) (1) Upper (2) lower and (3) guide channel retaining bolts

10 mm (0.39 in)

Fig. 12.30 Adjust glass upper edge clearance as shown

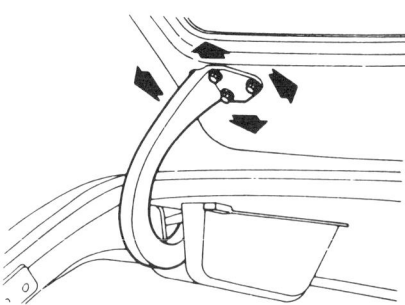
Fig. 12.31 Tailgate to hinge bolts adjustment

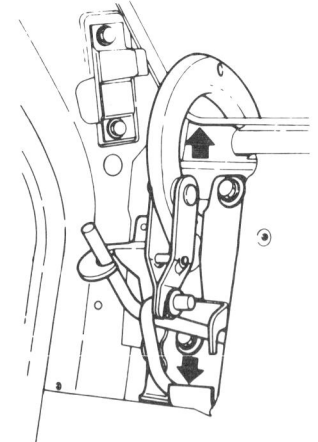
Fig. 12.32 Tailgate fore and aft adjustment

4   Refit in the reverse order.

23 Front door glass and regulator (Saloon and Estate) – removal, refitting and adjustment

1   Remove the inner trim panel (Section 20).
2   Use a screwdriver blade and turn the outer moulding retainer clips 90° and remove. Do not use excessive force.
3   Relocate the regulator handle and lower the door glass to gain access to the regulator/glass securing screws. Support the glass in this position and remove the screws.
4   Lift the glass and remove the regulator unit through the inner panel aperture.
5   Refitting is a direct reversal of the removal procedure.
6   To adjust the glass alignment, loosen the guide channel just sufficiently to enable it to be repositioned to suit. Retighten the bolts on achieving the correct alignment.
7   Check that the glass can be raised or lowered without binding before refitting the trim panel.

24 Rear door glass and regulator (Saloon and Estate) – removal, refitting and adjustment

1   Remove the inner door trim (Section 20).
2   Using the regulator handle, lower the glass sufficiently to gain access to the regulator/glass attachment screws through the inner door panel aperture.
3   Unscrew and remove the glass/regulator attachment screws and also the sash (rear window channel) retaining bolts. Lower the glass.
4   Detach the clip from the front of the centre sash and prise the outside moulding back to gain access to the sash retaining screw at the top.
5   Remove the sash screw, tilt the sash forward, slide it free and then lift the door glass out.
6   To remove the regulator unscrew the attachment bolts, and withdraw the regulator through the inner panel aperture.
7   Refit in the reverse sequence to removal. Any adjustment to the glass fitting can be made by resetting the sash position to suit. Loosen the retaining bolts/screws, adjust sash and retighten the bolts/screws.
8   Check that the glass can be raised and lowered without binding before refitting the trim panel.

25 Door glass and regulator (Coupe) – removal, refitting and adjustment

1   Refer to Section 19 and remove the door trim.

2   Use a screwdriver blade and turn the outer moulding retainer clips 90° to remove. Do not use excessive force.
3   Relocate the regulator handle and lower the glass sufficiently to enable the upper stoppers to be visible through the aperture in the inner panel.
4   Support the glass and remove the glass/regulator attachment bolts, and the rear and front stoppers.
5   The glass can now be lifted clear.
6   To remove the regulator, unscrew the retaining bolts and withdraw the unit through the inner panel aperture.
7   Refit in the reverse order and if necessary, adjust the glass.

Adjustment
8   To adjust the glass horizontally or vertically, loosen the upper stopper and adjust accordingly. The front height alignment can be adjusted by loosening the upper stopper and repositioning it to suit. If adjustment needs to be made inwards or outwards, loosen and reposition the guide rail to suit. The correct position is gained when the clearance between the upper side of the door panel (outside) and the glass is set as 0.43 in (11 mm). Turn the upper adjustment bolts accordingly to achieve this clearance. The clearance for the glass upper edge should be as shown (Fig. 12.30) and is adjusted via the lower adjusting bolts.
9   Check all bolts/screws for security and ensure that the window operates freely and correctly before refitting the trim panel.

26 Tailgate lock and cylinder (Estate) – removal and refitting

1   Raise the tailgate and remove the trim, carefully prising it free and then peel back the dust sheet.
2   Slacken the tailgate lock retaining bolts and remove the lock and striker plate.
3   Remove the cylinder by prising the retaining clip free and withdrawing the lock cylinder from the outside.
4   Refit in the reverse sequence.
5   Tailgate adjustment can be made by loosening the hinge to lid bolts and re-aligning the tailgate as required or alternatively by loosening the hinge to body bolts which will necessitate removing the rear portion of the headlining for access. The tailgate striker and catch plates can be immediately adjusted to suit.

27 Back door lock and cylinder (Coupe) – removal and refitting

1   Open and support the back door.
2   Detach the finisher in the boot.
3   Unscrew and remove the door lock retaining bolts and detach the lock unit.

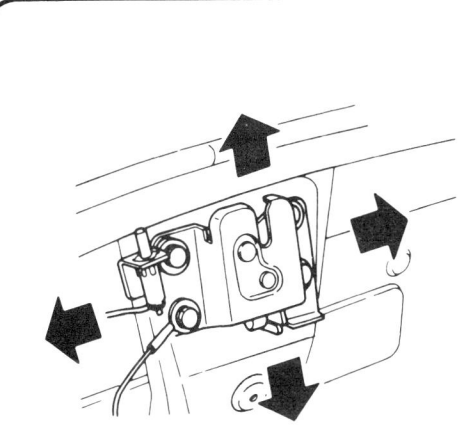

Fig. 12.33 The Coupe rear door lock unit showing possible adjustment position

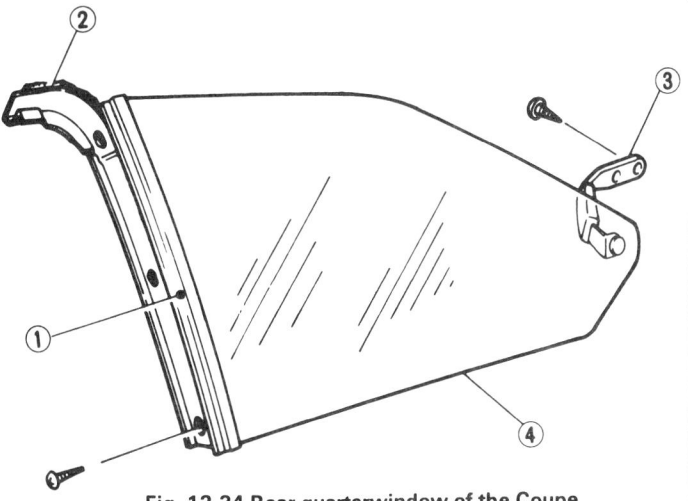

Fig. 12.34 Rear quarterwindow of the Coupe

| 1 | Sash | 3 | Handle |
| 2 | Retainer | 4 | Glass |

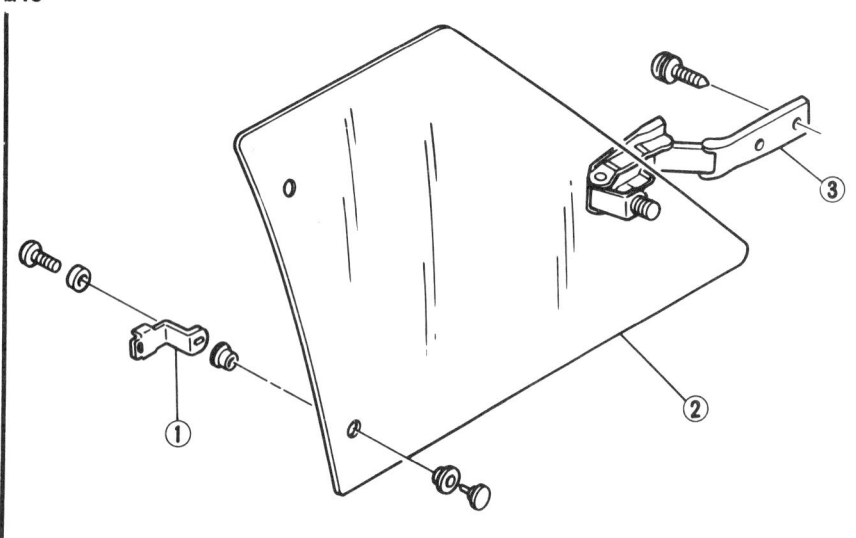

Fig. 12.35 Rear quarter window (two door Saloon)

1   Window hinge
2   Glass
3   Window handle

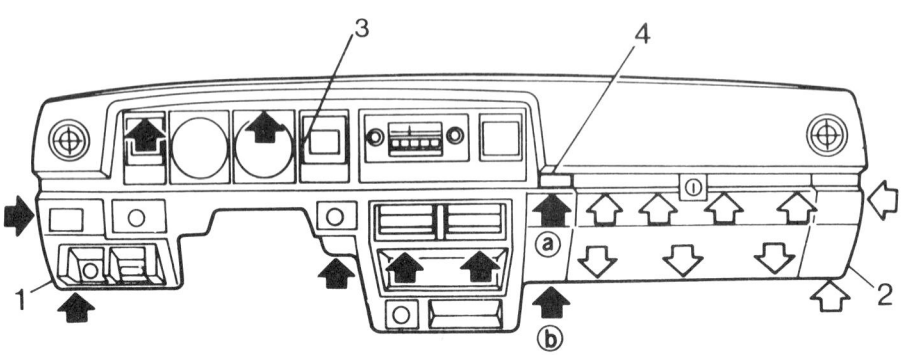

Fig. 12.36 Facia panels

| 1   Facia 'A' | 2   Facia 'B' | 3   Instrument panel | 4   Finisher (A) |

◀ Facia A securing screw positions
◁ Facia B securing screw positions

Fig. 12.37 Instrument panel removal

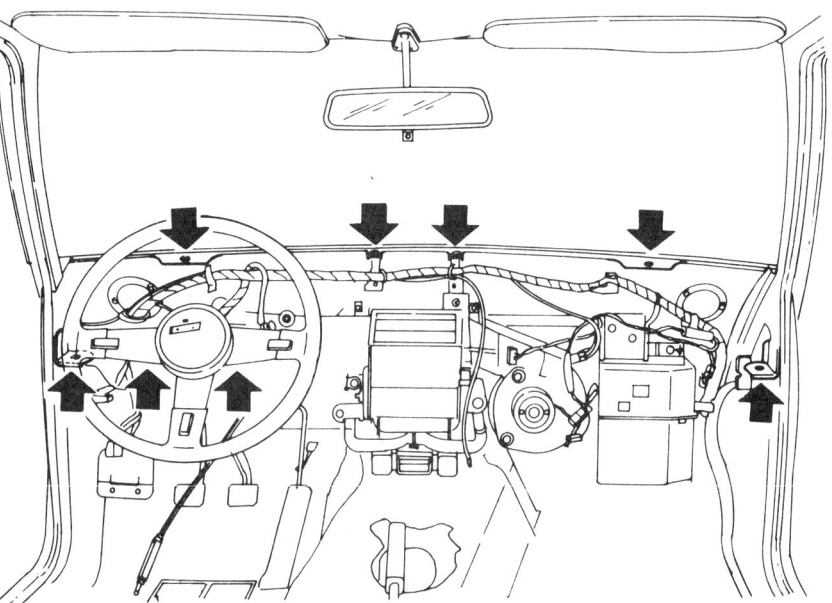

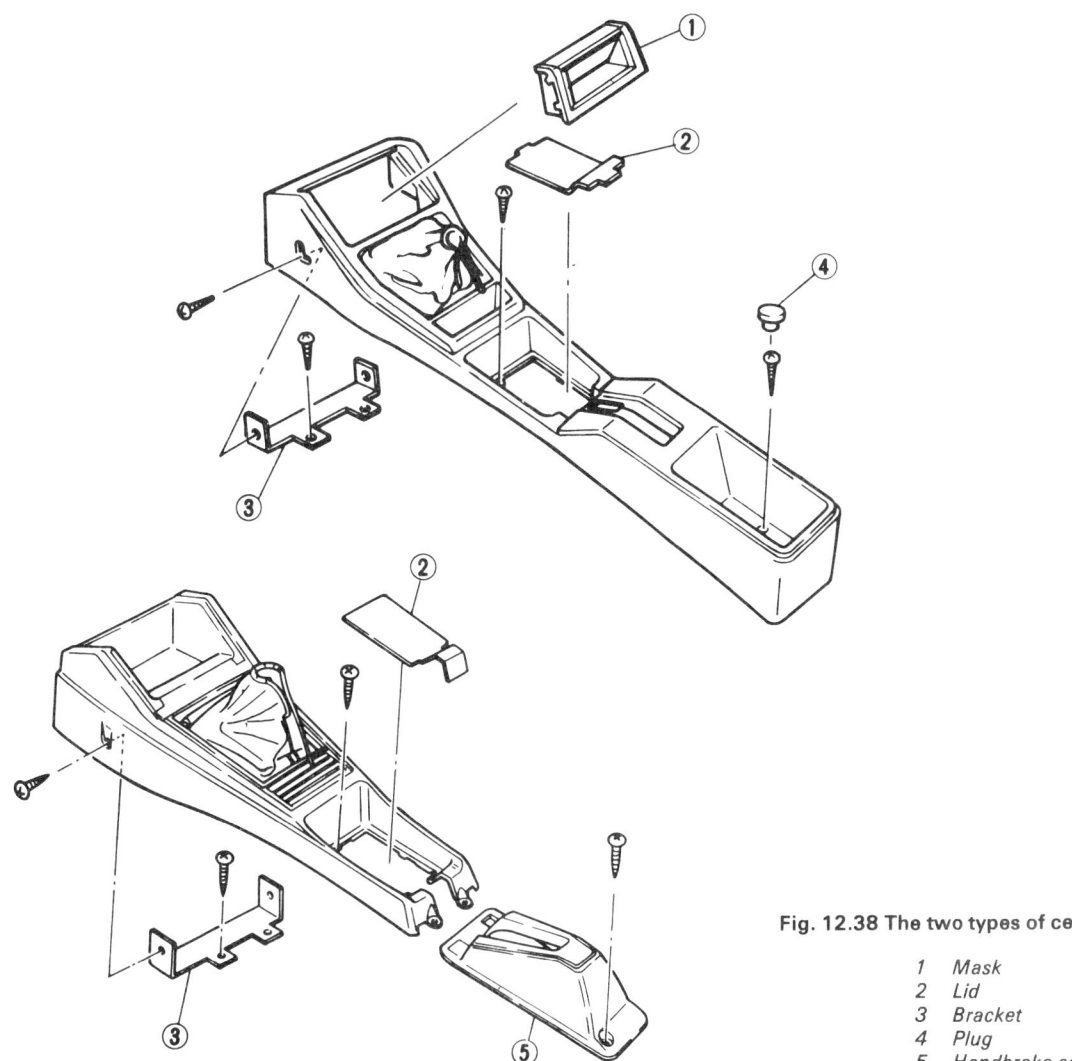

Fig. 12.38 The two types of centre console box fitted

1   *Mask*
2   *Lid*
3   *Bracket*
4   *Plug*
5   *Handbrake cover*

4   The lock cylinder can be removed by undoing the retaining screws and pushing the cylinder free from inside.

5   Refitting of both units is a direct reversal of the removal sequence, although the back door may have to be readjusted as described earlier.

28 Rear quarter window (Coupe and Two door Saloon) – removal and refitting

Coupe

1   Open the quarter window and prise free the weatherstrip from the sash/retainer.

2   Unscrew and remove the sash and retainer.

3   Loosen the quarter window handle retaining screws and withdraw the window.

4   Refit in the reverse sequence but renew the retainer sponge seal if it is defective.

Two door Saloon

5   Open the rear side window, unscrew the glass and handle retaining screws and withdraw the window.

6   Refitting is a reversal of the removal procedure.

29 Facia panels – removal and refitting

1   The facia panel is divided into two sections these being on the driving side 'A' and the passenger side 'B', see Fig. 12.36.

Driver's side 'A'

2   To remove the driving side 'A', first detach the battery earth cable.

3   Unscrew the wiper switch retaining screws and remove the switch.

4   Pull out the ashtray from its location.

5   Pull the heater control knobs off the levers and then withdraw the control facia panel. This is best removed by inserting a thin screwdriver blade into the fan lever slot and prising out the right-hand side of the heater facia panel but take care not to mark the panel facia.

6   Pull the radio knobs free and remove the nuts and washers.

7   Detach the manual choke knob and the side defroster control knob.

8   Remove the finisher 'A' (Fig. 12.36).

9   Unscrew and remove the nine facia retaining screws from the positions marked with black arrows.

10 Detach the wire harness connectors as follows:

    (a)   Indicator switch
    (b)   Cigarette lighter
    (c)   Clock
    (d)   Rear window demister switch
    (e)   Centre illumination

11 Withdraw the driving side facia panel.

12 Refit in the reverse order but check that all electrical connections are good on reassembly and check operation of each component on completion.

Passenger side 'B'

13 To detach the passenger side facia, open the glove box lid and

remove the lid stopper screw.

14 Unscrew and remove the passenger facia securing screws. There are nine in all and their positions are shown in Fig. 12.36.

15 Remove the two driving side facia securing screws from their central positions (marked (a) and (b) in the illustration). Withdraw the passenger side facia.

16 Refit in the reverse sequence to removal.

30 Instrument panel – removal and refitting

1 Refer to the previous Section and remove the right and left-hand facia panels.

2 Detach the speedometer cable from its location at the rear of the speedometer.

3 Detach the radio aerial cable.

4 Disconnect the respective body/instrument harness connectors.

5 Disconnect the heater control cables, and the heater earth harness connection.

6 Unscrew the respective instrument panel retaining screws and withdraw the panel – carefully.

7 Refitting is the direct reversal of removal but make sure that all electrical connections are fully secure.

31 Central console – removal and refitting

1 Refer to the illustration (Fig. 12.38), unscrew and remove the retaining screws at the front side faces.

2 Prise the tray from the rear section to expose the rear retaining screw, and remove it. On some models there may be a further screw at the rear as shown beneath a plug.

3 Engage 4th gear and pull the handbrake lever back. Lift the console unit clear of the gear lever and handbrake.

4 Refit in the reverse sequence.

Metric conversion tables

Inches	Decimals	Millimetres	Millimetres to Inches		Inches to Millimetres	
			mm	Inches	Inches	mm
1/64	0.015625	0.3969	0.01	0.00039	0.001	0.0254
1/32	0.03125	0.7937	0.02	0.00079	0.002	0.0508
3/64	0.046875	1.1906	0.03	0.00118	0.003	0.0762
1/16	0.0625	1.5875	0.04	0.00157	0.004	0.1016
5/64	0.078125	1.9844	0.05	0.00197	0.005	0.1270
3/32	0.09375	2.3812	0.06	0.00236	0.006	0.1524
7/64	0.109375	2.7781	0.07	0.00276	0.007	0.1778
1/8	0.125	3.1750	0.08	0.00315	0.008	0.2032
9/64	0.140625	3.5719	0.09	0.00354	0.009	0.2286
5/32	0.15625	3.9687	0.1	0.00394	0.01	0.254
11/64	0.171875	4.3656	0.2	0.00787	0.02	0.508
3/16	0.1875	4.7625	0.3	0.01181	0.03	0.762
13/64	0.203125	5.1594	0.4	0.01575	0.04	1.016
7/32	0.21875	5.5562	0.5	0.01969	0.05	1.270
15/64	0.234375	5.9531	0.6	0.02362	0.06	1.524
1/4	0.25	6.3500	0.7	0.02756	0.07	1.778
17/64	0.265625	6.7469	0.8	0.03150	0.08	2.032
9/32	0.28125	7.1437	0.9	0.03543	0.09	2.286
19/64	0.296875	7.5406	1	0.03937	0.1	2.54
5/16	0.3125	7.9375	2	0.07874	0.2	5.08
21/64	0.328125	8.3344	3	0.11811	0.3	7.62
11/32	0.34375	8.7312	4	0.15748	0.4	10.16
23/64	0.359375	9.1281	5	0.19685	0.5	12.70
3/8	0.375	9.5250	6	0.23622	0.6	15.24
25/64	0.390625	9.9219	7	0.27559	0.7	17.78
13/32	0.40625	10.3187	8	0.31496	0.8	20.32
27/64	0.421875	10.7156	9	0.35433	0.9	22.86
7/16	0.4375	11.1125	10	0.39370	1	25.4
29/64	0.453125	11.5094	11	0.43307	2	50.8
15/32	0.46875	11.9062	12	0.47244	3	76.2
31/64	0.48375	12.3031	13	0.51181	4	101.6
1/2	0.5	12.7000	14	0.55118	5	127.0
33/64	0.515625	13.0969	15	0.59055	6	152.4
17/32	0.53125	13.4937	16	0.62992	7	177.8
35/64	0.546875	13.8906	17	0.66929	8	203.2
9/16	0.5625	14.2875	18	0.70866	9	228.6
37/64	0.578125	14.6844	19	0.74803	10	254.0
19/32	0.59375	15.0812	20	0.78740	11	279.4
39/64	0.609375	15.4781	21	0.82677	12	304.8
5/8	0.625	15.8750	22	0.86614	13	330.2
41/64	0.640625	16.2719	23	0.90551	14	355.6
21/32	0.65625	16.6687	24	0.94488	15	381.0
43/64	0.671875	17.0656	25	0.98425	16	406.4
11/16	0.6875	17.4625	26	1.02362	17	431.8
45/64	0.703125	17.8594	27	1.06299	18	457.2
23/32	0.71875	18.2562	28	1.10236	19	482.6
47/64	0.734375	18.6531	29	1.14173	20	508.0
3/4	0.75	19.0500	30	1.18110	21	533.4
49/64	0.765625	19.4469	31	1.22047	22	558.8
25/32	0.78125	19.8437	32	1.25984	23	584.2
51/64	0.796875	20.2406	33	1.29921	24	609.6
13/16	0.8125	20.6375	34	1.33858	25	635.0
53/64	0.828125	21.0344	35	1.37795	26	660.4
27/32	0.84375	21.4312	36	1.41732	27	685.8
55/64	0.859375	21.8281	37	1.4567	28	711.2
7/8	0.875	22.2250	38	1.4961	29	736.6
57/64	0.890625	22.6219	39	1.5354	30	762.0
29/32	0.90625	23.0187	40	1.5748	31	787.4
59/64	0.921875	23.4156	41	1.6142	32	812.8
15/16	0.9375	23.8125	42	1.6535	33	838.2
61/64	0.953125	24.2094	43	1.6929	34	863.6
31/32	0.96875	24.6062	44	1.7323	35	889.0
63/64	0.984375	25.0031	45	1.7717	36	914.4

1   Imperial gallon = 8 Imp pints = 1.20 US gallons = 277.42 cu in = 4.54 litres

1   US gallon = 4 US quarts = 0.83 Imp gallon = 231 cu in = 3.78 litres

1   Litre = 0.21 Imp gallon = 0.26 US gallon = 61.02 cu in = 1000 cc

Miles to Kilometres		Kilometres to Miles	
1	1.61	1	0.62
2	3.22	2	1.24
3	4.83	3	1.86
4	6.44	4	2.49
5	8.05	5	3.11
6	9.66	6	3.73
7	11.27	7	4.35
8	12.88	8	4.97
9	14.48	9	5.59
10	16.09	10	6.21
20	32.19	20	12.43
30	48.28	30	18.64
40	64.37	40	24.85
50	80.47	50	31.07
60	96.56	60	37.28
70	112.65	70	43.50
80	128.75	80	49.71
90	144.84	90	55.92
100	160.93	100	62.14

lbf ft to kgf m		kgf m to lbf ft		lbf/in^2 to kgf/cm^2		kgf/cm^2 to lbf/in^2	
1	0.138	1	7.233	1	0.07	1	14.22
2	0.276	2	14.466	2	0.14	2	28.50
3	0.414	3	21.699	3	0.21	3	42.67
4	0.553	4	28.932	4	0.28	4	56.89
5	0.691	5	36.165	5	0.35	5	71.12
6	0.829	6	43.398	6	0.42	6	85.34
7	0.967	7	50.631	7	0.49	7	99.56
8	1.106	8	57.864	8	0.56	8	113.79
9	1.244	9	65.097	9	0.63	9	128.00
10	1.382	10	72.330	10	0.70	10	142.23
20	2.765	20	144.660	20	1.41	20	284.47
30	4.147	30	216.990	30	2.11	30	426.70

Index

**Printed by
Haynes Publishing Group
Sparkford Yeovil Somerset
England**